SALES
MANAGEMENT

SHAPING FUTURE SALES LEADERS

SECOND EDITION

JOHN F. TANNER, JR.
Baylor University

EARL D. HONEYCUTT, JR.
Elon University

ROBERT C. ERFFMEYER
University of Wisconsin – Eau Claire

Library of Congress Cataloging-in-Publication Data

Tanner, Jr., John F.; Honeycutt, Jr., Earl D.; Erffmeyer, Robert C.

    Sales Management / John F. Tanner, Jr., Earl D. Honeycutt, Jr., and Robert C. Erffmeyer

    Includes Index

    ISBN: 978-0-9897013-5-8 (paperback)

    ISBN: 978-0-9897013-6-5 (hardcover)

       1. Sales Management, 2nd edition. I. Shaping Future Sales Leaders. II. John F. Tanner, Jr., Earl D. Honeycutt, Jr., and Robert C. Erffmeyer

Editor: Laurie K. Dobson

Copy Editor: Juliet George

Book / Cover Design: Anna Botelho

Indexer: Judi Gibbs

To those who value the scholarship of sales management,
whether they are faculty, students, or practitioners,
and to Karen, my wife, for her love and support
—Jeff

To Laura, Travis, Andrea, Cole, Raine, and Carter.
—Earl

To the wonderful women in my life, Gretchen and Hannah
—Bob

BRIEF CONTENTS

CONTENTS

PREFACE TO THE SECOND EDITION

How firms manage their selling functions has evolved significantly over the past few decades. Technology, in the form of labor saving devices and the Internet, has had a tremendous effect on sales management. Simultaneously, the buyer-seller relationship has been impacted by customer contact centers, customer relationship management technology, greater cultural and generational diversity, increased emphasis on ethics and social responsibility, and myriad other factors. Most sales leaders would state that selling is today a more complex process that has changed how sales teams are led.

We want students to understand these changes and how today's sales managers actually manage their sales personnel. But in spite of what we knew about what was going on in the field, we discovered that sales management textbooks had changed little over the years. For example, no new major textbook had entered the market in more than two decades. As a result, we published our first edition because we believed it was time for a new approach. Based upon adoptions, and the comments we received, we were correct.

Our goal is to offer a book that prepares students for the exciting challenges related to leading sales organizations in today's hyper-competitive global economy. To do this, we provide students with a basic theoretical foundation that will enable them to adapt to an evolving economy, while we seek to balance theory with the practical applications they will need to know in order to lead top-performing sales teams.

What Makes This Book Different?

The emphasis of this textbook is to relate how sales management gets done. You will see the following cutting-edge material integrated not only into the textbook and end-of-chapter questions and problems, but also in the accompanying instructor's manual, test bank, PowerPoint slides, and a website. All instructor materials are conceptualized and written by the authors.

Sales Manager Profiles

Unique to our book are the chapter-opening profiles featuring actual sales managers. The profiles explain the day-to-day challenges faced by these practicing sales managers, which reinforce the chapters in which they appear. We also provide these profiles so students can get a sense of the world sales managers live in. Our goal is to engage and inspire students to explore possible sales management careers, as well as to provide a voice for sales managers who helped shape this textbook.

Technology Coverage

CRM and knowledge management technology are two software applications that can dramatically affect how both salespeople and sales managers spend their time. The question is: How do sales managers and their reps make the most of these systems? Not only will you find an entire chapter devoted to using technology to manage sales organizations, but you'll also find technology woven throughout the book that includes a number of short cases at the end of chapters, and a full-length CRM case found just after Chapter 15.

Culture and the Global Sales Environment

Like technology, new trade agreements and changing political environments have greatly impacted the global sales environment. Sales executives understand that overseas markets are growing faster than established economies, and these markets are or will become the firm's "bread and butter." As firms shift more focus to high-growth markets, they are counting on their sales managers to find ways to capture market share abroad via the day-to-day interactions they have with their firms' global partners and sales representatives—who likely grew up or live in other cultures. Because the sales environment has truly become a "flat world," we offer "Global Sales Management" features that address the chapter topics on a global scale. Chapter 15 also offers a major section that explains how to understand and manage buyers and salespeople from different cultural backgrounds. Global sales management is also integrated into each chapter, the discussion questions and problems, and the test bank, resulting in more complete coverage than other sales management texts.

Ethics

Many textbooks largely emphasize the law in their ethics chapters, and our ethics chapter also covers the legal aspects of sales management. However, you will find additional coverage of people's ethical beliefs and why they believe what they do. For example, can you really "train" sales representatives in terms of their ethics? What is the difference between a gift and a bribe? We also include three ethics-related cases that require students to analyze and make recommendations to guide appropriate salesperson behavior. This is especially important when their salespeople don't have the same ethical or cultural backgrounds as managers do—a common situation in global markets. In addition to a stand-alone ethics chapter, an "Ethics in Sales Management" feature is woven into each chapter of the book.

Sales Forces Structure

In the past, devoting a few paragraphs to distributors and manufacturer's reps might be all that was needed to cover the topic of outsourcing. Now, however, it is commonplace for a company to outsource its prospecting to a call center service bureau, to have an in-house contact center work with independent field salespeople, and to outsource customer service to yet another service bureau—all in addition to managing self-service channels via the web. As a result, the topics found in selection or training chapters should look very different in terms of today's best practices from that of 20 years ago. You'll still find chapters devoted to recruiting, selecting, socializing or "on-boarding," and training salespeople in our text, but the content more closely reflects the reality of the many different positions and multi-channel sales force structures that exist within the realm of selling today.

Leadership

Leadership concepts and practices have evolved as professionals and academics alike recognized that leading is more than motivating the sales force. Leadership is not just about getting someone to do what you want, but among other things, it is about what a leader does for her or his followers. The material in this book lies at the forefront of sales leadership thought and practice. Not only does the book present best practice material when it comes to U.S. leadership, but includes guidance about what sales executives and representatives abroad view as good leadership.

New Cases

In response to requests for ways to "engage" today's students, each chapter offers an in-class scenario that can be used or modified to fit your instructional needs. We also provide two short "caselets" at the end of each chapter that can be assigned after a short lecture or discussion to drive home and reinforce the chapter's important points. Lastly, we offer 12 all new, full-length, cases after Chapter 15. The topics and actual case situations were generated by situations encountered by sales managers and sales personnel who related the information to the authors. As might be expected, information that identifies the company has been changed. Unlike most sales management books, there are 12 new cases in this second edition and textbook adopters will have access to our website where 10-12 additional cases along with suggested solutions are available.

Managing Your Career

A new section has been added at the end of each chapter to remind the student how the information on sales management practices will help them be higher performing salespersons and more effective sales managers. Many first edition adopters informed us that their students ask: "This is interesting, but why is it important?" Our goal with the new section is to explain how this knowledge will immediately impact the new salesperson, and, in the all-too-soon future, when many students will quickly move into sales management!

New Pedagogy

Sales management instructors have told us that they want to flip their classroom because they are concerned that students aren't reading the book and coming to class prepared. Instructors often encounter students who ask for a copy of slides before class. As educators, we know that some students see this as a shortcut to reading or to active listening and involvement in class discussions. To improve student engagement and to respond to faculty who want to flip the classroom, we altered our PowerPoint slides to a format that requires students to take a more active role. You can hand them out prior to class or post them electronically, confident that the classroom experience will be enhanced. There are also teaching notes in the instructor's manual that will help increase student engagement.

ACKNOWLEDGMENTS

No book is solely the work of its authors. Although we take full responsibility for any errors or omissions, we could not have accomplished this project without help from the following outstanding individuals. We greatly appreciate and acknowledge their contributions.

Because we wanted a book that reflected the best practices that lie at the forefront of sales management, we involved both successful sales executives and consultants. These people reviewed outlines, made suggestions on topics to cover, and gave us access to their thought processes and their companies' practices. This group of executives, managers, and consultants include:

Jill Amerie, Xtreme Xhibits by Skyline, Inc.

Jeffrey Bailey, Oracle Corporation

Melaney Barba, Liberty Mutual

Bill Bencsik, Bencsik Associates, Inc.

Tracey Brill, Pharmaceuticals Co.

Charles Cohon, Prime Devices Corp.

Tait Cruse, Northwestern Mutual

Bruce Culbert, Pedowitz Group

Miles Curro, Covidien

Jason DeAmato, Island of Sales

Susan Denny, Cisco

Antoine Destin, Hormel Foods Corporation

Haley Earley, Konica Minolta Business Systems

Bill Febry, Cardinal Marketing

Dana Geisert, TEKsystems

Mary Gros, Teradata

Bill Haas, LabCorp

Tricia Jennings, Merck & Co., Inc.

Mike Kapocius, Takeda Pharmaceuticals

Kurt Knapton, ResearchNow

Richard Langlotz, Konica-Minolta

Kelvin Lewis, Coca-Cola

Candice Mailland, 3M Company

Evin Martinez, San Diego Padres

Will May, AppDynamics

Eric McMillan, 3M Company

Rich Merklinger, Ethicon, Inc.

Kurt Mueller, Hormel Foods Corporation

Ram Ramamurthy, Sri-lIST, Inc.

Ellen Rebne, Graybar

Karl Sherrill, Senn Dunn

Tom Sherrill, Edward Jones

Katherine Twells, Coca-Cola Company

Kevin Yoder, AstraZeneca

Several faculty members also provided input into the design and content of the book. We especially appreciate the early input of Andrea Dixon at Baylor University. Also, Randy Moser at High Point University, and Jerry Kollross at the University of Wisconsin–Eau Claire who provided valuable advice and support to the author team.

A number of students pretested the book and provided us with feedback on its content, including Jeb Phillips and Hunter Hendrickson. Research assistance was provided by Travis Tanner and Mandy McGowan. Jeri Weiser was instrumental in conceptualizing some of our graphics and in reviewing different parts of the manuscript. Bonnie Krahn's outstanding work on the slides helped our thoughts be better visualized.

We very much appreciate Noel Capon at Wessex Press for taking this project on, and the job Laurie Dobson did as the book's development editor. Other members of the team who deserve our thanks include Anna Botelho (Anna B. Type & Graphics) and Juliet George (copyeditor). We would like to thank three other supporters of collegiate sales education: Gerhard Gschwandtner, CEO of *Selling Power Daily Report*; Howard and Sally Stevens at HR Chally; and The Sales Education Foundation. They are all true advocates of college sales education. We greatly appreciate their assistance and their support of all college educators teaching sales-related courses.

ABOUT THE AUTHORS

JOHN F. (JEFF) TANNER JR. is Professor of Marketing and the Executive Director of Baylor University's Business Collaboratory. He joined the faculty at Baylor in 1988, upon completing his Ph.D. at the University of Georgia. He has published over 70 scientific research articles, and presented over 200 conference papers or posters. Tanner's work has appeared in the *Journal of Marketing, Journal of the Academy of Marketing Science, Journal of Personal Selling & Sales Management*, and others. Dr. Tanner is also author or co-author of 15 books, including the leading sales text *Selling: Building Partnerships,* Ninth Edition (McGraw-Hill, 2014), and *Principles of Marketing: How Marketing Gets Done* (Flat World Knowledge, 2013). His newest book, *Analytics and Dynamic Customer Strategy: Big Profits from Big Data* (Wiley, 2014), is aimed at marketing execs.

Dr. Tanner has served as a visiting professor at ITESM (Mexico), Universite de Montpellier and the IAE/Caen (France), University of West Indies (Trinidad & Tobago), and TABC (Malawi). An active consultant to companies such as SAP, Cabela's, and Teradata, as well as the federal government, he also serves on the board of directors of several companies and non-profits.

Dr. Tanner and his wife, Karen, breed and race thoroughbred horses at Jett Creek Farm.

EARL HONEYCUTT is Emeritus Professor of Marketing at Elon University, N.C. When he retired in 2012, he was Martha and Spencer Love Professor of Marketing and University Distinguished Scholar. Dr. Honeycutt earned his Ph.D. at the University of Georgia where his dissertation investigated sales training. Since then he taught undergraduate, MBA, and doctoral seminars as a tenured professor at UNC—Wilmington, Old Dominion University, and Elon University.

Prior to entering academia, he served as a B-52G flight officer in the United States Air Force and retired from the Air Force Reserve as a Colonel (0-6). After earning his MBA, he worked in B2B sales and marketing for an electronics division of TRW, Inc.

Dr. Honeycutt has published more than 200 articles in myriad outlets, and he received recognition for best papers from the *Journal of Personal Selling & Sales Management, Marketing Education Review,* and *Journal of Marketing: Theory & Practice.* Dr. Honeycutt has also co-authored textbooks in the areas of B2B marketing, global sales management, and cross-cultural selling.

Over the past two decades he led numerous study abroad trips for his students to Australia, Belgium, China, England, and the Philippines, and taught classes in Japan.

When not working on academic pursuits, Dr. Honeycutt, his wife Laura, their son Travis, daughter-in-law Andrea, and three grandchildren travel to Costa Rica and spend time at their home in Wrightsville Beach, N.C.

 **ROBERT C. ERFFMEYER** earned his Ph.D. in Industrial/Organizational Psychology from Louisiana State University in 1981, and worked in various human resource positions in the areas of selection and training. He returned to LSU to complete a post-doctorate in marketing, and has worked in marketing and sales training for Deere & Company, Wausau Insurance Companies, and other organizations. He is a professor at the University of Wisconsin–Eau Claire, where he teaches marketing, sales and sales management courses to undergraduate and graduate students.

Dr. Erffmeyer has been actively involved in MBA on-campus and distance education efforts for 20 years. He is the MBA Director for both the University of Wisconsin—Eau Claire and the University of Wisconsin Consortium MBA Program, an online graduate program comprised of four University of Wisconsin AACSB accredited business schools. He is also the Director of Distance Learning Programs in the UW-EC College of Business.

Dr. Erffmeyer helped to establish the Great Northwoods' Sales Warm-Up—a three-day sales competition held annually at UW-Eau Claire. He is the chapter advisor for Pi Sigma Epsilon, a national sales fraternity for university students.

He has been a visiting professor in the Asian Studies Program at Kansai Gaidai University in Osaka, Japan, and has lectured in China and Viet Nam.

Dr. Erffmeyer has served in numerous officer and board positions in the Society of Marketing Advances and the Marketing Management Association. He served two terms as President of SMA and is a Fellow of the Marketing Management Association. He was the first recipient of the *Marketing Education Review* Award and has received other teaching award recognitions.

Dr. Erffmeyer has published over forty articles in outlets such as the *Journal of Personal Selling and Sales Management, Marketing Education Review, Journal of Marketing Education, Industrial Marketing Management,* and the *Journal of Business Ethics.* He has served on the editorial review boards for the *Journal of Personal Selling and Sales Management, Journal of Research in Interactive Marketing* and on the Advisory Board for the *Journal of Advancement of Marketing Education.*

Dr. Erffmeyer and his wife Gretchen, reside in Eau Claire, Wisconsin, with their daughter, Johannah. They enjoy traveling, biking, and kayaking in the Northwoods.

Strategic Planning

PART ONE

O f all the functions in an organization, none has changed as much in the past decade as sales management—except, perhaps, purchasing! The Internet, mobile technology, globalization, a greater focus on ethical behavior, and a host of other social, economic, and political changes have altered selling and sales management to such an extent that the textbook had to be written over from scratch.

No other function in the organization has the same impact on a firm's strategy as sales management. Salespeople talk directly with customers, testing the company's strategy with every sales call. Information gathered from customers by salespeople feeds directly into company strategy. These and other factors make sales management a critical part of an organization's success.

This book presents sales management in six parts. The first part, *Strategic Planning*, orients you to the role of sales in the strategy of the organization. Part Two, *Sales Leadership*, defines the leadership roles needed to create the right sales culture. Part Three, *Analyzing Customers and Markets*, examines the market, recognizing the importance of using technology to understand customers. Part Four, *Designing and Developing the Sales Force*, contains three chapters that focus on the organizational issues of sales force design and the recruiting, selecting, and training of salespeople. In Part Five, *Process Management*, the emphasis is on supervision, goal setting, motivation, and compensation issues. Finally, Part Six, *Measurement, Analysis, and Knowledge Management*, considers not only performance evaluation, but also internal and external cultural issues—and how those affect sales management.

Successful companies don't become that way by accident. They became successful because they had a plan and executed it well. The beginning of a company is its purpose, and from that purpose flows its strategy. That's why Part One, *Strategic Planning*, illustrates how the sales force and the sales function fit into the company's strategy, and how the sales force serves the company's mission.

Chapter 1, *Introduction to Sales Management*, introduces you to the activities of sales managers and sales force leaders, placing the sales force into the strategic picture of the firm. This chapter also serves as an overview of the rest of the book.

Chapter 2, *The Sales Function and Multi-Sales Channels*, explores the selling function further, examining the different types of salespeople and sales organizations that are used to reach customers. In addition, we continue the dialogue regarding strategy, relating how each of these sales force alternatives can serve a company's strategy.

1

INTRODUCTION TO SALES MANAGEMENT

LEARNING OBJECTIVES

After completing this chapter, you should be able to:

- Define the strategy hierarchy and understand how a firm's sales and marketing strategies affect its overall strategy.

- Identify the different types of selling strategies and how the selling process varies across those types.

- Describe the sales management process and the responsibilities and activities of sales managers.

What should we make? What should we sell? At what price? To whom? What kind of people should we hire, and how will we manage their work? These are the questions that define a company's strategy. In turn, the answers to these questions define the company. Yet, in the minds of a company's customers, salespeople define the company. Why? Because salespeople are often the only face of the company that customers ever see.

In essence, this book is about how corporations convert strategic questions and answers into sales practices that affect customers. Today, people recognize that aligning a firm's sales practices with its sales strategy, and its sales strategy with its corporate strategy, is central to success. Thus, in this chapter, we not only introduce the basic sales management process, but we also show how a firm's sales force is central to the broader marketing strategy the firm pursues.

Sales Manager Profile: Candace Mailand

IF SOMEONE HAD TOLD ME when I was going to university that my first job out of school would be in sales, I would have said, "Not a chance." My goal was to secure a position in advertising or public relations. Everything that I had been doing, from the courses I selected to the organizations that I was involved in on campus, was done with this goal in mind. The very last occupation that I would have considered was sales. Why? Well, because in my mind's eye, I held a number of negative, stereotypical images of what a salesperson looked like and behaved, and I didn't perceive it to be a very scrupulous profession.

So what did I do? I took a job in sales.

Sales was my first position after university, especially after I discovered—after a number of interviews—the pay scale, or lack thereof, for entry-level people in the advertising and public relations (PR) fields. To say, at that time, that I was motivated somewhat by money is an understatement. Despite working while I was going to school, I still had accumulated a number of school loans, and that debt, as well as my need to put a roof over my head and gas in my car, motivated me to accept a position with 3M. It was one of the best decisions that I made in my life.

When I interviewed for sales positions, a commonly asked question was, "Are you willing to relocate?" I was definitely open to new experiences, and after growing up in Iowa, I was ready to see a bit more of the world. Never did I expect that my first assignment would be in Philadelphia.

I was 21 years old, living in a part of the country where I had no family or friends, and was entirely on my own. That first year was a challenging one. I spent three weeks shadowing senior sales representatives and, after that third week, I was given a product catalog, a price book, a customer list, and a sample bag, and told to go out and sell. I didn't know any basic sales techniques, or possess any negotiating skills except those that were innate, let alone know what territory management was or even how to read a map. In those days, GPS didn't exist.

It wasn't until six months later that I returned to corporate headquarters to participate in a sales training program. By that time, I had already gone through the school of hard knocks and made many mistakes along the way, but it was by making those mistakes that I learned. By the time I was relocated to New York to manage a key account territory, I felt almost like a seasoned professional. Or so I thought. I still had many lessons to learn, and I feel that I continue to do so each day—even after 30 years with the company.

After a couple of years in New York, I relocated to Chicago to handle national accounts and two years later, I relocated to our corporate headquarters in St. Paul, MN, as a sales development trainer. I spent a total of six years in the field.

Was I a phenomenal sales representative? No. There were others who I admired for their ability to spin a story and negotiate. What I had going for me was my work ethic, my ability to connect with people, the time I took understanding my customers' businesses and the customers that they served. I developed strong connections with my customers and they soon came to learn that I was reliable, honest, and wouldn't compromise what I knew to be ethically right. I also didn't forget who wrote my paycheck, and I have always had a sense of loyalty to this company that believed in me and gave me a start after college. To this day, I go to work every day believing that 3M doesn't owe me a job. I earn the right to work here each and every day.

CANDACE MAILAND
Sales Innovation Manager
3M

After coming to corporate headquarters as a trainer, I soon transitioned into many other different roles—marketing and sales-related—eventually becoming a marketing operations manager and, later, a national sales manager. My career path at 3M was in a state of constant change, and yet it was change itself that I embraced—almost thrived on it for lack of a better description. For it is through change that we continue to learn, and evolve and grow personally and professionally. Some people don't respond well to change. That has never been an issue for me.

So many career moves so quickly might faze some, but I've always been comfortable leading teams—especially having been a rep and carried the bag. It is because of my experience in the field that I feel I was a more effective marketer. With every job I've ever had, there's always been a process I followed, doing a deep dive into understanding how things have been done and what the processes are, and then beginning to ask myself, "what if." This process focus has enabled me to quickly grasp what needed to be done, what could be done, and how to succeed.

Now, as the leader of 3M's Frontline Sales Initiative—3M's collaborative partnership with universities that offer sales education programs—I identify and recruit talented college students into sales positions. I believe hiring and developing people is the most important thing a sales manager can do. I am truly committed to making sure the people who are hired through my efforts are well prepared and set up for success. When I look back on my career, I would say that one of the most rewarding things for me is in seeing how successful many of those that I've hired out of school have been. It's not because of me—I just opened a door. They walked through it, but perhaps I played just a little part in helping jump-start things for them.

Sales management offers a career that can be filled with opportunity. Life is often a full circle—to start in sales and now be in the position of bringing top talent into sales straight out of college—is intrinsically very rewarding. The talent on university campuses today is truly amazing, and some of that talent resides right here at 3M. I'd say that the company is in very good hands. ■

One of the oldest truisms of business is that "nothing happens until someone sells something." Clearly, without salespeople selling the output of businesses, some businesses would cease to exist. Nonetheless, many people believe the sales profession is not a noble endeavor. Visions of cheesy, aggressive, badly-dressed product-pushers dominate their view of sales. Professional buyers know better, though. These buyers rely on salespeople to bring them solutions to the business problems that challenge them. Product knowledge, technical expertise, and business acumen are all required to satisfactorily serve the customer and the company's needs.

Companies also know better. Richard Langlotz, vice-president of Konica-Minolta Business Systems, says, "Our salespeople who recognize that our business is more than pushing products and is more about building partnerships actually sell two to three times as much as those who just push products. We can't afford to keep product pushers around."

Yet, year in and year out, executives say that the sales position is one of the hardest positions to fill.[1] Sales is also one of the most expensive activities a company undertakes, consuming more than 20 percent, on average, of a firm's revenue.[2] For all of these reasons, managing the sales force is one of the most important jobs in a company.

As a career opportunity, starting in sales is an excellent choice. Starting salaries for salespeople are significantly greater than for other positions (about 20 percent greater than other marketing positions).[3] Many CEOs, such as Mark Hurd of Oracle, got their start in sales, and along the way, sales managers tend to earn more than their counterparts in other areas. Further, the predictions are that the jobs in sales will grow at a much faster rate than other professions.[4] The future for sales and sales force management is pretty bright!

From Sales Rep to Sales Manager

While we will discuss types of sales management and leadership positions later, some discussion is needed about the sales management career to reach the right perspective. Sales managers are *not* super salespeople—in fact, many of the characteristics of successful salespeople, such as the ability to work independently, may not be useful characteristics for sales managers. Pat Metz, sales manager for Abbott Laboratories, realized being a sales manager was different the first day after his promotion from salesperson. His boss ordered him to fire a salesperson he had never met. That's when he realized that being a sales manager means "you're a manager of people."[5]

Sam Mays of Konica-Minolta Business Systems discovered that his gift for selling did not transfer to sales management. After several years as a sales manager, doing a poor job and hating every minute of it, he was demoted by his boss. "It was the best move for everyone," says Mays. Within a month, he was back on top of the sales lists and much happier. Mays now laughs about it. "When I was promoted, the company lost a good salesperson and gained a bad manager; now the company has a good salesperson again, and the opportunity to hire a better manager."

Being a sales manager means coaching salespeople so they can improve; developing strategies and delegating the responsibility for implementation to others; trying to figure out how to motivate people, some who are nearly twice your age; and convincing others in the organization that what is right for the sales force is right for their departments, too. Because being a sales manager can be so different than being a salesperson, sales success is not the primary reason for promotion. In fact, research has consistently shown that sales success is a poor predictor of success as a sales manager.[6] Companies have to have the right skill set and abilities in a sales manager—skills and abilities that differ from those for sales.

A case in point: One day, while still a sales rep, Jill Amerie (now president of Skyline Displays) ran into her sales manager, who had tears running down her face. Her manager said she was frustrated with the members of her sales team—including Amerie—because they didn't listen to her. "They've seen that I was successful [as a salesperson], so I don't understand why they just don't do exactly what I did so they'll be successful," her boss told her.

Amerie pondered this statement and replied, "Have you asked them if they want to be just like you?" She says the experience still resonates with her today as she mentors her own team. That's why she prefers to call herself a sales mentor, rather than a sales manager. "My advice to other sales mentors who were former sales representatives is not to lose sight of where you came from," she says. "Remember what it was like when you were the sales rep and use those positive and negative experiences to make you a better mentor/manager. Take time to learn about your team. Learn what motivates them. Learn what their passion is and coach them on how they can integrate that passion into their career."

This is a book about sales force management—or sales management, for short. We define **sales management** as the set of activities required to lead, direct, or supervise the personal selling efforts of an organization.[7] This definition has several important aspects. The first aspect relates to what sales managers do to manage sales*people*. Our primary objective of the book is to explain this function of managing salespeople. However, because strategy is so crucial, we also discuss many of the day-to-day tasks that sales managers perform to further a firm's strategy for meeting its goals. Having laid this foundation, we developed a framework for the rest of the book.

ETHICS IN SALES MANAGEMENT   **Fake It to Make It?**

After graduating college with a finance and economics degree, Tait Cruse sent his résumé to Northwestern Mutual. A year later, they called, hired him, and put him to work in Dallas. "Everything seemed fine for about eight months, but suddenly it all crashed," recalls Cruse.

Driving into work, he was run off the road and totaled his car. The night before, his girlfriend had broken up with him, telling him he was going nowhere and had no career. He walked from the accident to the office, realizing that he was failing. With no leads, no appointments, and nothing to do, he just sat there all day and reflected, reaching some important conclusions.

"First, I realized that I should have been committed from day one to being successful. I hadn't been committed to the training, to the sales process, and to my customers. I realized I needed to be a student of people, relationships, and sales."

Cruse goes on to say that he was carrying a "fake it until you make it mentality." To him, this meant he wasn't being true to himself—that he was pretending to be something he wasn't. And that wasn't ethical—it wasn't right. Cruse realized that, while he could inflate the number of calls he made or exaggerate the quality of those calls when talking with a manager, he was really only hurting himself. "I had the 'fake it until you make it' mentality, and I wasn't making it."

"I had to ask myself if I was passionately pursuing helping people or only worried about my quota. I realized that, if I focused on truly helping people, then the quota would take care of itself." But he also had to keep this passion in front of him. "I had to write my goals down, track my activities, and make sure that I was doing the right things so that I could help as many people as I could."

He went to his boss at 5:30 that evening and described the factors he thought he needed to focus on to be successful. "My boss was surprised, and he told me that he was actually in the process of writing me a letter telling me I had 30 days to bring my numbers up or I was going to be fired. I asked him for a year to prove myself." A year later, Tait Cruse was the top rep in the country among those with under two years of experience. "When I became focused on helping others, I freed myself to be honest and ethical. That is what turned my career around as a salesperson; that is what is making my career as a sales executive successful."

The Parameters of the Firm's Strategy: The Mission Statement

A **strategy** is a plan designed to accomplish a mission. A **mission** is a set of objectives. In military terms, a mission might be the objectives set for a unit—a brigade, for example—for a campaign, or for a longer-term goal, such as Operation Enduring Freedom, the coalition forces' mission for building peace in Afghanistan. Because most companies are in business for the long haul, they tend to think of missions in longer terms, rather than as a single campaign. Often companies summarize their goals in a **mission statement**, such as those found in Exhibit 1.1. (You can usually find a company's mission statement by looking at its public financial statements or going to its website.) Corporate planners, including a variety of upper-management personnel from areas such as finance, manufacturing, and sales, are responsible for creating the mission of the organization and articulating the mission statement.

Mission statements should reflect a company's core values, serve to inspire the members of the organization, give purpose to their actions, and guide them when making decisions.[8] A good mission statement does more than simply organize the company's objectives; it also serves as a standard against which decisions and actions can be compared, to ensure that they are the right decisions and actions for the organization. Once the mission's objectives are set, strategy can be created.

EXHIBIT 1.1	Sample Mission Statements
AstraZeneca	The people of AstraZeneca are dedicated to: • Discovering, developing and delivering innovative pharmaceutical solutions. • Enriching the lives of patients, families, communities, and other stakeholders. • Creating a challenging and rewarding work environment for everyone.
Chick-Fil-A	Be America's Best Quick-Service Restaurant.
Coca-Cola	To refresh the world in body, mind, and spirit. To inspire moments of optimism through our brands and our actions. To create value and make a difference everywhere we engage.
Hilti	***Enthusiastic customers*** We create success for our customers by identifying their needs and providing innovative and value-adding solutions. ***Build a better future*** We foster a company climate in which every team member is valued and able to grow. We develop win-win relationships with our partners and suppliers. We embrace our responsibility towards society and environment. We aim to achieve significant and sustainable, profitable growth, thus securing our freedom of action.
IBM	At IBM, we strive to lead in the invention, development and manufacture of the industry's most advanced information technologies, including computer systems, software, storage systems, and microelectronics.
NCR	We are the new NCR: Leading how the world connects, interacts, and transacts with business. Our people offer a broad perspective that enables our customers to reach their goals and transform their business models. Our size, scale, and stability instill confidence in the marketplace.

The Strategy Hierarchy

A firm's corporate **strategy** encompasses its plans and goals for the entire organization. The corporate planners are responsible for creating the mission of the organization, such as the mission statements described in Exhibit 1.1. Corporate strategy will also address questions, in a general sense, such as what markets and sourcing options (such as manufacturing) the company should engage. For example, corporate planners might choose to outsource sales by hiring distributors versus hiring a sales force. Or the firm might outsource its manufacturing function and focus the bulk of its efforts on marketing the products.

Once the company's strategy is formulated, it is then communicated to the firm's various business units—marketing, sales, manufacturing, and others—whose leaders create their own plans to support the corporate strategy. The flow of strategy from the organizational level to the unit level is called the **strategy hierarchy**, shown in Exhibit 1.2. Note that the firm's marketing plan is likely to precede its sales plan. This order does not imply that sales executives do not participate in the process until after the firm's marketing plan is done. Rather, marketing and sales should work together to create an overall marketing strategy.[9] Then the sales leadership team must create action plans specifically for salespeople to carry out the strategy. A key factor in reaching plan objectives is then getting salespeople to buy into the plan; if there is too much separation from those who create the plan from those who execute it, there is a greater probability of the plan being improperly executed, leaving goals unreached.[10]

Microsoft's corporate strategy flows to each functional area, including sales, which then determines the sales strategy needed to support that corporate strategy.

EXHIBIT 1.2   Strategy Hierarchy

An abbreviated example of how strategy might be different at different levels of the organization.

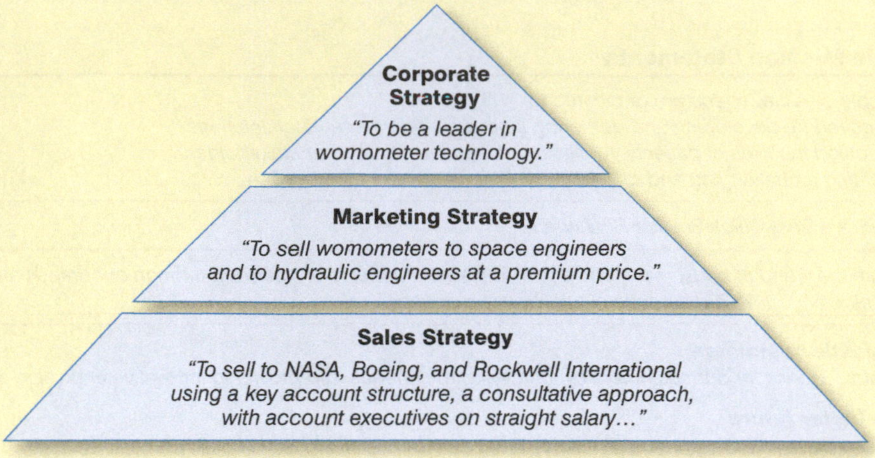

Corporate Strategy
"To be a leader in womometer technology."

Marketing Strategy
"To sell womometers to space engineers and to hydraulic engineers at a premium price."

Sales Strategy
"To sell to NASA, Boeing, and Rockwell International using a key account structure, a consultative approach, with account executives on straight salary…"

At the marketing level, planners have to answer the following four questions with much greater specificity than was done at the corporate level:

- What markets do we serve with what products?

- What types of relationships do we form, and with whom?

- What level of investment will be required, and how will we locate and allocate the needed resources?

- What are the detailed objectives and action plans?

What Markets Do We Serve with What Products?

In certain situations, the product defines the company. Consider, for example, Salesforce.com, which was built around sales automation technology. At other times, a natural market such as a geographical area might define a company. An example might be steel mills in Pennsylvania, located near iron ore and coal deposits needed to manufacture steel. Yet, when market conditions changed, both Salesforce and the mills had to carefully consider what markets they wanted to serve and with what products. Salesforce had to add social media and marketing automation technology to its lineup in order to compete. Steel mills had to address global competition and, in some instances, begin making other products, such as fiberglass. These changes required carefully considering potential markets.

The implications of a firm's product and market choices can be dramatic. Consider IBM, Apple, and Dell. All three companies used to sell personal computer (PC) products, but with very different product and market strategies. IBM ultimately chose to leave the PC market and focus on services; Apple, with products like the iPad, has become a dominant player in several new electronics markets; and Dell discovered that, to continue to grow, it had to focus as much on markets for products that include computers (such as airport kiosks for printing boarding passes).

The challenge is to find a **sustainable competitive advantage**, something that gives a company an edge in the market over time. Expertise, technology, or a patent that is difficult to copy can provide a competitive advantage. If the product is easy to copy and not patented, others will imitate it. If the advantage is based on price, the most efficient company wins. Finding a sustainable competitive advantage is perhaps the most difficult aspect of any strategic plan.

If the strategic planner creates a product-market grid like the one shown in Exhibit 1.3, a company can grow in four ways. First, a firm can seek increased **market penetration**; that is, it can try to gain more market share with its existing products. Market penetration is often about trying to find more customers like the ones who are already buying your products. Finding new customers is an important task for salespeople, and vital to the ongoing success of a firm. SAP, a company that makes software for business operations, has acquired several smaller companies in order to gain the products needed to attract new customers—customers who can then purchase the full line of SAP products.

EXHIBIT 1.3 Achieving Growth via Products and Markets

	Current Markets	New Markets
Current Products	*Market Penetration* HP creates "full line contracts" to encourage customers to buy all HP products.	*Market Development* Intel sells computer chips for use in John Deere tractors.
New Products	*Product Development* Dell adds consumer electronics such as cameras.	*Diversification* Carlson Marketing expands from selling promotional trips to promotional products, such as cups and caps.

Second, a company can grow through **product development**, which involves creating new products in order to increase business with the company's existing customers. Another term for this strategy is **account penetration**, because it involves selling more products to the same accounts. Salesforce is following this strategy, not only by adding social media marketing automation tools, but also by introducing general accounting and finance software that will put the company into competition with Oracle and SAP.

Third, a company can try to find new markets, employing the **market development** approach. Potential new markets can include new countries or new industries in which to sell the company's existing products. An example is the computer-chipmaker Intel. Intel found a way to increase its sales by putting computer chips in John Deere tractors. Today, the same type of chips used to measure the pressure of car tires now measures the pressure of tractor tires.

Fourth, **diversification** involves combining new products and new markets. For example, Carlson Marketing Group began as a travel agency selling trips to companies that wanted to reward their top salespeople or favorite customers by sending them on exotic trips. Carlson then expanded into other areas, such as the market for promotional products.

Risks associated with diversification are far greater than those accompanying other market expansion approaches, because it requires developing *both* new products *and* new markets. The company cannot leverage its existing relationships with its customers, and it may not be able to leverage its existing technology. Indeed, the annals of business history are littered with failed diversification attempts. When the strategy works, however, it can pay off tremendously.

What Types of Relationships Do We Form and with Whom?

Companies do not operate in a vacuum—they have suppliers, customers, and competitors who operate in a network. Touch one and, like ripples on a pond's

Service technicians that repair products, such as these solar panels, are part of the total product offer, and their service may be more important in the purchase decision and ownership satisfaction than the product itself.

surface, others are affected. A strategic plan should consider the network of relationships within which the company operates or wants to operate. This network includes its relationships with (potential) investors, bankers, suppliers of raw materials or components, sources of personnel (like your university), government regulatory agencies, and many more. For example, with which distributors will the company attempt to form close relationships so that its products have a greater likelihood of success? What customers are better served through transactional strategies and transactional channels? These are the types of questions that must be answered as part of a company's relationship strategy.

Relationship strategy is growing in importance, in part because more firms are in the business of providing services than ever before. Further, this growth in services occurs because sustainable competitive advantages are more likely to be gained by providing intangible resources such as expertise and relationships—things that are hard to imitate. Called the **service dominant logic**, the idea is that being in business is essentially about serving the needs of others.[11] Whether or not the company actually makes a tangible product, the real advantage lies in how the organization serves its customers' needs. Therefore, all companies, in all lines of business, should try to gain a service advantage.

Frequently, a service advantage is a function of the quality of relationships with customers. Relationships are the vehicle by which needs are understood—the stronger the relationship, the more that is known by both parties about both parties. The more that is known, the better able one is to serve the other. Consider the fashion industry. At the retail level, products are often similar. Stores that sell to college students, for example, will have similar styles. These stores are competing for a share of the average college student's expenditures on clothing. Some students claim that they spend $500 per month on clothing. A more reasonable average figure might be $200. At $200 per month, or $2,400 per year, the average college student will spend more than $10,000 before graduating, given that the average time to graduate is now four and a half years. Now walk into any store near campus. Do they treat you like a $10,000 customer? Yet the average college student's **customer lifetime value**, or the sum of all of the purchases made over a customer's lifetime, is worth a significant amount.

What these figures illustrate is that your lifetime value to that local store is worth far more than the average single purchase. Consequently, you might think stores would realize that building a stronger relationship would be an effective strategy. Few retailers, though, invest in such a strategy; contrast that with companies that rely heavily on salespeople, particularly operating from a service-dominant logic perspective and you can see that those salespeople are far more likely to invest in relationship strategies.

Customer Relationship Management (CRM) is the process of identifying and grouping customers in order to develop an appropriate relationship strategy so that the organization can acquire, retain, and grow the business. A firm's sales and marketing teams are responsible for customer relationship management. **Customer acquisition strategies**, or plans to obtain new customers, can include marketing activities such as telephone prospecting and attending trade shows to identify potential customers. **Customer retention strategies**, or plans designed to keep customers, might include making quarterly visits to current customers or inviting them to technology shows to see the firm's newest products. **Growth strategies** are plans that are designed to increase sales to the same customers. (Recall the earlier discussion on account penetration.) These strategies might include offering special discounts to customers when they make larger purchases.

What Level of Investment Will Be Required, and How Will We Allocate the Needed Resources?

Another important aspect of strategic planning involves finding the capital, or resources, necessary to accomplish the firm's plan. Resources include money, of course, but can also take the form of human and social capital. **Human capital** refers to the people that make up an organization. For example, a firm that has more highly skilled salespeople will have a greater degree of human capital that can be invested into sales strategies.[12] **Social capital**, or the ties that the firm has with others, can also be drawn upon as a resource.[13] At its simplest, social capital is who owes you a favor or who can be asked a favor. An historic example dating from the early 1980s concerns Chrysler. At one point, the firm was within days of declaring bankruptcy when David Kearns, the CEO of Xerox Corporation, called Lee Iacocca, the CEO of Chrysler. Kearns asked Iacocca how many cars must be sold for the company to stay afloat—Chrysler, after all, was a good Xerox customer. Iacocca told him, and he responded by placing an order for that many. The social capital between the two firms saved Chrysler long enough for other financing to be put into place and return the firm to solid footing.

For the sales executive, human capital decisions include determining how many salespeople the firm needs, what skills and experience they must have, and what training they require. Other decisions might include whether to hire inside salespeople to work in a call center or to outsource that activity and who should handle customer service (a sales rep or a customer service rep).

What Are the Detailed Objectives and Action Plans?

Review again the mission statements in Exhibit 1.1. What is NCR's business? Coca-Cola's? IBM's? Notice that these mission statements do not fully answer questions about what products the company will produce or what markets they will serve. Nor do the statements answer questions about the firm's objectives and plans. Again, marketing and sales leaders are tasked with making these objectives and plans more specific. For example, a strategic plan might include such objectives as achieving a market share of 10 percent by the end of the year, or sales of $500 million in the firm's fourth quarter.

One set of criteria for establishing objectives is the **SMART** format. According to the SMART acronym, firms' objectives should be:

- **S**pecific
- **M**easurable
- **A**chievable, yet challenging
- **R**ealistic
- **T**ime-based

For example, an objective to simply "increase market share" is not *specific* enough. As a manager, you need to ask yourself how much the company needs to increase market share. If the objective is to increase customer loyalty, then loyalty must be *measured*—perhaps by recording the number of your customers' repeat purchases. If the objective is to double market share, then you need to determine whether such an ambitious goal is *achiev*able or even *realistic*. Finally, the objective needs to be *time-based*. Will it be met in the next month, year, or decade?

SMART objectives can motivate managers and salespeople alike. These objectives can also be used to hold managers accountable. After all, without deadlines and other specifics, managers might claim they have achieved the firm's objectives when, in fact, they have not. **Milestones**, or important short-term objectives, can help mark the company's progress toward achieving its long-term objectives. Milestones can also be used to determine when the plan is off course so that adjustments can be made. For example, a company may set a goal to become the market leader, though it currently ranks fifth. Milestones may be goals, such as taking over the third spot in the market one year and moving up to second the following year. The ultimate goal is still to be first, but milestones help the company determine whether it is on track to reach the ultimate goal.

Along with setting objectives, a good strategic plan features detailed action plans, or steps that will be taken in order to accomplish those objectives. Effective action plans specify who will undertake each activity and when that activity will occur. At this point, the firm's strategy begins to involve salespeople and the sales process.

Selling Approaches

A recent study of more than 1,500 sales executives found that 55 percent have no formal sales process or sales model in their organizations.[14] This finding is disturbing, because it means that a lot of companies just throw salespeople out into the field and hope they will figure out how to perform their jobs. Moreover, how can sales supervisors manage salespeople if there is no standard approach? How can one rep's performance be compared to that of another? Of course, a manager can simply look at sales levels and tell if one rep is doing better than another. But how would that manager help either rep improve performance and results?

GLOBAL SALES MANAGEMENT   Transforming Sales Organizations

There's no question that the world is changing—and that the world of selling is no different. Social media, the Internet, and other data sources are combining to empower buyers, which makes selling in today's global environment very different.

SunGard, a leading provider of software and technology services around the globe, found its sales force stuck in old ways of doing things. To make matters worse, there was no one old way; the company had grown by acquisition and over 160 acquisitions meant over 160 old ways of doing things. To build a single system meant making sure the company's salespeople understood buyers' needs and their decision processes. Transformation also meant changing everything in sales management, from hiring and selection, to training and development, to compensation and motivation. Within a year's time, it meant replacing 25 percent of the sales force—but benefits included a doubling of sales by those new salespeople. Now the company is fast on its way to accomplishing a sales plan of $1 billion in revenue.

GE Healthcare Global Solutions' challenge was a bit different. The selling process was a good one; the challenge, or so they thought, was figuring out the right strategy—given all the various global healthcare systems. Then Fran Dierskmeier, general manager, stumbled across an article that suggested a more provocative approach to customers would work. He recognized that, if hospital executives failed to see the challenges facing them, they'd never recognize the value in the GE Healthcare service. But this approach would look very different based on the country's healthcare system; no single approach would work. Where it works, though, it works well, cutting the sales cycle in half.

Heather Baldwin (October 17, 2013), "War Stories of Success", *Selling Power Magazine*, 24; Henry Canaday (October 17, 2013), "Selling the New SunGard Way," *Selling Power Magazine*, 17–20.

A company should have a standard sales method. However, because customers make buying decisions differently, there will obviously be variations in the selling techniques successful salespeople use.[15] That said, most markets are comprised of buyers who tend to make decisions in similar ways. Buyers can be grouped by how they make decisions, and formal sales processes can be designed for each group.

Contemporary research shows four basic models of selling: transactional, problem-solving or consultative, affiliative, and enterprise selling. The first method, **transactional selling**, is designed to get the sale over with as quickly and as easily as possible. The key to success is making as many calls as possible to as many people as possible; little thought is given to the lifetime value of customers. An example might be life insurance salespeople who have only one product to sell—once a buyer has bought it, there is nothing else to sell, so the salesperson moves on. Simple products also tend to be sold this way: The buyer is well aware of the options and can decide without a lot of help.

Consultative salespeople help buyers identify and solve problems. They work to fully understand the buyers' needs, then ensure that the product solves those needs. In this instance, the consultant is showing buyers how to use the product.

Affiliative selling is based on a friendship between the salesperson and the individual buyer. Tupperware and Premier Jewelry parties rely heavily on affiliative selling, but affiliative selling also occurs in business settings. For example, if all products a buyer is considering are the same, but post-sales service is critical, the buyer will be inclined to purchase products sold by a friend who can be counted upon. An example is heavy mining equipment, for which there are only a few manufacturers. Distributors of the equipment all carry a similar lineup of machines. If a machine goes down, mining operations might come to a halt, costing the company thousands of dollars a day. In such a situation, trust is likely to be more important than product specs, so a mining company's buyer will tend to purchase machinery from a trustworthy friend.

Consultative selling involves identifying and solving a client's problems; for this reason, it is also called **needs-satisfaction selling** or **problem/solution selling**. The process typically involves asking prospective clients a number of questions in order to determine their needs and then presenting solutions to those needs.[16]

A consultative form, **challenger selling**, has emerged recently, based on a study of strategies employed by more than 2,500 salespeople.[17] A small group uses its collective industry and customer knowledge to challenge a customer's way of operating, thereby providing greater value by helping the customer identify previously hidden or misunderstood opportunities or threats.

Enterprise selling is a business-to-business (B2B) concept that reflects, at its best, a strategic partnership between buying and selling organizations. The strategy is based not only on person-to-person relationships, but also on company-to-company relationships. An account manager (salesperson) initially captures, maintains, and grows a customer's business. However, the account manager's firm knows that the entire enterprise is needed to satisfy the customer. Moreover, the customer is not just one person, but an entire company (or at least a large portion of it). For example, when GE sells jet engines to Boeing, engineering departments in both companies work closely to design the engines for the final plane, with implications for fuel systems, control systems, and fuselage design. Further, the process has implications for both companies' finance departments, which must work together to ensure that both organizations have enough capital at the right times. A GE account manager coordinates all joint efforts. When engaged in enterprise selling, a GE salesperson will, at times, utilize affiliative selling, transactional selling, and consultative selling—all within an enterprise-level strategy. The salesperson's choice of selling model, in this case, depends on how the buyer needs to buy at that time. Regardless of the model of selling, a sales call conforms to a basic structure. In the next section, we review that structure and identify how it varies for each selling model.

The Selling Process

The eight steps of the sales process, as illustrated in Exhibit 1.4, are prospecting, pre-approach, approach, needs identification, presentation, handling objections, closing, and implementation/follow-up. Note that, at times, these steps may occur in that sequence. In other situations, salespeople may find that the steps occur in a different order, or repeat, or that some may be skipped. We'll discuss how these work when we discuss each step in more detail.

Prospecting

Prospecting involves identifying potential customers for a particular product or service. A **prospect** is a **MAD** buyer, or someone with the **M**oney to spend, the **A**uthority to buy what you are selling, and the **D**esire to buy it (although the buyer's desire might not be specifically for *your* product, at least he or she *has* a desire). The process of finding prospects involves several steps. The first step is to identify a **lead**, or someone who appears to have the characteristics of a prospect. That is, the person *appears* to have a need (desire), money, and authority. The salesperson must still qualify the lead—determine that the person has the money, authority, and desire—later.

Pre-Approach

During the pre-approach stage, which precedes the salesperson's talking with the customer, the salesperson tries to learn everything possible about the account. Perhaps, using contact management software, the salesperson can explore the account's history with the firm to predict the customer's needs. Or, using the Internet or by searching a third-party database (Hoover's or Dun & Bradstreet), the salesperson can examine the account's financial strength and future strategies. The salesperson might also try to find out what can be learned about the industry in which the account operates.

While the pre-approach stage can take a significant amount of time, a salesperson might do little, if any, pre-approach planning in the prospecting stage. That's

EXHIBIT 1.4   Eight Steps in the Selling Process

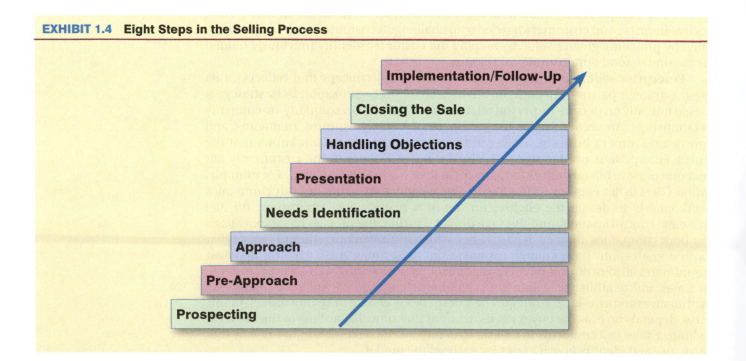

because the needed information is held by the buyer (versus, say, a database). Later in the process, pre-approach planning (also called pre-call planning) becomes more necessary to ensure that progress is made toward an eventual sale. Note that a well-prepared salesperson is more likely to gain trust. Preparation signals that the salesperson is knowledgeable, competent, and cares about the customer.

Approach

The approach step can be difficult. At this stage, the salesperson must ask the buyer to commit to a meeting without really knowing what he or she needs or wants. To obtain this commitment, the salesperson must make an opening statement to get the buyer's attention, creating that desire for a conversation. A good opening statement causes the buyer to focus on the salesperson, dropping all other activities or thoughts. For example, a salesperson may say something like, "Hi, my name is Dana from BPT Partners, and our firm is helping companies increase sales by upwards of 20 percent. May I have a few minutes to explore whether BPT could do that for you?" This statement is a good one, because the seller focuses on the potential for increasing sales. Alternatively, if the seller says, "Hi, my name is Dana and I'd like to sell you CRM software," the focus is entirely on the seller's goal. This statement is not likely to get that salesperson anywhere.

How does the approach differ when the salesperson and buyer meet for the third or fourth time? A good opening statement is still needed to get a time commitment from your customer. (The thirtieth sales call can probably begin with more of a social greeting.)

Needs Identification

The next step is the needs-identification step in which the salesperson confirms that the prospect has money, authority, and desire. The needs-identification step is comprised of three important elements. The first element is the use of SPIN®, New Base®, or other questioning techniques to determine the customer's needs. Questioning can take quite a while in a complex, custom-sales situation—such as Teradata salespeople face when selling specialized computer systems for database storage—or just a few minutes when selling a simple product. For example, using SPIN:

Seller: (**Situation Question**)	How do you currently store all of the data you get each day from your stores?
Buyer:	*They are stored in the transactional system at each store until we pull the data we need to run specific reports.*
Seller: (**Problem Question**)	Do you ever encounter problems because you can't get some data quickly enough?
Buyer:	*Yes, sometimes executives ask questions and it might take a few days to get them an answer.*
Seller: (**Implication Question**)	How has that gone over?
Buyer:	*They're not very happy about it when it happens. I think it has hurt us get the budget we need to build a better analytical process.*
Seller: (**Needs-Payoff Question**)	So—a data warehouse that would allow you to consolidate all data into one place—would that solve your challenge?
Buyer:	*Yes, I really think that would help.*

The second element is the identification of the decision process elements facing the customer (authority to purchase). The third is gaining pre-commitment. A **pre-commitment** is an agreement that all of the customer's needs have been identified, a budget has been identified, and the decision process is known. In other words, the pre-commitment sets the "rules" for the sale and confirms that the buyer is MAD (has money, authority and desire). In a transactional sale, there may be no needs-identification portion to the sales call. In many instances, the buyer already understands what is needed, or the needs are so similar across customers that the salesperson can simply focus on the presentation.

Qualifying the lead for MAD status is important; failure to do so can have many negative consequences. The most obvious consequence is that the salesperson wastes time with someone who may like the product but isn't allowed to make that decision. SRI-IIST is a business that scans documents for electronic indexing. Byron Williams, salesperson for SRI-IIST, had just such an experience. "I spent several hours with the office administrator of a law firm, even doing several sample jobs at no cost, only to find out the decision had to be made by the managing partner. I had to start over with her, so it took twice as long to sell this account as it should have." Williams notes that he could have made another sale somewhere else, too, had he started with the managing partner.

Presentation

During the presentation, the salesperson describes the product and how it meets the buyer's needs. Now the salesperson is playing by the rules—presenting how those needs can be met and providing the right information to the right people so a decision can be made. A sophisticated product such as a Cessna Citation executive jet has many features—so many, in fact, that a salesperson could put the buyer to sleep by explaining everything the plane does. Thus, during the presentation, the seller focuses on only those features that buyer needs.

One approach to presentations is to string together a series of **FEBAs**, or statements of Feature, Evidence, Benefit, and Agreement. Using this approach, the salesperson begins with a characteristic or feature of the product. For example, a pharmaceutical salesperson might say something like "Placron reduces cholesterol to safe levels." Then evidence is provided: "As you can see in this clinical study, the reduction has been to well under 200 in about 85 percent of all patients who did not respond to competitive drugs." Note that the evidence is written or visual. Whenever possible, the salesperson should offer tangible evidence that is credible. (A clinical study is usually completed by an objective third party and published in a journal or as a monograph. It is thus both credible and tangible.) The salesperson then ties that feature back to the need mentioned by the customer; in this case, "So as you noted, you would have fewer patients with difficulty lowering their cholesterol." Describing how a feature satisfies a need asserts a **benefit**. Finally, the salesperson asks the customer if the product meets the need, gaining agreement: "Is this the type of cholesterol-reducing program you are looking for?"

One advantage of the FEBA approach is that the potential buyer participates in the process; the presentation is not just one-sided. Furthermore, the salesperson is checking to ensure that the customer agrees that the product will meet the company's needs. This reduces the likelihood of a customer raising objections, which we discuss next.

Handling Objections

Objections are reasons a buyer gives for declining to buy your product. They can occur any time during the sales call, not necessarily during or immediately after the presentation. For example, a salesperson might hear an objection as soon as introductions are made: "You are with what company? Oh, you guys are terrible—I hate your products!"

Most objections, though, come near the end of the sales call. Even with good needs-identification and strong FEBA statements, customers sometimes realize they left out a need earlier, they conclude that the product won't meet their needs, misunderstand something the seller says, or simply do not want to buy the product at the present time. No matter what reason lies behind the objection, the salesperson should probe to determine what lies at the root of the concern and then seek to resolve it. In some instances, the concern is legitimate; only when the product's other benefits outweigh the concern should the buyer go ahead and make the purchase.

Closing the Sale

A salesperson asks the buyer for the sale during the **close**, but that's not the only time the salesperson asks for a commitment. When a salesperson asks for an appointment, permission to make a presentation, or some other commitment, the request is for a form of closing.

Closing the sale should be a natural part of the selling process and no surprise to the buyer. At this point, the buyer has already said several times that the features of the product meet the stated needs, a budget has already been discussed, and an implementation schedule for the product's delivery has been developed. When the seller asks for the order, the asking should be a logical conclusion of the selling/buying process.

In addition to asking for the order, though, a good close accomplishes several other objectives. The decision should be reinforced by the seller and the implementation schedule confirmed. In this way, the buyer leaves the meeting feeling secure in her decision and aware of what will happen next. In addition, a good salesperson always thanks the buyer for the business and asks for a referral.

If the salesperson reaches the close of the sales call but is turned down, a "thank you" is still appropriate. Most experienced salespeople are disappointed with a rejection, but they have learned not to take it personally. One way to view such a situation is that the buyer is not saying, "No, not ever," but rather, "No, not now." Like an athlete who lost a game but has the rest of the season, these salespeople know that there will be more decisions made by that buyer, so it is important to still treat the buyer with respect and lay the groundwork for future sales.

Implementation/Follow-Up

Following the close and, assuming a sale has been made, the customer has to accept delivery of the product. The salesperson's job may then be to ensure that the customer has a good experience with the product. This responsibility might include training the buyer on how the product works, explaining how to obtain service, and informing the buyer of any related policies or procedures.

Follow-up does not stop with the initial training, however. Richard Langlotz, now a vice-president for Konica-Minolta Business Systems, realized that he could achieve his quota by simply selling current customers a new system. Therefore, he instituted a practice of regular follow-up to ensure that the products were still meeting customers' needs, that there were no service or billing problems, and that everything was going smoothly. His regular follow-up set him apart from competitors who would sell and then forget their customers. As word of his service spread, he found it easier to sell to new clients, too.

The Selling Process versus the Selling Approach

The selling process is a constant cycle of prospecting, presenting, and closing. Whether the model is transactional, affiliative, consultative, or enterprise, the basic process is similar. As we explained, in a transactional situation, little time is spent on needs identification. You might simply have to ask customers which products they need and how many of them. The emphasis in the selling process is on the presentation, and a key to being successful is to make as many presentations as possible.

Similarly, affiliative selling may not require a long needs-identification process. The selling process takes place within an ongoing relationship-building process. More emphasis is given to follow-up because it is during this step that the relationship with the customer is built. Consultative selling emphasizes the needs-identification stage. The complexity of the buyer's situation will make it necessary for the salesperson to spend a great deal of time, relatively speaking, on understanding the situation and needs. With enterprise selling, the seller will engage in consultative, affiliative, and transactional selling at different times and with different products. The result is that the emphasis shifts, depending on the situation within the account.

These different models, and their variations on the process of selling, create many challenges for sales leaders. Executives and managers have a number of responsibilities in order to create, prepare, and lead an effective sales force. In the next section, their responsibilities are introduced, many of which merit a full chapter later in the book.

Sales Leaders

There are different levels of sales managers. Near the bottom of the organizational chart, field sales force managers directly manage the firm's salespeople and may even have some customers to handle. (Most experts agree that sales managers should only manage, not sell.) At the top of the organizational chart, sales executives lead the company's sales efforts, sometimes across several different sales organizations. A sales executive might also be responsible for choosing the company's distributors, deciding how the firm's products are sold on the website, and making other broad sales-related decisions. How the responsibilities of a sales leader are divided up and organized can vary with the size of the organization, the industry in which it operates, or the scope of the market. Levels in the organization can include local, regional, or other operating units. For example, Exhibit 1.5 shows two sales organizations' charts, illustrating how companies can vary; Konica-Minolta has several levels of managers, while Elk really only has two. For our purposes of understanding the roles and responsibilities of sales managers and leaders, we focus on both ends of the spectrum, beginning with those tasks and responsibilities typically carried out by a sales executive.

The Sales Executive

The first responsibility of the sales executive is to lead the sales force in achieving its goals. In doing so, the executive also sets the policies the firm's sales managers and salespeople must follow. In general, though, sales executives complete four activities —planning, organizing, implementing, and monitoring.

PLANNING We've already discussed how sales executives are involved in the overall strategic planning process. However, they are also responsible for making specific sales plans. Basically, the sales executive must take the company's strategic plan and devise an appropriate plan to meet the objectives set forth in the strategy.

The sales plan might include **quotas**, or minimum levels of acceptable performance. For example, the executive might assign a quota directly to each salesperson.

EXHIBIT 1.5   **Examples of Two Sales Organizations**

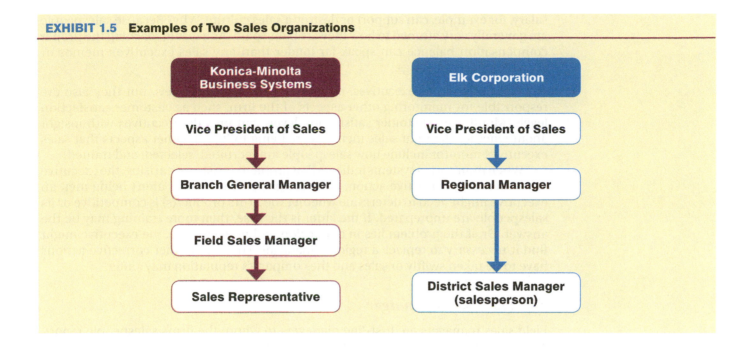

More likely, though, the executive will assign regional, or divisional, quotas, and allow the sales managers in those areas to set quotas for the individual salespeople they supervise.

The executive will also outline a general sales strategy to achieve those objectives. These general strategies will specify the sales approach—transactional, affiliative, consultative (or challenger), or enterprise—that will be used in each market. For example, the sales executive might allocate how much effort will be dedicated to any particular product or market. Product-positioning strategies, such as the key features emphasized for each product, will be determined by the firm's marketing strategy. However, the sales executive must translate that strategy into a sales strategy. This translation might involve creating guidelines about which customers to call and how to open sales calls and structure presentations.

ORGANIZING Organizing involves determining what type of sales force will be utilized. (The types of sales positions are detailed in Chapter 2.) For example, the executive might determine that one product should be the responsibility of a field sales force, whereas another product should be sold by telemarketing. Organizing also includes creating policies and strategies regarding how salespeople should be hired and trained. Recruiting and selecting the right people for the different sales positions is also critical to a company's success. (We will discuss all of these sales management aspects in later chapters.)

IMPLEMENTING Rolling out the plan to the sales force is a key activity for the sales executive. The plan must be communicated in such a way that sales managers and salespeople can implement it without constant supervision by the executive. Implementation also means creating the right sales environment, or culture. The executive is responsible for making sure that salespeople operate ethically and engage in selling practices consistent with the company's mission and desired image. Creating the right culture involves keeping a delicate balance. For example, if you pressure salespeople to close a deal at any cost, they are more likely to use unethical and possibly illegal methods. At the same time, however, sales targets have to be met or the company suffers.

Choosing a compensation method for salespeople is critical when it comes to implementing a sales plan. The balance between a salesperson's commission and salary, for example, can support or destroy a sales culture. Why? Because salespeople are generally very attuned to how they are being paid. As a result, reaching the proper compensation balance can speak far louder than any sales executive's memos or exhortations at meetings.

MONITORING Sales executives, of course, monitor sales levels, but they also are responsible for monitoring other aspects of the firm, such as customer satisfaction levels. Monitoring customer satisfaction levels can provide executives with insight about whether the right sales methods are being followed. Other aspects that sales executives monitor include how salespeople are recruited, selected, and trained.

When monitoring systems indicate that problems exist or are arising, the executive must then take corrective action. For example, if sales quotas aren't being met, an executive might need to determine whether the firm's product(s) is competitive or its salespeople are unprepared. If the latter is the case, then more training may be the answer. Or, if the problem lies in one region and nowhere else, the executive might find it necessary to replace a regional manager. These and other corrective actions have to be taken swiftly or sales and the company's reputation may suffer.

The Field Sales Manager

Field sales managers are first-line managers to whom the firm's salespeople report. The primary responsibility, though, for all sales managers is to achieve a sales quota. The sales manager achieves that sales quota by implementing the plans, policies, and procedures set forth by the sales executive. Thus, the executive determines the general profile of the salesperson to be hired, whereas the field sales manager conducts the actual interviews and makes the final hiring decision. Or the executive creates a compensation plan whereas the field sales manager makes specific salary recommendations for each salesperson. Similarly, the executive sets overall sales targets, and the sales manager allocates a sales quota to each salesperson.

Sales managers are also responsible for either directly training salespeople or ensuring that they undergo training. For example, by traveling with the salesperson in the field, observing the rep in action, and providing coaching, the sales manager can evaluate the rep's performance and offer suggestions for improvement. The sales manager must also understand what motivates each salesperson. Many people pursue sales careers because the earnings can be lucrative. But more people pursue sales careers for other reasons: the desire to help others, to work independently, or compete with other salespeople.[18] The sales manager's job is to adapt, or frame, the firm's policies in way that motivates each individual salesperson, and that also creates the culture sought by the sales executive.

The sales manager also plans, organizes, implements, and monitors for that particular sales team. As illustrated in Exhibit 1.6, the sales manager carries out similar tasks under the guidelines established by the sales executive.

Both sales managers and sales executives rely on technology to keep them informed as to what is happening in the field. Technology can be used to monitor a

EXHIBIT 1.6   Examples of a Sales Executive's and a Sales Manager's Duties

Activity	Sales Executive	Sales Manager
Plan	Set overall sales targets for each product.	Set quotas for each salesperson for each product.
Organize	Decide what type of people to hire for sales positions.	Interview and hire specific people for sales positions.
Implement	Determine the compensation plan.	Identify each person's motivators and find ways to reward good performance for each person.
Monitor	Track sales by region—take corrective action such as additional training if sales are too low.	Observe each salesperson's actions in the field and offer suggestions for improvement.

salesperson's performance, but it can also be used to identify trends in the market-place. These trends can then be incorporated into plans. Technology is also an important factor in increasing sales performance while managing costs. We focus on technology in Chapter 6, although technology is ubiquitous in the management of salespeople; thus, the topic permeates the rest of the book.

Managing Your Career

In a recent survey of college graduates, almost three-fourths indicated they wished they had spent more time focusing on career preparation during their school years.[19] To help with your career preparation, you will find this section at the end of each chapter. Our goal is to help you identify ways to learn and master the chapter material by applying it to your own career. Some aspects, of course, can't really be appreciated until you're in the field, but make the most of this opportunity.

Many students focus on important aspects for a first position, such as salary and training, only to find that they don't really like the job, company, or industry. Annie Fuller graduated with a specialized degree in sports sales, only to find that, as much as she liked sports, working in the industry didn't fit well with how she liked to sell. Many of the sales were transactional, whereas she liked solving bigger problems and getting to know buyers over time. Now she's interviewing with companies that use consultative approaches.

Frank Spikes (not his real name) joined a big-name company right after graduation, but found that the company's mission statement wasn't being lived up to in the field. Now he's working at a smaller company and is much happier, even though he's working much harder.

Finding the right position is about finding the right fit—a match with the right company—and is as much about matching a company's mission as it is the company's sales approach. What's also true, though, is that both Annie and Frank have plans. While their first positions may not have fit perfectly, they have SMART goals for themselves, against which they can mark their progress.

Summary

Sales force management is one of the most important positions in most companies, given the importance of the sales function to a company's success. Sales is a growing profession, highly compensated, with great prospects for the future.

Sales leaders participate in the creation of a firm's strategy. Strategy starts with the development of objectives, usually beginning with a mission statement to describe the firm's overall reason for being. The hierarchy of strategy begins with the corporate strategy, from which are developed the marketing and sales strategies.

A marketing strategy determines what products are sold to which customers, and at what price level. These decisions are then used to create a sales strategy. Companies seek to grow through one or more strategic approaches: market development, market penetration, product development, and account penetration. Salespeople then must develop customer relationship strategies in order to maximize customer lifetime value.

Salespeople take one of four approaches when selling: transactional sales strategies, affiliative selling, consultative or needs-satisfaction selling, and enterprise selling. Irrespective of the approach, the selling process generally follows eight steps; however, the relative length or importance of each step varies depending on which approach is used.

Key Terms

account penetration   9
affiliative selling   13
benefit   16
challenger selling   13
close   17
consultative selling   14
customer lifetime value   10
customer acquisition strategies   10
Customer Relationship Management
   (CRM)   10
customer retention strategies   10
diversification   9
enterprise selling   13
FEBA   16
growth strategies   10
human capital   11
lead   14
MAD   14
market development   9
market penetration   9

milestones   12
mission   6
mission statement   6
needs-satisfaction selling   13
objections   16
pre-commitment   16
problem/solution selling   13
product development   9
prospect   14
prospecting   14
quotas   18
sales management   5
service-dominant logic   10
SMART   11
social capital   11
strategy   7
strategy hierarchy   7
sustainable competitive advantage   8
transactional selling   13

Questions and Problems

1. In this chapter, we calculated the average lifetime value of a college student to that of a clothing store. Why is the lifetime only 4.5 years? Don't you expect to live longer than that? Estimate your lifetime value to Starbucks (if you never visit Starbucks, then pick a fast-food restaurant that you do visit). Then estimate your lifetime value as a car owner. Is the concept of lifetime value of equal importance to your car dealer as it is to Starbucks? What is the growth strategy of both?

2. How might the sales process vary for the following products?
    a. Large specialty computers, such as active data warehouses, that cost millions of dollars
    b. Cars used by companies for salespeople and service representatives
    c. Stubb's barbecue products (sauces, marinades, and rubs) sales to a grocery chain
    d. Electrical parts sold to a wholesaler who has electricians as customers

3. Go to your school's website and find the mission statement. Assess your school's mission statement and compare it to another university. Is one better than the other? If so, why?

4. What is your mission statement? How will that impact your choice of career and first job? How would you use SMART to set goals for your job search?

5. What does a "service-dominant logic" mean to salespeople? Why would that concept be important to a salesperson or a sales organization?

6. "Nothing happens until a salesperson sells something." This statement has been around for decades. What does it mean? How does it relate to the strategy hierarchy?

7. "I want to be the best salesperson this company has ever had." Is that a SMART goal? If not, re-write that statement into the SMART format.

8. Write down your goals for this semester's classes using the SMART format.

9. Some business experts have recently written that the strategy hierarchy creates problems. One is that there is too much separation from one level to the next, particularly between those who create strategy and those who execute it. What are the likely consequences of such problems and how would you overcome them? Be specific—what specific steps would you take?

Role Play

Graduation Time

You are about to graduate and are interviewing for jobs. You come across an opportunity to sell for AT&T. Your job would be to sell cell phones and cell phone services to businesses. Another opportunity to sell is with Enterprise, a car rental and leasing company. Your job would be to visit companies and convince them to sign a corporate contract as their exclusive car rental or vehicle leasing company. If you have the opportunity, you can visit the website of either company to learn more.

Assignment

Break into pairs, with each student choosing one company. You are the sales manager for that company. Take a moment and think about issues reflective of a service-dominant logic in each situation. From that reflection and other concepts discussed, identify three characteristics that, as a sales manager, you would want each new salesperson to have. Then take turns interviewing the other for a sales position.

Caselets

Caselet 1.1: *The Idli Bowl*

The Idli Bowl is a fast-food restaurant based on southern Indian food. The basis of the food is the idli, a soft rice cake, on which the customer can add toppings like sambar (a spicy Indian sauce), tikka masala, and other Indian foods. In two years' time, the company opened two locations in Austin, Texas, but expansion was limited due to the owner's lack of capital. Ram Natarajan, the founder of the company, then hired Cathy Swift to sell franchises. Cathy, after a successful career selling Subway franchises, sold 12 franchises in the company's third year.

Ram thought that was a good first year, but his goal was to have 200 franchises in the next two years. Ram hired five more salespeople and asked Cathy to manage them. Ram would then do franchisee training, franchisee support, and corporate marketing. Quickly, a number of problems arose: Salespeople were calling on the same prospects, which led to confusion. By contrast, other prospects were not getting called upon even after requesting information from The Idli Bowl. After six months, the sales staff had sold a total of twenty-two franchises. Worse, two of the salespeople quit, and ten franchisees wanted out of their contracts, saying they had been misled as to what the company offered.

At this point, it was pretty clear that there were problems. What might those be? What should Ram do to save his business?

Caselet 1.2: *Materials Handling, Inc.*

Materials Handling, Inc. was the brainchild of two sorority sisters, Gabby Gonzalez and Markie Meeks. Gabby, an engineering major, created a modular system for materials handling that integrated easily with a software system that Markie, a computer science major, developed. Through their university's entrepreneurship program, they were able to secure some start-up funding and introductions to potential buyers that led to enough initial business that the two formed the company upon graduation. But sales came to a halt—neither one knew really how to sell the system, and finding new buyers proved difficult.

Markie felt that the key was software and argued that they should find salespeople from software companies who could talk to information technology buyers. Gabby, though, felt that the real value lay in how the system moved goods, so she thought shipping and logistics managers were the right target. But both agreed that buyers had to see the system in operation to really understand the value. And once buyers installed the system in at one warehouse, they would want to apply it throughout the entire manufacturing process—not just within the finished-goods warehouse.

Markie and Gabby realize that they need help. They're going back to the university's business program to get the help they need. What would you say to Gabby and Markie to help them develop their business more effectively?

References

1. Manpower (2013). "Manpower Group Annual Talent Shortage Survey Reveals US Employers Making Strides to Build Sustainable Workforce." Accessed February 19, 2014. *http://press.manpower.com/press/2013/talentshortage2013/*.
2. Dwyer, Robert F., and John F. Tanner, Jr. (2005). *Business Marketing: Connecting Strategy, Relationships, and Learning*, 3rd ed. Burr Ridge, IL: McGraw-Hill.
3. U.S. Department of Labor, Bureau of Labor Statistics, *Occupational Outlook Handbook*, *http://www.bls.gov/oco/ocos020.htm*, last modified Aug. 4, 2006.
4. Lorenz, Mary (2013). "Death of a Sales Skill? Survey Highlights Industry Recruiting Challenges," The Hiring Site. Accessed February 12, 2014. *http://thehiringsite.careerbuilder.com/2013/01/22/sales-survey-highlights-industry-recruiting-challenges/*; SHRM Online Staff (2013). "U.S. Sales-Job Forecast Points to Better, but Cautious Hiring Outlook,." Accessed February 12, 2014. *http://www.shrm.org/hrdisciplines/staffingmanagement/Articles/Pages/US-Sales-Job-Hiring-Forecast.aspx*.
5. Marchetti, Michele (2006). "Moving on Up," *Sales and Marketing Management*, 158(1), 24.
6. Zival, Leyla (1995). "Why the Best Salesperson is Not the Best Sales Manager," *Journal of Managerial Psychology*, 10(4), 9-20; Richard and Janet Spitzer (2011). "Transitioning from Sales Rep to Sales Manager," Ezine@rticles. Accessed February 12, 2014. *http://ezinearticles.com/?Transitioning-From-Sales-Rep-to-Sales-Manager&id=6719205*.
7. For a discussion on sales management as control systems, see René Y. Darmon and Xavier C. Martin (2011), "A New Conceptual Framework of Sales Force Control Systems," *Journal of Personal Selling & Sales Management*, 31(3), 297-310 and Guangping Wang, Wenyu Dou, and Nan Zhou (2012). "The Interactive Effects of Sales Force Controls on Salespeople Behaviors and Customer Outcomes," *Journal of Personal Selling & Sales Management*, 32(2), 225-244.
8. Treace, John (2012). "How Core Values Drive Performance," *Proofs* 95(5), 20-21.
9. Le Meunier-FitzHugh, Kenneth, and Nigel Percy (2011). "Exploring the Relationship Between Market Orientation and Sales and Marketing Collaboration," *Journal of Personal Selling & Sales Management*, 31(3), 287-296.
10. Malshe, Avinash and Ravipreet Sohi (2009). "Sales Buy-In of Marketing Strategies: Explorations of Its Nuances, Antecedents, and Contextual Conditions," *Journal of Personal Selling & Sales Management*, 29(3), 207-225; Anonymous, "How Hierarchy Can Hurt Strategy Execution," *Harvard Business Review*, 88(7/8), 74-75.
11. Aspara, Jaakko, Sami Kaialo, and Joel Hietanen (2013). "Sales Activity Systematization and Performance: Differences Between Product and Service Firms," *Journal of Business & Industrial Marketing* 28(6), 494-505; Le Meunier-FitzHugh, Kenneth, Jasmin Baumann, Roger Palmer, and Hugh Wilson (2011). "The Implications of Service-Dominant Logic and Integrated Solutions on the Sales Function," *Journal of Marketing Theory and Practice*, 19(4), 423-440.
12. Wei, Yinghong Susan), Saeed Samiee, Ruby P. Lee (2014). "The Influence of Organic Organizational Culture, Market Responsiveness, and Product Strategy on Firm Performance in an Emerging Market, *Journal of the Academy of Marketing Science* 42(1) 49-70.
13. Kozlenkova, Irina V., Stephen A. Samaha, Robert W. Palmatier (2014). "Resource-Based Theory in Marketing," *Journal of the Academy of Marketing Science*, 42(1) 1-21.
14. Dickie, Jim, and Barry Trailer (2006). "The Impact of CRM and Sales Process: Monetizing the Value of Sales Effectiveness," White paper published by CSO Insights. *http://www.csoinsights.com/*.
15. Autry, Chad, Michael Williams, and William Moncrief (2013). "Improving Professional Selling Effectiveness Through the Alignment of Buyer and Seller Exchange Approaches," *Journal of Personal Selling & Sales Management*, 33(2), 165-184.
16. Griswold, Nelson (2012). "Do or Die: Create a Consultative Practice," Employee Benefit Adviser 10(2), 26-28.
17. Adamson, Matthew and Brent Dixon (2011) *The Challenger Sale: Taking Control of the Customer Conversation*, Boston: Portfolio Publishing.

18. Tanner, John F., Jr., and George W Dudley (2003). "International Differences: Examining Two Assumptions About Selling," in *Advances in Marketing*, William J. Kehoe and Linda K Whitten, eds., *Society for Marketing Advances*, 236-239.

19. Today *Waco Tribune Herald* (February 12)

THE SALES FUNCTION AND MULTI-SALES CHANNELS

LEARNING OBJECTIVES

After completing this chapter, you should be able to:

■ Explain what the sales function includes and how salespeople affect a firm's supply chain.

■ Identify how the sales function is carried out through various channels.

■ Explain how effective sales management efforts can align a firm's sales strategy in a multi-channel environment.

How companies sell their products and services in the marketplace—via the Internet, direct mail, retail stores, distributors, telemarketing, field salespeople, or some combination of all of these—is one of the most important decisions a firm will make. In most situations, choosing a sales force will be the most expensive option. Consequently, it is important that when a sales force is chosen, it is managed well.

Sales Manager Profile: Kelvin Lewis

ONE OF THE MOST CHALLENGING and rewarding roles in any organization is that of the sales manager. The responsibility is laced with key guiding principles to ensure that the vision of the enterprise is realized. The sales manager is the conduit, both internally and externally, managing resources and relationships upstream and downstream, while building salespeople's capabilities. The position requires casting a vision and strategy, influencing the system, and building a winning culture.

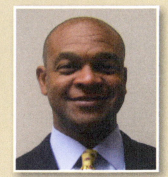

KELVIN LEWIS
National Sales Leader
Coca-Cola

The path to leadership roles in any organization, I believe, starts with a vision with the end result in perspective, understanding your personal brand, recognizing the cultural fit within the organization, demonstrating progression in the required behaviors and/or competency model, and gaining sponsors at every level who advocate and accelerate your career. Successful managers are people who get things done. A human resources director once told me that you should think and behave in the manner of the position you aspire to hold. For example, if you would like to lead a sales or marketing organization, then think about the impact of your decisions on a line salesperson, manager, or director on the enterprise. Ask yourself, "How will my decisions impact the organization two or three levels upstream? How myopic or how broad is my view? How can I motivate and influence outcomes when I have no direct interaction, at ground level, with the customer?"

Efficient sales leaders have processes that allow them to track, rank, and publish the performance and/or behaviors of the team they are leading. Additionally, leveraging an effective distance-coaching model ensures that appropriate behaviors are influenced beyond tracking and publishing performance. Vital to coaching success is knowing your people and operating appropriately (directing, motivating, counseling, or teaching) for each situation.

One example involved Super Bowl XXXXV. The preparation for the event began in March of 2010, nearly a year before the cold winter in Texas descended upon the Dallas-Fort Worth metroplex. In anticipation of the "Big Game," Coca-Cola expected some 400,000–500,000 people to visit Dallas and Fort Worth. An additional amount of volume was calculated into our forecast to account for the sales. At that time, 35 people served on our large-store team, with five reporting directly. The vision and strategies were communicated, resources were allocated to influence, and the winning culture was defined. Our team set out to engage every major retailer within a five-mile radius of the AT&T Stadium, with the intent of painting the town red with Coca-Cola.

While expecting to spar with our primary competitor by distinguishing our products and adding value in the soft-drink space, we also knew that we would compete with other consumer-goods companies for shelf space, and that we needed to have a strong value-add argument. Our primary value message is anchored on the flagship brands, commitment to service, volume to meet demand, an effective price point, and gross profit per square foot.

Our managers were instructed to prioritize key accounts, as well as positions within each account, that we would own, and to execute against those priorities while maintaining balance toward our day-to-day activities. Fortunately I led a mature and seasoned group of leaders. I was, therefore, able to focus on my customer peers with routine checkpoints with my leaders. Additionally, flawless collaboration was required with our product supply teams, marketing teams, distribution teams, merchandising teams, point-of-sale teams, and commercialization. A routine cadence of communication was established upstream to our Market Unity Vice President (MUVP), which updated him on our progress—leading to weekly progression updates during the final six weeks.

I found that my leadership coaching style shifted from motivating and teaching six months out from delivery, to directing and motivating as we approached the stretch run. Specifically, the major retailer across from AT&T Stadium was challenged with space for product based on the demand that would be generated. As our lead manager experienced obstacles, I pushed back to determine his types of barriers. Eliminating knowledge and motivation as barriers, the coaching session pivoted to the skill set for communicating the value-added features. He then connected with the customer, created a win-win outcome by aligning priorities and stakeholders, and moved forward with the necessary elements to execute the plan. The results were mutually beneficial. As the national media came to town, Coca-Cola won recognition from CNBC for having one of the finest "Big Game" displays network personnel had ever seen in a retail environment. Overall, we met our goal—an additional 500,000 cases sold above our forecast for the week—in which my large store team accounted for approximately 60 percent of the volume and a lion's share of the gross profit. ∎

The Sales Function

When Herbert Ruppman woke up one cloudy morning, he quickly grabbed a pencil and some paper and started scribbling madly. His wife sleepily asked what was wrong, and he quickly replied that he had seen a vision in his sleep, a vision for a new breakfast food—a wonderfully healthy and tasty concoction. He and his wife made hundreds of pounds of the breakfast cereal and then waited for orders to roll in. And waited. And waited.

Of course, orders just don't roll in. Contrary to what the Ralph Waldo Emerson is supposed to have said, no matter how good a mousetrap you invent, customers won't beat a path to your door to get it. In fact, mousetraps were once the most-often patented product, yet we still use the same basic model. Someone, in some way, must first go sell the better mousetrap to them. William Keith Kellogg knew this. Kellogg was a great salesperson, as he recognized what people wanted and found many ways to show and convince them that he had it; as a result, the Kellogg's brand name is familiar around much of the world.

The **sales function** includes locating potential buyers, persuading them, and consummating the transaction. Not to be confused with the selling process, the sales function can be undertaken by salespeople, but can also be carried out in other ways. For example, a company might run advertisements to attract customers to its website, where they can purchase its products. The firm's service department might then take care of any post-sales issues these customers have. In all likelihood, however, a firm's sales force will be responsible for providing market information to the firm's strategic planners by capturing and sharing information about potential customers, as well as information about competitors. Other likely sales force tasks include creating the sales forecasts used to schedule the firm's manufacturing, inventory, and shipping functions. These responsibilities indicate the salesperson's key role in the supply chain.

You may love and search out Kellogg's cereal now, but when William Kellogg founded his cereal company, he had to convince people to buy his products.

The **supply chain**, as illustrated in Exhibit 2.1, is the complete process of events and people needed to bring a company's product to the customer. Most students initially think that salespeople only push products forward into the supply chain. But salespeople can also play an important role in managing the supply chain itself. This role can be passive, as is the case when a salesperson turns in a sales forecast. A **sales forecast** is simply what the salesperson expects to sell in a particular period of time. Other employees in the supply chain then use that forecast to determine what needs to be ordered and delivered to customers. In this case, the sales forecast influences what happens in the supply chain, but the salesperson is not actively influencing the chain's activity.

EXHIBIT 2.1   An Example Supply Chain

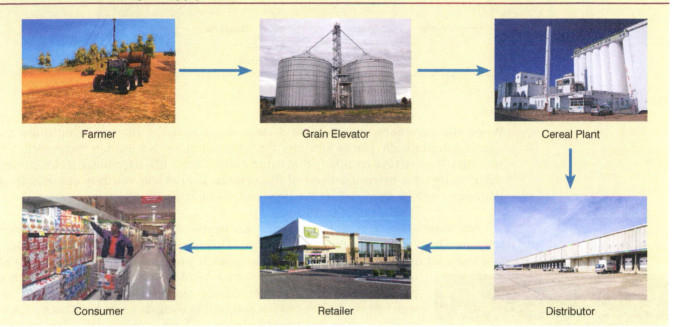

Farmer   Grain Elevator   Cereal Plant

Consumer   Retailer   Distributor

Taking an active role, though, means that the salesperson actively seeks to influence what the supply chain does. The salesperson might need to marshal resources—both inside and outside the firm—in order to consummate the sale or serve the customer. For example, a buyer needing special payment terms will require the salesperson's help in securing those terms from the company. Or the salesperson might need to arrange expedited delivery in order to meet a buyer's needs. Bell Helicopter's salespeople take an active role in their firm's supply chain management. Because each helicopter sold by Bell is customized, salespeople involve engineers in their sales calls so that the final product meets the customer's exact specifications.

With the advent of technology, however, more functions are being automated, including the selling function. Today, more customers want to be able to buy over the Internet, or by phone, or by other methods. Companies are turning to a multi-channel approach as a result.

Selling in a Multi-Channel Environment

When a company is selling in a **multi-channel environment,** it is using a number of methods, or channels, to accomplish the selling function, as illustrated in Exhibit 2.2. The variety of ways to use the Internet, for example, is actually increasing.[1] **Electronic Data Interchange (EDI)** takes advantage of the Internet by directly connecting the customer's inventory management system with the seller's order entry system.

EXHIBIT 2.2   Sales Channel

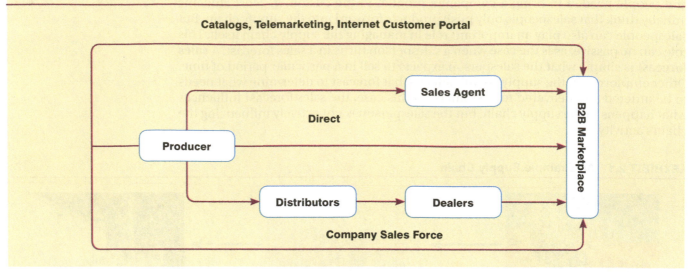

When the inventory management system notes that the buyer's inventories are low, it automatically places an order for replenishment. No human intervention is required. Walmart is a company that extensively utilizes EDI to manage its inventory, particularly as it drives cost out of the system. Every time you buy something at Walmart, the EDI system notes the need to replenish the store's inventory.

Alternately, the customer can enter an order on a special website in much the same way you might use Amazon.com. This special **customer portal**, though, is a site that only customers can enter because it provides them with customized information—such as their order history, shipping status, and other personalized data. Or the customer can use **reverse auctions** on the web by posting their needs and letting companies bid on that sale; the company with the lowest bid wins. [2] These auctions are called reverse auctions because sellers are bidding. This is just the opposite of what happens on eBay where sellers post items and buyers bid. Save33.com, for example, is an eBay for reverse auctions.

Customers may want to order from a catalog by calling a toll-free number. Dell, for example, has mastered multi-channel sales to its business customers. A business buyer can order a Dell product on the web either through Dell's small-business site, by calling a toll-free number, or requesting a personal visit by one of Dell's salespeople. Carphone Warehouse, a U.K.-based company that sells to thousands of stores across nine European countries, turned to multi-channel sales strategy to enhance customer service. [3] Both found that using many channels well gives them a competitive advantage, because not every company balances multiple channels well.

CP-Plus is an annual trade show held in Japan. Trade shows are just one channel companies use to reach customers. Booths are staffed by salespeople, as well as engineers, executives, and others. While showing an exhbit may cost a million dollars, the cost per contact can be much less than the cost of a sales call at the customer's office.

But it's just not price that matters to consumers. Companies today have come to realize that a competitive advantage can be created by selling the *way* a customer wants to buy. Of course, a company can create a competitive advantage by being the only one to have *what* the customer wants to buy. Customers buy to satisfy needs, of course, and the product itself fulfills some of their needs, but others, such as the need for convenience, are fulfilled by how the product is bought.

A key issue, then, for salespeople is how to provide value to customers. As we have explained, salespeople, especially field salespeople, are expensive—the most expensive way to reach customers, in fact. All other channels—the Internet, call centers, retail stores or distributors, catalogs, trade shows—are cheaper. (Keep in mind that call centers and distributors also have salespeople, but at a lower cost than field salespeople.) So salespeople have to provide additional value to the customer, or the customer will refuse to pay the premium needed to cover the cost of the salesperson.

Because salespeople are the most expensive option to reach customers, companies pursue two strategies to reduce costs without sacrificing performance. The first strategy is to "purify" the sales job, or shift non-selling activities to lower-cost alternatives. For example, creating a website that allows customers to track their own orders can eliminate phone calls to the firm's salespeople, freeing up their time for more selling activity. ResearchNow, a company that supports marketing research activities, frees up selling time by providing salespeople with a sales support team. The team helps prepare sales proposals and then manages the project once it is sold, leaving the salesperson free to make additional sales.

The second strategy is to outsource selling activity. **Outsourcing** means hiring another company to carry out a task or set of tasks. Outsourcing can be a challenging proposition. There are many ways to outsource the selling function. In the next section, we'll explore the different types of salespeople, or sales jobs, that represent these two strategies—purifying the position and outsourcing.

To Outsource or Not to Outsource the Sales Function?

Hire salespeople as employees or hire a company to sell for you? For most companies, the choice is not that simple.[4] There are, however, advantages and disadvantages of employing company salespeople or contracting with independent representatives. In a later chapter, we'll discuss how many salespeople are needed and formulas for determining whether it is more economical to outsource or hire company employees. Here, though, we focus on the broader strategic issues.

In general, there are a number of advantages to having company-employed salespeople. First, the company can exert greater control over their efforts, telling them what to sell and enforcing requirements to carry out non-selling activities. For example, if the salespeople are company employees, then they can be required to attend training sessions. Second, there is also greater control over who is hired to represent the company. Finally, a company salesperson will focus on only the company's products, whereas an outsourced representative might be free to sell many companies' products. The latter might spend less time selling the firm's individual products or product line.

GLOBAL SALES MANAGEMENT   **Entering New Markets**

Are orders or inquiries coming through the web from new markets, and you want to start selling in new countries? For many companies, outsourcing the sales function is the best way to begin selling in new markets in other countries. "You want someone with local knowledge," says Judy Bayer, strategy director for Teradata based in the United Kingdom. "They have to know the market, know the culture, and know some potential customers." At least at the beginning, that means outsourcing the sales function to local distributors or manufacturers' agents.

China and India are particularly attractive markets; after all, each has over one billion residents. But the reality is that they are actually comprised of many smaller markets. While each may be sufficiently large to support a sales organization, the situation is far more complex than it appears at first glance. According to Ram Ramamurthy, president of the Indian Institute of Sales Training, "India and China are so big that each country really represents many countries, not just one. Local knowledge and local relationships are so important, because you'll need to localize the sales strategy depending on where you are in India or in China." His company helps match companies wishing to enter the market with the right distributors or sales agents, depending on need. "The right local partner makes all the difference," he emphasizes.

With an outsourced sales force, the firm's selling and sales management costs can be shared with other manufacturers, thereby reducing the cost per sales call.[5] In addition, the outsourced sales force has established relationships with customers—relationships that can benefit the manufacturer. Both of these benefits can then yield greater coverage of the market for the manufacturer. In fact, outsourcing is especially beneficial when entering new markets, as you can see in this chapter's "Global Sales Management" box. The question for the sales executive is whether outsourcing is right for that company's situation. First, we will explore the different types of outsourcing; then, we will briefly examine the types of company sales positions.

Types of Outsourced Salespeople

A common solution to the sales question is to hire a manufacturer's representative or agent. The **manufacturer's representative** or **manufacturer's agent** is an independent contractor who does not take ownership of the product and does not maintain an inventory. Many reps will sell for several non-competing principals, a **principal** being a manufacturer. For example, in the furniture business, a rep might sell furniture for one principal, lamps for another, and decorative accessories for yet another. The same buyer needs all three types of products, so it saves time for the buyer to meet with one salesperson instead of three.

Another option is to engage a distributor. **Distributors** sell for many manufacturers, much like manufacturer's reps do. The difference is that distributors take ownership of the products, sell them on consignment, or otherwise maintain an inventory of them. Hilti, for example, sells fasteners and other construction products through distributors. These distributors sell Hilti's products directly to contractors at their job sites, or the contractors can visit the distributors' locations to purchase and pick up the products they want. Distributors carry many products made by many manufacturers, some of which compete with one another.

These hand-trucks (the dollies on the front of the vehicles) are held onto the vehicles by a patented system sold by Hand Truck Systems (www. handtrucksystems.com) through distributors.

A **broker** represents either a buyer or a seller, and sometimes both. A broker can carry an inventory of products, but does not take ownership of them. Brokers are common in the furniture business as a way of buying from overseas: a U.S. company can work through a broker to locate furniture manufacturers in China, for example. Brokers are not only used in international settings, though. They are common in industries such as the market for domestic produce, too. Grocery stores, for example, need to buy the best produce they can get, as quickly as possible, so it stays fresh. Buyers of produce often find it easier to go through a broker than trying to find sellers themselves.

Purifying the sales job, as mentioned earlier, often means moving non-selling activities to other people or to other channels such as the web. Another strategy is to break the sales process down into parts and outsource only parts of the process. For example, Intrep (*www.intrep.com*) is a company that only calls potential prospects and schedules appointments for company salespeople. GC Services (*www.gcserv.com*), however, operates at the other end of the spectrum, providing only customer support services for other firms. A company could use both Intrep and GC Services in addition to its own company-employed salespeople.

Types of Company-Employed Salespeople

Whether a company outsources some or all sales tasks, there are different types of sales positions possible. Unlike the types described earlier, these positions can be part of an outsourced sales force or kept within the company. In addition, companies can have one salesperson who covers a territory, or a team could be working together, as in the case of ResearchNow, with different types of salespeople teaming up to handle accounts.

One distinction that should be made concerns the inside versus outside, or field, salesperson—a distinction that has nothing to do with outsourcing. An **inside salesperson** is someone who sells at a company's facilities, either by telephone or in person. Jeff Moss, for example, was hired by IBM straight out of college to sell on the telephone. Moss handles four accounts that generate a total of $1 million in revenue for IBM. Although he might visit each account three or four times a year in person, Moss is considered an inside salesperson. Inside salespeople can include those who sell in a distributor's location as retail sales reps. Other inside salespeople, like Moss, work in a **contact center** or **call center**, an office where customers communicate with salespeople only by telephone or electronically by e-mail or live chat. (The term *call center* is now somewhat archaic, as it pre-dates the use of the web to talk to customers, but the terms are used interchangeably.) In some contact centers, a representative might handle as many as four chat conversations and a voice conversation at the same time. Contact centers can be either outbound, inbound, or both. An **inbound center** call center handles calls that customers initiate, while salespeople initiate the contact in an **outbound center.** Most outbound centers handle inbound contacts. A **field representative**, however, sells at the customer's location. Many distributors have both inside and outside salespeople, as do companies like IBM, Dell, and others. At Oracle, field representatives work with inside salespeople as a team. The inside salesperson finds new accounts for the field rep to contact.

The choice of inside or field is a function of several issues, such as cost. Inside salespeople cost less, especially on a per-call basis. A field salesperson may see only three to ten people a day; the rest of the field person's contacts are by phone or e-mail between calls. An inside salesperson can visit with many more people and without the costs of travel. Other reasons, such as a need to see and handle a product, or to build personal relationships, might influence the choice toward a field salesperson.

In addition to the inside or outside distinction, salespeople can be **account managers**—meaning that they take responsibility for building sales within specific accounts, or accounts within a specific area. The latter type of account manager is more commonly called a **geographic rep**. Jeff Moss is an account manager because he is responsible for whatever is sold from IBM to his four accounts. However, he is a **vertical market rep**, meaning that his accounts all operate in the same industry—in this case, the health care industry. Unlike the world of geographic reps, a vertical market territory consists of accounts from the same type of business, such as banking, finance, the government, and other sectors.

Some account managers have only one customer—usually a large corporation—that spans the globe. These global account managers usually have the support of geographic reps in certain areas to help cover the needs of the customer. By contrast, other salespeople can have limited responsibilities and serve mainly as support salespeople. For example, some might primarily prospect for new customers, whereas others might handle service and repeat business for existing customers. Still other support salespeople might specialize in a particular product line or technology. They might be brought in to a sales call only when an account manager thinks it is necessary. For example, when Moss needs an expert in customer relationship manager software, he calls in an IBM specialist who sells only CRM applications. Moss can't be expected to know everything about each product. That's why IBM uses specialists—salespeople who have a special expertise and only sell to an account when an account manager calls for them.

There are also different sales positions based on the product being sold, how it is sold, and where it is sold. For example, **retail sales representatives** sell to consumers who come into stores. Like inside selling at a distributorship, these salespeople work directly with consumers and rely heavily on product demonstrations. Some work solely on commission, such as in high-fashion, cosmetics, electronics, and furniture industries.

Trade representatives sell to organizations in the supply chain—usually to retailers. Hilti, the fastener company, has its own salespeople (trade reps) who sell its products to distributors. These salespeople also help the distributors with their marketing efforts—especially when it comes to selling to big customers. For example, Tempur Sealy International makes and sells mattresses. One of the top retailers for Tempur-Pedic mattresses is Gallery Furniture in Houston; the salesperson who handles that account is a trade rep.

Missionary salespeople sell to people who recommend, or prescribe, a product to others but do not personally use it. Pharmaceutical salespeople are missionary salespeople. They call upon doctors who, in turn, prescribe the representatives' medications to patients. So are furniture salespeople who call on architects, and textbook salespeople who call on your professors. Missionary salespeople are sometimes called detailers, or **detail reps,** because their primary activity is to detail, or describe, the product.

A company is not likely to have missionary salespeople, retail salespeople, *and* trade salespeople. However the firm *could* have a mix of inside, outside, outsourced, and company salespeople. Further, account managers of various types as well as specialists can all work in a team, serving the same customers. Add this complex picture to a multi-channel environment, and the potential combinations appear astounding and confusing. Decisions about what types of salespeople to use in certain situations will be discussed in greater detail in Chapter 7; however, understanding how to integrate all of these possible combinations so that customers are served properly and the company makes money is the topic of the next section.

Aligning the Organization

You order a book from Barnes & Noble's website but receive the wrong book. You then try to return it at your local Barnes & Noble store, but the store won't refund your money. Instead, personnel at the store say to send it back to the website. Aren't the store and its website the same company?

Yes, they are the same company, and actually Barnes & Noble does a good job of providing seamless integration. **Seamless integration** occurs when a firm's customers can easily shift their transactions across the company's various channels. The goal of multi-channel sales strategies is to allow customers to choose the method of doing business that makes the most sense for them. "Doing business" refers not only to buying products the way they want to, but also taking care of their billing, service, and shipping the way they prefer. Unfortunately, seamless integration is probably more of a goal than a reality for most organizations, as the cartoon in Exhibit 2.3 illustrates.

For example, you can buy a ticket directly at an American Airlines ticket counter, over the telephone, at AA.com, or through a travel agent. You will pay a premium to have a live person involved in the transaction; for example, it might add $15 if American handles the transaction over the phone and $25 if in person. American passes on their costs to the consumer because self-service over the web is the cheapest for everyone. That said, consumers *do* have the ability to choose the communication channels they most desire. No matter which channel you choose, your information is available. The American Airlines agent can pull up all the necessary information and handle your requirements, or you can visit a kiosk at the airport and do it yourself.

Imagine, then, the challenges that arise when you have only one account, Mercedes-Benz, and you are using an enterprise selling strategy. Mercedes spends more than $50 billion per year in total purchases, the company has offices literally all over the world, and 3,000 or more of its employees may be authorized to order products from your company. A buyer in Bogota, Columbia, might want to have a

EXHIBIT 2.3   Seamless Integration

Seamless integration occurs when all of areas of the company—from its online presence to the salesperson, to delivery, to customer service, and to the repair technician—have all of the customer data they need so that customer interaction is informed, consistent, and appropriate.

salesperson from your company personally take her order, but track the order's shipment on the web herself. If a problem arises, the buyer might want to call and resolve the problem over the phone or via another method, such as e-mail. And she expects the responder at your firm to be able to provide information about the account and the purchase. If your company succeeds in providing that information, your customer is experiencing seamless integration.

Achieving Alignment

You, as the account manager for Mercedes-Benz (or another company), must track all of this activity in order to make the right sales pitch to re-win the contract every time it comes up, even if you are based in Detroit and not Bogota. Moreover, you have a responsibility to make sure that every part of your organization services this account appropriately. Getting all functional areas of a firm to work together, including the company's various salespeople—its inside reps, geographic reps, and customer service reps, and the rest—is called **alignment**. Achieving alignment is a major challenge in all organizations.[6] However, as the multi-channel environment and sales organizations become more complex, achieving alignment becomes more difficult. As a result, the challenges associated with achieving alignment continue to grow.

TECHNOLOGY AND ALIGNMENT Technology can aid in aligning functional areas and multiple sales organizations. Certain types of software, as we discuss in Chapter 6, can make customer data, inventory information, financial data, and other forms of information available to all of the areas of the organization that require it for serving the customer. American Airlines has a reservation system, for example, that can be accessed at a ticket counter, by a ticket agent working in a call center, or by

If Mercedes Benz was your customer and needed service in a truck plant in another country, the buyer may want to resolve the issue via e-mail, phone, chat, or text. You'll need service channels to respond based on how the customer wants to handle the problem.

the customer over the web. Each American representative knows immediately if a customer is a Platinum Executive flyer (someone who travels more than 100,000 miles per year with American) or an infrequent traveler. Not only does the agent have information on the current flight, but historical passenger information also appears on the screen, showing whether that passenger was recently delayed due to a storm or lost a bag. The agent can then use that information to offer something—such as an upgrade to first class—in order to make up for what happened, even before the customer asks.

ALIGNING A COMPANY'S PROCESSES AND GOALS Alignment is not achieved by just having the right information, though; a firm's objectives must also be aligned so that its processes result in the right outcomes. For example, a credit clerk in charge of extending credit to the firm's customers might have all the necessary information to accept or reject their credit applications. But suppose the company rewards the clerk's performance based on customers' payment of bills. If this is the case, the clerk is likely to have such high credit standards that the firm will lose some sales—sales it otherwise would have made to customers who have only good, but not great, credit. Or a shipping manager who is paid for having the highest shipping completion rate is not likely to drop everything to help you expedite a particularly important order, even if it is for a big customer like Mercedes-Benz.

Thus, alignment requires that people in various areas work together and independently toward the same goals. For example, there are times when an account manager and a shipping manager have to meet to settle on a strategy for a particular account—times when their two functional areas have to work together. However, there are also times when the two managers have to work independently toward the same goal. The sales manager need not look over the shipping manager's shoulder to see what deliveries are scheduled first. The shipping manager works independently of the sales manager, but under policies and procedures tied to goals that both share.

SALES AND ALIGNMENT Salespeople would like to think that customer satisfaction is important to everyone in the firm. Do you think it is? Paul Greenberg, author and CRM guru, describes visiting a call center in which a large banner reading "Customer Satisfaction is Our Goal!" was hung. Next to the banner, however, was a large digital clock showing the average length of the center's calls. Customer service reps manning the phones in the center were under strict orders to keep every call under three minutes. So which objective do you think was more likely to be closely monitored and met? Customer satisfaction or length of the call? Yes, you guessed it—length of the call. If resolving a customer's needs took five minutes, the CSR would try to finish the call in three minutes or less, even though customer dissatisfaction resulted.

Three minutes, in that case, was a **metric**, or performance measurement, used to determine if an objective was being met. A firm's metrics have to be aligned so that its work processes will be aligned. Employees will find ways to meet the firm's metrics because their evaluations link to their compliance. Consequently, alignment requires having the *right* metrics.

We will discuss more about metrics in Chapter 14. Suffice it to say here that alignment is, perhaps, more important to the salesperson than to anyone else in the organization. A salesperson has to make promises to the customer that other people in the organization fulfill. Every time a salesperson tells a customer, "You'll receive your order on Tuesday," that salesperson is relying on an order-entry clerk, a shipping scheduler, and the credit clerk to make it happen. If any one of these people fails, then the customer's shipment is delayed and the salesperson's promise is broken.

Because alignment is so critical to sales success, the sales leadership of an organization has to take proactive steps to ensure that alignment occurs. Although everyone in an organization might, in theory, recognize the importance of customers to the firm's health, each person in each department has a budget to watch and will get in trouble if more is spent; each person has a set of metrics to achieve and risks getting fired after failure; and each person has problems and demands that must be resolved that may have nothing to do with the customer. A key function of the sales executive is to work with other areas of the firm to ensure that leaders in those areas (like the leader in the call center we just mentioned) understand how their metrics and budgets support—or sabotage—the company's larger goals of sales and customer satisfaction.

For companies that have purified their sales positions, alignment is becoming a bigger issue. Once upon a time, the salesperson was the only person interacting with a customer. Today, customers are encountering **customer-facing personnel**—people who have frequent and direct contact with customers. These people may or may not have been trained to sell to customers, yet they are expected to say and do the right things to make sure that the customer is persuaded that the solution is a good one.

ETHICS IN SALES MANAGEMENT   Suggestive Selling

You select a new suit at the department store, and a salesperson recommends a complementary shirt or blouse. At dinner, you see a different type of wine listed by each entrée. Both of these examples are forms of suggestive selling, a type of selling intended to increase the overall sale by adding on accessories or accompaniments.

Long a mainstay in retailing and restaurants, suggestive selling is now finding its way into customer service. A customer calls to get help with a product and the customer support person is supposed to suggest an add-on or a service policy. Whether that is a wise strategy is up for debate; research suggests that suggestive selling may actually harm intentions to purchase, but retailers have long argued that it is effective. But is it ethical when the customer's purpose in calling is to get help or to cancel? After all, the customer called to get service, not to inquire about accessories.

That answer is, of course, that it depends. The real question concerns appropriate and inappropriate sales strategy. When customers' needs are not being met, when customers are bullied or manipulated, or when customers are not getting accurately informed, ethics are violated no matter the setting. Traditionally, such behavior has been associated with used car salespeople, but recent cases include hotel chain "service" staff who try to sell vacation packages, clothing and electronics retailers, and some cell carriers. So when a customer calls with a service request, make sure that the request is handled promptly and completely.

But is it okay to try to re-sell to the customer who calls to cancel? Of course. Again, the first priority is to understand the customer's needs. Did the product fail to meet those needs? Or was it the right product, but broken or used incorrectly? Any channel can become a sales channel if the customer's needs are met.

Libby Dowd (2013), "Upselling Strategies," *Dancewear Retailer News* (12)7, 34–36; Magnus Söderlund (2013), "Positive Social Behaviors and Suggestive Selling in the Same Service Encounter," *Managing Service Quality* (47)6, 305–320.

Managing Your Career

If there is only one take-away from this chapter, it would have to be that there is no single sales job; rather, there are many types of selling. Whether or not someone enters sales as a job or as a career, making decisions about who should do what, whether to hire an employee or a contractor, and how to assemble the right balance will always be a part of management. Students, in many ways, make these decisions now. How do you assign functions within a group? Who will do what to help prepare for a test? Or do you manage that all by yourself? The reasons you would prepare alone—versus with others—for a test are not fundamentally different from the reasons why a company may choose from among sales options.

Summary

Selling in the multi-channel environment means that salespeople and sales managers have to integrate their activities with the other channels through which the company sells. The selling function can be accomplished through other channels, such as the web or call centers. Many salespeople also have to take an active role in the supply chain.

The multi-channel environment means that buyers want to purchase through the channel that is most convenient, and to get service in the most convenient way. These channels may not be the same; there are different ones for purchasing and for service. Channels can include EDI, customer portals, reverse auctions, and others.

A multi-channel environment may also mean outsourcing some or all sales activities. Some types of outsourced salespeople are manufacturers' reps, distributors, and brokers. Companies can employ their own contact centers or outsource them.

Whether or not some sales positions are outsourced, achieving seamless integration is important. Customers want to be served appropriately, no matter which channel they choose. Further, sales managers have to work toward alignment across all functional areas of the organization.

Key Terms

account managers   33
alignment   35
broker   32
call center   33
contact center   33
customer portal   30
customer-facing personnel   37
detail rep   34
distributors   32
Electronic Data Interchange (EDI)   29
field representative   33
geographic rep   33
inbound center   33
inside salesperson   33
manufacturer's agent   32

manufacturer's representative   32
metric   36
missionary salespeople   34
multi-channel environment   29
outbound center   33
outsourcing   31
principal   32
retail sales representative   33
reverse auctions   30
sales forecast   29
sales function   28
seamless integration   34
supply chain   29
trade representatives   34
vertical market rep   33

Questions and Problems

1. In many companies, there is little trust and collaboration between the marketing departments and sales forces. Some salespeople believe that marketing costs money without generating enough leads to cover the costs; some marketing managers believe salespeople are overpaid and want all the credit for any sale, in spite of what marketing has done. What effect would such conflict have on the firm's ability to accomplish its strategy and objectives? Why isn't it enough to just say the company needs them to get along?

2. At EMC, a computer storage company, the joke is that EMC stands for "Everybody Makes Calls," as in *everybody makes sales calls*. Similarly, at the offices of the Miami Heat (the professional basketball team), every employee is given a list

of season ticketholders to regard as her or his customers. What benefits could result from having everyone in the company call on customers? What possible problems could arise from such a policy?

3. At Conexco, field salespeople call on major accounts, and the call center handles medium-sized accounts, but small accountholders place orders through the website. Each channel is operated as a separate profit center, meaning that each channel manager is evaluated on how well each channel performs in delivering profit. What are some potential problems with this approach? What are the benefits? What needs to happen to maximize benefits and minimize problems?

4. Some have argued that technology will, ultimately, replace salespeople. Others believe salespeople will always have a place. What do you think? Why?

5. In some companies, customer service is carried out by the salesperson. In others, it is the responsibility of a separate department. When would a separate department make more sense? When would it not?

6. When you choose insurance for your automobile, you can select from any number of options. How many channels can you list through which you can buy car insurance? Identify a couple of companies for each channel. Are there some that seem to use a lot more channels, or do they seem to focus on just one channel? Pick two very different companies and consider why they would focus on such different strategies. Which would you prefer, and why?

7. How do salespeople affect the supply chains of their firms?

8. Would you trust someone more if you knew your salesperson was an employee of the company that made the product or an employee of a company representing many different product lines? Would it matter to you whether that salesperson was paid a commission? What types of products might change your response?

Role Play

Pet Business Today

Pet Business Today is a small, family-owned magazine that serves pet stores and small animal veterinarians. With about 5,000 subscribers, the magazine has increased subscriptions by 10 percent over the past two years, and the family expects to gain more. Advertising sales, though, which really bring in the revenue, have been stagnant. So far, owner Frank Scarpetti has tried to do all of the advertising sales himself, in addition to serving as editor. But today, Sandy Lake is calling on Frank to convince him to let her company do the advertising sales for him. Her company, Lake Sales, will also take over the subscriber management. Two statistics indicate plenty of room for growth: there are more than 5,000 independent pet stores and 70,000 vets in the United States.

Assignment

Break into pairs, with one person taking on the role of Frank and another Sandy. Frank should develop a list of objectives (using the SMART format from Chapter 1), as well as a list of concerns regarding outsourcing the selling effort. Sandy should develop a particular sales format (telephone, field, etc.) and prepare a list of advantages for that format. Once prepared, then role play the sales call Sandy makes to Frank.

Caselets

Caselet 2.1: *Maxfield Promotions*

Sharna Maxfield looked at the numbers and blinked. Her company, a small promotional products agency with three salespeople, had grown little over the past year. Sales were up only eight percent, but customer complaints had doubled. Over the past quarter, 12 new customers were added, but 15 had switched suppliers.

A promotional products agency typically represents many manufacturers. One manufacturer, for example, might make cups and glasses, while another might make shirts and jackets. All of these products are then printed or embroidered with the client's name and advertising message. Salespeople are typically paid a 10 percent commission on each sale, earning an average of $10,000 per month. Each rep who earns that much adds another $25,000 in profit margin to the company, which is used to pay expenses and benefits, and to cover Sharna's salary.

Sharna had considered adding a salesperson, but no new salesperson would work for straight commission, at least not until sales were high enough to cover expenses. Sharna estimated that would require paying the salesperson a salary of $5,000 per month—a major investment when the company's net income (after paying Sharna's salary) was averaging only a little over $10,000 a month.

The company averaged 40 large customers (each billed $20,000 per year) per salesperson. Small customers, taken together, accounted for about $20,000 per month in revenue per rep, with each rep managing 100 small customers.

What alternatives for growth might Sharna consider? Can you think of some multi-channel options she might pursue?

Caselet 2.2: *ProMedia Technology*

ProMedia Technology is a software company that sells to companies of all types. The software packages help marketers and public relations (PR) professionals manage media. Products include:

- Financial project tracking, an application that tracks and allocates costs to projects, and also enables budgeting through "what-if" scenario planning.

- Media buying and tracking software, which automates routine media buying.

- Creative management, which stores and makes available various creative illustrations.

- Lead management, an application that tracks leads by media channels and develops return on investment (ROI) models.

- The PR tracking application, an add-on to the media research service, scores the effectiveness of various media placements and provides an ROI on PR.

Companies can buy any or all of the applications and pay a monthly rate based on an annual subscription. Subscription rates vary by size of the account, and are priced either by the number of users (such as the financial project tracking), or by the number of pages (such as the creative management application), or both (such as the media research service).

As manager of the company's sales force of 12 people, you report directly to the CEO, who also happens to be the sole owner and founder of ProMedia. Over coffee last week, he mentioned that the company's growth of less than 10 percent for the past two years was stifling product development. He had to either find a way to grow faster or reduce costs; otherwise, some start-up company might leapfrog over ProMedia's offerings. He's thinking that cutting the sales staff in half and going with two inside salespeople might be the best route, and wanted you to report back on some options. Realistically, what options do you have? What do you think is the best option, knowing that the goal is to cut sales costs by 25 percent or grow sales by more than 15 percent?

References

1. Sarin, Shikhar, Trina Sego, Ajay Kohli and Goutam Challagalla (2010). "Characteristics that Enhance Training Effectiveness in Implementing Technological Change in Sales Strategy." *Journal of Personal Selling & Sales Management* (30)2, 143–156.
2. Liu Zhongcheng, and Li Hongyu (2013). "Research on Pricing Strategy of Online Reverse Auction Based on Complete Information," *International Business & Management*, 6(2), 71–76.
3. Jones, Gareth (2013). "Carphone Warehouse Harnesses the Power of Mobile Medium to Facilitate Multi-Channel Assistance and Drive Sales," *Marketing Week*, 34(21), 43.
4. Zimmerman, Andrea (2011). "Research at the Marketing-Finance Interface: Does it Pay to Outsource Marketing?" *AMA Summer Educators' Conference Proceedings*, 22, 53.
5. Pass, Michael W. (2012). "Outsourcing the Sales Function: The Influence of Communication and Customer Orientation," *Journal of the Academy of Marketing Studies*, 17(2), 99–119.
6. Goetz, Oliver, Ann-Kristin Hoelter, and Manfred Krafft (2013). "The Role of Sales and Marketing in Market-Oriented Companies," *Journal of Personal Selling & Sales Management* 33(4), 353–372.

PART TWO

Sales Leadership

In Part One, you were introduced to the concepts of mission and strategy, as well as the multi-channel reality that is sales today. You also have an idea of how complicated those channels can be, with salespeople who are company employees calling on independent distributors, or contact centers supporting field salespeople who, in turn, support manufacturer's agents. Somehow, these channels must also be integrated with the company's web channels and any other channels they may choose.

Simply managing in this reality is insufficient; leadership is also required. In Part Two, we explore sales leadership, beginning with Chapter Three, *Leadership and the Sales Executive*.

Are leaders born or made? What would it be like if you wanted to be a leader or were thrust into that position and you weren't sure if you were one of the born leaders? Yet we all know people we think are natural-born leaders. Can anyone lead? Can anyone manage? We don't claim that one chapter will enable everyone to become a leader or a manager. This chapter does identify those actions that separate leadership from management, but not necessarily leaders from managers. After all, as you will see in the chapter, managers must lead and leaders must manage—and there are things you can learn to do that will make you a better leader or manager.

In today's reality, ethics are extremely important. Chapter Four, *Ethics, the Law, and Sales Leadership*, explores the role of sales leadership in creating an ethical sales climate. First, we explore the more common approaches to ethics, such as the Golden Rule and the Protestant work ethic, that individuals can adopt. Carefully considering one's own approach to ethics is a good first step, but it takes more than one's good intentions to create an ethical climate. The chapter discusses policies and procedures that a sales leader can enact and enforce that should yield the proper climate, as well as considers legal issues that will confront sales managers. The right for a company to exist is a privilege extended by society. That is one reason sales executives must create the right ethical climate—so that their firm can serve its customers well.

LEADERSHIP AND THE SALES EXECUTIVE

LEARNING OBJECTIVES

After completing this chapter, you should be able to:

- Understand the historical development and different approaches to examining leadership.
- Recognize the contributions made by contemporary leadership approaches.
- Identify issues that today's sales leaders face.
- Use the information in this chapter to develop your own leadership skills.

Effective leadership is vital to guiding your sales organization. Are leaders born, or can leadership skills be developed? If they can be developed, what is the best way to do this? Can everyone be a leader?

Although there are many definitions for the term "leadership," having sales personnel with leadership skills to guide your sales organization is critical. A sales organization with these skills can overcome many challenges in a competitive workplace.

CHAPTER 3

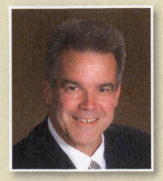

KURT MUELLER
Senior Vice President
of Sales
Hormel Consumer
Products Sales

Sales Manager Profile: Kurt Mueller

FROM HIS DAYS IN COLLEGE, Kurt Mueller knew he wanted to work with people. After a brief exposure to social work and management, he decided that sales would best meet his interests.

After graduating, Mueller progressed through a number of sales positions with Hormel Foods. Once in sales, he saw the unlimited options of growing his career—not only in sales, but in other areas of the company. He started as a sales representative and advanced through several other sales positions, including district sales manager. He then advanced to a series of marketing positions where he led the successful launch of several new consumer products. In his last position, as Senior Vice President of Business Planning, he took on both marketing and sales responsibilities, including the hiring and training of their sales team members. Through the course of his career with Hormel, Kurt has been responsible for a staff ranging from eight to 108 members, a force that has generated more than one billion dollars in sales.

In his management positions, Mueller has made a point to understand everything—from the challenges of inventory and scheduling, loading, and filling orders to the strategy behind marketing a product, the importance of understanding the analytics supporting what success looks like, to selling the actual products that Hormel markets.

Mueller describes his leadership style as a combination of empowerment and mentorship. It has evolved over time, with insights gained from previous bosses and mentors as well as through formalized training programs and reading.

In order for an individual to be successful, he believes, she must be empowered to make decisions independently. "I work to ensure that my team members understand the positions of all the parties involved in a decision, and to secure everyone's 'buy-in.' This gives them the opportunity to claim ownership in the decision-making process, expands their experience, and prepares team members to take on additional roles of responsibility during the course of their careers."

Mueller also believes that a leader needs to fully understand the business challenges facing their employees through a mentoring relationship. "It is important for each team member to fully understand the business and area of his or her responsibility. As a leader, if you don't know it, you should work to understand it." One of the ways he does this is by being accessible. "I manage with 'an open door policy,' meaning that I encourage members of my team to feel free to visit with me at any time to discuss any issues they may have." In addition, he maintains a regularly scheduled weekly meeting with his direct reports. "This allows me to coach and provide guidance on the business as well as career discussions. It allows me the opportunity to build a relationship of trust."

Looking ahead, Mueller believes that leaders will need to work harder to maintain meaningful communication with their team members. "With face-to-face and direct communication being replaced with e-mails and text messages, it will be a bigger challenge for leader to keep the culture of their group intact, and not fall victim to technology overloads." ■

What is Leadership?

The topic of **leadership** receives a great deal of attention these days. It seems that you can almost always find a headline discussing the leadership of a country, a company, or an organization. Sometimes it is because a positive, notable event has occurred—for example, a company has successfully launched a new product or service, or reached an important milestone. Oftentimes, however, it is because of just the opposite: something negative has occurred because of a lack of leadership. For example, perhaps, a customer or a group of customers was treated poorly, or a product or service did not function as expected.

People agree that every organization needs good leadership—and, especially, good sales managers. How does an organization achieve good leadership? Is it a trait that you identify when hiring employees? Is it a skill that can be developed in current employees? Can good managers be good leaders, and are the two one and the same?

In an effort to answers such questions, formal investigation has been going on for years. As a result, today, there are nearly as many definitions of leadership as there are researchers who have studied the topic. Researchers generally agree, however, that leadership is a process whereby an individual influences other group members to move toward or achieve a common goal. Four key points are implicit in this definition: *Leadership is a process*—not a trait, or characteristic, of a person. *Leadership involves influence. Leadership occurs in a group. Leadership involves movement toward a goal or goals.*

Leading versus Managing

Based on the previous definition, ask yourself: If a sales manager attempts to persuade employees to accomplish a shared goal, is he engaging in leadership, or just **management**? Harvard Business School Professor John Kotter, widely regarded as an authority on leadership, has tried to answer this question. In the late 1980s and early 1990s, Kotter spent several years interviewing, observing, and analyzing questionnaire data from nearly 200 leaders in business organizations. He noted that leadership can be defined two ways: *as a process* that helps direct and mobilize people and ideas, and referring to a person in *a formal position* whose job is to lead a group. The first definition describes a leader; the second describes a manager. *Leaders* are involved with establishing direction, aligning and communicating direction, and motivating and inspiring. *Managers* are involved with planning and budgeting, organizing and staffing, and controlling and problem solving.[1] A summary of these differences is presented in Exhibit 3.1.

EXHIBIT 3.1   Leadership Practices versus Management Practices

Leadership Practices

- *Direction*—development of a vision to guide the organization in the future
- *Aligning people*—communication and community building to support the organization's goals
- *Motivating and inspiring*—working to overcome political, bureaucratic, and economic setbacks by appealing to human needs, values, and emotions

Management Practices

- *Planning and budgeting*—setting and achieving targets, allocating appropriate levels of resources
- *Organizing and staffing*—structuring and staffing the organization with needed people
- *Controlling and problem solving*—monitoring the implementation of plans and making needed adjustments
- *Predictability*—results in an orderly, predictable pattern of results

Based on John P. Kotter, "What Leaders Really Do," *Harvard Business Review*, (Dec., 2001), Vol. 79, Issue 11, 85–96.

Kotter identified a number of similarities between leading and managing. They both include deciding what needs to be done and working with people to make sure action is taken. However, leadership focuses on change, while management focuses on results that keep things working efficiently. An organization needs both if it is to prosper. With only strong leadership (without strong management), the firm's executives might advocate change for change's sake. ("Let's try a different approach to this issue.") By contrast, with doses of heavy management (and no leadership), the organization might become too bureaucratic and produce order for order's sake ("We've always done it this way.")

It was Kotter's opinion that, in years past, most organizations did not need many people in leadership positions. However, with the advent of complex technology, increasing educational opportunities, changing demographics, and the intricacies of operating in a global marketplace, this is no longer the case. More change requires more leadership. Compounding this situation are the following research findings:

- Respondents from two-thirds of companies surveyed indicated they had too many people with strong management skills but weak leadership skills.

- More than 95 percent indicated having too few people with both strong leadership and management skills.

- More than 80 percent of respondents indicated that their firms did less than a very good job of attracting, developing, and motivating people with leadership potential.[2]

- Only 37 percent of sales leaders say they possessed sufficient leadership skills upon assuming their first leadership position.[3]

- Two-thirds of sales vice presidents indicated that fewer than 60 percent of their sales managers were meeting expectations.[4]

- Only 18 percent of HR professionals rated their leadership bench strength as strong or very strong, and only one in three organizations report that leaders had high quality, effective development plans.[5]

Given the challenges that exist in today's marketplace, organizations need their employees to be both good managers and good leaders. Much of the remainder of this book will focus on management skills. This chapter, obviously, focuses on leadership. We'll begin this process by examining the findings of some past leadership researchers, in chronological order, and reflect on the contributions they have made. As we review each of the different approaches, consider how to apply their contributions to your leadership style.

Understanding Leadership: An Historical Perspective

Over the years, a number of different approaches to studying leadership have developed. As shortcomings of each theory were identified, a new, improved perspective developed. In this section we'll describe some of the major approaches, some shortcomings of each, and how this has led to a better understanding of leadership. Exhibit 3.2 outlines these approaches.

The Trait Approach: "These are the Traits You Need to Be a Leader."

Is there one trait that makes a person a good salesperson or sales manager? Would it be the ability to communicate with people and motivate them, the ability to analyze information and prioritize it, or some other trait? During the first part of the 20th century, many researchers examined the traits or characteristics that leaders shared. Often referred to as "The Great Man Theory of Leadership," it examined (primarily

---

EXHIBIT 3.2   Leadership Research Approaches

Trait Approach—1900s to 1940s; 2000s

"These are the traits you need to be a leader."

- Leaders are different from followers.
- Leaders tend to display more intelligence, self-confidence, determination, integrity, and predictability.

Behavioral Approach—1950s to 1960s

"This is how leaders behave."

- Leaders should use a combination of behaviors focused on group relations (consideration) and tasks (initiating structure).
- Group-level supervision is preferred to supervising employees at the individual level.
- Groups report more satisfaction with higher levels of consideration.

Situational Approaches—1960s to 1970s

"Assess the situation and fit behavior to it."

- Leaders are different from followers.
- Group-level supervision is preferred to supervising employees at the individual level.
- Groups report more satisfaction with higher levels of consideration.

Contemporary Perspectives of Understanding Leadership—1980s to 1990s

"Motivate your followers through your leadership."

- Leaders should work with all group members to help them develop their leadership skills.
- Good leader/member relationships result in increased job satisfaction, productivity, and decreased turnover.
- Leaders should strive to be role models.

Emerging Theories of Leadership—1990s to 2000s

"Develop your followers."

- Leaders should be proactive, work to be good listeners, and build on the contributions of others.
- Leaders should work to support and advance each individual.
- Leaders should be humble, diligent, driven to produce sustained results, and ambitious for their organizations—not themselves.

---

male) leaders such as Thomas Jefferson, Abraham Lincoln, Napoleon Bonaparte, Mahatma Gandhi, and Martin L. King, Jr. The assumption was that people were born with certain traits that lent themselves to the development of leadership skills and, consequently, were more likely to become leaders. Identify the traits and you can then identify a person who either will be, or is, a leader.

Initially, these traits included a wide array of characteristics such as height, intelligence, dominance, and social skills. After a massive review of hundreds of trait studies, R.M. Stogdill criticized them for lacking universality.[6] He demonstrated that a leader with one set of traits in one situation was not a leader in another. He did observe that leaders differed from followers in that they had the following traits: intelligence, alertness, insight, responsibility, initiative, persistence, self-confidence, and sociability.

For years, further investigation into the trait approach languished. However, during the 1990s and into the twenty-first century, a more sophisticated statistical analysis procedure, called *meta-analysis,* was developed. Meta-analysis allows the results of different studies to be compared. Using this procedure, researchers re-analyzed earlier data to identify differences between leaders and followers. They made strong cases that **leadership traits** explain what makes some individuals leaders.[7, 8]

P.G. Northouse[9] examined the major trait studies and offered a summary of the major characteristics with a positive relationship to leadership. They include:

- **Intelligence**—Higher verbal, perceptual, and reasoning skills are important. However, a leader's general intelligence should not greatly differ from her followers, or it can be counterproductive.

- **Self-confidence**—The ability to be certain about one's competencies and skills helps produce self-confidence. These skills assist the leader in conveying appropriate and sincere messages that influence followers.

- **Determination**—Leaders demonstrate the ability to get the job done. They must have drive, dominance, and persistence for achieving their goals.

- **Integrity**—Leaders must demonstrate honesty and trustworthiness. Followers don't want to be deceived, and need to see these traits in a leader's actions.

- **Sociability**—The ability to interact in a comfortable, outgoing, and pleasant manner in social relationships is critical. Demonstrating good social skills helps leaders develop strong relationships with their followers.

The trait leadership approach can be observed in the success of Mary Jurmaine and her company Realityworks. As Jurmaine faced the challenges of a young family, limited job prospects, and a husband about to be laid off from his position as an aerospace engineer, Jurmaine's sheer determination to succeed blossomed. Utilizing her husband's engineering skills, the couple developed a computerized, lifelike, infant for use in simulating the challenges of caring for a newborn. (Their simulator is used in high school parenting education classes.) Jurmaine was responsible for the firm's public relations, advertising, and sales. She was so successful that the product received coverage in *USA Today, People, Forbes, The New York Times,* and on *The Oprah Winfrey Show.* Her strong determination trait has certainly been a leadership asset for Realityworks.

The trait approach has several limitations. Most notably, it lacks a universal list of traits. Furthermore, it's not evident as to which trait is more important than another and how they interact with one another. For example, can a shortage of one trait be compensated for with an excess of another? A person's traits, and the strength of each, change over time; however, the effect of changes does not appear to reverse a person's leadership ability.

Even with these shortcomings, the trait approach does offer several useful applications. Some organizations will look closely at these traits and incorporate them in their selection criteria when they recruit and select individuals for employment. Students interested in a sales leadership position should work to develop these traits and reflect them in their résumés.

The biggest beneficiary of this research is the area of training. Knowing what characteristics and experiences matter most in developing better leaders is very important. Using this information, organizations can help develop employees' leadership skills. The "Global Sales Management" box for this chapter elaborates on this benefit.

The Behavioral Approach: "This is How a Leader Behaves."

Unable to overcome the limitations of the trait approach, researchers pursued a new school of thought. World War II was ending, and there was an invigorated interest in studying leadership. Instead of focusing on leaders' characteristics, this approach examined how a leader interacted, or behaved, with his subordinates. In other words, the approach looked at different **leadership styles**. Three groups of researchers pursued this approach, with complementary findings.

Researchers at Ohio State University identified two dimensions of behavior: *consideration* and *initiating structure.*[10] Consideration behaviors dealt with maintaining good social interaction and relationships with a group's members, and building respect and trust within a group. The second dimension, initiating structure, dealt with behaviors that focus the group on accomplishing its task. These behaviors included giving direction, keeping people focused, and staying on schedule. It was

GLOBAL SALES MANAGEMENT   Identifying Global Business Leaders

World politics, communications, and technology have helped fuel the growth of multinational commerce around the world. This globalization has resulted in increasing interdependence on technology, economic, and social/cultural issues across countries. Perhaps the most challenging issues come from developing a better understanding of social/cultural influences. Business leaders now must understand and appreciate the cultural differences that come with operating in different environments.

Companies such as the Center for Creative Leadership and Development Dimensions are helping business leaders understand how leadership, and the factors that contribute to it, vary depending upon the culture. These firms have selection tools that can be used to help identify individuals with high leadership potential, as well as areas needing development for aspiring leaders. Both companies can also provide leadership development experiences for individuals, groups, and companies. A poor choice in identifying leaders can have a monumental impact on a business. Ramifications can lead to a good product or service that has no buyers. As multinational business growth continues, so will the demands on identifying cross-cultural leadership talent.

Much of the early research on identifying leadership traits was conducted in U.S. companies with U.S. employees. Yet today, many high-potential growth opportunities for businesses have locations in Asia, in countries such as China, Japan, Singapore, South Korea, New Zealand, and Australia, as well as in Europe and South America,. Therefore, using North American leadership measures for employees who have grown up in other parts of the world has significant drawbacks. We can't assume that experiences present in aspiring leaders in Dallas are the same as those growing up in Shanghai, Tokyo, or Bombay.

Fortunately, today there is a growing understanding of the cultural differences between what leadership traits and behaviors are considered important depending upon where you live. For example, Anglo countries (e.g., the United States, England. and Australia) value leaders who are competitive and results-oriented, but are less attached to their family groups when compared with other countries. They want leaders to be motivating, visionary, not autocratic, and considerate of others. Leaders should be team-oriented and autonomous. Countries such as China, Japan, and Singapore (from the Confucian Asian cluster) place higher value on results and encouraging the group working together, as opposed to having individual goals. They tend to have higher levels of loyalty and devotion to families than other countries. Their leader is described as a person who cares about others, but who uses status and position to make independent decisions without the input of others.

While there are many differences between cultural groups, it might be surprising to note there are some universal, similar findings on leader characteristics. Most agree that effective leaders are high in integrity, are charismatic and value-based, and have good interpersonal skills. Additionally, an ineffective leadership style is characterized as asocial, malevolent, and self-focused, no matter where the leaders are located.

Based on House, R. J., Hanges, P.J., Javidan, M., Dorfman, P.W. and Gupta, V. (Eds.), (2004). *Culture, leadership and organizations: The GLOBE study of 62 societies*. Thousand Oaks, CA: Sage.

theorized that each dimension was independent of the other—that is, that a leader could exhibit a high amount of consideration and a low amount of initiating structure or vice versa. Conversely, the leader could exhibit either a low or high amount of both behaviors. Leaders exhibiting a high amount of both behaviors were thought to be preferred.

A second group of researchers at the University of Michigan's Survey Research Center examined the behavior of leaders from highly productive work groups and groups with low productivity. They found that leaders of the productive groups were more *employee centered* rather than *production centered,* and that they exercised supervision at the group level, rather than at an individual level.[11] In other words,

The Behavioral Approach to leadership focuses on the dimensions of a leader's concern for people and a concern for production.

these leaders were less likely to micromanage individual employees; they concentrated, instead, on the efforts of the group as a whole.

Building on the foundation laid out by these early researchers, a third behavioral approach was developed by Blake and Mouton.[12] Initially called the Managerial Grid, it was later renamed the Leadership Grid.[13] This approach relies heavily on the previous findings dealing with the importance of leaders' demonstrating *a concern for people* and a *concern for production*. Individual and group assessments of a leader's style results in a score that is displayed on a grid. The axes for the grid reflect the leader's concern for people and concern for results (originally, for production) and are scaled 1-9. Each corner of the grid portrays a different leadership style: Impoverished Management (1,1—Low concern for people, low concern for results); Country Club Management (1,9—low concern for results, high concern for people), Authority-Compliance Management (9,1—high concern for results, low concern for people), Team Management (9,9—high concern for results and people). An additional style, Middle of the Road Management, was in the center of all the others (5,5—a midpoint of both axes).

All three behavioral approaches share an intuitive appeal. They describe behaviors that leaders need to exhibit on both a social level and a task level. If you were to subscribe to these leadership approaches, you would want to engage in behaviors addressing both the social needs of individual group members and those focused on accomplishing the task. The more you can display behaviors that demonstrate "consideration," the more satisfaction your group should report.

An example of this leadership style can be observed in Meg Whitman, formerly the CEO of eBay, now at Hewlett-Packard (HP). While at eBay, Whitman managed the company as it grew from 30 to 13,000 employees. She knows that her style balances the dimensions of working with people (the "number one job of a CEO," she says) and being able to focus on the tasks related to current challenges at hand.[14]

All three behavioral approaches have been criticized on several grounds. None of them identified one best way to lead. Testing the theories has consistently indicated that leadership depends upon the characteristics of the situation—not just those of the leader. Additionally, the theories lacked empirical evidence linking leadership styles with effectiveness. Though they implied that leaders with a high concern for both people and production are the most effective, this has never been demonstrated across all situations.[15]

Situational Approaches: "Assess the Situation, then Fit Behavior to It."

The lack of empirical evidence linking trait and behavioral approaches with the effectiveness of leaders underscored the importance of examining *the situations* that leaders faced. As a result, instead of focusing on leaders' traits and behavior patterns, research shifted to improve the understanding of different situations and how leaders should best respond.

The pioneer in this area was Fred Fiedler,[16] whose **contingency theory of leadership** incorporated both an assessment of the leader's style and characteristics of the situation. As did his predecessors, Fiedler considered a leader's style along the dimensions of relationships (concern for people) and task orientation (concern for production). Fiedler believed that a leader's style was stable—not open to major changes. In other words, only the situation could change, and this, in turn, impacted the leader's effectiveness. Evaluation of each leadership situation was based on three characteristics each considered either favorable or unfavorable in contributing to the leader's effectiveness. The dimensions were:

- **Leader-member relations**—Were the relations between the leader and group members good or poor?

- **Task structure**—Were the steps to solving the problem structured, or was the approach to solving the problem unclear?

- **Position power**—To what extent did the leader have formal authority to reward or punish the followers?

Task-oriented leaders will be most effective in either well-structured settings or disorganized settings (in which they can provide structure to their followers). Relationship-oriented leaders are generally more effective in situations that the model considers less favorable. Such a leader can work to develop strong relations and use them effectively as the group tackles a less-structured, more ambiguous task.

Because the demands of different situations are not identical, they will require leaders with different skill sets. This line of thought led to the concept of *organizational engineering*, where efforts are made to match tasks to people with the prerequisite skills for success.

Fiedler garnered applause for his pioneering efforts, but his model was not without weaknesses. For example, no one has yet replicated some of his initial findings. Additionally, because Fielder's position was that a leader's style was stable or not likely to change, the model doesn't consider the fact that a leader could learn from past experiences and adapt his style to the situation.[17]

A second leadership approach that incorporates the leader with the characteristics of the situation is the **situational leadership** model offered by Hersey and Blanchard.[18] Contrary to Fiedler's approach, where the style of the leader does not change, this model assumes that the leader can adapt her behavior to the constraints of the situation. In order to determine how to respond to a group, the leader must diagnose the group's level of task competency and commitment on a continuum from "developing" to "developed." Once this diagnosis has been made, the leader must then adapt her behavior along two dimensions: directive behaviors (task-oriented) and supportive behaviors (relationship-oriented). Depending upon a group's level of development, the leader should utilize one of four leadership approaches when working with the group. These styles include:

- **Directing**—providing a high degree of direction and a low degree of support to the group's members. In other words, the leader simply instructs members on what to do.

- **Coaching**—providing a high degree of direction and support to the group's members. In other words, the leader helps structure the group, and works with its members.

- **Supporting**—providing a low degree of direction and a high degree of support to the group's members. In other words, the leader works with members, but gives them the opportunity to make their own decisions.

- **Delegating**—providing a low degree of direction and support to the group's members. In other words, the leader gives members much authority.

The Situational Leader® approach is a popular training program for leadership. A version of the program has been developed specifically for sales leaders. Its popularity reflects the fact that it is easy to understand and offers guidance about which style(s) a leader should incorporate, depending upon the level of followers' development. Although this seems easy for sales managers to use, questions remain as to whether or not the data backs up the theory's assumption. For example, do leaders truly have the ability to diagnose the level of development of their followers?

The situational approach to leadership encourages leaders to adjust their style depending upon the characteristics of the situation they face.

Introduced in the 1970s, a third contribution to the situational leadership approach focuses on the level of involvement in decision making that a leader should obtain from group members. The **Vroom and Yetton Model**[19] examines each situation in terms of its structure, available information, and how important the decision's acceptance is to its implementation. It then proposes the level to which followers should be involved in the decision making. Group decision making has both benefits and drawbacks: When followers are allowed to make decisions, they typically will be more committed. Moreover, they might have additional information that the leader does not possess, which can help them make better decisions. Making group decisions often takes more time and, as anyone who has ever been involved in a group decision knows, it can lead to conflict when a clear course of action is not evident.

In sum, the situational approach advocates no one "best style." As a leader, you need to consider the characteristics of the situation and adapt your behaviors to each unique challenge. Consider Johan Hjertonsson, who received a call at home from his boss, the CEO of consumer product giant Electrolux. Hjertonsson's boss told him that "things weren't moving fast enough" and that sales were falling. He wanted Hjertonsson to fix the problem as soon possible. Faced with this challenging and changing situation, Hjertonsson adapted a leadership style that included the use of tight timetables. He also sought input from many parties, and used both "carrots and sticks" with his team to make things happen—fast. His success can be seen in the multitude of new products introduced by Electrolux.[20]

Contemporary Perspectives of Understanding Leadership: "Motivate Your Followers Through Leadership."

The next two approaches to understanding leadership appeared in the 1980s and 1990s. Neither focuses on the situation. Instead, they emphasize the relationships that exist between leaders and individual group members. These approaches theorize that, if a leader fosters the development of the members of the group, the members will grow and, in turn, move toward shared leadership roles.

The first such theory is the **leader-member exchange (LMX) theory**, which has evolved over the course of the last 25 years.[21, 22] The focus of LMX is on the unique relationship that exists between a leader and each group member. This relationship is referred to as a *dyad*. The theory proposes that, as a result of these interactions, two different relationships can develop: *in-group* and *out-group* exchanges. In situations in which the leader and a member develop high levels of interaction, support, trust, and respect, the member is considered part of the in-group. In situations in which that type of interaction fails to develop, an out-group relationship develops. The out-group relationship is based more on the formal roles of the organization, whereby a leader assigns job responsibilities and ensures that the follower completes them. These relationships are characterized as being more formal, or impersonal. As a result, followers are less satisfied and productive.

The distinction between in- and out-group membership is measured through the use of a questionnaire that addresses the level of affection, loyalty, contribution to work, and respect.

Further development of this approach resulted in the concept of *leadership making*.[22, 23] This approach suggests that every leader should work to have as many in-group relationships as possible with their followers, and few or no out-group relationships. Leadership making recognizes, however, that such leadership qualities as trust, respect, and the ability to make a contribution to one's job, develop over time.

According to the **transformational leadership theory,** a leader is someone who is determined and has the charisma to inspire, change, or otherwise transform their followers.[24, 25] Transformational leaders do this by stimulating their followers intellectually, encouraging them, and supporting their development. Leaders give personal attention to their followers and make each of them feel valued and important. As a result, their followers trust and respect them and want to be like them.

Research has generally supported many of the tenets of transformational leadership and found evidence that it positively correlates with job satisfaction and better performance on the part of employees. However, transformational leadership takes a very broad-based view of how a leader should act. It does not prescribe how a leader should act in a particular situation.

To adopt this style of this leadership, a sales manager would focus on building trust and respect among all employees. In some situations, that might mean focusing on improving a relationship with a member of the sales force, and in another, it might mean helping a member lay out the activities needed to be successful in a sales call. Over time, followers develop increased job satisfaction, become more productive, and take on actions similar to those of the leader. Michael Brown, the vice president of sales for Kodak, exemplifies this style. "How you recognize and treat salespeople is something I've focused on," says Brown. "You need to communicate with them en masse, but also on a one-to-one basis." Even during tough times, Brown keeps them motivated by constantly communicating his vision to his team. They trust him and support him, because they feel like he's one of the members of the team.[26]

Emerging Concepts of Leadership: "Develop Your Followers."

Several leadership approaches popular with the general public might be thought of as having somewhat of a "self-help" orientation. Three approaches, developed in the 1990s and early 2000s, fall into this category and have also found acceptance in the business community.

The late business professor Steven Covey gained worldwide recognition for having developed the **principle-centered leadership** approach. Covey outlined his approach in his book *Seven Habits of Highly Effective People*.[27] The seven habits (and an additional eighth, added in 2004) are briefly outlined below:

1. **Be proactive.** You can either take an active or a passive role in your environment. Take responsibility and initiative in your actions.

2. **Begin with the end in mind.** Make plans for where you want to go.

3. **Put first things first.** Manage your time and schedule your priorities in order to execute your plan. (See #2.)

4. **Think win-win.** Adopt a philosophy based on cooperation.

5. **Seek first to understand, then to be understood.** Be a good listener. Learn to diagnose before you prescribe.

6. **Synergize.** Respect differences and build on the contributions of others.

7. **Sharpen the saw.** Practice self-renewal, including the four dimensions of your nature: physical, social/emotional, mental, and spiritual.

8. **Find your voice and inspire others to find theirs.** Look for the potential in people.[28]

Central to the principle-centered leadership approach is listening and understanding different points of view. Understand first, then be understood.

Although not designed to be a theory, Covey's "principles" have won wide acclaim from individuals and organizations alike.

In the 1970s, the **servant leadership** approach grew from the writings of teacher and management consultant Robert Greenleaf.[29] Greenleaf believed that leaders should serve their followers. By serving their followers, they set an example. Some observers have commented that this approach has its origins in the teachings of

Jesus Christ. It emphasizes collaboration, empathy, and the ethical use of power. It was never designed as a theory.

A number of characteristics of the servant-leader have been identified: listening, empathy, healing, awareness, persuasion, stewardship, commitment to the growth of people, and building community.[30] A growing number of companies have embraced these concepts and include service to others as an integral part of their culture. Embedded in the mission statements of companies such as Starbucks, Men's Wearhouse, ServiceMaster and Southwest Airlines are examples of this approach. Additionally, a growing number of colleges and universities are requiring students to participate in service learning projects, believing the practice to be an important part of higher education. The "Ethics in Sales Management" box below discusses the importance of ethics in leadership and includes the five principles leaders should strive to incorporate.

ETHICS IN SALES MANAGEMENT   **The Principles of Ethical Leadership**

A popular concept emerging from leadership researchers and theorists is that leaders need to act ethically and lead ethically. Drawing from a number of theorists, Peter Northouse has observed a movement which advocates that leaders are those who build a more just and caring society. In order to promote the good of their followers, leaders must act ethically to influence others and engage them in accomplishing mutual goals.

Northouse has summarized five principles of **ethical leadership** that can be seen throughout history. These principles include respect, service, justice, honesty, and community.

- Respect—Leaders must treat others, and their decisions, with respect.
- Service—Leaders serve others through coaching, mentoring, teambuilding, and helping others.
- Justice—Leaders treat others with fairness and in a just and impartial manner.
- Honesty—Leaders need to be honest and open in all their actions.
- Community—Leaders should pursue goals for the good of the group.

When sales managers influence others through their leadership actions, they have the obligation to act in a manner that incorporates these guiding principles.

Does taking an ethical approach to leadership work? Next time you are in an office of someone you consider a leader, look around and see if, in addition to some sales awards, it doesn't also have some civic awards and citations, as well.

Based on Peter G. Northouse, "Leadership Ethics," *Leadership: Theory and Practice*, 6th edition, (2012), 377–395.

The **Level 5 leadership model** was set forth by another former business professor, Jim Collins.[31, 32] Collins sought to identify the characteristics of "good" companies versus "great" companies, based on a number of financial performance measures over a 15-year period. Some of those identified as great companies included Abbott, Kimberly-Clark, Walgreens and Wells Fargo. Collins discovered that leaders of great companies shared several common traits: They were modest, willful, humble, and fearless—and that they set up their successors for greater success, and were diligent.

The five-level hierarchy describes the skills and abilities individuals should possess as they move from using characteristics attributed to their positions as formal leaders into the more skilled and esteemed Level 5 leadership positions. The model proposes that an individual's level of skills builds successively on the skills and abilities of those from the previous level(s). Several concepts from earlier leadership research can be observed in the framework. For example, the first two levels reflect the need for leaders to have certain traits to be successful. Leaders operating at Level 1, termed the Highly Capable Individual, are hardworking and display the knowledge, skills, and abilities needed to master their particular job. At Level 2, the Contributing Team member level, leaders bring interpersonal skills that allow them to work effectively with others in groups. To be ranked in the hierarchy's three highest levels, individuals need to increasingly incorporate more transformational leader characteristics into their leadership repertoire. The Level 3 leaders, labeled the Competent Manager, have the skills needed to organize followers and resources to achieve goals. Level 4 leaders, the Effective Leader, can convincingly articulate a vision and motivate followers to achieve it. The Level 5 leader, or Level 5 Executive, is capable of executing all of the previous skills with a style that demonstrates humility and determination. Although the model is conceptually intuitive, additional research is needed to confirm Collin's hierarchy.

The Level 5 concepts have come under criticism because, over the years, some of the firms identified as higher-level performers have faltered,[33] e.g., among them Circuit City. Collins responded with new research, noting that great firms could change over time, but could also return to their past levels of high performance.[34]

For over 85 years, Marriott has fostered a culture that puts taking care of and developing their employees first. The Marriott sales force is consistently ranked as one of the best.

Leadership Challenges for the Sales Executive

Today's sales management leaders face many challenges when leading their organizations. Having good leadership at all levels of the organization can make the difference when it comes to meeting and exceeding these challenges. Sales executives frequently cite the following leadership challenges:

- **Recruiting and selecting good employees.** Finding and hiring the right person for your organization is vital to its future growth. The impact of a bad hire can be significant in terms of lost good will and sales, as well as training costs.

- **Keeping good employees.** Once you have identified good employees, you must work to ensure that they want to continue working for you and not be hired away by another firm.

- **Executing virtual leadership.** Sales managers may go for long periods without any physical proximity or face-to-face contact with their employees. Communicating effectively via phone, e-mail, text messaging, and other electronic methods with their employees is, therefore, essential.

- **Diversity in the sales force.** Customers usually don't share the same cultural backgrounds. Having a diverse sales force better positions a company to understand its existing customers and attract new ones.

- **Removing limitations facing females.** Women occupy CEO positions at many companies, including PepsiCo, Xerox, eBay, Archer Daniels Midland Company (ADM) and Kraft Foods. During the past ten years, more than half of the top winners in the National Collegiate Sales Conference were women. Making sure women are an integral part of every level in your organization is essential.

- **Avoiding ethical miscues.** Although the bar has been raised, ethical miscues will inevitably occur. Making sure, through training and good leadership, that they aren't happening in your organization is a constant challenge.

- **Maintaining motivated sales teams.** By nature, sales involves rejection. Sales leaders need to create and sustain an environment that maintains high levels of individual and group motivation.

Today's sales leaders face a constantly evolving array of challenges, including removing barriers faced by female employees.

- **Integrating technology in sales.** Integrating technology into sales and sale management processes will oftentimes provide the edge for the in- rather than out-company.

Managing Your Career

Kurt Mueller, who was interviewed in the opening of the chapter, has interviewed hundreds of college students aspiring to enter the workforce. He offered some suggestions for those either in, or about to be in, that process:

- **Being a good communicator is key to being a good leader.** Develop your skills by taking classes, or through involvement with activities. Learn how to be accessible to your team.

- **Becoming a leader will take time, and your style will evolve.** Be patient in your goal of getting to management. After school, many people have a goal of getting immediately into a management position.

- **Remember that getting there too soon will not prepare you for the challenges associated with managing people and processes.** Success early in your career as a manager is a great barometer of your future success in management and your ability to advance your career.

- **Make sure you have a full grasp of what your job entails.** A full understanding of the scope of the area you will be managing will increase your odds of being successful in your management role. If you don't have that full understanding, make it a priority to fully understand your scope of responsibility when you start working on your new assignment.

- **Don't make wholesale changes** until you fully understand the area you are managing, and earn the respect of your team, so that members believe you understand and are making changes that are beneficial to the area.

- **Be open to criticism and capitalize on the positive feedback given to help you improve.** It is human nature to strive for success. It is also very rewarding to see success breed success, and to be a part of that success. As you advance your career, remember that those working for you want to be a part of your success.

- **Slow down and enjoy the ride as you build your career.** As the old saying goes, "Rome was not built in a day." It is not how fast you can get to a management role; it is how prepared you are when you get to a management role, so you can see your career blossom to multiple managerial roles during the course of your career.

Summary

So—is there a best way to be a leader? Over time, the answer to that question has evolved. No doubt that, after reviewing the leadership research, today it would seem there is no one best way to lead a sales force. A person who wants to be an effective sales manager will have to focus on a variety of behaviors. Being a good manager does not necessarily make you a good leader, and vice versa. Oftentimes, it isn't a matter of finding a best theory or approach; it is a matter of finding one with which you feel comfortable and works best for you.

The trait approach would suggest that certain traits are the earmark of someone with leadership characteristics or potential. These traits include self-confidence, determination, and sociability. The behavioral approach distinguishes between leaders on the basis of their concern for people versus production, or task behaviors.

The nature of the situation dictates how leaders should behave, according to the situational approach. Depending upon the characteristics of a situation, a leader should display a corresponding level of social and task behaviors. The more contemporary approaches to situational leadership encourage leaders to motivate their followers. Developing their trust and respect helps improve their job-related satisfaction and performance.

Lastly, new emerging leadership approaches offer a set of principles for leaders to embrace. According to these approaches, sales managers who aspire to be leaders should work to support their sales people and derive satisfaction when their sales people are successful and advance. We point out that, regardless of which leadership concept a person utilizes, there is no shortage of challenges for the next generation of sales executives.

Key Terms

behavioral approaches   48
ethical leadership   54
contingency theory of leadership   50
leadership   45
leader-member exchange (LMX)
   theory   52
leadership practices   45
leadership traits   47
leadership styles   48

Level 5 leadership   54
management   45
management practices   45
principle-centered leadership   53
servant leadership   50
situational leadership   51
trait approach   46
transformational leadership   53
Vroom and Yetton model   52

Questions and Problems

1. Think of one person you know who is an effective leader. What actions or traits does the person demonstrate? What behaviors does he or she engage in? Now do the same for an ineffective leader.

2. What behaviors or actions can you engage in to help develop your leadership skills while you are still in school?

3. What is the difference between managing and leading? Give some examples of each for a sales manager. How are the two concepts interrelated?

4. If leadership can be developed, how well are organizations doing? Identify their strengths and/or weaknesses.

5. What traits are considered important for a leader's success? What are shortcomings of the trait approach to leadership?

6. Describe the central tenets of the behavioral approach to leadership. Provide examples of each in a sales-management situation.

7. According to situational theorists, what characteristics of a leadership situation need to be considered? What is organizational engineering?

8. What are in-groups and out-groups? Why is it beneficial to develop more in-group relationships?

9. What types of activities do transformational leaders engage in? Describe someone you believe displays these characteristics.

10. What is the focus of Covey's Principle-Centered Leadership? How can you apply these principles to your situation as a student? As a sales manager?

11. Visit the websites for ServiceMaster, Starbucks and Men's Wearhouse. How is the servant leadership approach conveyed in the mission statements of these firms? What servant-leadership behaviors might a sales manager adopt?

12. Describe the principles of ethical leadership. Give examples of how a sales manager could demonstrate them.

13. How would you describe the leadership behaviors exhibited by a person in Collins' Level 5? What behaviors can you personally improve to approach this level?

14. What are the most important leadership challenges you believe today's sales executives face, and how do you think they are doing?

15. Why is understanding leadership across countries difficult?

Role Play

Highpoint Springs

Highpoint Springs is a company that has bottled water for the past 50 years. A family-owned local bottler, Highpoint Springs was positioned perfectly for the bottled-water boom. The company has grown from a local bottler serving the immediate area to a regional bottler with distribution in eight states. The original owner, Harold Johnson, retired about five years ago, as his two daughters, Kelsey and Koral, took over. Over the past several years, they have seen their sales steadily grow—including their carbonated, flavored spring waters.

The sisters have been closely following the growth of the energy drink segment. Three years ago, they developed their own energy drink, branded Blitzen. Sales have gone beyond their wildest expectations. Initially, the salespeople employed were experienced Highpoint employees; over time, new hires with limited experience have been added to the salesforce.

New strategic plans call for growth into areas with a younger client segment (including university towns) and require an expansion of the sales force. The youngest sales managers have been assigned to recruit at campuses to fill the newly created positions.

High Point Springs' HR department includes standard questions for all screening activities; however, the sisters have always advocated for hiring people with leadership skills. They insist that leadership be a trait that can be identified in each candidate. They believe this trait helps the salesperson develop a good rapport and trust with their clients, and that it positions the company for future growth, as well. Kelsey sits in on all hiring decisions, and interviewers/managers must be prepared to show how and where each candidate has exhibited leadership qualities.

Assignment

Break into groups of three. Two people play the role of the sales managers with the recruiting assignment. They should develop a list of at least four or five questions that will be used to identify leadership traits in each candidate. Kelsey has instructed you to develop questions so that responses will reflect candidates' leadership potential, and wants your rationale for including each one. You must convince her of the value of using your questions in the interviews.

The third person is assigned the role of Kelsey, who has also developed her own list of questions. The two sales managers need to convince her that their questions should be used.

Caselets

Caselet 3.1: *The Natural*

Ty Hanson was completing his third year working for Jackson Kramer Clothing. Things had really fallen in line for him since joining the company. During his first year, he was among the top five rookie salespeople. For each of the last two years, his high sales levels were rewarded with a trip to the President's Club meeting in Hawaii. His outgoing personality served him well, as he found that he actually enjoyed making cold calls and making new contacts. He had found his groove.

Reflecting about his time in school, Ty described himself a bit of a goof-off. He always enjoyed himself and never worried too much about his studies, as long as his work was "good enough" to get by. He could rally to pass tests and get decent grades when he wanted. His friends enjoyed his jovial, outgoing, and laid-back style. Ty was always fun to be around. He thought it was personality that helped him land his job.

Ty's achievements at the company had not gone unnoticed. He nearly always met or surpassed his sales, profitability, and customer service goals. In addition, he had enjoyed his training and leadership development experiences with the company. People often told him he was a natural leader. Not surprisingly, his manager Kay Kimble had encouraged him to consider a new sales management position that was opening.

During a past meeting, Kay called Ty in and was helping him to prepare for his interviews with some additional sales executives. "Ty, you've done the training and are showing good prospects for being a terrific salesman," she said. If you are interested in becoming a leader at JK, you need to have some idea about how you'll get there. So when they ask you, in your interview, about your style of leadership, what will you tell them?"

Ty thought a moment and then commented: "Style of leadership? Hmmm, I've never thought much about it. I've just done things."

As Ty left the office, Kay offered the following comment and suggestion, "If you don't think about your leadership style, how can company management get a handle on what it is? Why don't you take some time and think about it?"

Put yourself in Ty's position. Based on what you know about different leadership approaches, how would you describe your leadership style?

Caselet 3.2: *Love It or Hate It?*

Lisa Yang and Megan Quick graduated from college together and accepted job offers from the same company. Lisa took a position in Seattle and Megan went to work in the firm's Chicago office.

They had the opportunity to renew their friendship at the company's training program at the end of their first year. During their time together, they shared stories about successes and failures and compared notes on a variety of things, including their managers' leadership approaches. Lisa enjoyed her morning meetings with her manager, which were often held at a coffee shop near her office. Lisa loved a great cup of coffee to get her day off to a good start. Megan, on the other hand, enjoyed a morning workout before she made it to her office. Her manager was a veteran whose fondness for fitness carried over into her civilian life. Lisa listened to Megan sing the praises of her sales manager, Emily Littlejohn. Megan commented that Emily's employees affectionately called her "Lieutenant." "We come in and Lieutenant tells us what to do," Megan said. "I never have to wonder what's up or how to deal with a problem. She tells me what to do. She is super results oriented. You always get pats on the back, and she has a whiteboard in the office that lists the progress that the sales team has made."

Lisa wondered about a manager who told you what do to so much. "Wow, Megan, your manager sounds like she is still back in the service with her troops—not like the leader of your sales team. I think she'd drive me nuts!"

"What do you mean?" Megan questioned. "She seems like the perfect leader. What else should she be doing?"

Put yourself in Lisa's shoes. What should she tell Megan about what alternative leadership behaviors "Lieutenant" practiced outside her office?

References

1. Kotter, John P. (1990). *A Force for Change: How Leadership Differs from Management.* New York, NY: The Free Press.
2. Kotter, John P. (1988). *The Leadership Factor.* New York, NY: The Free Press.
3. Burwinkel, Jeffrey, Richard S. Wellins, and Bradford Thomas (2006). "The Rapid Arrival of the Under Prepared: Sales Leadership Forecast, 2005-2006." White paper published by Development Dimensions International, Inc. (DDI).
4. Wellins, Richard S., Charles J. Cosentino, and Bradford Thomas (2004). "Building a Winning Sales Force," White paper published by DDI.
5. Lang, Annamarie, and Bradford Thomas (2013). "Where Are Your 'Ready-Now Leaders'?" White paper published by DDI.
6. Stogdill, R.M. (1948). Personal Factors Associated with Leadership: A Survey of the Literature. *Journal of Psychology,* 25, 35–71.
7. Lord, R.G., C.L. DeVader, and G.M. Alliger, (1986). "A Meta-Analysis of the Relation Between Personality Traits and Leadership Perceptions: An Application of Validity Generalization Procedures," *Journal of Applied Psychology,* 71, 402–410.
8. Kirkpatrick, S.A. and E.A. Locke (1991). "Leadership: Do Traits Matter?" *The Executive,* 5, 48–60.
9. Northouse, P.G. (2012). *Leadership: Theory and Practice,* 6th ed. Thousand Oaks, CA: Sage Publications, Inc.
10. Fleishman, E.A. (1953). "The Description of Supervisory Behavior", *Personnel Psychology,* 37, 1–6.
11. Katz, D., N. Maccoby, and N.C. Morse (1950). *Productivity, Supervision, and Morale in an Office Situation.* Ann Arbor, MI: University of Michigan, Institute for Social Research.
12. Blake, R.R., and Jane Mouton (1964). *The Managerial Grid.* Houston, TX: Gulf Publishing Company.
13. Blake, R.R. and A. McCanse (1991). *Leadership dilemmas: Grid solutions.* Houston, TX: Gulf Publishing Company.
14. Lashinsky, A. (2006). "50 Most Powerful Women: Building eBay 2.0," *Fortune,* (154)8, Oct. 16, 161–164.
15. Yukl, G. (1994). *Leadership in Organizations,* 3rd ed. Englewood Cliffs, NJ: Prentice Hall.
16. Fiedler, F.E. (1967). *A Theory of Leadership Effectiveness,* New York, NY: McGraw-Hill.
17. Vroom, V.H. and P.W. Yetton, (1973). *Leadership and Decision-Making* (Pittsburgh, PA: University of Pittsburgh Press.
18. Hersey, P. Blanchard K.H. (1969). "Life cycle of leadership," *Training and Development Journal,* 23, 26–34.
19. Vroom, V.H. (1976). " Leadership" in Dunnette, M. D., ed. *Handbook of Industrial and Organizational Psychology,* Chicago: Rand McNally.
20. Sains, A. and S. Reed (2006). "Electrolux Redesigns Itself," *Business Week* Inside Innovation supplement, (4011) November 27, 12–15.
21. Dansureau, F. G.B. Graen, and W. Haga (1975). "A Vertical Dyad Linkage Approach to Leadership in Formal Organizations," *Organizational Behavior and Human Performance,* 13, 46–78.
22. Graen, G. B. and M. Uhl-Bien (1991). "The Transformation of Professionals into Self-Managing and Partially Self-Designing Contributors: Toward a Theory of Leadership-Making," *Journal of Management Systems,* 3(3), 33–48.
23. Graen, G. B., and M. Uhl-Bien (1995). "Relationship-Based Approach to Leadership: Development of Leader-Member Exchange (LMX) Theory of Leadership Over 25 years: Applying a Multi-Level Multi-Domain Perspective. *Leadership Quarterly,* 6(2), 219–247.
24. Bass, B.M. (1985). *Leadership and Performance Beyond Expectations.* New York, NY: The Free Press.
25. Bass, B.M. (1997) "Personal Selling and Transactional/Transformational Leadership," *Journal of Personal Selling & Sales Management,* 17(3), Summer, 19–28.
26. Ehmann, L.C. (2006). "A Team of Winners," *Selling Power,* 26(9), November/December, 40–43.
27. Covey, S.R. (1989). *Seven Habits of Highly Effective People: Restoring the Character Ethic.* New York, NY: Simon and Schuster.
28. Covey. S.R. (2003). *The 8th Habit: From Effectiveness to Greatness.* New York, N.Y: The Free Press.
29. Greenleaf, R. (1977). *Servant Leadership,* Ramsey, N.J.: Paulist Press.
30. Spears, L.C., (1995). Reflections on Leadership: *How Robert K. Greenleaf's Theory of Servant-Leadership Influenced Today's Top Management Thinkers.* New York, NY: John Wiley & Sons.
31. Collins, J.C. (2001). *Good to Great: Why Some Companies Make the Leap...and Others Don't.* N.Y.: Harper Collins Publishers.
32. Collins, J., and J. Porras (2004). *Built to Last: Successful Habits of Visionary Companies.* New York, N.Y.: Harper Collins Publishers.

33. Collins, J.C. "Good to Great to Gone," (2009). *The Economist,* July 7, 2009. Accessed 3/1/2014. *http://www. economist.com/node/13980976.*

34. Collins, J.C. (2009). *How the Mighty Fall: And Why Some Companies Never Give In.* N.Y.: Harper Collins Publishers.

ETHICS, THE LAW, AND SALES LEADERSHIP

LEARNING OBJECTIVES

After completing this chapter, you should be able to:

■ Identify the more common ethical dilemmas that face salespeople, sales managers, and sales executives.

■ Distinguish between those organizational policies and practices that support ethical behavior and those that enable unethical behavior.

■ Explain how principled leadership can foster a firm's ethical principles and corporate culture.

■ Be able to develop an appropriate course of action when you're personally faced with an ethical dilemma.

Does the profit motive create opportunistic values and morals? Does greed drive every salesperson to engage in unethical behavior whenever possible? Of course not. Nonetheless, the sales profession has developed a reputation for being unsavory, yet any sales professional who is in business for the long haul knows that unethical sales practices and unethical salespeople can't last. Even without legal safeguards and judicial recourse (not to mention the potential for negative word-of-mouth and reduced future sales), most salespeople are still good people. They do the right thing because they want to, not because they have to. In this chapter, we will explore ethics in the sales profession and the actions that sales managers can take to support ethical behavior by their employees.

Sales Manager Profile: Kurt Knapton

KURT KNAPTON HAS REACHED THAT pinnacle that many strive for—to be CEO of a multi-million dollar company. He must have stabbed a lot of people in the back, climbed over a lot of dead careers, and thrown ethics to the wind, right?

Wrong.

Those who know Knapton know just how wrong perception that is. "I was Chief Revenue Officer for e-Rewards, an online marketing research company that rewarded people for doing surveys. We began early in the dot.com craze and managed to survive it, though at one point, we were down from 70-plus employees to just me and another guy." But by building a reputation for delivering value with values, he was able to rebuild the company to some $75 million in sales.

Then he stepped out of the role—and out of business. For two years, he worked with Project Restore Hope, a nongovernmental organization (NGO) devoted to serving orphans and others in Sierra Leone, Africa. In fact, project administrators still display his photo on the website (*www.restorehopeproject.org*).

After living and working in Africa, he got a call from the board of his old company. "They had gone through a series of acquisitions and the company was now global. But the CEO, who joined as part of one of the acquisitions, was ready to retire—so the board of directors called me and asked if I'd come back." The timing was right for his family, so it was back to e-Rewards, currently known as ResearchNow—this time as CEO.

Knapton recalls, "When I got back, I quickly realized the culture was different." In the process of assimilating the acquisitions, the culture had shifted to a "work-hard, play-hard" mentality, with a number of negative effects. The most obvious was that the value-with-values equation was out of whack.

At the very beginning of e-Reward's existence, Knapton said, "although I was doing sales, I wasn't the salesperson. So I could put a flag in the ground and state that, if a client was unhappy, we'd refund all of its money on a project." A salesperson wouldn't have that authority, but as Chief Revenue Officer, Knapton did. "Our business is about repeat business. So it was better to refund the money and keep the integrity of the relationship." Important to him was the idea of refunding as "a form of honesty" and that, with integrity preserved, "everything would be aligned. I wanted to have an organization that would say who you are and what you stand for, and do that continually; under-commit on performance, but not on value and values—then over-deliver." Somehow, that work-hard, play-hard culture was interfering.

So Knapton began making the company's values visible again. He discussed them in company communications and team meetings. Then he began publicly praising those who provided examples by living up to those values. Employees who fell short were counseled privately and expected to shape up, but if someone stepped across a company policy line, consequences ensued.

"For example, we try not to poach employees from competitors and, if we do hire someone from a competitive company, we have that new employees sign a statement, promising that they will not use information taken from the previous employer—and acknowledging that they will face termination." If a salesperson for a competitor prints out customer records, for example, and then joins the ResearchNow staff and uses those records to make sales calls, ResearchNow will fire the employee. "We operate in 40 countries," Knapton emphasized, "and such behavior may be considered entirely appropriate in another country, but it

KURT KNAPTON
Chief Executive Officer
ResearchNow

isn't aligned with our culture or our policy. We have to demonstrate that we live out our values all of the time."

Knapton goes on to say that, "When I began my career, I thought I could separate my corporate self from my personal self. I've since learned that I have to be true to myself if I'm going to be honest with anyone else." Whenever you're looking to join a new organization, he suggests that you ask about the values in its process, and then find out from insiders how real they are. Do employees know the company's values, and does the company live by them? "Make sure those values are compatible with yours," he advises, "because, when the personal goals of your career align with the value system and goals of an organization, everyone wins." ■

I n the business world, the issue of ethics is a constant. True, there are periods of time when unethical or illegal activities grab the headlines, and people wonder if business is becoming more ruthless and less honest. The reality is, though, that research shows workplace misconduct and pressure to engage in unethical behavior to be at an all-time low.

At the same time, however, buyers are putting more emphasis in their purchasing decisions based on how ethical salespeople and the companies they represent appear to be.[1] Ultimately, though, the question is whether or not *you* will do the right thing when faced with an ethical dilemma.

What exactly is the right thing? Is the Golden Rule, "do unto others as you would have others do unto you," the best guide? Or is "do whatever is legal, whether it is right or not," all that companies require of salespeople and their managers?

For the sales executive, there are many dimensions of "doing the right thing." Questions can involve the right thing to do for customers, salespeople, shareholders, vendors, and many, many others.

Ethics are moral principles of right and wrong that guide people's behavior. What is and isn't ethical varies from culture to culture. In terms of business, it can vary from industry to industry. What is believed to be ethical can also change over time; for example, it was once considered unethical for doctors and lawyers to advertise their services. Today, many doctors and lawyers are still reluctant to do so, but the practice has become more widely accepted. (We are all familiar with television and radio commercials touting the LASIK skills of doctors and the big awards attorneys have won for their clients.)

Problems arise, however, when people's values conflict with what they see going on around them. When the problems are large enough, responses to them are then codified into law. For example, there are laws regarding how prices can be set, laws that proscribe how long a buyer has to rethink a purchase (such as when buying a car), and still other laws that govern salespeople's behavior. All were created to stop practices that people thought were problematic.

Causes of Unethical Behavior

While problems may arise that lead to changes in the law, some people choose courses of action that they know to be unethical—whether legal or illegal. Research shows that these choices may be a function of financial strain, business opportunity, and rationalization.[2] While financial strain may be obvious, opportunistic behavior is simply choosing self over others, irrespective of the ethical conflict.

Rationalization can include denial of injury, denial of responsibility, blaming the victim, and condemning the condemner.[3] Factors that can reduce rationalization include leadership.[4] In particular, leadership that promotes moral idealism, or the degree to which an individual subscribes to principles of behavior based on morals, can lead to higher ethical behavior choices and less rationalization.[5] Of course, not everyone agrees about what is ethical and how people should and should not behave. As a result, different salespeople and sales managers have different ethical philosophies. In the following section, we review some of these approaches to ethics.

Approaches to Ethics

We mentioned a couple of approaches to ethics in the introduction to this chapter—among them the Golden Rule and the policy of doing as much as the law allows. Other common approaches include the Conventionalist Approach, the Market Imperative, the Protestant Ethic, the Libertine Ethic, and the Utilitarian Ethic.[2] Exhibit 4.1 summarizes them. Next, we discuss each.

EXHIBIT 4.1   Approaches to Ethics

Approach	Summary	Pros and Cons
Golden Rule	Treat others as you would like to be treated.	• Personalizes ethical decisions, making it easy to determine what to do. • Fails to account for situations in which "others" are in conflict.
Conventionalist	Acts are okay as long as legal or if "everyone is doing it."	• Fails to account for gray areas, in which acts are not specified as either "legal" or "illegal."
Protestant Ethic	Do what you can defend to a committee of peers.	• What's "ethical" is based on the intended, not actual, outcome. • Can lead to more concern about doing what can be defended than what is right.
Market Imperative	The market will determine what is right.	• Provides clear responsibilities for individuals. • Can devolve into a "might is right" scenario.
Libertine	Do what you want, as long as no one gets hurt.	• Outcomes are important, and a responsibility for others is assumed. • Can lead to problems when others are harmed indirectly, or when harm is not obvious.
Utilitarian	Do what has the best outcome for all involved.	• Outcomes, and honorable intent, are important; requires taking responsibility for others. • It's unclear who gets to decide what outcomes are "best."

The Golden Rule

The Golden Rule is familiar to most schoolchildren: *Do unto others as you would have them do unto you.* To treat others as you want to be treated seems to be considered the natural order of things. After all, isn't putting someone else's needs on par with your own needs only fair?[6] The challenge arises when there are multiple "others" and their needs or wants conflict with one another. For example, assuming you do not want to be cheated, you would, therefore, not cheat your customer. But when you are the buyer, you want to buy as much as you can at the lowest price. So do you offer your product at the lowest possible price? Dropping prices damages your company, and you and your manager get into trouble. You wouldn't want to be in trouble, so you don't want your manager to be in trouble. So who comes first—your customer or your manager? Thus, the Golden Rule often works well in situations with only two parties, but because most salespeople are responsible to several different people who all want different things, the Golden Rule does not always help.

Furthermore, the Golden Rule assumes that the way you want to be treated is the way others want to be treated, too, when maybe that's not the case.[7] For example, you may not want a salesperson to call your friends, so you don't give out references. Then a friend gets mad after learning that you've been using this great new product for weeks and wants to know why you didn't just have the salesperson call her.

The Conventionalist Approach

The Conventionalist Approach is entirely different, suggesting that people should take any and all actions allowed by law or by common practice.[8] In a sense, this approach is a variation on the saying, "Everybody's doing it, so it must be okay,"—a common rationalization for unethical behavior.[9] Thus, people shouldn't feel the need to act on a higher principle than other people, if they follow the Conventionalist Approach.

The problem with this approach is that it really doesn't consider what's ethical and not ethical. For example, if someone were harmed by a practice considered to be the norm, then the practice would still be considered okay according to the conventionalists. For example, not selling homes in certain areas to people of color was once considered standard practice in the real estate business. But the negative, unethical outcomes of the practice were precisely why laws were passed to ban it. Another way to view the Conventionalist Approach to behavior is as follows: "Do it until they say you can't." But that does not make the behavior right.

Recently, it seems a similar philosophy has arisen in the business world—one that is based on the expression, "It is easier to ask for forgiveness than permission." Although such a philosophy might be appropriate when it comes to dealing with red tape that can slow down doing what is right, some have observed salespeople and managers using this expression as an excuse to engage in questionable activity. Giving free service to a customer when company policy prices that service at several thousand dollars is an example. There may be a good business reason to do so, but failure to ask permission may not be considered forgivable. Problems arise when the outcome damages someone, such as a customer or the company, as in the free-service case, when the company lost out on sales revenue it is due.

The Protestant Ethic

Most students associate the term "Protestant Ethic" with "Work Ethic." However, when discussing approaches to moral choices, these terms are not the same. The Protestant Ethic is an approach to considering an ethical dilemma and can be summed up as follows: "Could I satisfactorily explain this choice to a committee of my peers?"

Such was the case in the early development of the Protestant church. If you were a Protestant accused of a sin, you had to appear before a committee of your brethren that was charged with deciding upon your punishment. A similar question related to this approach is the following: "Could I explain the action to my spouse, or to the public?"

You can probably see how the Protestant Ethic can end up mirroring the Conventionalist Approach. Pick the right committee (don't put any customers on it, for example), and you can probably explain away anything. In addition, your explanation could focus on your intent, rather than on your actions, but the committee would have to consider your intent to be more important. (Recall that the origin of the Protestant Ethic lies in understanding sin; thus, your intent is very important.) Providing evidence that your intent was honorable, though, can be difficult.

Suppose a customer's shipment of a product is delayed. If the firm's sales rep has some of the product on hand, it could be given to the customer to tide her over until the shipment arrives. The problem is that the customer might consider the product the sales rep supplied to be free, whereas the sales rep's manager might consider the handout to be a form of stealing on the salesperson's part. Even though the rep's intentions were honorable, the final decision would be made by a committee of peers.

The Market Imperative

The Market Imperative stems from philosopher and economist Adam Smith's classical economics approach to capitalism. The imperative states that the market requires a person to act in his or her own best interest. Similar to Darwin's approach to understanding the natural world, Smith believed that the notion of "survival of the fittest" dictated the economic world. This perspective is also somewhat similar to Nietzsche's "might makes right" philosophy—that the strongest deserve to rule. However, all of us know that modern civilizations have decreed that such an approach is not appropriate. Laws are created to protect the defenseless, and one's strength does not determine one's rights.

The Protestant Ethic can be traced back to the Pilgrims who brought with them to America a system of peer-review of any potential ethical breaches.

Nonetheless, isn't the purpose of an organization to maximize the wealth of its shareholders? This vision of an organization's purpose is true if you accept Smith's view of the market. The salesperson, therefore, works for the organization, and the organization's needs must come first, according to this ethic. A counter-argument to the Market Imperative is that the corporation is an entity that is granted the right to exist by society. Therefore, the corporation must be governed by what is best for society *in addition to* maximizing shareholder wealth. Moreover, what is best for society must balance the interests of the different people and groups within it—those of shareholders, employees, and customers alike. Smith, though, might argue that these three groups should fight it out to see which comes out on top. As a result, sometimes labor wins (with passage of labor laws, for example), sometimes customers win (as was the case when the Consumer Rights Act of 1962 was passed), and sometimes companies win (as was the case when the Robinson-Patman Act—a law protecting retailers from powerful manufacturers—was passed).

The Libertine Ethic

According to the Libertine approach, ethics are based on the principle of individual freedom. Specifically, customers should be free to make their own decisions, as they best see fit. The Libertine Ethic grew to prominence in the 1960s, and is best expressed as the notion that one should be free to do whatever one wants, as long as no one else gets hurt.

On the face of it, the Libertine Ethic appears to work very well with sales. A salesperson can do whatever he wants, as long as no one (the customer) is harmed. So, for example, if the salesperson manipulates the selling situation in a way that eliminates or narrows down the customer's choices, the adverse effect on the customer would clearly make such an action unethical. What about bribing customers with kickbacks? At first glance, according to the libertine view, bribery would appear to be okay. After all, bribery doesn't influence the buyer's *ability* to choose—just his willingness to do so.

As you can see, if bribery is acceptable, there must be drawbacks to the Libertine Ethic. After all, fairness isn't just what is fair for the customer; it must also be fair for the competition—and a bribe eliminates competitors unfairly. Furthermore, a

The libertine philosophy grew in popularity during the 1960's, stemming from the hippie movement, and essentially reflects a philosophy that any behavior is okay as long as no one gets hurt.

bribe isn't fair in a B2B setting, because the person doing the buying personally benefits from the bribe for a purchase made for his company. The difficulty with the Libertine Ethic is similar to the limitation of the Golden Rule's sales application; it identifies as important only the two actors in the transaction—in this case, the person selling and the person buying. Conflicts among others are rarely considered, much less resolved. Still, the Libertine Ethic, like the Golden Rule, holds appeal for many situations.

The Utilitarian Ethic

The Utilitarian Ethic, like the Libertine Ethic and the Golden Rule, focuses on outcomes—on doing what results in the best outcome.[10] There are different forms of the Utilitarian Ethic (Situational Ethics, the Bentham/Mills Proportional Ethic, and others). All of them, however, come down to the basic question of whether or not an action's positive consequences outweigh its negative consequences.

The difficulty of this approach becomes immediately apparent: after all, who gets to decide the value, or weight, of the positive and negative outcomes? Of course, it has to be the person making the decision about whether or not to engage in the act—in this case, the salesperson. The salesperson's temptation, therefore, would be to minimize the weight given to the negative outcomes experienced by others, and maximize the value of the positive outcomes she, herself, experienced.

Hence, we return to the Golden Rule: The salesperson must consider the customer's needs to be as important as her own. Ultimately, however, we know she not only has to consider her own needs and the needs of her customer, but also the needs of the organization and society. They, too, come into play. This means that neither the Golden Rule nor the Libertarian Ethic adequately addresses all situations a salesperson faces.

The Salesperson as a Boundary Spanner

Is sales among the most unethical professions? Actually, there are people in many professions who are more likely to exaggerate, which is another form of **manipulation**. According to several studies conducted by noted psychologist George Dudley, politicians (no surprise there), psychologists, preachers, and professors are more likely to exaggerate than are salespeople. So are web designers, architects, and others.[11] Another study found that business students are more likely to engage in unethical behaviors than are sales professionals.[12] Salespeople are unique, however, in that they are **boundary spanners**—meaning that they operate both outside of and within an organization's boundaries. That is, they work within their companies, but they also work outside of their companies with customers. As boundary spanners, salespeople encounter ethical dilemmas—internally with other employees and externally with customers.

If salespeople are boundary spanners, who, then, do they ultimately represent? The organization employing them, obviously. However, in a very real sense, they also represent their customers. You can probably see how a salesperson might represent a customer. For example, if the customer needs an order expedited, it is the salesperson who argues the customer's case to the firm's shipping department.

Does the salesperson represent different people within the company? At times, yes. Suppose a company's sales managers want certain products produced faster in order to make more sales. Now suppose personnel in the company's manufacturing department want slower production, in order to reduce the risk of turning out defective items. With whom should the salesperson side in this case? After all, if the products are defective, the salesperson will be hearing customers' complaints.

Also, doesn't the salesperson, in some respects, represent her own family? Suppose not enough of the product is produced, and the salesperson doesn't make her quota. Obviously, her performance will suffer, she will earn less money, and her family will have less income.

As you can see, trying to understand ethics from a simple dyadic (seller/buyer) perspective or from an organizational perspective (doing whatever you want as long as it is best for the company) doesn't work. In the real world, things are obviously more complex than that.

Representing multiple parties simultaneously causes salespeople difficulty, and problems can ensue when the salesperson emphasizes one party's needs over another's. When selling is done right, however, great things can happen. The "Ethics in Selling" box describes one such situation.

ETHICS IN SALES MANAGEMENT   A Legacy of Integrity

When Jim Keller retired after 30-plus years of sales, he had the traditional retirement party. The only difference is that his customer hosted it! For almost all of Keller's career, he called on one client: FedEx. And when it was time to say good-bye, it was his client who wanted to honor him with a going-away reception.

Not that all of those years were smooth. Keller once lost his job because he wouldn't do what his manager told him to do, which was to lie to the customer (FedEx). He says he nearly lost it again when the customer, angry over a problem that was taking a long time to solve, wouldn't talk directly to Keller, even when he was in the room. But Keller "stepped into the man's face and said something to the effect of, 'I'm here to take my beating, now let's get it over with so I can go to work fixing your problem.'" What his customer learned was that Keller could be trusted to do what he said he would, and that, as the CIO of FedEx said at Keller's retirement, he "bled purple" (FedEx's corporate color).

Keller actually worked for several companies in his career, even though FedEx remained his customer over the years. To build the kind of legacy he left with FedEx, Keller says there has to be a balance between 1) doing right by the customer, 2) making money for the company, and 3) treating salespeople with respect.

Too often, we're told that you should be ethical because it is good business to be ethical. Doing things the right way, though, is something Keller believes you should do just because it is something you should do. Sometimes, being ethical can cost a salesperson the job. FedEx doesn't know (at least, not until now) that Keller once lost his job because he was ethical. They just knew they could count on him.

Common Ethical Issues Facing Salespeople

In this section, we examine ethical dilemmas salespeople most commonly face with regard to their customers. Then we examine the dilemmas they mostly commonly face with regard to their firms.

ETHICAL ISSUES ASSOCIATED WITH THE SALESPERSON'S CUSTOMERS Exhibit 4.2 summarizes the more common ethical issues salespeople face with customers. When a salesperson lies about a product—making claims for it that are not true—the salesperson is guilty of **misrepresentation**. Misrepresentation can lead to lawsuits, the recovery of damages by injured parties, and other negative consequences. A recent case involving misrepresentation of real estate, for example, meant that the sale was reversed, and the seller had to pay the buyer for damages and expenses.[13]

Misrepresentation is not the same as **puffery**, an allowable exaggeration, as long as it is vague and general, with no specific facts. For example, a salesperson

---

EXHIBIT 4.2   **Common Ethical Issues between the Customer and the Salesperson**

Misrepresentation: The salesperson exaggerates benefits or minimizes problems, leading a customer to draw erroneous conclusions about a product or service.

Bribery: The salesperson attempts to influence a buyer unfairly by offering a gift or money.

Privacy: The salesperson fails to protect the privacy of another customer by giving the customer's confidential information to another customer; the salesperson invades the customer's privacy with spam or unwanted calls.

---

can be reasonably expected to claim that his firm's product is the best because "best" is a general term, meaning different things to different people. However, if the salesperson claims the product will process 200 packages per hour, and it only processes 100, then that stated claim is misrepresentation.

Bribery, another common temptation (and illegal; we'll discuss bribery laws later), is any offer of a gift that secures undue influence. Consider the following cautionary tale: When a company purchased a Xerox product at a certain price level, the person buying it received a free round-trip ticket to fly anywhere in the U.S. This offer would pose no problem if the people buying the copiers had given the tickets to their companies to use for business travel, but no mechanisms were in place to ensure that this happened. Competitors and customers alike complained that the free airline ticket amounted to bribery. As a result, Xerox pulled the plug on the promotion. What is interesting about this example is that Xerox executives, not salespeople, created the promotion. This example illustrates how sales managers can unwittingly put their salespeople at risk by devising poorly conceived sales strategies.

As you can probably tell from the Xerox anecdote, offering customers overly expensive entertainment and gifts can get companies and their sales reps into trouble. Pharmaceutical companies once gave lavish trips to doctors—weekend hunting trips, for example, during which time they would listen to a half-hour presentation about a new drug. Would you want to know that the medicine you take was chosen on the basis of which company offered the best hunting trip? Thankfully, the practice was halted by government regulations.

GlaxoSmithKline, a pharmaceutical company, was investigated in China for bribing government officials and doctors in order to boost sales. While the company admitted no wrongdoing and pledged cooperation with the government, such investigations can take many months and tie up management's attention, leaving critical business needs unmet.[14]

So that there can never be any question about undue influence resulting from gifts or entertainment, some companies, such as IBM and Walmart, will not allow their employees to accept so much as a cup of coffee from a vendor.

These examples don't mean that it's always wrong to reward your customers for being loyal, to say thanks with a small gift, or to spend funds to entertain them. The question is how it is done and whether or not it's excessive. For example, as a thank-you to its customers, Kurt Knapton's (profiled at the start of this chapter) ResearchNow provides salespeople with a catalog of gifts to choose from. However, the salespeople are given guidelines regarding what they can give in various situations. In addition, the company's marketing staff determines what holiday gift to give customers at the end of the year. This approach eliminates guesswork for the salesperson as to what gift is appropriate for which customer and when.

What about an offer from a customer to a salesperson? A student once reported that his father had accepted a month-long vacation on a private Caribbean island from a customer—his only customer. Was this simply a gift from one friend to another, or an attempt to generate special offers, lower prices, and the like?

Recall that, earlier, we pointed out that a bribe can harm the competition. Salespeople are sometimes tempted to hamper their competitors in other ways, though. Julie Featherston, a sales representative for Revlon, described how her competitors would sometimes move Revlon's products off of store shelves and interfere with displays she had set up. When it happened in one part of her territory regularly, Featherston brought it to the attention of the store managers there. The managers determined who the guilty party was and removed that company's products from their stores. Salespeople also have access to a lot of confidential information which needs to remain confidential. It's not usual for buyers to want to know what their competitors are doing and to try to obtain that information from salespeople. For example, a buyer in one store might ask Featherston how well Revlon's products sell in a competing store. If Featherston says, "Walgreens sells an average of five cases of Revlon products per store," she just gave Walgreen's confidential sales figures to the competitor. The competitor might also be reluctant to do business with Featherston in the future, because she obviously can't be trusted to keep trade secrets confidential. Similarly, salespeople sometimes pressure buyers to give them information about their competitors. For example, customers sometimes find themselves in situations in which they know about new, soon-to-be-released products, but are asked by the makers to keep the information private until market announcements are made. During that time, it would be inappropriate for a customer to share such knowledge with a salesperson employed by another vendor.

The issue here is privacy. Sales professionals often find that personal privacy, as well as commercial confidentiality, brings ethical dilemmas. Privacy laws apply to some sales-related activities. (Recall the controversy that the National Security Administration got into over using phone records, even though individuals' names were not attached. What few realize is that companies like Sprint and AT&T track customers' call patterns—the same thing—but not anonymously—and for the purpose of making additional offers.) The Federal Trade Commission requires financial institutions that collect personal information to have a privacy policy. Any company with a privacy policy must abide by it, whether or not the firm is a financial institution. Salespeople have to recognize that they are bound by these policies, too. No one wants their private information published or shared with others without permission.

Another issue is not following established policies that your customer's company sets. For example, Valero requires all salespeople calling on the firm to register with its purchasing office before making a visit to the company's corporate headquarters. Even a visit to drop off supplies or a sales proposal means the salesperson has to register. If the salesperson doesn't comply, he can be banned from doing business with the company. What Valero is to trying to do via this policy is to prevent **rogue purchasing**—the practice of purchasing products from non-approved vendors.

In summary, most students, when asked, say that they would neither accept nor offer a bribe. Yet, as you can see, rarely are ethical issues as obvious as a buyer saying, "Here—take this bribe and give me a cheaper price." Ethical issues are generally much more complex and subtle.

ETHICAL ISSUES ASSOCIATED WITH THE SALESPERSON'S COMPANY Not all ethical issues are associated with the salesperson's customers. Salespeople can also find themselves either tempted or pressured to engage in unethical activity within their own companies. Exhibit 4.3 summarizes such issues.

EXHIBIT 4.3   Common Ethical Issues Involving the Salesperson's Company

Stealing: The salesperson fails to work a full day, stealing time that she is paid for; the salesperson pads his expense accounts.

Claiming Credit: The salesperson steals other people's leads; the salesperson misrepresents the location of a customer in order to receive credit for an order belonging to someone else.

Sexual Harassment: The salesperson experiences unwanted sexual offers or inappropriate physical contact.

Generally, everyone can agree that salespeople shouldn't steal from their companies—say, by taking office supplies home for their own personal use. But more subtle forms of "stealing" can occur. Consider the salesperson who spends money on office supplies while traveling, although company policy prohibits reimbursement for those expenses. In this case, the salesperson might be tempted to recover the money for the supplies by inflating other allowable expenses. Or consider a salesperson who takes a day off without telling anyone. These types of behaviors can be considered stealing; in the latter case, the salesperson is stealing time (or salary).

In some situations, in which salespeople do not have defined territories, stealing "leads," or contacts, from other salespeople can be a problem. Jeff Hostetler, sales director at Tele-Optics, a telecommunications firm, likens the behavior to "wolves fighting over a chunk of meat." Consequences can be dramatic. "Not only will reps kill each other, but they will kill the business, too," Hostetler says.[8] But even designating a **protected territory**—meaning that only one salesperson can sell in that territory, so that it is protected from others—can create challenges. We've heard stories of reps changing a company's name on an order (for example, using initials instead of the full name) when the customer belongs to someone else, as well as shipping products to their own customers' addresses, but then taking the products to other customers— even though those other customers actually belong to another rep. In both instances, these salespeople manipulated shipping information so that they could get credit for the sale, even though the customer actually belonged to another salesperson. In either case, it is stealing—and wrong.

Sexual harassment, unwelcome sexual advances, sexual jokes and so forth, even if unintentional, can obviously occur within a salesperson's company, as well as among one's customers. Overall, however, sexual harassment is rare. One study found that the average company experiences just over one case of sexual harassment per year.[9] Nonetheless, companies need to prepare their employees, including their salespeople, to deal with unwelcome sexual advances.

Creating an Ethical Sales Climate

A recent study of salespeople in France found that high-performing salespeople are far more likely to leave a company if the ethical climate of that company is poor. A firm's **ethical climate** is the degree to which its corporate culture supports ethical business practices. (Or, stated in the obverse, an unethical climate is the degree to which unethical business practices are tolerated or encouraged.) From this study, we can conclude that high-performing salespeople prefer high ethical standards and want to work for companies that support such standards.[9] Although the culture of the firm is the subject of another chapter, suffice it to say here that a company's sales leaders are responsible for ensuring that its salespeople operate in an ethical environment.

A company outlines its standards for ethical behavior in its **code of ethics**. According to the Ethics Resource Center, a nonprofit educational organization with a mission of fostering ethical practices among individuals and institutions, more than 90 percent of U.S. organizations have written ethics codes.[15] A code of ethics is established in order to:

- provide salespeople and other employees with guidelines and standards for conduct;

- help salespeople inform others that they intend to conduct business in an ethical way;

- support salespeople's intentions to remain ethical, offering salespeople an "out" when under pressure. In other words, make it easy for them to say, "I

can't do that because it's against my company's policy, and I would get fired";
and

• attract high-quality salespeople.

Therefore, the first step to creating an ethical climate is to set standards and list them in a code of ethics. Many companies now post their codes on their corporate websites, in part to guide employees, but also to attract high-quality employees and customers.[16] Companies are not the only groups with codes of ethics; professional organizations also set codes for their members. For example, Sales and Marketing Executives International has a code for its members, as does the Direct Selling Association (comprised of companies like Mary Kay, Premier Jewelry, and other companies that sell direct to consumers). Of the 12 standards set forth by the Direct Selling Association, nine focus squarely on the salesperson. Codes of ethics exist for purchasing, too; the Institute for Supply Management (formerly the National Association of Purchasing Managers) has a code of ethics for its members. The Caux Round Table offers a code for businesses that operate internationally, covering many aspects of company activity—not just selling.

GLOBAL SALES MANAGEMENT   **Global Codes of Ethics**

Excessive imbalances in trade and the disparities between developed and developing nations create a number of problems in the world. Countries with greater economic power can easily abuse those with less by building sweatshops, using child labor, and other practices designed to take advantage of people in these countries. Even companies that want to do the right thing sometimes find themselves criticized for their business practices in other countries, because what is considered ethical in one country is not in another. To provide guidance for companies operating globally, the Caux Round Table (CRT) was developed.

The CRT was founded in 1986 by Frederick Phillips, the former chair of Phillips Electronics, and Olivier Giscard d'Estaing, the former vice-chair of INSEAD, an international business school. In 1994 they introduced the CRT Principles, codifying the most comprehensive set of responsible business practices that exists today, with the goal of promoting "moral capitalism."

While there are many CRT principles, several are particularly important to sales organizations:

• The value of a business to society is the wealth it creates for shareholders and employees, as well as the marketable products and services it provides to consumers at a price commensurate with quality.

• Businesses should respect international and domestic rules, and avoid behavior that, even if legal, has adverse consequences to society. Thus, salespeople have to consider the impact of their behavior on society, rather than the legality of such behavior.

More recently, the CRT released The Mountain House Statement, a position paper on ethics that combined the thinking of leading Islamic, Jewish, and Christian scholars. Specifically written to identify commonality among the three faith traditions and to combat mistrust, hostility, and stereotyping, the paper specifies very practical lessons for ethical global finance and business. But this paper is not just an academic exercise. Companies such as Nissan, Coca Cola, and others have signed on, making the principles a business reality.

But what about at the salesperson level? Can these corporate- and country-level ethics really help salespeople make better decisions? Organizations such as Sales and Marketing Executives International have created codes specifically to guide salespeople and their leaders. And others have worked to integrate these with other codes so that leaders can be guided across countries, professions, and situations. Where laws are not available, these codes can guide individuals through the tricky ethical waters of multi-cultural business.

Ning Li and William Murphy (2012), "A Three-Country Study of Unethical Sales Behaviors," *Journal of Business Ethics* 111(2), 219–35; Dinah Payne and Milton Pressley (2013), "A Transcendent Code of Ethics for Marketing Professionals," *International Journal of Law & Management* 55(1), 55–73; www.cauxroundtable.org (2014).

An important aspect of these codes is clarity of writing. The more specific the codes, the greater assistance they can be to salespeople and sales managers. Salespeople and sales managers don't have to worry about whether a decision is right or wrong if the decision is spelled out in the code.

The U.S. **Federal Sentencing Guidelines** (FSG) were enacted in 1987 and updated in 2007 in response to an increase in white-collar crime, specifically crimes committed by businesses. The FSG is a set of suggested guidelines requiring all sales organizations to develop programs for preventing, detecting, and halting unethical or illegal misconduct by employees. If a company's employee engages in illegal behavior, the company is liable if it has not followed the FSG; however, if that company follows the guidelines, it can avoid severe penalties. In this case, the legal system assumes the company did all it could to prevent the behavior, and that the employee simply acted on his own accord.

These guidelines include:

- developing a clear and complete code of ethics capable of reducing misconduct;

- securing top management's support for high ethical standards, and charging an executive-level officer of the company with responsibility for establishing and managing a compliance program;

- establishing and managing a compliance program that includes mandatory training and regular communication;

- creating internal auditing systems to monitor behavior and detect misconduct;

- consistently enforcing standards and punishing violations; and

- reviewing and modifying the compliance program on a regular basis to demonstrate a focus on continuous improvement.

As you can see from our discussion of the Federal Sentencing Guidelines, simply establishing a code of ethics is not enough. Sales leaders must also clearly and regularly remind salespeople of what is considered ethical and what is not, as well as monitor their behavior. Further, sales leaders can't say one thing and do another. When unethical dealings are identified, the personnel involved have to be punished, and the punishment has to be consistent across people and situations.

IDENTIFYING AND RESPONDING TO ETHICAL BREACHES How are unethical dealings identified? Many times an unethical event or incident is not identified unless an employee or customer reports it. When an employee reports unethical or inappropriate behavior, it is called **whistle-blowing**. Whistle-blowing is the primary method by which companies identify breaches of policy.[17]

Another method is to use technology. Edward Jones, the stock brokerage firm, uses sophisticated statistical modeling techniques that help the company's compliance department identify when an investment representative (IR) is engaged in questionable behavior. Such behavior might include buying and selling stocks in an account far too frequently, only for the purpose of earning commissions. A compliance department employee might, in this case, call the customer who owns the account in order to determine if she really wanted to make those transactions or if the IR had acted independently.

DUE PROCESS SYSTEMS FOR RESPONDING TO ETHICAL BREACHES Once a breach is identified, four types of due process systems are used to evaluate and respond to ethics violations complaints: (1) investigation and punishment systems, (2) grievance and arbitration systems, (3) mediator/counseling systems, and (4) employee board systems.[18] As you will see shortly, some of these systems are better at punishing violators than they are at reinforcing ethical behavior or improving a firm's policies.

Compliance investigation and punishment systems, led by an upper manager, are created to investigate potential violations, determine guilt, and assess punishment to the guilty. In many companies, the Human Resources (HR) area will handle the investigation and suggest punishment, if needed. Or HR may guide the manager who conducts the investigation. This person can be an ethics officer, but is probably more likely to be a line officer (in sales, a sales manager). That's why HR gets involved; the sales manager has probably had little training in investigation of problems (such as how to pursue a sexual harassment claim). Recall the Federal Sentencing Guidelines; proper training of management limits culpability for the company, but does just the opposite for a manager. If a manager has been trained, there is no excuse for not getting it right. Whether or not you've been trained, get assistance from HR if you are presented with an ethics issue.

Extravagant gifts, such as a free trip to an exotic beach locale, are viewed as bribes and can be illegal in the United States.

In this system, there is no intentional examination of the appropriateness of policies or potential biases in the company's policies that might be—at least partially—responsible for the violation's occurrence; only the behavior is considered. For example, a company may have an explicit policy against the use of samples after a purchase is made. But if inventory is low and a customer has to wait too long for delivery, couldn't a few samples tide them over? While the behavior may make sense, the system has to consider the behavior that went against the policy—not the policy's lack of flexibility.

A **grievance and arbitration system** is similar, in that guilt and punishment are investigated and discussed by progressively higher levels of management and labor—the difference being that labor (such as a union) is involved. If management and labor cannot agree on guilt or on the amount or type of punishment, then an outside arbitrator resolves the case. Again, however, the appropriateness of the company's policies and practices are not considered, and HR should be involved. Grievance and arbitration systems generally require that more procedures, or due process, be followed than do compliance and punishment systems. On the upside, the extra amount of due process gives people a sense that they are being treated more fairly. The downside is that the system can be expensive and slow, and that it requires employees to have labor contracts with their companies, which most salespeople don't have.

The mediator/counselor system is somewhat different, in that the goal is not punishment so much as it is determining what is right—both now and into the future. In **mediator/counselor systems**, a manager (typically an ethics officer or someone from HR) investigates, leads discussions, and builds consensus about the potential guilt of an accused person, as well as the need for any changes in the organization's practices or policies. This system is widely accessible to employees and typically fast and inexpensive. The degree of due process administered, though, depends on the mediator/counselor's expertise, and may vary. If a consensus is not reached in the mediator/counselor system, then some other form of governance—such as compliance investigation and punishment—has to finish the job.

An **employee board system** operates in much the same way as a mediator/counselor system, except that a board of the accused's peers takes on the mediator/counselor role. These people are formally able to make decisions about the violation, as well as offer formal recommendations for change. The process—as one might expect—is slow and cumbersome, making it expensive. On the positive side, the system typically offers high levels of procedural fairness and is widely accessible to employees. Furthermore, it allows not only for investigation of violations and determination of guilt, but it can also bring about changes in the organization's policies.

DEALING PERSONALLY WITH ETHICAL BREACHES What choices does a person have when faced with pressure to engage in questionable tactics? Essentially, if your boss or someone else in charge at your company pressures you, your choices are these:

- quit;

- try to talk them out of it, perhaps by bringing up the ethics concern or by showing a better strategy;

- agree;

- agree, but then do something else;

- threaten to expose the unethical request; or

- report the unethical request through company channels for anonymous reporting.

Of course, one choice is to quit and leave the organization. However, quitting is not always possible, at least not right away, without a significant sacrifice being made.[19] After all, quitting might mean having to take a pay cut, move to another city, or otherwise burden your family with a loss of income and stability. Thus, leaving might seem like the obvious, simple solution, but life is rarely that simple.

Another choice is to just say no—that is, to refuse to engage in an unethical tactic. Taking a stand and trying to influence policies is a moral high ground that few people are willing to take. Yet once such a stand is taken, a salesperson is likely to find many others willing to support it. Taking a stand is more likely to be effective when the organization has a code of ethics and an ethics officer responsible for enforcing the code. The salesperson or sales manager faced with the challenge can refuse to follow along and put the blame on the ethics code, a tactic that can help alleviate the stress associated with such situations.

Organizations with a code of ethics often have reporting mechanisms allowing victims to report ethics violations. Usually, an ethics officer is available to hear concerns about violations. The victim can simply threaten to inform the ethics officer or the violator's manager. If threatening does not work, then the victim can file a complaint.

Sometimes, the victim can negotiate for an alternative course of action. Assuming the pressure is coming from above, what is the manager's objective? More sales of a certain product? If the victim can identify an alternative and ethical course of action to achieve that objective, and the objective is ethical, then the manager is likely to allow the victim to proceed with that action.

Another alternative is to appear to agree with the tactic, but then choose to remain ethical. The risk here is that if the manager encouraging the unethical behavior is caught, the victim might also be culpable. For example, suppose your sales manager tells you to tell a customer that a product is safe to operate underwater when really it isn't. You say okay, but then choose to tell the customer the truth. If your customer then inadvertently operates the product underwater, is hurt, and sues, you might be in trouble. Why? Because as far as your company knew, you promised your manager you would tell the customer the product, indeed, worked underwater. To defend yourself against such a charge, you must document whatever actions you took (or in the above example, your advisory communications with the customer).

Sales-Related Laws

In the field of selling and sales management, several laws apply. There are laws addressing how salespeople treat customers, and labor laws that apply to sales managers' treatment of salespeople. We will briefly review both sets of laws; Exhibit 4.4 summarizes them.

EXHIBIT 4.4   Some of the Laws Affecting Sales

Law	Comments
Uniform Commercial Code	Defines key elements of a sale, such as what is a "sale" and a "warranty."
Business Defamation	State laws that govern what businesses (and salespeople) can say about competitors.
Gramm-Leach-Bliley Act	Federal law regarding privacy policies.
CAN-SPAM Act	Federal law prohibiting spam and governing how companies can contact customers; related is the Do-Not-Call registry.
Foreign Corrupt Practices Act	A U.S. law that makes bribery and other activities illegal in other countries for American companies.
Civil Rights Act	Governs hiring practices, among others, for sales managers.
Robinson-Patman Act	Federal law regarding fair pricing.

THE UNIFORM COMMERCIAL CODE In the United States, one of the most important sets of laws salespeople must follow is the **Uniform Commercial Code**, or **UCC**, because it is the legal guide to commercial practices. For example, the UCC determines who has the ability to make a binding agreement for a company; this person is called an **agent**. Not all salespeople are agents, though a company cannot escape the consequences of misrepresentation by salespeople simply by claiming they are not agents.

Another important element is that the UCC defines the term **sale** as the transfer of title from the seller to the buyer in exchange for a consideration (money). The date of a title transfer can be very important in determining who is responsible for what and when. For example, if the motor quits on a car as the buyer is driving it off the lot, who is responsible?

Another factor that determines who is responsible is the warranty. A **warranty** is an assurance by the seller that the product or service will do what it was sold to do. The warranty might also outline how any performance issues the product may present must be resolved. Warranties can be both written and *implied*. For example, when you buy a car, it's implied that the car to be at least drivable. As agents of their companies, salespeople can even create warranties through their statements to customers. A chemical company was once held liable for a product that did not do what the salesperson promised, even though the company's own printed brochures contradicted the salesperson's claims.[20] Laws in Canada and in European countries are often tougher about what can be said about a product. Even puffery is illegal in Canada.

OTHER IMPORTANT LAWS Other laws affect salespeople, too. For example, **business defamation** occurs when salespeople (or other company representatives) make unfair or untrue statements to customers about a competitor, its products, salespeople, or other aspects of that organization. These are state laws and, therefore, vary from state to state, but in general involve false public statements about a firm's products, salespeople or other employees, service levels, and any other actions. What is public may be open to interpretation, but if a salesperson defames a competitor's

Laws are passed, such as here in the State of Hawaii legislature, when ethics alone are insufficient to halt practices that harm vulnerable populations.

product to a customer, those comments can be used to prosecute both salesperson and company. Typically, if a business is found guilty, the punishment is to pay the victim an amount equal to estimated business losses due to the defamation.

We mentioned the issue of privacy earlier, but sales leaders must be aware of another law governing privacy policies. The Gramm-Leach-Bliley Act requires companies to notify their customers regarding privacy policies. Importantly, although the law was written to protect information provided on credit applications or posted on the web, it does not distinguish between sources of information. Therefore, a salesperson who gathers any information from a customer is under the same obligation regarding that information as is the company regarding any credit information gathered from the customer at the time of the sale.

The CAN-SPAM act is a law that many salespeople may be violating without any intention. This law requires companies to clean up their e-mail lists and only contact those with whom they have an ongoing relationship. Salespeople who spam people with blanket e-mails sent to everyone on their customer lists are breaking the law. In addition, salespeople can create other problems with blanket e-mail, such as putting every customer's e-mail address into the address lines for all other recipients to see. Customers may not want their e-mail addresses publicized, and might consider it a violation of the privacy policy. All it takes is for one customer, angered about being spammed, to forward the list to a competitor. Now the rep is really in trouble! The best advice is to either send each e-mail separately and personalize it, or let your marketing department conduct e-mail campaigns.

Similar is the Do Not Call (DNC) list maintained by the Federal Trade Commission. This registry allows individuals to place their phone numbers off-limits to telemarketers. Now, only companies with whom the individual has a business relationship are permitted to call them. So your credit card company can still place a marketing call to your number, but a credit card company with which you have no connection may not call—assuming you've registered your number.

An important law for salespeople who operate in other countries is the Foreign Corrupt Practices (FCP) Act. This law requires salespeople to live up to the law of the United States, even if the laws in the country where they operate are more lenient. If Lebanese law allows bribery, for example, a salesperson representing an American company cannot offer a bribe in Lebanon because it is against the law in the United States. Violations can result in large fines for the company and the persons involved. Interestingly, although Italian and German laws do not allow bribes in those countries, they do allow companies to not only use bribes in other countries, but to expense those bribes when calculating Italian or German taxes! Exhibit 4.5 shows the top 10 countries for bribe offers, according to Transparency International, a nonpartisan organization committed to helping end worldwide corruption.

Jens Jensen, a sales representative for Dow Chemical, sells ion-exchange resins in Malaysia, Singapore, Brunei, and Thailand. These resins take minerals out of water to prevent chemical buildup in pipes, boilers, heaters, and other water-using machinery. Jensen notes that many companies in the region close their deals by providing kickbacks to key decision makers. He, however, can't offer kickbacks. Not only is it against Dow's corporate policy, but it would be in violation of the FCP act. Instead, he focuses on building friendships with buyers, thus leveraging the fact that people all over the globe like to do business with friends. As a result, Jensen has become very successful.

EXHIBIT 4.5   World's Top Bribe Payers

	2006	2011
1.	India	Russia
2.	China	China
3.	Russia	Mexico
4.	Turkey	Indonesia
5.	Taiwan	United Arab Emirates
6.	Malaysia	Argentina
7.	South Africa	Saudi Arabia
8.	Brazil	Turkey
9.	Saudi Arabia	India
10.	South Korea	Taiwan

Least Likely?	2006	2011
1.	Switzerland	Switzerland
2.	Sweden	Belgium

Transparency International survey of more than 3,000 executives, reported annually at www.bpi.transparencyinternational.org

Tying agreements are also illegal under anti-trust laws such as the Sherman Act of 1890. A salesperson cannot force a buyer to buy some products in order to get others that are protected by patents. For example, a company cannot force buyers to buy five games in order to get the latest Xbox when it comes on the market.

Both state and federal laws provide buyers with cooling-off periods, during which they may cancel a purchase without penalty. These laws do not apply to sales made at the seller's location, such as a store, but do apply to most purchases made in your home (including your dorm room), at the state fair, or any other location. Not all products are included; in some instances, even local ordinances can apply, and laws vary with the city or state in which a transaction took place.

Laws for Sales Managers

Most of the laws sales managers need to worry about address labor issues—fair pay, appropriate employee selection and retention, and the like. (Many of these laws will be covered later, when we discuss recruiting and selecting salespeople.) In addition, there are laws regarding the reporting processes and legal requirements for regarding sexual harassment claims against firms. The 1964 Civil Rights Act prohibits workplace sexual harassment, and a company can be held liable even if the harassment is done by a customer. If a company forces a salesperson to continue to call on an account in which harassment (either unwanted contact or negative work environment) occurs, the firm can be found guilty of contributing to that harassment. At the same time, however, if a company has a procedure for preventing sexual harassment, and the worker does not avail himself or herself of those procedures, the company is not liable.[21]

Another set of laws that affects sales leaders are market laws designed to promote fair competition. The Foreign Corrupt Practices Act, mentioned earlier, is one of those laws. Another is the Robinson-Patman Act, together with anti-trust acts, which forbid **price discrimination**— defined by the law as a seller giving unjustified special prices, discounts, or services to some customers and not to others. Differences in pricing are acceptable if there are differences in the quality of the product, or service delivered, or if the prices have to be different to meet the prices offered by competitors in particular markets, or if the cost of doing business varies with different markets. For example, buyers of large quantities can be given discounts for their purchases, because they cost less per unit to process and ship.

Some prices, including car prices, are negotiated. Does this mean that the Robinson-Patman Act is violated when one person pays one price for a car and another person pays a different price? Why doesn't an airline have to charge the same price for every seat on a flight? The answer is that every customer had the same opportunity, either to negotiate the price, or to buy on the date that a certain price was valid.

Anti-trust laws also prohibit certain forms of non-competing agreements. For example, two competitors cannot agree to divide up a geographic area in order to create a monopoly within each separate territory. A company can hire another company to be an exclusive dealer in a particular area, but that same company cannot conspire with a competitor to create a monopoly.

We've also discussed whistle-blowing and responses individuals can take if asked to do something illegal or unethical. There are also laws protecting the whistle-blower. A whistle-blower who is treated badly by a company can win literally millions in compensation for damages. The largest claim, to date, is $77 million—won by a whistle-blower who notified federal prosecutors of a scheme to bribe doctors to prescribe a particular medication. In 2013, the most a whistleblower received was nearly $49 million, on top of the more than $500 million in fines and settlements paid.[22]

As you can probably tell, sales executives are very concerned with all laws that apply directly to salespeople's activities. But if a salesperson does something wrong, was it only the fault of the salesperson, or is the company also guilty? As mentioned earlier in this chapter, the Federal Sentencing Guidelines specify that a company must create policies and procedures to ensure that salespeople act appropriately— and policies and procedures that can be used to demonstrate that the company acted appropriately. Such policies and procedures include creating a code of ethics, conducting training so that salespeople and sales managers know what is right and wrong or legal and illegal, and other practices. If a company has successfully developed such policies and procedures, judges are more likely to assume that the salesperson is at fault, not the company; however, if a company is found to have created a culture that encourages illegal activities, then under the FSG, the consequences can be huge. TAP Pharmaceuticals, for example, had to pay more than $875 million in fines because the federal government determined that the firm's salespeople acted in accordance with a company culture that encouraged deception.[23]

Managing Your Career

Ethical temptations for students seem fairly common and obvious. Advice for resisting is also simple—don't cheat on exams, don't turn in someone else's work as your own, and so forth. But other questions might seem less obvious. For example, is it okay to interview with a company you have no intention of joining? If you get an offer from one company but really want another, is it ethical to accept the first, knowing you'll renege if the dream job comes along?

The reality is that you are building your reputation now. Whether you show up for class on time, honor your promises to your peers and your professors—these become pages of your ethical history. Your reputation is built on choices that mark you as a person of integrity; it also includes how you respond to situations that might challenge your sense of right and wrong. Think for a minute about your faculty. You know which professors favor athletes unreasonably, which ones may demean poorer-performing students, and the like. At the same time, faculty members also quickly realize which students show integrity, and when recruiters ask, your instructors will share that information.

Summary

While there are many approaches to developing ethics guidelines, common ones are the Golden Rule, the Conventionalist Ethic, the Protestant Ethic, the Market Imperative, the Libertine Ethic, and the Utilitarian Ethic. These different approaches might lead to different choices by individuals as they face dilemmas involving ethics.

Salespeople, as boundary spanners, may find themselves faced with many ethical challenges because they have to represent both the company and their customers. Common ethical issues specific to sales can include misrepresentation, bribery, and encouraging rogue purchasing.

Companies and sales managers can reduce unethical behavior by creating the right ethical climate. Codes of ethics are also useful tools, not only because they can provide guidance to salespeople as they face ethical challenges but also as companies create the right kind of ethical climate. Companies can also create different forms of systems for identifying and responding to ethical breaches. These systems create mechanisms for whistle-blowing, compliance investigation, and punishment. Such systems might include grievance and arbitration systems, mediator/counselor systems, or employee-board systems.

Laws also govern salespeople's and sales managers' actions. Such laws include the Uniform Commercial Code, which defines when a sale occurs, the limitations of warranties, and other important elements in selling. Also important are state laws governing business defamation, the CAN-SPAM act, the FTC's Do Not Call registry, and the Federal Corrupt Practices Act. Managers also have to worry about labor laws, such as those protecting employees from sexual harassment.

One challenge is whether the company should be liable or whether an individual was operating alone. The Federal Sentencing Guidelines specify actions—such as creating codes of ethics and conducting training programs—to demonstrate that companies have taken all of the necessary steps to create the right culture.

Key Terms

agent   77
arbitration system   75
boundary spanners   68
bribery   70
business defamation   77
code of ethics   72
compliance investigation and
   punishment systems   75
employee board system   75
ethical climate   72
ethics   64
Federal Sentencing Guidelines
   (FSG)   74

grievance and arbitration systems   75
manipulation   68
mediator/counselor systems   75
misrepresentation   69
price discrimination   80
protected territory   72
puffery   69
rogue purchasing   71
sale   77
sexual harassment   72
Uniform Commercial Code (UCC)   77
whistle-blowing   74
warranty   77

Questions and Problems

1. Which of the ethical approaches best fits you? Which one is least like you? Why?

2. Different approaches to ethics were discussed in this chapter, with a focus on the salesperson's actions. Now consider what buyer actions might be considered appropriate or inappropriate behavior under each of the different approaches. Are buyers held to the same standards for honesty and ethics in purchasing transactions?

3. Likewise, consider each of the different approaches and review the ethical challenges faced by sales managers. How might a sales manager's response to an ethical challenge differ under the different approaches?

4. Is it okay to interview with a company you have no intention of joining? If you get an offer from one company, but really want another, is it ethical to accept the first—knowing you'll renege if the dream job comes along? Would your answer change if you adopted the Golden Rule versus a Libertine or Conventionalist approach?

5. Jim Stradinger, a sales manager for Holland 1916, argues, "Do what's right for the customer and everything else will take care of itself." Discuss the pros and cons from each perspective: the perspectives of the sales representative, customer, and sales manager. Which of the ethical approaches is most represented by Stradinger's comment?

6. The Federal Trade Commission has generally ruled that puffery is acceptable. What is not acceptable is deception that is subjectively interpreted as injurious to consumers—that is to say, the claim can be interpreted in a way that harms the buyer. Review the following claims. Are they puffery or deceptive misrepresentation?
    a. This sinus medication was developed by a scientist to alleviate his own sinus headaches!
    b. There is no other wrench like it!
    c. You can't buy a faster printer in this price range.
    d. I've sold lots of other customers this same product at the full list price.

7. Which of the following are legal practices and which might be considered illegal? If you determine that not enough information is provided, what would make the practice legal or illegal?
    a. A salesperson offers a discount to a small drugstore if the store will set up a special display of his product at its entrance.
    b. A salesperson sends two bottles of wine, valued at $100 each, to a customer as a thank-you gift after making a large sale.
    c. The buyer asks the salesperson out for drinks after work.
    d. A buyer provides a salesperson with a competitor's proposal, including pricing information.

8. As a sales manager, you find yourself faced with the following situations. Identify the ethical or legal issue in each and discuss how you would handle the problem. (All of these were experienced by former students.)
    a. Your boss, the regional sales manager, forwards several ethnic jokes and lewd e-mails to you and your entire sales and support staff. Two of your salespeople complain to you.
    b. A customer has called and asked you to send someone else to his office as he does not want to be called on by his currently assigned salesperson. When you ask why, it is because he doesn't want someone of that sexual orientation calling on him.

c. You've asked a salesperson to create a training session for the entire sales team, a task that will require the salesperson to spend about $60 on materials that company policy expressly prohibits salespeople from charging on their expense report. She agrees, then submits an expense report with the $60 listed as entertainment of a client—an acceptable expense. You notice it on the expense report; she hasn't said anything about it, but you know she was conducting the training session on the day in question and couldn't have entertained a client that day.

d. The company has introduced a new product and requires all salespeople to memorize a demonstration script. To encourage salespeople to learn it, a contest was developed by your boss to award a new HDTV to the best presentation of the demonstration. Two salespeople come to you and say, "Let's just let Beverly represent our team, we don't have time for this. We need to be out selling."

9. Look at the "Global Sales Management" box describing the Caux Round Table principles. Which model of ethics would you say most aptly describes those principles? What is the impact on salespeople and sales managers if they ascribe to the CRT principles?

Role Play

Crosby Chemical

Crosby Chemical manufactures and sells chemicals to distributors, which then sell to companies that use those chemicals in the manufacture of their own products. Today, Fran, the Crosby salesperson, is calling on Jackie of Jackson Distributing— Fran's largest account. At issue are several concerns: (1) Fran's fastest-growing account, Epsom Derby Inc., is taking market share away from Jackson, and Jackie knows that Fran is selling to Epsom Derby; (2) a large bid is coming up at Ottumwa Engineering and both Epsom & Jackson are bidding; and (3) prices, in general, have been rising faster than inflation, putting margin pressure on distributors. Also of concern is that Crosby's regional vice president used to be the salesperson selling to Jackson Distributing; and the Crosby exec called Fran, wanting to know why the account seemed to be unhappy and not growing.

Assignment

Break into groups of three. In each group, one person is Jackie, the owner of Jackson Distributing, and another is Fran, the salesperson who is responsible for the Crosby account. Don't worry about matching gender to the names in the case. Discuss strategies for how to handle Jackson (the client) and how to respond to Crosby's regional vice president. The role of the third party is "the devil's advocate," and this person's job is to suggest unethical strategies to each person. The devil should call time-out and whisper suggestions to each person, who must then act out that suggestion. The other person then listens to the unethical suggestions and responds with implications of those choices and then presents alternatives.

Caselets

Caselet 4.1: Putnam Pulp & Paper Co.

When Emily Hernandez was promoted to sales manager for Putnam Pulp & Paper Co., she was extremely proud. Her sales performance, first as an inside salesperson, then as an account executive, had always been in the top three of her company. Further, she had built a solid reputation for integrity. But within a very short time, she realized there were some issues on the team she took over.

"I've had three complaints this morning for the same thing," she thought to herself. "Why would customers think we could waive the delivery fee?" Moreover, this wasn't the first time she got this complaint, and these complaints over the delivery fee involved several members of her sales team.

Worse, she wasn't sure what to do about some incidents that had occurred during team meetings. When Beverly Drea brought in a big order, Paul Baker exclaimed, "What did you have to give away for that?" with a smirk, and everyone laughed, except Beverly. When Paul announced his large order, someone catcalled that all those evenings at the strip club had finally paid off. That was probably the mildest comment she heard; several others were more direct, implying that salespeople were either spending lavish amounts (and not reporting it on expense reports—she had checked) or using sex to get clients. There was absolutely no evidence to either claim, and Emily believed she actually had a sales team with solid sales skills; they didn't have to rely on shady techniques.

But the delivery fee complaints worried her. What should she do?

Caselet 4.2: *Callahan Car Parts*

Tommy Callahan took over the manufacturing firm Callahan Car Parts after his father died of a heart attack. The company had 12 salespeople, each responsible for a region of parts stores. The firm also has two account executives who handled the big parts retailers—either NAPA or O'Reilly's. Callahan's three manufacturing plants in the U.S. were unionized, but its sales force was not.

The company has never had many complaints about its salespeople. However, one of its competitors had been hit with a multimillion-dollar fine for resale price maintenance (setting minimum prices its distributors could charge for its products). The competitor's lack of policies prohibiting the practice was cited as a contributing factor, which made the fine much larger than it would have been otherwise.

Tommy trusted his salespeople, but he knew that, without an effective ethics policy and a procedure for investigating complaints, Callahan's was at risk. So he asked three of his senior salespeople, the firm's VP of human resources, and the company's attorney, to form a committee and set up policies and procedures.

The sales staff, however, revolted. "We're honest people—we don't need this!" they claimed. Worse, one of the senior salespeople told Tommy privately that if the policy were truly effective, it might identify some real problems Tommy would rather not learn about!

What type of approach to monitoring, investigating, punishing, and improving ethics policies should Tommy suggest to the committee? What should he do to get salespeople to support the need for clear ethics policies?

References

1. Anonymous (2014). "Workplace Misconduct at an All-Time Low," 2013 National Business Ethics Survey, *http://www.worldatwork.org/adimComment?id=74683*, accessed June 24, 2014.
2. Kaynak, Ramazan, and Tuba Sert (2012). "The Impact of Service Supplier's Unethical Behavior to Buyer's Satisfaction: An Empirical Study," *Journal of Business Ethics*, 109(2), 219-226; Ou, Wei-Ming, Chia-Mei Shih, Chin-Yuan Chen, and Chi-Wei Tseng (2012). "Effects of Ethical Sales Behaviour, Corporate Reputation, and Performance on Relationship Quality and Loyalty," *Services Industries Journal*, 32(5), 773–787.
3. Agnihotri, Raj, Adam Rapp, Prabakar Kothandaraman, and Rakesh Singh (2012). "An Emotion-Based Model of Salesperson Ethical Behaviors," *Journal of Business Ethics* 109(2), 243-57; Gallagher, Chuck (2013), "Sales and Service Ethics: When Good People Make Bad Choices," *Sales and Service Excellence*, 13(11), 24–25.
4. Serviere-Muñoz, Laura and Michael Mallin (2013). "How Do Unethical Salespeople Sleep at Night? The Role of Neutralizations in the Justification of Unethical Sales Intentions," *Journal of Personal Selling & Sales Management*, 33(3), 289–306.

5. Schwepker, Charles Jr., and Roberta J. Schultz (2013). "The Impact of Trust in Manager on Unethical Intention and Customer-Oriented Selling," *Journal of Business & Industrial Marketing*, 28(4), 347–56.

6. Donoho, Casey, Timothy Heinze, and Christopher Kondo (2012). "Gender Differences in Personal Selling Ethical Evaluations: Do They Exist?" *Journal of Marketing Education*, 34(1), 55–66.

7. Tullberg, Jan (2011). "The Golden Rule of Benevolence versus the Silver Rule of Reciprocity," *Journal of Religion and Business Ethics*, 3(1), 1–20.

8. Jackson, Peggy (2012), "My Personal Take on Business Ethics," *Review of Management Innovation & Creativity*, 5(17), 22–32.

9. Gaus, Gerald (2013). "Why the Conventionalist Needs the Social Contract (and Vice-Versa)," *Rationality, Markets, and Morals*, 4, 71–87.

10. Serviere-Muñoz, Laura and Michael Mallin (2013). "How Do Unethical Salespeople Sleep at Night? The Role of Neutralizations in the Justification of Unethical Sales Intentions," *Journal of Personal Selling & Sales Management*, 33(3), 289–306.

11. For a defense of the Utilitarian Ethic, see Andrew Gustafson (2013), "In Defense of the Utilitarian Business Ethic," *Business and Society Review*, 118(3), 325–360.

12. Dudley, George, and John F. Tanner, Jr. (2005). *The Hard Truth About Soft Selling: Restoring Pride and Purpose to the Sales Profession*. Dallas, TX: Behavioral Sciences Research Press.

13. Nill, Alexander, and John A. Schibrowksky (2005). "The Impact of Corporate Culture, the Reward System, and Perceived Moral Intensity on Marketing Students' Ethical Decision Making," *Journal of Marketing Education*, 27(1), 68–80.

14. Colby, Allyson (2012), "Nothing but the Truth," *Estates Gazette*, 1248, 61.

15. Anonymous (2013), "GlaxoSmithKline Executives Face China Bribery Probe," BBC News Business, *http://www.bbc.com/news/business-23265958*; Pratley, Nils (2014), "Inquiry into Alleged GlaxoSmithKline Bribery in China Has Led to Pay Fudge," *The Guardian, http://www.theguardian.com/business/2014/feb/27/glaxosmith-kline-alleged-bribery-china-pay-fudge.*

16. Fournier, Christophe, John F. Tanner Jr., Lawrence B. Chonko, and Chris Manolis (2010), "The Moderating Role of Ethical Climate on Propensity to Leave," Journal of Personal Selling & Sales Management 30(1), 7–22.

17. Sharbatoghlie, Ahmad, Mohsen Mosleh, Taha Shokatian (2013), "Exploring Trends in the Codes of Ethics of the Fortune 100 and Global 100 Corporations," *Journal of Management Development*, 32(7), 675–89.

18. Lee, Gladys and Neil Fargher (2013), "Companies' Use of Whistle-Blowing to Detect Fraud: An Examination of Corporate Whistle-Blowing Policies," *Journal of Business Ethics*, 114(2), 283–95.

19. Joseph, Joshua, Lee Van Weer, and Ann McFadden (2000). *Ethics in the Workplace*. Washington, DC: Ethics Resource Center.

20. Much of this section is based on Richard P. Nielsen (2000). "Do Internal Due Process Systems Permit Adequate Political and Moral Space for Ethics Voice, Praxis, and Community?" *Journal of Business Ethics*, 24(1), 1–27.

21. Much of this section is based on Richard P. Nielsen's work, including "What Can Managers Do About Unethical Management?" *Journal of Business Ethics*, (1987), 6, 309–320: "Negotiating as an Ethics Action (Praxis) Strategy," *Journal of Business Ethics* (1989), 9, 383–390: and "Dialogic Leadership as Organizational Ethics Action (Praxis) Method," *Journal of Business Ethics*, (1990), 9, 765–783.

22. Castleberry, Stephen B., and John F. Tanner, Jr. (2014). *Selling: Building Partnerships*, 9th ed. Burr Ridge, IL: McGraw-Hill.

23. Tycko, Jonathan (2013), "Top Whistleblower Settlements of 2013—To Date," *National Law Review*. Accessed March 22, 2014. *http://www.natlawreview.com/article/top-whisleblower-settlements-2013-to-date.*

24. Haddad, Charles, and Amy Barrett (2002), "A Whistle-Blower Rocks the Industry," *Business Week* (June 24), 126–130.

PART THREE

Analyzing Customers and Markets

Now that you understand that sales leadership strategies are influenced by ethical and legal values, you will be better prepared for this part, which focuses on sales strategies and information technologies for managing customer relationships. Sales firms and their sales leaders invest time and energy in serving their best customers at a profit. Sales technology permits the sales leader to identify profitable customers and understand their needs. The more accurate the customer information that firms possess, the easier it is to manage customer relationships.

Chapter 5, *Business-to-Business (B2B) Sales and Customer Relationship Management*, discusses how business-to-business salespersons sell to, and serve, buyers. Selling firms expect their salespersons to understand buyer needs and goals in order to provide value and form long-term relationships with their best customers. Business relationships can vary from transactional to strategic, depending upon the level of trust and cooperation between the two firms. We explain how salespersons get to know their customers and gauge the roles played by individuals in the buying firm. By identifying who will influence and make purchase decisions, a B2B salesperson can share pertinent information and use appropriate influence strategies. Selling firms compute customer lifetime value to prioritize customer service levels, and employ information technology to monitor and manage customer relationships.

Information technology is also useful in managing customer relationships, which is the focus of Chapter 6, *Leveraging Information Technologies*. Imagine, for example, that General Motors (GM) is your customer. GM buys more each year than do most countries, and they may need products shipped to hundreds of locations all over the world. How do you keep up with that—or with the hundreds of people who may be involved in various purchase decisions? Or what if your territory was banks in New York? You might have thousands of customers! This chapter examines those technologies that help salespeople manage their markets—whether their market is one account or thousands.

The sales strategy and customer relationship approach that a firm selects determines the structure of the sales force, as continued in Chapter 7. To increase sales success, the sales force structure must align with the sales strategy. There are many organizational options sales leaders can choose to meet buyer needs. In turn, the sales structure and desired service levels impact the type of individual that is hired and the skills and knowledge taught in training and development programs.

BUSINESS-TO-BUSINESS (B2B) SALES AND CUSTOMER RELATIONSHIP MANAGEMENT

LEARNING OBJECTIVES

After completing this chapter, you should be able to:

- Recognize how people make organizational purchasing decisions.

- Describe and explain the three buying situations.

- Identify the different roles played by buying center members.

- Understand individual forces that influence the B2B buying process.

- Comprehend how buyer-seller relationships are established and maintained.

- Explain success factors that apply to buyer-seller relationships.

- Discuss seller performance factors that lead to successful customer relationships.

To succeed in today's highly competitive marketplace, a firm's sales force must deliver long-term customer value. This is especially important in business-to-business (B2B) sales. Why? Because B2B buyers are large customers in comparison to most firms that engage in retail or business-to-consumer exchanges. For example, retailers like Walmart or Target serves millions of customers annually. B2B firms like Boeing and Airbus have several hundred customers—among them airlines, organizations, governments, and wealthy individuals located in many geographical areas of the world. When Boeing or Airbus loses a single sale of 20 or 50 aircraft, the company experiences a significant loss in sales revenue. To minimize lost customers, a firm's managers and sales team must understand what is important to B2B buyers; that is, how and why they purchase what they do. They must also formulate a sales strategy that expands the firm's relationships with its most profitable buyers. As selling firms better understand and build trusting relationships with their buyers, they will succeed more with their sales efforts.

JASON DeAMATO
CEO, Island of Sales
and Author of
The Pocket Guide
for Sales Survival

Sales Manager Profile: Jason DeAmato

WHEN ASKED ABOUT FORMING AND maintaining relationships, sales consulting executive Jason DeAmato states that the quality of their customer relationships is the foundation upon which they build their entire business. He says:

A sale is not about forcing something upon a customer. Rather, it is about understanding a customer's needs and providing a solution. Without a solid relationship, you will not uncover true needs. The deeper you build a relationship, the more information you will uncover about a customer's needs. Needs are more complex than "I want good value,"—which can mean different things to different people. Only when trust is established will total disclosure reward the seller. We also want our customers to know that we care about them—first and foremost. We want long-term relationships and to make human connections with our customers in every way. When a salesperson becomes a true consultant and puts the customer's needs first, successful building of healthy business relationships results.

The first thing we teach our new salespersons is to use the "B3 Rule:" Be Yourself. Be Loved. Be Remembered. We designed this easy to follow mnemonic so that salespeople will not over-think the process. You cannot build a relationship if you are not yourself. You want to be LOVED! Being "liked" is good, but being loved is what you should aim for! And lastly you must be remembered. If your customer ends a phone conversation without remembering your name, you didn't do your job. We also teach people to engage and ask genuine questions. Of course this starts with hiring people that have a sincere people approach and who truly want to form relationships.

Buyers' receptivity to forming sales relationships varies, depending upon personality and social style. Expressive people are more open to relationships and want to connect. Analytical people make decisions based upon facts and figures. The key is knowing clients well enough to understand what they want when it comes to relationships. Our customer base is a mix of personalities; therefore, we have to be experts at matching social styles and building relationships accordingly.

Island of Sales uses a custom CRM system to track everything. Our CRM was built in-house and has a section for notes on crucial information about a customer that would be needed to maintain a strong relationship. This is also vital information for new salespersons when we reassign a sales territory or pass accounts between salespersons. If the CRM is not well detailed, the new salesperson is at a huge disadvantage.

Salespeople who leverage a CRM system give themselves a big advantage. We see highly-talented salespeople who believe that they can remember all the details about every customer. But when you build and manage a portfolio that has over 100 customers, this skill becomes impossible. Salespersons should build CRM notes about their customers as if they were handing over their portfolio tomorrow.

In Jason's experience, keeping detailed notes about buyers allows salespersons to find greater success in building and sustaining deep relationships with their customers. ■

Understanding B2B Purchasing Decisions

Business relationships occur between people, so it is important to remember that personal relationship skills are essential to making sales and concluding successful commerce. Forming and maintaining a relationship with a B2B customer is a complex undertaking that requires a highly skilled sales force and constant interaction and support from the firm's other functional groups—especially the salesperson's manager. Understanding buyers also requires an information technology system that's easy for people to use and provides salespersons and sales managers with accurate and near-real-time information that is needed to serve their customers. Chapter 6 discusses the technical aspects of CRM systems in greater detail.

Technology allows today's sales teams to increase their efficiency while improving buyer service levels.

The Buyer's Decision-Making Process

B2B buyers tend to engage in a specific process when making a purchase decision. This process is shown in Exhibit 5.1. The first step is recognizing that a problem or need exists that can be resolved by making a purchase. In a commercial situation, the buying firm may view the situation not as a problem, but as an opportunity that can be exploited for a profit by making a purchase. For example, when considering the purchase of new manufacturing machinery, replacements that exhibit greater production capacity will reduce production costs and increase company profits.

EXHIBIT 5.1   The Buyer's Decision-Making Process

Problem Recognition   >   Information Search   >   Evaluation of Alternatives   >   Purchase Decision   >   Postpurchase Evaluation

Once a decision is made to search for a product or service, buyers must decide upon the specifications of the needed product or service. They then begin to search for possible alternatives offered by sales vendors. These offers are then evaluated based upon price, adherence to the buyer's stated specifications, quality, and delivery time. When a vendor passes certification that they can provide the needed product or service, they are placed on an **approved vendors' list**. As the product is needed, orders are placed. The new product or solution is then evaluated based upon the buyer's original criteria—price, delivery, and so forth. As long as the buyer is satisfied with the product's value, future purchases are made.

Organizational Buying Situations

The first buying situation is based upon whether the purchase event is completely new, current business that is up for re-bid, or a routine purchase. Each of these buying situations impacts the relationship formed and the amount of information that is shared between the buyer and seller. A **new buy** occurs when a complex or expensive product is purchased for the first time. In many organizations, a new-buy product/ service is a rare occurrence. For individual buyers and sellers in organizations, however, new buys happen more frequently. When a new-buy situation occurs, the buyer engages in all eight buying steps shown in Exhibit 5.2. However, if the selling firm and buyer already have a relationship, the amount of information shared regarding the new product is greater, and the level of testing and scrutinizing for approval is lower. The opposite conditions will apply to sellers who have a limited relationship with the buyer—or none.

EXHIBIT 5.2   The Buy-Grid Framework: Participation in the Buying Stages of the B2B Buying Process

	New Buy	Modified Re-buy	Straight Re-buy
1. Recognize problem	Yes	Perhaps	No
2. Determine product characteristics	Yes	Perhaps	No
3. Determine product specifications	Yes	Yes	Yes
4. Search for suppliers	Yes	Perhaps	No
5. Evaluate proposals	Yes	Perhaps	No
6. Select supplier	Yes	Perhaps	No
7. Specify quantity needed	Yes	Yes	Yes
8. Review the supplier/products performance	Yes	Yes	Yes

A **modified re-buy** is the purchase of a product or service after the buyer—for important reasons—has considered different vendors or product changes. For example, a manufacturing firm that previously purchased a fleet of Ford trucks to deliver automobile parts to independent repair facilities might consider switching to Toyota trucks in order to benefit from higher gas mileage and lower maintenance costs. When this happens, the company engages in a modified re-buy. A selling firm that has a strong relationship with the manufacturer will be aware of any changing needs, and will have more time to work out a solution for the customer. In contrast, sellers with weak relational links are most likely to learn about the change in purchase specifications when and if the buying firm issues a **request for quotation** (**RFQ**)—a formal request by the buyer for a sales quotation. More experienced salespeople generally participate in new-buy and modified-re-buy purchase decisions, because these situations are often high-dollar sales and long-term in nature. Thus, a good relationship and a high level, and amount, of information about the buyer is needed to successfully negotiate with the firm.

Last is a **straight re-buy** situation, where the buying firm moves directly from need recognition (Step 1) to ordering (Step 7). Today, many routine purchases or straight re-buys are made through automated electronic data exchange (EDI) systems or the exchange of electronic information between buyer and seller for purchase orders, confirmations, and invoices. For example, suppose a company routinely buys printer paper and office supplies. As the firm's employees consume these supplies, the company's inventory management system tracks stock levels and, when inventory reaches the reorder point, the system electronically transmits an order to the supplier. At a large manufacturing firm like Chrysler, supply analysts use a "production control portal" linked to the company's suppliers and shippers to monitor the status of the orders, and send out alerts when there appears to be a potential problem with inventory levels, deliveries, and so forth.[1]

Clearly, straight re-buy situations do not require a live salesperson to call upon the buyer—yet, it was a salesperson who got the seller's product(s) on the buyer's approved vendors' list, set up the electronic reorder system, and finalized the contract during a new-buy or modified-re-buy situation. Furthermore, by maintaining a positive relationship with the buyer, the seller increases the probability of extending the original contract with a new agreement.

An **in-supplier**, or an approved vendor that has established a relationship with the buyer, will often try to convert all the buyer's purchases to a straight re-buy situation. If the seller can successfully do so, it can strengthen and extend the business relationship. By contrast, an **out-supplier**—a vendor who has no (or only a transactional) relationship with the buyer—will attempt to initiate a modified re-buy situation in order to create an opportunity to capture the business. For example, an out-supplier will raise questions in order to persuade the buyer that the current product being purchased is not the best one, or that a new technology or feature found in the out-supplier's product is superior. Unlike in-suppliers, out-suppliers must often offer price concessions to buyers to persuade them to do business with them.

Understanding the Buyer's Criteria

An important model for the sales force to understand is the multi-attribute matrix. Buyers utilize a **multi-attribute matrix** to evaluate vendors by assigning an importance weight to categories like price, product conformance and quality, delivery time, and manufacturing capacity. That is, a buyer might compare all vendor offerings by assigning an importance ranking of .5 for quality, .3 for delivery, and .2 for customer service. Then, the buyer rates each seller in terms of that category on a scale, say 1-10, and multiplies the weight times the rating. All the sellers' scores for all the categories are then summed up and compared. As seen in Exhibit 5.3, a multi-attribute matrix allows buyers to more objectively compare two or more vendors. In this example, Vendor A's offering receives the highest multi-attribute rating and will likely be selected as the supplier of the product.

EXHIBIT 5.3   A Multi-Attribute Matrix Comparison

Attribute	Weight	Vendor A	Vendor B
Quality	.5	9 = 4.5	7 = 3.5
Delivery	.3	8 = 2.4	9 = 2.7
Customer Service	.2	10 = 2.0	8 = 1.6
Totals	**1.0**	**8.9**	**7.8**

For certain important categories, all vendors would probably have to meet a minimum standard for their product or service to be considered. For example, sellers might have to quote a price that is below a specified ceiling amount. For the remaining features, the buyer might allow a strong performance on one dimension to compensate for a weaker performance on another. In this case, a moderate rating on one important feature will be pulled upward by stronger ratings on other categories, even when these features are less important. Salespeople who understand a buyer's weights and ratings can use this information to alter the weights (convince the buyer that other features are more important), or improve the ratings (show that the product's/service's performance is higher than the buyer originally thought). It is easier for a salesperson to modify product/service weights or ratings when a high level of trust exists between the two firms.

Buying Center, or Group, Purchases

An autonomous purchasing decision occurs when one person single-handedly moves the firm through all eight stages of the purchase process. However, it is more likely that a group of employees in the firm—either a **buying center** or a **decision-making unit** (**DMU**)—is involved in the purchase process. These employees play a variety of "roles" in the process.[2] The **initiator** starts the purchase process by recognizing a need. For example, the purchasing manager

The sales force must understand the needs and goals of buyers.

concludes that the current copier requires maintenance too often and produces poor-quality copies. Or a design engineer may specify the need for a product to replace an existing component in an air-conditioning unit that is failing at a significant rate. At the other end of the process is the **decision maker**, or the person/committee making the final purchase decision. Sales managers have long been taught to help their sales reps identify and meet with the "economic decision maker" or the person who holds ultimate purchase decision authority. To help identify the decision maker, a sales manager instructs her sales people to ask the customer to explain the buying process to them. When the purchase is large, the salesperson can also find out who is on the buying committee and then ask who chairs the group. In some cases, the decision maker isn't a member of the buying center at all; for example, a **controller** may approve or set the budget for the purchase.

The **purchaser** is any person who actually buys the product. The purchasing role can be played by anyone in the firm—the person who will use the purchased product, or his manager. The purchasing agent's role is to be responsible for the firm's making objective buying decisions. Purchasing agents may assume multiple roles in the decision, such as coordinating meetings, sharing information, ensuring that the firm's purchase process is followed, and even finalizing the purchase of a product or service. There is no absolute job description for someone who holds the purchasing agent title, but people who do are normally involved in more than simply ordering the product. Consequently, sales managers need to coach their salespeople to be careful not to confuse roles and titles.

Today's salespersons must also be aware of, and use, social media to further their goals. First, Linked-In can be utilized to gather information about a purchasing agent or other buying center members prior to visiting the buying firm. Salespersons and sales managers must understand that the purchasing agent can monitor their company's webpage, and this tells them which salespersons have been doing research. Second, it is important for every sales firm to have an up-to-date website that buying center members can utilize to find information pertinent to their needs. If salespersons are told that buying center members cannot find important information, this omission should be communicated to the sales manager who will raise the issue and ask for an update by the IT department or manager.

Influencers are individuals who affect the decision maker's final choice—through recommendations about which vendors to include or which products will best satisfy the organization's needs. The number of influencers expands as major purchases are considered that involve more departments and personnel. A case in point: a mining machine sales firm experienced "pushback" from a mining company when it came to buying a new type of machine. Careful questions by the salesperson revealed that the mining company's maintenance department vetoed purchasing a different machine brand because they would have to learn how to repair a new machine and maintain additional parts inventory.[3]

Users are part of the buying center because their jobs require that they implement and evaluate what was purchased. Users may also attempt to influence the decision and, at times, influencers represent users' perspectives by considering the users' needs or abilities to implement the purchase decision. For example, a decision maker may choose one product over another because of the users' familiarity with the selected product, thus shortening the user's learning curve when implementing the new product.

Gatekeepers control information, either in the form of knowledge or access into, out of, or between members of the buying group. They can actively influence a decision by determining the level and amount of information reaching the decision maker. Sometimes gatekeepers unintentionally exclude or over-emphasize information that impacts the purchase decision. There are two types of gatekeepers: **screens**, who decide who is given access to members of the buying center, and **filters**, who control the flow of information. Secretaries who decide which salespeople can communicate with executives and managers are one type of screen. A purchasing agent who demands that all salespeople check in with the purchasing office before visiting anyone at the account also acts as a screen.

An example of a buying center in action is a plant manager who informs the CEO that a piece of manufacturing equipment is costing more to repair than to operate, and suggests that it is time to purchase a new one. In this scenario, the plant manager acts as an initiator. The CEO meets with the chief financial officer (CFO) and inquires whether there is money in the budget to buy a new piece of equipment. The CFO sets a budget for the purchase. The CEO then asks the plant manager to request proposals from three vendors. In this instance, the plant manager is also acting as a gatekeeper. If the plant manager prefers a particular vendor, he may try to make a stronger case for that vendor, and becomes an influencer. When a proposal is made and the CEO decides to buy the recommended equipment, this makes her the decision maker. If she instructs the plant manager to order the equipment, the plant manager is the purchaser. The plant manager will also be the user, since his department installs and uses the equipment. Thus, as can be seen in this example, roles can and do shift as one person plays multiple roles. The number of stakeholders participating in a buying center usually ranges from three to 12,[4] and this number may be increasing.[5] In cross-cultural buying centers, the number of participants can reach 30![6]

Note that at no time in our plant-equipment purchase example was a committee formed, nor was there an official designation of specific roles. A common misconception by new sales personnel is that, with the formation of a buying committee, someone assigns specific roles to individuals. Actually, the buying center is a dynamic group of individuals whose membership changes over time. There may be a formal buying committee for certain high cost decisions, but—more frequently— the decision process is informal and less structured.

Team Selling and Multi-Level Selling

In today's business environment, which is focused on customer relationships, buyers expect higher levels of service from sales organizations. One way to provide higher service levels is to form sales teams that are comprised of highly skilled members of the selling firm. An **extended selling team** is a group of specialists from the major areas of the sales organization who interact with their counterparts in the buying center. Buyers report a number of advantages derived from a sales team: quicker responses to buyer's questions, an ability to speak with one's counterpart who understands the technical language, and a capability to work as a group to offer multidisciplinary solutions to complex buyer problems. Depending upon the situation, extended selling teams can be formed for short or long periods. For example, an extended selling team may be formed to navigate through a modified re-buy scenario with a buyer, and then may disband. Or an extended selling team can be formed to manage all long-term interactions with a major account like IBM.

At Omni-Cell, a market leader of automated pharmaceutical distribution systems, the salesperson is expected to make four to five visits with prospective customers— normally hospitals—to learn their business models and establish relationships. It is important for the salesperson to plan the calls, ask the buyers open-ended questions, and determine the firms' needs.[7] At that point, the regional sales director accompanies the salesperson and, in consultation with the client, helps assemble an expert team. For example, a pharmacist may be added to the team to evaluate and advise how drugs can be more efficiently and safely handled throughout the supply chain. Likewise, a nurse may be called upon to interview and advise how the client's nursing staff can be trained and motivated to utilize automated systems that safely distribute and protect pharmaceutical products.

In many firms, the account manager serves as the official team captain. This means that the salesperson must demonstrate leadership and an ability to plan, coordinate, and communicate with sales team members from diverse functional areas within the firm. For example, an extended selling team may be comprised of select personnel from engineering, finance, quality control, manufacturing, management information systems, and customer service. In addition, a vice president from a functional area may serve as the executive member of the team—weighing in with other top-level managers to expedite important requests made by the buying organization. Since buyers form centers to reduce risk, improve decision making, and increase technical expertise, the selling firm may also form a selling center to interact with the buying center and offer the highest levels of service to the customer.[8]

Although essential, team selling faces coordination, communication, and compensation challenges. For example, when multiple parties within the extended sales team interact with members of the buying firm, promises may be made that remain unknown to the remainder of the sales organization. Also, once a sale is made, a customer is lost, or customer satisfaction decreases, the sales manager is not certain who to credit or blame.[9] Extended team selling is utilized almost exclusively for large, major accounts that make high-volume purchases and generate sufficient profits to cover the higher expenses of team selling.

As a result of these ambiguities, managing selling teams is a complex undertaking for sales managers. First, when a sales manager creates a sales team, it is important that recruited members are adaptable, able to work together, and willing to put the good of the group above their own individual needs. Second, they must undergo sales training that covers topics such as team selling and relationship marketing. Third, as a sales manager, you must clearly communicate the team's goals and coach the various team members who may perform below expected levels. Last, a team's compensation package must include a component that motivates the members to cooperate, so that the group's goals will be achieved.

Team compensation can consist of a significant commission or bonus tied to a group's meeting its goals, and managers of the group are expected to evaluate individual contributions to the team. For example, a customer-service manager at Cisco will have different team-selling responsibilities than will a supply-chain manager, even though they serve on the same team. Since all sales team members must contribute their expertise for the group to succeed, Cisco requires sales team members to regularly (weekly or monthly) evaluate their teammates.

Sales firms also form multi-level teams from different areas of the organization to sell to their counterparts in buying firms. That is, **multi-level selling** occurs when two or more personnel from a selling firm make a sales call to their functional counterparts at the buying organization. This occurs when a salesperson calls upon the purchasing agent at the buying firm, while a vice president of engineering calls upon the buyer's vice president of engineering, and a quality assurance supervisor visits with the buyer's chief of quality control. From a protocol perspective, sales firm members call upon their counterparts at equivalent levels of the organizational chart. As necessary, the executive team member can negotiate price agreements, policy deviations, and expedited shipping dates to win the order and establish a deeper relationship with the buying partner.

In certain industries, including computers and telecommunications, customers purchase electronic components that are manufactured by two or more suppliers. Recently, firms began forming **marketing alliances** in which two or more companies combine their technologies, unique resources and skills, and products in order to market total systems to final users. Alliances allow selling firms to combine resources that create and deliver value to buyers in response to market opportunities. Marketing alliances are most effective when mutual trust, interdependence, and cooperation exist in the partnership. Salespersons can enhance their value in a sales alliance setting by exhibiting high levels of product, market, and buyer knowledge (competence trust) and demonstrating caring and integrity (benevolent trust).[10]

A marketing alliance was formed by Parke-Davis, a pharmaceutical division of Warner Lambert, who introduced the drug Lipitor to reduce cholesterol. Parke-Davis combined its sales efforts with Pfizer, a pharmaceutical firm with a large and experienced sales force, and the two sales forces worked together to maximize sales of Lipitor. A few years later, Pfizer purchased Warner Lambert.[11]

A **value-added reseller** (**VAR**) purchases products from one or more manufacturers and assembles these products into a system before delivering the package to specialized buyer segments. A VAR might purchase a computer system from Dell, add software from SAS, and have their technical staffs merge, test, and install the system for the end user. When a VAR delivers a complete package, buyers call their purchase a **turn-key operation**. VARs may also handle customer service and repair issues. Alternatively, if one of the manufacturers partners with the value-added reseller, then the manufacturer may assume responsibility for repair and customer service.

B2B Customer Relationship Management

Recall from Chapter 1 that customer relationship management (CRM) is the process of identifying and grouping customers in order to develop an appropriate relationship strategy, so that the organization can acquire, retain, and grow the business. Progressive firms have known for years that the key to successful business is keeping customers satisfied by developing a deeper understanding of their buyers' needs and producing products and services that they truly need and want. This is often easier for business-to-business firms to do, because their sales forces are very in-touch with their customers. They also have relatively fewer buyers to deal with than, say, retailers do. Having fewer customers allows sellers to more readily explore and uncover what products or services buying firms need.

However, in the past, many B2B sellers were less willing to track the needs of their customers and customize products for them—in part because they lacked accurate information about what their buyers wanted—since that knowledge was not readily available. Things are much different today: Salespeople and managers can gather a lot of information about their customers simply by looking on their websites. Industry-wide and firm-specific news is accessible with the click of a computer mouse. Sellers today are also more willing to customize their products for business-to-business buyers, because new technology like CRM software has made it more feasible to determine the profitability of these customers over a specific time period. In other words, the selling firm knows in advance if taking the trouble to customize a product for the customer is worth the extra effort. Many global firms, including Dow Chemical, Clorox Co., and Kforce, utilize CRM software to analyze the profitability of short- and long-term sales and compensate their salespersons.[12] As seen in the "Sales Technology" box, there are at least 10 reasons to adopt a CRM system.

Other advances in information technology, like e-mail and EDI, have made it much easier for sellers to communicate with their buyers, predict their purchasing needs so as to forecast future sales, and more accurately understand buyer behavior through data mining. Firms that **data mine** examine information collected in their CRM databases. The bulk of this information is gathered by salespeople, and may include: purchase dates, incentives offered to the buyers, products/services purchased, selling prices, a buyer's position in an organization, number of sales visits between buys, and samples and promotional materials requested by the buying firms. Having such information allows both sales representatives and their managers to identify important relationships or "connections" that might not be readily apparent.[13] For example, sales managers at a large pharmaceutical company learned which sales approaches were most effective via data mining—something they did not know before.[14] Managers are also able to conduct competitive analyses that result

TECHNOLOGY IN SALES MANAGEMENT   **10 Reasons to Adopt and Implement a CRM System**

1. Increased sales team productivity.
    CRM helps reduce cost, increase sales, and increase market share.

2. Build stronger customer relationships.
    CRM efficiencies allow salespersons to spend more time with customers.

3. Reduced costs.
    CRM increases accuracy and effectiveness.

4. Enhanced communication.
    CRM improves communication with sales manager and other key managers.

5. Easier access to lead intelligence.
    CRM provides the complete file for anyone speaking with a potential buyer.

6. Improved organization.
    CRM makes it easier to identify, and to service, accounts needing attention.

7. Deeper view of customer.
    CRM provides a complete picture of customers.

8. Improved sales reporting.
    CRM offers current information that can be used for reports and forecasting.

9. Closer cooperation between sales and rest of firm.
    CRM allows near real-time information to be shared with the sales team.

10. Improved customer satisfaction.
    CRM helps satisfy buyer needs, build loyalty, and keep buyers satisfied.

Based on "10 Reasons Why Your Sales Team Should Adopt CRM Technology," Accessed February 23, 2014.
http://www.trackvia.com/blog/technology/10-reasons-why-your-sales-team-should-adopt-crm-technology.

in higher sales revenues, lower order-entry errors, and the increased acquisition of new customers.[15]

From a technological perspective, an information-based CRM system connects the organization's entire operations to function as a 24-hour nerve center, sharing information in real time[16, 17] by sending information that alerts appropriate managers about change in demand. Consider the following example: a buyer requests that an order be delivered by FedEx and this is entered into the CRM system. When the CRM prints shipping labels, they are FedEx labels. The system also records when the delivery company picked up the shipment, and provides tracking numbers to confirm that the shipment arrived safely. The seller's Intranet also permits the buyer to log into the site securely and check production schedules and delivery dates.

Cisco is a company that uses an information-based CRM system to enable its sales team. First, the CRM system at Cisco provides a single source of information for the extended selling team. In effect, the system increases accuracy and decreases confusion by allowing Cisco sales, marketing, and/or customer service team members to access historical purchases, part numbers, sales revenue, who sold the product(s), when the purchase occurred, and whether a service contract is on file. A recent study concluded that utilizing a CRM system resulted in higher levels of internal collaboration, a better understanding of buyer needs, and perceived higher performance.[18]

In short, CRM technology helps firms become more market- or customer-oriented.[19] Firms practice market orientation when their business processes and functions are aligned to maximize their effectiveness in the marketplace. As Exhibit

5.4 shows, a market-oriented selling firm places the buyer at the center of all the strategic decisions it makes. In effect, the seller becomes **customer-centric**. We discuss more about sales information technology, including CRM technology, in Chapter 6.

EXHIBIT 5.4   A Customer-Centric Firm's View

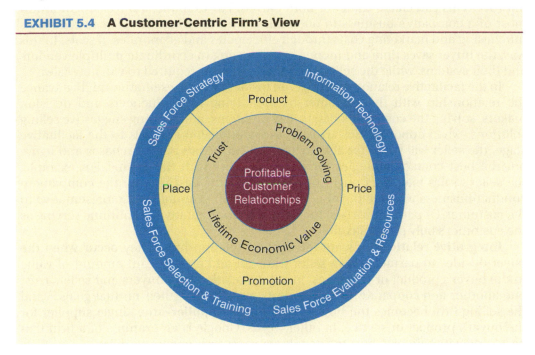

The Nature of B2B Relationships

Different B2B buyers and sellers have distinct types of relationships with one another at different times. Exactly how a buyer and seller relate to one another will depend upon how the buyer extracts—or gets—value from the relationship. After all, the buyer is often in the "driver's seat," so to speak. Sales managers must understand business relationships in order to devise strategies and direct their salespeople to move profitable customers to deeper relationships. It is management, not the salesperson, who decides which customers are worth the investment of additional time and resources.

In a **transactional relationship**, the buyer-seller relationship can be adversarial when either party views the situation from a purely economic perspective. In this case, important and powerful buyers might play the sellers off against one another to get lower prices or free services. For example, a buyer might inform the salesperson that the selling firm must lower the product or service price if he or she is to continue to doing business with the firm. Otherwise, a competitor will receive either a larger portion or all the business. This does not mean that transactional situations are good or bad. Rather, in certain industries in which a product is viewed as a commodity, there is a known market price for the product, and the buyer and seller work together to reach an agreement that benefits both parties.

But it's not only buyers who play games. Salespeople have been known to play games with their buyers. They might, say, ship products manufactured for established buyers to new, more profitable customers, and make the original customers wait for a later shipment of the products. In transactional relationships, communication and contact are funneled through a "bow tie" arrangement between the salesperson and the buyer. This means that all information and contact occurs between the salesperson and the buyer; however, the information and requests are then communicated by the purchasing agent or salesperson to related areas within their firm. Although sellers and buyers may begin to establish trust and share information in a transactional relationship, their early relationships are greatly influenced by established business practices within each firm.[20]

In a **facilitative relationship**, trust and cooperation between seller and buyer improve. This can create value for both parties. For example, a buyer might award most of a company's business to one selling firm, allowing the seller to reduce its purchasing and marketing costs through efficiencies and economies of scale. In this way, the buyer saves time and money by not having to coordinate multiple vendors and their systems, while the seller minimizes expenses required to win new sales.

In the facilitative relationship stage, an inside sales representative might advance the relationship with the customer by identifying the influencers and decision makers, solving the customer's day-to-day problems, and offering suggestive selling solutions, when opportunities arise. As the relationship expands to the facilitative stage, the seller will be better able to analyze the buyer's past purchases and figure out the best contact strategies for doing business with that firm.[21] For example, the seller's sales managers might determine that the best way for the company to conduct business with the buyer is by assigning an external sales representative to the customer. Or perhaps it's best for an inside representative to continue serving as the customer's only point of contact.

Integrative relationships are the deepest relationships. They occur when the buyer decides to partner with a seller who can add a significant amount of value to the buyer's product or processes. In a deep relationship, buyers and sellers trust one another and cooperate to reduce costs and advance their mutual goals,[22] and the selling firm becomes the buyer's **sole source supplier**—the single supplier for the buyer's product or service, in other words. Google is an example of a firm that partnered with Yahoo! to become its sole source search-engine supplier.

In integrative relationships, both partners also search for new ways to deliver and add value to one another's products and processes. (See Exhibit 5.5.) In certain integrative relationships, a sales manager might decide to replace an outside salesperson with an inside sales representative who might actually go to work in the buyer's office.[23] IBM is one company that stations on-site consultants, or representatives, at their buyers' sites to help solve computing problems.

EXHIBIT 5.5 **Differences in Key Variables Based Upon the Stage of the Buyer-Seller Relationship**

Relationship	Transaction >	Facilitative >	Integrative
Trust	little trust	increasing trust	broad trust
Communication	buyer-seller "bow-tie"	a few departments begin communicating	direct communication between all departments
Value	"win-lose"	buyer: lower prices seller: lower costs	"win-win" for both
Commitment	few expectations beyond current contract	growing commitment by buyer & seller	long-term expectations of partnership
Feedback	little expectation of feedback	growing acceptance of feedback	honest feedback expected and sought
Sales Programs	little opportunity to cross-sell, up-sell	may switch to inside salesperson	expansive opportunity to cross-sell, up-sell
Profits	little concern for supplier profits	more concern	acknowledgement that supplier must make reasonable profit
Competitive Advantage	little, other than current buy	growing competitive advantage	customized offering

When business partners trust one another, they depend on one another to achieve a goal. However, not all sales organizations receive the same level of trust from their partners because trust is earned by making and keeping promises.[24] At Schering-Plough Pharmaceuticals, sales managers expect their sales representatives to bring integrity and honesty to their jobs in order to establish trusting relationships with physicians. Building this relationship can take from six to 18 months.[25] Without trust, the buyer will likely be reluctant to share information that the salesperson needs to recommend solutions to the buyer's problems.[26] Serving customers can vary significantly across cultures, as seen in the "Global Sales Management" box.

GLOBAL SALES MANAGEMENT   **Offshoring of Customer Service Centers**

Most B2B buyers expect their customer service requests to be resolved by competent workers in their home countries. However, a number of Fortune 500 firms have shifted their customer care centers offshore to increase profits, as offshore call centers are estimated to be 20-25 percent less expensive than domestic service centers in the U.S. Although there are short-term savings to be realized, caller complaints have centered on: communication problems, cultural disconnects, and security concerns. U.S. firms responded to this "push-back" by trying to locate call centers in cultures closer to the U.S. such as New Zealand and Canada. But how do sellers handle their best customers—those considered key or major accounts? According to one study, U.S. firms have kept local customer service centers for their most profitable customers, while shifting the less profitable customers overseas. These decisions follow economic theory in regard to maximizing profits, but what is not known is the impact this level of service will have on firms wanting to move their customers with growing sales and profits into deeper facilitative or integrative relationships?

Based on Earl D. Honeycutt, Jr., Vincent P. Magnini, and Shawn T. Thelen (2012), "Solutions for Customer Complaints about Offshoring and Outsourcing Services," *Business Horizons*, 33–42.

Customer Lifetime Value (CLV) Strategies

The goal for sales representatives and their managers is to establish and maintain mutually beneficial, long-term relationships with their *most profitable* customers. Firms that follow a CRM strategy work to provide distinct service levels to customers, based upon their expected **customer lifetime value (CLV)**. Recall that customer lifetime value refers to the profitability of partnering with a buyer for an extended period of time.[27] This involves computing the CLV for each buyer—its future profitability, that is.[28] In fact, CLV is the most effective metric for managing future customer profitability.[29]

The selling firm can compute CLV by knowing or projecting three criteria: (1) the probability of future purchases, (2) future marketing costs, and (3) future contribution margins. Depending upon the CLV of customers, selling firms can allocate resources based on the profitability of sales to them, propose the correct product to the correct buyer at the correct time, and earn and retain profitable customers. Exhibit 5.6 shows how a firm might set its sales strategies based upon customer lifetime value.

Once the customer's CLV is calculated, salespeople and their managers then develop distinct service levels, approaches, and strategies for the customer, based on its CLV. Exhibit 5.7 shows how a seller making one sale to a customer receives $18,000 in customer lifetime value. But if the seller works to make the buyer a long-term partner, the account could potentially generate a CLV of nearly $275,000 over five years, due to lower marketing costs and additional customers being referred by the seller.

EXHIBIT 5.6   Planning a Firm's Sales Strategy Based Upon Customer Lifetime Value (CLV)

	Low Percentage of Purchase Share	High Percentage of Purchase Share
High Lifetime Earning Value	• frequent sales force visits • monthly visits • direct mail/telemarketing • optimal contact: bi-weekly • high potential customer value	• constant sales force interaction • weekly visits • direct mail/telemarketing • optimal contact: weekly • highest customer value
Low Lifetime Earning Value	• extended sales force visits • yearly intervals • direct mail/telemarketing • optimal contact: quarterly • low-value customer	• infrequent salesforce visits • six-month intervals • direct mail/telemarketing • optimal contact: bi-monthly • low-potential customer value

EXHIBIT 5.7   Computing a Buyer's Customer Lifetime Value (CLV)

	One Year	Three Years	Five Years
Average Sales	$20,000	$24,000	$30,000
Sales Orders Per Year	1	1	1
Referrals	0	2	4
Number of Referrals That Buy	0	1	2
Gross Sales/Year/Customer	$20,000	$72,000	$150,000
Referrals That Become Customers	0	20%	25%
Gross Sales Referrals	0	$28,800	$150,000
Computed Customer Value	$20,000	$100,800	$300,000
Minus Marketing Expenses	($2,000)	($13,600)	($25,500)
Net Lifetime Customer Value	$18,000	$87,600	$274,500

The Stages of B2B Customer Relationship Management

Firms that adopt a CRM strategy tend to follow three distinct stages. Initially, CRM sales managers view the system as a driver of income. Having accurate information about buyers allows the sales force to **up-sell** more expensive products and **cross-sell** new products to existing buyers who haven't purchased the products before. For example, at Cisco, a salesperson may gather information from customers by asking the following questions:

1. What does your computer network currently look like?

2. What is the design of the network?

3. Where does your company want to be in a year? In five years?

After gathering the information, the salesperson determines how Cisco's products can be matched to the buyer's needs and how many years it will take for the buyer to receive a financial return on the product(s) purchased. By following this process, Cisco boosts revenue and profits by selling at a higher level to its current customers.

In the second stage, sales managers recognize that CRM allows their sales representatives to manage customer relationships to earn higher profits. For example, a sales executive might decide to primarily contact customers from which the firm earns less profit via less costly Internet, telemarketing, or mail campaign methods. This will give sales representatives more time to call upon more profitable clients and lower the firm's overall selling costs.

In the third stage, sales managers understand that CRM drives customer lifetime value. Thus, sales managers encourage their salespeople to offer customized solutions to their most profitable buyers. The sales managers then work to coordinate activities with the firm's sales, customer service, and marketing groups to retain buyers with the highest CLV.

Buyers will perceive a salesperson who has product and application knowledge, advocates for the buyer, and calls upon the buyer at the appropriate time and in the correct medium (in-person, phone, or e-mail) as a professional sales consultant who adds value to their firms.[30] An excellent example of a "credible consultant" is Michael Gerrity of Action Packing Systems. Gerrity once promised a customer an overnight delivery of 30,000 labels. To keep his promise, he remained in contact with FedEx throughout the night, drove to the Boston Airport at 5:00 a.m. to collect the shipment, and personally delivered the order to the customer at 7:30 a.m. to meet an eight o'clock deadline.[31]

Maximizing Value for the Buyer

Buyers look for value and satisfaction in their purchases. This value can be computed as:

$$\frac{\text{Benefits}}{\text{Costs}} = \frac{\text{Functional Benefits} + \text{Emotional Benefits}}{\text{Monetary Costs} + \text{Time Costs} + \text{Energy Costs} + \text{Psychic Costs}}$$

Salespersons can increase their product's or service's value in the minds of the customer by: (1) increasing product/service benefits, (2) decreasing buyer costs, or (3) doing both. For example, the selling firm, through the salesperson, can maximize the functional benefits of its offering by ensuring that the product exceeds the buyer's expected satisfaction level. Emotional benefits are maximized through trust and through shared successful business relationships. Although it may not be possible to lower the buyer's monetary costs, the seller can reduce the buyer's time and energy costs through electronic reordering, with high-quality products that exceed expectations, and by assuming additional service duties—such as monitoring the buyer's inventory and communicating directly with the buyer's manufacturing and quality control personnel when problems arise. Likewise, the seller reduces the buyer's "psychic" costs by exhibiting high levels of honesty, trust, and dependability.

The reward for creating customer value is that buyers purchase larger amounts for longer periods, and are less likely to leave the business relationship. This goal can be achieved by eliminating causes of dissatisfaction and increasing the buyer's **drivers of delight**; that is, factors that exceed the buyer's expectations. Most sellers can list four or five categories that account for 80 percent of buyer dissatisfaction; among these are perceived value, customer service, responsiveness, and quality. Two or three other factors cause increased satisfaction.[32] Remember that buyers invest, rather than purchase, and a salesperson's job is to provide information that justifies this investment.[33]

Building trusting relationships leads to sales success.

Risk and the Organizational Buyer

Sales managers can also help their salespeople establish trust and form deeper relationships by reducing the risk faced by the firm's customers. For example, when a professional buyer decides to order a computer system, a major piece of manufacturing equipment, or a healthcare system for the workforce, the potential risk is high. The purchase price is significant and problems associated with such products may be difficult to correct. However, if a sales manager in a computer manufacturing firm can convince the company's executives to offer a "no-questions asked" return policy for newly released products, then the seller has substantially minimized the buyer's risk. The easiest and least expensive way to reduce risk is by sharing information. A CRM system provides common information within the sales organization that can improve the probability of higher customer service levels occurring.

Consider the following example: the buyer calls the seller's customer service department to report that a shipment arrived damaged. The customer service representative apologizes for the problem, opens the buyer's CRM account to record this service failure event, and places an expedited replacement order. This report is almost immediately available to the salesperson, his sales manager, the firm's customer service manager, production manager, and shipping team leader. A replacement order is readied for overnight shipment to the customer, and an e-mail is sent to the salesperson confirming that the replacement order will arrive the next day. The salesperson calls the buyer to confirm that the problem has been corrected and to thank her for the company's continued business. In addition, the seller's representatives provide the buyer with excellent product information via sales presentations, product demonstrations, or product trials at every meeting. In a trustful, customer-centric relationship, partners lessen risk by sharing valuable information with one another.

Sales managers are primarily concerned with the outcome of the relationships their salespeople have with customers—namely, higher sales and higher profits. However, to take these relationships to their highest levels and extract maximum customer lifetime value, sales managers must also be concerned about the importance of the outcome for their customers. As we have said, ideally, both buyers and sellers work to attain mutually agreed-upon relationship goals by forming a trusting relationship and willingly resolving problems.[34]

To sum up this section, let's refer back to comments from the chapter's opening profile sales manager. Jason DeAmato feels that to gauge the quality of the relationship, the company must rely on the instinct and follow-up of company salespersons. There is no relationship barometer. This is why hiring highly instinctual salespeople is such an important step in setting up a business for success. Being open, honest, and confident helps keep the relationship on track. In many ways, business relationships mirror personal relationships. There must be open and honest communication. Paying attention and making sure you have the confidence to communicate within strained relationships brings many relationships back on track at an even stronger level. Jason DeAmato feels that 99 percent of the time relationship problems are a result of failed communications somewhere along the line.

Important Salesperson Behaviors

Sales managers should encourage sales representatives to practice the following key behaviors that create and maintain positive relationships with their customers:

- **Foster a long-term perspective**. CRM success depends on the salesperson's passionate interest in, and constant efforts toward, establishing and maintaining long-term relationships. The sales force cannot generate sales unless the buying firms possess a true need. At Cisco, sales managers encourage their representatives to take a long-term perspective by assigning each buyer a single sales contact. This assures the buyer that the seller is available to support the buyer's needs.

- **Being honest and sincere.** Both qualities are important in business relationships. To retain trust, the buyer must be told the truth, even when a promise cannot be met. Cisco salespersons are encouraged to take the time to get to know their buyers, show genuine interest in them, and truly address their needs. It is obvious to the buyer, from this behavior, that Cisco is not simply looking to make a quick sale.

- **Understanding customer needs and problems.** A good CRM program requires fully informed and knowledgeable sales representatives. For example, Medtronic requires senior managers to attend medical operations and discuss how the company's products work. This serves as an example to the company's sales representatives. The idea is for everyone in the company to gain an intimate understanding of what customers need and how Medtronic's products can meet those needs.[35]

- **Meeting commitments.** To build trust and maintain a relationship, the salesperson must keep all commitments made to the buyer. This requires support from the sales firm and the salesperson's manager, to ensure the buyer is not let down. In this way, buyers come to believe that the selling firm and its salespeople are committed for the long-term and will serve them at a higher level than would other competitors. As a Cisco salesperson told one of the authors, "This is the name of the game." Cisco salespersons call and update buyers on the status of their information request or purchase. After all buyer-seller discussions, the Cisco salesperson researches questions and concerns raised by the buyer, and shares the research findings with the buyer.

- **Providing after-sales service**. The salesperson must respond positively to buyers' concerns and problems. Many customer-centric firms have established high-quality customer service centers that resolve buyers' problems quickly and efficiently. Even so, the salesperson must be made aware of customer concerns expressed to his or her firm's customer service center, and ensure that the buyer receives valued service and remains satisfied. For example, all of Cisco's sales quotes contain an after-sales service contract supported by a "Follow the Sun" service center setup. This means the customer can call Cisco anytime day or night. Depending upon where the sun is shining, a service center in Virginia, California, Australia, India, or Belgium will take the call, consult the CRM system, help troubleshoot the customer's problem, order replacement parts, or send in a certified local partner to any non-functioning equipment the buyer may have. Cisco believes that selling a product without after-sales service is not responsible selling.

Why Business Relationships End

Business relationships unravel or come to an end when one or both parties feel their partner is too complacent, their goals no longer match, their cultures have diverged, or one or both parties have behaved irresponsibly. This can include acting in a way that is not trustful, dishonesty, looking out for only their own interests, sharing confidential information with others, and/or taking unfair advantage of information shared by a partner. When such behavior occurs, one or both parties conclude that it is not in their best interests to maintain the business relationship.[36]

When a problem occurs with your best customers, you should meet personally with them to be sure all of their issues are understood and addressed.

Salespersons, who act as boundary spanners, can be "lightning rods" whenever anything goes wrong. (Recall that we discussed boundary spanners in Chapter 4). After all, it is the salesperson's job to bring the selling and buying firms together to conduct business for mutual benefit. As a result, the salesperson is often blamed for the loss of the relationship with a valued partner. When a salesperson makes a promise—that she will have parts air-freighted to the buyer to maintain production, for example—this commitment must be honored, or the buyer will rightly assume that the seller cannot be trusted and does not have the buyer's best interests at heart. In fact, research confirms that the strength of the buyer-seller relationship plays an important role in reducing buyer defection.[37]

The trouble is that salespeople cannot control everything that occurs at their firms. Sometimes the selling company itself is responsible for "cracks" in the relationship with a B2B partner. For example, a manufacturer might promise the salesperson that a product will be delivered to the customer on a specific date; whereupon, the salesperson passes the information to the buyer. But when the product doesn't arrive on time, who do you think the customer will blame? The salesperson, of course!

Even if it is not the salesperson's fault, it is often best to have him or her resolve the buyer's conflicts instead of, say, the firm's service center. In other words, for the relationship to be maintained, it is the salesperson who should—optimally—break the "bad" news to customers. However, sales managers can help in situations such as this by taking speedy actions to remedy the misunderstanding.[38] For example, Bill Bencsik, President of Bencsik Associates, Inc., located in Florida, makes a special effort to correct misunderstandings that lead to broken relationships. Benscik feels that it is important to communicate with the buyer as soon as possible, and to meet personally over dinner, whenever possible. According to Bencsik, moving quickly to resolve misunderstandings shows how much the salesperson values the relationship with the buyer and, when successful, can make the partnership stronger—because he went the extra mile for his customer.

Managing Your Career

Few new salespersons have worked in, or have an extensive knowledge of, B2B sales. In contrast, many college graduates have worked in retail sales at some point in their lives. This material provides you with a deeper understanding of how B2B sales work that not even those in B2B sales fully grasp after a year or so on the job! Understanding how B2B markets work—at professional buying centers, with requests for quotations, in qualification of vendor sellers, and through customer relationship management selling behavior—will bring order to what you do in your first sales job, and help you master your responsibilities more quickly.

There are times when selling firms claim that they are customer-centric, but you will be able to tell if this is true from what you learn in this chapter. If the firm claims it puts its customers first, are you being pushed to make a quick sale? When you interview, are you asked questions about how much money you want to earn? Such questions should raise a warning flag that the seller is more interested in making a sale than addressing the long-term needs of the buyer. Mastering the B2B CRM material also allows you to interview more competently and decide if the job for which you are interviewing is a good fit—one to which you want to devote a large amount of your waking time, trying to succeed. In short, knowledge is power!

Summary

Buyers tend to engage in a specific process when making a purchase decision. The buying process is based upon whether the purchase situation is completely new, current business that is up for re-bid, or a routine purchase. Each of these buying situations impacts the relationship formed and the amount of information that is shared between buyer and seller.

Buyers use specific criteria, as shown in the multi-attribute matrix, to objectively evaluate sales offers. A multi-attribute matrix allows the salesperson to list and prioritize the importance of the buyer's criteria, ranking price, delivery, and quality. When a group of employees in the firm—either a buying center or a decision-making unit (DMU)—are involved in the purchase process, these employees play a variety of roles in the buying process. They act as initiators of the purchase, influencers, the decision maker, the purchaser, the gatekeeper, the financial controller, or perhaps a combination of these roles. Buying centers are dynamic. That is, the group of individuals who comprise them changes over time. Certain decisions might involve a formal buying committee. More frequently, however, the decision-making is informal and less structured.

More and more firms are adopting a customer relationship management strategy to profitably serve their current and future business partners. CRM systems allow the seller to collect information through a data-base system that helps them better understand and fulfill a buyer's needs. For a B2B relationship to be nurtured and grow, both partners must act in a trustworthy manner and work to resolve the inevitable problems encountered in any relationship. However, a customer relationship means different things to different people. Not all firms want a "partner" for every purchase. Lastly, firms understand that it is not economically feasible, or even desirable, to turn every customer into a long-term partner.

Key Terms

approved vendors' list 89	marketing alliance 94
buying center 91	modified re-buy 90
controller 92	multi-attribute matrix 91
cross-sell 100	multi-level selling 94
customer-centric 97	new buy 89
customer lifetime value (CLV) 99	out-supplier 90
data mine 95	purchaser 92
decision maker 92	request for quotation (RFQ) 90
decision-making unit (DMU) 91	screen 92
drivers of delight 101	sole source supplier 98
extended selling team 93	straight re-buy 90
facilitative relationship 98	transactional relationship 97
filter 92	turn-key operation 95
gatekeeper 92	up-sell 100
influencer 92	user 92
in-supplier 90	value-added reseller (VAR) 95
integrative relationship 98	

Questions and Problems

1. Define customer lifetime value (CLV). What three factors comprise the formula for computing CLV? Why is CLV the most effective metric for managing future customer profitability?

2. Go to Multimedia Education Resource for Learning and On-line Teaching (MERLOT) at *http://www.imrtn.com/lifetimecalc.asp* and compute two lifetime customer values (CLV) based upon a one-year customer experience and a five-

year relationship. First, assume you will sell $25,000 two times per year to your new customer, but for only a single year. The customer will not provide you with any referrals. What is the computed value of a satisfied customer for a single year? Second, run the same calculation, but make these new assumptions: The customer continues to buy $25,000 twice a year for five years; in addition, the customer provides two referral customers that result in one additional customer. Based upon this information, recompute the total value of a satisfied customer. What are the financial differences between a one-year and five-year customer? How can sellers increase their profitability by computing and adhering to the expected CLVs?

3. What actions can a sales manager propose, other than lowering the price, to increase value for the customer?

4. A bank wants to purchase a new PC-based computer system. As the salesperson calling on the bank, it is your job to identify and provide the correct information to each party in the buying center. Therefore, what roles would you initially predict for the following parties: bank president, IT manager, teller, customer service manager, and branch manager? What characteristics or personal interests might influencers have? How might the size of the bank influence the purchase? That is, compare and contrast the different purchase decisions for a bank that wanted to purchase 25 PCs and had one location and $5 billion in assets—versus a larger bank with 125 locations and $500 billion in assets?

5. Discuss the differences between a new buy, a modified re-buy, and a straight re-buy situation with respect to process time, amount of information required, and the role of the salesperson. What impact will having a relationship with the buyer influence the roles played by the in-supplier and the out-supplier?

6. Use the multi-attribute matrix below to compute the assigned list of attributes for a machine lathe for an engineering firm. Machine A costs $22,000 and Machine B costs $25,000. In regard to quality, warranty and service, A is rated as average while B is judged as being above average.

Purchase Criteria	Weight	A	B
Price	.5		
Quality	.2		
Warranty	.2		
Service	.1		

7. What advantage does a salesperson have who can correctly identify the decision maker in a buying center? How should the sales manager go about coaching his or her reps to find out who this person is?

8. Define multilevel selling. Give an example of a marketing alliance, and explain how such a partnership benefits both parties.

9. What is a value-added reseller (VAR)? How should VAR sales managers coordinate their service and repair issues with their manufacturing partners?

10. Why have more and more B2B firms shifted to a relationship marketing strategy? What are the benefits of shifting to a CRM strategy? How does the shift to CRM impact the sales team, sales manager, and other departments in the selling firm?

11. What are the three levels of B2B customer relationships? How do they differ?

12. What actions should a sales manager take when a firm adopts a CRM strategy? What sales force skills are driven by a CRM strategy, and how does it affect

the skills applicants need, the training program, and the way the sales team is coached and rewarded?

13. What types of behaviors lead to the demise of a business relationship? How can a sales manager minimize the loss of profitable partners? What role should a sales manager play in terms of dealing with dissatisfied partners? Why?

14. Some sales firms have attempted to form and maintain relationships with all their customers. Is this a wise strategy for a selling firm to pursue? Why and why not?

15. Is all business "good," or is there business you should not want to pursue?

Role Play

Managing a Sales Team at Piedmont Manufacturing

Shahid Karim is the sales manager for Piedmont Manufacturing, a company that produces B2B goods for global customers. A major customer, RD2 Solutions, approached Piedmont's senior sales rep, Maddie Goodman, to set up a meeting to discuss its purchase of a new line of machinery, as well as the affiliated contract for installing and servicing these machines. Karim appointed a selling team comprised of Goodman and the following individuals (and specialties): Henry Wong (design engineering) and Emily Justus (customer service manager). Karim has scheduled a meeting to discuss the team's goals, plus to seek out the team's concerns and suggestions about forthcoming meetings with counterparts at RD2 Solutions. Karim must appoint a team leader and compile a list of questions his colleagues would like answered at the buyer-seller meeting. Also, Karim must decide how to evaluate the contribution of each team member. That is, what criteria should he use to assess the performance of each team member, even though they bring different skill sets to the team?

Characters

Shahid Karim, sales manager at Piedmont Manufacturing

Maddie Goodman, senior sales rep

Henry Wong, design engineer

Emily Justus, customer service manager

Assignment

Break into groups of four, with each student in the group playing a character. Do not be concerned about matching the gender of the character; simply substitute your first name for that of the character. Prior to the group phase, work individually to summarize a list of concerns and questions that you believe to be important to your area of responsibility at Piedmont Manufacturing. Then, meet as a group and role play the meeting between Shahid, Maddie, Henry, and Emily. Your goal is to conclude the meeting with an agreed-upon list of questions to be discussed. Also, work together as to select the team leader, decide how the team will be evaluated, and determine the reward structure for acknowledging each member's contribution to the team's success.

Caselets

Caselet 5.1: *Managing Buying Dynamics at Hughes Aircraft*

Dan Francis is a sales manager for WRT Electronics, and his team of sales engineers call upon original equipment manufacturers located primarily in Los Angeles, California, and Tucson, Arizona. Hughes Aircraft is a large manufacturer with multiple government contracts for supplying helicopters, communications equipment, and weapons systems to all braches of the U.S. military. WRT functions as a subcontractor, providing electronic components for nearly all these systems and platforms.

In the most recent visit to the satellite communications component division in Los Angeles, sales engineer Ford King was told by the purchasing manager, Carly Moore, that WRT would be in a bidding war with two other suppliers, and that price would drive the negotiations. Moore's position was that all components must meet military specifications; thus, they are commodities. After going to lunch with Moore, King met with Ravi Das, chief design engineer for the project. Das told King that conformance to standards was crucial for winning the large contract. In the last meeting of the day, King met with Ron Jones, who heads up quality assurance at Hughes in Los Angeles. After meeting with Jones for an hour and asking questions about Hughes' needs, King was informed that any problems with quality would result in immediate disqualification as a "preferred vendor," and that the orders would be split between the other two vendors. King immediately called Dan Francis to ask for advice.

Dan Francis is a sales manager with 20 years' B2B experience, he knows that participants in the buying center play distinct roles, and are motivated by different outcomes. Sitting in freeway traffic in Orange County on his way home, Francis tries to make sense of the conflicting messages his sales engineer had received from three managers at Hughes. What strategy should he recommend to King when he visits the Hughes account again in two weeks?

Questions

1. How can Dan explain Carly's, Ravi's, and Ron's motivations to Ford King—based upon the different buying roles they play?

2. Can Dan explain each buyer's weight, using the multi-attribute model?

3. What actions should Dan offer Ford King to successfully manage this major account? Why did you make these recommendations?

Caselet 5.2: *Forming a Relationship at Green Solutions, Inc.*

Serika Lee is a sales rep for JJ Associates in Raleigh, North Carolina, and one of her accounts is Green Solutions, a green energy company located in near-by Chapel Hill, North Carolina, and home of the UNC Tar Heels. JJ Associates provides all needed materials, such as solar water heater kits, tankless water heaters, high-quality metal roofing, insulation, and solar panels. Green Solutions utilizes all these products to provide their customers with alternative energy solutions for new construction and for existing homes.

Serika has called upon Green Solutions for about three months, and has sold the company a smattering of products. From talking with the president and chief engineer, Serika understands that, when a product is needed, Green Solutions' purchasing department simply calls all the suppliers in a 100-mile radius and asks for price and delivery for the needed product. Thus, there does not appear to be any loyalty between Green Solutions and its suppliers. Serika knows that purchase levels are unlikely to increase unless some type of relationship is established. She wonders how this process can be implemented to help her increase sales to this account.

Questions

1. What criteria should Serika Lee evaluate to determine whether Green Solutions is a good candidate for moving into a deeper relationship?

2. If appropriate, what are the next steps Serika Lee should take to build rapport and trust with the officers of Green Solutions?

3. Is it possible to form deeper relationships with all accounts, and—if this is not possible at Green Solutions—how should the account be handled?

References

1. Anthes, Gary (2006). It's All Global Now," *Computerworld*, February 20.
2. Jackson, Donald W., Janet E. Keith, and Richard K. Burdick (1984). "Purchasing Agents' Perceptions of Industrial Buying Center Influence: A Situational Approach," *Journal of Marketing*, 48:4 (Autumn), 75–83.
3. Bonoma, Thomas V. (2006). "Major Sales: Who Really Does the Buying," *Harvard Business Review*, July-August, 172–181.
4. Jennings, Richard G. and Richard E. Plank (1995). "When the Purchasing Agent is a Committee: Implications for Industrial Marketing," *Industrial Marketing Management*, 24:5 (October), 411–419.
5. Trailer, Barry and Jim Dickie (2006). "Understanding What Your Sales Manager is Up Against," *Harvard Business Review*, July-August, 48–55.
6. Honeycutt, Earl D. and Lew Kurtzman (2006). *Selling Outside Your Culture Zone*, Fort Worth, Texas: Behavioral Science Research Press, Inc.
7. Ruff, Richard (2011). "How can sales reps create value and differentiate themselves from competitors?" *Sales Training Connection* September 1. Accessed February 15, 2014. *http://salestrainingconnection.com/2011/09/01/how-can-sales-reps-create-value-and-differentiate-themselves-from-competitors/*.
8. Moon, Mark A. and Susan Forquer-Gupta (1997). "Examining the Formation of Selling Centers: A Conceptual Framework," *Journal of Personal Selling & Sales Management*, Spring, 31–42.
9. Brewer, Geoffrey (1998). "Lou Gerstner Has His Hands Full," *Sales & Marketing Management*, May, 36–41.
10. Kusari, Sanjukta, Steven Hoeffler, and Dawn Iacobucci (2013), "Trusting and Monitoring Business Partners Throughout the Relationship Life Cycle," *Journal of Business-to-Business Marketing*, 20:3, 119–138.
11. Cohen, Andy (1998). "Top of the Charts—Pfizer," *Sales & Marketing Management*, July, 41.
12. Badal, Jaclyne (2006). "A Reality Check for the Sales Staff," *Wall Street Journal*, October 16, B3.
13. Magnini, Vincent P., Earl D. Honeycutt, Jr., and Sharon K. Hodge (2003). "Data Mining for Hotel Firms: Use and Limitations," *Cornell Hotel and Restaurant Administration Quarterly*, 44:2 (April), 94–105.
14. Graettinger, Tim. "Digging Up $$$ with Data Mining? An Executive's Guide," *The Data Administrator's Newsletter*, TDN.Com, Accessed July 8, 2007. *http://www.tdan.com/view-articles/5263/*.
15. Dickie, R. James (1999). "The Sales Effectiveness Challenge—Are We Solving the Right Problem?" *CSO Forum White Paper*, Boulder, Colorado.
16. Goldenberg, Barton (2007). "Real Time CRM the New Way of Doing Business," *Sales & Marketing Management*, June, 34–37.
17. Lee, Dick (2000). "Smarketing! Is CRM Technology Ready to Support the New Sales/Marketing Discipline"? *Sales and Marketing Automation*, January, 51–56.
18. Rodriguez, Michael and Earl D. Honeycutt, Jr. (2011), "Customer Relationship Management (CRM)'s Impact on B to B Sales Professionals' Collaboration and Sales Performance," *Journal of Business-to-Business Marketing*, 18:4, 335–356.
19. Shapiro, Benson (1988). "What the Hell is Market Oriented?" *Harvard Business Review*, November-December, 2–7.
20. Wilson, David T. (2000). "Deep Relationships: The Case of the Vanishing Salesperson," *Journal of Personal Selling & Sales Management*, XX:I (Winter), 53–61.
21. Kumar, V. (2006). "Customer Lifetime Value is the Path to Prosperity," *Marketing Research*, Fall, 41–46.
22. Kalwani, Menohar and Narakesari Narayandas (1995). "Long-Term Manufacturer-Supplier Relationships: Do They Pay Off for Supplier Firms"? *Journal of Marketing*, 59 (January), 1–16.
23. Wilson (2000).
24. Dorsch, Michael J., Scott R. Swanson, and Scott W. Kelly (1998). "The Role of Relationship Quality in the Stratification of Vendors as Perceived by Customers," *Journal of the Academy of Marketing Science*, 26:2 (Spring), 128–142.
25. Stewart, Thomas A. and David Champion (2006). "Leading Change from the Top Line," *Harvard Business Review*, July-August, 90–97.
26. Liu, Annie H. and Mark P. Leach (2001). Developing Loyal Customers with a Value-Adding Sales Force: Examining Customer Satisfaction and the Perceived Credibility of Consultative Salespeople," *Journal of Personal Selling & Sales Management*, XXI:2 (Spring), 147–156.
27. Kumar (2006).
28. Ibid.
29. Ibid.
30. Johnson, Julie T., Hiram C. Barksdale, Jr., and James S. Boles (2001). "The Strategic Role of the Salesperson in Reducing Customer Defection in Business Relationships," *Journal of Personal Selling & Sales Management*, XXI:2 (Spring), 123–134.

31. Anonymous (2007). "Proof of Delivery," *Sales & Marketing Management*, May, 46.
32. Kotler, Philip (2003). *A Framework for Marketing Management*, Upper Saddle River, NJ: Prentice Hall.
33. Sales Horizons, LLC: Effective sales training affordably priced. Accessed February 15, 2014. *http://www.saleshorizons.com/Sales_Strategy.php.*
34. Leek, Sheena, Peter W. Turnbull, and Pete Naude (2006). "Classifying Relationships Across Cultures as Successful and Problematic: Theoretical Perspectives and Managerial Implications," *Industrial Marketing Management*, 35:7 (October), 892–900.
35. George, Bill (2003). *Authentic Leadership*, San Francisco: Josey-Bass.
36. Jones, Thomas O. and W. Earl Sasser (1995). "Why Satisfied Customers Defect," *Harvard Business Review*, 73:6, 88–99.
37. Johnson, Barksdale, and Boles (2001).
38. Palmatier, Robert W., Rajov P. Dant, Dhruv Grewal, and Kenneth R. Evans (2006). "Factors Influencing the Effectiveness of Relationship Marketing: A Meta-Analysis," *Journal of Marketing*, 70:4 (October), 136–153.

LEVERAGING INFORMATION TECHNOLOGIES

LEARNING OBJECTIVES

After completing this chapter, you should be able to:

- Explain how common technologies used today influence sales forces and the way they are managed.

- Explain what sales force automation technology is and its uses.

- Explain what a customer relationship management system is and the challenges related to implementing one.

- Describe what sales managers can do to encourage their employees to adopt an effective utilize technology.

An engineer makes a comment on Twitter about an upcoming conference and gets a reply that includes an invitation to see a company's new product at the conference. She visits the booth and sees a demonstration, after which she receives a phone call from an inside salesperson asking what she thought about the product. The inside salesperson makes an appointment for an account exec to visit her, but also makes a product recommendation. She decides to buy the product and goes online to place her order. She then gets an e-mail confirmation from the field salesperson, who schedules a visit to train her to use the new product after it arrives. In this instance, the customer interacted with the selling company through at least five channels—Twitter, trade shows, phone calls (inside sales), personal visits, and online. How much did technology help her salesperson close the sale?

In this chapter, we explore the role technology plays in sales and sales management. Most technology supporting salespeople is not obvious to the customer, yet today's salesperson would be much less productive without it.

EVIN MARTINEZ
Manager
Partnership Services
San Diego Padres

Sales Manager Profile: Evin Martinez

I MANAGE SPONSORSHIP FULFILLMENT for the San Diego Padres. The main purpose of my job is to create a meaningful connection between my client's brand and our fans. Sports marketing provides a unique platform for brands to advertise to a team's fans, and we are continuously finding better and different ways to deepen that connection through technology.

I landed this incredible job because I studied sales in college. While studying sports sponsorship and sales at Baylor University, I worked firsthand with professional sports teams, including a summer internship with the San Antonio Spurs. Upon graduation, I joined the San Diego Padres, in San Diego, California, as manager of partnership services.

My job requires me to fulfill sponsorship agreements for the San Diego Padres' sponsorship accounts. I oversee everything that is in the contract and make sure that these elements are executed throughout the season. To accomplish our sponsors' goals, I work with several other departments in the organization, such as entertainment, ballpark operations, ticket sales, and marketing. Effective communication with other departments and with my clients is very important in order to be successful in my role. I rely heavily on technology such as the Internet, e-mail, texting, phone calls, media-tracking tools, Photoshop, and digital photography.

One of my primary focuses is to provide top-quality customer service to my clients. The best way to provide top-level customer service is to stay organized and manage accounts effectively. There are several tools that we use to help us stay organized. The most important tool that we use to stay organized is our CRM System. We use an in-house CRM system to track information on all of our prospects and clients. We have a customized notes section that is tailored specifically for the sponsorship department, since some of the information that we need to track is more detailed than what other departments in the company need. We also keep track of our product inventory in CRM and assign the inventory to the appropriate client. Inventory can mean seats and suites, but it can also mean signage, sponsorship opportunities, and other possible things to sell. For example, if we have a concert after a game, there are several sponsorship packages for that concert that can be sold that are part of inventory. We also list if a piece of inventory is "pitched business" in order to avoid overselling. Having a record of pitched business is extremely helpful because there are several pieces of sponsorship inventory that are not unlimited.

High-quality service and a meaningful partnership with a sponsor start at the very beginning of the sales process. Our sales representatives are trained to first research the prospective client in order to better understand their business before a conversation with that company ever takes place. We rely heavily on Internet technology to thoroughly research the company using tools such as the company's website and its social media pages. There is a list of key questions that we try to answer through this research; we ask how the company makes its money, who belongs to its target audience, how it differentiates itself from the competition, and more. Once we have answered most or all of these questions, we enter that information in our CRM system.

After the research stage is complete, we set the meeting. The sales rep will take a tablet computer into the meeting, using it to show a short presentation showing our brand, what other partners do in the ballpark, and other examples of ways to advertise through the San Diego Padres.

One unique part about selling inventory at an event space or a sports stadium is that the inventory list is constantly changing. Depending on our prospect or client, we can tailor inventory to fit their brand specifically. Most of our clients like to see visuals of how we can incorporate their brand into our venue. In order to create these visuals, we enlist the help of our Creative Services department to help us mock up current inventory or spaces in the ballpark to incorporate the client's branding on the current inventory. The Creative Services staff takes photos of the current space or sign with a digital camera and then uses Photoshop to create the image with the prospect's branding.

We also use a technology called Fortress, which is a point-of-sale system. The Fortress system allows our customers/fans to pre-load money and their game tickets on their membership cards. The card is accepted at all concession stands and the team store. Having the ability to store tickets and money on one card enhances the fan experience, allowing convenient transactions when they are at the ballpark. This is a helpful tool for our concession partners, allowing faster and more frequent transactions, but it also helps us forecast concession needs and make special offers to fans.

Another form of technology that we are using in the ballpark is Geo Fencing. This technology is being used to communicate to fans through their smart phones and the Major League Baseball app, "At Bat." Fans will have the capability (if they opt in) to receive special offers—exclusive to guests in the ballpark—from our corporate sponsors. Fans will also receive notifications letting them know which concession lines are shorter, and if there are any special offers in the concessions areas that day.

At the end of the term (baseball season), the sponsorship department is responsible for providing sponsors with a sponsorship recap. We include research in the recap that shows how the sponsors' advertising scored with our fans and with the San Diego market. We use technology such as Repucom and Scarborough, as well as research done by Dr. Kirk Wakefield. Repucom is a media tracking technology that shows the sponsor how often, and how visibly, their signage was shown on television. Scarborough is a market research company that measures shopping patterns, media usage across platforms, and lifestyle trends of adults. We use Scarborough data drawn specifically from the San Diego Market. Dr. Kirk Wakefield helps us construct fan surveys and analyzes the results of those surveys to show how our fans perceive the sponsor's brand, versus how non-fans perceive it. This research is imperative in order to show our sponsors that their sponsorship was successful and helped their brand image. The results that we gain from measurement technology become a major part of our renewal conversations and make it much easier for the account manager to explain why sponsorship works and how it impacts the sponsor's business—to secure that sponsor's partnership for another season. ■

Sales technology has dramatically changed the way salespeople sell. Today, technology drives how salespeople plan their days, how they contact customers, how they manage all the information they must collect, and much more. Moreover, new technology applications are being developed continually. Some applications affect the sales executive or sales manager without much benefit for the salesperson; others address only the needs of the salesperson.

In this chapter, we explore different types of sales technology. Some of the most common forms of technology used by salespeople include things familiar to you: smart phones, laptops, tablets, pad computers, and so forth. First, we discuss these technologies—how they have changed sales forces and the way they are managed. We then discuss software applications, including knowledge management, sales force automation, customer relationship management, and enterprise resource planning software. Finally, we discuss how sales managers can encourage their employees to get the most of out of the technologies available to them.

Commonly Used Technology

Today's college student stays in touch with friends and family through technology in ways that seem incredibly foreign to their grandparents. The same is true of salespeople. Just for prospecting alone, Kaitlin Atkinson, for example, is likely to contact potential buyers through Twitter, LinkedIn, and even Facebook.[1] Once she's gotten their interest and can schedule a call, her pad computer then serves as a demonstration device, enabling potential clients to see what her company can offer. Social media channels continue to serve as a way to stay in contact with her customers once they've purchased.

Today's sales force relies upon digital media to communicate with customers. Salespeople who use social media, for example, are more likely to achieve their sales quotas. Very few, however, have received any training on how social media and digital communication (such as e-mail) can help their sales.[1]

Smart phones, pad computers, and laptops turn any place into a virtual office. With any of these devices, a salesperson can access the Internet, access presentation materials, or access customer records. Mike Kunz, sales executive with St. Louis-based Kunz and Associates, believes that these technologies will lead to more virtual office-based salespeople in the future. In fact, it is because of these technologies that the cost of a sales call has declined over the past decade, even though salaries have doubled. Salespeople can visit with more clients in less time, and the visits are more effective, because of technology.[2]

Sales Management Software

Salespeople and their managers use different types of software applications to solve their problems. Some of these technologies are designed to manage the ever-growing body of knowledge they have to process. Others are designed to automate functions, making it less costly and time-consuming to serve customers. Exhibit 6.1 briefly describes a number of more advanced software applications designed to support sales functions.

This salesperson is using her pad computer to share information with a customer.

Knowledge Management, Proposal Writing, and Pricing Software

Salespeople sometimes have to manage as many as 5,000 products. Not only have companies replaced printed catalogs with online catalogs, companies can add information to the catalogs to increase their use in the field. For example, links to case studies showing how customers have used products to solve common problems can help salespeople determine sales strategies. In addition, proposal materials can be included for cutting and pasting into proposals, saving salespeople valuable time. This online application is a form of **knowledge management.**

Of course, customers want that information, too. Many knowledge-management systems have mechanisms to enable customers to access portions of the knowledge base. The **knowledge base** is the data contained in the system; it can consist of product specifications, tell how to troubleshoot problems with products, or identify and locate knowledge, such as who to call in certain situations.

Some knowledge-based information isn't available to customers, but only to the firm's sales reps and other employees. This information can include things like answers to service questions, even if they are not frequently asked; how to handle customer service issues; and so forth. For example, Dell maintains a knowledge base of employees who have expertise troubleshooting certain applications, including a record of who was able to fix what problems. Then if the problem arises again, Dell's customer service reps can call these employees for help.

Companies are even building knowledge bases around selling practices. For example, if a salesperson sells a product to a funeral home, that sale is entered into the knowledge base. The next rep to try to sell to a funeral home can then access the knowledge base to find out how the sale was closed. If a proposal was created for the funeral home, it might become part of the knowledge base, and the rep can then copy appropriate portions of it. In fact, proposal-writing software was one of the first knowledge management applications created for salespeople and their managers. The idea was to create a library of successful proposals from which they could select portions and create new proposals. Octant (*octantsoftware.com*) and PropLibrary. com are two providers of proposal library and management software.

Pricing software was another early knowledge management application created for sales purposes. Job-costing, or putting a price together on a custom job, can be very difficult, particularly if there are many components to the job. Pricing software made sure that all components were accounted for, resulting in a more accurate estimate of the job's cost. Octant's software provides pricing features, but there are other packages specific for job-costing. Most of these are industry-specific; for example, Pem Software (*pemsoftwareinc.com*) serves the construction industry.

Each industry has its own special software. For example, real estate agents use software that enables them to easily create brochures on properties for sale, whereas salespeople for contract manufacturers use animation software to show how components work in machinery.

Sales Force Automation

Sales force automation (SFA) was one of the first types of information technology used by salespeople and their managers. SFA systems automate salespeople's contact management, scheduling, and reporting functions. **Contact management** is the use of customer databases to keep track of customer information, calendaring to schedule customer activities such as sales calls, follow-up, and so forth.

The applications enable salespeople to not only record basic account information, such as who to contact and with what address or phone number, but also important data such as notes from each sales call. Competitors' sales to the account can also be recorded—information that can be quite useful to marketing managers, product planners, and other people in the salesperson's organization.

In the past, salespeople would send handwritten or typed call reports to their managers, listing the customers they had called upon, what was discussed, and any items needing follow-up. Now, sales managers simply access the same data system used by their salespeople. After each sales call, or at the end of the day, the salesperson downloads call notes into a central system. Summary reports can be created, outlining the salesperson's activities for the day, week, or month. The manager can also track salespeople's activities by the types of call they make and suggest strategies to improve their productivity. We'll discuss reporting more in Chapter 14 when we explore how managers evaluate a salesperson's performance.

Being able to access sales reports instantly can not only help managers evaluate and coach their salespeople at critical points, but also improve a firm's sales forecasts. We'll discuss forecasting in detail in Chapter 13, but, for now, think of the sales process. By knowing where each account is in the process, and knowing the probability of a sale based on which stage each account is in, a manager can estimate sales for the next week, month, or quarter.

Another benefit to managers, and to their companies, is the retention of customer records. Companies without SFA systems can encounter problems when salespeople resign. If the salesperson takes these records to the next job, or simply throws them away, the next salesperson won't have much of a knowledge base. That lack of knowledge makes it harder for the new salesperson to get up to speed. Customers suffer, too. For example, they might have expected their salesperson to call or service them at certain times, or otherwise be familiar with their accounts. But without the data, the new salesperson is likely to fall down on the job.

For the salesperson, the benefits of an SFA system can include improved customer interaction, because more information about each customer is readily available. This is especially important in large territories. Without an SFA system, keeping track of who wants what can be pretty difficult. DeVon Labrum, Juniper Systems' vice-president for sales, says his company uses SFA to not only keep track within sales territories, but across the entire sales force.

Salespeople using SFA systems also enjoy automatic reminders, called **ticklers**. Ticklers remind them to complete certain tasks. For example, if a customer tells the rep to call back in a month's time, the salesperson makes a note in the account, and the SFA system automatically notifies him in one month to call back. SFA systems can also help salespeople manage their time more efficiently, even creating schedules for them that minimize their driving times.

Eric Williams uses an SFA tool to manage his real estate business. His real estate company, Legacy Land and Ranch, focuses on selling large tracts of farm and ranch land around the world. His agents create accounts for both buyers and sellers in the system. When one of Williams' agents lists a property, the file on the seller is also tied to other files on the property, such as topographic maps, Portable Document Format (PDF) scans of brochures, satellite photos of the property, and other important information. These files can then be sent by the SFA system to prospective buyers based on parameters such as buyers' desired price range or property type.

The use of SFA is not without issues and challenges. Some of the challenges involve getting salespeople to use the system, which we will discuss later. Other

---

insightpool   Brand Bundles   Segments   **Reporting**   @insightpoolHQ

Confirm these messages, or click to edit the content.

Regular messages will appear first and followup messages will appear second.

1. Hey Lisa, more fuel for Atlanta becoming THE capital of marketing tech http://bit.ly/1a2SNXU help us spread! -Adam

2. Hey Mimi, more fuel for Atlanta becoming THE capital of marketing tech http://bit.ly/1a2SNXU help us spread! -Adam

3. Hey Chuck, more fuel for Atlanta becoming THE capital of marketing tech http://bit.ly/1a2SNXU help us spread! -Adam

4. Hey , more fuel for Atlanta becoming THE capital of marketing tech http://bit.ly/1a2SNXU help us spread! -Adam

5. Hey Miriam, more fuel for Atlanta becoming THE capital of marketing tech http://bit.ly/1a2SNXU help us spread! -Adam

6. Hey Jacqueline, more fuel for Atlanta becoming THE capital of marketing tech http://bit.ly/1a2SNXU help us spread! -Adam

Insightpool is a targeted social media software tool that helps companies reach potential prospects and engage in a real conversation. Buying an application or service like this will be integrated into the company's technology roadmap so they can plan for integrating it with other software.

issues relate to the ways managers should use the system. For example, how closely should sales managers monitor their salespeople's activities? Salespeople frequently enjoy working independently. If using the technology results in supervision that is too close for comfort, some good salespeople may leave the organization. Perhaps more importantly, a salesperson often needs to adjust her approach in the field, depending upon what customers are indicating they want.[3] But if technology is used to "script" a sales pitch or sales approach, this flexibility will be lost. In other words, greater technological control might result in less autonomy for the salesperson, which in some situations might not increase sales.

However, when customers' needs are similar and the selling process is the same for each of them, technology can be a tool for ensuring that salespeople stick to the script. Inside salespeople frequently use scripts generated by SFA systems; even customers' responses to questions can be programmed into the script, so that the dialogue the reps use sounds spontaneous.

Although SFA systems have automated some tasks, allowing salespeople to better manage their time and their territories, alone it has proven to be insufficient for larger organizations and companies following a multi-channel strategy. What began as SFA has since morphed into CRM software, with SFA just one of many applications within the broader CRM package.

Customer Relationship Management Software

Customer relationship management (CRM) is more than a software package; it has been described as a philosophy, a strategy, and even a way of life, because it encompasses the types of relationships you want to create with your customers.[4] CRM software enables more effective communication, integrating salespeople's customer communication with other channels, such as websites, e-mail campaigns, direct mail, and others. The philosophy, though, is that companies should strategically create the right kinds of relationships with customers. These relationships then become the foundations for customer service, product creation, product delivery, and everything else the company does to add value for the customer. Thus, CRM software has to integrate with all of the company's other software systems and cannot just automate salespeople's activities.

CRM software is not just used in situations where companies employ a sales force. Retailers such as Cabela's, Target, Kroger, and others use CRM software to track the purchases and activities of their customers; they just don't use the SFA applications. Each time you use a frequent buyer card at any of these stores, your purchase goes into your database, along with other data they may collect through surveys, web browsing histories, or purchases from data sources like Facebook or marketing research firms.

CRM data should be visible to those who need it. For example, Konica-Minolta Business Systems is a complicated business, with many customer-contact personnel. In this situation, not only do the field salesperson, the call center salesperson, and a marketing manager need information about each buyer, but so does a technical-support person, a dispatch center for field-service calls, the shipping department, and the billing department. When each of these people talks with the customer, information from the dialogue has to be captured and added into the system. Ideally, the customer should come away with the feeling that the company "knows" her and will take care of her. From the company's perspective, each conversation gives a salesperson an opportunity to learn more about that customer, so that the company can do a better job of serving her. As the "Global Sales Management" box illustrates, the same challenges of getting information to the right people at the right time are even greater when the sales team is scattered across the globe.

GLOBAL SALES MANAGEMENT   Global Issues in Sales Technology

You want to adopt a new sales tool, one that is technology-based. But you've got sales teams on six continents, representing 22 languages. What single software product has a user interface for each of those languages?

The reality is that none do. Most businesses operate globally in one language—most often in English—but software from the major vendors is often written with user interfaces in other major Western languages, Japanese, and Chinese.

Language aside, there are many other challenges.

"One challenge is simply getting everyone to agree on definitions of terms," says Tim Pavlovich, director of sales for Dell's OEM Partner Program in Europe, the Middle East, and Africa. "It seems simple enough when you say a prospect is a prospect, but when you start generating forecasts, or evaluating a region's performance based on data they put into a software system, you had better have agreement on what the terms in the system mean."

"In my experience," says Pavlovich, "you've got two aspects to manage: the relationship and the sales opportunity." His sales team uses CRM to map decision-making processes at his customers' businesses, develop sales and account management plans, and then execute against those plans. Use of the same CRM platform (his company uses Salesforce.com) helps keep account plans on track across countries, but only when the data mean the same thing. Moreover, he has to consider factors such as currency exchange rates, local culture and language, and other factors that affect the value of the system.

Nils Opperman, director of marketing and sales for BookRix, agrees that operating in multiple countries creates many technology challenges. "Our customers in Russia, for example, tend to have very poor technology, which makes interacting with our customer websites very challenging. And some technologies you have in the States—such as Pages at Amazon—Amazon in Germany not only doesn't have, they don't even know anything about it." Technology you think would be global often isn't.

Still, they both agree that sales force automation tools, knowledge-base software, and social community platforms (think Facebook for a company) help sales organizations manage global sales teams serving global customers. "We use our CRM platform to manage pricing, service-level agreements, and other elements of the sale. The key is making information available when reps need it—which may occur in the middle of the night for another rep or manager. With good information, we can make sure we serve the customer in the proper fashion," says Pavlovich.

The more commonly used CRM software for companies with salespeople are Salesforce.com, Microsoft Dynamics, Oracle's offerings, and those from SAP. Other than Microsoft Dynamics, these are sold as "hosted" applications, or **software as a service** (**SaaS**)—more commonly referred to as operating in the cloud. What the **cloud** means is that the makers of the software host the program, and all of the data, on their own servers. Salespeople of other companies then access the data via the Internet. In other words, the salespeople's firms' entire customer databases reside on servers owned by Salesforce.com or SAP, rather than at the customers' own locations.

The cloud has several benefits over software purchased and either kept only on laptops or company servers. First, the vendor (Salesforce, SAP, etc.) is responsible for making sure the software is always up and working. The vendor can also make updates and fix minor bugs globally, cover the full system, and all customers immediately benefit. By contrast, when the software resides on the customer's computers, new software to fix bugs has to be sent to the customer, who has to stop everything and install the new software. Also, with the cloud, salespeople can easily access customers in real time anywhere they can get on the Internet. This may or may not be the case for resident software like Dynamics, which depends on the salesperson to download, or "sync" new data periodically from a company computer upon which the software is installed. Not all CRM software is hosted, nor is all hosted software used for CRM applications, but CRM software for sales applications is more likely to be hosted.

However, when the software goes down, as has happened to Salesforce, it goes down for everyone at the same time.

WHAT CAN A CRM SYSTEM DO? Contact management is an important function of CRM software, but it is only one of many. Exhibit 6.1 lists some of these functions, and shows how different people in the organization might make use of those functions. CRM software enables customers to interact with the company via all channels in a seamless fashion called **omni-channel marketing**. Via a CRM system, important data such as shipping information, for example, can be made available to the salesperson in the field, a customer service representative in a call center, or even, perhaps, to the customer via the Internet.

EXHIBIT 6.1   Sales Tools and Uses of SFA/CRM by Job Role

CEO
- Sales forecast

VP of Sales
- Sales forecast
- Identify/share best practices
- Track performance—by salesperson, product, etc.
- Capture win/loss data for strategic planning/pricing
- Create or use models to understand segments

Sales Manager
- Sales forecast
- Identify big-impact opportunities
- Identify coaching and training opportunities by examining win/loss ratios by rep and by stage of sales process
- Monitor activities by account or by rep relative to results

Sales Representative
- Access to customer data
- Access to pricing formulas and product information for better proposals
- Integrated access to other relevant information (shipping, billing, etc.)
- Faster access to leads

Multi-channel marketing, though, occurs when different parts of the company operate independently. For example, Walmart.com is a separate business unit from the stores, so if you bought something on the website, you can't return it to the nearest store if it's the wrong size. From the customer's perspective, it is like doing business with separate companies. Sometimes, when companies have multiple product lines, each with their own sales force, customers have the same complaints. We'll discuss this more when we discuss sales force structures but for now, recognize that one goal of CRM software is to enable omni-channel strategies, not multi-channel strategies, by providing a single view of the customer for all in the organization to see.

A critical feature of a hosted version of CRM is the ability for salespeople and sales managers in multiple divisions or locations to access the same customer information. **Opportunity management**, which is the process of identifying prospective customers or sales opportunities and shepherding those potential customers through the sales process, is accomplished more effectively when salespeople and managers can access the information. For example, Andy Haffke, director of sales operations for LexisNexis, reports that his company uses its CRM system to identify opportunities that span different business divisions. The software can notify salespeople when their accounts are making purchases from other divisions, thus enabling salespeople to consider whether there are additional sales opportunities for these accounts. Another key component of CRM software is that it enables managers to create predictive models using customer data. Using statistical procedures called **data mining**, analysts, marketing managers, and sales managers can build statistical models to get a better understanding of the company's customers. More advanced modeling is likely to require sophisticated statistical software like SAS or IBM's SPSS, but Salesforce.com, SAP, and others have the ability to create simple models. These models can be used to determine the best approach for certain customers, which customers should be targeted, how offers for products and services should be priced, and even what features should be included in a new product design.

For example, long before CRM technology existed, pharmaceutical salespeople would target doctors for sales calls based on how many prescriptions they wrote. In other words, doctors who wrote more prescriptions were called upon more often. Having a CRM system makes this information much more accessible to reps. Rather than having to figure out who to call upon at what intervals, they can spend more time making actual calls.

CRM software can also manage e-mail sent by a firm's marketing department, track the activity of customers on the company's website, and incorporate information collected from customers at trade shows. Salespeople then have information about how their customers responded to the company's different marketing activities. This information can also be useful when it comes to finding new sales leads.

Campaign management is yet another feature of CRM systems. **Campaign management** is a rules-based method to determine which message to send to a buyer at what time. CRM systems offer campaign management because it can track customers' responses to various offers. For example, Axcess Capon, the publisher of this book, can send an e-mail to professors about this book when it first comes out. Those who respond positively to the e-mail might then get a visit from an Axcess Capon salesperson. Those who do not respond may get a second e-mail with a somewhat different offer or a survey asking them for their opinions. Based on factors such as class size (which affects how many books will be sold), the professor's response, and other factors, different rules are put into action. Professors with bigger classes are likely to have a salesperson drop by their offices. Professors with smaller classes are more likely to get a call from a representative via telephone. Campaign management helps companies like Axcess Capon determine which campaigns are more effective.

Exhibit 6.2 illustrates how a rules-based campaign might work. This example is fairly simple. In reality, campaigns can be far more complex. For example, they might begin with a salesperson visiting a customer's office, or with the customer visiting the company's booth at a trade show, or browsing the company's website. The point is to engage the buyer through the channel that makes the most sense for that person, both in terms of the cost and timing of the contact, and information needed by the buyer in order to move the sale along.

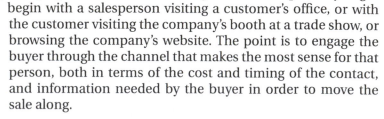

With CRM systems like Pipeliner Sales, sales leaders can keep abreast of how well their entire sales team is doing, while individual salespeople use the same application to manage their own business.

CRM APPLICATIONS One of the more vital CRM applications is segmentation. **Segmentation**, or the process of grouping customers into homogeneous groups, has long been associated with marketing. What makes CRM segmentation different is that each customer is actually classified or placed into a segment. The San Antonio Spurs have purchased a database called Personicx (developed by Axciom), which categorizes people into different lifestyle segments. The club then augments that information with fan information in its own database, which gives Spurs salespeople a much better understanding of the personality and lifestyle of season ticket holders when a salesperson calls on them. For companies that sell to other businesses, segmentation tools are likely to be statistical models based on industry types, company sizes, and other factors that might influence the buyers' purchasing practices.

Once a customer is placed in a segment, the value of the customer can then be determined. Customer lifetime value (CLV) analysis is a CRM tool that calculates the

EXHIBIT 6.2   An Example of Simple Rules-Based Campaign

In this example, actions are based on buyer response. If the buyer clicks on a button contained in the e-mail to visit the website, an e-mail is then sent back to the buyer, suggesting a call to the contact center. Based on the outcome of that call, a sample is sent, or other information is provided by a salesperson. Many campaigns are far more complicated, with branches to different actions based on account size or CLV.

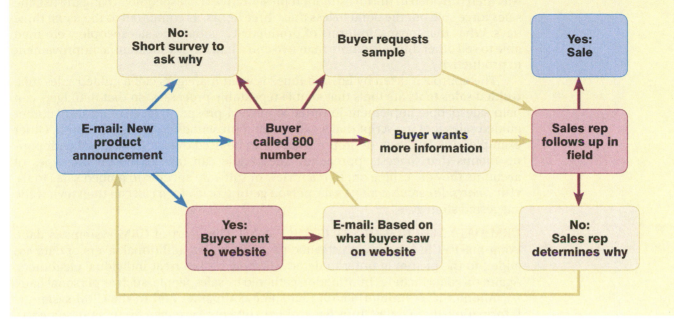

value of a customer to the firm for a period of time. (Recall the example in Chapter 1 about how much clothing a student buys while in college.) Theoretically, you could calculate each customer's value for the remainder of that customer's lifetime, but as with any forecast, the farther you go into the future, the less accurate your forecast will be. Most companies now forecast CLV for a shorter period of time, such as three to five years.

Once CLV is calculated, it can be summed across an entire market segment. Effort can then be spent on acquiring and retaining more-valuable customers and even specific customers. This concept of focusing on more-valuable customers is not new. Pharmaceutical companies have long been dividing doctors into four levels: A-level doctors prescribe the most of a company's drug, and B doctors the next, while C doctors rarely prescribe the drug, and D-level doctors never prescribe it. Salespeople might spend most of their time on A doctors, half as much on B doctors, and visit C doctors only if convenient or they had nothing else to do. D doctors would never be visited. What makes CLV different is that it is forward-looking. In some industries and settings, understanding the full buying potential of the customer over time is more important than knowing how much they buy today, because companies want to capture as much of a continuous revenue stream as possible.

Think about how much information on buyers a salesperson collects on a daily basis. A salesperson can almost build a lifestyle model of each buyer in a business-to-business setting. This additional information can then be matched to the customer's lifetime value, allowing the firm to create more effective sales campaigns, design better products, price products more strategically, and so forth. CRM spreads customer information beyond just the salesperson's head, making it available to all decision makers who can use it.

CRM data collected by an entire sales organization can also help individual salespeople with their accounts. By mining the data, sales managers can create predictive models that their salespeople can use to close more business. A case in point: When Edward Jones, a financial services company, was about to sell a new Chicago O'Hare Airport bond issue, the company's CRM department built a predictive model that identified a list of people most likely to buy the bond. This list was then provided to the investment representatives (salespeople). Using the list, the sales force sold out the bond in less than three hours, as compared to the usual three days. What that means, in terms of productivity, is that the salespeople were then able to sell other things for more than two and a half days, a substantial improvement in productivity.

The approach taken by Edward Jones is what managers call a guided sales tool. **Guided sales tools** are tools that enable repeatable processes, so that managers can help salespeople implement in order to move a prospect closer to a sale. Another guided sales tool is a script that a call center representative can use verbatim. Other examples are databases of proposals that can be used over and over, and with pop-up menus that suggest approaches salespeople can take based on the types of accounts they are calling on. (For a review of software specific to guided sales tools, visit *smartsellingtools.com*.) A salesperson getting ready for a call can then review the suggested strategy.

CRM DATA: WHERE DOES IT COME FROM? The heart of CRM systems is data. What makes CRM more sophisticated than SFA is that additional layers of data are added to the picture in order to determine how best to treat individual customers. Again, this data includes information gathered by salespeople, such as personal data.

Another layer of information that some companies add to the CRM system is information that comes from **back office** software systems—systems designed to automate functions like accounting, shipping, inventory control, manufacturing, and other activities the customer doesn't see. From these databases and software systems, the CRM system would capture and use information as simple as billing addresses and payment histories, or as complex as combined total shipments to every location for that company. Such data may seem simple, but when companies have many divisions and many different names, just putting it all together can be difficult. For example, 3M may buy as 3M, Minnesota Mining & Manufacturing, 3M Medical Systems (a division of 3M), and so forth.

A third layer of information can also be added to the information that salespeople collect. That layer is information purchased from other sources. In the pharmaceutical industry, marketing research companies often purchase data from pharmacies about the number of prescriptions doctors write. This gives a firm's salespeople significantly more accurate information on doctors' prescribing habits.

OneSource is a company that mines information from its database of businesses in order to provide leads to other companies. Experian is a similar company that has a database of some 16 million businesses. These two companies can create models to identify leads, which sales organizations then purchase. Both systems can also be integrated with the CRM software that these organizations use.[5] Dunn & Bradstreet, Standard & Poor's, and other companies offer various other kinds of databases on companies. The additional data can tell the salesperson such things as a company's size, executives' names, contact information, and more, even though the salesperson hasn't yet made a call to that account.

All of this information is intended to provide what is called a "360-degree view" of the customer, or a complete picture of who that customer is and what motivates his or her purchases. Not only is the salesperson then better armed for a sales call, but the marketing person can also create more effective advertisements, stronger trade show programs, and better e-mail campaigns targeted toward the customer. All of these sales and marketing efforts should be more meaningful to the buyer, which should then increase the effectiveness of all of the firm's sales and marketing activities. Exhibit 6.3 illustrates the various sources of information and how the firm might use them.

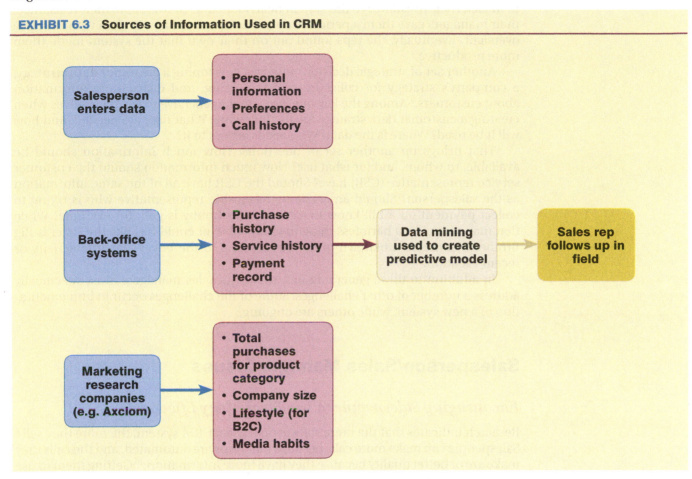

EXHIBIT 6.3   Sources of Information Used in CRM

The Challenges of Implementing CRM Systems

Using CRM software is not without its challenges; nor is it a solution to all of a company's selling problems. In fact, it can create a number of problems or issues, not all of which are simple to solve. One of the biggest challenges becomes who "owns" the relationship with the customer. As we've noted, once a CRM system is installed, many members of the firm can contact customers in addition to the customer's salesperson.

Take, for instance, a university. Most likely, a university will have a fundraising department for the entire university, another for its athletic department, and yet others for each of its academic units. An individual donor might receive "sales" offers from all three independently, and give to all three separately. Companies with multiple divisions selling products and services to the same buyers face the same question. Ultimately, the question of who owns the relationship should determine what offers are made, and when. If athletics owns the relationship, then gifts to the athletic department should be solicited first, for example.

As you can probably tell, the salesperson loses an element of control over how each account is sold, what is sold, and when once a CRM system is installed. Many salespeople may see this as threatening their role if they are used to being a customer's sole contact with the firm. Although research shows that sales technology does make salespeople more productive, it also makes them feel like their jobs are less secure.[6] A case in point: When Harris Interactive, one of the largest marketing research companies in the world, installed a CRM system, the company asked its salespeople to hand over all of their files so the data could be entered. They weren't happy about it. In fact, their resistance to the system nearly killed it. To overcome their resistance, their managers gave them a period of time to adapt to the new system without close oversight. Eventually, the reps found out on their own that the system made them more productive.[7]

Another set of strategic decisions involves developing a **customer data strategy,** a company's strategy for collecting, storing, using, and distributing information about customers.[8] Among the key questions managers have to ask themselves when creating a customer data strategy are the following: What data are needed, and how will it be used? Where is the data? Who needs access to it?

That brings up another set of questions: How much information should be available, to whom, and for what use? How much information should the customer service representative (CSR) have? Should the CSR have all of the same information as the salesperson? Should an accounts receivable representative who is trying to collect payment on a bill know that the buyer's hobby is golf, for example? While that may seem like a harmless thing to know, a buyer could feel like the seller is Big Brother if someone unknown to the buyer refers to the buyer's favorite activity or recent vacation.

In addition to these general issues, the firm's sales managers must specifically address a number of other challenges. Some of the challenges occur in implementation of a new system, while others are ongoing.

Salesperson/Sales Manager Issues

Encouraging Salespeople to Use Technology Effectively

Research indicates that the more salespeople use a CRM system, the more they sell.[9] Salespeople can make more calls because functions are automated, and the calls they make are of better quality because they have more information.[10] Getting them to use it, though, as well as other technology, can be quite a challenge. 3M, for example, has found that salespeople's reluctance to use the system is the biggest barrier to CRM effectiveness. To some extent, the challenge may be generational, with older salespeople being less likely to use new technology. Another issue may be success; salespeople who have been successful without technology may not perceive the need for implementing it. These are challenges endemic to any technology-adoption situation, not just CRM; salespeople can be slow to adopt other software, such as proposal management.

There are tactics that sales leadership can implement to get salespeople to use the system. These tactics include communicating the benefits of technology to the salespeople and sales managers, eliminating opportunities to conduct work without the technology, and creating reward/punishment systems for using the system.

TRAINING Training is very important. A critical issue identified in the research is having sufficient training; too little training actually results in a decrease in a salesperson's performance. Salespeople who have to use a program or technology, but don't know how, waste too much time trying to figure it out. Research also indicates that, because they simply do not know how to make use of the system, they make poor decisions about their time. The result is fewer sales calls and lower sales, the opposite of what you want from sales technology.

Training isn't a once-and-done project, either. While initial training is important, ongoing training can secure more effective use of the system. Ongoing training, according to Ram Ramamurthy of DG Vault, is as much about how to get the most out of the system as it is about what buttons to push. He regularly presents the sales staff with ideas for using the information in the system, as well as its more advanced features. Salespeople now eagerly attend these training sessions, because they know they will learn something that will enhance their performance. We'll address training with greater detail in Chapter 9.

MANAGEMENT SUPPORT When SFA or CRM software is not used by the sales force, sales managers may be part of the problem. In a study of sales executives, one of the participating execs stated that he believed technology had little to offer in the future. Yet this same sales executive was not using the system he had to its fullest capability; many applications were going unused. The researchers concluded, among other things, that sales leaders do not always fully comprehend the value of a CRM system or have the skills needed to gain full benefit.[11]

Managerial support is critical to salesperson adoption. If managers expect salespeople to use the software, salespeople are far more likely to adopt it.[12] When managers fail to adopt the software themselves, and to support it, they create a significant barrier to adoption. Salespeople who want to use the software then report being stymied in reaching the productivity gains they expect from the software.[13] What is less important is peer use; salespeople are not as likely to use software just because their peers do.

Managers can run into some ethical challenges when they implement software. The "Ethics in Selling" box identifies some of these challenges, though the list is by no means complete.

ETHICS IN SALES MANAGEMENT   **Technology and the 24/7 Salesperson**

Technology has made all of us available 24/7. You expect your professor to respond instantly to an e-mail or text; your customer may expect the same of you. But what's really fair? Spencer Ryan, as a salesperson for Stryker, expects to be called anytime, day or night. "My job is to assist trauma surgeons when they are in surgery, and trauma doesn't wait for regular business hours." In taking the job, Ryan knew what he was facing.

But with the ubiquity of smart phones and pad computers, all business professionals are finding it harder to turn things off and just be off. "I find myself answering e-mails when they come in, which could be during dinner or during *American Idol*," laughs Sandy Kennedy, an account exec with Spherion. This pressure to respond is called the "tyranny of the urgent," because that phone call or e-mail seems more urgent than anything going on. Research says that technostress, or the stress associated with technology—such as the 24/7 nature of smart phones—adds to salespeople's stress and actually reduces their ability to use technology effectively in their job.[16]

One common scenario occurs when companies ask their salespeople to learn new technology on their own time and without pay. According to Bruce Culbert, a leading technology consultant, making such a request is a poor decision from the purely practical standpoint of getting the technology adopted. But the pushback from the sales force is always about the fairness of the request.

"A related issue," says Culbert, "is raising quotas because of the increased productivity that should happen." He cautions against accepting a software vendor's glowing predictions that productivity will improve to justify raising the sales force's quota. "One way to get the technology adopted quickly is to let salespeople enjoy the benefit. Raising the quota kills that opportunity." It is also questionable from an ethics perspective.

Technology can be a boon for sales organizations, but the implementation of technology can present its own ethical dilemmas. For business technology to be implemented ethically, management cannot lose sight of the people issues. Salespeople and customers have to be treated properly, creating a win-win for all.

TECHNICAL SUPPORT In addition to training and managerial support, post-implementation technical support is also important. Salespeople need easy access to help, because problems can arise in the field; there is no one right there with them to answer questions. For example, Tricia Jennings has her office in her home. As a sales manager for Merck, a pharmaceutical company, she spends most of her time making sales calls with her salespeople or working at home on reports. When she encounters problems with the system, there isn't anyone in the next office to ask for help. Good technical support is important to ongoing use, after the initial training.

COMMUNICATING THE BENEFITS When a new system is launched, salespeople have to be sold on its benefits. Some companies have created systems that benefit marketing or sales management, but provide few benefits for salespeople. According to Paul Greenberg, a leading CRM consultant, a lack of real benefits for salespeople can doom a system to failure. He also says, though, that even when the benefits are real, they must be communicated to the sales force. Otherwise, using the system may be seen as just another task or responsibility added to the bottom of an already long list of things to do.

Kristin Johnson, of Wallace Welch & Willingham (WWW) Insurance, encountered a sales force that was still happy with spreadsheets and index cards. The best salesperson, at least in terms of sales, refused to adopt the new system. "He told me," says Johnson, "'You can have all of the new guys change, but I'm not.'" Other salespeople then started asking why they had to use the system. This problem could have been averted had she communicated more completely with the sales team when launching the system.[14]

The system can only be as good as the data that drives it. Quality use requires the system to have quality data put into it. At the same time, there is some evidence to suggest that overuse can result in lower performance.[15] There are many possible explanations for such a fact, one of which is that some salespeople find it difficult to make calls unless they are completely and totally prepared.[16] These salespeople spend far too much time getting ready—through over-using CRM software, for example—so much so that they don't have as much time for making calls.

MAKING THE TRANSITION Making the transition when launching a new system requires eliminating ways to work around it, as well as rewarding good use and penalizing bad use. Even the best system has a learning curve, and the steeper (or more difficult) that curve, the more likely that salespeople will try to revert to their old ways of doing things.

Rewarding good use can also aid in the adoption of the new system. 3M, for example, created incentive systems to reward salespeople with small prizes for inputting their account data when the company launched a new system for the first time. The key is that 3M needs the data in the system, but not at the expense of salespeople making calls; if they spend too much time putting the initial data in, their performance will suffer for a short period. The incentives encourage salespeople to put the data in over a month's time—in the evenings or other downtime—so that it doesn't affect their selling performance.

Penalizing failure to use the system can also encourage effective use. David Dubroff, with Cypress Care, put a system in place whereby salespeople's expense checks are delayed one month if they have not kept the system up to date. Lockhart Industries uses the CRM system for order entry, but unless an account buys something, the file may or may not be current.

Technology Roadmaps

Technology selection is not a once-and-done process; rather, companies recognize that long-term planning is needed in order to make wise choices in technology. Yes, some technology may not even be known when the plan is made, but making adjustments to a plan is much better than buying into the latest craze.

Factors sales leaders consider when building out a technology roadmap include the following:

- **Business needs**, such as decisions regarding which technology is needed to accomplish sales objectives, so there can be prioritization of technology choices.

- **Absorptive capacity**, or how well the sales force can handle change. In addition to change wrought by technology, the sales leader also has to consider other sources of change, such as new products, organizational changes, and so forth

- **Technology maturity,** or the general technology familiarity and current usage level. Salespeople who are already adept at using technology are more likely to be able to handle faster rates of change.

- **System integration**, or the need to be able to select tools that will work together. A company may choose, for example, a social media campaign management tool to meet immediate needs, but a roadmap highlights plans for how that system may ultimately tie into the CRM system, a web-browsing data-capture application, and so forth. Without the roadmap, they may select a system that won't integrate well with future purchases.

The roadmap includes what is to be purchased, and when, as well as general guidelines for the workforce and budget requirements for successful implementation. Thus, a complete roadmap includes training budget estimates as well as technology budget requirements.

Managing Your Career

You are likely to be a digital native, or someone who grew up with digital technology, such as smart phones, computers, and the like. As a result, you already have familiarity with and trust in, digital technology; the thought of life without it seems so foreign and strange as to be nearly incomprehensible.

That means you are more readily adaptable to new technologies that your company or school may adopt. Being a digital native also means, though, that you've used technology for purely personal reasons, rather than professional. Now is the time to not only clean up your Facebook page, blog, and Instagram, but also build your LinkedIn profile, create a Twitter handle for professional use, and the like.

Summary

Technology has greatly changed how salespeople are managed, and how they manage their time and their territory. Technology as common as PDAs, cell phones, wireless broadband, and laptops turn any location into a virtual office.

Salespeople use special technology, though, like knowledge management software, to manage the complex myriad of information ranging from which technician knows how to fix certain problems best to the details of all the products they must sell. Specialized proposal-writing and pricing software is also used.

Sales force automation software was among the first software used by salespeople, and includes contact-management applications that enable salespeople to maintain detailed records on their customers. Software designed to support customer relationship management strategies evolved from SFA applications and includes many features designed to enhance customer communication and management reporting.

Data for CRM systems can come from back-office software systems, through third-party providers, and from salespeople. Implementing CRM systems is fraught with challenges—such as deciding who owns the customer relationship, overcoming salesperson resistance to the system, and improving the quality and quantity of data.

To improve salesperson acceptance and usage, many firms rely on training; management support; technical support; and building, and communicating about, benefits to the salesperson. Such activities make the transition to new technology easier for salespeople and their managers.

Key Terms

absorptive capacity   127
back office   122
campaign management   120
cloud   118
contact management   115
customer data strategy   124
customer relationship management (CRM)   117
data mining   119
guided sales tools   122
knowledge base   115

knowledge management   115
multi-channel marketing   119
omni-channel marketing   119
opportunity management   119
pricing software   115
sales force automation (SFA)   115
segmentation   120
software as a service (SaaS)   118
technology roadmap   126
ticklers   116

Questions and Problems

1. A salesperson says, "This CRM software is like Big Brother. My company and manager watch every move I make! As long as I make my quota, why can't they leave me alone?" As a sales manager, how would you counter an argument like this?

2. In addition to contact information, like name and address, what other information would you expect to see in a salesperson's database?

3. One student argued that he didn't want companies to know what he ate for breakfast, what television shows he watched, what magazines he read, or what websites he visited. Another student said she wanted companies to know that information if it meant she got better products and services as a result. What information about you is okay for salespeople to put in their databases? What information would you like to keep private? As a sales manager, how would you manage this private/public balance?

4. How should a sales manager deal with salespeople who are resistant to technology? Does age of the sales force matter in these decisions? Or does the age of the salesperson matter? Why or why not?

5. The "Ethics in Sales Management" box in the chapter discusses several ethical issues in the use of technology. Identify two such issues raised in the box, and discuss how you would handle such situations if you were a sales manager with a sales executive pushing for such ethically questionable practices.

6. Create a chart, listing the benefits of CRM for sales executives in one column, sales managers in the next, and salespeople in the third. Who does CRM serve the most? How do those differences in benefits create challenges in managing such technology, and in making sure the software gets fully used?

7. One barrier to full use of CRM software is that sales managers don't understand how they can use CRM for any more than just tracking salesperson activity or performance. As a result, they expect their salespeople to learn and use it more fully than they do themselves. If you were a sales executive, how would you overcome this barrier?

8. You encourage your salespeople to use social media to find new potential buyers, to learn what's on their buyers' minds, and for other such applications. You follow your salespeople on Twitter and LinkedIn, and you've seen some disturbing tweets and posts. One salesperson tweeted, "How much beer can I drink? Find out after the sales meeting Monday! #blitzedagain #coparty." Another posted a beach-and-bikini profile photo on LinkedIn. These are just a few examples of what has bothered you, but the company has no policies on social media usage. What do you do?

9. Re-read the "Ethics in Sales Management" box. What are the ethical issues in those examples? Would your perspective of what is fair change if the sales staff was paid straight salary, versus straight commission? Why or why not?

Role Play

MacNamee Manufacturing (MNM)

For this role play, you will need to divide into groups of three. MacNamee Manufacturing (MNM) makes manufacturing equipment and software, and provides maintenance, and training to fiberglass producers around the globe. Hardware, software, and maintenance are offered by the solutions division; consulting and training are offered by the services division. Consulting usually involves supply chain management, plant layout, and materials handling design work. Typically, both divisions are involved with the same accounts, as it requires consulting and training to complete any major project. The solutions division, though, spends more time with a client—because most upgrades don't require significant consulting or training, and maintenance is ongoing. The solutions division employs 48 salespeople; the services division has 36.

The company is now implementing a complete CRM system—a significant improvement over its SFA-only system. The people of the marketing department, which manages the company's exposure at trade shows, special events, and technology shows (events staged in major cities, where the company showcases its new products and invites customers), are really excited about the new software. It gives them the capability for e-mail campaigns, customer tracking, and so forth. Customers will soon be able to log into the system to track the status of service calls and delivery of new products, place orders, and much more. Further, if there is special negotiated pricing (and there usually is), that is the only pricing that a customer sees.

Assignment

Divide into groups of three. One person is the VP of marketing, another is the VP of sales for solutions, and the third is VP of sales for services. The three of you will now conduct a meeting to determine who owns an account. Before you conduct your meeting, determine the reasons your division should take charge of an account (marketing, services, or solutions?), including what communication is provided to an account, who should access and track overall sales performance in an account, and who should develop strategies for an account. Should the assignments differ for current accounts versus prospective clients? If services or solutions owns the account, how does that affect what marketing staff members do or say at trade shows, in e-mail campaigns, or in advertising? And when conflicts in strategies or pricing decisions occur, how should they be resolved?

Caselets

Caselet 6.1: *Bainbridge*

Mike Jensen, the vice president of sales for Frisco Solutions, was exasperated. Jensen spent nearly a half million dollars on new software, including the cost of flying all of the Bainbridge salespeople to a nice resort for two days of training. Yet after six months, it hadn't increased sales. In fact, in some regions, sales had even declined. And—if the numbers were to be believed—in those regions with declining sales, salespeople were averaging fewer sales calls, which could explain their poor performance.

According to Leslie Horne, the IT director, those regions with higher sales actually used the software more. But in the regions with flat or slow growth, salespeople weren't using the software much. Worse yet, their sales managers were hardly using it at all. Horne told Stubbs that one manager had not logged onto the system in over a month. "What kind of training did you do for the managers?" she asked. "It looks like some managers are using the system incorrectly, and others aren't using it at all!"

With that, Jensen felt the bottom drop out of his stomach. He had not done any specialized training for sales managers, who had taken the same training given for reps. Now, with no money left in the budget, he didn't know what to do. Nonetheless, it was clear that the sales managers weren't using the system properly—if at all—and, therefore, neither were the reps. "We could create an online training program for the sales managers out of the IT budget," Horne suggested. "But it will take more than training now."

Jensen wondered—should he create penalties for not using the new program, or rewards for using it? And how could he make sure managers got trained?

Caselet 6.2: *Zeron Corporation*

Zeron Corporation sells vitamins, mineral supplements, and veterinary products to horse trainers. The company has just over 100 salespeople who call on trainers at horse tracks, rodeos, horse shows, and other places where they gather. These salespeople also call on feed stores, to sell products through the stores.

Zeron's salespeople have gathered e-mail addresses for about 30 percent of its 200,000 accounts. Of those 60,000-plus e-mail addresses, probably 45,000 are for feed stores, but the company isn't sure. The company has created a website for its feed store clients, so that store managers can re-order Zeron products at wholesale rates, without having to contact their salespeople. (New stores have to be set up with accounts by salespeople, who verify that they are, indeed, stores and qualify for wholesale pricing.) The company also has a website for trainers, also allowing them to order products directly, at business prices (which are lower than suggested retail, but higher than wholesale). In addition to the 60,000 e-mail addresses by Zeron's salespeople, the company has another 60,000 e-mail addresses gathered from its website—and a way to know whether these additional addresses belong to trainers or feed stores.

Zeron's VP of sales would like to create a campaign strategy encouraging smaller customers to always order via the company's website. Moving some customers to the website for orders would give the firm's salespeople more time to focus on larger accounts. But, because customers sometimes buy from several vendors, knowing which customers are big and which customers are small can't be determined by looking just at their purchases of Zeron products. A potentially large account can look small if the customer only buys a few products from Zeron.

If you were a sales manager for Zeron, how would you go about developing a rules-based campaign covering all 120,000 e-mail addresses?

References

1. Emily Buratowski (2013), "Social Media's Impact on Today's Business Interaction," Baylor Business Collaboratory White Paper, *www.baylor.edu/business/collaboratory*.
2. Fidelman, Mark (2013). "Study: 78% of Salespeople Using Social Media Outsell Their Peers," *Forbes*. Accessed March 25, 2014. *http://www.forbes.com/sites/markfidelman/2013/05/19/study-78-of-salespeople-using-social-media-outsell-their-peers/*.
3. Tanner, John F., Jr., and Shannon Shipp (2005). "Sales Technology within the Salesperson's Relationships: A Research Agenda," *Industrial Marketing Management*, 34(4), 305–312.
4. Castleberry, Stephen B., and John F. Tanner, Jr. (2014). *Selling: Building Partnerships*, 9e, Burr Ridge IL: McGraw-Hill/Irwin.
5. Greenberg, Paul (2008). *CRM at the Speed of Light*, 4e, New York, NY: McGraw Hill Professional.
6. Canady, Henry (2006). "Leading to Sales," *Selling Power*, (November), 88–93.
7. Holloway, Betsy Bugg, George Deitz, and John Hansen (2013), "The Benefits of Sales Force Automation (SFA): An Empirical Examination of SFA on Quality and Performance," *Journal of Relationship Marketing*, 12(4), 223-242; Johnson, Devon S., and Sundar Bharadwaj (2005). "Digitization of Selling Activity and Sales Force Performance: An Empirical Investigation," *Journal of the Academy of Marketing Science*, 33(1), 3–18.
8. Cotteleer, Mark, Edward Inderrieden, and Felissa Lee (2006). "Selling the Sales Force on Automation," *Harvard Business Review* 84(7/8), 18–19.
9. Tanner, John F., Jr. (2014). *Analytics & Dynamic Customer Strategy: Big Profits from Big Data*, New York, NY: John Wiley & Sons.
10. Eggert, Andres, and Murat Serdaroglu (2011). "Exploring the Impact of Sales Technology on Salesperson Performance: A Task-Based Approach," *Journal of Marketing Theory and Practice*, 19(2), 169–186.
11. Rodriguez, Michael, and Earl Honeycutt (2011). "Customer Relationship Management (CRM)'s Influence on B to B Sales Professionals' Collaboration and Performance," *Journal of Business & Industrial Marketing* 18(4), 335–356.
12. Jelinek, Ronald (2013). "All Pain, No Gain? Why Adopting Sales Force Automation Tools is Insufficient for Business Performance Improvement," *Business Horizons*, 56(6), 635-642; Ahearne, Michael, Ronald Jelinek, and Adam Rapp (2005). "Moving Beyond The Direct Effect Of SFA Adoption on Salesperson Performance: Training and Support As Key Moderating Factor," *Industrial Marketing Management*, 34(4), 379–88.
13. Schillewaert, Niels, Michael J. Ahearne, Ruud T. Frambach, and Rudy K. Moenaert (2005), "The Adoption of Information Technology in the Sales Force," *Industrial Marketing Management* 34(4), 323–336.
14. Buehrer, Richard E., Sylvain Sénécal, and Ellen Bolman Pullins (2005). "Sales Force Technology Usage–Reasons, Barriers, and Support: An Exploratory Investigation," *Industrial Marketing Management*, 34(4), 389–98
15. Beasty, Colin (2006). "Barriers to CRM Success," *CRM Magazine*, (May), 32–35 [quote on 35].
16. Ahearne, Michael, Narasimhan Srinivasan, and Luke Weinstein (2004). "Effect of Technology on Sales Performance: Progressing from Technology Acceptance to Technology Usage and Consequence," *Journal of Personal Selling & Sales Management*, 24(4), 297–310.
17. Dudley, George, and Shannon Goodson (2010). *The Psychology of Sales Call Reluctance*, 4e, Dallas, TX: Behavioral Sciences Research Press.

Designing and Developing the Sales Force

In Part Three, you learned how sales firms form relationships and manage those relationships better by using technologies. In this part, we provide guidance for designing the sales force structure, hiring qualified salespersons, and training them to meet both employer expectations and customer needs.

Chapter 7, *Designing and Organizing the Sales Force*, examines the options that sales managers and firms have when *designing and organizing the sales force*. Sales managers understand that, to keep and maintain profitable buyers, customers must be able to buy what they want, from a convenient channel, when they want it. However, sales force design is a fine balancing act between desired service levels and cost. Today, sales firms offer products and services through multiple channels that include: a company sales force, manufacturers' representatives, distributor and wholesaler partners, and—directly—to large-end users. Customers are normally organized around geographical, product, market, functional, or combination criteria. Sales leaders constantly monitor and modify the sales force structure as markets and buyer expectations change.

Chapter 8 looks at *Recruiting and Selecting the Right Salespeople*. Once the territory is designed, the firm must determine what characteristics are necessary for success in the sales position. Then, firms select sources of potential sales candidates and put them through an organized selection process that includes: formal applications, testing, reference checks, interviews, and physical exams. Sales managers handle the entire selection process in some firms, while human resource managers play a role in generating, testing, and interviewing applicants in larger companies. Unless a formal selection process is followed, new hires may prove to be unqualified as salespersons, and loss of personnel or "turnover" occurs. While some turnover is inevitable, high levels result in high costs, low morale, and dissatisfied buyers.

Chapter 9, *Training and Developing the Sales Force*, is an overview of how the sales force is trained and developed for success on the job. Sales managers play a critical role in ensuring that their sales force receives the training they need to be successful in the field. Some smaller firms, or those with few new hires, may depend heavily on informal sales training methods, such as on-the-job training, while larger organizations may offer formal training programs. Regardless of the company, sales managers need to understand the planning that goes into developing a training program, the issues related to the development and the delivery of training, and how to evaluate the effectiveness of their training investments. The advent of many new technologies is creating opportunities for sales training that is available in an on-demand, in-the-field capacity.

Once the sales force is properly designed, appropriate human resources specialists are hired to implement the needed knowledge and work requirements, and salespersons receive training to ensure that proper skills, knowledge, and attitudes are present. Managers must lead the sales force to success. Part Five offers guidance for leading individuals and teams, setting goals, and motivating and rewarding salespersons.

DESIGNING AND ORGANIZING THE SALES FORCE

LEARNING OBJECTIVES

After completing this chapter, you should be able to:

- Explain how a firm's goals affect the organization of its sales force.

- Understand that a sales force can be organized in multiple ways that match the way customers want to buy.

- Explain the advantages and disadvantages of different sales force organizational structures.

- Describe the various reporting relationships sales forces typically have.

- Understand the advantages and disadvantages of outsourcing a firm's sales force.

Salespeople directly impact the satisfaction and long-term relationships their organizations have with their customers. To increase the satisfaction levels of their buyers, firms must structure their sales forces so that their customers can purchase what they want, when they want it, and from the channel or channels that are most convenient for them. Although many firms continue to employ geographical, product, market, or functional sales force structures to serve the marketplace, buyers also utilize electronic, multi-channel, or hybrid supply chains. As a result of these changes, selling firms use inside salespersons (discussed in Chapter 2), sales alliances, and sales teams (discussed in Chapter 5), and other methods to serve their buyers, as well. Ultimately, a well-designed sales territory results in stronger customer relationships, higher sales efficiency, more balanced pipelines, and more accurate sales forecasts.[1] This chapter explains the myriad options firms must navigate to successfully serve their customers.

HALEY EARLEY
Branch Sales Manager
Konica Minolta Business
Solutions U.S.A., Inc.

Sales Manager Profile: Haley Earley

AS I WORKED MY WAY through college studying kinesiology at Northwestern State University in Louisiana, I had no intention of getting into sales. My original goal was to go into physical therapy, but as I neared the end of my undergraduate program and looked at more years of study, I decided I didn't want to stay in school forever—and I wanted to start making some real money. Given my course of study, I thought the best place for me would be pharmaceutical sales and, to get there, I had heard they recruit from copier companies. I interviewed with Minolta Business Systems, but I didn't get hired.

Even back then, I had a hard time with the word "no." A couple of weeks later, I saw a posting on Monster.com for another sales position with Minolta. I called the manager I had interviewed with, told him that I still wanted a sales position, so he gave me another chance, and they hired me the second time.

Twelve years ago, I took the job, thinking it was going to be a stepping-stone to pharmaceutical sales. In fact, over the twelve years I've been with this company (now called Konica Minolta Business Solutions, or KMBS, after a merger), I've been recruited to join pharmaceutical sales teams several times, but I am very happy with my Konica Minolta family. I don't think I could find a better opportunity for income, freedom of action, and great people to work with.

When I started, I was a "down the street" rep, selling copiers up and down the street. Minolta had just gotten into digital equipment, and it was certainly not our shining moment. Products were very different, especially from the customer's perspective, because of the way digital versus analog products work. The new products had some kinks to work through, but I learned a lot, KMBS learned a lot, and we adjusted and grew.

After about 18 months, I was promoted into a digital color specialist role. Digital color was just beginning to be affordable, and could be used for production print (high-volume/high-quality printing work). That's where I really learned the production print and graphics art market—in fact, that's where I met my husband. From him, I've learned about the printing market, and we've grown a lot within that world, and the company has grown. One lesson I gained in that position was just how important it is to learn and understand a market from the customer's perspective. Our business can't be about selling copiers; it has to be about helping customers grow their businesses, solve their problems, and overcome their challenges. As a specialist in color printing equipment, I was able to do that.

When I joined Minolta, it was a much simpler time in that all salespeople were assigned specific zip codes in which they could sell. We had one major account representative who sold to government agencies and larger customers. Our average sales were somewhere between $4,000 and $6,000 per device. About a year later, after I was promoted to branch sales manager, our focus as a company had to change. What we were doing just didn't fit with what our customers needed. Konica and Minolta merged, and then bought Danka, which created transitions in the way we run our business. Our leadership has changed and, as a result, the direction and goals have changed. I've learned you have to be comfortable with change and willing to adapt to changing company goals and initiatives.

Today, our average sale is closer to $12-15,000 per device, and the client list focuses on larger companies. We still take care of our smaller customers and service them like they're bigger, but that's not the client we're prospecting for in an effort to add to our portfolio. My deep experience in the color production print market, though, is a prime example of what we have to do now in order to compete effectively. Now, things are much more complicated, because my salespeople have to know and learn so much—not just about our company and the different products, but they have to be very knowledgeable about clients, their businesses, and how we fit with their needs. They can't just memorize product features; they have to learn and understand much more.

Our company is in the process of organizing salespeople by vertical markets (industries). For example, a legal rep is an expert on the legal field and is able to better understand a law firm's business. I have a logistical challenge in my market (East Texas and Northern Louisiana, including Shreveport) because we're very spread out. I don't have a major metropolitan area, and that makes verticalization more difficult. My reps still cover an assigned geography, but I've also assigned each salesperson a specific vertical market. I have most health care with one rep, most government and education with another, and so forth.

The salesperson's biggest challenge in making the transition from selling hardware to selling in a strategic fashion in a solutions environment is the mindset. They have a good account base, so they can easily go into an account and just update what the customer has. It's harder for the rep to have the discipline to go in, dig deep, and understand all of what the customer needs and how Konica-Minolta can help them. That means they have to have more patience, and not just go in and close the quick sale, but do the full assessment and, in the end, do the best thing for all involved.

Changing that culture, getting my sales team to buy into that, has been the hardest part of this transition, because the sales cycle is longer. One of the things I've done with newer reps is to go out with them on their larger accounts. I try to be out in the field 90 percent of the time; I can't sit in my office. I coach and develop newer reps through the assessment process, to uncover needs for customers that they may not see right away. Tenured salespeople—those who've been with us a long time—have an ingrained hardware mentality and are successful with that. Actually, the better I get the new reps up and running, the more it helps the more tenured reps, because that internal competition moves the whole team along. When the tenured reps see rookie reps do a better job of selling to needs, instead of pushing hardware, the more tenured reps get on board.

We had a kick-off meeting just last week that signaled a push for more strategic development in accounts. One of my senior reps didn't take it as seriously as he should, so I took him aside to discuss his role as a leader and how the rookie reps look up to him. As someone who leads our team in sales, he had to understand that others will look at him and watch how he's conducting his business to gain success. Putting in place those leadership roles and responsibilities helps our more experienced reps make the transition we have to make to be successful in a changing market. In our branch, we all have assigned job titles, specific territories, and job descriptions. One of my more enjoyable tasks, though, is making sure everyone understands what his or her role is, in addition to what the job description says. That senior rep needed to understand that his title responsibilities included leadership.

Recently, I was asked to stand up and give a speech on how our smaller branch sells so much production print, because we had outsold much larger markets. I just said we get up and go do it! But the reality is, I've been blessed. We have a great team, we work closely with service and administration, and we work hard as a branch to keep that team synergy going. When everyone knows their roles and responsibilities, especially those outside the formal job description, we can all work together more effectively as a team. ∎

How a Firm's Goals Affect the Design of Its Sales Force

The opening profile about Haley Earley and Konica Minolta Business Solutions U.S.A., Inc., shows that the organization of a company's sales force is best driven by its strategic goals. The seller's organizational structure dictates how many salespeople will call on the buyer, and it has an impact on how familiar the sales force will be with the purchaser's strengths, weaknesses, and buyer base. The way the seller company organizes its sales force also defines the type of customers the firm's sales representatives will call upon, the array of products they will sell, and the sales activities they engage in daily. This, in turn, drives the selection, training, evaluation, and compensation decisions made by the company's sales managers, as shown in Exhibit 7.1. Ideally, the firm's sales reps should be organized in a way that allows them to best respond to purchasers' needs and problems.[2]

Normally, a company's goals are set at the corporate level, and then are implemented via the firm's marketing and sales plans. Thus, the setting of sales goals flows from higher to lower levels of the organization. In the end, sales managers are responsible for organizing the sales force so that sales goals are accomplished and the sales force operates as efficiently as possible. These plans are communicated to, and approved by, company executives. Organizational sales structures serve a number of purposes that include:

- Serving buyers effectively in ways they want to be served:
  - contacting the buyer at preferred times;
  - allowing the customer to order when and in a way that best meets the buying company's needs;
  - providing high-quality customer service levels;
  - developing an appropriate relationship level with different types of customers, depending upon their value to the firm; and

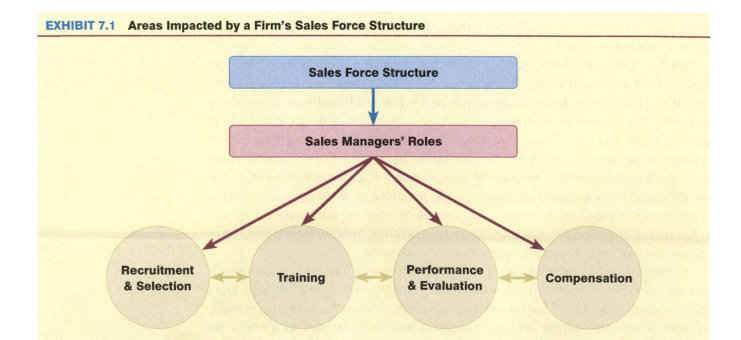

EXHIBIT 7.1 Areas Impacted by a Firm's Sales Force Structure

- Operating efficiently as measured by cost and customer satisfaction:
  - achieving a competitive advantage as measured by the firm's market share, profits, and buyer feedback; and
  - offering customers stability and sales continuity over time, as measured by customer-retention levels.

Firms may mistakenly design their sales structures around their current sales-people and managers, rather than in response to the firm's sales activities.[3] Decisions such as this are made when a sales force is already in place, when the firm changes its mission or products, or when the firm merges with, or takes over, another firm. Rather, the best way to design a sales structure is to determine the necessary sales activities to be performed to achieve the firm's goals, followed by the sales structure that affords the highest levels of service to buyers at the lowest overall cost. Then, once the sales structure is decided, salespersons and managers can be selected, trained, and managed to become experts in their assigned duties.

Organizing the Members of the Firm's Sales Force

As we explained earlier, although many customers continue to buy through a company's regular sales force, today they also purchase through multiple personal, electronic, or third-party channels. For example, Merrill Lynch reaches customers daily at its offices, over the Internet, and through telemarketing calls. This multi-channel sales activity increases the complexity of organizing the sales force. In light of these complexities, how do sales managers and sales executives determine how to best organize their sales forces? Let's begin by looking at some of the factors they have to consider.

The Size of the Sales Force

When firms design their sales organizations, a major decision is how many sales-persons are needed to serve existing and potential customers. Economic theory suggests that a firm should continue to hire salespersons as long as the marginal revenue of doing so exceeds the marginal cost. Said differently, sales managers should hire additional salespersons as long as the new salesperson generates more revenue than expenses. However, it is difficult to practically apply this economic theory, since the added costs and revenue derived from hiring one additional salesperson are seldom known with certainty to the sales manager. Therefore, sales managers utilize two methods for computing the number of salespersons they should hire and maintain: the breakdown and workload methods. (See Exhibit 7.2.)

The **breakdown method** is relatively simple to compute. Sales managers need only divide the forecasted sales revenue by the average sales dollars per salesperson. For example, if a firm forecasts that the sales force will sell $20 million next year and, on average, a salesperson sells $2 million, the firm would need 10 salespersons to accomplish this level of sales. However, experienced sales managers understand that sales forecasts are often inflated, and that not all salespersons are equally productive. That is, one or two salespersons will sell $6 million each; whereas, three or four salespeople might sell $1 million or less each year. Sales managers may use the breakdown method for computing a sales force's size when the firm wants to achieve a certain total sales revenue figure, and the main goal of the company's sales personnel is to close sales—rather than, say, develop relationships with, or service customers. For example, if a sales manager was directed to generate $45 million in sales this year, and an average salesperson generates $3 million in revenue, then 15 salespeople would be needed to reach the sales goal.

A second method for computing the appropriate number of salespersons in an organization incorporates the firm's strategy and work expectations into a **workload method**. For example, how many salespersons are required to visit existing accounts, based upon the customers' wishes, to convert non-buyers to buyers, and perform other duties—such as customer service and finding new customers—assigned by the sales firm? A workload computation consists of three steps:

1. computing the total sales call workload

2. determining the amount of work performed by each salesperson

3. factoring in additional work responsibilities

The first step in the workload method requires that, based upon current or potential sales, all current buyers be placed into A, B, or C categories. "A" accounts have the highest value, "B" accounts have high potential value, and "C" accounts are of lowest value. According to the firm's sales strategy, "A" category accounts are to be visited weekly, "B" accounts monthly, and "C" accounts are called upon quarterly and serviced by inside telephone salespersons. Thus, as shown in Exhibit 7.2, there are 22 "A" accounts that require approximately 50 annual calls (50 x 22 = 1,100 calls); 53 "B" accounts that a salesperson will call upon 12 times (12 x 53 = 636); and 104 "C" accounts that require four annual visits (4 x 104 = 416). Totaling this workload requirement (1,100 + 636 + 416) results in 2,152 total sales calls by the outside sales force.

In step 2, the sales manager computes the work expectation for an average salesperson. That is, how many sales calls can a salesperson reasonably be expected to complete in a year? The sales manager can compute this number by multiplying the total number of calls per day by the number of days worked outside the office per week by the weeks worked annually. For example, if the average salesperson makes

---

EXHIBIT 7.2   Breakdown and Workload Methods for Determining Sales Force Size

Breakdown Method: $\dfrac{\text{Forecasted Sales}}{\text{Average Sales per Salesperson}}$ $\dfrac{\$20 \text{ million}}{\$5 \text{ million}}$ = 4 salespersons

Workload Method:

Step 1: Compute Total Number of Calls to Current Customers

Category of Account	Number of Accounts	Calls per Year	Total Calls
A	22	50	1100
B	53	12	636
C	104	4	416

Step 2: Compute Total Calls Made Per Salesperson

Salespersons will average 3 calls per day.	3
Salespersons will work outside office 4 days per week.	4
Salespersons will work 45 weeks per year.	45

   3 x 4 x 45 = 540 sales calls per year for each salesperson

Step 3: Compute Total number of Salespersons

$\dfrac{\text{Sales Calls to Service Existing Accounts}}{\text{Sales Calls Made Per Salesperson}}$ $\dfrac{2152}{540}$ = 3.98

Adjust For Other Workload Factors

15 percent to call upon new accounts and 10 percent for customer service duties = 25 percent

$\dfrac{3.98}{.75}$ = 5.33 salespersons needed to service existing accounts, call on new accounts and provide customer service

three calls per day and spends four days per week on the road, this works out to 12 completed sales calls per week. Few salespersons work 52 weeks annually—due to vacation time, training, and holidays. A reasonable estimate is 45 weeks, since most U.S. workers are on the job about 220 to 225 days per year. Multiplying 12 calls per week times 45 weeks worked (12 x 45) results in 540 annual sales calls made per salesperson.

To calculate the total number of salespersons needed, divide the total number of calls the sales force must make (2,152) by the total number of calls completed by an average salesperson (540). That is, 2,152 divided by 540 tells us that approximately four full-time salespersons (actually 3.98) are needed to call upon all existing outside accounts. The final step requires computing additional sales-related activities the salesperson will also be expected to complete. Let's assume each salesperson will be directed to devote 15 percent of work time calling on new accounts and 10 percent will need to be committed to making customer service calls. This means that each salesperson spends 75 percent of the time (100 percent minus 25 percent = 75 percent) on existing accounts. By dividing 4 by .75, we calculate that 5.33 salespersons are needed, based upon all projected workload activities computed by the sales manager. Sales managers utilize the workload method for determining a sales force's size when the market is large and complex, and when sales success depends upon interacting and building relationships with customers.

Specialists versus Generalists

Sales managers like Haley Earley at Konica Minolta understand that, when selling a complex service like digital copier technology, it is difficult to be an expert in all aspects of the product line. Thus, a specialized sales force can give the firm the advantage of selling expertise. That said, the sales forces of many companies are not specialized. Their salespeople sell the firm's sole product or entire product line to a discrete group of customers that use the product(s) similarly. Consider Karl Strauss Brewing Company of San Diego, whose sales reps sell all nine of the firm's beverages—including Red Trolley Ale, Off the Rails, and Wreck Alley Imperial Stout, among others, to retail accounts.

Conversely, other firms find it necessary to employ the efforts of a specialized sales force. For example, computer manufacturers often organize their sales forces by consumer, B2B and by education markets, because each market purchases and utilizes the products differently. Likewise, sales managers also understand that—based upon internal and external conditions—partnering with distributors, sales agents, and resellers can improve the effectiveness and profitability of their own sales organizations. A specialized sales structure offers the firm expertise advantages over those of a generalist sales force. That said, the sales manager must safeguard against a number of potential problems caused by overspecialization. First, all sales efforts must be coordinated and integrated to address and satisfy buyers' needs. This is necessary because, as a firm increases the specialization of its sales force, the addition of personnel—both inside and outside of the company—interacting with the buying firm increases the complexity of its operations. Second, the sales function must be integrated and coordinated with other organizational functions: accounting, finance, production, engineering, quality control, customer service, and so forth. As discussed in Chapters 5 and 6, CRM systems help firms communicate and coordinate effectively between a company's functional work areas.

Geographical, Product, and Market Structures

Sales force structures can be as simple as this: a generalist salesperson sells all products manufactured by a firm in a discrete geographical area to a specialized salesperson who works with a team of experts to sell certain products to specific markets. Let's consider each type of sales organizational structure.

Geographic territories can increase the travel distances for the sales team.

A firm that employs a **geographical sales structure** depends upon physical boundaries to organize its sales force with customer accounts. When the sales force is organized geographically, the sales force interacts with buyers as generalists. For example, B.W. Wilson Paper Company, which was formed in Richmond, Virginia, slowly expanded its geographical sales territories across geographical lines to North and South Carolina, West Virginia, Washington, D.C., and Maryland. Depending upon the number of accounts located within a geographic entity, a salesperson is assigned a specified group of customers within a state, region, or nation, a single city, a county, or even a zip/postal code.

Firms may favor a geographical sales organization because it is relatively easy to design, minimizes duplication of effort, and ensures a specific salesperson is assigned to each customer. Geographical sales structures also address a number of concerns for the sales firm. First, customer visits can be more efficiently scheduled, based on their geographical location. Second, as sales in a geographic territory increase, the territory can be divided and an extra salesperson added to the force. On the other hand, if sales should shrink, two or more small territories can be combined.

However, there are a number of potentially negative aspects of geographical sales organizations. Geographical sales territories work best when the selling firm's product line is simple. This means that the salesperson can reasonably be expected to master all the products sold by the firm and advise the potential buyer about their unique features. Let's look again at B.W. Wilson Paper Company, where salespersons sell all paper and industrial products to commercial printers, publishers, and government print facilities located in their geographically assigned territories. The geographical territories option can also be inefficient. If you analyze most geographical territories, the sales are concentrated in one or more cities or areas, leaving large areas of the territory with only a few profitable customers. Examples of geographical, product, and market organizational charts are shown in Exhibit 7.3.

When a firm's product lines are broad and complex, it might be more effective to organize sales activities around a product or division—to specialize the sales force, in other words. An example of a sales force that sells broad and complex product lines is Applied Industrial Technologies (AIT), which distributes more than two million specific products to 156,000 customer accounts in categories that include bearings, power transmission components and systems, industrial rubber products, linear components, tools, safety products, general maintenance, and a variety of mill supply products.[4]

In a **product sales structure**, the firm organizes its sales activities around related product lines or manufacturing divisions. For example, General Electric offers home and business solutions in the areas of aviation, capital, energy management, health care, oil and gas, power and water, and transportation to markets worldwide (*www.ge.com*). It's simply not feasible for a salesperson to be an expert in each of these areas of technology and customer usage, as many of the large categories are defined by sub-categories. By specializing by product line or division, the salesperson can become an expert in that one area.

There are also a number of limitations to product specialization. First, a firm may unknowingly send two or more salespersons to the same account, thus confusing the buyer. A noteworthy example is Xerox, which at one point had three independent sales forces that sold computers, copiers, and office equipment, respectively. Xerox became aware, based on customer feedback, that its sales representatives from the different forces: (1) called upon the same accounts; (2) had little knowledge of, or interest in, each other's products; (3) confused buyers who had a genuine need for the company's products; and (4) did not cooperate by providing leads and sharing information with one another.

EXHIBIT 7.3   Geographical, Product, and Market Sales Force Structures

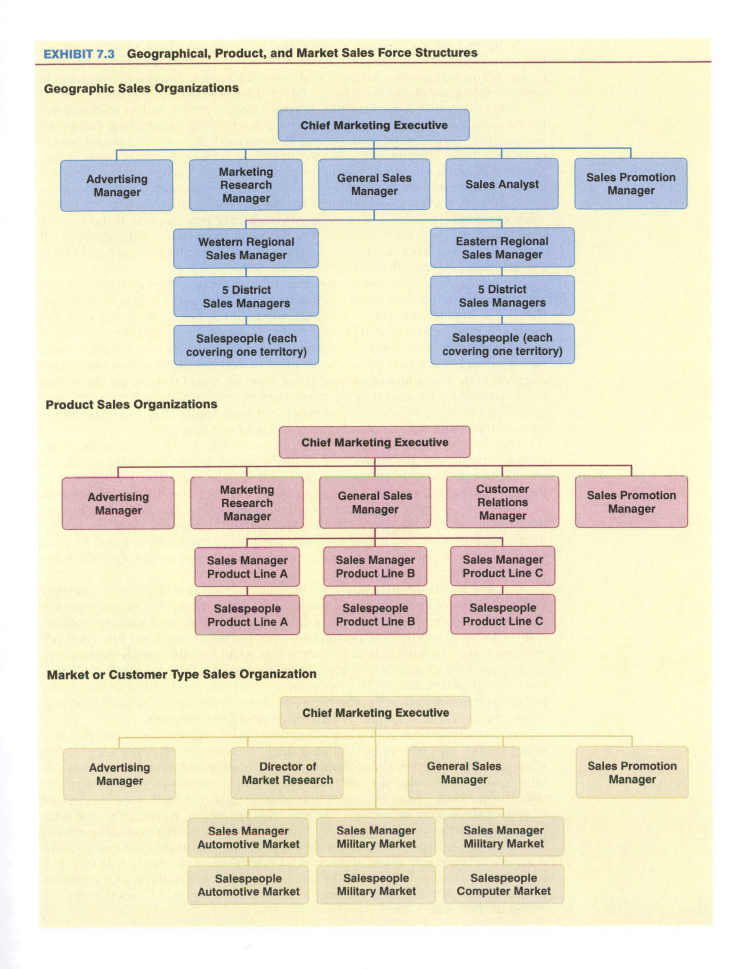

Geographic Sales Organizations

- Chief Marketing Executive
  - Advertising Manager
  - Marketing Research Manager
  - General Sales Manager
    - Western Regional Sales Manager
      - 5 District Sales Managers
        - Salespeople (each covering one territory)
    - Eastern Regional Sales Manager
      - 5 District Sales Managers
        - Salespeople (each covering one territory)
  - Sales Analyst
  - Sales Promotion Manager

Product Sales Organizations

- Chief Marketing Executive
  - Advertising Manager
  - Marketing Research Manager
  - General Sales Manager
    - Sales Manager Product Line A
      - Salespeople Product Line A
    - Sales Manager Product Line B
      - Salespeople Product Line B
    - Sales Manager Product Line C
      - Salespeople Product Line C
  - Customer Relations Manager
  - Sales Promotion Manager

Market or Customer Type Sales Organization

- Chief Marketing Executive
  - Advertising Manager
  - Director of Market Research
  - General Sales Manager
    - Sales Manager Automotive Market
      - Salespeople Automotive Market
    - Sales Manager Military Market
      - Salespeople Military Market
    - Sales Manager Military Market
      - Salespeople Computer Market
  - Sales Promotion Manager

To fix the problem, Xerox assigned a single salesperson to sell all three product lines to accounts. As a result, customer service levels and total sales increased. However, the reorganization led to higher short-term turnover, because some salespeople were not interested in, or able to learn and sell three separate product lines.

Firms that utilize a **market sales structure** assign representatives to customers based upon their markets—telecommunications, military, automotive, computer, and so forth—or by how the product being sold was used, say by individual consumers or by B2B firms. By employing a market or industry-type sales force organization, the firm is better able to apply the marketing concept and be more customer-centric. That means the sales force learns more about customers' specific business needs and offers customized solutions by recommending the right applications to solve customers' problems.[5] Organizing by customer type appears to be gaining momentum in today's marketplace. For example, many B2B manufacturers sell similar products to commercial and governmental buyers who purchase and utilize the product(s) in very different ways.

Organizing by market also appears to be an effective strategy when a seller wants to penetrate a new market. A market structure allows a selling firm to vary the allocation of its sales efforts to specific industries by adding to, or reducing, the number of salespersons slotted in one area. For example, at one time pharmaceutical manufacturers like Pfizer added a large number of salespersons to sell to physicians, hospitals, and health care providers. In some markets, pharmaceutical firms have assigned more than one salesperson to the same physician to intensify the selling effort. Organizing by market or customer type also permits the sales firm to offer specialized training and develop individualized sales approaches and applications by industry—unlike what is possible in other sales force structures.

The disadvantages of market sales structures are similar to those faced by product-specialized sales forces. Because businesses in the same industry, or market, are often located in different parts of the country, selling expenses are higher than for geographical sales organizations. Also, when a buying firm has several divisions or offers a wide variety of products, multiple salespersons may end up calling on the same buyers. As we have explained, this results in potential buyer confusion, duplication of effort, and higher sales expenses. Pfizer eventually reduced its sales effort, because physicians and hospitals complained about multiple sales efforts for the same product![6]

In a **functional sales structure**, the selling process is divided into two or more steps that are performed by specialists. For example, a company may have one salesperson open a new account. But as soon as the buyer makes the first purchase, the account is turned over to another salesperson who manages the account. For firms that sell to grocery stores or retail outlets, the sales effort might include one salesperson who establishes a store's account; a second sales professional who manages the store's stock and its orders, and resolves customer service issues; and a third sales-support person who merchandises the company's products by setting up in-store shelf and point-of-purchase displays and mailing out promotional materials.

A potential problem with using a functional sales organization is coordinating multiple sales reps who would call on a single customer. A customer relationship management (CRM) system can simplify coordination problems and allow the entire sales team to know what the others discussed and promised—no matter who last talked to the buyer. Sales managers may also struggle to coordinate the activities of two or three sales specialists: the one who opens the account, the one who manages customers, and the one who conducts customers' merchandising efforts. That is, once a salesperson opens an account, the sales manager must ensure there is a smooth "hand-off" to the other account manager(s). One way to help ensure a smooth transition, and make sure the salesperson who opened the account remains dedicated to it, is to reduce his or her commission if the company loses the account within the first year.

A firm utilizes a **combination sales structure** when its sales force is organized based on a mixture of product, market, and geographical factors. Combination sales structures work best when the market is large, the product mix is complex, and customers require different applications. An example of a combination sales force organization is the Lenovo approach. Lenovo sells sales force CRM systems to automotive parts manufacturers in the Midwest. A combination sales force structure connects the benefits of product and market structures. But combination sales structures can be expensive and result in duplicate sales efforts, too. Such a structure tends to work best for larger firms that serve many diverse and specialized markets.

As you can probably tell, sales managers face different trade-offs with different sales structures. Exhibit 7.4 outlines the major pros and cons of each sales structure.

EXHIBIT 7.4   The Pros and Cons of Different Territory Structures

Territory Structure	Pros	Cons
Geographical (generalist approach)	Simplicity Efficiency No Duplication	Unbalanced Territories Product and Market Knowledge More Difficult for Reps to Master Broad Product Lines Coordination Issues
Product (specialist approach)	Better Rep Product Knowledge Better Rep Product-Application Knowledge	Duplicate Sales Effort
Market (specialist approach)	Better Rep Customer Knowledge Better Rep Product-Application Knowledge Better Rep Market Knowledge	Duplicate Sales Effort More Complex to Work With Product Managers
Functional (specialist approach)	Job Expertise Achieved by Reps	Coordination Issues
Combination (specialist approach)	Better Rep Customer Knowledge Better Rep Market Knowledge	Economies of Scale Issues More Complex to Manage Duplicate Sales Effort

Key Account Structures

Firms today provide their key accounts (which may also be called national accounts) with extra attention and service levels by assigning special salespeople to them. **Key accounts** consist of customers that are large in terms of their sales revenue and profitability and that are strategically important for the future of the sales firm. An excellent example of a key account is Walmart, which purchases and distributes a significant amount of Procter & Gamble products, both nationally in the United States and throughout the world. Because key accounts are so important to manufacturers, they are given higher levels of service, a more experienced sales force, and private channels to communicate with sales firm executives. IBM reports that its largest customers generate 75 percent of its revenues.[7] Key account relationships also exemplify the **80/20 Rule**, which states that 80 percent of a firm's total business and profits are derived from 20 percent of its customers.

Recently, B2B buyers have reduced the number of approved sellers they work with in order to cut costs—and to form closer relationships, and work more closely, with retained vendors. As a result, many suppliers now sell larger volumes to fewer key accounts.[8] This shift can be both good and bad: it can lead to lower costs for the supplier, because there are fewer accounts to service. However, the supplier is also more likely to face pressure from the buyer to lower its prices, so the buyer doesn't switch its business to another firm.[9] To keep from entering into a "downward spiral," sellers must be prepared to offer the buyer something other than low prices that its

GLOBAL SALES MANAGEMENT   **Sales Structures in Global Markets**

Sales assignments can vary tremendously in global markets.

When a firm implements a global sales force, sales managers have multiple factors to consider. In global markets, sales force organizations and practices vary by country. A country's cultural context greatly influences the type of organizational sales force structure a company selects. Foreign salespeople and sales managers from the firm's home country (known as expatriates) can work well in low-context countries, like Germany, where oral and written communications are direct. By contrast, local salespeople perform more efficiently in Japan and China, due to the language and cultural knowledge they possess. Firms such as Procter & Gamble learned that local hires who understand both the market and the local culture work best in the growing China market.

Even though organizational alternatives are available, sales firms still employ geographical territories to structure their overseas sales forces. For example, Caterpillar organized Central America into a single region for a U.S. expatriate salesperson to manage. On the other hand, global firms that offer broad product lines, have large sales volumes, or operate in large, developed markets tend to favor customer or product assignments. In smaller markets, like those found in developing areas such as Southeast Asia, it is not economically feasible to structure the sales force by product or customer—thus, geographical assignments are more common.

Lastly, global firms often utilize cultural components, including languages, to organize their sales forces. That is, a firm might divide the nation of Belgium by language—French to the south and Flemish in the north—and combine Austria and Germany because each nation speaks German. Likewise, global firms might combine the Central American countries into a single geographical territory if the sales in those countries are small, and if their languages and cultures are similar. However, sales force managers must remain sensitive to the fact that, although nations might lie geographically close to one another, a country can be distinct in terms of its culture, customs, and values.

Based on Honeycutt, Earl D., John B. Ford, and Antonis Simintiras (2003). *Sales Management: a Global Perspective*, London, UK: Routledge.

competitors can't offer—that is, higher levels of service, greater product value, or both.

Sellers today understand that large, strategic accounts require higher levels of service and deeper buyer-seller relationships. Thus, sellers must develop a strategy for serving large, strategic accounts. Many firms begin their key account management programs by utilizing the existing sales force. Because key account buyers require significantly higher service levels than smaller, non-key accounts, sellers must restructure their sales force to best meet the needs of their strategic partners. Firms can manage national or key accounts through their existing sales force structure by assigning company executives to the accounts, or by creating a separate sales force or sales division. We discuss each option next.

EMPLOYING THE EXISTING SALES FORCE STRUCTURE Firms may initially manage national or key accounts through their existing sales forces. In this way, the sales force structure is simplified, and all accounts are managed under a single organizational structure. However, a number of disadvantages rise to the surface when using the regular sales force to serve key accounts. For example, a territory-based salesperson might focus on closing sales, rather than on fostering long-term relationships. This short-term view is prevalent when salespeople are motivated by constant sales-quota pressures. Plus, a territory-based salesperson is unlikely to understand the broader, overall needs of the key account. For reasons such as these, many firms decide to structure their key account sales operations differently.

ASSIGNING COMPANY EXECUTIVES Assigning sales and marketing executives to manage key accounts makes sense for smaller firms that cannot afford a separate sales effort. The drawback of assigning executives at small firms to singly manage key accounts is that the added assignment can take a lot of time, which leaves the executives less time for their principal duties, including overseeing the firm's sales force. Large firms like Cisco assign their 15 most important accounts to individual executives—with each responsible for managing the relationship of one key account. The Cisco account executive also coordinates the sales team to meet the needs of the key or major accounts. By virtue of their influence and power, company executives at both large and small selling firms can ensure their firms address the needs of key account buyers.

BUILDING A SEPARATE SALES FORCE/DIVISION As sales firms grow in size, they often create separate sales structures to serve their most important customers. This can take the form of having a senior salesperson visit the buyer's headquarters and then assign regular sales force members to service local accounts. Or a parallel sales force structure can be formed and managed. For example, a firm can establish a separate key account division to which it promotes the most successful and experienced sales reps. Establishing a separate sales force/division offers the benefit of integrating key account marketing and sales operations under one organizational structure. However, establishing distinct sales channels for major accounts is more costly, and results in duplication of effort for the sales organization. Lastly, should one or two large customers be lost to competitors, the financial viability of a separate sales force or division could be in jeopardy!

Telemarketing and Computerized Sales Structures

Recall that **telemarketing** is the use of telecommunications technology by an inside salesperson to communicate with an established or potential customer to sell products or services. For business-to-business firms, telemarketing is growing at a rate of nine percent per year, and it accounted for $650 billion in sales in the most current reports.[10] Firms have switched to telemarketing to service small accounts, pre-qualify customers, set up appointments for the outside sales force, notify customers about upcoming trade shows, and handle incoming sales calls. As sales firms rely on telemarketers to conduct sales activities for smaller accounts and to support the field salesperson, the sales manager must devote more time and effort to coordinating the interactions of inside and outside sales personnel. In a number of instances, sales firms have moved their telemarketing operations offshore in order to lower costs. However, as customers subsequently complained about the level of service they received from service providers at offshore call centers, sales firms slowed or stopped offshoring their telemarketing and customer service centers, as discussed in the accompanying "Global Sales Management" box.

GLOBAL SALES MANAGEMENT   Some Offshore Call Centers Return Home

Sales managers often encounter problems coordinating the strategies of their sales forces and their overseas customer service support groups.

At first, firms that built and staffed offshore call centers were praised for their cost-cutting acumen. In fact, the offshoring of services—to include telemarketing and customer service—is proving to be a global phenomenon: French-speaking Europeans are serviced by residents of former colonies in Africa, German speakers by Eastern Europeans, Scandinavians by workers in the Baltic region, Portuguese by Brazilians and residents of former colonies in Africa, and Japanese by citizens of northern China.

But the offshoring movement to lower-cost countries was quickly met by buyers who complained about miscommunications, cultural gaffes, lack of professionalism and product knowledge, and the agents' inability to solve problems. In response, firms invested more time and money training their offshore agents and retaining the best telemarketing salespersons they could afford. Some firms purchased better voice-recognition software to make communication with customers easier and faster. Still other companies went so far as to purchase software designed to help sales managers recognize buyer dissatisfaction levels during telephone calls.

Despite these efforts, many firms moved call centers back to their home countries because, in the buyers' eyes, lower-cost offshore centers equated with lower-quality service. In fact, one study found that many U.S. citizens "hang up" or refuse to speak to call center representatives when they believe the telemarketer is located in another country.

Based on Ali, Sarmad (2006), "If You Want to Scream, Press..." *The Wall Street Journal*, October 30, R4; Thelen, Shawn T., Vincent P. Magnini, Tayna Thelen, and Earl D. Honeycutt, Jr. (2009), "Elements of Service Ethnocentrism," *Services Marketing Quarterly*, 30:1, 1–17.

There are two basic forms of telemarketing sales structures that firms employ: incoming and outgoing. An incoming telemarketing group operates within a firm's pull strategy. That is, the firm employs advertising and promotional messages to end-users to "pull" or create buyer demand to call an 800 number and consult with an in-house telemarketing salesperson. Sales companies also utilize toll-free phone numbers that allow small accounts to contact the seller and place orders that fulfill their needs. An outgoing telemarketing group performs a variety of activities that involve pushing a firm's product line by calling current or potential customers to try to uncover needs and close the sale. Telemarketing is favored by firms because of its lower cost, higher call rate per day, and overall profitability that can be generated. Sales managers understand, however, that telemarketing salespersons require different skill sets, training, compensation, and motivation than do field sales personnel.

Telemarketing salespeople who work in a functional sales organization might prospect for, and qualify, sales leads; set sales-call appointments; and handle customer satisfaction issues. Telemarketers are normally organized similarly to field representatives—by geography, product, or markets. As Exhibit 7.5 shows, a firm has the option of shifting the functional responsibility for servicing customers between its inside salespeople and its field salespeople.

EXHIBIT 7.5   The Sales Process in a Hybrid Selling Structure

Vendors		Lead Generation	Qualifying Sales	Pre-Sales	Close of Sale	Post-Sale Service	Account Management	Customer
	Field Sales/ Agent				X		X	
	Telemarketing		X	X		X		
	Direct Mail/ Computerized Sales	X						

Computerized sales, generated via the Internet and telephone, are increasing annually for most firms. According to one study, B2B e-commerce is double B2C e-commerce, and is expected to achieve $559 billion in U.S. sales by 2013.[11] Computer sales experts counsel that moving more buyers online is key to increased B2B success. That said, it is essential that B2B computerized sales are user-friendly and relevant. In a recent study, B2B buyers reported that ordering online remains a challenge in the areas of product, price, channel, and back-end complexity.[12] Thus, sales firms have more work to do to make computerized sales more "buyer friendly."

As you might expect, the Internet sales process can vary greatly. For example, Prentice Hall allows university bookstores to go online to interact with OASIS, a free Internet-based system that enables the placing and tracking of book orders 24 hours a day, seven days a week. In addition, bookstores can look up price and availability, and request copies of invoices, credit memos, and statements. If customers need to speak with a person, there is an 800 phone number they can call to reach an inside salesperson.

Another computer option, mentioned earlier, allows firms to be linked to an Intranet and order standard products as they are needed. Buyers order either when they are notified via e-mail by a just-in-time or EDI ordering system, or when their stock reaches a designated level. No live salesperson is needed, because the buyer orders from an approved vendor at a pre-negotiated price. Computerized sales systems are significantly less costly for the seller.

Firms that use computerized sales to either service buyers placing reorders or to attract new buyers have to keep in mind that customers are being inundated by e-mails and automated sales calls. Much of the e-mail that buyers receive is **spam** ("junk" or unsolicited electronic messages). Salespersons should ask permission to send e-mail messages to buyers; otherwise, only personal electronic messages that are relevant should be sent to current or potential buyers. That is, make sure that you have permission to send "blanket" e-mail sales messages to buyers. The CAN-SPAM

Act became law in 2003; it sets conditions for sending e-mail to current clients and potential buyers:

* The subject lines of e-mails should not be misleading.

* The "From" line should contain a functioning e-mail address.

* The body of the message should list a valid physical postal address.

* There should be conspicuous instructions to opt out of future mailings.

If these requirements are not followed, firms face penalties of up to $2 million or more imposed by the U.S. government.[13]

As far as telephone messages go, the federal law allows firms to make telemarketing calls under specific conditions. Sales firms that make telemarketing calls to business locations are not in violation of the Federal Trade Commission "No-Call" regulation; telemarketing calls are expressly permitted when a business relationship exists. However, it is a violation of the Telephone Consumer Protection Act (TCPA) for firms to make pre-recorded telephone calls via automatic computerized dialers (also known as Automatic Dialing and Announcing Devices, or ADAD) and to fax spam to any fax location.[14] Therefore, sales managers should keep in mind that, although business telemarketing calls may be legal, unwanted and intrusive telemarketing calls are likely to negatively impact an existing or potential business relationship.

Reporting Relationships within a Firm's Sales Force

There are a number of ways a sales force's reporting relationships can be set up in a firm. In a **line organization**, all salespeople, from the highest to the lowest levels, report to a single manager. For example, a field or inside salesperson reports to her sales manager; her sales manager reports to the district sales manager; the district sales manager is supervised by the regional sales manager; and the regional sales manager reports to the national sales manager. To carry this line organization further, the national sales manager reports to the firm's vice president of sales and marketing, and the vice president of sales and marketing then answers to the president of the firm.

There are advantages and disadvantages to line structures. Line structures are advantageous because the chain of command is clear. For example, if the president and the vice president of sales and marketing feel that it is necessary to modify the firm's sales strategy, this action can be implemented quickly and easily through the firm's line structure. A disadvantage of the line structure is that, as firms adopt customer relationship strategies, salespeople need greater authority to make quick decisions to keep customers satisfied. To make quicker decisions, companies and sales managers must flatten the sales organization—if not the actual reporting structure itself—and then flatten the decision making that occurs within it. That is, authority must be pushed down to lower-level salespeople who can be more responsive to buyers' needs.

Firms also must decide how other sales activities—like sales selection, sales training, buyer research, and customer service—fit into the structure. When a sales support activity falls outside of the line structure, the organization operates a line and staff structure. A **line and staff sales structure** entails using a line structure for the firm's core sales functions, and then placing its support activities—like sales training and customer service—into centers or departments that reside outside of the line structure. For example, a salesperson would report directly to his district manager in a line organization. However, when undergoing training, he would be supervised by the firm's sales training manager, who is a staff member. Remember that staff managers report to, and are delegated authority by, line managers. The geographical, product, and market sales force structures shown in Exhibit 7.3 all provide examples of line and staff structures.

Span of Control

The **span of control** refers to the number of individuals who report directly to a sales manager. There is no rule for an "ideal" span of control; however, Exhibit 7.6 offers guidelines for sales managers. Technical sales and industrial products—both of which require customized customer solutions—result in narrower spans of control (fewer employees reporting to a sales manager), whereas routine trade sales and telemarketing activities allow a broader span of control (larger numbers of employees reporting to a sales manager).[15] For example, as the exhibit shows, the recommended number of salespeople reporting to one sales manager in a technical sales setting is seven, while a sales manager can supervise 12 to 16 trades salespersons who are involved in more routine sales duties.

EXHIBIT 7.6   Recommended Span of Control Ratios

By Selling Task		By Product Type	
Technical Sales	7:1	Industrial Products	6:1
Missionary Sales	10:1	Consumer Products	8:1
Trade Sales	12–16:1	Services	10:1
Telemarketing	12–18:1		

Adding Independent Sales Reps to the Sales Structure

Recall that **independent sales representatives**, or agents, often sell on behalf of manufacturers or other sellers in territories where no company sales force is present. These agents receive commissions for all sales they make within an assigned geographical sales territory. As agents, they neither take ownership of the products nor maintain inventories. A manufacturer's representative traditionally sells a number of related, but noncompeting, product lines that are similar in quality and price. For example, in the furniture business, a rep might sell furniture for one principal, lamps for another manufacturer, and decorative accessories for yet another. The retail buyer needs all three types of products, so it is more efficient for the buyer to meet with a single salesperson instead of three. One study found that 50 percent of North American companies utilize sales agents for product, geographic, or market-oriented sales. Intel, Texas Instruments, Hunt Wesson, and Cirrus Logic are companies that switched from in-house sales forces to sales agents. Moreover, as we also discussed in Chapter 2, there are times when firms outsource their entire sales forces.

The relationship between company sales managers and agents in general is complex. First, a selling firm can contract with a manufacturer's agent or a wholesaler's sales force to manage accounts in geographical regions. For example, a manufacturer might have a company sales force that manages larger, more profitable territories, while also contracting with agents to service less-developed, less-profitable geographical territories. Many insurance firms utilize a combination of company and independent sales agents to sell their products.

Second, because agents are "independent," a company sales manager has little direct control over them—other than dissolving the agency relationship. As a result, the sales manager must motivate the agents by appealing to their self-interests. For example, the sales manager might structure the compensation system for the agents based upon measures other than simply sales revenue generated. This may include measures that are related to growing the company's existing accounts and building higher-quality relationships with customers.

As we mentioned, when firms enter new territories with low or unknown sales volumes, it is common for manufacturers to use sales agents. This appears to be a prudent business decision for sellers, because selling costs are only incurred (in the form of sales commissions) when products or services are sold. For example, a manufacturer that decides to expand into a new region—but lacks the financial resources to hire, train, equip, and manage a company sales force—will likely contract with an independent sales agency that may also be called a broker or manufacturer's representative.

Independent salespeople offer firms the following advantages:

- an "in-place" or existing sales force;
- established buyer relationships;
- little (or no) fixed costs;
- experienced sales personnel;
- lower costs per sales call; and
- long-term stability in the territory.

However, given these many benefits, firms that hire independent sales reps often complain that they do not receive equal time for their products. Or agents are blamed for shifting their sales-call focus to another product line when a buyer's need is not easily identified. Independent sales reps are also criticized for opening fewer new accounts, not following up on leads, representing too many manufacturers, and communicating poorly with their partner firms. That said, there's a tendency for manufacturers to take credit for positive sales outcomes accomplished by their agents, and to assign blame for negative outcomes when they lack control over the outcomes. For example, if a sales agent is making a high level of sales, the manufacturer will assume that a company sales force will work even better at a lower cost, and the agency will be dropped. This suggests that a sales agency will likely be criticized when its performance is either too high or too low.

Any written agreement a selling firm has with an agent should clearly articulate the expected level of feedback the firm wants regarding its customers, the customers' inventory levels, the customer service level the agent will provide to the firm's customers, and how the agent will represent the firm at trade shows.[16] Otherwise, conflicts like those listed in Exhibit 7.7, are likely to occur. For example, the manufacturer might want the agent to focus on selling the firm's products at premium prices, whereas the sales agent's goal might be to maximize sales revenue by selling the firm's products at discounted prices.

Sales agencies understand that, once their client's sales revenues reach a certain level, the client might sever their business relationship and hire its own

---

EXHIBIT 7.7   **Sources of Conflict between Firms and Their Selling Agents**

Conflict	Explanation
Goal Divergence	This conflict occurs when the objectives of the agent and the seller differ. For example, the seller might want the agent to focus on getting a high price for products, whereas the sales agent might want to maximize sales revenue by offering discounts and remaining flexible on prices.
Domain Dissension	This conflict relates to a disagreement about who owns a particular domain, like the territory served, expected duties, and the target market.
Reality Perceptions	This conflict is often observed in the very nature of human relationships: one party feels slighted, while the other believes it acted in good faith.
Abuse of Power	One partner may threaten to change, or actually change, a policy without consulting with the other. When challenged, the more powerful partner simply tells the other "that's the way it is."

Russell S. Winer, *Marketing Management*, 2nd edition, Upper Saddle River, NJ: Prentice Hall, 2004.

sales force. In effect, the sales agents are so successful that they put themselves out of business. Because both agents and the firms that contract with them realize that their relationship can change over time, it's a good idea to incorporate provisions for modifying the agreement that created the partnership in the first place. That is, in addition to clearly stating how each partner will support the other, it is also essential to discuss and agree upon how the partnership can be amicably dissolved. Agreements between agents and manufacturers normally offer specific provisions for how the partnership can be ended, how much notice is required, and how each party will behave toward the other. It is also common practice to split commissions for a specified time period, such as one year, after the company sales force assumes responsibility for a territory's customers. Even so, ethical dilemmas can arise between the parties, as illustrated in the accompanying "Ethics in Sales Management" feature.

ETHICS IN SALES MANAGEMENT   Ethical Dilemmas with Partners

John Orlando is a national sales manager for Exitron, a manufacturer of electronic chips utilized in alarm systems, appliances, irrigation timers, and industrial machinery. Currently, Wiles & Associates represents Exitron as a manufacturer's rep in California. When Wiles agreed to represent Exitron, both parties signed an agreement that stated that either party could terminate the relationship by sending a written notice to the other party at least 90 days prior to ending the partnership.

Exitron's recent sales in California have been phenomenal, and Orlando calculates that the cost of servicing the accounts would decrease by 25 percent by switching to a company sales force. Exitron's attorney advised Orlando to send notification to Wiles & Associates by overnight express mail—exactly 90 days from the termination date. John Orlando feels badly about not personally meeting with Mr. Wiles, thanking him for the service his company has extended to Exitron, and offering to split the sales commission for the next year. Exitron's attorney advises that nothing in the partnership agreement requires this "golden handshake," and that such an action would set a bad precedent and financially impact Exitron's bottom line. Orlando wonders, in this instance, what the difference is between being legal and being ethical.

Epilogue

After weighing his options, John Orlando decided his best course of action was to meet with the managers at Wiles & Associates, thank them for representing his products in their territory, and offer a phase-out of commissions. His actions were well-received by Mr. Wiles, and Orlando believes that—should sales decline significantly in this region at some time in the future—Wiles would once again partner with Exitron.

Company Salesperson or Sales Agent?

When it is important to control the sales effort, when the product or its related technology is new, and when buyers need a high level of sales service, most firms and their sales managers conclude that it is in their best interests to hire, train, organize, and manage a company sales force. This way, the company can exert greater control over the sales force's efforts, such as what will be sold, when, and how. The firm also has greater control over who is hired to represent the company. However, when the potential sales revenue is low in a territory, or will take years to become substantial— and highly qualified sales agents currently operate in the area—an attractive alternative is a contract sales force.

So, at what point, exactly, should a sales agent and a company sales representative be switched? The simplest way to determine this is to do a **break-even analysis** that compares the fixed and variable costs associated with the two types of representatives. A break-even analysis can be conducted by using a mathematical formula (see Appendix 7A) or an economic diagram, as shown in Exhibit 7.8. First, the total cost of the agent (TC^a) line begins at zero and increases linearly as the agent sells additional

Sales firms often hire sales agents instead of in-house personnel because of cost, expertise, and contacts.

units of the product. Second, a company salesperson receives a straight salary component and an additional commission for each unit sold. As a result, the firm's costs for maintaining the company salesperson in the field is highest at lower sales volumes, but increases more slowly as sales levels grow.

As Exhibit 7.8 shows, the total cost of the salesperson (TC^{SP}) starts on top of the horizontal fixed cost line, because the salesperson is paid a salary; other fixed costs must be expended, even when there are no sales in the territory. At a specific unit of sales volume, there is a point of indifference (Q*) where the two sales options cost the selling firm exactly the same amount. Prior to reaching the break-even point, the agent is the least costly option for the sales firm. However, once the break-even point has been crossed and sales continue to increase, it is more economically advantageous for a sales firm to operate a company sales force in a territory. Conversely, when sales revenue decreases to the left of the switch over point Q*, then the sales manager would need to consider changing from a company salesperson to an agent.

Firms understand that sales agents may be the best solutions for given situations. For example, National Semiconductor and Advanced Micro Systems each employ a contract sales force, because their products are used in most industries and it is not feasible for a company sales force to cover the entire market. Likewise, using agents to sell services like advertising is logical, because nearly anyone can advertise. However, sales agents are not practical in all sales situations. For example, pharmaceutical companies use in-house sales forces because of ethical and accountability issues.[17]

Manufacturers and wholesalers have recently begun outsourcing their sales responsibilities to independent companies. For example, firms routinely outsource their telemarketing functions to independent telemarketing companies that have call center and telemarketing expertise. Likewise, insurance companies have found that independent sales reps are less expensive than hiring, training, and retaining company salespersons. As we have discussed, "the jury is still out" on the outsourcing of a firm's sales-related responsibilities. Companies that partner with other firms to perform their sales functions must decide whether to stick with the partnership, depending upon the level of sales, profitability, and buyer satisfaction achieved by the independent or outsourced sales firms.

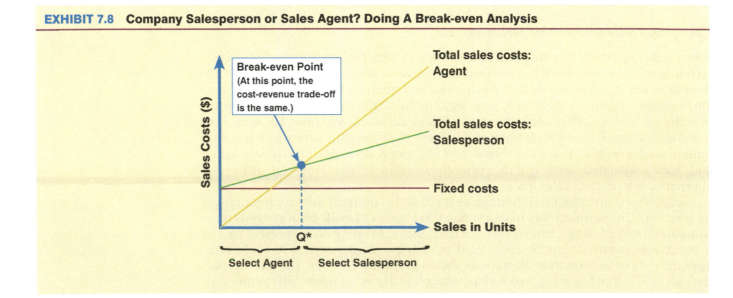

EXHIBIT 7.8   Company Salesperson or Sales Agent? Doing A Break-even Analysis

Managing Your Career

Understanding the reasons behind how your sales activities are organized provides a "big-picture" view of your position in the company. Your firm can organize the sales force any way it chooses, but it should do so in such a way as to provide outstanding service to its clients and potential clients at the lowest cost. If the current sales force structure is not serving customers well, or is costing too much to operate, you will know that the sales force will be reorganized—and how the changes will impact your responsibilities. The chapter also provides you with important information about what clients look for in a supplier; how they work together in a buying center; how to behave as a salesperson depending upon the sales situation; how to serve clients who purchase in multiple supply-chain channels; and how to minimize buyer-seller conflict. Possessing and using this knowledge will lead to greater success and less stress on the job as you begin, and as you move up through, the sales organization.

Summary

The way the sales force is organized and managed is a major aspect of a firm's strategic sales plan. When the sales force is organized geographically, the representatives interact as generalists, with buyers located in their territory. Conversely, by organizing along product, market, combination, or functional structures, buyers receive additional specialized service from the sales force. Sales managers must consider line and staff, span of control, specialization, coordination, and integration factors when deciding upon the best way to organize the sales effort. In addition to structuring their field representatives, firms also have to decide how to structure their other selling groups, such as their key account, telemarketing, and computerized sales functions and groups.

When the sales territory is unproven, or when the selling firm cannot afford to hire, train, and manage its own sales force, the firm can partner with sales agents or manufacturers' representatives. Sales agents are less controllable than company salespeople, and misunderstandings between a firm and its agents can sometimes lead to conflicts between the two. Sales managers can perform a break-even analysis to compare the fixed and variable costs associated with the two types of sales representatives. There are times, however, when sales agents are not practical in a particular selling situation, no matter how large the cost differences. A clear example discussed in the chapter is that of pharmaceutical firms utilizing their own sales forces to ensure that their sales members follow ethical and accountability guidelines.

Key Terms

breakdown method   137
break-even analysis   151
combination sales structure   143
computerized sales   147
80/20 Rule   143
functional sales structure   142
geographical sales structure   140
independent sales representatives   149
key accounts   143

line and staff sales structure   148
line organization   148
market sales structure   142
product sales structure   140
spam   147
span of control   149
telemarketing   145
workload method   138

Questions and Problems

1. Explain why firms organize their sales activities into a specific structure. How important is the sales structure for a business's strategic plan?

2. Using the following information, perform a breakdown and workload computation to predict how many salespersons XYZ, Inc., will need to service its customers. Forecasted sales for next year are $110 million, and an average salesperson sells $9 million annually. Also, the XYZ sales manager has categorized existing accounts into 41 "A," 105 "B," and 225 "C" customers. "A" accounts are visited weekly, "B" accounts monthly, and "C" accounts every other month. Salespersons are required to make four calls per day, and to be in the field four days per week. Because of vacation, training, and holidays, each salesperson works 48 weeks a year. In addition to calling upon existing accounts, salespersons are assigned a ten-percent quota of calling upon new accounts and devoting five percent of their time to information gathering duties.

3. Why does specialization lie at the heart of organizing the sales force? That is, what is the principal advantage of a specialized sales force?

4. Compose a table with five rows and four columns. List the five potential ways to structure a sales force in the left-hand column and then discuss the advantages and disadvantages of each sales structure in the middle and far right columns.

5. What are the three principal ways to manage national or key accounts? What is the best option for a smaller firm? For a large multi-divisional firm?

6. Explain team selling. What role does the salesperson play? What other functional areas are likely to be represented on the team? Why?

7. Many firms have moved their customer service and telemarketing operations offshore. How have many U.S. citizens responded to offshore sales and customer service representatives? How do you explain this reaction? What actions could a sales manager take to improve customer acceptance of offshore service?

8. What should sales managers coach their salespersons to do prior to sending blanket e-mail messages to customers and potential customers?

9. What is spam? What four conditions does the CAN-SPAM Act impose on the sender of e-mails? Integrate these four conditions as you compose a sales e-mail strategy for communicating with buyers.

10. What influences do line and staff organizations and span of control have on the final structural decision with regard to decisions being made, and on routine vs. non-routine sales calls?

11. Compare and contrast the advantages/disadvantages of utilizing an independent sales agent and a company sales force.

12. Draw a break-even analysis diagram and assume that Q^* is 500 units. If the forecasted sales for the territory is 450 units a month, which sales structure—an independent agent or a company sales force—would be most economical? What other factors, other than costs, might influence your decision?

Role Play

Structuring the Sales Effort at Eno River Software

Chandra Singh is the sales manager at Eno River Software (ERS), a firm that produces custom B2B software for manufacturing equipment. Examples include software for the robotic assembly of automobiles, the mixing of precise chemical solutions at pharmaceutical and chemical plants, and the testing of assembled and manufactured goods for their quality and reliability. Eno River's sales efforts have been handled by a manufacturer's representative firm, VL Associates, owned by Vince Latham.

Latham was a computer science professor who consulted with Eno River in the early days of computing, when software solutions for manufacturing problems were first being developed. Latham left academia after several ERS programs were developed, and he offered to handle the sales efforts for Eno River. This arrangement has worked well for ERS for 10 years as sales increased; however, about a month ago, ERS made the strategic decision to transition to a relationship-marketing approach for its best customers.

Singh is trying to determine whether ERS is receiving the best support from VL Associates, because its agents also sell hardware and peripheral computer equipment—made by other companies—to ERS customers. VL Associates receives an eight percent commission on all sales of ERS products. Last year, the sales revenues for ERS were $200 million. Besides the obvious cost of outsourcing its sales effort, ERS believes that the relationships it has with its best customers are not deepening because of the current sales agency arrangement. Singh wants to do what is best for both VL Associates and ERS; thus, she has scheduled lunch one week from today with Vince Latham to discuss the agency relationship. The outcome of the meeting will determine the sales structure that Singh recommends to ERS's CEO and board of directors.

Characters in the Role Play

Chandra Singh, Sales Manager at Eno River Software

Vince Latham, Owner and Principal of VL Associates

Assignment

Break into groups of two, with one student playing each character. Do not be concerned about matching the gender of the character with the actual gender mix of the student group. Prior to meeting, work individually for a short while to list the advantages of each option for organizing ERS's sales force. Then role play the meeting between Chandra and Vince. Each party should present what they believe are the costs and benefits of the current sales agency relationship. At the conclusion of the meeting, Singh and Latham need to agree about the changes that should be made to meet ERS's new strategy. Alternatively, Singh should recommend and logically justify that the contract with VL Associates be terminated and a new sales structure established for ERS. Remember that most sales agent contracts require a three-to-six-month termination notice.

Caselets

Caselet 7.1: Should National Insurance Reorganize Its Sales Force?

Ed Patarski is the Sales Vice President for National Insurance Corporation (NIC). NIC offers life, hospitalization, and disability insurance to both small and large companies—primarily in the southwestern United States—through its company salespeople. Each salesperson currently receives a small, fixed salary and a commission that is based on closed sales within a geographical territory. Over the past decade, the turnover rate for NIC's salespeople increased from less than 20 percent to more than 50 percent annually.

Patarski had the firm's accounting department conduct a financial analysis regarding the total cost of hiring new salespeople, including the cost of advertising to attract applicants as well as interviewing, training, and licensing them. He's surprised when the figure he receives amounts to more than $6 million dollars per year! With a turnover rate exceeding 50 percent, Patarski quickly concludes there is a tremendous amount of waste associated with the firm's current sales structure.

Consequently, Patarski is considering partnering with independent sales agents, located in all of the company's current sales areas, because of their marketplace knowledge, market status, similarity of goals and values, and ability to create win-win situations for all parties involved in transactions. However, to make this a reality, NIC's sales managers would need to contact the agents operating in the various sales territories and convince them of the benefits of partnering with National. Patarski also understands that utilizing this new market channel would make NIC's current salespeople unhappy, because the independent reps would compete—at least indirectly—with them. Still, as Patarski considers the money NIC could save, and how the independent reps have strong reputations and sales histories in their local areas, he knows partnering with independent salespersons is probably the way to go.

Questions

1. What are the benefits of partnering with independent reps, as opposed to a company sales force? Can a case be made for finding a way to retain Patarski's current salespeople instead of hiring sales agents to replace them?
2. Why would the turnover rate be significantly lower for NIC if it hired sales agents?
3. What type of resistance might NIC encounter from its current sales reps if it hired sales agents?
4. Can NIC integrate an independent rep strategy with its existing company sales force? How?

Caselet 7.2: *CMI Considers Offshoring Its Call Center*

Continental Manufacturers International (CMI) produces high-quality electronic components for original equipment manufacturers (OEMs). Currently, CMI pays about $5 million a year to operate a customer service center for its dealers and distributors located worldwide. CMI sales manager Tameka Smith has been reading about her competitors' opening call centers in India, the Philippines, and in remote parts of Canada. Smith is reluctant to offshore CMI's call center, but her department is being pressured to lower its total costs.

To learn about her options, Smith contacts NCS International, which provides global site selection services specifically for the call center industry. She discovers that utilizing offshore call centers will lower her department's cost per call by 75 percent—a huge savings for CMI. But Smith is concerned about the negatives she has read about in industry publications and newspapers. For example, other firms have initially experienced the euphoria of saving money, only to learn—later on—that buyer satisfaction and repeat purchases dropped significantly. As Smith waits for a flight to Chicago, she ponders how she can make an offshore call center work for CMI.

Questions

1. Even though CMI's cost per call would decrease, what other costs should Smith consider when making her decision?
2. Do you think some of the countries Smith is considering for offshoring the firm's customer care center would result in potentially less caller dissatisfaction than others? Why?
3. What primary criteria would you recommend that Smith consider when evaluating potential offshore locations?
4. Are there other possible options Smith should consider in regard to this major shift in customer service responsibilities? List three or more options, by priority.

APPENDIX 7A

COMPUTING THE POINT AT WHICH TO SWITCH OVER FROM A COMPANY SALESPERSON TO A SALES AGENT

1. To compute Q*, a number of factors must be known or estimated:
   a. the fixed costs for the salesperson or sales force in an area. This may include straight salary, automobile cost, and cell phone costs.
   b. the variable costs, such as cost of goods sold and commissions.
   c. the forecasted sales for the salesperson or sales team.
   d. the ability to compute contribution margin, or the selling price minus the variable costs. This leaves the amount from a sale that is left to pay off the firm's fixed costs.
   e. An estimation of the time the agent spends on your product, in comparison to time spent by a company salesperson. This is abbreviated as "R." Since agents sell multiple products, the agent cannot spend time exclusively on a single product.

2. Q*, or the break-even point, can be computed by using the following formula:

$$Q^* = \frac{\text{Fixed Costs}}{\text{Contribution Margin}_{SP} - R \times \text{Contribution Margin agent}}$$

Compute the break-even point, based upon the following information:

Product sales price is $225; the manufactured sales cost is $110.

A sales agent receives a commission of 6 percent of the sales price.

The company salesperson receives $3,000 monthly salary and a 2 percent commission on total sales. Additional fixed costs = $800 a month for an auto and $150 for a cell phone. The sales agent spends 30 percent of his or her time selling the firm's products.

Fixed Costs = $3,000 + $800 + $150 = $3,950

Con Margin$_{SP}$ = $225 – $110 – $4.50 = $110.50

Con Margin$_{AGENT}$ = $225 – $110 – $13.50 = $101.50

Adding numbers to formula:

$$\frac{\$3,950}{\$110.50 - .3 \times 101.50} = \frac{\$3,950}{80.50} = 49.068 \text{ units per month}$$

If Q* is 49 units, and the sales manager forecasts that a company salesperson (or team) can sell 60 units per month, the forecasted sales is greater than Q*. Therefore, from an economic perspective, the company should replace the sales agent with a company salesperson. Conversely, if forecasted sales were 45 units per month for a company salesperson, the company should retain the sales agent in the territory.

References

1. Anderson, Steve (2010). "The Best Practices of High Performing Sales Teams," Performance Methods, Incorporated. Accessed March 28, 2014, and April 4, 2014. *www.performancemethods.com.*
2. Ledingham, Dianne, Mark Kovac, and Heidi Locke Simon (2006). "The New Science of Sales Force Productivity," *Harvard Business Review,* September, 124–133.
3. Honeycutt, Earl D., John B. Ford, and Antonis Simintiras (2003). *Sales Management: A Global Perspective.* London, UK: Routledge.
4. Jordan, Jason (2006). *2006 World Class Sales Force Benchmark Executive Summary,* The HR Chally Group. Accessed May 9, 2008. *www.chally.comlbenchmark/index.html.*
5. Jordan (2006).
6. Herper, Matthew (2007). "At Pfizer, Brutal Cuts and Big Changes," *Forbes.* Accessed January 22, 2014. *www.forbes.com/2007/01/22/pfizer-changes-layoffs-biz-cz_mh_0122changes.html;* "Sales rep mirroring declines," Accessed April 2, 2014. *www.pmlive.com/pharma_news/sales_rep_mirroring_declines.*
7. Marchetti, Michele (2001). "IBM's Marketing Visionary," *Sales & Marketing Management,* September, 52–62.
8. Sharma, Arun (1997). "Who Prefers Key Account Management Programs? An Investigation of Business Buying Behavior and Buying Firm Characteristics," *Journal of Personal Selling & Sales Management,* Fall, 27–39.
9. Piercy, Nigel F., and Nikala Lane (2006). "The Hidden Risks in Strategic Account Management Strategy," *Journal of Business Strategy,* 27: 1, 18–26.
10. Libey, Donald R. (2004). *Libey-Concordia Economic Outlook: Extrapolations and Implications for the Direct Marketing Industry,* MMIV:5 (July), Philadelphia, PA: Libey-Concordia. accessed July 1, 2014, *www.libey.com.*
11. "Building a World-Class eCommerce Business," Forrester Research, January 7, 2013.
12. Oracle (2013). *2013 B2B Commerce Trends,* April. Accessed April 5, 2014. *www.oracle.com/US/Products/Applications.*
13. Clarke, Irvine, III, Theresa B. Flaherty, and Michael T. Zugelder (2005). "The CAN-SPAM Act: New Rules for Sending Commercial E-mail Messages and Implications for the Sales Force," *Industrial Marketing Management* 34:4 (May), 399–415.
14. *www.ag.state.rnn.us/Consumer/YLR/AutoDialers.asp.* Accessed August 1, 2007.
15. Honeycutt, Ford, and Simintiras (2003).
16. Zoltners, Andris, Prabhakant Sinha, and Greggory Lorimer (2005). *The Complete Guide to Accelerating Sales Force Performance,* New York, NY: AMACOM, a division of the American Management Association.
17. Anonymous (2004). "Making the Case for Outside Sales Reps," Association of Independent Manufacturers' Representatives, Inc., *www.aimr.net.* Accessed June 7, 2007.

RECRUITING AND SELECTING THE RIGHT SALESPEOPLE

LEARNING OBJECTIVES

After completing this chapter, you should be able to:

■ Understand why having a formal selection process improves the quality of newly hired salespeople.

■ Discuss why it's important to analyze the skills a salesperson needs to succeed, and include that information in a job description.

■ Name the sources from which salespeople can be recruited, both within and outside of the firm.

■ Explain the five steps of the selection process.

■ Explain why it's important to have a diverse sales force.

■ List common recruiting mistakes and ways to avoid them.

Successfully recruiting salespeople is one of the most important functions performed by sales managers. Informed sales managers understand that, when a firm conducts its selection and recruiting practices haphazardly, the company will experience higher salesperson turnover rates, higher recruiting and training costs, dissatisfied and lost customers, and lower revenues. One sales-industry expert calculated that the sum of the various costs of hiring the wrong salesperson can exceed $300,000![1] By following the process presented in this chapter, sales managers can reduce the likelihood of making incorrect decisions, improve the probability of hiring successful salespeople, and reduce costly sales force turnover.

WILL MAY
Inside Sales Manager
AppDynamics

Sales Manager Profile: Will May

WILL MAY IS AN INSIDE sales manager at AppDynamics, an application intelligence company that specializes in providing insight into the performance of critical web and mobile applications. He manages two teams in Plano, Texas, although the company is headquartered in San Francisco. A graduate of Baylor University, May completed the professional sales program there.

AppDynamics, like most firms, has a specific process for finding and hiring the best salespersons. May notes that AppDynamics has many funnels for finding qualified applicants. These include in-house and out-sourced recruiters who work with professional sales programs and electronic platforms like Glassdoor and Indeed.com. The goal for both recruiters and electronic platforms is to get qualified applicants to look over the job descriptions and—if they feel there is a match and interest—to apply for the jobs. Additionally, individual sales managers do their own recruiting through their networks, LinkedIn, and other recruiting events. A promising applicant receives a direct introductory call from one of the recruiters or one of the managers to evaluate his or her personality, intelligence, fit, and interest in the position. The recruiters and managers are trained to look for certain key words like "tech sales," "1-5 years experience," and "Application Performance Management." Those applicants who pass this initial screening are forwarded to a hiring manager, who initiates an introductory phone call to discuss the position and gauge the applicant's qualifications. If this call goes well, the applicant is invited for an on-site visit and interview. At the on-site interview, applicants meet both managers and sales reps. Prior to the formal interview, the manager meets with another manager or vice president to jointly go over the résumé to agree upon the applicant's important skills and potential red flags. Peer sales reps, who will also interview the applicant, are coached in how to determine whether the applicant will fit in and succeed at AppDynamics.

After the personal interview, the managers and sales representatives who participated in the interview "huddle" and share their observations/evaluations. Successful applicants are then asked to take an external vendor test that measures analytical and verbal abilities, and compares the results to the baseline scores of AppDynamics' top salespersons. For some positions, the AppDynamics management team brings candidates back on-site to present a demo of the AppDynamics solution to the hiring managers. Managers are also expected to check references on more experienced sales applicants. For job seekers straight out of college—many of whom are graduates of professional sales programs—the hiring managers look for positive references from sales professors.

AppDynamics managers then meet to discuss applicants who they are serious about hiring, and consider each potential hire based upon a scorecard of criteria that includes: intelligence, drive, coachability, and character. Managers rate each applicant on each of the four functional areas. Once there is a meeting of minds about bringing an applicant on board, this decision is communicated to the finance and human resources colleagues who put the formal offer together. Normally, the sales manager calls to make the offer—explaining that the human resources staff will forward the formal paperwork—and gives the applicant a specified time period to respond to the job offer. ■

Successful Hiring Requires a Process

By investing quality time and effort—upfront—into a structured recruiting and selection process, a sales manager can determine the most appropriate type of individual needed for the job, attract sufficient numbers of applicants, and select the best-qualified person for the position. Aside from the huge costs related to hiring the wrong person, why is this so important? It's important because companies are discovering that every competitive advantage they have—except better employees—can be duplicated by their competitors.[2] As a result, the successful recruitment and selection of salespeople has become a higher priority for sales managers.[3]

A comprehensive recruiting and selection process consists of five inter-related steps:

- determining the number of salespeople needed;

- identifying the unique skills, knowledge, and attitudes a salesperson needs to do the job successfully;

- attracting a sufficient number of applicants to form a pool of potential new hires;

- conducting an interview process that accurately assesses the applicants' qualifications for the position; and

- offering a sales position to one or more applicants.

Although larger firms may utilize human resource professionals to assist with the recruiting and selection process, in many organizations the task falls primarily upon the shoulders of sales managers. Therefore, sales managers should not view the selection and hiring of a new salesperson as a "knee-jerk" reaction, but rather that of following a methodical hiring process that produces a stream of revenue and return on investment.[4]

Planning to Hire

Sales managers and firms, at times, may view the selection of representatives as a process to be initiated once there is a sales opening. But, ideally, a firm should have a sales selection process in place—one that considers such factors as the firm's strategy, predicted sales force turnover rate, the growth or shrinkage of sales territories, and the promotion and retirement of sales personnel. This is important because the longer a territory goes without a competent salesperson working it, the more revenue the company can lose to a competitor. Moreover, good salespeople are hard to find, and turnover rates are generally high in the profession—because many potential candidates have negative perceptions about working in sales. In a few industries, including life insurance, the turnover rates of salespeople can exceed 300 percent a year. This means that the average salesperson is hired and leaves the firm after just four months on the job! By contrast, Exhibit 8.1 shows that the 2012 turnover rate for U.S. Industries was just a little over 15 percent. That's why many sales managers make recruiting an ongoing process and try to have a list of potential applicants on hand in case a sales position opens up.

EXHIBIT 8.1   2012 Total Turnover by Industry

Industry	Percent
Utilities	6.5
Manufacturing & distributing	12.8
Not-for-profit	15.2
Banking & finance	16.5
Insurance	10.8
Services	15.6
Healthcare	15.7
Hospitality	33.7
All industries	15.2

Based upon *www.compensationforce.com/2012/09/2012-turnover-rates-by-industry.html*. Accessed 3/23/2014.

Calculating the Turnover Rate

The **turnover rate** is the annual percentage of salespeople who leave the firm for both controllable and uncontrollable reasons, which are shown in Exhibit 8.2. The turnover rate can be computed as follows:

$$\text{Annual turnover rate} = \frac{\text{Number of salespeople who left the firm during the year}}{\text{Average sales force size during the year}}$$

$$= \frac{4}{25} = 16 \text{ percent}$$

A far more difficult task for the sales manager is determining *why*, exactly, salespeople are leaving the firm. To accurately understand this aspect, sales managers should ask themselves a series of pertinent questions:

- **Who is leaving the firm?** Are they primarily men, women, minorities, the young, or the old? If a larger percentage of salespeople in one category or another are leaving the firm, what's driving the decisions made by these people?

- **How long has the average salesperson worked for the company?** Are new salespeople seeking opportunities elsewhere after a short period of employment with the firm? Or are older, higher-performing workers leaving?

- **What is the level of performance within the sales team?** Are the highest performing salespeople departing? This is important, because the loss of a "sales star" to a rival firm is usually felt more deeply. High-performance salespeople are also more difficult to replace.

- **What specific reason(s) did the salespeople give for resigning?** Are they going elsewhere for higher salaries, better working conditions, management positions, or increased responsibility?

EXHIBIT 8.2 **Controllable and Uncontrollable Reasons for Sales Force Turnover**

Controllable	Uncontrollable
Retirement	Relocating
Promotion	Marriage
Transfer	Death
Termination	Quitting
Territory changes	Returning to college Changing career

Usually, firms require their sales managers and human resources personnel to jointly investigate these questions. Recent studies report that insufficient compensation and rewards, lack of growth opportunities, and feeling unappreciated account for most voluntary turnover.[5] While these facts may reveal unpleasant truths about an organization, without such an analysis, the sales manager cannot attempt to address the root causes of turnover. For example, if the turnover rate is high among newly hired reps, a sales manager might look for ways to improve the training and onboarding they receive. Perhaps mentors can help them increase their self-confidence during the first year(s) on the job. By contrast, if more senior salespeople are leaving the firm, it may be that alternate career plans can be developed to encourage them to remain. If a large percentage of salespeople is moving to positions in career fields outside of sales, perhaps the firm's current recruiting and selection process isn't painting a realistic view of what a sales job really entails.

That said, a zero-percent turnover rate should also concern sales managers who understand that some level of sales force turnover will occur, no matter what policies are followed. Being human, salespeople will leave their jobs for myriad personal reasons—for example, to live in a warmer state, to get married or have children, to work a more convenient schedule, or to return to college or graduate school full-time. Sales managers should also examine their firm's turnover rate in comparison to industry standards. This allows the sales manager to better understand whether turnover is higher or lower than those of competitors, and whether it's related to the firm's environment or market forces. For example, if a sales manager finds that her company has a turnover rate of 22 percent, whereas the industry average is only 10 percent, she should consider issues like the firm's working conditions, pay, training, and the career stages of those salespeople who are leaving the firm.

Computing a turnover rate provides the sales manager with a starting point for understanding how many salespersons left the firm, or were terminated, during a defined time period. Next, we consider how a sales manager identifies the characteristics that job applicants should possess in order to succeed in the open sales position.

Conducting a Job Analysis

What personal characteristics or "objective profile" do sales managers seek when they look for candidates to fill an open sales position? Several studies report that enthusiasm, organizational ability, verbal skills, and general sales experience are important predictors of future sales success.[6] Other sales managers believe that it is important for candidates to have successful experience in the same industry.[7] Sales jobs vary tremendously, so it is important for each firm to determine the characteristics that lead to the best representatives for the organization's purposes. Determining these characteristics or abilities requires the sales manager or human resources specialist to conduct a job analysis.

A **job analysis** is an objective examination of the duties, activities, and behaviors of people employed in a sales position. When sales managers lack the technical expertise, or do not have the time, to conduct a job analysis, they should contact a human resources specialist or consultant for assistance. A comprehensive sales position job analysis provides the hiring manager with an understanding of: (1) what a salesperson currently does on the job, and (2) how the salesperson should, ideally, spend his or her time. The person performing the job analysis should interview current salespeople and their sales supervisors. A job analysis can also include conducting field observations, keeping field diaries, looking at sales reports, and seeking feedback from customers. By observing how the more successful members of the sales force prioritize their time and activities, sales managers can identify successful or "best-practice" on-the-job behavior.

Misunderstandings about what's expected of a person on the job underscore the importance of performing an accurate and current job analysis before taking actions to fill an open sales position. For example, a misunderstanding could occur if a sales manager tells a prospective salesperson that the job she seeks involves forming a deeper relationship with the president of a purchasing firm, when—in reality—the buying firm expects the salesperson to be available 24/7 to expedite and process orders. When the expectations salespeople have about their jobs don't match the realities they face, their turnover rates will increase.[8]

Writing a Job Description

After conducting a comprehensive job analysis, a **job description**, like the one shown in Exhibit 8.3, is prepared. The job description for a salesperson should address:

1. the nature of the products and services the salesperson will sell.

2. customer type(s) and the frequency with which they should be called upon.

3. the salesperson's specific tasks and responsibilities.

4. the relationship(s) between the salesperson and other people in the sales organization.

5. the intellectual and physical demands of the job.

6. environmental factors affecting the sales position, such as the amount of travel required.

7. the compensation method used—for example, whether the salesperson will be paid a base salary plus commission or whether the position will be commission-only.

EXHIBIT 8.3   **Job Description–Southeast U.S. Territory Manager**

- Responsible for acquiring new business and developing partnerships at original equipment manufacturers (OEM) in southeastern U.S.
- Coordinates sales, contracts, technical support teams, and internal sales assistants. Conducts long-range planning of OEMs to assure account penetration, customer satisfaction, sales growth, and profitability.
- Develops and plans account strategies and activities for assigned accounts to include: selecting accounts, selecting products for buyers, identifying buyer influences and concerns, introducing new products, making sales presentations, and negotiating contracts.
- Relays customer and competitor feedback to management.
- Attends and participates in industry sales conferences and trade shows.
- Required to operate independently and travel 50 percent of the time.
- Must possess strong knowledge of industry products and sales tactics, demonstrated organizational and planning skills, exceptional verbal and written communication skills, and computer proficiency.
- Bachelor's degree or equivalent in business or engineering required. Prefer an MBA degree and minimum of five years of related sales experience working with OEM firms.

Once a job description has been written and approved by management, the document can be utilized to develop a statement of job qualifications. For example, based upon the identified job qualifications, the sales manager lists the necessary skills, knowledge, attitudes, and experience required of applicants. It should be clear that, without an accurate and current job analysis and a job description that lists job qualifications, the sales manager will have trouble selecting the best person from a pool of applicants. This initial stage of the process—that is, determining the qualifications for a new hire—is the most exacting part of the sales selection process.[9]

Sales managers make a mistake when they attempt to minimize the costs of recruiting salespeople, in the false belief that training them can correct their individual weaknesses. This hiring strategy is fraught with danger, because short-term training seldom corrects a new hire's core deficiencies. The new salesperson must possess specific attributes and the sales manager must ensure—through the selection process—that the individual hired possesses those attributes.

Finding and Recruiting Applicants

Recruiting is the process that firms use to find and hire the best-qualified candidate for an open sales position. This recruiting step in the selection process is based upon accurate information gathered in the planning stage while forecasting turnover, conducting a comprehensive job analysis, and writing an accurate and concise job description. The sales manager must also determine an appropriate number of applicants needed for the open position(s). To arrive at a suitable number of applicants, sales managers can employ the following formula:

$$\text{Number of applicants needed} = \frac{\text{Number of open sales positions}}{\text{Percent of applicants selected} \times \text{percent of acceptances}}$$

To estimate the number of applicants to be generated in the recruiting step, let's assume that a firm needs to hire two salespeople; that traditionally, ten percent of applicants who apply with the firm are offered a sales position; and that 80 percent of them accept the offer. This would lead you to the following solution:

$$\text{Number of applicants needed} = \frac{2 \text{ open positions}}{.10 \text{ selected} \times .80 \text{ acceptances}} = 25$$

As you can see from this analysis, 25 applicants are needed to generate two quality hires. The number of applicants necessary to satisfy the total open sales position requirement is directly influenced by the total number of open sales positions, the percentage of applicants offered the position, and the percentage of applicants accepting the job offer. The number of applicants needed to ensure a successful job search can be reduced by generating higher-quality candidates and offering employment packages that result in higher acceptance rates.

Sales managers often have a difficult time generating a large enough pool of highly qualified applicants from which to fill an open sales position. When too few or low-quality applicants are generated, it's likely there is a problem with the sources utilized to find them. As a result, most firms look at several origins, including both internal and external candidate sources.

Recruiting Internal Applicants

Internal applicants are potential candidates for open sales positions who currently work for the company—perhaps as engineers, product managers, customer service representatives, buyers, or manufacturing managers. Many companies first look within their firms to find outstanding candidates. Managers already know a great deal about internal applicants in terms of work habits, personality, and ability to assume more responsibility—information that is seldom known about external applicants. In any case, they may find themselves in a quandary: whether it is best to hire an external salesperson and teach product knowledge or to hire an internal employee who knows little about selling. One study of the pros and cons of hiring "from within" versus externally suggested that internal hires are more successful.[10] That said, internal candidates seldom possess sales experience, and managers from the firm's other functional areas will likely view internal recruiting less positively than the sales department. For example, when a first-rate engineer is selected for an open sales position, the engineering manager must subsequently initiate a job search to fill the open position created by the transfer. However, in industries in which buyers prefer purchasing from salespeople with strong engineering or scientific backgrounds, recruiting internal candidates with a technical background can be the better route to follow.

External Applicants

Internal sources may not produce the quantity or quality of candidates desired by the firm. In these instances, a company must turn to external sources to identify applicants for open sales positions. **External applicants** are candidates for sales positions who are generated from a variety of sources, including referrals, advertisements, private recruiters, educational institutions, job and career fairs, trade shows, and e-recruiting.

REFERRALS There is a saying, "It's not what you know, but *who* you know." Many sales managers look to referrals as first applicants. When current salespeople provide a sales manager with the names of friends or acquaintances who are seeking sales jobs, networking has occurred. **Networking** is the practice of forming relationships and consulting with other salespersons, executives, educational institutions, and friends to learn about positions that may or may not be publicly advertised. For example, members of the sales force are sometimes aware of competing salespersons who have expressed a desire to be considered for future openings with the firm. Applicants can also network with individuals and career centers at the college or university they attended, or with current employees at firms they are interested in joining through websites like LinkedIn (*www.linkedin.com*), Facebook (*www.facebook.com*), and

---

ETHICS IN SALES MANAGEMENT   **Should a Sales Manager Recruit from Her Competitors' Sales Force?**

Alora Myers is sales manager for ChemWorld, Inc., a firm that represents the largest chemical manufacturers in the world. ChemWorld sells to large, medium, and small manufacturers in Texas, Louisiana, Arkansas, and Oklahoma. Two weeks ago, John Phillips tendered his immediate resignation to accept a sales management position in San Diego, California. Since John was ChemWorld's top salesperson, Myers is very concerned about finding a competent replacement who can quickly "get up to speed." Yesterday, Jen Smith, head of purchasing at a major account, informed Myers that Jim Cooper, the top salesperson at AMC Chemical—ChemWorld's biggest competitor—casually mentioned that he was seeking a better situation. Myers would like to speak with Cooper, since he is the top salesperson at AMC, but she is not sure if this would be ethical. She discussed her dilemma with the HR director, who told her, "The important point is who contacts whom. If Cooper contacts you, you are obligated to speak to him." Do you agree or not with Myers about a possible ethical dilemma if she considers hiring a competitor's best salesperson? What are the reasons for your position?

Ryze (*www.ryze.com*). Many firms pay salespeople a bonus for referring applicants who join the firm and remain with it for a specific period of time (three to six months). Such incentives help motivate salespeople to provide their firms with qualified leads, as well as to help the people they referred succeed once hired.[11]

Your customers can also be a good source of referrals. That is, you can ask customers with whom you have a good business relationship to refer highly qualified candidates who they come across in the course of doing business. However, take a look at the "Ethics in Sales Management" box and—based upon the scenario—consider whether you would actively pursue competing salespeople for an open position.

ADVERTISEMENTS A universal method of finding sales applicants is by advertising in newspapers, magazines, and/or online. Technically and highly qualified applicants can be reached through trade publications, or in special issues of newspapers like the *USA Today* or the *Wall Street Journal*. Advertisements assume various forms, but most contain a format of information that includes:

1. the title of the job opening.

2. minimum job qualifications.

3. preferred job qualifications.

4. location of the sales territory.

5. expected travel time in the field.

6. discussion of pay and benefits.

7. statement of core company values.

8. who to contact within the hiring firm, and how.

Exhibit 8.4 shows some of the different kinds of advertisements sales managers run to generate interest in the positions they're trying to fill. **Blind advertisements** offer only a limited amount of information about the sales position and, therefore, tend to generate an applicant pool with a wide range of experience and qualifications. Often, these jobs pay sales commissions only, rather than a regular, fixed salary. The sales managers hiring for commission-only jobs prefer blind ads, so as not to disclose any potentially negative information—because they would prefer to talk with candidates personally, in an effort to stress the more-positive aspects of the job. That said, few college graduates gravitate toward opportunities publicized by blind ads!

Advertisements that elicit a large pool of job seekers are ineffective unless a sufficient number of applicants qualify for a personal interview. Conversely, generating too large an applicant pool can result in costly screening activities. The goal of a sales position advertisement is to generate sufficient numbers of *qualified* applicants for an open position, so that managers can interview and select highly qualified applicants. In most cases, the more precisely the advertisement describes the minimum acceptable requirements, the higher the probability of attracting qualified applicants.

PRIVATE RECRUITERS For more complex sales positions, like technical and international sales, career counselors or "headhunters" from private recruiting firms are utilized to locate and conduct initial applicant screening. Examples of professional recruiting firms that specialize in sales positions include: Porter Group, Inc. (*www.portergroup.com*), Sales Ladder (*www.sales-jobs.theladders.com*), and Sales Recruiters, Inc. (*www.salesrecruiters.com*). Career counselors often specialize by industry or company and maintain a pool of applicants who want to move to higher-paying and/or more challenging sales positions. Firms turn to professional recruiters to identify sales managers and sales executives—more so than for finding entry-level salespersons.

EXHIBIT 8.4   Examples of Open and Blind Advertisements

REGIONAL SALES MANAGER

Bogen Communications, Inc., a leader in institutional and commercial sound, telephone paging, and business communications, is currently seeking aggressive individuals to be a Regional Sales Manager in our Eastern Regions.

Must have strong history of sales success, selling through systems contractors and design community, with solid knowledge of Commercial Audio/Pro Sound markets and products. Extensive travel within the region is also required. Responsibilities include: manage individual sales region to achieve business objectives by motivating, training, selling and managing all Bogen customer types to meet the objectives of the region.

Bogen provides a competitive compensation and benefits package. Please take a look at our web site www.bogen.com.

If you are willing to work hard, you meet the above description, and thrive on building and maintaining excellent customer relationships and winning, send, fax, or e-mail your résumé and salary requirements in confidence to:

Bogen Communications, Inc., Human Resources Manager, 50 Spring Street, Ramsey, NJ 07446. Fax 201-995-2061. E-Mail: hr@ bogen.com.

An Equal Opportunity Employer

An Example of a Blind Advertisement for a Sales Position

SALES POSITION

Firm expanding territory. Salary and commission opportunity for selling technical products to small businesses. Appointments furnished. Sales experience preferred. Call (201) 555-4303.

Sales managers at times criticize professional recruiters for being expensive and not identifying long-term employees. In many cases, the recruiting firm receives a significant percentage of the first year's salary as compensation for finding and screening the new salesperson. This means that sales managers must weigh each of these factors, in a cost-benefit analysis, before signing a contract with a recruiting firm.

However, for busy sales managers at larger firms, private recruiters can save the manager significant time and frustration. To improve the likelihood of success, sales managers must provide private recruiters with specific applicant skill information that is derived from the job analysis and job description. Firms tend to reuse the same private recruiting firm when high-performing job candidates are hired and retained.

Photo Credit: dboystudio / Shutterstock.com

Sales managers use different recruiting sources—including job fairs and open houses at educational institutions.

EDUCATIONAL INSTITUTIONS Colleges and universities can be excellent sources of applicants for firms seeking entry-level salespeople. This is because college graduates have demonstrated an ability to complete projects, solve problems, and remain focused on achieving long-term goals. Research shows that sales recruiters prefer collegiate applicants who are enthusiastic about selling, think outside the box, can work in a team setting, and demonstrate initiative.[12] Many colleges and universities maintain well-organized placement or career management centers that actively work to link graduates with potential employers.

College graduates normally require basic sales training and mentoring. However, a number of colleges and universities offer undergraduate professional sales majors. Students who major in professional sales are required to complete courses in sales management, professional selling, CRM, and business-to-business marketing, plus serve as interns in sales. Firms like ADP and Oracle are hiring new salespersons from University Sales Center Alliance (USCA) schools—a consortium of sales centers located at universities throughout the United States.[13] One study found that professional sales graduates were in high demand and earned significantly higher salaries than did marketing majors.[14]

JOB FAIRS/CAREER CONFERENCES AND TRADE SHOWS Job fairs are career conferences jointly conducted by trade groups, student organizations, universities, cities, or business consortiums. Firms with current or potential position openings can participate in the fairs and have sales and/or human resources representatives on hand at their booths to meet and talk with applicants. In effect, job fairs provide firms with an opportunity to conduct initial screening interviews with a large number of potential candidates and to identify a pool of individuals for formal interviews.

At trade shows, manufacturers and vendors sometimes post signs advertising open positions for distributors and sales agents. Salespeople also actively seek sales jobs at high-tech trade shows by handing out their résumés and asking that they be passed on to the appropriate hiring manager in the firm. Smart job seekers take the opportunity to ask trade show personnel questions to learn what it would be like to work at different firms. Recruiting at both job fairs/career conferences and trade shows can be accomplished at very little cost to the company.

E-RECRUITING E-recruiting is becoming increasingly common, particularly since firms can quickly and economically generate a large pool of candidates using this method.[15] Potential applicants can go to a firm's website where job openings are posted on an electronic bulletin board. Job data banks are available at such sites as: *www.monster.com*; *www.acareerinsales.com*; *www.marketingjobs.com*; and *www.careerbuilder.com*. Firms regularly post their job openings on websites, including Facebook and ZipRecruiter.[16]

Because the response to online ads can exceed expectations, firms may utilize key words to electronically evaluate and sort qualified from unqualified applicants. This process reduces the time managers must personally devote to the task. Of course, it is the total cost of generating applicants—finding interested personnel and screening the applications—that managers must consider when computing the cost of acquiring a pool of applicants for open sales positions. As we have pointed out repeatedly, the quality of the applicant pool is significantly more important than the size of the pool.

Selection Procedures

Once a pool of applicants for a sales position has been identified for further consideration, it is important to follow a formal interview process. An objective selection process allows the sales manager to assess the qualification levels of the applicant pool and gain essential information that is needed to select the best person for the job. The five stages of the selection process include:

- having the candidate complete an application form;
- testing the candidate;
- personally interviewing the candidate;
- verifying the candidate's background information; and
- conducting a physical exam (when appropriate).

Application Forms

An **application form** is an electronic or paper form that requires the job candidate to provide a standard list of information about his or her background, education, and work experience. Although most sales applicants initially submit an electronic or paper résumé, for a number of excellent reasons, applicants are required to complete an application form. First, completed application forms provide managers with consistent information about candidates' formal education, former positions, start/stop dates, levels of responsibility, and supervisors. Also application forms have to be signed by the candidates, thereby granting the firm legal permission to verify the information they provide.

Second, completing an application form requires the job candidates to read and follow directions, respond to questions, and express themselves—offering sales managers an initial impression of each applicant. Companies utilize software to scan electronic application forms for identifying applicants with pertinent skills or interests, as explained by Will May and AppDynamics in the sales manager profile at the beginning of this chapter. Also, firms use screening software to check application forms submitted online for misspellings and improper grammar usage.

Third, sales managers can use the information gleaned from applications to develop personal interview questions. For example, a sales manager wanting to find out how well applicants planned during their college or university days might formulate a question as follows: "I see that you majored in art history [or any subject] when you were a student at the University of Georgia. What motivated you to choose art history as a major for your undergraduate studies?" Likewise, application forms provide sales managers with the opportunity to find inconsistencies in dates or other questionable entries that can be probed during personal interviews. An example of one area that may need further exploration during the personal interview is why someone has frequently changed employers. Studies show that a person's length of employment at one firm strongly influences how long the applicant will remain employed with a new firm.[17]

Application forms should not ask questions about an applicant's marital status, gender, religion, race, age, or handicaps. Firms and sales managers soliciting this information can be accused of illegal discrimination. Exhibit 8.5 outlines the various U.S. legislative acts that define and prohibit discrimination. These legal standards are enforced by the Equal Employment Opportunity Commission (EEOC) and the Office of Federal Contract Compliance (OFCC). Firms can, however, inquire about an applicant's military service, because they must generally report this information to the U.S. government as a condition of doing business with the government. A few applicants might deliberately add unrequested information about marital status, race, or gender on their application forms in an effort to establish a reason for not being hired. To avoid complaints of discrimination, the company should immediately inform these applicant(s) that any additional information of the sort added to the application form will result in the applicant being disqualified for further consideration.[18]

Testing

Firms test applicants to try to confirm what they have learned about candidates during the interview process. That is, testing offers managers another perspective on the applicant. A **psychological test** is a method of sampling small, representative sets of behavioral responses gathered under uniform conditions. The samples are then scored, based upon pre-determined rules or formulae.[19] A range of psychological tests, available to sales managers, includes personality, intelligence, ability, and aptitude tests.

Personality tests are designed to measure traits that motivate sales applicants—such as their empathy and ego. Since it is difficult to identify specific traits for a sales position, personality tests are the most difficult to validate. Examples of personality tests include the Multiple Personal Inventory and the Gordon Personal Profile.

Firms use **intelligence tests** to estimate the quality of information acquired and used by the applicant. Instruments such as the Wonderlic Personnel Test can be completed in 12-15 minutes. This test measures applicants' memory, reasoning, and

EXHIBIT 8.5 **U.S. Legislative Acts Prohibiting Employment Discrimination**

Civil Rights Act of 1964	Prohibits discrimination against any individual with respect to compensation, terms, conditions, or privileges of employment, because of race, color, religion, sex, or national origin.
Age Discrimination in Employment Act (1967)	Prohibits discrimination against an individual between 40 and 70 years of age, with respect to their compensation, terms, conditions, or privileges of employment.
Equal Employment Opportunity Act (1972)	Amends the Civil Rights Act of 1964 and empowers the Equal Employment Opportunity Commission (EEOC) to prevent any person from engaging in any unlawful employment practice.
Rehabilitation Act of 1973	Requires firms that employ 50 or more workers, and that bid on federal contracts in excess of $50,000, to affirmatively hire and promote handicapped workers.
Vietnam Era Veterans Readjustment Act (1974)	Requires employers with federal contracts or subcontracts of $100,000 or more (after 2003) to provide equal opportunity and affirmative action for Vietnam-era veterans, special disabled veterans, and veterans who served on active duty during a war, campaign, or expedition.
Uniform Guidelines on Employee Selection Procedures (1978)	These guidelines are based upon, and supersede, previously issued guidelines on employee selection procedures. They have been built upon court decisions, the previously issued guidelines, and practical experience of the agencies, as well as the standards of the psychological profession.
Americans with Disabilities Act (1990)	Prohibits discrimination against qualified individuals with disabilities with regard to job application procedures, hiring, advancement, discharge, compensation, job training, and other terms, conditions, and privileges of employment for firms with 15 or more workers.

verbal ability. Another intelligence test is the Otis Self-Administering Test of Mental Ability. A few firms also ask sales applicants to list their SAT Reasoning Test scores.

Ability tests are designed to estimate the current capacity of an applicant to effectively perform specific tasks, such as reasoning. For example, the Customer Contact Aptitude Series (CCAS), measures the core reasoning abilities related to sales and customer service positions. **Aptitude tests,** like ability tests, measure whether an applicant has an interest in or an ability to perform certain tasks—like selling. The Campbell Interest and Skill Survey (*www.pearsonassessments.com/tests/ciss.htm*) is one such test. An applicant's aptitude test scores can be compared to the scores of the firm's current successful salespeople who have also taken the test. Obviously, then, aptitude testing is less appropriate for applicants who have no sales experience.

Testing experts recommend that, rather than relying upon a single test score like the SAT, sales managers should base their hiring decision on college grades, which are a more recent measure of a person's aptitudes.[20] In other words, grades show not only what the applicant has the ability to learn, but what she or he actually worked on and did learn.

There are also additional tests that predict success in specific sales positions. One such test, pioneered by a subsidiary of International Risk Management Institute (IRMI) of Dallas, Texas, identifies the traits a salesperson needs in order to be successful. Early in the interview process, the applicant completes a 15-20 minute exam that identifies traits. The results of the test provide interviewers with the common traits top (and bottom) sales candidates have, as well as "red flags" or concerns about the individual candidate being tested. An IRMI spokesman claims that the exam goes beyond personality testing and determines whether candidates have the "thinking orientation to be good in sales and like it."

Sales managers favor the system, because it not only prevents them from hiring people with the wrong personalities for sales jobs, but it also generates questions that allow them to customize the interview process for those candidates who are a good

Many sales firms require applicants to complete formal tests to identify traits that have been shown to lead to sales success.

fit. The managers are also provided with appropriate answers for each question, to which they can compare candidates' answers.[21]

Regardless of the test administered, a firm must ensure it is "valid." That is, the test must differentiate applicants based upon who will be successful and unsuccessful on the job. If a test routinely indicates that men, women, minority, or other members of society are less qualified, it's possible the test is biased. There are statistical procedures for validating these tests. If challenged to defend its tests in a legal venue, based upon one of the legislative acts shown in Exhibit 8.6, the firm will be required to provide specific information to the courts.

Sales managers are often skeptical about the likelihood of tests to predict the future sales success of candidates—and with good reason: Research has shown that no one personality or mental ability test will determine a salesperson's success.[22] This finding supports the recommendation that testing should be utilized as a confirming factor in the selection process—not an eliminating factor.[23] No applicant should be denied employment based upon a personality or mental ability test when all other factors paint an entirely different picture of the applicant.

EXHIBIT 8.6 Examples of Questions Asked on Different Sales Hiring Tests	
Personality Test Questions Applicants are asked to respond on a scale with anchors of "strongly agree" to "strongly disagree."	1. I get stressed out easily. 2. I put others first.
Intelligence Test Questions Respondents answer each question as true or false.	1. Two of the following numbers add up to 13: 1, 6, 3, 5, 11. 2. A pie can be cut into more than 7 pieces by making only 4 diameter cuts through its center.
Ability Test Questions In question 1, the answer is one-half of the previous number of .125, which is presented as a multiple-choice response. In question 2, Grace should aim her kick at point B. This is presented as a multiple-choice response.	1. What number comes next in the following sequence? 16, 8, 4, 2, 1, .5, .25 2. Grace wants to kick a ball to John. At what point below should Grace aim her kick? Grace John X X A B C D
Aptitude Test Questions Applicants are asked to respond on a scale with anchors of "strongly agree" to "strongly disagree."	1. I like to study and solve math or science problems. 2. I like to lead and persuade people and sell ideas and things.
Emotional Intelligence Test Questions Applicants are asked to respond on a scale with anchors of "strongly agree" to "strongly disagree."	1. I do not get angry when verbally attacked. 2. In my life, the stress never ends.

The Personal Interview

The personal interview is considered by many people to be the most important stage in the hiring process. Managers rely heavily upon it, especially because testing applicants can be expensive. During **personal interviews**, job candidates appear before the firm's sales managers and other employees. Firms understand that multiple interviewers at both the managerial and peer levels result in a more accurate overall assessment than those provided by a single interviewer. Next, we discuss the different types of interviews sales managers typically conduct.

STRUCTURED INTERVIEWS A **structured interview** means that, prior to meeting with applicants, the sales manager or interview team prepares a list of questions along with a range of acceptable answers, like the ones shown in Exhibit 8.7. The questions and answers are designed to cut across an applicant's background, work experiences, formal education, sales experience, and hobbies. In a structured interview, all applicants are asked the same questions.

Structured interviews have several advantages. First, if the sales manager is new at interviewing applicants, a structured interview offers confidence and "structure" to the process. Second, this approach ensures that important areas are covered during the interview, because managers have a prepared list of questions to ask. Finally, standard questions make it easier to record and compare applicants' responses. With multiple interviewers, a structured interview more readily allows them to compare their notes and discuss the answers applicants provided.

One concern about structured interviews is that less-experienced sales managers may simply follow the questions on the list and fail to probe for responses that deviate from the expected answers. For example, the interviewer might focus on reading the questions and recording the applicant's responses, rather than critically evaluating the applicant. After asking a question, a sales manager needs to evaluate the answer, probe further when necessary, and take sufficient notes with which to compare candidates later. According to one study, structured interviews predict—twice as reliably—how well a person will perform on the job.[24]

Sales managers view the personal interview as the most important aspect of the hiring process.

SEMI-STRUCTURED INTERVIEWS A **semi-structured interview** allows sales managers to ask a series of open-ended questions that applicants can address in their own words. An example of a semi-structured question might be: "Why are you interested in a sales position?" Then, after the interviewee answers, "I enjoy the freedom and travel," the sales manager can delve more deeply by asking: "What do you enjoy specifically about business travel?" The belief is that a semi-structured interview

EXHIBIT 8.7   Structured Interview Questions and Answers

Questions:	Listen For:	List & Rate Answer +/–:
What has been your proudest achievement?	Cites examples of his or her selling success.	
Have you ever gone against others to do something you believed was right?	Yes, offers a clear example.	
What do you like about being in sales?	Independence, unlimited earning potential, helping others.	
How do you persuade reluctant buyers?	By finding and satisfying the buyers' need(s).	
Why do you want to work for this company?	He or she can help the firm grow and/or satisfy buyers' needs.	
With what kind of boss do you work best?	A boss who allows freedom, communicates expectations, and helps as needed.	
Some people like to plan their day's activities in advance. How do you do this?	Offers a specific, detailed strategy.	
What have you found to be the best way to change someone else's mind?	By appealing to the person's needs, feelings, and concerns.	
What is the best way to develop your specific life goal?	By focusing on family, and by contributing to the firm and society.	
You have a buyer who wants to buy immediately, but you are not sure the product is right for buyer. What do you do?	Would not sell the product until certain it is what the customer needs, and that he or she will be truly satisfied with it.	

allows the interviewer to gain insight about the applicant as the discussion moves along a natural, logical course. Some firms extend the semi-structured interview by asking detailed questions about actual situations. For example, the interviewee might be instructed: "Tell me about a time when an irate buyer called you, what had upset the buyer, and how you successfully handled the situation." The sales manager or interviewer must identify areas that require more probing and be able to redirect the discussion should it veer off course. Firms use the semi-structured format more often when interviewing candidates for higher-level sales management jobs. The goal in this situation isn't to try to assess whether the candidate has given the "right or wrong" answers, but to gain a sense of his or her overall strategic sales vision for the firm. A semi-structured interview is more likely to lend itself to this purpose.

OTHER TYPES OF INTERVIEWS Firms often employ role playing or field exercises during the interview process. In a **stress interview**, the interviewer places the applicant in an unstructured situation to see how well he or she will perform. For example, an applicant might be asked to sell the interviewer an item—a pen, ashtray, or piece of furniture—to demonstrate his or her selling skills. The basic premise is that, if the salesperson makes a solid attempt to sell whatever she or he is asked to sell, then there is a higher likelihood the applicant does not suffer from call reluctance.

A myriad of role-playing techniques can be used in a stress interview.[25] For example, the interviewer can behave as a customer might—ignoring the applicant; being rude and obnoxious or inquisitive; or sitting in silence, waiting for the applicant to react. It is important for sales managers to have a pre-determined range of acceptable responses in mind when conducting role plays. In other words, sales managers need to decide what the applicant must or must not do to pass the stress interview. For example, they might agree to eliminate applicants who negatively respond to confrontational "customers" (in this case, the interviewers). A sales manager should understand, however, that if an interview is too stressful, the applicant might become discouraged and look elsewhere for employment. Firms that use stress and role-play interviews often do so in conjunction with either structured or semi-structured interviews.

A sales applicant may also need to be prepared for a group or panel interview. In the **group interview**, a several applicants for the position are placed in a group or open forum and encouraged to ask questions. Applicants are favored who ask insightful questions rather than sitting quietly. A second type of **panel interview** involves placing a single applicant before a panel of two or more company representatives. In effect, the interviewers play off each others' questions and the applicant's responses. It is important for the applicant to maintain composure in this situation, and to maintain eye contact with all members of the panel.[26]

Another form of stress or "surprise" interview is the field observation or "ride-along." A **field observation** allows an applicant to travel with, and observe, a salesperson making calls on current and potential clients. Each applicant for sales positions at Prentice Hall is required to ride along with a current sales rep for a day. This activity gives sales force applicants a realistic view of the job for which they are applying. Is it the type of job the candidate wants to do every day, for example? Firms can also have applicants attend a social function to gauge their fit with the sales team, or ask candidates to brainstorm a problem with the sales team. Exercises such as these allow sales managers to observe how applicants behave and interact in the day-to-day business environment.

Background Verification

The past performance of a candidate is, of course, a potential indicator of the person's future performance. The problem is that candidates may exaggerate or even lie about their past performance. In fact, one study reported that human resources managers *routinely* observe job candidates exaggerating their educational requirements, salaries, or time working for former employers.[27] That's why it's so important for sales managers, human resources personnel, or independent background-checking firms to verify the information candidates list on their application forms.

One way to gauge the honesty of applicants is to ask judgment-neutral or factual questions[28] on the application form. These are questions about the applicant's starting and ending dates of employment, position(s) and ranks held, accounts managed, level of sales, sales training completed, and, where permissible, salary earned. If background checks uncover the applicant has given false information, this raises concerns about the applicant's basic honesty, trustworthiness, and reliability. (One of the authors of this book watched a former student lose a job offer for a sales position by claiming that his final collegiate grade-point-average was 3.20 when, in fact, it was 3.18!)

Sales managers also need to contact the references listed by candidates they are seriously considering hiring, but should understand that applicants have, most likely, referred them to individuals who will only say positive things about them. It is also helpful to require applicants to provide different categories of references: business references, such as former clients or employers; financial references, like banks and financial institutions; and educational references, such as professors or counselors. To get a more independent assessment, you can ask a reference if she or he knows anyone else you can contact—someone who is familiar with the candidate's work. Many firms routinely conduct credit checks from providers such as Equifax. Firms that hire salespeople who are responsible for handling money are more likely to conduct credit and more extensive background checks. Many, if not most, firms today search applicants' names online to uncover examples of immoral or illegal behavior.

Physical Exam

The final stage of the selection process is the physical exam. Firms used to require drug tests and physical exams as part of their normal hiring procedures, but the Americans with Disabilities Act (ADA) of 1990 prohibits pre-employment physicals. However once the job offer has been extended, the employer can require all applicants to complete a medical exam that focuses on job-related physical requirements. It is not permissible for the firm to ask whether the applicant *has* a disability or to ask about the severity of an obvious disability.[29] A job offer may not be made conditional upon the results of a medical exam.[30] However, the firm can legally ask the following type of question if there are certain physical abilities related to the job: "The job involves lifting 25-pound boxes on a regular basis. Is this something you would be able to accomplish?"

Making the Job Offer

Once all applicants have completed the interview process, the sales manager or interview team normally ranks each applicant in terms of fit and potential for contributing to the firm. Then, the sales manager contacts the top applicant to make a job offer. The sales manager should call the top applicant and ask if she or he is still interested in a sales position with the company. If the answer is "yes," then the sales manager should describe the position's responsibilities and make the job offer.

Sometimes, applicants attempt to delay accepting the position, especially if they are highly competent, have interviewed with several firms, and are waiting on more than one job offer. That's why, after talking with the applicant on the phone, the sales manager should send the finalist a first-class letter containing a formal offer of employment. The letter should also clearly state a deadline for accepting the position, as well as include the salesperson's responsibilities, starting salary, allowable moving expenses, formal training dates, time before his or her first performance review, when he or she will first be eligible for a raise, and the number of vacation days he or she has been allotted.

This completes the standardized process sales managers utilize when hiring new salespersons for their firm. As Exhibit 8.8 shows, the sales manager uses applications forms, tests, formal interviews, background checks, and physicals to ensure the applicants meet the standards established earlier in the process. Should an applicant not meet a standard, as shown in Exhibit 8.8, they are rejected. Even after being hired, managers must remember to evaluate the performance of new hires and then add that information to the standards they seek when hiring future sales personnel.

Transitioning New Hires

Because of the strategic importance of hiring high-quality salespersons, the sales manager must often go beyond simply making the best candidate a job offer. For example, allowing high-level job-offer recipients and their spouses to tour the area in which they will be working can provide them with a clearer understanding of their life if they accept the career opportunity. Sales reps, like all employees, want to feel respected and assured that the company is a good fit for them. Showing that your company is a unique or exciting place to work can also help seal the deal. Emphasizing the selling points of the job itself, and the career development opportunities that it provides—as well as selling the firm's image and brand—can increase the appeal of the sales opportunity.

Once a candidate accepts the job, the sales manager's role shifts to building the new sales hire's commitment to the company and enhancing his or her ability to succeed on the job. It can also be helpful to ask what persuaded the person to say "yes" and what she or he thought of each company contact and the hiring process.

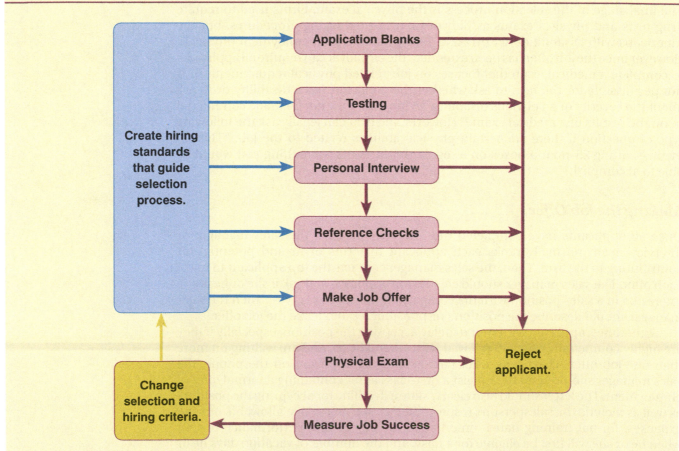

EXHIBIT 8.8   **Model for Selecting New Salespersons**

Many companies send job and company information that can ease the new hire's transition. Firms also send welcome packages of company materials: pens, paper, and company logo shirts. If there is a transition time before the first day of work, a company should invite the new salesperson to social events and talk regularly by phone to maintain enthusiasm for the new position. Once the new hire is on the job, a recent study suggests that firms should have a well-structured onboarding program that includes mentors and in-person group training, a meaningful first-day program, and testing at the end of the onboarding program that includes additional help to bring the new hire up to speed.[31]

Why a Diverse Sales Force is Important

The current growth of the U.S. population is being driven by racial and ethnic minorities. In 2012, the estimated Hispanic population of the U.S. was 53 million individuals. More than 19 million people in the U.S. are Asian, and 40 million are African American. Over the past decade, Asian population growth rates exceeded Hispanic increases, which outpaced African-American growth. Hispanic population increases were driven by two factors: immigration and, perhaps more importantly, domestic births. Much of the Asian increase was attributable to immigration. Given these demographic trends, sales managers and salespersons need to understand that more than 110 languages are spoken in the U.S. today, and that, by 2043, Anglo Americans will comprise the minority of the U.S. population.[32]

A sales manager must remain abreast of the changing marketplace and how a demographic shift increases the need to hire a more diverse sales force—one that reflects the buying community being served. To increase the diversity of a firm's sales force, and to prosper in a changing marketplace, firms and their sales managers must:

- institute recruiting and selection procedures that do not discriminate against candidates based upon nationality, ethnicity, age, and/or gender;

- offer opportunities for older salespersons to work later in their lives; and

- recognize that not all families are traditional, which results in differing employee needs for parental leave, on-site childcare, job sharing, switching between full- and part-time responsibilities, and adoption support.

A number of firms have increased their partnerships with the National Black MBA Association and Historically Black Colleges and Universities in order to increase the level of recruitment of high quality minority candidates.

The need to hire a diverse workforce is even more important today, because many businesses are expanding globally to either remain or become more competitive. As the "Global Sales Management" box shows, buyers report that firms staff their global sales forces with representatives who do not offer the level of service needed by the buying organization. However, in their defense, sales managers face complicating factors when selecting a global salesperson—including culture and language. During the selection process, applicants raised in another culture may respond differently than do local candidates. For example, in collectivist or group-oriented cultures, the applicant will not try to sell him- or herself. If the candidate was raised in a culture with high "power distance," or the belief that managers are of superior status, he or she is unlikely to ask the hiring manager questions and may speak only when spoken to by

Good sales managers understand the many benefits that derive from hiring a diverse sales force that mirrors the marketplace.

the higher-status sales manager. Lastly, in some cultures, it is considered aggressive or rude to look directly at someone for long periods of time. A U.S. sales manager might mistakenly believe that a candidate who looks away during the interview is being evasive.[33]

In the final analysis, however, a firm's sales effort is no better than the weakest member of the sales team. It is up to the sales manager to ensure the best-qualified candidates are hired for open sales positions—both domestically and abroad—regardless of their age, gender, culture, marital status, race, or religion.

GLOBAL SALES MANAGEMENT   **What Role Does Hiring Play in Buyer Satisfaction?**

Buyer perceptions of salespersons in Australia, Canada, France, Germany, the United Kingdom, and the United States are not very flattering. That is, buyers have described salespersons as being unwilling to listen and take "no" for an answer, lacking product knowledge, and acting pushy and deceptive! Global buyers, in general, hold negative attitudes toward sales—judging from the percentage of respondents to a study who agreed that they would not be proud to call themselves a "salesperson." This figure differed by country, with more than 50 percent of respondents in France and the U.K. agreeing, and more than 40 percent of buyers in Germany and Canada aligning with the statement. German salespersons were most likely to provide buyers with the support needed, while Australian buyers felt they received the lowest support levels. Buyers from all six countries suggested the following for salespersons:

1. Be prepared for each meeting and understand the client's business.
2. Listen to buyers' needs and provide solutions.
3. Create "win-win" solutions.

Many respondents perceived that salespeople lack the temperament, desire, and core skills needed to succeed. Fortunately, temperament and desire can be identified and confirmed during the selection and interview process. The study should be a wake-up call for global businesses, to ensure that they hire well-qualified sales reps who can properly assess and address buyer needs.

Based upon Mitchell, Simon, Bradford Thomas, and Paul Hughes (2007). *Is the Sales Force Delivering Business Value?* Development Dimensions International, Inc.

Avoiding Common Hiring Mistakes

Finding and hiring the "right" person for an open sales job is difficult unless the sales manager adheres to a comprehensive recruiting and selection process. Sales managers should be especially careful to avoid making the following mistakes:

RUSHING TO HIRE SOMEONE Sales managers often fall into the trap of hiring someone quickly to cover open sales territories, and don't look hard enough at candidates' actual capabilities and interests. Not only will such an approach result in hiring the wrong representative, it is likely to result in the sales manager's recruiting of people with similar backgrounds, educational attainment, or social interests as him- or herself—rather than diverse employees. Moreover, if the wrong person is hired, and then quits or fails shortly thereafter, this leaves the sales manager in a worse position than if she or he had taken time to conduct a proper search initially.

FAILING TO CONDUCT A PROPER JOB ANALYSIS Sales managers are busy with day-to-day activities. Still, they must find time to evaluate the jobs they're trying to fill, so as to identify essential skills, knowledge, and activities that the new hire should possess to succeed. This is especially true if the products, the way the firm sells, or the company's customer base, are changing.

NOT GENERATING A SUFFICIENTLY LARGE APPLICANT POOL The goal is to have a large enough group of qualified individuals from which to select the best applicants to be interviewed and hired. Too often, sales managers interview only a handful of applicants, because doing so requires less work and consumes less time.

POOR INTERVIEW PLANNING Oftentimes, sales managers interview candidates "off the cuff." This can often result in a poor set of interviews being conducted or a set of interviews that aren't easily comparable. Another pitfall occurs with multiple firm interviewers involved—and no one taking the time to coordinate and train them to properly interview candidates.

NOT CONDUCTING A COMPREHENSIVE INTERVIEW Too often, sales managers ask a few questions and then decide whether or not they will hire the candidate. They believe, incorrectly, that their own experiences as successful sales representatives allow them to make accurate hiring decisions on the spot.

NOT PERFORMING A BACKGROUND CHECK A recent study found that as many as 20 percent of applicants fabricate facts and accomplishments on their résumé and application form. When a sales manager fails to check a candidate's facts prior to offering a sales job, this increases the likelihood of hiring someone of dubious character. Always conduct a thorough background check.

Evaluating the Success of the Firm's Sales Force Recruiting and Selection Efforts

Because recruiting and selection consume so much of the firm's resources and sales managers' time, it is imperative that an evaluation of applicant sources be performed as shown in Exhibit 8.9. In effect, an evaluation allows the sales manager

EXHIBIT 8.9   Evaluating Applicant Source Matrix—Evaluation Criteria

Sales Applicant Sources	Strategic or Opportunistic Hire?	Number of Applicants Generated	Number of Applicants Hired	Percent Retained After Three Years	Cost	Number of Times Used	Percent with Above Average Performance After Two Years
Internal Applicants • Technical • Non-Technical							
Referrals • Internal • External							
Advertisements • Newspapers • Magazines							
Private Recruiters							
Educational Institution • Four-Year • Two-Year							
Electronic Websites • Internal • External							
Job/Career Fairs							

to determine the effectiveness of each applicant source. The matrix can be tracked on a spreadsheet program, and sales executives can utilize the information derived from the matrix to evaluate the managerial skills of field sales managers who are responsible for selecting and hiring new salespersons.

Managing Your Career

Before you graduate from college, you will more than likely search for a sales job. The material taught in this chapter explains the recruiting and selection process you will encounter in your job search. As a result, you will not be surprised if the hiring firm asks you to take a test, puts you into a multiple-person stress interview, or requests that you ride along with a current sales rep. You will know what to expect, feel more comfortable during the interview, and most likely perform at a higher level. Later, when you become a sales manager, the information in this chapter provides you with guidance for correctly setting up an interview process that is legal, ethical, thorough, and successful. Hiring new sales personnel is one of the most important actions undertaken by a sales manager. Anyone can hire a new salesperson, but the most successful sales managers are consistently able to hire the best sales applicants!

Summary

Hiring a salesperson is an extremely important undertaking by the firm. The five steps related to hiring are: determining the number of salespersons needed; identifying the skills, knowledge, and attitudes salespersons need to succeed; attracting a sufficient number of qualified applicants; performing an interview process that accurately assesses applicants' qualifications; and offering one or more applicants a sales position. In smaller firms, sales managers are generally responsible for these activities; however, in larger firms, human resources personnel may perform one or more of these activities.

By conducting a thorough job analysis and writing an accurate job description, a sales manager can accurately identify the qualifications needed to do a job. The exact job qualifications can then be posted in advertisements designed to generate applicants. A variety of sources are utilized to generate applicants: referrals, advertisements, job fairs, universities, and web job sites. The interview or selection process includes application forms, testing, personal interviews, background checks, and physical exams.

The personal interview is the most important part of the recruiting process. Sales managers can use structured, unstructured, and semi-structured interviews, but structured interviews have been proven to be most effective. Other personal interview techniques include role plays, panel and stress interviews, and field observations.

Common mistakes that sales managers make when managing the hiring process include rushing to fill an open sales position, failing to perform an accurate job analysis, generating too few applicants, devoting inadequate time preparing for formal interviews, conducting an abbreviated interview, and omitting background checks on finalists. Making any one of these mistakes will result in the manager hiring the wrong applicant.

Key Terms

ability tests   171
application form   169
aptitude tests   171
blind advertisements   167
emotional intelligence   171
external applicants   166
field observations   174
group interviews   174
intelligence tests   170
internal applicants   165
job analysis   164
job description   164

job fairs   169
networking   166
panel interviews   174
personal interviews   172
personality tests   170
psychological tests   170
recruiting   165
semi-structured interview   173
stress interviews   174
structured interviews   172
turnover rate   162

Questions and Problems

1. Should a firm's selection process be initiated whenever there is an opening? Or should the process be on-going? Would the hiring effort vary by firm size or industry?

2. Suppose a firm typically employees 15 salespeople. During the course of the year, two salespeople leave the firm for higher-paying jobs, one salesperson is fired, and one salesperson retires. Using this numbers, calculate the turnover rate of the firm's sales force for the year.

3. Why should sales managers investigate reasons for turnover? Why is it important to compare a firm's turnover against industry turnover rates?

4. What benefits are likely to be gained by conducting a job analysis? What options does a sales manager have to analyze how a salesperson performs the required duties? How is the information gathered, and how is a job analysis utilized?

5. How are job descriptions and statements of job qualifications related? Why is it difficult to determine the necessary qualifications for a new hire?

6. How many applicants should be recruited if a firm needs to hire three salespeople, and 20 percent of applicants are offered a job, but only 50 percent accept the offer?

7. What are the advantages and disadvantages of recruiting internal versus external candidates for sales positions? Discuss the four types of tests that firms rely upon when screening candidates. Why is it important for firms to validate the tests they use?

8. Why is the personal interview the most important step in the sales selection process? What are the advantages and disadvantages of structured and semi-structured interviews? What can a sales manager learn about a candidate by conducting a stress test or a field observation?

9. Why is it important to conduct a background check on a candidate prior to offering him or her a sales position? What specific information should be verified by a background check? Can a firm require a candidate to take a physical exam prior to being offered a sales position?

10. Why is it important for sales managers to try to increase the diversity of their sales forces?

Role Play

Rushmore Industries Plans for Salesperson Interviews

James Ford manages the sales effort at Rushmore Industries (RI), located in Rapid City, South Dakota. In two weeks, six finalists will visit the Rapid City office for personal interviews, as candidates for an open sales position. Ford realizes that the personal interview is, perhaps, the most important component of the selection process, and that—in order to be as objective as possible—he must have a plan to minimize subjectivity and bias during the interviews. Ford prefers to use a structured interview process. That is, he will review a list of 10-12 standardized questions he has utilized in the past, making sure they are in line with the duties of the open position. He knows he must also meet with his colleagues on the human resources staff to ensure that the selection process is conducted within the confines of existing laws. Ford has also asked Jennifer Grawey of the marketing office to conduct an unstructured interview with all six applicants. Lastly, Ford wants each applicant to ride along with current salespersons, to provide a stress situation component that offers a different viewpoint of each applicant. The question is: how should all of these activities be planned and coordinated?

Characters in the Role Play

James Ford, sales manager at RI

Jennifer Grawey, marketing manager at RI

Shandiz Butler, human resources director at RI

Assignment

Break into groups of three, with each student in the group assuming the role of one character. You may change the first name of the character to your own, if that is more comfortable for role-playing. Prior to meeting as a group, work individually to complete your plans for conducting structured, unstructured, and ride-along interview components for each of the six finalists for the sales position at RI. Then meet and role-play the meeting between James, Jennifer, and Shandiz. Your objective is to conclude the meeting with an interview plan that is both logical and legal, and that answers the questions: Who? What? Where? When? and How?

Caselets

Caselet 8.1: *Southwestern Industrial*

Raine Tavener is regional sales manager for Southwestern Industrial, a supplier of industrial products for manufacturers of computer peripherals located in five southwestern U.S. states. Although Tavener's region has met its total sales and profitability goals during the past three years she has been sales manager, she is concerned about her region's turnover rate. The first year she was sales manager, the turnover rate was 16 percent, rising to 18 percent the second year, and increasing to a 23 percent rate the third year.

Each of the salespeople who resigned offered legitimate reasons for leaving. A few were old enough to retire; one or two found higher paying jobs; and, unfortunately, two salespeople just did not meet standards, and had to be let go. Tavener would like to reduce the annual turnover rate to below the industry average of 12 percent per year. She plans to analyze the situation over the next few weeks, talk to others—both inside and outside the firm—and present a proposal to upper management for revamping the recruitment and selection process.

Questions

1. What recommendations would you offer Raine Tavener for evaluating the current recruitment and selection process at Southwestern Industrial?
2. How would it help to compare the performances of all salespeople who either resigned or were let go?
3. Would it be helpful for Tavener to know how each salesperson was originally recruited? Why?
4. Should Tavener scrutinize the notes from the former salespeople's personal interviews, or study their pre-employment test scores? Assuming these items were available, what insight might they provide her?
5. How would you recommend that Southwestern recruit and select new salespersons?

Caselet 8.2: *Celestial International*

Gang "Jerry" Shu is a Chinese-born American, originally from Beijing—where he earned his undergraduate business degree. After emigrating to the U.S., he earned an MBA at Stanford University. Shu is currently the Asian regional sales manager for Celestial International, overseeing a sales force comprised of local hires (salespeople from the country in which they sell). One of Celestial's reps in Singapore recently left the firm to attend graduate school at the country's prestigious National University—creating a job vacancy. Shu recently traveled to Singapore to interview the three finalists generated by a Singaporean search firm. The candidates were:

1. Wu Lo Chin, a Chinese Singaporean with a B.S. from Nanyang University in Singapore. Although Chin has no sales experience, he has good connections in the Chinese business community. Chin answered seven of the ten structured interview questions correctly, made a satisfactory attempt to sell an expensive pen when asked, and told Jerry Shu that the job with Celestial was his "dream job."

2. P.C. Agarwal, an Indian Singaporean with a B.S. in chemical engineering from the University of Madras. Agarwal brings with him two years of newspaper advertising sales experience. However, he answered only five of the ten structured questions satisfactorily, and declined to sell a pen to Jerry Shu. Agarwal appeared arrogant, and admitted he was considering several job leads.

3. Ali Mohammed Najand, a Malaysian with Singaporean citizenship, has an MBA from the Malaysian International University in Kuala Lumpur. He provided correct answers to eight of the ten structured interview questions and made a solid attempt to sell the pen to sales manager Shu. However, one thing that bothered Shu was Ali's lack of eye contact and his subservient behavior, exemplified by his answering questions by saying, "Sir, I would…" or "Sir, the best way to…"

The territory that Celestial's new salesperson will cover serves a mixture of Chinese (85 percent), Malaysian (10 percent), and Indian (5 percent) businesses. Based upon the limited amount of information you have, which candidate do you believe Shu should hire? Why?

Questions

1. How helpful would a job description/qualifications be in this situation?
2. Given that the territory is predominantly Chinese, how should this influence Shu's decision?
3. Can you identify factors that might disqualify any of the finalists?
4. What explanation might you offer for Ali's behavior during the interview? What is your recommendation for Shu? Please justify your decision.

References

1. Shamis, Barry (2007). "Have You Ever Thought About the Cost of Hiring the Wrong Salesperson?" Accessed 5/27/2007. *www.salesrephire.com.*
2. *The Chally World Class Sales Sales Excellence Research Report (2007).* Dayton, OH: The HR Chally Group. Accessed 7/4/2014, *http://www.httraining.co.uk.*
3. Burton, Scott E. (2002). "The Realization of Human Capital Advantage through Recruiting and Selection," Development Dimensions International, Inc. White Paper, 1–7.
4. Salz, Lee B. (2014). "The Test That Most Executives Fail," *Sales & Marketing Management,* February 17. Accessed March 24, 2014. *http://www.salesandmarketing.com/content/test-most-executives-fail.*
5. Mitchell, Simon, Bradford Thomas, and Paul Hughes (2007). *Is the Sales Force Delivering Business Value?* Development Dimensions International, Inc.
6. Marshall, Greg W., Daniel J. Goebel, and William C. Moncrief (2003). "Hiring for Success at the Buyer-Seller Interface," *Journal of Business Research* 56, 247–255.
7. McMaster, Mark (2001). "Ask SMM," *Sales & Marketing Management,* December, 58.
8. Naumann, Earl, Scott M. Widmier, and Donald W. Jackson (2000). "Examining the Relationship Between Work Attitudes and Propensity to Leave Among Expatriate Salespeople," *Journal of Personal Selling & Sales Management,* Fall, 227–241.
9. Churchill, Gilbert A., Jr., Neil M. Ford, Steven W. Hartley, and Orville C. Walker, Jr. (1985). "The Determinants of Salesperson Performance: a Meta-Analysis," *Journal of Marketing Research,* (May), 103–118.
10. Campbell, Tricia (1999). "Finding Hidden Sales Talent," *Sales & Marketing Management,"* March, 84.
11. Soltis, Cheryl (2006). "Got a Good Hire? Your Reputation May Be on the Line," *The Wall Street Journal,* September 26, B8.
12. Raymond, Mary Anne, Les Carlson, and Christopher D. Hopkins (2006). "Do Perceptions of Hiring Criteria Differ for Sales Managers and Sales Representatives? Implications for Marketing Education," *Journal of Marketing Education,* 28 (April), 43–55.
13. Simon, Baylee (2006). "The Paper (Money) Chase," *Sales & Marketing Management,* July/August, 38-40, 42–43.
14. Weilbaker, Dan C. and Michael Williams (2006). "Recruiting New Salespeople from Universities: University Sales Centers Offer a Better Alternative," *Journal of Selling & Major Account Management,* 6:3 (Summer), 30–38.
15. Piturro, Marlene (2000). "The Power of E-cruiting," *Management Review,* 89:1 (January), 33–37.
16. Anonymous (2007). "Recruiting with Facebook," *The Week,* February 2, 5.
17. McMaster (2001).
18. Gable, Myron, Charles Hollon, and Frank Fangello (1992). "Increasing the Utility of the Application Blank: Relationship between Job Application Information and Subsequent Performance and Turnover of Salespeople," *Journal of Personal Selling & Sales Management,* (Summer), 39–55.
19. Dudley, G.W. (2007), "Sales Selection: Mental Testing," Working Paper, Dallas, TX: Behavioral Science Research Press, Inc.
20. Dunham, Kemba J. (2003). "More Employers Ask Job Seekers For SAT Scores," *The Wall Street Journal,* October 28, B1, B10.
21. Harris, Alana (2000). "Reducing the Recruiting Risks," *Sales & Marketing Management,* May, 18.
22. Churchill, Ford, Hartley and Walker (1985).
23. Dudley (2007).
24. Engle, Robert (1998). "Multi-Step, Structured Interviews to Select Sales Representatives in Russia and Eastern Europe," *European Management Journal,* 16:4, 476-484; Mak, C. (1995), "Successful People Selection in Action," *Health Manpower Management,* 21, 12–17.
25. Menkes, Justin (2005). "Hiring for Smarts," *Harvard Business Review,* 83:11, (November), 100–109.
26. About.com. Accessed December 25, 2007. *www.jobsearchtech.about.com/interview.*
27. Harris, Jim and Joan Brannick (1999). *Finding and Keeping Great Employees,* New York, NY: American Management Association.
28. Peck, David (2007). "Is Checking References During the Hiring Process a Waste of Time?" *Sales & Marketing Management,* April, 12.
29. Swift, Cathy Owens, Robert Wayland, and Jane Wayland (1993). "The ADA: Implications for Sales Managers," National Conference for Sales Management *Proceedings,* 146–148.
30. Shepherd, C. David, and James C. Heartfield (1991). "Discrimination Issues in the Selection of Salespeople: a Review and Managerial Suggestions," *Journal of Personal Selling & Sales Management,* Fall, 71.
31. Bradt, George (2012). "Survey Highlights Successful Onboarding Strategies for Salespeople," June 13, Accessed March 24, 2014. *www.forbes.com/sites/georgebradt/2012/06/13/survey-highlights-successful-onboarding-strategies-for-salespeople/.*
32. United States Census Bureau (2013). "Asians Fastest-Growing Race or Ethnic Group in 2012, Census Bureau Reports," June 13. Accessed March 26, 2014. *www.census.gov/newsroom/releases/archives/* population/cb13-112.html.
33. Honeycutt, Earl D., and Lew Kurtzman (2006). *Selling Outside Your Culture Zone,* Dallas, TX: Behavioral Science Research Press.
34. Harris and Brannick (1999).

TRAINING AND DEVELOPING THE SALES FORCE

LEARNING OBJECTIVES

After completing this chapter, you should be able to:

- Identify factors that help determine what types of training are needed by sales personnel.

- Summarize the inputs needed to design and deliver an effective sales training program.

- Explain why it's important to assess the effectiveness of a firm's sales training and what's involved in the assessment.

- Distinguish the elements that contribute to effective and ineffective training programs.

Hiring the most talented individuals to work for your organization is only the first step toward employing a successful sales force. After salespeople are hired, they need training to deal with the challenges of the job and workplace. A poorly trained sales force will be less likely to meet the needs of potential customers, thus opening the door to your competitors. The impact of losing customers—and their business—ultimately affects every department in an organization. Sales managers need to take steps to ensure that their sales forces have the skills and abilities to be successful on the job. This chapter examines how sales training efforts help to accomplish this task.

Sales Manager Profile: Eric McMillan

ERIC MCMILLAN
Area Business Manager
3M

IT IS DIFFICULT TO PREDICT where our experiences will take us. Eric McMillan started his university experience in chemistry classrooms and labs, studying the relationships between different dynamics and materials. As part of a summer internship, he was given the opportunity to go outside the lab and interact with the users of the products of the lab. There, he saw a different relationship—the one between the products made in a lab and the end users. That's when, he says, it really all "came together" for him. Since then, his work with 3M has offered a variety of experiences and taken him to a variety of places within the organization.

McMillan started in sales and technical service, and then had his own territory, where he worked developing channel members and industrial facilities to help them become more efficient and grow. From his work in the field, he moved to headquarters and transitioned into various sales training positions, where he was responsible for developing and delivering training for new and experienced sales personnel.

The training of the new and experienced reps was exciting and rewarding for McMillan. He enjoyed the opportunity to provide training and problem-solving skills that helped them start and expand on a successful career with 3M. "Each group has its own challenges. New reps have a great deal to learn, so there should be a balance of developing a strong foundation versus 'informational overload.'" As might be expected, experienced rep training can follow a totally different process and can be much more critical. Sales trainers have to balance between providing information on new areas, and enhancing and developing the existing skill sets of each experienced rep.

McMillan continued to work in training and development when he accepted a position as a Lean Six-Sigma Black Belt. This positioned him well for his current job as an area business manager with a sales team. The challenges of being a sale manager are many. When asked what he considers his highest priority as a sales manager, he has a quick response. "Continuous training, development, and coaching is part of the DNA of the 3M Company. It has been shown that effective coaching improves sales productivity. As the manager of my sales team, it is my highest priority. These activities are continuous and ongoing. I see a similarity between the best professional athletes and the best sales people. Professional athletes practice daily. Sales professional need to, also. With my team, we have practice, preparation, and then execution. You need to do this every day to remain relevant and real."

McMillan's sales team is spread out across a large city and part of another state. "It is nearly impossible to be with them all at once. While I prefer to coach in a face-to-face setting, we have to do what will work, so we often use field work opportunities and the phone on an informal basis. I'm talking with them daily, which opens an opportunity to coach. The number of contacts you have with the team is important; it helps develop individual skills and drives the growth of the team."

On a more formal basis, he meets individually with each sales rep for a monthly coaching meeting, and each quarter for a quarterly coaching meeting, along with the field work that he schedules with each team member. They typically review and work on key CRM activities that drive success. In addition, they schedule joint calls around key accounts and initiatives. "Training and coaching is an individualized activity; there is no 'one size fits all.'" Good coaching takes time. McMillan notes that one of the challenges sales managers face is to make sure to prioritize coaching as a top priority. "You have a large number of external activities you need to do, but coaching has to be part of your everyday activity."

When asked about suggestions for guiding new reps through a successful transition into the field, he is again drawn to understanding relationships—not chemical reactions this time—interactions he has noted between successful reps and their behaviors. "Newly hired reps should take some time to observe and note what the practices are of the 'best of the best.' Try to understand what they do to be successful and start trying to integrate those behaviors into your practices." Sounds like a good formula. ■

How Important is Sales Training?

Have you ever dealt with a salesperson who wasn't knowledgeable about the product or service that he was selling and in which you were extremely interested? It probably wasn't a reassuring experience. Organizations that utilize sales training do so because they see a number of benefits from this investment: trained sales representatives are more knowledgeable about their firm's products and services, the markets in which they operate, and the selling process than are their untrained counterparts. As a result of sales training, representatives are able to better understand their customers and deliver better service to them. This typically results in higher sales for the company, and higher incomes for the sales reps, who experience greater job satisfaction because they're successful.

Tim Owens, an agent for Northwestern Mutual Life Insurance, exemplifies this. Because of the sales training Owens has received, he understands the expenses associated with long-term care for a person suffering from a chronic illness or a disabling condition. As a result, Owens is able to show how a long-term insurance product may be of value to a Baby-Boomer-aged client. After graduating from college, Kellen Busey Richter went to work for TEKsystems, a leading technology staffing and services company. Because of the training she received, Richter knows how to provide valuable advice and personalized service to her clients when they are planning new technology projects. Their sales training has made them more successful, and both Owens and Richter are satisfied with their careers and are less likely to leave their organizations. Owens' and Richter's sales managers have benefited from the training, too, because they have to spend less time supervising the two salespeople.

When you think of it, would you want to have a relationship with a company that doesn't make an investment in the ongoing training of its sales personnel? Organizations that see sales training as "too expensive" or "too time consuming" seem to be ignoring its benefits. Another important component is how long it takes to get a new salesperson up to speed. One study of the insurance industry, for example, yielded this finding: the average company spends as much as $120,000 (in terms of lost sales opportunities, recruiting, training, development costs, and so forth) to get a new salesperson up to speed.[1] Lots of different numbers are thrown around in making an estimate on the value of sales training. However, by and large, most companies know that training their salespeople is critical—not only to their success, but to their very survival—as the following statistics show:

- Nationwide, across all industries, more than $164 billion is spent annually on formal training efforts.[2]

- Compared with all other areas of training, sales training receives the most funding, exceeded only by professional or industry-specific training. Funding spent on sales training exceeds management and supervisory training.[2,3]

Kudos go to the top sales training programs.

- Top-performing global companies typically invest in more than 57 hours of training per employee. Training for sales personnel exceeds that 1.5 week/year amount.[2]

- Ninety-four percent of sales personnel report that sales training helps them do their jobs better.[3]

Every year, *Selling Power* magazine publishes a list of the "50 Best Companies to Sell For" in the U.S. manufacturing and service industries.[4] The list includes only companies with sales forces greater than 500 people. The three criteria used to determine inclusion on the prestigious list are sales force compensation, career mobility, and training. The compensation category is a summary of average starting salaries, incentive pay plans, availability of company cars, and other benefits—such as health insurance—that representatives receive. The career mobility category considers the number of performance reviews that sales representatives receive, a firm's sales force turnover, and number of salespeople promoted. The training category includes both how much time a company invests in developing the initial selling skills and product knowledge of its representatives, and the follow-up training they receive. When you think about it, to a certain extent, training is the crux of these three criteria. After all, both a salesperson's compensation and career mobility are acutely affected by how well the person has been trained. With good training, a salesperson is more likely to maximize her performance, earn more money, and have greater career mobility.

Exhibits 9.1 and 9.2 show the companies on *Selling Power's* "50 Best Companies to Sell For" list, ranked in terms of their training scores during the time period 2010-2012. Only companies that made the list in each of the years 2010, 2011, and 2012 are included. In addition to those listed in the table, 10 other manufacturing and 11 other service companies were included over this period. To be included in this listing is considered quite an accomplishment.

EXHIBIT 9.1   Training Rankings of the "Best Manufacturing Companies to Sell For," 2010–2012

Company	2010	2011	2012	Total
Hilti	1	3	1	5
Forest Laboratories	3	1	2	6
3M	2	2	3	7
Nalco	4	4	5	13
Reynolds and Reynolds	5	5	6	16
Shaw Industries	6	6	1	19
Xerox	7	7	8	22
Ecolab	8	8	9	25
Hormel Foods	12	9	4	25
Microsoft	9	10	10	29
Parker Hannifin	10	11	11	32
Sanofi-Aventis	11	12	12	35
Johnson Controls	13	13	13	39
Thermo Fisher Scientific	14	14	14	42
Watson Pharmaceuticals	15	15	15	45

(Ten other companies were ranked during this period. Only the top 15 are included here.)
"50 Best Companies to Sell For," *Selling Power*, October/November/December, 2010-2012.

EXHIBIT 9.2   Training Ratings of the "Best Service Companies to Sell For," 2010–2012

Company	2010	2011	2012	Total
ABF Freight System	2	2	2	6
Applied Industrial Technologies	3	3	3	9
Heartland Payment Systems	1	4	4	9
Cintas	8	1	1	10
FedEx	5	5	5	15
Iron Mountain	6	6	6	18
CA	4	9	9	23
US Postal Service	7	8	8	23
ARAMark	11	10	10	31
First Data	12	12	12	36
Lawson Products	13	13	13	39
Career Builder	14	15	16	44
Northwestern Mutual	15	16	17	48
UniFirst	16	17	18	52
CDW	18	18	20	56

(Twelve other companies were ranked during this period. Only those making the list for the last three consecutive years are included here.)
"50 Best Companies to Sell For," *Selling Power*, October/November/December, 2010-2012.

The Training Process

The sales training process will be different for each firm—depending upon its size, resources, and the markets in which it operates. A small organization is likely to have neither the resources nor the level of specialization that a multinational organization has. In smaller firms, district or regional sales managers might be in charge of their firms' sales training. However, no matter what size firm they work for, one thing all sales managers have in common is their responsibility to help train their sales teams. This training can take the form of simply providing feedback and assistance to a salesperson on a training issue, or it could involve the teaching of a course. As Mike Kapocius, a regional sales manager for Takeda Pharmaceuticals, notes, "Training doesn't end when the class is over. Training goes on all the time." This is supported by research, which has found that for sales training to be effective, managers must provide follow-up training to their representatives to reinforce what they've learned.[5]

Regardless of an organization's size or the resources it has, the process sales managers should follow to develop an effective sales training programs is the same. A four-stage **sales training cycle,** from planning to delivery, is outlined in Exhibit 9.3. Identifying the topics to be covered and who to include in training are the first questions that must be addressed. After determining the firm's sales training needs comes the planning. What should be included in the content, who will staff the program, and what training format should be used to deliver it? Once the planning is complete, the program must be delivered in a manner that best facilitates learning. Evaluating the training effort at individual and organizational levels is the fourth stage. We will discuss each of these stages in more detail.

Identifying the Firm's Sales Training Needs

Most companies provide their new salespeople with training. More senior members of sales forces generally receive training to update them on their firms' new products and other market developments. Both of these situations would seem to warrant

EXHIBIT 9.3   The Sales Training Cycle

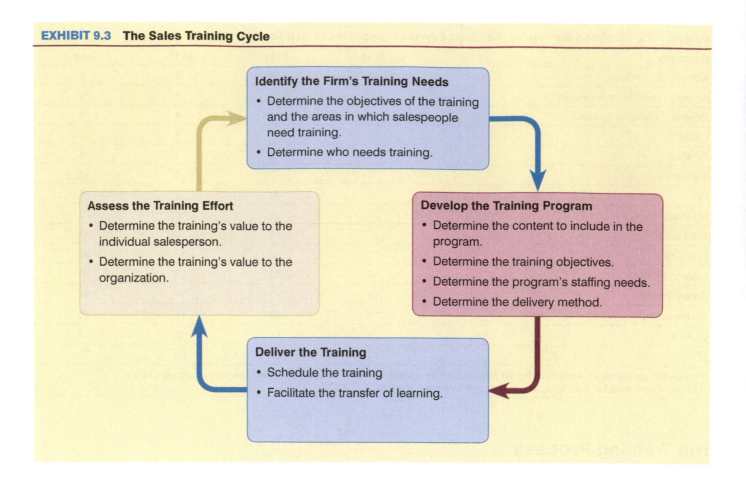

training. The latter situation would seem to be warranted when there is a difference between the outcomes the members of a firm's sales force are achieving versus what their sales managers want them to achieve. Wouldn't training correct the situation?

The fact is that training is not the solution for all of the problems a sales force faces. Moreover, sales training programs can be expensive and time-consuming. Before jumping to the conclusion that sales training is the "fix" you need, you must ask yourself, "Is additional training for the sales force the most appropriate response to the situation?" For example, low levels of compensation, morale, motivation, and job satisfaction among representatives might be problems no amount of training will remedy.

DETERMINING SALES TRAINING OBJECTIVES Assuming the sales training appears to be warranted, most experts recommend that sales managers consider three levels of information during the training planning stage: information from the organizational level, the task level, and the individual level.[6] Exhibit 9.4 offers a perspective on this process. The sources of information used to determine the training needs at all three assessment levels is displayed in Exhibit 9.5. The information can be collected through informal means, such as input provided by sales managers, upper management, training personnel, or customers; through formal means, such as customer surveys; or through performance measures like sales volumes, the turnover rates among representatives, and so forth.

At the **organizational level**, this information should reflect the firm's mission statement, strategic initiatives, and upper management's mandates, as well as the company's sales and marketing objectives.[7] **Task-level** information can be generated from sales managers' and trainers' observations, input from customers, and from commercially available training programs. **Individual-level** information is available from sales reps' performance reports, sales manager's observations of their representatives' performances, customers, and sales reps' self-reports.

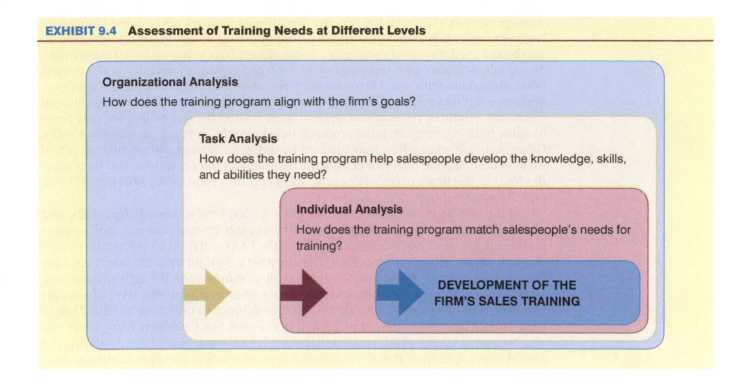

EXHIBIT 9.4   Assessment of Training Needs at Different Levels

Organizational Analysis

How does the training program align with the firm's goals?

Task Analysis

How does the training program help salespeople develop the knowledge, skills, and abilities they need?

Individual Analysis

How does the training program match salespeople's needs for training?

DEVELOPMENT OF THE FIRM'S SALES TRAINING

EXHIBIT 9.5   Sources of Training Needs Information

Input from:
- Sales managers
- Job incumbents
- Upper management
- Training personnel
- Customers

Performance Measures
- Sales volumes
- Customers service levels
- Customer complaints
- Turnover rates
- Number of sales calls conducted
- Profitability

Other
- Organizational objectives
- Sales training goals
- Observations of salespersons' skills
- Commercially available sales training programs

Determining Sales Training Needs

Based on Erffmeyer, Robert C.; Russ, Randall K. and Joseph F. Hair, Jr. (1991). "Needs Assessment and Evaluation in Sales-Training Programs," *Journal of Personal Selling & Sale Management*, (11)1, 18–30; and Honeycutt, Earl D., Jr. (1996), "Conducting a Sales Training Audit," *Industrial Marketing Management*, Vol. 25, 105–113.

The broadest level of analysis—**organizational analysis**—should reveal which of the firm's short-term and long-term strategic goals are being met, and the activities that need to be done to meet them. Wausau Insurance, which provides insurance to business owners, illustrates why it's so important for a firm to match its corporate strategy with its sales training process. Because of mergers and related changes in business structures, Wausau's corporate strategy changed, too. Instead of focusing on small- and medium-sized companies, Wausau began focusing on larger companies. As a result, Wausau's sales representatives, who had typically worked with the owners of small- and medium-sized firms, found themselves working with much larger firms, and more sophisticated, challenging clients. These clients required more complicated insurance products. Wausau's strategic change started the ball rolling for new types of sales training, ranging from proposal development to team presentation skills. Other strategic goals a firm may uncover by doing an organizational analysis might include reducing the turnover among the company's representatives, and increasing the level of the firm's overall sales or sales of certain products, by offering different types of sales training.

At the task level, the focus is on identifying what level of **knowledge, skills, and abilities (KSAs)** are needed for a firm's sales jobs. Job descriptions are good sources for this information. A job description will list the KSAs and tasks a salesperson should do, with whom, why, and how often. The information might indicate that, on a daily basis, a sales representative must be able to collect information through an interview, analyze data on a spreadsheet, and determine what products and level of support would be best to offer to a client via a written, electronic, or oral presentation. This, in turn, should affect the content presented in the training. Customer complaints can also be a great source of information to help drive sales training plans. Analyzing the complaints might show that the firm's sales reps who lack knowledge about products or services don't take the time to follow-up with customers, or that customers don't like some of their sales tactics. To remedy this, the firm might need more content training, sales process or service training, or more insight about the nature of their customers and what they expect.

Antoine Destin knows the challenges and importance of conducting a good needs assessment. In his previous position, he was the sales training manager at Hormel Foods. "Determining the sales training needs of a sales force is a big challenge. Your programs have to meet the needs of three parties: management, middle managers, and the salesperson. If you aren't able to provide a product that everyone agrees to and thinks has value, you don't have a good training program," Destin explains. "Everyone has to 'buy in' to the program." Input from Hormel's sales managers is gathered during in-field visits and on-site training sessions. Input from Hormel's sales force is gathered via training conference calls with new hires. If you don't correctly identify your needs, no training program will solve your problems.

DETERMINE WHO NEEDS SALES TRAINING The last level of the needs assessment is the individual level. Not all salespeople need the same sales training program. Their needs may vary, depending upon their experience levels and the needs of the markets in which they sell. Sometimes, groups of sales representatives who need training can be easily identified, such as newly hired or newly promoted representatives. However, there will also be times when all members of a sales force need training. This might be the case when a company, or its competitors, launches a new product or service, enters a new market, or adopts a new technology. A good needs assessment will provide an idea of what training is needed, so that sales trainees get what they need to be successful—rather than too much information (which is likely to result in their boredom) or too little information (which is likely to result in their becoming frustrated). Similarly, companies with global sales forces must take into account the needs of their salespeople abroad in their sales training planning. Both Wyeth Pharmaceuticals and Hitachi Data Systems are companies that are doing so, as the "Global Sales Management" box in this chapter illustrates. Sales managers who fail to consider the cultural differences related to training their salespeople around the world face disastrous consequences.

GLOBAL SALES MANAGEMENT **The Challenges of Training a Global Sales Force**

You've heard it before: "Think globally, but act locally." This saying hits home when it comes to sales training. As much as companies would like to standardize their sales training in one country and send it out to others, it just isn't a good idea. As we learned in Chapter 3, leadership behaviors valued in one country may not be valued in another one. Companies have learned that, while it is acceptable to develop a standard sales platform in one country, they must let it be adapted to take into account the cultural, regulatory, geographical, and economic differences that exist across borders. "One size doesn't fit all" in sales training.

How do companies provide a consistent sales training program to a globally dispersed sale force, yet offer some degree of local customization? Richard Creasy is Wyeth Pharmaceutical's director of marketing development, global training, and instructional design, and it is his job to figure out how to solve that challenge. Creasy notes that advanced early planning of the sales training program and frequent communication are needed between the home office training unit and the firm's global affiliates. Once a program is developed at the headquarters unit, it goes out for localization of content and approval by the affiliates. "Our affiliates are the only ones who understand, and can address, the important issues in their region—including everything from regulatory considerations and drug price controls to reimbursement requirements and cultural differences." Wyeth believes that their localization model allows them to move fast and deliver consistent sales training that meets each of their constituents' needs.

Hitachi Data Systems, based in Santa Clara, California, takes a similar approach to developing training for its global sales force. In an effort to establish worldwide consistency, the headquarters team develops the core of each training program. A local training expert then adapts the program to each geographical area. The expert might add localized content, success stories, examples, and hyperlinks so that it more closely aligns with the culture and selling style in that area, and then help to deliver the training content to the designated location. Terri Casady, who heads the Hitachi training unit, notes that, "The challenge with global sales training is that the audience comprises such a huge, dispersed group...that has unique needs. Even though it is important to develop standardized training...it is equally important that we have people in the field who are empowered to deliver their own training that addresses those immediate needs—and in a manner and style their geographically dispersed sales force prefer."

Boehle, Sarah (2010), "Global Sales Training's Balancing Act," *Training*, (47)1, 29–31. Canaday, Henry (2010), "Students of the Marketplace: How to train a global enterprise sales force," *Selling Power*, (30)6, November/December 2010, 25–27.

To be sure, identifying specific individuals who need training can be time-consuming for a sales manager who is responsible for a large number of sales personnel.[8] As a result, it's not surprising that this step is often minimized, overlooked, or simply neglected. In fact, a survey of sales vice presidents reported that 34 percent of all companies said that skipping the step represented a critical deficiency in their sales training programs.[9] However, information to help identify individuals can be drawn from a variety of sources. The sources range from quantifiable performance appraisal data and customer satisfaction or CRM data, to more subjective information collected from training-needs surveys taken by sales managers and salespeople themselves. The latter can help build support for training programs, because those who are most likely to receive the training are the individuals who identified the need for it.

After an individual's training needs are identified, these should be included in an individual training and development plan for the person. The plan should include training courses the representative should take at scheduled career milestones, such as an advanced training course once the person has achieved a certain amount of experience. It could also include training from outside vendors, such as a software training course for a representative who struggles to use a particular type of software product. Or it could include job rotations to ensure that the representative has an opportunity to be exposed to a variety of selling experiences. Unfortunately, the attention that is needed at this stage is often minimized, overlooked, or simply neglected. A survey of sales vice presidents reported that 54 percent of companies who were shifting their sales approach—and 34 percent of all companies—identified assessing individual training and development needs as a critical deficiency of their sales training programs.[10]

Designing and Developing the Training Program

WHAT CONTENT IS NEEDED? Exhibit 9.6 reflects the content areas that sales training programs cover. Product knowledge and sales skills training lead the way. Although it wasn't identified in this survey, ethics training is becoming more common. The "Ethics in Sales Management" box in this chapter describes recent developments in this area.

The results of a **training assessment** need to be tailored for the target group undergoing training. Most companies identify several groups of sales personnel in need of different types of training. These generally include programs for new hires, ongoing programs for established sales representatives, sales management training, and professional or career-development programs. Training programs for new hires will often include an orientation to the company, steps and behaviors used in the selling process, product and market information, procedures used to monitor the progress of a sale, and the use of sales-related software and technology. Additionally, some organizations will include instruction on networking, or how to develop new sales contacts, and instruction on time management. Many companies will bring in a group, or "class," of new hires, to a central or corporate location and train

EXHIBIT 9.6 Topics Commonly Covered in Sales Training Programs

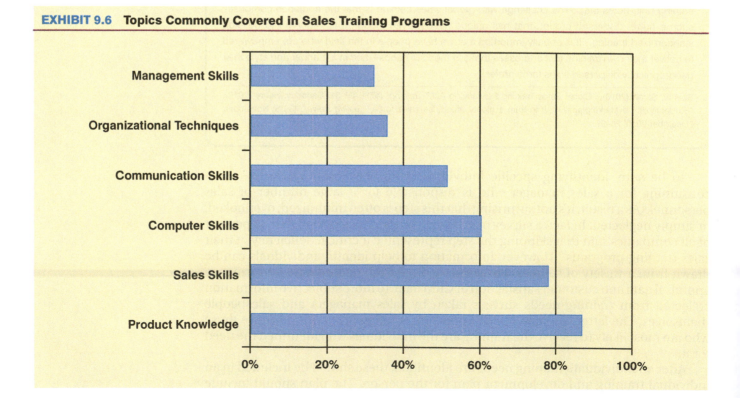

ETHICS IN SALES MANAGEMENT   Can You Teach Sales Ethics?

Can sales ethics be taught? Most sales educators would agree that understanding the underpinnings of ethical sales issues can be taught—with the caveat that acting ethically is something that only the salesperson can decide to do or not. It wasn't too long ago that companies avoided talking about ethics in their sales training programs for fear that their sales people might pick up some bad habits. Times change, and attitudes gradually do, too.

The most recent findings of the Ethics Resource Center's National Business Ethics Survey of the U.S. Workforce, in 2013, brought good news about the state of ethics. Respondents indicated that observed misconduct (of various kinds) was reported at 41 percent, its lowest point in the 19-year history of the survey. This was attributed to the continued increase in the number of companies providing ethics training to 81 percent of sales personnel. Two-thirds of the respondents indicated that ethical conduct was included in their performance measures. Additionally, 74 percent of the respondents indicated that their companies communicated internally about disciplinary actions when wrongdoing occurred. One area of concern noted was that, when ethical misconduct was observed, it was most likely to occur at the management level. This finding fit with findings from sales training research.

Over the last decade, a great deal of research has been conducted on sales ethics. One finding, consistently echoed in much of the research, is the importance of the sales manager as the role model for sales reps. If the sales manager demonstrates ethical behaviors, the likelihood of his or her sales reps demonstrating ethical behaviors is high. If the sales manager dismisses or minimizes ethical behaviors, then the likelihood of the sales reps' cultivating unethical sales behaviors is higher.

Sales ethics training specialists recommend that ethics training involve a review of a company's code of conduct and group discussions involving members of the sales force and sales management teams. The discussions should focus on specific business ethics dilemmas such as selling out-of-date products, sending gifts to customers, the value and the timing of gift giving, presenting false or misleading information about products, selling unproven solutions, exaggerating the extent of support that a firm can offer customers, and filing inaccurate expense reports.

While most ethical training is still conducted in the classroom, an interesting new training method is gaining popularity. **Gamification** is the use of interactive computer games that encourage employees to learn ethical behaviors by role playing them in a simulated office environment. The developer, Adam Sodowick of True Office, notes that the use of stories and interactivity engages people in solving problems, and motivates them to complete the training. In addition, he reports that people are better able to remember the matter presented in this format than other forms of training. Just like other games, this one also keeps a score that reflects how well the participant handled the ethical situations they had to confront.

Hansen, John D., and Robert J. Riggle (2009), "Ethical Sales Person Behavior in Sales Relationships," *Journal of Personal Selling & Sales Management*, (29)2, 151–166. Schwepker, Charles H., Jr. and David J. Good (2007), "Sales Management's Influence on Employment and Training in Developing an Ethical Sales Force," *Journal of Personal Selling & Sales Management*, (25)4, 325–339. McClaren, Nicholas (2010), "The Personal Selling and Sales Management Ethics Research: Managerial Implications and Research Directions from a Comprehensive Review of the Empirical Literature," *Journal of Business Ethics*, (112)101–125. *National Business Ethics Survey of the U.S. Workforce (2014)*. Arlington, VA: Ethics Resource Center (ERC). Rodier, Melanie (2012). "A Game Called Compliance," Accessed March 15, 2014. *http://www.wallstreetandtech.com/regulatory-compliance/a-game-called-compliance/240004357?printer_friendly=this-page.*

them together. Depending upon the start date of a new hire, a salesperson is likely to undergo training shortly after beginning her job, or wait several months until enough new hires are in place to form a class. Many companies have incorporated online programs that typically focus on product knowledge. This training can begin immediately after salespeople begin their new jobs.

New hires are also likely to begin **on-the-job training (OJT)**, job shadowing, or "ride-alongs" with experienced sales personnel. This helps expose new

One of most important tasks for sales managers is the training of their sales force.

representatives to a company's sales practices, products, and customers immediately. The idea is that the new hire will learn to model the behavior of the more experienced representative. Therefore, it is critical that the representative being "shadowed" is a good role model who is willing to train the new representative. Refresher courses for more experienced salespeople tend to cover certain advanced sales skills, including how to work with larger or more complicated customers, or advanced products and services. As we have mentioned, some companies position these courses at specific points in sales reps' careers to help prevent turnover among their salespeople.

One content area that has, and will continue to be, an important training area is integrating the use of technology into the sales process. Many people enter into sales professions because they enjoy interacting with people—as opposed to technology. However, most salespeople quickly realize how technology-driven applications, such as CRM software, can enhance their sales performance. Other useful technology applications include contact management, sales call scheduling, travel route-planning software, and in-house templates that automatically fill in commonly used letters, presentations, proposal information, and other forms of documentation, so that the sales rep only needs to customize it to fit his current client.

Sales managers have learned that technology can provide real benefits without resulting in additional work. Sometimes, salespeople end up rejecting, or not using, the technology their sales managers provide them.[11] This usually occurs when there is a poor fit between the technology and what the salespeople needed— not because the technology itself is flawed. Trainers have learned several lessons from their early efforts to teach salespeople to use new technology (some of which didn't meet with success). First, the trainers must ensure that sales personnel see the potential benefits of the technology so that they will accept and use it.[12] The trainers must also thoroughly train the sales force to use the technology—both in the field and out—and provide them with adequate technical support and follow-up training if they need it.

The last category of training focuses on the overall **professional development** of sales personnel. This might include training related to professional speaking, account management, analytics, team selling, negotiating contracts, and other advanced training conducted as part of an industry-wide seminar, for example. Category management, or managing how many different brands a retailer should carry and display, is an area in which salespeople are receiving training. In addition, a firm's sales training programs might include enrolling in summer institutes or graduate courses offered by colleges, universities, and professional associations.

Sales representatives aren't the only people who need different types of training, though. Sales managers need training, too, especially as they transition from sales-representative to sales-management positions. Historically, the training needs of this group have taken a backseat to the needs of the new sales force members and, oftentimes, only larger organizations have provided formal training in this area. However, recent studies indicate that more organizations realize the value of providing training for their sales managers.[13, 14] The content included in the majority of training programs for sales managers is incorporated into many of the chapters of this book. Topics include transitioning into management and coaching (Chapter 10), recruiting and interviewing (Chapter 8), conducting performance appraisals (Chapter 14), and business-to-business account management strategies (Chapters 5 and 13).

DEVELOPING THE OBJECTIVES OF SALES TRAINING: CHANGING IDEAS INTO ACTION After the topics of training have been identified, the trainer needs to develop the learning objectives of the program. This will help them properly develop, execute, and evaluate the program. Educational psychologist Benjamin Bloom outlined three different categories of intellectual behavior important for learning, often referred to as **Bloom's Taxonomy**. The behaviors can be categorized as: cognitive, affective, and psychomotor behaviors. These correspond to the KSAs which we described earlier, and are useful to trainers when they are writing their training objectives—that is, what they want their trainees to do in order to learn what they need to know.[15, 16] The goal is to accurately describe the intent of your sales training programs in terms of these various behaviors. Exhibit 9.7 shows the range of activities and behaviors that should be incorporated into a training program's objectives, based on Bloom's work.

EXHIBIT 9.7   Using Bloom's Taxonomy (Categories) to Develop Effective Objectives

Cognitive/Knowledge Categories	
Category (ranging from lower-to higher-level skills)	**Examples and *Key Words***
Remembering recalling and restating learned information	Describe the pricing policy to a customer *list, recognize, describe, identify, name*
Understanding interprets and translates what has been learned; explaining ideas or concepts	Summarize the pricing policy; explain the benefits of a new product to a customer *summarize, interpret facts, infer causes, explain, classify, compare*
Applying using information in another familiar situation	Implement the policy for a client *administer, assess, calculate, interpret, apply, prepare, solve*
Analyzing breaking information into parts to explore relationships	Differentiate how the pricing policies affect different types of buyers *analyze, compare, distinguish, illustrate, infer, explain*
Evaluating make decisions based on reflection, criticism, and assessment	Assess the viability of the pricing policy *judge, assess, revise, recommend, convince, support, decide*
Creating generating new ideas, products, or ways of viewing things	Create a pricing policy *design, construct, devise, propose, develop, formulate, forecast*

Affective/Attitude Categories	
Category (ranging from lower-to higher-level skills)	**Examples and *Key Words***
Receiving inputs aware of and attuning to inputs	Listens to others and remembers the name of an introduced person *asks, describes, identifies, selects, replies*
Responding to inputs active participation on the part of the learner	Participates in a discussion and can make a presentation *answers, discusses presents, reports, writes*
Valuing establishes a worth for an idea, behavior, idea	Proposes a plan or a solution that is sensitive to the needs of multiple parties *explains, initiates, justifies, proposes, selects, shares*
Organizing organizes values into priorities and resolves conflicts between them	Prioritizes needs of customer, co-workers and the organization *compares, defends, explains, formulates, generalizes, modifies, integrates, relates*
Internalizing values has a value system that controls their behavior	Revises judgments and changes behavior in light of new information; values people for who they are *acts, discriminates, influences, practices, proposes, qualifies, revises, serves, solves*

Based on Anderson & Krathwohl, 2001, *A Taxonomy for Learning, Teaching and Assessing: A Revision of Bloom's Taxonomy of Educational Objectives.*

Trainers should be sure to include activities beyond the lowest-level skill sets (i.e., incorporating more than just remembering in their objectives). Ultimately, training programs should show a progression of higher-level competencies and require related activities (i.e., analyzing data to make determinations, evaluating proposals to identify the most worthy one, and creating new plans). No doubt, you recall some of your earlier collegiate courses which might have included heavy doses of memorization (i.e., remembering terms on a multiple-choice test). Compare the behaviors needed to succeed in those courses to those required for your upper-level courses. Managers function at the upper level—analyzing cases, writing business plans, and presenting persuasive arguments.

STAFFING THE TRAINING PROGRAM Once decisions about the content and desired outcomes of a proposed program have been determined, managers need to address a number of questions about the **staffing** of the program. These include internal versus external resources, time pressures, and cost considerations.

Internal versus External Staffing Resources Should the trainer come from within the company, or would it be preferable to hire an outside trainer or a training vendor? This will depend on whether the firm's internal talent has the KSAs to assemble and present the program. For example, is the firm's sales process so unique that the insights and credibility an internal trainer can provide outweigh the benefits of hiring an external firm? Generally, an internal trainer (one within the firm) will have more credibility than an outside trainer. There are cases, however, when an outside trainer is likely to have more credibility. For example, if a firm purchases a new information technology application, salespeople are likely to find outside trainers employed by the developer of the technology a more credible source of training.

Is there a dedicated sales training team within the firm that can direct the effort? Or is there a large number of people who need immediate training, which precludes using internal resources? Depending upon your answers to questions such as these, it might be more feasible to hire an outside vendor to conduct your training. Many companies today are doing just that. In fact, each year, U.S. companies spent a little less than 10 percent of their budgets on vendor-provided sales training.[17] If the training isn't extremely company specific—that is, if it is "generic" enough—it's possible that it can be conducted by a number of outside vendors. A number of capable vendors, including Wilson Learning, Dale Carnegie, Sales and Marketing Executives, and the Center for Creative Leadership, offer a range of programs, from general sales training to presentation and personal development skills. These are designed for companies that may not provide any in-house training. Larger firms often seek out these vendors for more specialized training, such as in negotiation, category management, or leadership development that surpasses what in-house training programs can offer. Or perhaps an outside technology partner such as A. C. Neilson or IRI is needed to help facilitate the delivery of the program via webinars, blogs, on-line learning, and so forth. Most companies use a combination of instructional approaches. A survey of sales companies found that 68 percent use sales managers, 58 percent have an in-house instructor, 54 percent use an outside instructor, and 20 percent indicate that the instruction is done on the computer.[18]

Time Pressures How frequently is the training needed? If it is a recurring program that is offered at regular intervals, it may warrant in-house development. Is the program needed on a regular basis or only once? Because developing a training program from scratch internally can be time-consuming, offering such a program only once might not be justifiable. Also, can the program be rolled out gradually, or must it be done within a short time period? When training is needed immediately and the firm's in-house resources are limited, using an external firm is likely to be beneficial. Finally, how involved should sales managers be in the training? Training programs that require the insights of a firm's sales managers might be better handled internally. If, indeed, sales managers are selected to participate in the training, will they have the time and resources to commit to the training when it needs to be conducted? Making sure sales managers are available—and can dedicate the time needed to deliver the training—can sometimes be a challenge. In this case, using an outside vendor might be preferable.

Costs Not to be overlooked is the cost of developing and delivering the program. If inside staff members are going to handle the program, will there be additional costs related to researching the content of the program and creating the materials for it? Are additional staffing costs required? For example, how many individuals will be delivering the training? What will it cost for them to do so? Will they have to travel to the training site? Are there enough individuals needing training to warrant the company's developing and delivering the training, or will it cost less to utilize an existing vendor program? In other words, how does "outsourced" training compare, price-wise, to internal training? Addressing these questions will help you determine who is best positioned to staff the program.

SELECTING THE TRAINING DELIVERY METHOD There was a time when selecting the delivery format for a sales training program was very straightforward; it was generally face-to-face, or **instructor-led training**. Either the sales force traveled to a central site to receive training from an instructor, or the instructor traveled to a site closer to the students to deliver a program.

Instructor-led sales training can include many different components, including lectures, discussions, role plays, and presentations. It has the benefit of being very flexible and interactive. It also helps socialize participants and allows them to network with another. As a result, they can consult one another for advice and support once the training has concluded, which many of them find valuable.

Historically, instructor-led training has been the method firms favor when it comes to training their salespeople. It can sometimes result in heavy doses of one-way communication, however. (You have probably experienced a long, boring lecture where no one was paying attention.) This type of training also requires all participants to gather together at a particular training site, which can be expensive if representatives have to travel very far. Housing, meals, and missed selling opportunities are among the other costs companies incur by sending their representative to training.

Today, there are other alternatives to in-person, instructor-led training. The use of technology-based learning delivery methods now gives companies many delivery options. Traditional instructor-based classroom training remains the most popular, representing 54 percent of total training, followed by technology-based online delivery methods.[19] In years past, technology-delivered training was simple; it might involve sending trainees printed materials and/or audios and videos. Today, many companies provide their employees *on-demand (self-paced) training* that is available on the Internet.

Instructor-led conference calls are another alternative. So are **web conferences**. Web conferencing allows a presenter to deliver information remotely to trainees' individual computers. A **webcast** is a one-way flow of communication, suitable for quick, worldwide training needs. A **webinar**, typically, is de-signed for a smaller audience, incorporating a two-way flow of communication, with feedback from the receivers either via phone line and/or text messaging. VALIC, a member company of SunAmerica Financial Group, replaced its traditional class-room training with webinars to train its large network of agents, and realized large savings on travel costs.[20]

Two other delivery options are gaining increasing popularity in the sales training scene: podcasting and the use of wikis. **Podcasting** is the delivery of information to a salesperson's tablet or other, similar device. Some companies send podcast information to their

As webinars have become more interactive, so has their popularity for sales training.

The availability of online training resources allows for greater scheduling of sales training.

representatives on a daily basis. The information might include how a new product is being accepted by customers, or how competitors have reacted to it. Podcasts, typically, must be downloaded by participants, however, and do not allow for interaction with an instructor. **Wikis** are a quick-response training vehicle. (The name comes from the Hawaiian term *wiki*, which means "fast."). Wikis are websites that individual sales representatives are able to put up on short notice. A wiki allows all people who have access to a site to post material on it. Wiki participants act as instructors when they post information about how they were able to successfully sell to the firm's customers.

A key advantage of the newer approaches is their convenience; much of the coursework can be completed anytime and anywhere you have access to a personal computer or handheld device. As a result, firms don't have to pay for sales representatives to travel somewhere to receive training. The new learning software is more interactive, and can be tailored to the different needs of individual learners.

Exhibit 9.8 shows how frequently different general training methods are used.[21] The methods used for sales training, in particular, are similar. However, online education methods are used somewhat less often to train salespeople.[22] This might be because teaching interpersonal and communications skills is crucial in a sales training course, and this type of training isn't easy to transfer into an online learning format. Some companies are addressing this by incorporating a blended online (product and market knowledge) and in-person (selling skills) approach to training. Both IBM and Booz Allen Hamilton, a management strategy consulting firm, have adopted blended approaches in their sales training. "Not every topic lends itself to e-learning," comments Melissa Chambers, a learning strategist at Booz Allen Hamilton, which has integrated hundreds of e-learning modules into the company's 120 classroom courses. The company's combined approach gives it the benefits that distance learning affords, as well as classroom participation to reinforce the lessons trainees are taught online.[23]

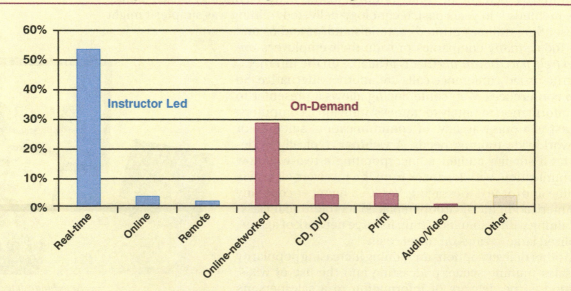

EXHIBIT 9.8   Percent of Training Time Delivered Using the Following Formats

Based on Rivera, Ray J. and Andrew Paradise (2006). *2006 State of the Industry in Leading Enterprises: ASTD's Annual Review of Trends in Workplace.*

Roger Anderson, Home Depot's director of learning agrees that online training should not be used in all situations. Anderson says that the training is great when sales reps need a standard set of information or "where you want all employees to hear the same message." But when you need to incorporate multiple skills for a complex job, face-to-face training is preferable.[24] A frequently used training format to handle this situation is a set of **role-playing exercises.** Role playing requires sales people to present information to a "client" (usually a sales trainer or another sales trainee) who has little understanding of the product and thus requires a basic presentation—or who has a great deal of understanding and, thus, requires a very sophisticated presentation. Additionally, the demeanor of the client can range from pleasant to anything but pleasant. The goal is for the presenter to overcome these challenges in real time.

Some firms are even using **avatars,** or computer representations of humans (like those found in the online game *Second Life*), as sales coaches. Danielle Paden, an account manager at CDW Corp., a technology products and service company, completed a sales training course with an avatar coaching her through a series of simulated phone interactions with clients. Paden was pleased with the realistic sales experience. This "futuristic" type of sales training offers a number of benefits: the simulation is based on the expertise of all the trainers; it provides consistent experience with a coach who does not tire; it is available any time of day or night; it can be duplicated for individual training for large numbers of trainees; and it can be repeated at the convenience of the sales person.[25]

So which training delivery method is most effective? A comparison of several instructor-led and self-paced training formats—used in a new product sales training program for experienced sales representatives—revealed little difference in the learning outcomes representatives achieved.[26] A better approach would be to consider the unique challenges of each training situation—perhaps the firm's training budget is limited, or there is a pressing need to train the firm's entire sales force quickly—and then choose the method that best fits the situation, depending upon factors such as these.

Delivering the Training

SCHEDULING THE TRAINING After all planning is complete, the logistics of the program need to be addressed. If the training is instructor-led, for example, additional decisions must be made about the location of the training—whether it should take place at a centralized location, such as the company's headquarters, or a decentralized location(s), such as the territories or regions in which the trainees are located. Sales managers have to consider the travel and lodging costs that would be incurred under the different scenarios, as well as the time trainees spend traveling as opposed to selling. On the one hand, a centralized site, such as a company's headquarters, is also likely to have a complete set of training resources and equipment. Centralized training also allows new sales representatives to network with other trainees from outside their districts and regions, as well as with the company's sales executives and in-house personnel. On the other hand, it usually involves a higher travel price tag than does a decentralized sales program. Coordinating and getting the resources and training equipment to a decentralized location can involve more work for trainers, however.

Making sure that trainees, presenters, and technical assistants have their schedules cleared, selecting a training location, and arranging for their travel and housing, are also part of training delivery. However, not only do the physical attributes of the training site need to be ready, but the psychological "readiness" of the trainees also needs to be in place. For example, the timing of the training in the sales cycle is important. Training salespeople during a slow selling time (as opposed to bringing them in for training when they are ending a sales period) will affect how psychologically ready they are to be trained. The time salespeople need to complete any pre-training assignments you have given them also needs to be considered. Researchers have found that individuals who have a predisposition about the importance of training will transfer more into the field than those who don't.[27]

FACILITATE THE TRANSFER OF LEARNING Part of providing excellent training is ensuring that what is learned in the training program can be retained and applied in the field. This is called **learning transfer.** To help facilitate this, educational researchers suggest trainers do the following:

1. Make sure that training and field conditions are as similar as possible.

2. Provide many opportunities to practice new skills.

3. Provide a variety of situations for applying the new material.

4. Identify the important features of the tasks.

5. Make sure the trainee has the opportunity to practice the new skills in the field.[28]

These suggestions incorporate Bloom's lower-level skill sets, as well as some of the higher ones. Learning and practicing the new behavior in a similar situation to their work environment is critical to ensuring that a transfer of learning occurs.

Assessing the Firm's Training Efforts

The last phase of a sales training cycle involves **assessing the results**. How effective was the firm's sales training? Were the objectives of the program accomplished? What were the gains of the program to the company? These sound like straightforward questions that should require simple answers. However, as Antoine Destin, former sales training manager of Hormel Foods Corporation, has commented, "Evaluating the effectiveness of training can be tough." Apparently, it's not just Destin who thinks so. When asked if their companies had a definitive method for measuring the value of their sales training, only 28 percent of sales trainers indicated they did.[29] This phase of training often receives the least attention, despite its importance.[30]

In addition, sales trainers can't lose sight of the fact that some managers view sales training merely as an expense. As one sales professional put it, "Unlike a capital asset—which can be reused or resold—training generally can't. Therefore, it is important that management clearly understand the value of this expense."[31] Clearly, evaluating the success of a firm's training effort is an area that deserves attention.

One popular assessment approach includes looking at certain reaction, learning, behavior, and return on investment (ROI) levels.[32] Despite some criticisms, this framework is intuitively simple and easy to apply. Exhibit 9.9 shows the different types of evaluation measures that sales trainers use, their reported importance to trainers, and frequency of use.[33] Next, we discuss each of the four types of assessment and their strengths and weaknesses.

DETERMINE THE VALUE OF SALES TRAINING TO THE INDIVIDUAL
Reaction (Level 1) This category addresses what a trainee thought of a program by asking the person to fill out an evaluation, or what some trainers call a "happy sheet." In other words, was the trainee happy with the training? This is the most frequently used measurement. Note that, in Exhibit 9.9, the four most frequently used methods— course evaluations, trainee feedback, training staff comments, and supervisory feedback—are all reaction measures. These ratings can be easily collected using end-of-course questionnaires. Unfortunately, the assessment measures that sales trainers considered most important weren't those most frequently collected.

Reaction measures have been criticized because they don't show if anything was really learned and applied back in the field. They only indicate if, and how much,

EXHIBIT 9.9 **Training Evaluation Measures Ranked by Their Importance and Frequency of Use**

Assessment Approach	Sales Trainers' Rankings		
	Importance	Frequency	Type
Trainee feedback	1	2	reaction
Supervisory appraisal	2	6	behavior
Self-appraisal	3	7	behavior
Bottom-line measurement	4	9	results
Customer appraisal	5	10	behavior
Supervisory feedback	6	4	reaction
Performance tests	7	5	learning
Training staff comments	8	3	reaction
Course evaluations	9	1	reaction
Subordinates' appraisal	10	12	behavior
Pre- vs. post-training measurements	11	11	learning
Co-workers' appraisal	12	13	behavior
Knowledge tests	13	8	learning
Control group	14	14	learning

Note: Sales trainers' ratings of each method's importance to them, and how frequently they used them, were ranked from 1 to 14.

Erffmeyer, Robert C., K., Randall Russ, and Joseph F. Hair, Jr. (1991). "Needs Assessment and Evaluation in Sales-Training Programs," *Journal of Personal Selling & Sale Management*, (11)1, 18–30.

participants liked the program. In addition, measures such as these may be unduly influenced by the training location (after a brutal winter, who wouldn't like the opportunity for training in a warm location?), the trainer's personality, and how much the trainee values being away from work. However, there is some value in collecting this information. If sales representatives like the training program, it stands to reason that they will be more motivated to participate and learn from it. In sum, a good reaction rating doesn't mean learning took place, but a negative rating reduces the chances that it occurred.

Learning (Level 2) This level involves measuring the amount of information participants mastered during the program. This can be done by testing them before and after the training, and comparing the results of the two tests. However, the measurement doesn't necessarily reflect if the material can be applied in a productive manner back in the field. Both the reaction and learning-level measures gauge the effectiveness of the training program at the individual level. To gain insight about the program's value at the organization level, the next two higher-level measures are needed.

Behaviors (Level 3) Level 3 measurements identify to what degree trainees applied the training principles and techniques they learned to their jobs—in essence, their learning transfer. The measurements can be collected by sales managers as they observe their sales personnel. They can also be collected from self-reports that trainees themselves complete in journals, or from their contact management, or CRM, entries. Research has shown that this level of evaluation has only a few shortcomings, and that it is particularly useful.[34]

Joint calls with a sales manager is a great way to evaluate the effectiveness of training and identify areas to work on.

DETERMINE THE VALUE OF SALES TRAINING TO THE ORGANIZATION

Results (Level 4) Level 4 measurements assess whether or not an organization achieved the objectives it sought by conducting the training. For example, did the program result in more sales of a new product that helped the company enter a new market? Or were fewer customer complaints received, which helped the company achieve a higher customer service rating in its industry? Measurements at this level tend to be conducted less often and, unfortunately, lend themselves to a few problems. A major problem involves determining whether the firm's objectives were achieved directly because of the training program or because of other factors—for example, competitors' actions, changes in the market, or changes in economic conditions.[35]

Because of the difficulties related to gauging Level 4 results, many managers assess the results of their training programs by using **utility analysis.** How "useful" was the training, in other words? Although this category isn't included in the original model, it seems like a natural extension of the fourth level. Utility analysis involves looking at the economic impact the training had by examining the cost-benefit tradeoffs of the training program. By looking at the program's benefits—that is, the retention rates of the personnel who have been trained, and the performance differences between trained and untrained employees—versus the training program expenses. In other words, sales managers use utility analysis to determine the *relative* usefulness of different sales training alternatives. They want to adopt training programs that minimize the firm's costs while maximizing the important outcomes the company seeks.[36]

Measuring the success of the sales training program is one of the toughest aspects of the sales trainer's job, notes former Hormel sales trainer Antoine Destin: "Evaluating the effectiveness of training is difficult. Sure, you can tell if participants liked it. But measuring it or showing a return on the investment is tough." To help measure this, in addition to verbal feedback, Hormel relies on written assessments the sales representatives complete after they undergo training.

Completing the Sales Training Cycle

The sales training cycle is not completed until the results of training are compared with the initial objectives laid out for the program. Ideally, the sales training objectives are met and the program is considered a success. If this is the case, oftentimes the training program will go forward with only minor modifications and updates.

At the other extreme are those programs that do not meet their initial objectives. What might have caused these shortcomings? As you might expect, few companies want to grant interviews about how their training programs didn't measure up. However, researchers investigating this area have found that the majority of companies that experience training shortcomings did not systematically set specific objectives for their training programs. Without these objectives to guide the development of their training courses, properly implementing and evaluating them will be difficult. Thus, the value of the firms' training investments would appear to be greatly diminished.[37]

Rather than an isolated event, sales training needs to be viewed as a systematic process of integrating the training curriculum into the sales force. The American Society for Training and Development regularly honors organizations for their award-winning training practices.[38] Exhibit 9.10 outlines these practices. The Professional Society for Sales & Marketing Training has identified a number of best practices for sales trainers.[39] Exhibit 9.11 consists of a "checklist" of some of these practices.

EXHIBIT 9.10   The Best Training and Development Practices of Companies

Companies that have received awards for their training programs share several characteristics. The programs:

- Include a front-end analysis of the performance, skills and knowledge gaps of a firm's employees using both internal and external metrics, such as customer satisfaction.
- Conduct analyses, surveys, and interview of clients, customers, internal business leaders, and employees to identify the learning needs and desired outcomes at the corporate, business-unit, and individual levels.
- Link a corporation's strategic objectives to the individual objectives of its employees.
- Incorporate learning objectives in employee performance evaluations and promotional decisions.
- Use career management systems to align the competencies of the firm's employees with its functions, track the degree of employee learning, support performance reviews, and enhance productivity.
- Hold managers accountable for complying with the individual development plans of their employees.
- Use corporate universities to provide a variety of learning models in creative and dedicated learning environments.

Based on Rivera, Ray J. and Andrew Paradise (2006). *2006 State of the Industry in Leading Enterprises: ASTD's Annual Review of Trends in Workplace.*

EXHIBIT 9.11   A Best-Practices Checklist for Sales Trainers

Needs Assessment

- Is the training tied to the organization's mission and vision?
- Can you understand the true nature of the problem/issue at hand, and what is needed to correct the problem?
- Is training the appropriate solution, or can the problem be corrected by other solutions, such as changing the firm's procedures, developing job aids, or modifying jobs?
- Have you determined the learning objectives that will result in the desired changes?
- Have you identified the knowledge and skills that will produce the desired new behaviors?
- Can you determine the cost/budget constraints and develop suggested solutions within these constraints?
- Can you identify the learning styles and needs of participants and incorporate them into the program's design?

Content Development

- Does the program incorporate adult learning principles into all aspects of the training?
- Does the content emphasize the essentials, not every possible detail?
- Does the program provide participants with the materials they need without overwhelming them?

Technology Proficiency

- Is the instructor up to date using the most current technology?
- Is the instructor able to utilize the technology that best fits the learning situation, rather than using technology for the sake of appearances?
- Can the instructor bring the course material "alive" via an effective presentation regardless of the technology used?

Personal Professional Development

- Does the instructor have an interest in participants' personal growth and learning?

Evaluation

- Does the instructor seek feedback to improve the program?
- Does the program include an evaluation process to capture information on the training's effectiveness, learning retention by participants, and the use of learning related to the firm's day-to-day business practices?

Based on Training Competencies, (2006), Professional Society for Sales & Marketing Training, Retrieved January 2, 2007, from *http://www.smt.org/i4a/pages/index.cfm?pageid=3325.*

Managing Your Career

This chapter and where you are right now have two elements in common: investments and perspectives. How you ever stopped to think about how much you have invested in yourself to get where you are? No doubt you (and perhaps your family) have made significant financial and effort investments for achieving your college education. Will you continue to get a good return on your investment after you graduate? You and they hope you will. Can you imagine how long a person can stay current in a chosen field without some form of continuing training and education?

As you talk with companies about internships and employment, find out how they will continue to build on your investment by providing training and development. Don't overlook a serious discussion of how a firm invests in the members of its sales force. Are educational opportunities included in an internship, or is it just learning a series of repetitive sales activities? Once hired, how do they handle training and development? Is it strictly "on-the-job" training, or is it more involved? You've made a huge investment in getting to this point in your career; make sure you find an employer who will help you continue to build on the good practices you've demonstrated.

The second element is your perspective. If you are driving down the highway, looking down at the pavement, it gets pretty boring. Look up and you'll get a different perspective by looking at the surroundings and how the landscape changes. While some training tasks may get boring, don't forget to look for the bigger picture. Ask yourself, "How can what I'm learning apply to my current and future situation? Why do they want me to know this information? How can I develop to add value to the things I do for my customers and my company?"

Summary

Every year, companies invest more in the training of sales personnel than for any other occupational group, including managers and supervisors. A firm's products, services, markets, customers, and technology change rapidly. Consequently, having a sales force that is knowledgeable about these changes is critical to an organization's ability to successful compete and survive. Regardless of the resources available to an organization, its sales training programs should follow four stages: identifying the firm's training needs, developing the training program, delivering it, and assessing its results.

Most organizations provide training for entry-level sales people that includes selling skills, product knowledge, technology skills, and—more frequently—sales ethics decision-making skills. Training for more experienced sales personnel typically will include advanced decision making, sales, and presentation skills for use with larger clients. Technology and ethics training are increasingly becoming more common for sale forces.

Once the content and trainees are identified, the training program needs to be developed. Sales trainers can use Bloom's Taxonomy to help them translate ideas into objectives that guide the development, and later evaluation, of the program. This classification framework can assist the planners in designing a program that might include only basic skills, or lead to a more complex program and address a wider range of behaviors.

The next two steps involve determining who will conduct the training and what delivery format best suits the program's needs. The roles that sales managers play in the training process should never be overlooked, because they are responsible for reinforcing sales training on a daily basis and, ultimately, are responsible for the success of their representatives. Factors, such as the frequency with which the firm's training program must be conducted, the degree of specialized content the program contains, technological requirements, number of trainees, and the delivery schedule will influence whether an outside vendor should be utilized to assist in, or deliver, an entire program.

Technology has expanded the methods companies can choose for delivering training to their employees. In-person, instructor-led sessions are generally very flexible and allow participants to interact and socialize with one another, but also entail added travel costs and scheduling challenges. On-demand, or self-paced, training can involve sending printed or electronic materials and/or audio and video recordings to representatives to watch or access online. Web conferencing, webcasts, and webinars offer even more training delivery choices. With good planning and development, the delivery of the training program is often thought of as one of the most straightforward parts of training. However, logistical issues and scheduling still must be dealt with for a program to succeed. Care needs to be taken to ensure that delivery of the material facilitates the ability of trainees to apply the content to their work environment.

Determining how successful a training program was is the final step in the sales training cycle. Most trainers use multiple measures to determine their programs' effectiveness. Kirkpatrick proposed a four-tier classification system, which includes reaction measures, learning measures, behavioral or performance measures, and results measures.[32] A utility analysis can be conducted to determine the cost/benefit ratios of programs. Behavior, or performance, measures offer the most valid form of assessment.

Organizations oftentimes focus on single aspects of sales training, rather than viewing it as an entire process. Firms that fail to develop meaningful training objectives tend to develop programs that don't meet their needs, or are impossible to assess.

Key Terms

assessing the results 202
avatar 201
Bloom's Taxonomy 197
gamification 195
individual level 190
instructor-led training 199
KSAs (knowledge, skills, and
  abilities) 192
learning transfer 202
OJT (on-the-job training) 195
organizational analysis 192
organizational level 190

podcasting 199
professional development 196
role-playing exercises 201
sales training cycle 189
staffing 198
task level 190
training assessment 194
utility analysis 204
webcast 199
web conference 199
webinar 199
wikis 200

Questions and Problems

1. What are the limitations of a survey such as the one used by *Selling Power*?

2. In what situations does it **not** make sense to conduct sales training?

3. What is the difference between the organizational, task, and individual assessments? What are the benefits of using them?

4. Describe the concept of a KSA and how it can be used in sales training.

5. One of your friends, a new college graduate, has accepted a sales position with a large firm. What topics do you believe should be included in a sales training course for her? Consider another friend who has accepted a position with a smaller firm that has four sales people. How will their two experiences differ?

6. What are some of the reasons a company would consider using someone outside of the firm to train its sales force?

7. Online courses are growing. What reservations might a person have for taking sales training courses online?

8. When does in-person sales training make more sense than on-demand sales training? When does on-demand sales training make more sense than in-person sales training?

9. What sales training format do you believe holds the most promise for the future? Why?

10. "An individual should never be assigned permanently to a sales trainer's position." Develop arguments to both support and refute this statement

---

Role Play

Blindsided

Melissa Moore was the human resources and training manager for Crane Company, a manufacturer of custom molds for the plastics industry. Moore was about to enter a meeting set up by John Rock, the vice president of sales for Crane. John was hired away from Crane's nearest competitor, and had been with the company for a little less than a year. The topic to be discussed was the ongoing training Crane Company's 200 field sales representatives across North America and Canada should receive.

Moore did her homework before the meeting, and was very well prepared. She had been with the company for 15 years, and had seen it grow from a small, single-location, regional company of 50 employees to the industry leader with 1,200 employees and five manufacturing facilities. She felt that her department had a strong ongoing sales training program, with two experienced professional sales trainers who conducted classroom lectures, guided role playing, and supplied the sales force with new product field training materials. She also felt that the sales training was in line with Crane's corporate vision and goals, based on conversations with her direct supervisor, Tom Jenkins, the firm's, vice president of human resources.

The sales training programs were comprised of small groups of eight to 10 field sales representatives who would rotate into the corporate office for three days of training seminars. On average, a salesperson received formal training twice a year (10 days annually, including travel time). Salespeople took assessment tests during training.

Moore believed the on-going sales training seemed to be successful, because there was very low turnover within the sales force, customer complaints about the sales force were minimal, and the company's overall sales had steadily increased over the years. There were no formal measurements of the ongoing sales training program, but she felt confident in its value, because the feedback she received from the sales force was always positive with regards to the training visits.

Five minutes into the meeting, Rock blindsided Moore by telling her that he believed Crane's ongoing sales training was no longer working, outdated, and lacked trainers with field experience. He went on to explain to her that he could no longer afford to have his salespeople out of the field for 10 days a year. He challenged her to utilize new technologies to deliver ongoing sales training more efficiently. He explained that he needed to increase sales, and how the time sales reps were spending in training was taking away time the time they needed to spend in front of customers. In addition to objecting to the time out of the field, he also gave Moore a copy of an expense report showing the average travel expenses incurred per salesperson (more than $2,000 a year) to attend training classes. A large percentage of training costs were expensed to each sales manager's budget, and the increasing cost of transportation (let alone meals and lodging) and time out of field, was cutting into the ability to achieve sales and profitability goals. Consequently, sales managers have historically been reluctant to ask for additional training from corporate. Rock stated that the expenses were out of line, and that he could use the travel expense money as a cost savings. The meeting ended when he stood up and said he wanted Moore to prepare a new sales training proposal, to be placed on his desk in two weeks. After Rock left the room, Moore sat there, wondering what had just transpired.

Assignment

Break into pairs or a group of three. One person will role play Melissa Moore. The second person will role play Pat Lee—the national sales manager. The third person will role play John Rock. Rock wants the other two to prepare a list of suggestions outlining the direction the company's new sales training program should take. Weigh the pros and cons of the different training methods available to Crane and present them to John, who you know is keen on cost savings.

Caselets

Caselet 9.1: *Finding a Sales Training Solution*

The Tri-State Hospital and Clinic has grown from its initial service area around River City into a major regional healthcare organization, offering a variety of health-related services. For three quarters of a century, the hospital and clinic has provided health care to families in its service area. It was rewarded with the loyalty of many families and companies that only dealt with Tri-State. Over the years, the hospital and clinic expanded geographically into the surrounding three-state area and introduced new healthcare services. The new and changing healthcare initiatives have brought Tri-State into a much more competitive marketplace than it has ever experienced. Many of Tri-State's established medical businesses—such as occupational therapy, ventilation therapy, shot clinics, and eye care—are challenged by new, more aggressive providers who are willing to charge a lower rate. Patients now seem more motivated by cost savings or special offers, rather than by loyalty.

In the past, different clinic services were sold by a representative of each unit that provided the service, with little oversight from other units. Of the dozen clinic employees who sell these services, only a couple do so on a full-time basis. The others do some selling as part of their other administrative responsibilities. These individuals are located at various locations across the Tri-State market area. Most have been with the clinic for a significant period of time.

A task force recently conducted a review of Tri-State's different business units, looking for ways to improve profitability. As a result of the task force's efforts, Jules Chan, head of business services, was asked to research the possibility of offering a sales training course to those employees responsible for selling. The thought was that there might be room for more cross-selling of the clinic services. Jules wasn't too much of a marketer, but with due diligence went to work trying to identify possible providers for a cross-selling sales training class. He is now in possession of three very different proposals. They include proposals from:

1. a nearby college that offered to provide a sales course, including 14 weeks of three-hour units of instruction via the Internet, taught by a local sales professional.

This proposal was the lowest cost and offered to provide the highest employee time-to-complete.

2. a two-day seminar, taught by a healthcare industry representative, who would fly in and teach a two-day program from an existing catalog of programs. This was the middle-cost proposal. The fee also would cover bringing all sales personnel to a central location for the two-day seminar.

3. a two-part program, involving a survey of current sales practices of the sales personnel, followed by a day-and-a-half program. This would include two instructors who would participate in role plays with all sales personnel. This was the most expensive proposal.

Questions

1. What are the advantages and disadvantages of each of the proposals?
2. Going back to the group that requested the review, which one proposal should Chan recommend? The group has requested a rank order and rationale for this decision.
3. After training is complete, what additional issues might face the clinic's sales personnel?

Caselet 9.2: *What's This Sales Training Really Worth?*

The *Farm and Horse Journal (FHJ)* has been published by the Haskins family for more than 50 years. Current publisher Samantha (a.k.a. Sam) Haskins is an accountant by training and an entrepreneur and horsewoman by spirit. The horse magazine category has nearly two dozen publications vying for the attention of this fiercely competitive and lucrative marketplace. With more than nine million horses in the U.S. alone, its direct and indirect economic impact is estimated by the American Horse Council at over $109 billion. The *Journal* generates income through print and online subscriptions, advertising sales, and a variety of specialty workshops and shows it produces. Most recently, it has been producing some video programs for horse/farm cable channels. With a sales force including 12 full-time and 20 part-time horse-loving individuals located across North America, the *Journal* publisher is considering overseas markets in Australia, and Central and South America.

Anna Rust has been worked for *FHJ* since she graduated from college 12 years ago with a degree in marketing and a minor in journalism. She has been riding horses since she was five, and working with them since she was 10 years old. Anna has managed the magazine's sales force for the past six years, overseeing its expansion from four salespeople to its present size.

In their most recent bi-weekly meeting, Sam growled at Anna, "I see you want me to pay for 40 new computer tablets, upgrades, phone charges, and a bunch of other do-dads for your salesforce. What's that all about—more trinkets? Then, on top of that, I've got the bill for your extra training costs!" Anna knew that Sam was always tight on spending, and a bit out-of-touch on technology, but didn't expect quite such a nasty exchange. Sam had never complained this much about an expense like this in the past, but the tech and training investment was enough to catch the publisher's eye.

Anna explained that, in the past, only the full-time sales reps had access to laptops, and most of those personal computers were three or four years old, were slow, and had little interactivity for high-speed connection from in the field. The new purchase would allow all sales reps to have access to the newest laptops and interactivity possible. Their extra day and a half of training (on the back of the company's annual employee meeting) covered topics such as using the laptops for social media, CRM work, limited video production, and creation of better sales presentations.

Sam rolled her eyes and said, "Sure, you bet. When I invest in a new machine on the production floor, they show me how it helps our bottom line. Now, it's your turn.

What's our plan to show me what I got for my money? Otherwise you and your crew are gonna be mucking out a lot of horse stalls to pay this off." Anna knew that this was a bit of an act—and yet also a bit of seriousness.

Questions

1. Can you recommend several ways that Anna can evaluate whether or not her sales training will be effective?
2. Which training evaluation method will be the most effective? Why?
3. Which will be the least effective? Why?
4. Ultimately, which would you recommend she use?

References

1. Wilhelm, R. (2003). "Investing in New Agents: A Cost Blueprint" (April). Windsor, CT: LIMRA International.
2. ASTD Research (2013). *2013 State of the Industry*. Alexandria, VA: American Society for Training & Development.
3. ASTD Research (2013). "The State of Sales Training 2012," [White paper] 4 (4), Alexandria, VA: The American Society for Training & Development.
4. "The 50 Best Companies to Sell For," (2010-2012), *Selling Power*, (29-31), October/November/December.
5. Ahearne, Michael, Ronald Jelinek, and Adam Rapp (2005). "Moving beyond the direct effect of SFA adoption on salesperson performance: Training and support as key moderating factors," *Industrial Marketing Management*, (34), 379–388.
6. Goldstein, Irwin L., and Kevin Ford (2001). *Training in Organizations: Needs Assessment, Development and Evaluation*, (fourth edition). Belmont, CA: Wadsworth Publishing.
7. Attita, Ashraf M., Earl D. Honeycutt, Jr., and Mark P. Leach (2005). "A Three-Stage Model for Assessing and Improving Sales Force Training and Development," *Journal of Personal Selling & Sale Management*, (25)3, 253–268.
8. Attita, et. al. (2005). Op. cit.
9. Wellins, Richard S., Charles J. Cosentino, and Bradford Thomas (2004). *Building a Winning Sale Force, A Sales Talent Optimization Study on Hiring and Development*. Winter. Pittsburgh, PA: Development Dimensions International.
10. Rivera, Ray J., and Andrew Paradise (2006). *2006 State of the Industry in Leading Enterprises: ASTD's Annual Review of Trends in Workplace Learning and Performance*, Alexandria, VA.: The American Society for Training and Development.
11. Robinson, Leroy, Jr., Greg W. Marshall, and Miriam B. Stamps (2005). "An Empirical Investigation of Technology Acceptance in a Field Sales Force Setting," *Industrial Marketing Management*, (34)407–415.
12. Ahearne, Michael, Ronald Jelinek, and Adam Rapp (2005). "Moving Beyond the Direct Effect of SFA Adoption on Salesperson Performance: Training and Support as Key Moderating Factors," *Industrial Marketing Management*, (34), 379–388.
13. Powers, Thomas L., Thomas E, DeCarlo, and Gori Gupte (2010). "An Update on the Status of Sales Management Training," *Journal of Personal Selling and Sales Management*, (30)4, 319–326.
14. Gordon, G.L., C. D. Shepherd, B. Lambert, R. E.Ridnour, and D. C. Weilbaker (2012). "The training of sales managers: current practices," *The Journal of Business & Industrial Marketing*, (27)8, 659–672.
15. Bloom, B. S. (1956). *Taxonomy of Educational Objectives, Handbook I: The Cognitive Domain*. New York, NY: David McKay Company, Inc.
16. Anderson, L. W. and D. R. Drathwohl, eds. (2001). *A Taxonomy for Learning, Teaching and Assessing: A Revision of Bloom's Taxonomy of Educational Objectives*. New York, NY: Longman.
17. "2013 Training Industry Report," (2013). *Training*, (50)6, 22–35.
18. Paradise, Andrew, (2007). *State of the Industry Report 2007*, Alexandria, VA: American Society for Training and Development.
19. "ASTD Research (2013). Op. cit.
20. Lang, Annamarie (2011). "A Virtual Success at VALIC," *Learning Circuits*, January, 1.
21. Rivera and Paradise (2006). Op. cit.
22. "2006 Training Report" (2006). Op.cit.
23. Aronauer, Rebecca (2006). "The Classroom vs. E-learning," *Sales & Marketing Management*, (158, October) 8, 21.
24. Ganders, George (2007), "Companies Find Online Training Has Its Limits," *Wall Street Journal*, March 26, B3.
25. Borzo, Jeanette (2004). "Almost Human: Using avatars for corporate training, advocates say, can combine the best parts of face-to-face interaction and computer-based learning," *The Wall Street Journal*, May 24, R 4.
26. Erffmeyer, Robert and Dale Johnson (1997). "The Future of Sales Training: Making Choices Among Six Distance Education Methods," *The Journal of Business & Industrial Marketing*, (12)3/4, 185–195.
27. Wilson, Phillip H., David Strutton, and M. Theodore Farris II (2002). "Investigating the Perceptual Aspect of Sales Training," *Journal of Personal Selling & Sales Management*, (22)2, 77–87.
28. Goldstein and Ford. Op. cit.
29. Galea, Christine, and Carl Wiens, (2002). "Sales Training Survey," *Sales & Marketing Management*, 154(7), 34–36.

30. Erffmeyer, Robert C., K. Randall Russ, and Joseph F. Hair, Jr. (1991). "Needs Assessment and Evaluation in Sales-Training Programs," *Journal of Personal Selling & Sales Management*, (11)1, 18–30.

31. Wilson et. al. Op.cit.

32. Kirkpatrick, Donald L. (1959). "Techniques for Evaluating Training Programs," *Journal of the American Society for Training and Development*, 13(11), 3–9.

33. Erffmeyer, et. al. Op.cit.

34. Leach, Mark P. and Annie H. Liu, (2004). "Investigating Interrelationships Among Sales Training Evaluations Methods," *Journal of Personal Selling & Sales Management*, (23)4 (Fall) 327–339.

35. Leach and Liu. Op.cit.

36. Honeycutt, Earl D. Jr., Kiran Karande, Ashraf Attita, and Steven D. Maurer, (2001), "An Utility Based Framework for Evaluating the Financial Impact of Sales Force Training Programs," *Journal of Personal Selling & Sales Management*, (21)3, 229–238.

37. Honeycutt, Earl D. Jr.; Vince Howe, and Thomas N. Ingram (1993), "Shortcomings of Sales Training Programs," *Industrial Marketing Management*, (22), 117–123.

38. Rivera, Ray J. and Andrew Paradise (2006). *2006 State of the Industry in Leading Enterprises: ASTD's Annual Review of Trends in Workplace.*

39. "Training Competencies" (2006), Professional Society for Sales & Marketing Training, Accessed January 2, 2007. *http://www.smt.org/i4a/pages/index.cfm?pageid=3325.*

Process Management

When you graduate and begin working, your first job is likely to be as a salesperson. Currently, more marketing majors go into sales than any other position. The point is that you will not start as a chief sales executive or even a sales manager. Your first encounter, then, with sales managers will be as the supervised.

Part Five begins with Chapter 10, *Supervising, Managing, and Leading Salespeople Individually and in Teams*. In this chapter, we get even more specific about those activities that make for effective management and leadership. You may not start out as a sales manager, but you can certainly use this material to assess the quality of sales management you are receiving!

Next, Chapter 11, *Setting Goals and Managing the Sales Force's Performance*, focuses on goal setting. Sales leaders set goals for individual salespeople, as well as for the entire sales organization. These goals are then tied to compensation plans, directing salespeople and sales managers to focus their activities on the right outcomes.

Following that discussion is Chapter 12, *Motivating and Rewarding Sales People*. Using the goal-setting processes outlined in the previous chapter, we move into systems designed to encourage and reward achievement of those goals. Thus, this chapter describes the compensation and motivation options that companies use to motivate and reward their salespeople.

SUPERVISING, MANAGING, AND LEADING SALESPEOPLE INDIVIDUALLY AND IN TEAMS

LEARNING OBJECTIVES

After completing this chapter, you should be able to:

■ Explain and describe the difference between sales supervision, management, and leadership.

■ Identify the skills and abilities that a person needs to develop to become a good sales manager.

■ Understand the elements of teamwork and how to successfully develop and work with teams, including those that are virtual.

■ Recognize the ethical challenges facing leaders and teams in the sales environment.

What does it take to manage and lead salespeople individually and in teams? Do you use the same skills for a new hire that you use with an established sales veteran? It's not the same answer for every person or every occasion. A new hire might require close supervision, whereas—when developing a sales proposal that involves gathering and analyzing large amounts of information from several sources—the supervision of employees might best be handled through delegation and teamwork. In other situations, the sales manager needs to take the lead and lay out the vision, or plan, for their sales force to follow. While there may be differences of opinion as to whether a sales manager supervises, manages, or leads his or her sales force, there is agreement that all these behaviors are needed in developing a successful sales organization.

Sales Manager Profile: Dana Geisert

AS THE DIRECTOR OF BUSINESS Operations, there are several things that you might expect someone like Dana Geisert to say about what she likes most about her job. If you thought it might be the reward package, working conditions, or some other tangible benefits that come with position, you would be wrong. "Seeing people change and develop, and knowing you had an impact on them, is why I do this job," she says. "There is nothing more rewarding than helping someone be a good performer so they can achieve their goal, whether that might be buying a new car, closing their first big sale, or reaching a financial milestone."

It seems like a sales career has always been in the cards for Geisert. One of her first jobs, when she was in high school and college, was working in a retail clothing store. "I found I was pretty good at it. I could make people happy and make money. I was hooked!" After college, she started her career with Computer Horizons Corporation (CHC) at a time when the IT talent pool was very limited. Companies would hire promising college graduates, regardless of major, and then provide them with training for the technology applications that the company used. CHC contracted to provide that training. "I had a phone book and a phone, and did a lot of cold calling to find those companies. Unfortunately, at times, our product wasn't always a good fit for the market. I quickly learned to listen and better understand what the customer wanted, and then realigned what we could provide," she commented. It must have worked, as she continued to open branches in 12 different markets across the U.S. over the next 15 years.

When TEKsystems acquired her division of CHC in 2007, Geisert went from using heavy doses of e-mails to communicate with her cross-country, virtual sales force to having them just outside her office. She recalls that one of her mentors asked her why she was spending so much of her time on her computer. "There is nothing that is going to happen on that computer that compares with what's going to happen out in those offices. Leave your computer at your desk and pull up a chair next to your people!" Some of the best advice over her career has come from her mentors, she noted.

Geisert believes that TEKsystems excels at training and coaching all of its employees. Evidently, others in the company agree; for the second straight year, it is ranked by *Fortune* as one of the top 100 companies to work for. Her own coach has helped her adapt and successfully lead the 13 sales people, 16 recruiters, and five administrative assistants who report to her. TEKsystems coaches Geisert and its other leaders to identify gaps between current performance and where they want to be, or should be. "I started out with a gap between 'wanting to be liked by all my employees' and 'making tough decisions,'" she recalled. Geisert learned that she had to get over the need to be liked, because—as a sales manager—you are bound to make decisions that someone is not going to like. As a sales manager, she sees that one of her most important jobs is to help people to identify and leverage their strengths and work on narrowing their performance gaps.

During her time with TEKsytems, Geisert's leadership style has evolved. "In this position, you have to learn to delegate. You can't make all the decisions, and, if you think about it, you don't want to make all the decisions either. We coach our recruiters and sales staff by asking questions that make them think through the situation, so they learn to make the right decisions. Salespeople, like me, by nature, can be a bit impatient. We tend to want to answer questions and then move on. If I want to develop my team, I know I need to slow down and ask them

DANA GEISERT
Director of
Business Operations
TEKsystems

questions, so they can figure out the answer. I try to have a balance of push and pull in my questioning. Some people need a little pull to get them there, and some need a push."

When asked how much of her time was spent coaching, Geisert responded, "Not enough; probably about 50 percent of my time. I don't get to spend as much as I'd like. It is the most fun and rewarding part of my job. While we do small bits of daily coaching, one larger part of what we do is called our four-week game plans. We think through the activities that we need to do for each rep's five largest customers over the next four weeks. Then we discuss how to prepare and accomplish those actions."

Geisert notes that an important part of her job is making sure that all members of her group work as a team. "We do tons of teamwork in our job. Teamwork is part of TEKsystem's core values. An important part of our selection process is spending time and effort in identifying people who will be good team members. Then we work on becoming better team players. If you aren't a good team member, you won't be successful." ■

In Chapter 3, we discussed leadership theories and different approaches to conceptualizing leadership. At this point, we will extend that knowledge base and explore new skill sets as you examine the activities of supervision, managing, and leading, and see how they fit into a sales manager's position. Additionally, we'll examine elements of how sales managers incorporate coaching in their daily activities. Finally, as part of this discussion, we will also examine mentoring and what elements help make teamwork effective—both in person and in virtual settings.

Supervising

Supervision is generally used today to refer to time spent working with employees to be certain they are aware of the responsibilities of their job and how to perform them correctly. Because of the independent nature of the sales job, most of the supervisory activities sales managers engage in occur when they're working with new hires. This seemingly simple and potentially time-consuming task should not be taken lightly, as it is a critical element of a sales manager's responsibilities. Supervision was an important element in a manager's position when "management" was first studied, and continues to be in the twenty-first century.

Today, the term *supervisor* is seldom heard, yet the act of supervising is no less important than it was a century ago. Sales managers—and sometimes sales trainers—spend time **supervising** people who are performing new tasks. They observe, and then offer suggestions for improving that performance, if needed. Their presence can help ensure that, if the salesperson needs assistance, he or she gets it. Whatever you want to call it, supervising involves lots of "hands-on" time. Mark Baranczyk recalls his time as the Midwest regional sales manager for MillerCoors, where he would spend about three days a week in the field with each of his sales representatives, providing personalized supervision. During this time, he reviewed the objectives of the call and helped out reps,

New hires are most in need of supervision to be sure they accurately perform their job.

as needed. If a call was going well, he'd hold back on participating during the visit, and offer a review of the representative's performance during a "curbside coaching and counseling" session. Sometimes, Baranczyk would know the representative was having difficulties achieving an objective with a client. During calls such as these, he would take a more active role—helping to answer questions, providing insight, and overcoming the client's objections. At times like these, Baranczyk used coaching skills to help the salesperson identify and correct any shortcomings they had identified. We present more information about coaching later in this chapter.

Sometimes managers don't supervise new hires; more experienced sales personnel do. Some companies refer to people such as this as **first-level manager**.[1] Another source of supervisory assistance sales managers use is technology. If a company is using a CRM system, a supervisor can track employees' daily activities. This information can provide a sales manager with insight about how employees are progressing with their customers, whether or not they are achieving their objectives during calls, and if they are using their time wisely.

Managing

More experienced sales personnel usually don't require supervision. They do, however, require that someone, like their sales managers, manage their work responsibilities, and those of other sales force members, in order to achieve the goals of their organizational unit. In this section, we look at activities involved with managing a sales force from two different perspectives: the sales manager's and the sales representative's.

Managing the sales force requires the sales manager to be skilled in several areas, including: **setting objectives**, **organizing** the tasks necessary to achieve them, **motivating** the sales force, and **problem solving**. Although the goals of the organization are set by executive officers, most managers are charged with setting the objectives of their units to meet the goals of the organization, and with developing a budget to support them. Wayne Nash is the national account sales manager for LDPI, Inc., a company that manufactures commercial lighting fixtures for hazardous, wet, and clean room applications. The company's sales goals are set by LDPI's vice-president of sales and marketing. Nash works with a regional sales manager, three sales engineers, and a large number of independent sales representatives and distributors located across the U.S. and North America. He is responsible for planning how the sales force will work to achieve the company's sales goals. He sets sales objectives for each sales unit and individual sales rep. He then allocates his budget in a manner that will support accomplishing the objectives he has laid out. If his company wants to increase its sales by five percent, Nash might, for example, look at marketing research showing potential market segments underserved by the company. To help educate potential buyers about LDPI's products, he could set aside resources to purchase advertisements in industry magazines, mail materials to a select group of customers, send personnel to participate in appropriate tradeshows, and offer a financial incentive for sales made to new customers in this new market segment.

The next set of management responsibilities focuses on organizing and staffing the sales force. The sales manager must make decisions about how to organize the work and who is going to handle each task. This may range from broader decisions, such as deciding how to organize the sales force (for example, by industry, geography, or product line), to more narrowly focused decisions, such as assigning specific salespeople to specific clients. It might also require making decisions about how to divide responsibilities for a team-based selling effort—for example, deciding who should handle outbound calls to qualify

Planning, analyzing, and organizing are all parts of managing a sales force.

prospects, who should meet and present products to clients, and who should follow up to offer them sales support.

Sales managers also typically play an important role when it comes to staffing. Oftentimes, they work very closely with their human resources departments, recruiting and selecting new sales force members. At other times, especially in larger organizations, they leave most of the recruiting and screening activities to their human resource departments, which then refer the top candidates to the sales managers for consideration and final hire—or no-hire—decisions.

Certainly, making sure sales representatives have an incentive to do their jobs well is also an important task for the sales manager to perform (see Chapter 12); so is training and developing sales representatives (see Chapter 9), as well as coaching them.

The last set of management responsibilities involves measuring and analyzing the performance of the sales force and, when needed, taking corrective action in order to meet the initial objectives. (This aspect is discussed in more detail in Chapter 11.) In essence, this is problem-solving. If LDPI was trying to capture wastewater treatment plants as potential new customers, for example, Nash would need to measure the extent of sales activities aimed at this group by determining how many inquiries resulted from the ads he placed, how many and what quality of prospects were identified at trade shows, and where potential customers were in the buying process. After analyzing the data, he might determine that—although LDPI had improved its visibility among these buyers—the company's representatives still needed to spend a greater amount of time familiarizing the buyers with the company. In order to help his representatives accomplish this task, he might encourage LDPI's marketing department to engage in new promotional activities, such as placing additional advertisements in other industry publications, attending industry trade shows, or using a small, outbound call center to make follow-up calls to trade show attendees.

If Nash learned that the sales force was requesting more information on the needs of the wastewater treatment industry, and the regulations governing it, he again would have to respond. Suppose, for example, that—after hearing reports such as this from the field—he learned that different chemicals are used in different climates (Florida versus Minnesota), and that different states have more stringent regulations than others. As a result of these differences, he might decide that further training of the sales representatives was needed immediately. It might be that, after overcoming these obstacles, he then learns that there are certain times of the year when municipalities are more likely to make a purchase. At this point, he might decide to offer reps a 60-day bonus plan during these times of the year, to motivate them to concentrate their efforts on these potential buyers. With each piece of information he gains, he *manages* his personnel and budget to accomplish the goals of his sales force.

Sources of Power

To accomplish their goals, sales managers need power, which can stem from different sources. While studying the workings of teams, two psychologists, French and Raven, developed a classification of **power bases** that team leaders used to reward or punish their team members.[2] The amount of power a leader had with their team varied depending upon the composition of each team and skill set of each individual manager or leader. Some of the sources of power may be the result of a formal structure, or they may also be acquired through informal structures. Exhibit 10.1 displays the bases of power.

Formal power is given on the basis of the position a person holds in an organization. It is the authority an individual is given to accomplish her job. The formal bases of power are legitimate power, reward power, coercive power, and informational power. **Legitimate power** is the power given to a particular position.

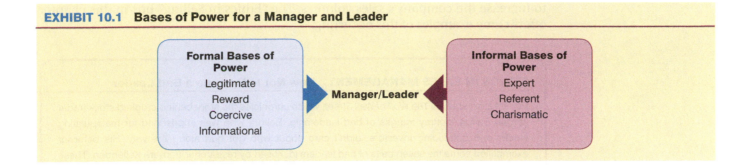

EXHIBIT 10.1   Bases of Power for a Manager and Leader

For sales managers, this typically would include the power to make decisions regarding issues of employment, budgeting, and any other decisions they need to make to accomplish the tasks under their responsibility. A national sales manager has more legitimate power than a regional sales manager, who will have more than a district sales manager.

Reward power is the ability to distribute rewards. The rewards might include providing reps with more desirable territories (perhaps involving less travel), different compensation levels, gifts, benefits, promotions, job titles, and accoutrements related to their work environment, such as, say, company cars, the latest technological devices, and nicer offices. Praise and recognition are also considered rewards, even more so when material rewards are not readily available. The opposite of reward power is **coercive power**. This stems from the ability of the sales manager to withhold rewards. It could also include making negative verbal comments to or about a salesperson. When coercive power is used, it typically builds resentment and resistance on the part of the recipient(s). As you might expect, it is the least effective form of power.

Informational power is power a leader derives from the ability to access and control information that other people don't have. If only the sales manager has a great deal of information about the sales process or sales organization, the representatives will be dependent upon the manager, and will have to contact her for assistance at multiple points during a sales cycle. Thus, the manager will have power over the representatives. More effective organizations encourage the sharing of information throughout the sales organization. Customer relationship management systems are designed for this very purpose, in fact. The more information sales representatives have, the more empowered they are to do their jobs.

Informal power is power that an individual has as a result of his skills, personality, or geniality. These bases are expert power, referent power, and charismatic power. People who possess informal power can actually exert more influence over other group members than a person with only formal power. **Expert power** is power based on a person's knowledge, skills, and expertise. Sales managers who are skilled in the various aspects of selling a product, solving customer problems, and managing their accounts have expert power. **Referent power** is based on the degree to which a person is liked due to her personality and interpersonal skills. A sales manager who is well-liked and admired, based on her personal attributes, will have a high level of referent power. When an individual is strongly admired—based on personality, physical attractiveness, and other factors—that individual may have what is referred to as **charismatic power**. Those with charismatic power over their group members are often able to induce them to accomplish the most. For example, sales managers with charismatic power might have the ability to revitalize and encourage their sales forces to succeed—even against seemingly insurmountable odds. However, if this power is used in a negative way, it can result in sales representatives' engaging in unethical sales practices. An example would be a manager who encouraged his sales force to misrepresent their firm's product characteristics to potential buyers, so as to increase the company's sales volumes. The "Ethics in Selling" box in this chapter offers some examples of this occurring.

ETHICS IN SALES MANAGEMENT   **How Not to Become a Bad Leader**

Recent films such as *The Wolf of Wall Street*, which chronicles the story behind crooked stock trader Jordan Belfort, portray images of bad leadership. Belfort, who was imprisoned for manipulating stocks and defrauding investors, didn't care about who got hurt along the way. His behavior exemplified some the seven traits of bad leaders identified by researcher Barbara Kellerman. These traits include being corrupt, insular, callous, intemperate, rigid, incompetent, and evil.

No one wants to become a bad leader. Successful leaders clearly communicate, plan well, and build strong working relationships and teamwork. Researchers, including Kellerman and Clinton Longnecker, have identified behaviors that result in bad leadership. Below are some tips on minimizing bad leadership behaviors and on maximizing good ones.

- Don't be arrogant or inflexible. Stay humble.
- Don't misrepresent the truth or become untrustworthy. Tell the truth.
- Don't lack vision or a plan. Provide a clear direction. Tell where things are heading.
- Don't be unwilling to listen. Equip your followers with the information needed to do their jobs, demonstrating a willingness to listen.
- Don't be erratic or unpredictable. Be consistent in your behavior.
- Don't claim the credit and avoid blame. Share recognition with all parties, and take responsibility when things don't go well.
- Don't limit employees' opportunities. Develop your employees to the fullest.
- Don't surround yourself with "yes" people. Seek input from experts in your area of weakness.
- Don't go it alone. Have a support system of people who can administer tough love.
- Don't be a workaholic. Stay balanced and understand what it takes to have a healthy work-life balance.

Based on Kellerman, Barbara (2001). *Bad Leadership: What It Is, How It Happens, Why It Matters?* Boston, MA: Harvard Business School Press. Kellerman, Barbara (2006). "Bad Leaders," *Leadership Excellence*, (24)9, September, 17. Longnecker, Clinton O. (2011). "Characteristics of really bad bosses," *Industrial Management*, (53)5, 10-15.

Which form of power is most effective for a sales manager to use? Without some formal power, sales managers have a very limited ability to direct the efforts of their sales representatives. However, sales managers with only formal power might find that their sales representatives are just minimally dedicated to their jobs. Those sales managers who are able to utilize more informal power bases, in concert with their formal power bases, will likely find themselves with sales reps who actually want to work for them.

As a sales manager, you need to think about the various power bases, and how you can develop and effectively use them. Bruce Hanson's past position was as a regional sales manager for RR Donnelly, a printing company with worldwide locations. In that position, Hanson utilized a variety of types of power. He had legitimate power, based on his position; reward power to affect the compensation his reps received; the ability to hand out praise to reinforce their behaviors; and, if needed, he could use coercive power to attempt to correct the actions of representatives. Lastly, he could utilize informational power—especially with newer hires—to help guide them through selling situations that required a great deal of insight and experience.

Hanson is also very knowledgeable about printing, and enjoyed working with his sales representatives. They looked to him for guidance. In other words, he has power as an expert. He made sure that he spent time not just working with his employees, but also socializing with them—whether it was over a meal, at a ballgame, or a company function. His representatives enjoyed working with him and, as a result, he also had referent power and charismatic power he could use to accomplish his managerial goals.

The Up-Close Perspective: Becoming the Boss

Using power is one area that new managers often struggle with as they transition into their new positions. Studies of new managers indicate that the assumptions they hold about becoming the boss often are not accurate.[3] Findings indicate that the skills required to be a good manager are different from those of being a star performer. Many sales managers are promoted because of their sales ability—not their management skills. Looking back on the first group of sales representatives he managed, Dave Anderson, who was a sales manager with an automotive dealerships company comments, "I am so, so sorry. I didn't know what I was doing." Anderson's comments are not that uncommon. Few new sales managers know what challenges lie ahead for them.[4]

A sales manager faces new challenges she did not face as a sales person.

Linda Hill's research on transitioning into managerial positions finds that it is often a difficult task because of new managers' misperceptions about their soon-to-be roles. The biggest misperception of many new managers is that their jobs will revolve around implementing their own ideas. In reality, they find that it is more about working together and combining everyone's ideas. Another misperception is that power will come from their position; instead, they find out that it comes more from their informal bases of power. Controlling people is not nearly as important as getting their commitment. And, finally, sales managers learn that it's not just about working one-on-one with individuals to keep things going, but about clearing the path of obstacles so that your team will make great achievements. Recognizing these common misperceptions can help new sales managers develop into their new roles.[5]

For new leaders, experts recommend making a low-key entry. This gives you time to learn the ropes, develop relationships, and benefit from the wisdom of those who have preceded you. It also allows your employees time to demonstrate what they know, and gives you a chance to show your appreciation for the contributions each of them make. As leadership expert Warren Bennis puts it, "It shows that you are a leader, not a dictator."[6]

One way to understand what traits are considered most important for sales managers to be effective would be to ask them. Research summarizing the opinions of sales managers on what traits they thought were most important is displayed in Exhibit 10.2.[7]

Once established in their positions, sales managers must always work to improve and expand their expertise in terms of their people management skills. There are volumes of books written on this topic. The following is a summary of suggestions of important behaviors that managers should demonstrate to their direct reports.[8] These are behaviors that a new sales manager should find actionable and would serve them well:

1. **Clarify the direction your business is taking**. Managers need to communicate clearly where the business is headed, why, and how employees will contribute to it. By discussing this, people have a better perspective of the issues facing the organization and how they fit in.

2. **Set goals and objectives**. Without goals and objectives, sales managers are just making assumptions about their progress. Goals and objectives should be set at both team and individual levels. Doing a good job of establishing them will also make your bonus and merit decisions clearer and easier to communicate to your individual representatives.

EXHIBIT 10.2   Characteristics of Effective Sales Managers

Variable	Definition "The sales manager…"	Ranking by Sales Managers	Ranking by Sales Representatives
Communication and listening skills	communicates and listens effectively.	1	1
Human relations skills	works with the sales team and develops rapport with team members.	2	1
Organization and time management skills	can organize and manage his or her own time and work activities.	3	5
Knowledge possession	is knowledgeable about the product, place in the market, and the industry.	3	1
Coaching skills	mentors reps to improve their skill.	5	7
Motivation skills	identifies motivating factors and rewards good performance.	6	4
Honest and ethical tendencies	is perceived as truthful, straightforward and ethical.	6	8
Selling skills	has sales experience	8	not listed
Leadership skills	encourages and inspires reps.	8	5
Willingness to empower	allows reps to take responsibility and action.	10	9

Adapted from Deeter-Schmelz, Dawn R., Daniel, J. Goebel, and Karen Norman Kennedy (2008). "What are the characteristics of an effective sales manager? An exploratory study comparing salesperson and sales manager perspectives," *Journal of Personal Selling & Sales Management*, (28)1, Winter, 12.

3. **Give frequent, specific, and immediate feedback.** This shows you are interested in the development of your representatives, how you think they are performing and, if need be, how to improve their performance. It will also make the performance reviews you administer go more smoothly.

4. **Be decisive and timely.** After you have the information you need, your salespeople expect you to make a decision in a timely manner. This helps your reps move forward instead of wondering how they should proceed.

5. **Be accessible.** If, as a sales manager, you expect your sales representatives to keep you informed, you need to be available when they need to see you. This can be done in person, by phone, or electronically.

6. **Demonstrate honesty and candor.** When sales managers communicate with their representatives, especially during performance appraisals, they should use language that is specific and not vague. Masking the truth doesn't help people develop.

The Sales Representative's Perspective: What It Takes to Be a Good Sales Manager

So what does it take to be considered a good sales manager by your sales representatives? Perspectives differ depending upon what position you are viewing things from. Exhibit 10.2 contains sales reps' ranking of traits.[9] When groups of sales representatives were asked to describe characteristics that help make a sales manager *good*, they were able to identify some common themes.[10,11,12] The following is a summary of the characteristics they identified to be a good sales manager:

1. **Flexible**—Good sales managers need to be able to balance the demands of handling business issues one minute, and then shift gears to direct and coach people the next. They have to work through people, and not do the job themselves.

2. **Good communicator and listener**—This means being available to give timely and frequent feedback. When sales representatives need help, it usually means they need immediate help—as opposed to feedback in a couple of days. Good managers have an open-door policy and don't mind being interrupted. They respond to e-mails the same day and return missed phone calls the day they come in.

3. **Works for the good of the team**—Good sales managers don't put their needs ahead of those of the team. They shift the spotlight from themselves, so that it focuses on their team and team members. They take satisfaction from the accomplishments of their groups.

4. **Considered trustworthy**—Over time, through actions and examples, a good sales manager is able to develop an atmosphere of trust. Sales representatives feel comfortable about sharing information with the manager, because they know the manager will help do what is best for them and respect their individual wishes.

5. **Can motivate and lead the team**—Good sales managers help their teams conquer the challenges they face by keeping their teams motivated via informal actions (for example, by offering feedback to their reps on a personal basis) and formal actions (for example, by recognizing their representatives publicly).

Leading

Research shows that a poor sales manager can literally cost a company millions in lost sales opportunities. (One research study places this number between $10 and $20 million annually.) For example, two-thirds of sales vice-presidents who were surveyed indicated that 40 percent of their sales leaders were not meeting expectations, and cited a lack of leadership and coaching skills as the source of their sales leaders' failure. Dissatisfaction with one's boss is, in fact, the number one sales representatives complaint.[13] Another study, conducted by The Forum Corporation, found that a firm's sales managers "figured prominently" in the success of their sales forces, and that sales forces whose managers think strategically, provide coaching and feedback to their salespeople, and create a motivating environment perform much better than others. The respondents noted, however, that sales managers were often promoted because they were high-performing sales representatives—not because of their managerial abilities.

The qualifications required by sales managers are changing, though. Firms are demanding a higher level of **leadership** and management skills than in the past. "We have changed the first-line sales manager's role to become more of a training and coaching/development role, versus a super sales rep," one survey respondent said. Given the extent to which a firm's success is determined by its sales managers, the remainder of this section examines a promising new leadership approach and skill sets new sales managers should develop.[14]

A New School of Managerial Thought?

In the last part of the twentieth century, leadership studies identified a classic, two-factor approach that focused on the tasks and relationship behaviors of leaders. These approaches were labeled **transactional approaches,** because they focus on an exchange, of some nature, between leaders and their followers, such as leaders giving promotions and bonuses to sales representatives who meet their sales goals.

More recently there has been a movement toward a **transformational approach** to leadership. "It (the transformational approach) is concerned with emotions, values, ethics, standards, and long-term goals, and includes assessing followers' motives, satisfying their needs, and treating them as human beings." Transformational leaders focus on the needs and motives of their employees, trying to help them reach their fullest potential.[15] These leaders also exhibit **emotional intelligence**.[16] Emotional intelligence includes one's ability to understand and manage the emotions of other people in light of their own. "The underlying premise is that people who are more sensitive to their emotions and the impact of their emotions on others will be more effective leaders."[17] Emotional intelligence includes self-management skills such as self-awareness, self-regulation, motivation, and the ability to relate to others through a leader's empathy and social skills. Leaders with high levels of emotional intelligence create environments that foster trust, reasonable amounts of risk-taking, and higher levels of productivity. Low levels of emotional intelligence in a work environment foster fear and anxiety.[18] Generally, as people mature, their emotional intelligence increases.

Researchers and companies like American Express, Nestlé, Pfizer, Hilton, and Johnson & Johnson see great potential in training their sales leaders to improve their emotional intelligence styles.[19, 20, 21] FedEx Express implemented training programs that developed the emotional intelligence capabilities of their new managers on a worldwide basis. They report increases in several metrics that measure core leadership competencies. One participant commented, "… I was limiting myself with a single leadership style…that was preventing me from reaching my full potential, particularly in stressful situations…[using my training,] I learned how to apply different leadership styles to meet specific situations…"[22]

What Leadership Competencies Do Sales Managers Need?

The studies we discussed in this chapter suggest that sales managers today need to focus on and develop better leadership skills than in the past. According to the responses of sales vice-presidents, many sales managers appear to be under-prepared to play this role.[23] The highest-performing sales organizations rely heavily on their sales managers to provide representatives with ongoing coaching and feedback. In fact, it is a key predictor of the success an organization will achieve. In addition to developing managers' coaching skills, two other leadership development methods— utilized increasingly over the past 20 years—are coaching and working in teams.[24] We look at these activities next.

Coaching

What image comes to mind when you hear the word *coaching*? Perhaps you envision someone involved in athletics or the arts. Can you imagine a performer or team trying to perfect a performance without the benefit of feedback? No doubt you have probably tried performing some activity without the advice of a coach or teacher. Contrast that performance with one in which you received feedback. As you probably know, the value of a coach can be significant.

Coaching salespeople is not that much different than coaching athletes or performers. Findings from a study of more than 1,000 firms showed that salespeople who meet at least one-half day a week, one-on-one, with their managers are 20 times more productive than other salespeople.[25] Some researchers believe that it's because "coachability" is such an important attribute for new reps to possess that they propose that it should be considered as part of the selection criteria when hiring a sales rep.[26]

As we mentioned earlier in the chapter, Mark Baranczyk, a regional sales manager for MillerCoors, spends about three days each week in the field with each of his sales representatives. During and after each of the sales calls, Mark coaches each of his representatives. This includes asking them questions about their performance, offering positive feedback and advice, perhaps setting aside time for practice, and setting future performance-related goals for them.

For sales coaching to be effective, a sales manager should follow several guidelines: [26, 27, 28, 29]

1. **Prepare and observe.** Let your sales representatives know you are joining them to observe them and offer your feedback. Make sure you understand the objectives of the calls they are making. Watch for nonverbal communication and listen carefully.

2. **Give feedback.** Avoid asking your sales representatives "yes or no" questions about how well they performed. Instead, ask them open-ended questions such as the following: "What other options could you have offered the customer when she objected to the product's price?" Be specific when pointing out a person's good selling skills and those that could be improved. Telling a representative, "You should take more initiative," is not as helpful as telling the person something like: "When the buyer didn't know if there was a good fit between the two systems, it probably would have been a good idea to ask her to explain where the fit was 'off' or ask her to try to use our product during a no-cost trial period." Focus on improving your reps' skills, rather than dwelling on things they did incorrectly. Provide the feedback as soon after the observation as possible.

3. **Be a role model.** Modeling or demonstrating the desired behaviors, and letting your representatives model that behavior, is a powerful way of coaching people. Explain how and why you did the things you did. Give your representatives the opportunity to use the same tactics you did.

4. **Follow-up.** Demonstrate to your representatives that you follow up—in other words, that you do what you say you will do. Develop an action plan with goals, measures of success, a timetable, and how the rep and coach will work.

5. **Build trust.** The relationships between sales representatives and their sales managers in which there are high levels of trust will be more productive than those relationships that lack trust.

Sometimes it doesn't matter how great a coach a sales manager is. It still might not be enough. An example might be a case in which a sales representative is excessively absent, misses appointments and deadlines, experiences numerous customer complaints, or is even involved in auto accidents. This could indicate that the salesperson's on-the-job performance is being impacted by other factors that no amount of coaching will cure. It might be that the salesperson just needs a little time off to deal with some pressing personal issues. However, when a pattern of these behaviors develops, it may be time for the sales manager to see if the salesperson needs professional **counseling**. The representative could be experiencing marital and/or family problems, financial stress, health issues, or engaging in substance abuse. In cases such as these, the sales manager should seek the confidential assistance of her or his human resources personnel. HR can help evaluate whether the representative needs professional help, and if so, help the person get it.

Mentoring

Many firms are encouraging sales managers to not only be a mentor, but to also have a mentor. **Mentoring** is a long-term relationship in which a senior person supports the personal and professional development of a junior person.[30] The mentor concept has its origins in Greek mythology. When King Odysseus was about to go to fight in the Trojan War, Mentor, an elderly friend, was charged by the king to watch over

Working with a mentor is one of the best developmental activities a sales person can have.

the hero's son, Telemachus. Mentor provided insights to his younger protégé that only an elder, more experienced person could.[31]

A mentor, then, is a person who acts as a teacher or trustworthy advisor. The mentor, typically, does not have a reporting relationship with the person they are mentoring. Their relationship can be formally established by an organization, or can develop more informally.

Camellia Poplarski is a regional sales director for the drug maker Eli Lilly. Eli Lilly is a firm believer in the merits of being—and having—mentors. Typically, a person being mentored benefits from being given the perspective of someone who has already "been there and done that." Mentors can help with everything from the proper procedures employees should follow to career advice. As Poplarski sees it, "It gives you a leg up, because you learn things that are not in any book." Mentoring helps younger representatives become more knowledgeable about the marketplace, the firm for which they are selling, and its products. Having a mentor program can also give a company an advantage when recruiting new sales reps.[32] Experts recommend that, if your organization does not have a formal mentoring program in place, you should seek out an individual and ask if they will serve in a mentoring capacity. It is recommended that this individual be several levels above you—and someone you trust and admire. Mentoring sessions are usually very informal and occur several times a year or when needed.

Traditionally, there were two times when it was thought best to participate in a mentoring relationship. The first was when someone was just beginning their career (they learned what to expect), and when senior sales personnel reached a plateau in their career (they benefited from offering their counsel to new hires). New approaches to implementing this junior/senior matching have recently surfaced.

GLOBAL SALES MANAGEMENT   Mentoring Around the Globe

The topic of mentoring is frequently found in articles and websites in the United States. But what about its value or popularity outside the U.S.? The Center for Creative Leadership (CCL) has reviewed and examined research on the value of mentoring as it is perceived by respondents in 33 countries. The most universal finding is that managers who provide career-related mentoring to their direct reports are rated as better performers in their jobs by their boss. Mentoring typically consists of providing career-related behaviors of sponsorship, coaching, and challenge to their charges.

Countries with the high correlation between mentoring and performance were noted as having the following characteristics:

- They encourage and reward improvement and excellence.
- They value training and development.
- They view feedback as essential.
- They value setting ambitious goals and challenging participants.

Researchers found that mentoring was considered a more valuable activity in some countries than in others. In countries with a high performance orientation, the relationship between mentoring and performance was even stronger. This relationship was particularly strong in the Americas—including Canada, the United States, Mexico, Venezuela, and Brazil. In addition, both Portugal and the Philippines were also noted for having a strong relationship.

Based on Gentry, Bill. (2013). "Mentoring Matters for Managers," Accessed March 20, 2014. *http://www.leading effectively.com/mentoring-matters-for-managers-infographic/*. Gentry, W. A., T.J. Weber, and G. Sadrii, (2008) "Examining career-related mentoring and managerial performance across cultures: A multilevel analysis," *Journal of Vocational Behavior*, (72)2, April 2008, 241–253.

One pharmaceutical firm paired its best sales people with new hires for a three-step process. In the first step, new hires observed the established sales people to observe all the nuances of a successful sale. In the second step, the roles were reversed, as new hires made the call and were coached by the senior rep. In the last step, the pair met regularly to review setbacks and accomplishments. Senior reps were compensated for their efforts by receiving a one percent commission on all revenue brought in by the new hire during the one-year program.[33] Another twist on this idea is reverse mentoring, with the pair sharing skill sets. For example, a senior rep may help in showing different parts of a sales call, and the junior rep may reciprocate by showing the senior rep skills where they may have more expertise—for example, how to use social media tools to increase sales.[34]

While anecdotal comments about the value of mentoring are often shared in the popular media, research evidence also supports this. Researchers have shown that sales managers who were mentored by managers inside their firms experienced less turnover and perform better than those sales managers with peer mentors, outsider mentors, or no mentors.[35]

The Ability to Organize and Work Effectively with Teams

Historically, sales representatives have worked independently. However, with the more complex products and services that firms are offering, the increased use of supply chain management, and a more global marketplace, more situations require sales personnel to work in **teams**. Some organizations now assign a sales team to their key, or national, accounts. International sales opportunities require sales personnel from different cultures and parts of the world to work interdependently on projects.[36] To develop better product solutions for the buyer, a team might be comprised of representatives from several functional areas, such as sales, product development, operations, and customer service.[37, 38]

Sales teams can be as small as two individuals or larger. Pfizer Oncology found that their product portfolio was more than one rep could handle. So they paired two reps with different specialties—but complementary knowledge—to call on doctors together. For the dyad to be effective, both reps must bring complementary strengths, trust, and great communication skills. Pfizer found that, with training, its teams learned how to successfully use the talents of both professionals.[39]

Greg Shortell is the president and CEO of Network Engines, a company that makes server applications to be installed on computer hardware, or to be packaged with it. Shortell says his company has moved from product-based sales to solution-based sales. "You need in-depth, specialized knowledge…that goes right through all the steps—from requirements to delivery—and different people have to fill those needs," he explains. For example, a "prospecting" representative might work to identify and qualify leads before handing them off to a "sales" representative who would establish face-to-face communications with prospective customers. At this point, a specialist involved with the development of the product would talk to the customers about the fit of the product with their firms. If a sale was completed, the client might then be turned over to a "customer service and follow-up" team member, responsible for ensuring that the products are delivered on time and meet customers' quality expectations.[40]

Sales managers need to work with sales teams to react to changes in the marketplace.

Just working with other people does not make your group a team, however. A team is a small group of people with complementary skills, who, as such, are able to collectively complete a project in a superior way. They are committed to a common goal. Members interact with each other and with the leader, and depend on each other's input to perform their own work. Those teams that are empowered to handle an ongoing task are considered **self-managed teams**. A **project team** is organized around a unique task of limited duration, and is disbanded when the task is completed.[41]

Sales managers working with teams will fare better if they take the time to structure and organize the teams when they are initially established. If they don't take that time to do so, the team will likely struggle. An initial orientation meeting, in which team members learn about each other's skills and the team's goals, is often a good idea. Team responsibilities, tasks, and leaders should be clearly assigned, so that everyone understands what is expected of them and who "owns" the different aspects of different accounts or projects. Another important element of successful teams is sharing client communications. Contact management systems can be used for this purpose. Sales managers also need to make sure the team has the right people with the right skills, and that it is only as large as it needs to be. Making sure that reward systems are in place to motivate the individual efforts of team members, as well as entire teams, is also important. In fact, poorly designed reward systems for teams are a frequent reason why they fail.[42]

Being a Team Member

Once you have a team up and running, what should you expect from the reps—and what is expected from you, as a member of a management team? Again, we will provide a short summary of some actionable behaviors that a new sales manager (and team members) should consider engaging in when working with their teams.[43]

1. **Get involved.** This is particularly important when someone falls behind on his or her commitments, especially because of important personnel issues, and in a crisis.

2. **Generate ideas.** Sales managers and team members who contribute innovative and creative ideas are rarer than those who don't.

3. **Be willing to collaborate.** You might not enjoy working with all your colleagues, but you need to be able to work with them for the benefit of the organization.

4. **Be willing to lead initiatives.** Future projects are full of uncertainties; being willing to take a risk is a valuable attribute.

5. **Develop leaders as you develop.** It is important to be personally involved in developing your employees.

6. **Stay current.** Know what is going on in the world, with your customers, and with their markets.

7. **Anticipate market changes.** Don't sit back, waiting for change to occur; plan for it.

8. **Drive your own growth.** Constantly seek out education and self-development opportunities through the activities and assignments you are engaged in, and in your personal relationships.

9. **Be a player for all seasons.** Be open to change in good times and in bad.

VIRTUAL TEAMS Oftentimes, sales managers assign personnel in different geographic locations to work in **virtual teams**. These people send and receive the majority of their communications electronically, as opposed to in-person. Some sales managers, such as Eric McMillan from 3M, work virtually with their representatives and also in-person with them. For others, such as Katherine Twells of Coca-Cola, whose sales personnel are widely dispersed, working at a distance is the norm. Twell uses e-mails, instant messaging, and weekly calls to communicate with his reps. Tips for working with virtual teams include:

1. **Selecting the technology that works best for the team.** Although some technologies might sound appealing, the majority of teams prefer to use an Intranet website with areas on team information and contacts, discussion, and information posting. When needed, they will hold a teleconference.

2. **Communicating frequently.** Most groups do so daily.

3. **Tracking down members who aren't participating.** This is especially important for the leader of the virtual team to do early in the life of the team, while norms are being set.

4. **Having agreed-upon ground rules for the team's interaction.** For example, require team members to answer e-mails within 24 hours, even if their replies are brief.[44, 45]

In his former position, Bill Febry was the national director for sales, managing the sales force for the Jacob Leinenkugel Brewing Company. Febry says sales managers should "educate, motivate, and inspire." However, he notes that he can't do that by e-mail: "As much as I'd like to see every one of my direct reports in person, when I can't, I make an effort to pick up the phone and speak with them personally, not in an e-mail, not with a recording on the voice mail." In other words, in even the best virtual teams, there's no substitute for personal contact. You can't solely manage people electronically—at least, not well.

The Future of Sales Management

Whether sales managers are supervising, managing, and/or leading, they will always face challenges. Business executives have identified five challenges for future leaders.[46]

1. **Incorporate globalization/internationalization of leadership concepts.** Sales leaders must be comfortable with, and knowledgeable about, doing business in the international marketplace (see Chapter 15).

2. **Increase the integrity and character of leaders**. Sales leaders of today need to be humble, team builders, good communicators. Transformational leadership works only when leaders have a solid moral character and a concern for others, and demonstrate these through their actions.

3. **Incorporate new ways of thinking about leadership.** Leadership is shifting from a focus of individual leaders toward developing the capacity of all group members.

4. **Integrate technology.** Technology changes how we live and work; how information is gathered, organized, and shared; and how we communicate. Leading a virtual team located in different parts of the country and globe is a reality. Leaders will clearly have to be much more engaged, and comfortable, with technology.

5. **Demonstrate return on investment**. Leadership development activities—just like other forms of training—must be able to demonstrate their effectiveness. Those aspiring to advance to sales leadership positions would do well to use these challenges to guide their future directions.

Managing Your Career

It's not often that all research findings say the same thing, but in the case of the value of mentoring in helping you develop a successful start to your career, opinions seem to be unanimous. Whether you receive advice from a more experienced person on what options lie ahead for you, or you give advice to a less-experienced person—both are considered great for your career.

If you can be a good role model, provide open and honest feedback, and are accessible to others, you already have traits associated with good mentoring. Where can you start? Think back to when you first arrived on your college campus. Were you a little lost and anxious about how things worked, and what to expect? Did you have older, more experienced, friends or siblings who shared their insights with you?

Most campuses would love to have you mentor arriving freshmen. Who knows more about your college campus, courses, and how to survive—and thrive—than someone like you? If you are willing to help, you are likely to find that the rewards of being a mentor are meaningful, and can have a significant impact.

Don't stop with the first week of school. Ever hear the term, "Big Brothers/ Big Sisters"? You can continue that relationship beyond that first week in your professional and social organizations. What do you get besides a "feel-good feeling?" Again, the research consistently notes that individuals who mentor are seen as having good judgment, good reputations, and credibility. They receive increased recognition, influence, visibility, respect, and admiration. Not a bad habit to start now and continue throughout your career.

Summary

In years past, many sales managers were promoted because of their excellent selling skills, with little regard for their management skills. Today, people know that sales managers with good managerial skills have a big impact on the success of firms. However, many organizations find that their sales managers lack these skills.

In terms of supervising their representatives, sales managers observe their representatives (more often, the new hires) and then give them suggestions for improving their performance. A sales manager's presence can help ensure that, if the salesperson needs assistance, he or she gets it. In some firms, more experienced sales personnel—called first-line managers—supervise new representatives.

Managing sales representatives is multi-faceted. Although the goals of a firm are generally set by its executive officers, most sales managers are charged with setting the objectives of their units to meet those goals, and developing the budgets to support them. Sales managers are also responsible for organizing and staffing their units, and for analyzing the performance of their representatives to make sure they are achieving their goals. Sales managers utilize a number of sources of formal and informal power to accomplish these tasks.

Research confirms that sales managers who have strong leadership skills, and develop their sales representatives, are more likely to have higher-performing sales forces than sales managers lacking those skills. Sales managers who adopt a transformational leadership style of management focus on the needs and motives of their representatives, and work to develop them. Sales managers with high levels of emotional intelligence have the ability to understand and manage the emotions of other people.

Other leadership skills valued more and more these days in sales managers are coaching, mentoring, and teambuilding. Coaching involves providing immediate feedback to your sales representatives in a positive way. Serving as a role model and demonstrating the behaviors you want your representatives to emulate is a powerful way to coach people. To successfully coach your representatives, they also need to believe they can trust you. Mentoring occurs when a senior member of a sales organization provides long-term career advice to a more junior member. This type of career guidance helps individuals gain new insights about their fit and contributions to the firm. The ability to build and develop sales teams is another skill set that sales managers are, increasingly, called upon to master. With sales forces becoming more geographically dispersed, and because products and services are growing too complex for a single individual to sell, sales representatives are, increasingly, working in teams to achieve their firm's sales goals. In even the best virtual teams, however, you can't solely manage people electronically. There's no substitute for personally contacting your representative—either in person or on the phone.

Key Terms

charismatic power   219
coaching   224
coercive power   219
counseling   225
emotional intelligence   224
expert power   219
first-level manager   217
formal power   218
informal power   219
informational power   219
leadership   223
legitimate power   218
managing   217
mentoring   225

motivating   217
organizing   217
power bases   218
problem solving   217
project team   228
referent power   219
reward power   219
setting objectives   217
supervising/supervision   216
self-managed teams   228
teams   227
transactional approach   223
transformational approach   223
virtual teams   228

Questions and Problems

1. Describe a situation in which a sales manager would engage in supervisory behavior. When can sales reps benefit most from supervision? Why should sales managers consider supervising a good investment of their time and efforts?

2. What activities are involved in *managing* a sales force?

3. How is a sales manager involved with organizing and staffing the sales force?

4. What bases of power available to a sales manager do you think are most effective, and why? What bases of power does your favorite instructor exhibit? What about your least favorite instructor? List some examples of instructors' behaviors that illustrate each type of power.

5. Management skills are something new sales managers need to develop. What are some specific behaviors that they should engage in? What misperceptions do new sales managers have about managing people?

6. Why is the concept of leadership of such importance to vice presidents of sales? What has caused their heightened concern?

7. How are transactional and transformational leadership approaches different? How might they be displayed in a sales manager's behaviors? What are some of the components of emotional intelligence? Who do you know that exhibits a high level of emotional intelligence?

8. Imagine a situation in which your sales rep just had a poor sales call. What coaching principles should you make sure you follow as you provide the rep with feedback? How would you initiate such a conversation?

9. What is the value of having a mentor? Explain why you would, or would not, want to have one as a sales representative. Why would a salesperson want to be a mentor if takes time away from selling to their clients?

10. Sales reps usually work independently. How would you encourage your reps to work as part of a team? What objections do you think they would have to doing so, and how might you counter them?

11. Consider the team projects you've worked on in school. What are some of the behaviors you like to see your team members engage in? Do you believe your team members would behave differently in virtual teams?

Role Play

Friend or Mentor? Deciding When to Take Action

Mara Tibby loved and hated company meetings in Capital City. It offered great food and enjoyable late-night activities, but always made the "Top 10 Worst Cities for Allergies." It was spring, and she was regretting leaving her allergy pills back home. She always got congested and a scratchy, sore throat at times like this. Tibby was headed down to the hotel lobby to buy some medicine and meet her former "rookie of the year"—star employee Jessica Dawson.

Over the past several years both, women had moved on within their company. Tibby had moved into another sales leadership position, and Dawson had moved out of the region into a position that handled larger accounts. However, the two women had managed to stay in contact with one another and have dinner together twice a year, prior to their semi-annual sales meetings.

Tibby had never officially been asked to mentor Dawson. However, over the years, Dawson had sought her advice when she had difficult decisions to make. Thus, the mentoring relationship between them seemed to naturally evolve. Lately, however, Tibby had heard that Dawson's performance seemed to be slipping a bit. Other sales managers were talking about how she had missed appointments and meetings and not met her deadlines. This certainly didn't seem like the person Tibby knew.

Dawson was sitting at the lobby bar when Tibby arrived. Tibby was taken by the fact that Dawson, who typically dressed smartly, looked a little less well-kempt, and was puffy-eyed. After they greeted, Dawson told the bartender, "I'll have another vodka tonic, and my friend will have a red wine." They finished their drinks and headed out to one of Tibby's favorite restaurants. Dawson ordered a bottle of wine as she announced to her mentor that she and her husband were splitting and that she needed a drink. "We just don't seem to have that much in common anymore. Maybe we never did." Other than the food, which was great, the dinner turned out to be a downer for Tibby, as she listened to Dawson's rant of personal issues, complaints about the lousy meal and service, and lamenting about how her marriage didn't work out.

After they finished their meal, the waiter asked about a dessert; Dawson quickly ordered an after-dinner drink. As they were walking back to the hotel, she mentioned that she was pursuing a new sales management position, and hoped that Tibby would be a reference. As they parted in the hotel lobby, they made plans to meet for breakfast before the first session meeting.

Tibby waited for Dawson for breakfast and, finally called her on her cell phone, but got a recorded message. She ended up eating breakfast alone. After the first meeting ended, she caught up with Dawson, who said, "Oh, I'm so sorry. My mom called this morning, and I had to deal with her problems. At lunch, can we talk more about that new position I mentioned last night?" Tibby couldn't help but notice that Dawson smelled strongly of mints.

Tibby knew about the new sales management position, and that her opinion about candidates would be sought. She began to reconsider recommending Dawson for the position.

Assignment

This can work for one or two scenes with two or three individuals.

Scene 1: Dawson finds Tibby at lunch, saying that she wants to pursue the new position, and that she faces some tough competition. Can she count on her for 100 percent support? Pick up the conversation at that point.

Scene 2: Later that afternoon, in the hotel hallway, the VP of Sales, who will decide on staffing for the new position, asks Tibby for her opinion on Dawson. Pick up the conversation at that point.

1. Where should Tibby's loyalties lie? What do you think is going on with Dawson?

2. As her informal mentor, should Tibby take it upon herself to ask Dawson about her performance and what's causing it to decline? Or should she mind her own business?

3. What other actions should Tibby consider taking?

Caselets

Caselet 10.1: *Using Mobile Technology?*

Dan Bernardez and Steven Jenkins work for the National Faculties Management Company (NFMC). NFMC was started by a group of engineers and a couple of software developers. Over the years, it has grown to be a nationwide provider of facilities management and energy conservation services. NFMC monitors energy consumption for each of its clients' buildings. Based on their findings, the company will identify areas of any facility that is in need of updates and repairs. The NFMC specialists can either conduct the repairs themselves or outsource it in a manner that would minimize any inconvenience for the building owner and/or the commercial tenants. Their client list ranges from small stores to shopping malls, and from doctors' offices to hospitals. Sometimes, the projects are one time-engagements; with others, the firm is contracted for multi-year monitoring services.

Bernardez had just returned from a week of travel, visiting several of his sales reps for some "ride-alongs" and coaching. He was enjoying his Saturday morning, playing a round of golf with Jenkins, who worked in the IS/operations side of the company. It wasn't uncommon for their discussions to vary from their golf game to what was going on at work. Today Bernardez was still wrestling with a situation he was having with one of the younger field sales reps, Austin Green. When Green started, he had adequate performance levels, and should have developed into a star performer. Unfortunately, now that he was on his own, he was falling short of his performance goals. To address this issue, Bernardez's past coaching had focused on increasing Green's input activities with new and existing clients.

As they sat in the clubhouse, Bernardez shared with Jenkins that he typically let reps set up his visit with them, with the expectation that he would join them on several calls to several different customers. On a recent call, Green picked up Bernardez at his hotel and they began a two-hour trip to the headquarters of a new client. When they arrived at the location, Green explained that the meeting wasn't until after lunch, so the two of them had a long lunch. This was followed by their one-hour call—with a presentation that explained the basics of how NFMC's services could benefit the client. After the call, they got back in the car and headed toward the office. When they arrived, Bernardez was surprised when Green said, "Well, that's it for today, Dan. I've got some personal things that just came up that I have to attend to. Sorry I gotta go."

Bernardez scratched his head and said, "You know, Steven, I've got my doubts about Austin. He seemed to have a lot of promise, but he just keeps coming up short. I can't quite put my finger on it. His records in our CRM system indicate he is active, but I just don't get what's going on—other than his time management skills this week, which were pretty sorry. He acted like he is accepting of my suggestions."

Jenkins had an idea. "Sounds like you've got your doubts on how he is spending his time. Did you know we have recovery GPS devices in every company car and cell phone? It is our legal right to use them on our equipment and not tell the user. Although we've never done it for anything other than for loss prevention, why don't you let me get the data on Austin's activities? You can see where he is and at what time. That way, you can really see if he is out making the calls."

1. What do you think about having Jenkins send the locations of Green's car to Bernardez? What are the advantages and disadvantages to proceeding with this idea?

2. What about his phone? What about the advantages and disadvantages of tracking him through cell phone GPS devices? What differences do you see between use of the car device and the phone device?

3. Discuss other options for Bernardez to help Green with his performance issues. What would your final recommendation be?

Caselet 10.2: *Sports League Web Services*

Sports League Web Services (SLWS) was founded by two college students who saw the need for professionally managed webpages for recreational sports leagues. With the addition of community fields and skating rinks, as well as well as indoor sports faculties, the growth of youth and adult league sports has mushroomed over the past 20 years. Typically, information about schedules was mailed to participants at the beginning of a sports season. After that, it was up to the team members to communicate with each other about issues ranging from weather delays or postponements, field changes, travel plans, and—in more competitive leagues—information about standings and tournaments. SLWS initially started with soccer and football leagues, but quickly expanded into baseball, volleyball, hockey, bowling, lacrosse, tennis, and equestrian organizations. If there was a league, the company would now service it.

With an annual contract, SLWS handles webpages for all teams in a league. Its range of services goes from hosting a basic webpage to developing a very detailed website—featuring uploaded photos, videos, and statistics, as well as weather forecasts. Once a league or team had used their services, the SLWS people thought that their clients loved them. The typical retention rate was 60 percent from season to season. Part of the reason for client turnover was because of the volunteer nature of the administrators of many leagues and teams. At one time, the company was the only provider for this niche market, but as that market expanded, the leaders found themselves facing more competition.

SLWS's internal sales teams is, typically, comprised of three different positions, staffed by four to six team members. The sales support member is typically an entry-level position that helps manage day-to-day operations, as well as searching for sales leads. Two to three field sales reps per team meet with the team/league administrators and demonstrate the product. The third position in the team is a webdesigner/data entry expert, who might work for two or three different sales teams. Sales team members are compensated based both on their individual performance and the productivity of their teams as a whole.

Ajay Singh is the sales manager for four sales teams. The sales goal deadline for his teams is fast approaching. He just received a phone call from Gwen Webster, who knows Singh through their joint volunteer work. Webster has just explained to him that she called his company last week, and that no one from the sales department had contacted her to discuss a new account. Singh knows that this account could be potentially lucrative. Singh apologized, and, after almost making the presentation himself, said that one of his account managers would contact her that afternoon. Singh discovered that her call was correctly logged into the CRM system for Team Four, and was surprised that neither of the two reps from the team had acted on this lead. Team Four's sales reps included Cody Miller, a competent, senior account rep, and Brad Hendricks, a newer, less experienced representative who was still developing.

Singh is wrestling with the decision as to which account manager he should hand the lead. He feels that someone as experienced as Miller should have already contacted Webster as a potential new client. However, he had a tendency to only go after larger, known accounts. Hendricks was always eager to "get the sale" and work with new accounts, but recently lost an account because the clients were not satisfied with the services of SLWS. Singh knows that a large sale for this team will push them over their sales goal and help assure everyone's bonus, including his.

1. What are the advantages and disadvantages of handing the lead to Brad Hendricks, the newer account manager?

2. What are the advantages and disadvantages of handing the lead to Cody Miller, the veteran account manager?

3. How would you make this decision?

4. How do you think your decision would affect the rest of the members on the team?

References

1. Priestland, Andreas, and Robert Hanig (2005). "Developing First-level Leaders," *Harvard Business Review*, (83)6, 111–120.
2. J.R.P. French, Jr., and B. Raven (1959). "The Bases of Social Power," in D. Cartwright (Ed.), *Studies in Social Power*. Ann Arbor, MI: University of Michigan Institute for Social Research.
3. Hill, Linda A. (2007). "Becoming the Boss," *Harvard Business Review*, (85)1, 48–56.
4. Hammers, Maryann, and Gerhard Gschwandtner, (2004). "Tap into the 7 Qualities of the Best Sales Managers," *Selling Power*, (24)4, May, 61–66.
5. Hill, Op.cit.
6. Bennis, Warren (2004). "The Seven Ages of the Leader," *Harvard Business Review*, (82)1, January, 46–53.
7. Deeter-Schmelz, Dawn R., Daniel J. Goebel, and Karen Norman Kennedy (2008). "What are the characteristics of an effective sales manager? An exploratory study comparing salesperson and sales manager perspectives," *The Journal of Personal Selling & Sales Management*, (28)1, Winter, 7–20.
8. Bossidy, Larry (2007). "What your Leader Expects of You–And What You Should Expect In Return," *Harvard Business Review*, (85)4, April, 58–65.
9. Deeter-Schmelz, Op.cit.
10. Hammers, Maryann, and Gerhard Gschwandtner (2004). "Tap into the 7 Qualities of the Best Sales Managers," *Selling Power*, (24)4, May, 61–66.
11. Goebel, Daniel J., Dawn R. Deeter-Schmelz, and Karen Norman Kennedy (2013). "Effective Sales Management: What do sales people think?" *Journal of Marketing Development and Competitiveness*, (7)2, 11–22.
12. Deeter-Schmelz, Dawn R., Karen Norman Kennedy, and Daniel J. Goebel (2002). "Understanding sales manager effectiveness: Linking attributes to sales force values," *Industrial Marketing Management*, (31), 617–626.
13. Wellins, Richard S., Charles J. Cosentino, and Bradford Thomas (2004). *Building a Winning Sales Force: A Sales Talent Optimization Study on Hiring and Development*. Pittsburgh, PA: Development Dimensions International.
14. Atkinson, Thomas (2004). *How Sales Forces Sustain Competitive Advantage: Sales Force Research Report*. Boston, MA: The Forum Corporation of North America.

15. Northouse, P. G. (2012), *Leadership: Theory and Practice*, sixth ed., Thousand Oaks, CA: Sage Publications, Inc., 185.

16. Goleman, Daniel (1998). *Working with Emotional Intelligence*. New York NY: Bantam.

17. Northhouse, Op. cit., 27–28.

18. Goleman, Daniel (2000). "Leadership that Gets Results," *Harvard Business Review*, (78)2, March/April, 78–91.

19. Deeter-Schmelz, Dawn R., and Jane Z. Hojka (2003). "Developing effective salespeople: Exploring the link between emotional intelligence and sales performance," *The International Journal of Organizational Analysis*, (11)3, 211–230.

20. Lassk, Felicia G., and C. David Shepherd (2013). "Exploring the relationship between emotional intelligence and salesperson creativity," *Journal of Personal Selling and Sales Management*, (33)1,Winter, 25–37.

21. Freedman, Joshua (2005). "Dr. Daniel Goleman on the Origins of Emotional Intelligence," Accessed March 18, 2014. *http://www.6seconds.org/2005/01/30/goleman-emotional-intelligence/*.

22. Freedman, Joshua (2014). "Case Study: Emotional Intelligence for People-First Leadership at FedEx Express," Accessed March 18, 2014. *http://www.6seconds.org/2014/01/14/case-study-emotional-intelligence-people-first-leadership-fedex-express/*.

23. Atkinson, Thomas (2004) Op.cit.

24. Hernez-Broome, Gina, and Richard L. Hughes (2004). "Leadership Development: Past, Present, and Future," *Human Resource Planning*, (27)1, 24–32.

25. "The Chally World Class Sales Excellence Research Report" (2007). [White paper]. Dayton, OH: HR Chally Group.

26. Shannahan, Kirby L.J., Rachelle J. Shannahan, and Alan J. Bush (2013). "Salesperson coachability: what it is and why it matters," *Journal of Business & Industrial Marketing*, (28)5, 411–420.

27. Craumer, Martha (2001). "How to Coach Your Employees," *Harvard Management Communication Letter*, Boston, MA: Harvard Business School Publishing Corporation, December, 1–5.

28. Rich, Gregory A. (1998). "The Constructs of Sales Coaching: Supervisory Feedback, Role Modeling and Trust," *The Journal of Personal Selling & Sales Management*.

29. Harvard Business School Press (2006). "Closing Gaps and Improving Performance: The Basics of Coaching," *Performance Management: Measure and Improve the Effectiveness of Your Employees*. Boston, MA: Harvard Business School Press.

30. Hernez-Broome, and Hughes, Op cit.

31. Bennis, Op cit.

32. Marchetti, Michele, (2005). "A Helping Hand," *Sales & Marketing Management*, (157)8, August, 12.

33. Ledingham, Dianne, Mark Kocac, and Heidi Locke Simon (2006). "The New Science of Sales Force Productivity," *Harvard Business Review* (84)9, 124–133.

34. Meister, Jeanne, C. and Karie Willyerd (2010). "Mentoring Millennials," *Harvard Business Review*, (88)5, 68–72.

35. Brashear, Thomas C., Danny N. Bellenger, James S. Boles, Hiram C. Barksdale, Jr. (2006). "An Exploratory Study of the Relative Effectiveness of Different Types of Sales Force Mentors," *The Journal of Personal Selling & Sales Management*, (26)1, 7–18.

36. Badrinarayanan, Vishag Sreendhar Madhavaram, and Elad Granot (2011). "Global Virtual Sale Teams (GVSTS): A Conceptual Framework of the Influence of Intellectual and Social Capital of Effectiveness," *The Journal of Personal Selling & Sales Management*, (31)3, Summer, 311–324.

37. Jones, Eli; Andrea L. Dixon, Lawrence B. Chonko, and Joseph P. Cannon (2005). "Key Accounts and Team Selling: A Review, Framework, and Research Agenda," *The Journal of Personal Selling & Sales Management*, (25)2, Spring, 181–198.

38. Arnett, Dennis B.; Barry A. Macy, and James B. Wilcox (2005). "The Role of Core Selling Teams in Supplier-Buyer Relationships," *The Journal of Personal Selling & Sales Management*, (25)2, Spring, 181–198.

39. Rutigliano, Tony and Brian Brim (2011). "Winning Sales: A Team Sport," *Gallup Business Journal*, (2/24/2011). Accessed March 18, 2014. *http://businessjournal.gallup.com/content/146237/winning-sales-team-sport.aspx*.

40. Kinni, Theodore (2007). "The Team Solution," *Selling Power*, (27)3, April, 27–29.

41. Polzer, Jeffrey T. (2004). *Creating Teams with an Edge*. Boston, MA: Harvard Business School Press.

42. Ibid.

43. Gordon, Jack (2005). "Do Your Virtual Teams Deliver Only Virtual Performance?" *Training*, (42)6, June, 20–25.

44. Majchrzak, Ann, Arvind Malhotra, Jeffrey Stamps, and Jessica Lipnack (2004). "Can Absence Make a Team Grow Stronger?" *Harvard Business Review*, (82)5, 131–137.

45. Bossidy, Op. cit.

46. Barrett, A. & J. Beeson, (2002). *Developing Business Leaders for 2010* [White paper]. New York, NY: The Conference Board.

SETTING GOALS AND MANAGING THE SALES FORCE'S PERFORMANCE

LEARNING OBJECTIVES

After completing this chapter, you should be able to:

- Describe how sales managers use goals to guide and control the efforts of their sales forces.

- Summarize the elements of an effective goal.

- Distinguish when different outcome and behavioral sales goals should be used.

- Identify different informational resources available to capture information used for making effective decisions on goals.

- Apply goal-setting theory in order to improve managerial and motivational practices.

Companies rely on their sales forces to generate the revenues they need to stay in business. Consequently, it shouldn't surprise you that more than 92 percent of companies with sales forces use some form of sales goals.[1] Setting and achieving a firm's sales goals is an extremely important and—sometimes—a daunting responsibility for sales managers. One study of sales leaders reports it as their number one challenge.[2] Goal setting is a powerful sales management activity when it's done correctly. But, when it's done incorrectly, few corporate actions have a more potentially devastating consequence.

CHAPTER 11

**ELLEN REBNE
Director of Communication
and Data Sales
Graybar**

Sales Manager Profile: Ellen Rebne

AS THE DIRECTOR OF COMMUNICATION and Data Sales, Ellen Rebne works with the 20 sales managers in her district to help implement Graybar's sales strategies and achieve their sales goals. Goal-setting isn't confined to the sales area. "As an employee-owned company, Graybar operates with a set of principles—and one of the principles underlying everything we do is that everyone must take responsibility for the company's performance and be accountable for their own results. As members of the sales team, we share our responsibility to deliver the top-line growth that Graybar needs to be successful." This could be quite an accomplishment, considering that Graybar's sales force is ranked by *Selling Power* as the 76th largest sales force in the U.S.

Every organization relies on achieving its sales goals in order to steer its future. At Graybar, the process of setting sales goals begins at the corporate level with a study of economic indicators in key markets. The process cascades through the sales organization, and includes sales management and sales personnel. The end result is a set of sales and margin goals for different industries for each sales rep. Sales results are published and reviewed monthly.

The sales manager plays a critical role as a coach in this process. Each sales manager helps identify activities that are going to help make that sales rep successful. If reps are below their goals, the sales manager helps them drill down and identify what the issues are. The issues may be with skill sets that help reps perform better in their sales roles (e.g., making presentations, frequency of customer contact, organization of their business cases) or with business issues (e.g., the rep doesn't have enough product knowledge to use to overcome objections, having difficulty getting access to the right people, etc.). It is the sales managers' responsibility to help ensure that their reps achieve their respective goals. In their role as coach, sales managers needs to set clear expectations, help reps develop the needed skill sets, and then hold them accountable to reach their goals.

The advent of technology is significantly impacting the way customers buy, and how sales reps need to sell. Customers' buying behaviors and expectations are changing, as well. Rebne notes, "Successful sales people and sales managers must continually evolve to understand and adapt to changes in the marketplace. For instance, online buying is growing. Effective sales reps understand this and use it to their advantage by becoming champions for the company's e-commerce capabilities. They realize that e-commerce is not a threat, but rather a tool that can increase Graybar's value to the customer and help grow sales.

Another challenge that most organizations face is the shifting demographics of their buyers. A sales representative today must learn how to sell to different generations and understand how to build relationships across all types of buyers. Most younger customers have different ways of communicating and working than do their older counterparts. A sales rep could be a rock star with one customer and struggle when using the same selling approach with another. Truly understanding your customers' preferences and adapting your approach to meet his or her needs is critical."

Rebne points out that one of the most important skills for reps is the ability to listen to the customers and determine what they perceive as value. "Focus on the things that matter most to customers, and make it easy for them to do business with you." Evidently, they must be doing these well, as Graybar was recently recognized by *Fortune* as one of the World's Most Admired Companies for the 13th consecutive year. ■

Goal setting isn't just picking a target; it includes monitoring salespeople, market conditions, and competitors' reactions; following up; and instituting corrective actions, if they are needed. Sales managers can use software to monitor which actions are working and which ones are not, and analyze those actions by territory and region. If corrective action is needed to achieve the firm's goals, they can see that those actions are taken before it's too late. This could include altering the sales messages related to them, focusing on different potential customers, and coaching salespeople who need help. When reps are having trouble achieving their goals, sales managers need to find out what types of problems the reps are encountering, and respond. At one end of the continuum, the action might involve refining the sales message that reps are delivering. At the other, it might involve suggesting to upper management that a major strategic initiative be reconsidered.

A **sales goal**, or **quota**, is a performance standard by which salespeople—sales representatives and sales managers alike—are measured. The primary purpose of having sales goals or quotas is to synchronize the direction and efforts of the sales force with the plans developed by a firm's top managers. Salespeople use goals to **benchmark**, or **target**, their own performances within a specified time period, and in most cases, they are compensated based on their meeting those goals. Another compelling reason to use goal-setting is because the achievement of those goals can, and should, be motivating—and in most cases is tied to compensation. The first half of the chapter focuses on the sales aspects of goals, and shows why this is such an important topic—not just for the sales force, but for the entire organization. The second half of the chapter concentrates on what sales managers need to do to set good goals that motivate their sales forces.

Why Are Sales Goals Important to an Organization?

Sales jobs allow for a great deal of discretionary effort and time on the part of sales representatives, especially when compared with managerial, manufacturing, and service jobs. Most sales representatives work independently and outside the immediate presence of their sales managers. Therefore, goals need to be in place to help motivate and guide their performance.

Sales personnel are not the only professionals with performance goals or quotas. Healthcare professionals operating in clinics have daily, weekly, and monthly goals in terms of patient visits. Service personnel are assigned a number of service calls they must perform during a set time period. Production workers in manufacturing have output goals. So why are achieving sales goals or quotas such a big deal?

The answer to this question can be found by examining how a firm's other departments are affected by how well the company's salespeople achieve their performance goals. As you no doubt realize, the success of the business hinges on successful sales of its products and services. Consider all the planning, financial, production, and marketing resources and efforts that go into producing what the sales force sells. An industry report notes

Setting goals gives direction of effort and motivation.

that about 80 percent of companies will spend two months or longer preparing their annual forecasts. The majority will simply use last year's, plus a certain percentage model, while about 30 percent will use external third party data.[3] Everyone depends upon the sales force to sell the company's products and services, and eagerly anticipates knowing how things are going. If sales are going well, everyone breathes easier; if sales aren't going well, then there is reason for concern.

Using Goals to Guide and Manage the Performance of a Firm's Sales Force

Sales goals serve a variety of purposes for the sales organization. Specifically, sales goals help to:

- **Motivate the sales force.** Having achievable goals can help motivate salespeople to do their work. Goals serve as benchmarks to help them gauge how well they are doing. Tying their goals to their compensation is a common practice in North America, though in some countries this is not a recommended practice.

- **Focus the selling efforts of the sales force.** Goals help direct the efforts of the sales force toward certain sales activities that a company wants them to engage in, such as focusing their efforts on certain products or services, or on target markets. For example, as more baby boomers retire and don't want to burden their children with medical expenses, many are purchasing long-term care insurance. Seeing this growing market segment, a company like Northwest Mutual Life Insurance might set a goal for its agents to contact their current life insurance policyholders, spend a certain amount of time with them to explain the product, and sell a specific number of new policies to these customers.

- **Assess the financial return on the firm's investment in its products and services.** Firms need to balance the expenditures they make on the goods and services they produce with the returns earned on them. In other words, companies want to make sure the effort they put into selling their products brings a good return. Imagine if Northwestern Mutual were to extensively promote its mutual funds product line to current life insurance policyholders below or above a certain income level—and then find this group to be a difficult sale. If the company didn't set a certain sales goal for the product, and then monitor how well the goal was being met, the firm might engage in repeated efforts to capture these market segments when it's not worth the effort. When sales are falling short of expectations—despite the efforts of a good sales force—it might be because the market is not receptive to the company's offerings. As a result, the firm's top managers might need to reformulate one or several of the marketing-mix variables. In the case of Northwestern Mutual, the company might redirect its efforts toward selling mutual funds to new customers. Perhaps Northwestern Mutual's existing insurance clients have, on the whole, already established relationships with other brokerage firms, and are reluctant to switch.

- **Compare the results achieved by salespeople in different sales territories and regions**. Gathering the results achieved in different territories and regions helps sales managers determine how the areas compare. They can then analyze the variations to determine what factors explain why sales are lower (or higher) in one territory versus another. For example, perhaps the number of competitors and strength of each in the territories are different. Or—perhaps—the characteristics of the buyers in a certain area, the geographical distance between them, or the skills and efforts of the salespeople working the areas, differ. Of course, as we have indicated, the performance of different salespeople can be compared, too. Performance variations are to be expected, to some extent, based on the experience and skills of individual representatives as well as differences in their territories.

GLOBAL SALES MANAGEMENT   **Tying Sales Goals to Sales Compensation on a Global Basis**

How difficult do you think it would be to make a company's goal and quota systems equitable across different territories? Goals for well-established, mature territories must be balanced against those set for markets where the same company is a new entrant to the marketplace. Instead of thinking just within one country, consider how that might be done for a company with sales personnel in multiple countries.

With the advent of the global economy, this is a challenge facing companies such as HP, Verizon, Intuit and Avaya. Verizon has 5,000 sales employees in 41 countries; HP works with more than 27,000 sales personnel worldwide; and Intuit has more than 900 sales employees in countries such as the U.S., Canada, the U.K., India, and Singapore. Coordinating the goals and supporting compensation systems that help achieve the business objectives for each unit has recently led to the creation of positions such as director of global sales incentive design, and deployment and director of global sales compensation.

Parrish Pullen, director of sales compensation and recognition at Intuit, notes that the work of his team "has an immediate impact on the company's performance." In order to coordinate these types of efforts, the team coordinates their work with sales operations, human resources, IT, and communications. The unit has to monitor economic conditions in different regions—with different cultural sales practices. Economic conditions in South and Latin American countries have often caused cyclical currency issues; Western Europe has unique labor laws and regulations; China has experienced a booming economy with rising labor costs; and even staying abreast of labor laws in California can be a challenge.

They also must consider some of the unique cultural sales practices, such as setting short-term versus long-term goals. For example, short-term goals set for a sales force in the United States might not be handled in the same manner in Japan, where there is more concern for goals that are more long-term.

Although business practices are becoming more standardized around the world, there is still variation. Sales personnel must ensure that goals and rewards are aligned with global environments and keep in mind that not all members of an international sales team will react to goals, and the incentives for meeting them, in the same way.

Cichelli, David J. (2013). "The Emergence of the Global Sales Compensation Manager," *Workspan magazine*, July, 53–56.

Different Types of Goals or Quotas

Goals are based on measures of performance that occur over time. A variety of measurements and time periods can be incorporated into goals. Regardless of what's being measured, however, the performance measurements, or **metrics**, should reflect what is most important in an organization's marketing strategy. Goals are often described as being either input- or output-based. **Input-based goals**, or **activity-based quotas**, relate to the observable selling efforts a salesperson must make; for example, the number of sales calls (phone or in-person) and presentations she must make and the number of sales proposals she writes. The number of new clients contacted by a representative is also an input goal. Input goals ensure that representatives are performing the firm's core selling activities. In the past, some of those measures have been reported by reps themselves, which made it more difficult to validate their accuracy. Use of CRM systems have helped to authenticate activities completed, and improve the validity of those measures.

Unfortunately, efforts alone don't always produce results. That's why output goals are important. **Output- (outcome) based goals** are the selling results a representative is expected to achieve. Examples include the number of orders the representative must receive and the revenues, sales volumes, and profits the rep must generate. Consider our hypothetical Pickerel Lake Industries (PLI), which develops software programs for online education and training. PLI is about to introduce a new product that customers might purchase, based on the company's marketing research. The company has determined the revenue the product needs to earn to cover its development, production, and marketing costs, and return a profit. The number of units, and the revenue associated with it, are then divided among PLI's different sales divisions, and then further divided among the individual sales representatives in the various divisions.

Sales volumes generated has traditionally been the most frequent measure companies use to set goals for their salespeople. The major advantage of this approach to setting sales goals is that the measures are easily counted and analyzed, and sales representatives understand them. A disadvantage is that a sole metric may not accurately reflect the entire effort needed to produce the sales, or to provide a complete picture of what is being sold. For example, a salesperson might have generated a large volume of sales—but very little profit—because the person was selling only items with small profit margins, or discounting the price. Clearly, when only output is measured, it can result in a situation in which salespeople ignore or minimize other behaviors, such as providing customer service, or selling more difficult higher-margin products.

As a result, many organizations will utilize a **combination of input and output goals**. This approach can ensure that certain customer service activities are being performed and a certain amount of profitable sales is being made. For example, after PLI establishes the revenue goals for its sales representatives, it then develops the behaviors (input goals) they need to engage in. The behaviors should not only result in making the company's financial targets (like the number of calls and presentations they need to make), but also in achieving the firm's other objectives—such as, say, "providing the best after-sale service in the industry." This might involve, for example, requiring them to make a certain number of service calls to their customers, based on the revenue each one generates.

A **pipeline analysis** shows how well a salesperson is maintaining a stream of customers at different stages in the sales process. There are various ways to visually display these metrics, so sales reps and sales managers can make a quick assessment of the rep's sales performance. Exhibit 11.1 provides an example of a **dashboard**, or a visual representation of various performance measures. Exhibit 11.1 shows some of the different types of measurements firms use to create their sales goals. Not surprisingly, the most frequently used measurement is revenue generated.[4]

At the other end of the continuum are metrics related to customer service. Surprisingly, fewer than 15 percent of companies surveyed indicated that their organizations included customer retention and satisfaction metrics in their goals.[5] If customer service is important, why isn't it measured and established as a goal? Could it be because customer satisfaction is difficult to measure? Does delivering good customer service simply mean a firm loses no accounts or experiences no complaints? Or is good customer service evidenced by a note from

Dashboards visualy display progress toward performance goals.

EXHIBIT 11.1   Typical Input and Output Goals Set by Firms

Input Goals		Output Goals	
Activities	**Volume**	**Number of Sales**	**Ratios**
Number of telephone calls in the last 30 days	Pipeline 30 day volume	Number of sales completed in past 30 days	Deals closed/deals proposed
Number of new client meetings in the last 30 days	Pipeline 90 day volume	Number in the past 90 days	Lead converted/qualified opportunities
Number of presentations and demonstrations in the last 30 days	Qualified pipeline volume	Qualified pipeline	
Number of proposals written in the last 30 days	Accounts lost	Accounts lost	

a customer to a manager, commending a sales representative for going above and beyond the call of duty?

Unfortunately, sometimes it is just easier to count the number of customer complaints you receive than gauge the service your customers are getting. Perhaps an example can help illustrate this: A few years ago, one of the authors' schools attempted to assess how successfully its marketing professors were advising their students. The school attempted to review mandatory course evaluations ratings, count committee and service work, and count research publications and presentations. However, there was no good metric for advising the school's students. Personally interviewing them about how well they were being advised wasn't practical, because of their large numbers and the large number of faculty members trying to advise them.

Nonetheless, an attempt was made to develop a measurement of some sort. Students received e-mail requests to fill out an advisor rating slip (with three questions), and deposit them at a central location after meeting with their advisors. Advisors were also given rating slips to distribute to their advisees. (There was some concern that students who had a poor experience with their advisors would not be given slips, which is why the slips were e-mailed to students.) However, at the end of the pilot semester, only six response slips were returned to the school, even though 1,100 students received them. The advising metric project was cancelled. As it turned out, simply counting the number of complaints the department received was far easier than undertaking such a project. Unfortunately, many—if not most—companies take the same approach toward measuring customer service. A more accurate, but time-consuming, approach would be to develop some form of customer satisfaction metric, (i.e., a combination of number of complaints, lost customers, referrals, customer satisfaction ratings). You may have noticed attempts to capture some of this information happening more frequently at retail locations, if you have been encouraged to complete post-purchase surveys about your shopping experience.

Expense quotas are used to keep the costs associated with a representative's sales in line with what the firm thinks the representative should spend in order to be successful as well as keeping the firm's expenses in line. The costs involved in putting on demonstrations, entertaining customers, sampling products to them, lodging, and other travel costs are among the many expenses sales representatives incur. Typically, the expenses are calculated as a percentage of a representative's sales. For example, if a representative from Deere & Company is expected to generate $4,000,000 in annual

The number of client contacts or presentations are examples of input goals.

sales of industrial equipment, then the representative would be expected to incur a certain percentage, say one to three percent of that amount, in expenses. The exact percentage will differ from industry to industry, and even from company to company. Representatives who go over the expense percentages allotted to them usually have to justify why they did so. However, salespeople whose expenses fall far short of the percentage allotted them might not be using all of the resources available to them, and could possibly be losing sales as a result. This, too, can create a concern for their sales managers. Expense budgets are usually adjusted upward annually, due to inflation.

Exhibit 11.2 displays a combination goal system for our Pickerel Lake Industries (PLI). Potential customers of PLI are reluctant to seriously consider purchasing the company's software until they see it demonstrated. The worksheet contains information on goals the firm has set for three sales representatives' sales volumes, net profits, number of demonstrations, and number of new accounts established for a certain time period. Experienced sales mangers know that only after analyzing all of the data can a clear picture of the representatives' entire performance come into focus.

EXHIBIT 11.2   Assigning Weights to Salespeople's Goals: A Worksheet

Metric	Goal	Actual (to be determined at end of sales period)	% of Goal	Weight	% of Goal x Weight
Sales Rep – Hannah Elizabeth					
Sales volume	$400,000		90%	3	
Net profit	256,000		94	4	
No. demos	10		140	1	
New account	8		120	1	
Total Score				9	
Goal score = (Goal x Weight points/weight of metric) =					
Sales Rep – Sydney Nguyen					
Sales volume	$500,000		112%	3	
Net profit	344,000		102	4	
No. demos	11		45	1	
New account	9		55	1	
Total Score				9	
Goal score = (Goal x Weight points/weight of metric) =					
Sales Rep – Moe Peterson					
Sales volume	$600,000		103%	3	
Net profit	380,000		84	4	
No. demos	9		67	1	
New account	7		86	1	
Total Score				9	
Goal score = (Goal x Weight points/weight of metric) =					

The last step in this analysis is determining which of the goals are more important than others. PLI has assigned weights reflecting the importance of each goal. Sales volumes have been assigned a weight of 3 and net profits a weight of 4. The number of demonstrations and new accounts have each been assigned a weight of 1. Multiplying the percent of each goal a representative ultimately achieved by the weight assigned to him or her yields the total weight for that factor. Adding those numbers and dividing by the number of weights (in this case, there are nine) produces the final performance score for each person.

Choosing the Right Metrics to Track

As Exhibit 11.2 indicates, adding metrics helped present a more complete view of each sales representative's contributions. So, if information from four factors is better than information from just one factor, wouldn't information from 20 factors be better than just four? Most companies have multiple product lines; others will have, literally, hundreds. Keeping track of sales with these parameters can create headaches. As one researcher noted: "Few quota-setting procedures integrate all these relevant factors, because too many parameters are required, making them extremely difficult to estimate."[6]

In fact, a study of sales management practices, senior sales executives said that they believe their firms track too many sales performance measures. Having too many measures made it more difficult to focus on the "critical few" metrics. As one sales management executive put it: "What gets measured gets done, but only metrics that get inspected have any significant impact." Historically, most practitioners agree that having more than seven to nine metrics becomes more difficult to manage,[7] and a frustration for those trying to achieve them.[8]

Choosing the Right Time Period to Track

Goals need to be completed within a prescribed time period. They can be yearly, quarterly, monthly, or even weekly or hourly. Surveys indicate that over 80 percent of sales organizations establish their sales goals on a yearly basis.[9] They then break down the yearly figure into quarters and, sometimes, monthly units. Sales organizations with short or rapid sales cycles, such as in-bound call centers or retail establishments, might use weekly or hourly units, for example. Companies with seasonal buying fluctuations may find that monthly goals don't accurately represent the activity that is going on, and may opt for a longer/seasonal approach.

What About Almost Meeting a Goal?

Should a salesperson be rewarded if he can achieve only 80 percent of a sales goal? What about 90 percent? Consider this course and your reaction to the following scenario: Over the semester, you are required to interview five sales managers. Your final interview is with a company you are really interested in joining one day. Unfortunately, at the very last minute, your interviewee has a family emergency, and has no time to reschedule before your assignment is due. Consequently, you submit your four interviews, and your instructor gives you a zero because your assignment wasn't complete. Would you have preferred a grade of 80 percent for your work completed?

For the same reason illustrated above, most companies do not take an "all or none" approach. A more typical approach is to reward salespeople for reaching the 90 percent mark (called a **threshold goal**); the 100 percent mark (**actual goal**); or 110 percent mark (**stretch goal**). Exhibit 11.3 shows how using this approach on a

EXHIBIT 11.3 An Example of How Threshold, Actual, and Stretch Goals Are Set			
Basic Sales Volume Goal	**Threshold Goal (90%) x Goal**	**Actual Goal (100%) x Goal**	**Stretch Goal (110%) x Goal**
Rep 1: $400,000	0.9 x 400,000 = **$360,000**	1 x $400,000 = **$400,000**	1.10 x $400,000 = **$440,000**
Rep 2: $450,000	0.9 x 450,000 = **$405,000**	1 x $450,000 = **$450,000**	1.10 x $450,000 = **$445,000**

Performance goals can include threshold, target, and stretch goals.

sales volume metric would make a difference. (The exact percentages of threshold, actual, and stretch goals will vary from company to company.)

Should Salespeople Be Involved in Setting Their Own Goals?

As a student, would you prefer to be able to discuss with your instructors how your assignments and grades should be determined? If you answered, "yes," you could probably guess that most salespeople feel the same way about their sales goals. Although not every organization solicits input from its sales force about the goals set for them (actually only about 18 percent don't), about 60 percent include bottom-up input in their goal setting.[10] The greater the number of accounts, the more likely sales management will use a top-down goal allocation approach. The fewer the accounts, the more likely sales personnel will be to participate (i.e., the bottom-up approach).[11]

Soliciting input from reps can improve the morale of a firm's salespeople by helping their managers better understand the obstacles they face. When the quotas are set and there's no changing them, it's de-motivating. Adam Faragilli describes a failed sales call where a veteran hibu sales rep, selling online marketing services associated with the Yellow Pages, broke down and cried for that reason.[12] One drawback of asking salespeople for their input is, of course, that they often have an incentive to **lowball**, or make their estimate low, so they can more easily achieve their quotas. Nonetheless, some firms use a combination of a top-down and bottom-up goal setting approach. With a little negotiation, a goal that both a sales manager and representative agree on can be reached.

When is a Sale a Sale?

When do you count a product or service as sold and include it as part of the individual's sales goal? This has been a controversial topic for some time. If a sale is counted toward a sales representative's goal when a customer places an order, what happens if the customer cancels or reduces the order later, after 30 or 60 days? To achieve their goals, salespeople have been known to ask their clients—or otherwise cut a deal with them—to purchase products immediately, with the understanding that they can later return them.

To take a conservative approach, one would count the sale when the product is either shipped or paid for. However, this can create a problem for an item with a long sales cycle—say, an item that might not be delivered for a number of months. Many B2B products fall into this category. For example, the sale of an airplane, a major software installation, or a highly customized product (such as a custom-built piece of industrial equipment or a personal yacht)— all would have long sales cycles. Some firms will deal with this problem by giving reps partial credit (e.g., 30 percent) when the order is placed and the remaining credit (e.g., 70 percent) when the order is shipped.

However the sale is counted, organizations need to develop, and clearly communicate, this information to their representatives. Also, no matter what method is chosen, unethical sales managers (and their representatives) will have an incentive to manipulate the system—particularly because sales managers' goals (and their bonuses) are based on what their reps earn. Drug maker Bristol-Myers Squibb found itself in such a predicament. Between 1999 and 2001, the company's sales managers offered the firm's wholesalers incentives to build up their inventories of the company's products, and recorded those deliveries as revenue. This allowed the company and its salespeople to meet their quarterly revenue goals. However, the U.S. Department of Justice and the Securities Exchange Commission later concluded that the "loading" of inventories onto wholesalers could not be recognized as revenues. The company was charged with overstating its revenues and fined.[13] The problems Bristol-Myers Squibb experienced show why sales managers (as well as a firm's top managers) need to have a strong sense of integrity.

Should Everyone Achieve Their Sales Goals?

Goals should be set with the expectation that salespeople will be able to achieve them.[14] If an organization was successful in hiring and training the best people available, this seems only reasonable. However, not every organization can hire the best, or support a good training program. Industry studies show that, in fact, most companies prefer to have the average quota exceed 100 percent, with the expectation that 60 to 70 percent of the sales force personnel will achieve their goals, and 30 to 40 percent will not.[15, 16]

So why don't more salespeople make their goals? In some surveys conducted with senior executives, the respondents believed that poor skills on the part of their sales forces and sales managers were to blame.[17, 18] Although a lack of skills or motivation on the part of sales personnel might be a contributing reason for not achieving sales goals, several other important factors also should be considered. These factors include:

- flawed sales projections, based on limited marketing research;
- estimates based on a new territory with limited market-based analyses;
- changes in a firm's marketing mix variables that result in inferior products or services;
- an increase in the cost of supplies, which is passed on to buyers in the form of higher product prices;
- promotional campaigns that don't produce the results projected;
- delays or other problems with the distribution of a firm's products;
- new competitors and competing products that enter the marketplace;
- environmental factors that affect customer demand, such as slumps in the economy, natural disasters, that cause customers to postpone or cancel their purchases;
- change in laws and regulations that prevent or restrict the use of products and services, or make them more expensive; and
- changes in the way firms do business, for example, as a result of new technology.

Do Goals Ever Get Changed or Altered?

According to sales executive surveys, most companies adjust their goals on a yearly basis to reflect changes that have occurred in the marketplace for their products. The intent is to set the goal only once a year, but the reality is that some goals will need to be adjusted.[19] In some cases, a company's sales might exceed its expectations.[20] As a result, the firm will increase its sales goals—and the goals its representatives must achieve. A number of factors might contribute to this—a competitor dropped out of the market, the firm's market research might have been flawed and underestimated sales, or a change in economic conditions may have helped bolster buying. The opposite can also happen, though, leading a firm to lower its sales goals. Experts caution that a company shouldn't adjust its sales too many times, or confusion among its sales force can result. Moreover, if the goals are being adjusted upward, sales people will often feel cheated.[21]

What Happens When Salespeople Do Not Achieve Their Sales Goals?

Sales managers need to understand that there can be a number of reasons why salespeople don't achieve their goals. This doesn't mean that it's the end of the line for a representative. Bill Febry, sales development manager at Cardinal Marketing, comments "The notion that sales managers can say 'Do it—or else,' is a relic of days gone by, stupid TV commercials, and bad movies. That type of approach just doesn't work if a sales manager wants to develop and retain a professional sales force." The rep's manager needs to find out why the person didn't achieve his or her goals, and help the person engage in activities that will result in success. Realize, too, that not every rep is going to meet every goal he or she is given each period. Even the best reps will miss some of their goals some of the time. It only becomes a problem when a rep continually or repeatedly misses his goals. We'll discuss more about this aspect in Chapter 14.

The Process of Setting Good Goals

Goals can truly be a double-edged sword. When set correctly, it can motivate a sales force to succeed. However, when set incorrectly, it can be de-motivating and lead to high turnover among salespeople—or tempt them to engage in unethical sales behaviors. In a series of studies, researchers found that difficult sales goals alone did not result in unethical behaviors on the part of a firm's sale force. However, they certainly helped set the stage for those behaviors. In addition, when sales representatives were given exceedingly high goals, they often focused primarily on activities that generated sales and delivered less customer service. The researchers also noted that a sales manager's tendency to tolerate—or not tolerate—unethical sales behaviors had a direct effect on whether their representatives would or would not engage in unethical sales behaviors.[22, 23, 24] The "Ethics in Sales Management" box in this chapter provides additional details about the unethical sales behaviors that can occur because of poor goals setting.

Recall from Chapter 1 that we discussed the importance of goal setting and use of the SMART characteristics for developing a well-written goal (one that's specific, measurable, achievable, realistic, and time-based). That acronym is a good starting point for discussing the procedures used to set goals. After more than 40 years of research on goal-setting theory, it is no doubt one of the most-researched, well-understood concepts in behavioral science.[25, 26] All of this study yielded two consistent findings about the use of goal setting:

- **Difficult goals lead to higher levels of performance.** Sales representatives will put forth more effort when their goals are somewhat difficult—versus too easy or too difficult.

- **Specific, difficult goals lead to higher levels of effort than do general ones.** Specific difficult goals—for example, calling upon eight clients a day—will lead to higher levels of performance on the part of salespeople.

Goal setting works because it impacts people's performance in four ways:

1. **Goals direct people's attention and efforts toward goal-relevant behaviors, and away from other less-relevant behaviors.** They provide focus and direction. For example, when a new product or service comes out, more effort (and reward) needs to be placed on selling it. That's why sales managers often set specific sales goals for new products and the rewards associated with meeting those goals.

2. **Goals have an energizing function.** Higher goals produce more effort than goals that are set at lower levels. Knowing what level of sales is expected of them gives salespeople a target for which to aim.

3. **Goals affect persistence.** Harder goals will prolong the expenditure of effort. Tight deadlines lead to a more rapid work pace than do loose goals. When there is plenty of time, it often seems no one is in a hurry. With a tight schedule, step-by-step completion dates must be met, which helps the work get accomplished.

4. **Goals affect people's problem-solving skills.** When faced with completing difficult goals, people will seek out new ways to accomplish them.

Challenging goals can help motivate sales personnel.

Based on goal-setting principles, here are some practical guidelines that sales managers should follow when setting representatives' goals.[27, 28]

1. Set goals that are easy for sales representatives to understand, difficult to achieve, and have exact deadlines for completion.

2. Important tasks—such as providing a high level of customer service—that are excluded as a goal may be ignored. If an action is important, then a goal for its accomplishment should be set.

3. Having too many goals can create stress. Keep the number of goals an individual is responsible for to reasonable number, such as three to seven. Clarify their importance, so that their priorities are understood.

4. Try to get sales representatives to commit to their goals by explaining how they have been set. For example, if the representatives' goals are six percent higher than they were the previous year, explain why.

5. Clearly indicate how the sales performance will be measured and rewarded.

6. Provide feedback to salespeople as frequently as possible, so they know if they need to redirect or increase their efforts. Encourage salespeople to use alternative approaches to sell to their customers, if their initial approaches don't work.

7. Make sure people know you have confidence in their ability to achieve their goals.

8. Selling effort, typically, increases up to a certain point, but will decrease as goal levels increase.

9. Failing to achieve a goal should not be viewed as failure. It should be considered progress on the road to success.

In short, goals should help motivate salespeople. The next chapter describes some other ways sales managers motivate their sales forces, in addition to setting goals for them.

ETHICS IN SALES MANAGEMENT   What Happens When Goals Are Set Too High?

Ever heard of a class where the instructor says, "A's in this course are rarely given."? Research and common sense indicate that setting goals that aren't achievable typically results in two events. People get de-motivated, frustrated, and often quit the task, class or job. And when someone doesn't have the luxury of quitting, then he or she may respond with activities such as cheating, lying, or some other undesirable behavior, in order to attain the goal.

Wells Fargo is the nation's largest retail bank, averaging more than six financial products per household—roughly four times the industry average. Branch employees are responsible for selling a variety of bank products and services. Some employees report that pressure to oversell to achieve quotas was unbearable—and led to ethical breaches, customer complaints, and labor lawsuits. According a report in the *Los Angeles Times*, employees would open unneeded accounts for customers, order credit cards without customers' permission, and begged family members to open ghost accounts so they could meet their quotas. They were told they would be "working for McDonalds" if they did not make their sales quotas. Some report having had to stay late, after hours, and/or report to special call sessions. One sales manager reported that, if his branch did not make its goals, "...you are severely chastised and embarrassed in front of 60-plus managers." Wells Fargo has denied the allegations in court filings, but declined to comment further.

Ease of access to Internet publicity has also made it easier for employees to report companies they perceive as having unrealistic sales goals. For example, the 300-location department store chain Dillard's was voted as the second "Worst Company to Work For," largely due to its goal-setting practices. One Dillard's sales representative commented that high turnover was the result of employees being paid on the number of sales made per hour instead of based on a commission. In a posting by a current T-Mobile employee, that company is berated for the pressure on sales personnel for achieving their quotas. The employee cited 15 different quotas she was expected to achieve and believes that "Each quota is treated like it directly threatens your job."

Goal setting and goal-directed behaviors are, indeed, powerful sales management tools that need to be implemented carefully to achieve the desired results.

Reckard, E. Scott (2013), "Wells Fargo's pressure-cooker sales culture comes at a cost," *Los Angeles Times*, Accessed March 15, 2014. *http://www.latimes.com/business/la-fi-wells-fargo-sale-pressure-20131222-story.html#page=1*. McIntyre, Douglas A., Ashley C. Allen, and Michael B. Sauter (2012). 24/7 Wall St., Accessed March 15, 2014. *http://www.foxbusiness.com/personal-finance/2012/08/10/americas-worst-companies-to-work-for/*. S., Ray (2013). "T-Mobile employee speaks up about the problems with the carrier," PhoneAreana.com, posted March 23, 2012. Accessed March 15, 2014. *http://www.phonearena.com/news/T-Mobile-employee-speaks-up-about-the-problems-within-the-carrier_id28368*.

Managing Your Career

It has often been said, "*The most important thing about goals is having one.*" In reality, why should you limit yourself to just one? Why not have a number of goals?

Have you already set some goals, or are you "still waiting" to be inspired? Do you have a goal for your academic achievements (beyond graduation)? If your current occupation is "student," you might consider one or more. Other goals often recommended for near-to-be-graduates might include getting an internship, volunteering, staying active and fit, participating in a club or activity group, having fun, or even getting to know a favorite instructor better.

Recall the earlier discussion about the benefits of goals? Goals help give you direction, focus, drive, and a sense of accomplishment. Without a goal, you really don't know where you are headed. Without a goal, you don't have a real plan. Without a goal, you don't have a timetable. Without a goal, you really don't know what you are going to be.

Ellen Rebne from Graybar encourages students to be sure they set both short-term and long-term goals. She recommends that you continually measure yourself to see if you are accomplishing the short-term goals that will eventually lead to your long-term goals.

Even if you don't think you achieved your goal, you no doubt learned something in trying to achieve it—more than from not trying at all.

Summary

Without a plan, it's hard to tell where you may end up. Because the success of businesses hinges on the successful sales of products and services, nearly all organizations with sales forces use sales goals. The primary purpose of having sales goals, or quotas, is to synchronize the direction and efforts of the sales force with the plans developed by a firm's top managers. Keeping the efforts and activities of the sales force aligned with the firm's marketing strategies helps ensure that the firm's sales resources are being spent wisely. In addition, it allows for comparisons to be made between different sales territories and sales personnel. The results of these comparisons can then be used to determine where the company's biggest opportunities and challenges may lie.

Different types of factors can be used to set sales goals. Input factors are the efforts a salesperson is expected to make to develop relationships with customers, meet with them, and make presentations and proposals to them. Output factors are the results of what a firm expects a representative's sales efforts to yield. They include metrics, such as the amount and profitability of sales. Many organizations utilize a combination of input and output goals to ensure that their sales representatives are engaging in customer service activities as well as meeting their output goals. Expense goals are used to motivate sales representatives to keep their selling costs to a reasonable amount. Finding the correct combination of goals—and not overwhelming sales representatives with too many types of goals—can be a challenging task for sales managers.

The majority of organizations tie the performance of salespeople to the compensation they receive, which is frequently based on the percentage of their goals they achieve. To help obtain their commitment to meeting their goals, sales managers often encourage sales representatives to provide input about what their goals should be, and the obstacles they face on the way to meeting them. A firm should adjust its sales goals only as needed, so as not to confuse or demoralize the company's sales representatives (especially if their goals are being increased). However, more than half of sales organizations indicate they usually make at least one adjustment a year. Many people mistakenly believe that, if representatives fail to achieve their goals, they are typically dismissed. Most sales experts and professionals agree, however, that the failure to meet a goal merely signals that a sales manager or sales trainer needs to help diagnose, and remedy, a salesperson's selling weaknesses.

Sales goals should motivate a firm's sales force. They should be difficult, yet achievable. When they are too difficult, salespeople are more likely to behave unethically to achieve them. By contrast, when salespeople understand why their goals have been set the way they are, and commit to them, their efforts and perseverance increase. Finally, giving their salespeople frequent and timely feedback about their progress toward their goals can help a sales manager increase or redirect their efforts.

Key Terms

Questions and Problems

1. Explain how e-commerce might affect selling and sales management practices in B2B organizations that are similar to Graybar.

2. Sam is a sales manager who prefers to use output measures for goals. Heather, another sales manager, prefers the use of input measures. Summarize the advantages and disadvantages of both approaches. What type of products/services lend themselves to each type, and why?

3. Customer service receives a lot of lip service and press, but when it comes down to using it as a sales goal, it presents some problems. Develop a possible customer service goal that could be used in a B2B setting.

4. Naperville, Illinois, located southwest of downtown Chicago, has undergone rapid growth. It is now the second largest city in Illinois, next to Chicago. As a sales manager, you knew the time would come when there were more potential clients than your present sales force could handle. Your organization has authorized splitting its two Naperville sales territories under your control into four. What type of goals do you think would be the most important to focus on, given the situation?

5. The sales goals for one of the territories you manage have been set at $5.1 million for this year. There are three sales representatives in this territory: José, who is one month out of training; Katie, who has five years of experience and is considered an average performer; and Norah, who has 12 years of experience and is a top performer. Set three goal levels for each representative and explain your rationale for each.

6. A number of factors can impact a salesperson's ability to achieve his or her goal. What are some of these factors?

7. As a student, you probably have had some courses requiring only one or two exams or research papers. Likewise, you've probably encountered some courses at the other end of the spectrum, during which many aspects of your performance were graded. The same situations could be said to exist in sales. As a sales representative, which end of the continuum would you prefer? As a sales manager, which end would you prefer? In each case, explain your rationale.

8. How well, and in what situations, do "all or nothing" goals work? What problems do you think a sales manager might encounter by rewarding salespeople who only partially meet their goals?

9. Are coaching and mentoring skills involved in goal setting? If so, explain where and how should they be incorporated?

10. As a sales manager, you know that goal setting can be motivational. If you are about to set goals with your sales force, what are some behaviors you want them to demonstrate?

Role Play

Black River Brewing

Ellah and Pete Tan couldn't help but smile as they read the news about how, on a nationwide basis, the big brewers' market share had once again been cut by sales of microbrewery beers. Call it timing or dumb luck, but this couple's love of brewing was timed perfectly. Every year, more and more brewers are entering the marketplace. Last year, an additional 450 brewers were opened in a field that already included 2,450 existing craft brewers. The Tans stopped brewing beer in their kitchen 10 years ago and opened Black River Brewing (BRB). Every year since then, their sales had grown. They now had a microbrewery in a beautifully refinished 100-year old building—nestled among the nearby modern office buildings. Their on-premises sales had allowed them to develop new seasonal brews, and to expand their distribution into other states. The work was evenly divided between the two partners. Pete loved to brew beer. Ellah's background in sales and marketing, and her outgoing style, seemed to open doors as the BRB brands expanded into new markets. She and Pete had always set aggressive sales goals and had the resources to pursue them. She had grown the sales efforts from one person to the present seven-person sales force. Their once city-sized market now covered eight states.

Assignment

Divide into pairs. One person should role play the BRB sales rep, Taylor, and the other, her sales manager, Ellah. Taylor's territory was recently split, and is located in the part of the country with a lower per capita interest in, and purchasing level for, microbrews. Taylor was hired three years ago, and was thought to be a rising superstar. Her background—working as an apprentice brewer at another microbrewery—was initially thought to be an asset. Taylor is a hard worker; however, she has developed a bit of an abrasive, "know-it-all" personality toward co-workers and Ellah. She is driven by compensation. Clients are generally pleased with Taylor, although a couple of smaller accounts have complained about some service issues.

Taylor will normally make sales goals, but has struggled with winning new clients. Sales goals were just announced by an e-mail from Ellah, and now Taylor is in town for a quarterly review. Nationwide sales for microbrews are up nearly 10 percent over last year. Ellah has increased BRB sales goals by 15 percent. Taylor feels like the BRB management has taken advantage of her by a recent realignment of her territory, and by putting her in the toughest part of the country. A fairer goal, she believes, would be an 11 percent increase. Her last e-mail to you about her new sales goal reflects that sentiment. "Once again, you folks have set an unrealistic goal for me. You have no idea how difficult it is to make this amount. You are unfairly increasing what I need to accomplish my goals without knowing how much work this requires on my part. I feel fully taken advantage of by this situation. I deserve better treatment than this. Policies and protocol are clearly lacking."

Ellah recalls last year's goal discussion being a bit like a wrestling match with a loud buzz saw. Taylor recalls that, to her, last year's goal discussion felt like trying to have a discussion while being made to walk the plank. Your goal setting meeting's success or failure depends upon you both.

Add another scene and a third person. Pete, the other owner of BRB, walks by the tap room office and gets pulled in on the discussion. Taylor says, "Pete, got a minute? What's your take on this situation?"

Caselets

Caselet 11.1: *Tough Times*

One of your younger reps, Joshua, needed a few minutes of your time this morning. He shut the door behind him as he came into your office.

He started by telling you a favorite saying his grandmother always told him: "Josh, tough times never last, tough people do." He related that, since joining Educational Software (ES) three years ago, it seemed like tough times. The recent recession had impacted school districts' ability to purchase the educational software ES sold. He understood that not everyone makes their sales goals, but after two years of not making his goal, knew it was time for him to be one of those who did. Couple that with the news that his spouse was diagnosed with multiple sclerosis (MS)—a disease that affects the central nervous system of young adults—with a typical onset between 20 and 40 years of age. While doctors say it is not fatal, over years the individual with MS will experience diminished muscle control and speech abilities, requiring more assistance. It is difficult to predict the impact MS will have on individuals, but Josh told you that this may be the last month they would be a two-career couple. His spouse soon would be staying at home, and the family would depend on Josh's paycheck. You knew the couple has a set of twins who are four years old, and another child who is seven years old. They were definitely facing some tough times.

Josh shared the dilemma he was facing with a potential sale and wanted your insights. He was, once again, short of his sales goal. However, he had one potentially large sale on the horizon that could put him past his goal. He had been working with the Sugarville School District on a large software sale. Sugarville had the highest per capita income in the state, which helped ensure that the public school district had the potential for investing heavily to equip its schools with current technology. People in Sugarville were known statewide for boasting about how good everything in their schools were. In reading the school district's RFP (request for proposal), Josh knew that Educational Software's Basic System would meet their needs. Unfortunately, such a sale would not push his sales over his goals. However, if he sold the more expensive ES Premium System, he would achieve his sales goals and, ultimately, bring home a larger paycheck. The problem was that the Premium System contained features and capabilities not included in the RFP. The school district had narrowed down the field of possible vendors to two. Tomorrow, Josh and a rep from ES's toughest competitor would each have 30 minutes to present their proposals to the Sugarville School Board, which would award the contract. He had been wrestling with what he should do.

"You know," he said, "if there ever was a time to push the limits, this seems like it. What do you think?"

Question

What advice will you give Josh?

Caselet 11.2: *Coasting?*

Sales awards for outstanding salesperson decorated the walls of Andy's office. With a closer look, a visitor would notice that most of them are from 20 years ago. Andy had quite a run when he first started selling insurance. Too bad it hadn't continued. Annuities from his earlier sales helped him make up for lack of income from new accounts. His agreeable nature made it difficult to find fault with him. But, unfortunately, he was now setting a different kind of record—the number of years of not making his goals. He was short on his input and output goals. This wasn't going unnoticed by many of the newer reps, who felt that Andy received special treatment and didn't contribute much to the agency. Andy says he loves his job and may never retire.

Questions

1. As his sales manager, how would you handle your next performance review meeting with Andy?
2. What would you tell the next rookie rep that asks you why Andy isn't required to make goals?

References

1. Cichelli, David J. (2003). "2004 Sales Compensation Trends Survey," [White paper]. Scottsdale, AZ: The Alexander Group.
2. Eddleman, Dave (2013). "What do sales leaders say is their #1 challenge? Setting quotas." [White paper]. Scottsdale, AZ: The Alexander Group. Accessed March 10, 2014. *http://www.alexandergroup.com/blog/sales-quotas/what-do-sales-leaders-say-is-their-1-challenge-setting-quotas/*.
3. WorkatWork and Better Sales Comp (2013). "2012 Quota Practices Study, Accessed February 14, 2014. http://www.worldatwork.org/waw/adimLink?id=70265.
4. "How Sales Forces Sustain Competitive Advantage," (2004). [White paper]. Boston, MA: The Forum Corporation of North America, 10.
5. "How Sales Forces Sustain Competitive Advantage," (2004).
6. Darmon, René Y. (2001). "Optimal Sales force Quota Plans Under Salesperson Job Equity Constraints," *Canadian Journal of Administrative Sciences*, (18)2, June, 87–100.
7. "How Sales Forces Sustain Competitive Advantage," (2004).
8. S., Ray, (2013). "T-Mobile employee speaks up about the problems with the carrier," PhoneAreana.com, posted March 23, 2012. Accessed March 15, 2014. *http://www.phonearena.com/news/T-Mobile-employee-speaks-up-about-the-problems-within-the-carrier_id28368.*
9. WorldatWork and Better Sales Comp Consultants (2013). "2012 Quota Practices Study, Executive Summary and Key Findings," Accessed February 14, 2014. *http://www.worldatwork.org/waw/adimLink?id=70265.*
10. WorldatWork and Better Sales Comp Consultants (2013).
11. Cichelli, David J. (2014). "2014 Sales Compensation Trends Survey Executive Summary," The Alexander Group. Accessed February 14, 2014. *http://www.alexandergroup.com/sites/default/files/images/documents/AlexanderGroup_2014SalesCompensationTrendsExecutiveSummary_010614Final.pdf.*
12. Faragalli, Adam (2014). "The Hibu Account Rep That Cried," Titan Web Marketing Solutions, Accessed April 15, 2014. *http://www.titanwebmarketingsolutions.com/the-hibu-account-representative-that-cried/.*
13. Taub, Steven (2005). "Bristol's Former CFO Indicted," CFO.com, June 16, 2005. Accessed April 15, 2014. *http://ww2.cfo.com/accounting-tax/2005/06/bristols-former-cfo-indicted/.*
14. Good, David J., and Charles H. Schwepker, Jr. (2001). "Sales Quotas: Critical Interpretations and Implications," *Review of Business*, (22)1, 2, Spring, 32–37.
15. Cichelli, David J. (2014). Op. cit.
16. WorldatWork and Better Sales Comp Consultants (2013). Op. cit.
17. "How Sales Forces Sustain Competitive Advantage," (2004).
18. Koprowski, Ron and Tom Atkinson (2005). "The Pressure Paradox," Forum Sales Practice [White paper]. Boston, MA: The Forum Corporation of North America, 1–5.
19. WorldatWork and Better Sales Comp Consultants (2013).
20. Galea, Christine (2006). "The Rising Tide Does It Again" *Sales & Marketing Management*, (158)4, 30–35.
21. Schwepker, Charles H., Jr., and David J. Good (2004). "Understanding Sales Quotas: An Exploratory Investigation of Consequences of Failure," *The Journal of Business & Industrial Marketing*, (19)1, 39–48.
22. Good, David J. and Charles H. Schwepker, Jr. (2001). "Sales Quotas: Critical Interpretations and Implications," *Review of Business*, Spring, 22, 1 & 2; 32–37.
23. Schwepker, Charles H., and David J. Good (1999). "The Impact of Sales Quotas on Moral Judgment in the Financial Services," *The Journal of Services Marketing*, Vol. 13, No. 1, 38.
24. Schwepker, Charles H., Jr. and David J. Good (2004).
25. Latham Gary P. and Edwin A. Locke (2006). "Enhancing the Benefits and Overcoming the Pitfalls of Goal Setting," *Organizational Dynamics*, Vol. 35, No. 4, 332–340.
26. Locke, Edwin A. and Gary P. Latham (2002). "Building a Practically Useful Theory of Goal Setting and Task Motivation – A 35 Year Odyssey," *American Psychologist*, Vol. 57, No. 9, 705–717.
27. Shalley, Christina E. and Edwin A. Locke (1996) "Setting Goals to Get Innovation," *R & D Innovation*, Vol. 5, 10, 16.
28. Fu, Frank Q.; Richards, Keith A. and Eli Jones (2009). "The Motivation Hub: Effects of Goal Setting and Self-Efficacy on Effort and New Product Sales," *Journal of Personal Selling and Sales Management*, (XXIX)3, Summer, 277–292.

CHAPTER 12

MOTIVATING AND REWARDING SALESPEOPLE

LEARNING OBJECTIVES

After completing this chapter, you should be able to:

■ Summarize how motivation has been conceptualized, and how the contributions of past studies can be incorporated into managerial activities.

■ Explain the different models of motivation, and how sales managers can utilize them.

■ Identify generational differences in motivation, and how to adapt motivational approaches for each group.

■ Describe how managers can utilize different motivational elements that are available to sales organizations.

■ Distinguish different situations in which financial and non-financial rewards should be used to motivate salespeople.

■ Illustrate how compensation systems can be utilized to address different motivational needs.

No two people act the same or are driven or motivated by the same things. Motivational factors often vary at different stages of a salesperson's career. In order to help guide the activities of their sales forces as a whole, sales managers need to be able to understand what drives their individual salespeople over time. As you read this chapter, you will learn different approaches to understanding motivation. You will also explore reward mechanisms—both financial and non-financial compensation plans—to help you guide, cajole, reward, and motivate your sales force to achieve its goals.

Sales Manager Profile: Rich Merklinger

RICH MERKLINGER KNEW HE ENJOYED teaching and coaching. But he also knew that a career in these areas might be a bit financially challenging with a growing family and changing career aspirations. After a little career realignment, he moved into a progression of sales positions with Ethicon, a subsidiary of Johnson & Johnson. In his positions, he found that he really enjoyed his leadership opportunities and educating and selling medical devices to hospitals, doctors, and nursing staffs. Prior to advancing to his current role, Rich spent time in field sales, division sales management, product marketing, sales training, and professional education. These roles prepared Rich for succession to the sales director position.

RICH MERKLINGER
Sales Director
Ethicon, Inc.

"Sales managers must be good leaders, trainers and motivators," Merklinger comments. "Salespeople are motivated by many different things, and the sales leader's job is to discover what those things are. Salespeople like compensation; money is a good motivator, but not for all. Some want promotions, others favor some status. Some are motivated by recognition, like their name on a scoreboard. Others like the sense of community—belonging to a good, strong company that promotes good causes. Lastly, there are those motivated by more intrinsic aspects of the position. They like the fact that what they are doing has 'people impact.' Johnson & Johnson products help people have healthier and better lives. They like to help make that happen."

Merklinger notes that, at Ethicon, sales reps have a total rewards package. Compensation is available is several forms. There is a salary base and an incentive compensation plan for efforts in growing and maintaining the business. For some roles, a bonus plan is also in place, as well as long-term stock incentives for those who qualify. In addition to health care benefits, Johnson & Johnson also offers pension and 401(k) plans, and provides a company vehicle when needed for field sales associates.

Recognition awards for outstanding performance tend to go a long way as a motivator. At Ethicon, a sales manager can use a rewards point system to recognize and reward important behaviors on the spot. Sales representatives can work with a more long-term perspective to earn a sales excellence trip designed for the top 10 percent of the sales force—the salesperson and a guest. As part of the trip activities they have different opportunities to interact with senior leadership.

"As a manager, I tend to use lots of non-monetary recognition to help motivate. Our region of the organization recently started a 'You Rock' campaign. Once a quarter, we recognized those who demonstrated 'above and beyond performance' with overnight delivery of a box. Inside the box was a rock paperweight branded 'You Rock' with a handwritten note letting the recipient know that their extra efforts were appreciated, and that he or she would receive rewards points. Everyone liked the surprise element and special recognition this program has offered."

"What motivates reps is also determined by their tenure and experiences. What really motivates a new sales rep isn't likely to have the same impact on a senior rep or an executive sales rep. Members of Gen X and the millennial generations have grown up with technology that provides instant feedback," Merklinger comments. "As a manager, I've observed that they really value quick recognition. For others, they may operate on more of a long-term perspective and value things that reflect that orientation. For example, they are more likely to be motivated by having an impact on actions that shape their future, their families, and the organization."

"Outside sales can be liberating," Merklinger points out, "or crippling—if you don't have good time management skills. You have to have self-discipline and be self-starting. As a manager, I don't talk with my direct reports every day. I trust them to 'do their thing.'" With the right motivation, along with clear goals and expectations, no doubt they will. ■

What Motivates Salespeople?

Done correctly, a sales manager's motivational activities can have a positive impact on the performance and outlook of sales representatives. But the reverse is also true: done incorrectly, the activities can actually de-motivate the sales force and be disastrous at both the individual and company levels. In this chapter, we'll approach motivation first, examining its different components and how they work. Then we'll look at different ways that sales managers motivate their sales forces. All of the theories have their shortcomings and, unfortunately, none can predict what people will do in the future; however, they do offer a starting place to understand how motivation affects all of us. We will also examine the flip side of this concept, which is understanding the different types of rewards that people are motivated to achieve— and how sales managers can exert impact.

Understanding which needs motivate people, and being able to fill those needs, might seem simple. However, in practice, both are complex and require skill in order to execute effectively—especially as your sales force grows. Let's take an example you should be familiar with. In an effort to understand what motivates the students in your class to attend a class session, your instructor may ask, "Why are you attending class today?" Possible responses from students might include:

- I want to learn how to become a sales manager.

- I'm concerned that, if I'm not here, I'll lose points.

- I needed a class to graduate, and this one fit my time schedule.

- I have a special friend who is also taking the class, and I like to be with that person.

- I heard the instructor was fun.

What if you were to pose the same sort of question to sales representatives: Why do they go to work, selling, every day? The possible responses you might hear include the following:

- I like to sell, and I enjoy my job.

- It pays the bills.

- My company's products help make people's lives better.

- Without this job, my family would not have insurance, and we need it.

- I'm in a sales contest, and I want to win the prize in front of my peers.

- My customers are counting on me to help them solve some of their problems at work.

As you can probably guess, what motivates people ranges widely. **Intrinsic motivation factors** are those items that are done because the person finds doing the activity a reward in itself. **Extrinsic motivation factors** are external to the job, and the work is done in order to obtain a monetary, physical, or social reward—or to avoid punishment. These factors include wages, incentives, awards, or a job title that reflects status. Those people who are motivated largely by intrinsic rewards truly love their work and take pride in the feelings of accomplishment it provides them. They have little concern or desire for economic or personal gains. Those people who are motivated primarily by extrinsic rewards are focusing on what they receive for their efforts. Their work is not of utmost importance; it's what they receive (or don't receive) for it that's important. Most people are motivated by a combination of intrinsic and extrinsic rewards; after all, it's great when you like your job and are rewarded for your work. Later on in the chapter, we will examine how sales managers balance the intrinsic and extrinsic rewards their sales personnel seek.

Motivation is a fascinating and complex topic. Sales managers need to understand what drives their sales representatives to action, how hard they are willing to work, and how long they are willing to persist. Some researchers have tried to explain motivation by identifying different *needs* of individuals, or the **content of motivation**. Three of these approaches and contributions for sales managers are outlined in Exhibit 12.1. Unfortunately, the content approach suffered from the "one-size-fits all" problem. To overcome that shortcoming, the focus shifted to understand motivation as the **process** of what someone does, for how long, and at what level of intensity. Exhibit 12.2 explains how the equity and expectancy approaches work, and how sales managers can use what they know about their reps to help motivate them.

Discovering what factors best motivate the sales force is an important part of a sales manager's job.

Generational Motivational Issues

Is there a difference between what motivates salespeople based on their ages? You might have noticed how people in their sixties respond differently to situations, as compared with people in their twenties. If you work with individuals from multiple generations, you've probably heard comments such as:

"We tried that two years ago. It won't work."

"It was a lot harder to do before technology came around."

No matter what concept or theory of motivation is developed, being able to motivate a sales force is complicated by the differences in motivation due to generational differences. For the first time in history, members of four different generations are working side-by-side in the U.S. The fastest growing segment of the workforce is under 27 years of age, with half of the workforce under 40. Younger workers are moving into important organizational positions, yet more workers continue working past retirement age. Nearly one in four households includes a family member involved in elder care. Teams composed of multigenerational members are becoming, more and more, the norm rather than the exception. Understanding these differences—and how to exploit their advantages and minimize their liabilities—will be a challenge sales managers must meet.[6]

Each generational group has experienced unique events and, as a result, each group has a different frame of reference or perspective on life. Because each generation has different sets of experiences, they have different values, expectations and motivations. We communicate in different ways, based on our generational

EXHIBIT 12.1 Understanding *What* Motivates Sales Representatives—Content Approaches

Maslow's Hierarchy of Needs[1] classifies people's needs by the following levels; when the needs in one level are met, factors in the next will motivate a person.

- *Physiological*—the most basic needs in order to survive: air, water, food, and shelter
- *Security*—the need to be safe from physical and psychological harm; the need for shelter
- *Social or Belongingness*—the need to have interaction, friendships, affection, and love with others
- *Ego*—the need to feel good about yourself, and to receive recognition, appreciation, and admiration
- *Self-Actualization*—the need to reach one's fullest potential

Sales managers can apply this concept by using reinforcements that meet needs at each level.

- *Physiological*—salary and bonuses
- *Security*—insurance (for example, health, life, disability) and retirement plans
- *Social or Belongingness*—programs that balance work with life and family commitments (e.g., flexible hours, job sharing, telecommuting, paid parental leave, on-site day care, and paid sabbatical leave)
- *Ego*—programs that recognize individuals for their sales efforts and accomplishments
- *Self-Actualization*—satisfaction with the balance between accomplishments at work and the balance with home life

McClelland's Needs Approach[2] suggests that people are motivated by varied amounts of three needs:

- *Achievement*—a desire to perform challenging tasks
- *Affiliation*—a need to be liked and avoid confrontation
- *Power*—a need to take charge

Managers can apply this concept by matching reps with rewarding aspects of their job.

- *Achievement*—important that a sales representative with a high amount of this drive have an interesting and stimulating job
- *Affiliation*—provide friendly relationships and avoid confrontational situations, or having to provide any negative feedback; these are the most effective leaders
- *Power*—offer tasks where they can lead, teach, or coach

Herzberg's Motivation-Hygiene, or Two-Factor Approach,[3] suggests that sales representatives need to have jobs with motivators present, and with hygiene factors absent or neutral.

- *Motivating factors* were found to be intrinsic to the job, and included: achievement, recognition for achievement, the work itself, responsibility, advancement, or growth.
- *Hygiene factors* were found to be extrinsic to the job and included: company policies and administration, supervision, relationship with supervisor, work conditions, salary, relationship with peers, status, and security.

Managers can apply this concept by considering the presence or absence of the groups of factors.

- Making sure that each sales representative finds his or her work interesting and challenging. As much as possible, the sales manager needs to build motivating factors, such as opportunities for achievement, recognition, enjoyable work, responsibility, and advancement into each representative's activities.
- Ensure that hygiene factors—such as company policies, working conditions, and their supervisory relationship—are not considered negative and are not working as de-motivators.

backgrounds and the technology that has been available to us. Exhibit 12.3 presents the personal and lifestyle characteristics distinctive to each generation.[7, 8, 9, 10]

All of these different events, technologies, and perspectives also impact us at work—especially in terms of how sales managers need to manage, assign work in teams, recruit, and motivate. Consequently, each generational group is motivated by slightly different drives at work. A sales representative from the Baby Boomer generation might value money or recognition most.

By contrast, a Generation X (Gen X) or Millennial (also called Generation Y) sales representative, although still wanting to be paid well, might put more value on having a good work-life balance. Sales representatives from the Matures appreciate more formal means of communication, while a Millennial desires an informal style. Exhibit 12.3 also summarizes characterizations of the work and motivational differences of each group.

Reflecting on these composites of living generations, consider each group and examine how managing a multigenerational sales force can affect you as a sales manager, team member, and leader. The benefits offered by a multi-generational sales force are significant, and include opportunities for competitive advantages.

EXHIBIT 12.2   Understanding *How* Sales Representatives are Motivated—Process Approaches

Adam's Equity Theory[4] proposes that sales reps weigh their perceived inputs and outcomes in comparison to others' and decide if their effort/reward ratio is equitable or fair, and then re-align their efforts to be rewarding.

- *Inputs*—their perception of their training, experience, effort, hardships they endured for work, and anything else they believe they contribute to the organization
- *Outputs*—their perception of their compensation, benefits, status, job security, job satisfaction, and anything else they receive
- *Balancing*—sales representatives' comparison of their input/outcome ratios in comparison with those of different people; the resulting ratio could result in three possible scenarios:
  1. *Equity*—input/outcome ratio is equal to others' input/outcome ratio; reps are motivated to keep doing what they do
  2. *Overpayment inequity*—input/outcome ratio is greater than that of others; sometimes reps will increase their efforts
  3. *Underpayment inequity*—input/outcome ratio is less than others'; reps either decrease their efforts, ask for more, find different points of comparison, or leave to find more equitable jobs

Sales managers can apply this concept by considering the reps' *perceptions* of their motivators, in comparison to their peers' motivators. Sales managers need to:

- Be attentive to comments regarding concerns about fairness.
- Ask salespeople to explain their perceptions of how they compare with a top performer (e.g., "What would a top performer be doing? How does their performance compare to yours?"). The resulting discussion should allow all parties to view the salesperson's perception of his or her input/outcome ratio.

Expectancy Theory[5] suggests that a salesperson will choose to behave in the manner that gives him or her the highest motivational force in order to maximize efforts the rep finds pleasurable and minimize those that are not.

- Reps value outcomes differently (e.g., recognition, out-of-town travel, etc.).
- Reps realize that different levels of effort are required for tasks. For example, if you prepare for a sales call, you should have a better presentation, and—we hope—a better chance at making a sale to a potential client than if you did not prepare.
- Performances have different likelihoods of producing outcomes. Some situations are more certain than others.

Sales managers can apply this concept by focusing on the highest motivators, or on how to raise the level of the lower ones. Sales managers should:

- Understand what value their sales reps place on different rewards. Providing rewards reps don't want does no one much good; focus on those they value.
- Help improve reps' performances. Make sure reps receive good training and are prepared, and align representatives to clients whose needs are consistent with the reps' abilities.
- Be sure to include other performance measures beyond just a sale (e.g., number of calls, presentations and proposals), and include an incentive system that can reflect different levels of performance.

Diversity of experiences and skills that individual members can contribute can create a more versatile workforce—with more resources to solve problems.

Matures

Raised during the Depression and World War II, they've worked through good times and bad. They have worked in a top-down environment, know how to follow rules, and appreciate more formal communication (i.e., personal or phone preferred over e-mail). They are hard-working, loyal, and reliable workers. They want to be respected, and want a meaningful title that reflects their importance. They are admired most by their Millennial counterparts and possess much wisdom—which they enjoy sharing with younger workers. Traditional forms of recognition (e.g., plaques, certificates, etc.) are valued. Allow them to make meaningful contributions, engage them in mentoring, and show respect for their experience.

Baby Boomers

Growing up, they experienced economic prosperity and periods of social consciousness (e.g., the eras of the civil rights, environmental, and other movements). They are the dual-career couples who work long hours and, as a result, have struggled to balance their family lives, which can include elderly parents as well as kids. They have expectations that others should, and will, work as hard as they do.

EXHIBIT 12.3   Generational Characteristics and Differences

	Matures	Baby Boomers	Generation X	Millennials
Year born	1922–1945	1946–1964	1965–1980	1981–Present
How many	75 million	78 million	45 million	80 million
Work place composition	5%	45%	40%	10%
Defining events and trends	Great Depression New Deal Labor unions World War II Korean War	Suburbia Space race Focus on youth Vietnam War Assassinations Equal opportunity for all Earth Day	MTV AIDS Personal computers Fall of Berlin Wall Challenger Wall Street frenzy	Gulf Wars Clinton/Lewinsky School shootings Corporate scandals 9/11 Iraq/Afghanistan Facebook Social media

Workplace characteristics	Organizational loyalty
	Respect authority
	Sacrifice
	Duty before fun
	Adhere to rules
		Idealistic
		Workaholics
		Time stressed
		Personal fulfillment
		Question authority
			Individual contractor
			Entrepreneurial
			Flexible
			Seeking work/life balance
			Media/info/tech savvy
			Sets own rules
				Multi-tasker
				Entrepreneurial
				Well-educated and well-
				  traveled
				Team-oriented
				Socially/politically
				  conscious
				Media/info/tech/ savvy

Work preference	Individual	Committee within unit	Matrix	Global

Diversity	Non-existent; white males
	  only
		Politically correct and
		  legislated
			Valued and sought out	Expected way of life

Work technology	Mimeograph machine Mainframe	Copiers Desktop	Paperless office Laptop	Wireless office iPhone, Android
Communications	Formal Memo	In person	Direct, via e-mail	Immediate, via instant messaging

Leadership style	Authoritative
	Command-and-control
		Benevolent dictator
		Participative
			Straightforward
			Everyone is the same
			  with equal input
				Relationship and team
				  building via group
				  meetings and
				  technology

Reward preferences and motivators	Larger office and other
	  perks
	Public recognition that
	  their contribution is
	  valued
	Money
		Promotion
		Opportunities for
		  leadership
		Money
			Workplace flexibility
			Latest technology
			Freedom to set own rules
			  and/or work on own
			  projects
			Opportunities for learning
			  and development
			Opportunities to work
			  with other bright,
			  creative people
				Workplace flexibility
				Latest technology
				Time off for travel and
				  philanthropic work
				Opportunities to work
				  with other bright,
				  creative people
				Opportunities to move up
				  and contribute

Cooperative teamwork (e.g., football) and verbal communication is preferred over texting. They value promotions, leadership positions, and public recognition of their accomplishments. As they age, flexible working arrangements that help them pursue time with family and individual interests increase in value for them.

Generation Xers

Raised by parents who both worked, they have shifted the workplace emphasis from materialism to a focus on family. They are moving into managerial positions and prefer independence over teamwork, and immediate communication over structured meetings. Computer use and multitasking is second nature. They value work opportunities that are changing and that allow for the opportunity to grow. Flexibility in working arrangements is critical, as family time is more important than time at work. Bonus days off may be valued more than the traditional monetary bonus.

Millennials

Generation Y is another term frequently used to describe this group[11] that will soon fill the largest segment in the workforce. Some have experienced tight job markets and moved home. They've been counseled to find a good job that is right for them. They follow the Xers in their requirement of a work/life balance. They have a high level of social consciousness and responsibility, and desire an employer who incorporates and displays these values in their work. Being individuals within a team is valued. These people like immediate feedback and rewards. They want meaningful work experiences, and mentors or coaches who can help them achieve their goals and contribute to their companies. Flexibility in their work environment is a must.

Reps from different generations are likely to be motivated by different rewards.

No doubt managing someone who is your parents' or grandparents' age—or being managed by them—might initially seem a little daunting. (Having someone their child or grandchild's age managing them may initially be a bit uncomfortable to them, also.) Sales managers, regardless of their age, need to understand different work styles, expectations, personal preferences, and motivators of all four generations in their sales forces. Keep in mind that everyone—no matter what the person's age is—has something valuable to offer a sales organization. It's a sales manager's job to figure out what that is. Listen to what different people have to say, ask questions, and determine what motivates them.

The Dos and Don'ts of Motivating Your Sales Representatives

The following section summarizes some of the suggestions sales manager can use to motivate their sales forces.

- **Hire self-motivated people.** The old adage—"Surround yourself with good people, and you'll never have any problems too big to achieve,"—would seem to fit. When you are hiring, be sure to look for individuals who demonstrate a "can-do" approach to work.

- **Show trust.** Sales managers need to demonstrate trust with their employees, and will gain it in return. Those managers who do not, won't get any in return from their salespeople.[12]

- **Capitalize on unique strengths of each member of the sales force.** Great managers discover the unique characteristics each employee has, then capitalizes on them.[13]

- **Encourage some salespeople to become experts.** Having someone designated as a specialist in an area demonstrates your trust, and helps recognize the person's specialized contribution to the team.

- **Empower salespeople to make their own decisions.** When you feel like you "own" some aspect of your work, you become more motivated to be responsible for it. Likewise, empowering salespeople to make decisions helps develop and motivate them.

- **Ensure that you offer rewards** that all members of your sales force value, regardless of age, gender, and years of experience.

- **Develop or remove negative talkers and deadbeats.** Nothing can put a damper on things faster than a full-time complainer whose attitude sours others. Coach those salespeople who are open to becoming more positive about their jobs, and dismiss those who aren't.[14] If a person is not the right fit for the job, help him or her realize as much.

When a once-high-performing sales representative is no longer demonstrating past levels of achievement, and performance has leveled out, the rep's career may have **plateaued.** This is not an uncommon event for someone who has had a successful career for a long period of time. In essence, the salesperson is still capable of performing at a high level, but might no longer be driven by the company's current mix of rewards.

 Peter Gundy, principal and director of sales compensation at Buck Consultants, recognizes that plateau. "You end up with salespeople who may not have that fire in their bellies anymore, so you have to find other ways of motivating them. Certainly, the challenge and thrill of the hunt are still part of the job," comments Gundy. He recommends mixing up their reward plans—to possibly include new responsibilities, such as training and coaching newer representatives. Alternately, you could alter your incentive offerings to develop a plan based on tenure, recognizing salespeople who earn 110 percent of their quota for a designated number of years in a row.[15]

Having a good understanding of what motivates salespeople is really half the solution. A good sales manager has to have, and build on, an underlying base of information. The second half of the solution involves ensuring that your salespeople are rewarded for their efforts. The next section discusses the various financial and non-financial rewards available to sales personnel, and insights that sales managers need in order to administer them.

Financial and Non-financial Rewards

Imagine that you just won a contest your instructor held as part of your sales management class, or in your personal selling class. How would you prefer to be rewarded for your efforts? Would you like your reward to be an award, extra points to improve your grade, a meal at a nice restaurant, public recognition, a day off from class, an opportunity to attend a training seminar, a weekend trip, or merchandise? With so many choices, how could your instructor go wrong? Let's consider a few things:

- If you've received about as many certificates or awards as your wall can hold, then another piece of paper or a trophy might really turn you off. But if you really need something of the sort to make your résumé look good, then such a reward might be great.

GLOBAL SALES MANAGEMENT   Motivating a Global Sales Force

We've all heard the expression, "Think globally, but act locally," in reference to many aspects of international business. But how might that be accomplished with offering the right rewards to motivate a sales force? After all, there are many different types of sales positions—requiring many different talents. And the market conditions in which these sales personnel operate change frequently; therefore, a compensation system that aligns a company's sales objectives is critical. And, to top it off, the system needs to be fair.

Consider a company with sales reps servicing a client that has locations in several countries. The client requires that the product be available in all of its locations. It seems reasonable that, if a company was convinced that its product was the preferred one in a country, consumers might be predisposed to buy it in another country. This leads to the question, "How should sales reps, located in different countries, get credit—and compensation—for this sale?" Now, multiply this situation times the number of countries where a company may sell, and you have a significant challenge.

The solution to this challenge involves developing a global compensation plan engaging multiple team members, including sales managers. Plans such as these are typically administered by a corporate human resources department, acting on the input of sales and marketing leaders. Designing such a plan includes making decisions about target compensation levels, the mix between base pay and incentives, individual versus group contributions, which performance measure to include, length of measurement periods, frequency of incentive payments, limits, how new hires are treated, and what earning levels are used for benefit programs such as 401(k) and other earnings-sensitive benefits programs.

As sales compensation expert David Cichelli notes "These principles do not exist independent of the values and preferences of a company. While the topics are universal, their application is unique to each company" and each country. "Numerous factors suggest the need for locally defined sales compensation programs including laws, philosophies, past practices, and cultural norms."

Research has shown that what motivates people to enter the sales occupation differs across the globe. While economic return may be a prime motivator in some countries, (e.g., Singapore, the U.K., and the U.S.), the "ability to use my special abilities" is a prime motivator in others (e.g., Australia, Canada, New Zealand, and Norway).

So, if what motivates salespeople isn't the same worldwide, then shouldn't compensation plans be adjusted to reflect the variances? The researchers noted that, although the same motivators are essentially important in all of the countries the study examined, managers need to consider individual country differences. This is particularly true when it comes to sales contests. For example, in some countries, such as Japan, recognizing the accomplishments of individual salespeople to a greater degree than recognizing the accomplishments of one's sales force as a whole is not considered to be in good form.

Cichelli, David (2012), "Seven Elements of an Effective Global Sales Compensation Framework," *workspan*, (Feb.), 27–30. Cichelli, David (2013), "Five Global Sales Compensation Trends," *workspan*, (Jan.) 39–42.

- If you've already nailed down the grade you want to get for the course, additional points won't help you much. However, if you're really struggling in the course, extra points might be wonderful.

- If you work at a fancy restaurant or a resort, then a fancy meal or a weekend stay might not be so valuable, because you have access to them already. But if you wanted to take someone special out, to thank them for the things they've done for you, this could be a good reward.

- Public recognition in class is nice. However, if you've already participated in a couple of activities that resulted your being recognized, you might be uncomfortable receiving more recognition. That said, if you thrive on positive feedback, you'll want even more.

As you can probably tell from this discussion, there are many ways to reward performance. There was a monthly column from *Sales & Marketing Management* magazine titled "What Motivates Me." Salespeople wrote to the magazine with their responses. Exhibit 12.4 shows what some individuals had to say about what motivates them.[16]

Not only do the rewards that salespeople desire differ from person to person, they also differ from country to country. The "Global Sales Management" box in this chapter examines the findings of researchers who looked at the importance of maintaining equity in rewards among different countries, and what motivates salespeople in different cultures.

EXHIBIT 12.4   What Motivates You as a Salesperson?

- "Achieving a team goal and all of us going on a four-day cruise."
- "Receiving a gift from the company president at a company-wide meeting."
- "The owner's verbal recognition."
- "A work environment that lets me work part of the day at home, to balance my family needs."
- "A trip to Hawaii for reaching a sales goal."
- "A personal gift, selected for me by the company president."
- "Sending me to a seminar that helps me become more productive."
- "A trip to a special spa."
- "Quarterly bonuses. The extra money helps with the bills."
- "Being selected for the President's club (and the ring or trip that comes with it)."

The Components of a Reward Program

With so many options that can be used to motivate sales personnel, the task for putting together a complete program, or **total rewards program**, initially might seem daunting. We use the term *total rewards* to include all options a sales manager should utilize to reward performance, rather than just compensation and benefits. Exhibit 12.5 depicts the different factors that affect sales managers' rewards choices.[18, 19] As you consider the different factors involved in a reward system, you can appreciate the complexity of administering them. Human resources personnel are likely to be involved in administering the program. Typically, top sales management executives will help structure components that are critical to salespeople. The programs need to be designed so that salespeople receive rewards that keep them motivated, but don't cause a financial burden to the firm. Of course, the plan needs to be in line with what others in your industry and area are paying. Otherwise, you risk losing reps to your competitors that offer better pay and benefits.

Now, let's look at each of the different reward factors used to motivate salespeople.

The **marketplace environment** includes factors such as the level of industry competition, the use of technology, the financial resources available to firms in the industry, the competition for sales personnel, and the level of training salespeople require. Companies with limited competition in the marketplace and desirable products and services are likely to have more resources available to them for rewarding their salespeople than companies selling undifferentiated products and services in highly competitive markets. Similarly, to recruit salespeople who live in high-cost locations, a firm might need to offer them higher compensation levels. Firms might also have to adjust their reward levels in order to retain and recruit for positions for which qualified or trainable salespeople are scarce. Kevin Powell, the president of Van Meter, Inc.—a wholesale distributor of electrical products—knows that to find a sales representative with a sales or business background, and some

EXHIBIT 12.5 Factors that Affect an Organization's Total Rewards Program

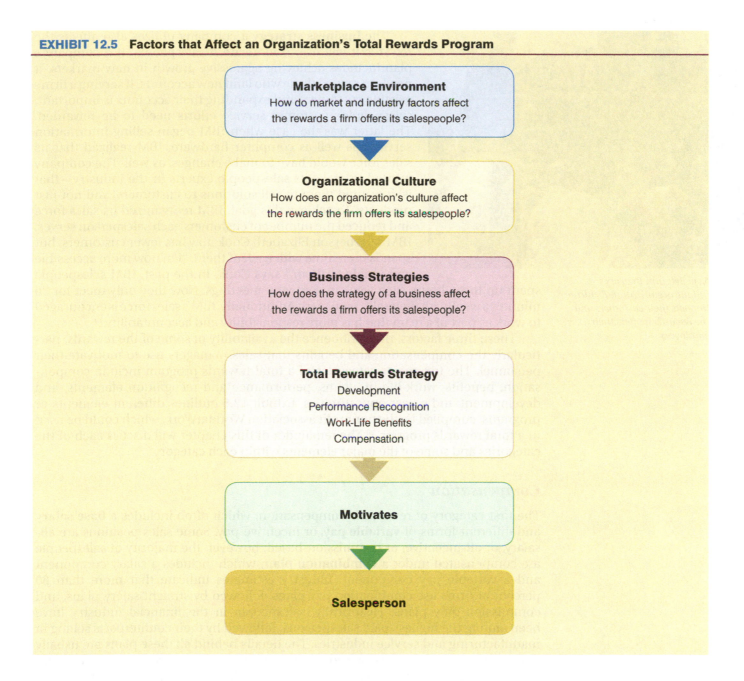

experience selling electrical products, he will likely have to pay the person more than someone who lacks as much.

Many organizations make conscious efforts to strengthen **organizational culture** by choosing certain rewards to offer their sales representatives. Take for instance, New Belgium Brewing Company, a Fort Collins, Colorado, firm that prides itself on its environmental responsibility, philanthropy, and the fact that it's a great place to work. (See their website at *http://www.newbelgium.com/Events/tour-de-fat.aspx.*) The company has its own water treatment plant and energy-producing wind farm, and it has taken the 3Rs—reduce, reuse, and recycle—to extremes. In addition to donating $1 for each keg it sells to the communities in which they were purchased, the company's leaders believe work should be fun. To keep things fun, it gives each of its employees a "cruiser bicycle" (one with fat tires) after they have been employed by the company for one year. After five years, the company rewards them with a trip to Belgium.

New Belgium Brewery's unique organizational culture impacts their customers and the rewards it offers their employees.

The **business strategy** a company utilizes also affects the rewards it will use to motivate it salespeople. If a company's plan includes achieving aggressive growth in new markets, it needs to reward those who land new accounts. If serving a firm's existing customers and expanding their accounts is important, salespeople's customer service efforts need to be rewarded. The latter was the case when IBM began selling information services as well as computer hardware; IBM realized that its sales force would have to make changes, as well. The company wanted to make its salespeople experts in the industry—that is, it wanted them to sell solutions to customers, and not just products. To achieve this goal, IBM reorganized its sales force and reduced the number of customers each salesperson serves. IBM salesperson Elizabeth Cook now has fewer customers, but spends more time with each of them. "I'm now more accessible and visible to them," says Cook. In the past, IBM salespeople spent up to six hours each week in company meetings. Now they only meet for 30 minutes a week with their sales managers. Additionally, IBM's sales force is encouraged to work as part of a team that has more responsibility and accountability.[19]

These three factors, then, influence the availability of some of the rewards, particularly the compensation and benefits that sales managers use to motivate their personnel. The five major categories of a total rewards program include compensation, benefits, work-life programs, performance and recognition elements, and development and career opportunities. Exhibit 12.6 outlines different elements or programs, compiled by the nonprofit association WorldatWork, which could be used in a total rewards program.[20] The remainder of this chapter will discuss each of the categories and some of the major elements within each category.

Compensation

The first category of rewards is compensation, which often includes a **base salary** and different forms of **variable pay,** or incentive pay. Some sales positions are all-salary, or all-incentive, or commission-based; however, the majority of salespeople are compensated under a **combination plan**, which includes a salary component and a variable pay component. Industry estimates indicate that more than 80 percent of firms use combination pay plans, followed by straight salary plans, and commission-only plans. Historically, salespeople in the financial industry have been among the highest-paid salespersons, followed by their counterparts selling in manufacturing and service industries. The details behind all these plans are usually developed at headquarters by top executives from sales, marketing, finance, and human resources. Sales managers are charged with making certain that the various programs are implemented in a manner to achieve company objectives, including personal development and sales goals.

As important a role as it plays, it seems surprising to find that, when asked what their company's compensation program was designed to do, only about one-third of employees could accurately describe it or explain its desired outcome.[21] Obviously, if you design a compensation program to motivate your employees, and truly use it as such, they need to understand how it works.

BASE SALARY A base salary is a fixed amount of compensation an individual receives. It will depend upon a combination of factors. A newly hired graduate's salary is likely to take into account the person's unique skills (such as languages spoken), past experiences (for example, whether she completed a sales internship, held a selling job, or participated in a local, regional, or the National Collegiate Sales Contest), and future potential. As we have explained, higher living costs in some locations can also influence the salary levels that firms offer their salespeople. Differential pay based

EXHIBIT 12.6 WorldatWork Total Rewards Inventory

Compensation	Benefits	Work-Life	Performance & Recognition	Development & Career Opportunities
Base Wages • Salary Pay • Hourly Pay • Piece Rate Pay **Premium Pay** • Shift Differential Pay • Weekend/Holiday Pay • On-call Pay • Call-In Pay • Hazard Pay • Bilingual Pay • Skill-Based Pay **Variable Pay** • Commissions • Team-Based Pay • Bonus Programs • Referral Bonus • Hiring Bonus • Retention Bonus • Project Completion Bonus • Incentive Pay *Short-term:* • Profit-Sharing • Individual Performance-Based Incentives • Performance-Sharing Incentives	**Legally Required/ Mandated** • Unemployment Insurance • Worker's Compensation Insurance • Social Security Insurance • Medicare • State Disability Insurance (if applicable) **Health & Welfare** • Medicare Plan • Dental Plan • Vision Plan • Prescription Drug Plan • Flexible Spending Accounts (FSAs) • Health Reimbursement Accounts (HRAs) • Health Savings Accounts (HSAs) • Mental Health Plan • Life Insurance • Spouse/Dependent Life Insurance • AD&D Insurance • Short Term/Long Term Disability Insurance	**Workplace Flexibility/ Alternative Work Arrangements** • Flex-Time • Telecommuting • Alternative Work Sites • Compressed Workweek • Job Sharing • Part-time Employment • Seasonal Schedules **Paid and Unpaid Time Off** • Maternity/Paternity Leave • Adoption Leave • Sabbaticals **Health and Wellness** • Employee Assistance Programs • On-site Fitness Facilities • Discounted Fitness Club Rates • Weight Management Programs • Smoking Cessation Assistance • On-site Massages • Stress Management Programs • Voluntary Immunization Clinics	**Caring for Dependents** • Dependent Care • Reimbursement Accounts • Dependent Care Travel Related Expense Reimbursement • Dependent Care Referral and Resource Services • Emergency Dependent Care Services • Childcare Subsidies • On-site Caregiver Support Groups • On-site Dependent Care • Adoption Assistance • After-School Care Services • College/Scholarship Information • Scholarships • Privacy Rooms • Summer Camps and Activities • Special Needs Childcare • Disabled Adult Care • Geriatric Counseling • In-home Assessments for Eldercare	**Performance** • 1:1 Meetings • Performance Reviews • Project Completion/Team Evaluations • Performance Planning/ Goal Setting Sessions **Recognition** • Service Awards • Retirement Awards • Peer Recognition Awards • Spot Awards • Managerial Recognition Programs • Organization-wide Recognition Programs • Exceeding Performance Awards • Employee of the Month/ Year Awards • Appreciation Luncheons, Outings, Formal Events • Goal-Specific Awards (Quality, Efficiency, Cost Savings, Productivity, Safety) • Employee Suggestion Programs	**Learning Opportunities** • Tuition Reimbursement • Tuition Discounts • Corporate Universities • New Technology Training • On-the-Job Learning • Attendance at Outside Seminars and Conferences • Access to Virtual Learning, Podcasts, Webinars • Self-Development Tools **Coaching/Mentoring** • Leadership Training • Exposure to Resident Experts • Access to Information Networks • Formal or Informal Mentoring Programs

continued

EXHIBIT 12.6 (continued) WorldatWork Total Rewards Inventory

Compensation	Benefits	Work-Life	Performance & Recognition	Development & Career Opportunities
• Incentive Pay (continued)	**Retirement**	**Financial Support**		**Advancement Opportunities**
Long-term:	• Defined Benefit Plan	• Financial Planning		• Internships
• Restricted Stock Options/Grants	• Defined Contribution Plan	• Services And Education		• Apprenticeships
• Performance Shares	• Profit Sharing Plan	• Adoption Reimbursement		• Overseas Assignments
• Performance Units	• Hybrid Plan	• Transit Subsidies		• Internal Job Postings
• Stock Options/Grants	**Pay for Time Not Worked**	• 529 Plans		• Job Advancement/ Promotion
	• Vacation	• Savings Bonds		
	• Holiday	**Voluntary Benefits**		• Career Ladders and Pathways
	• Sick Leave	• Long Term Care		• Succession Planning
	• Bereavement Leave	• Auto/Home Insurance		• On/Off Ramps Through Career Lifecycle
	• Leaves of Absence (Military, Personal, Medical, Family Medical)	• Pet Insurance		• Job Rotations
		• Legal Insurance		
	Health and Wellness (continued)	• Identity Theft Insurance		
	• Health Screenings	• Employee Discounts		
	• Nutritional Counseling	• Concierge Services		
	• On-site Nurse	• Parking		
	• Business Travel Health Services	**Culture Change Initiatives**		
	• Disability Management	• Work Redesign		
	• Return to Work Programs	• Team Effectiveness		
	• Reproductive Health/ Pregnancy Programs	• Diversity/Inclusion Initiatives		
	• 24-Hour Nurse Line	• Women's Advancement Initiatives		
	• On-site Work-Life Seminars (Stress-Reductions, Parenting, etc.)	• Work Environment Initiatives		
	• Health Advocate	• Multigenerational Initiatives		
	Community Involvement			
	• Community Volunteer Programs			
	• Matching Gift Programs			
	• Shared Leave Programs			
	• Disaster Relief Funds			
	• Sponsorships/Grants			
	• In-Kind Donations			

on this factor is called a **cost of living allowance** (COLA) or adjustment. (There are several Internet calculators that allow a person to compare the cost of living of one location versus another. The calculator at *http://cgi.money.cnn.com/tools/costofliving/costofliving.html* is one such online device.)

Some positions, particularly those requiring a salesperson to offer high support levels to a firm's customers, will be entirely salaried, or **straight salary**. For example, ThoughtWorks—a software company with headquarters in Chicago—eliminated commissions and placed its entire sales force on straight salary to encourage exceptional service to customers. With ease of access to information on the Internet, customers are becoming more educated and savvy consumers. With a wealth of information available to them online, customers may place a higher value on understanding the unique services applicable to them more than hearing about information they have already read about. Other firms following this approach believe it puts the customer's interest first (i.e., "The customer always comes first") above that of the selling company.[22, 23]

A straight salary plan also works well when a salesperson is just getting established and developing her own clientele, or **book of business**. It might also work in situations where it is difficult to trace what role in the sale each individual played (with large capital purchases, for example). The advantage of this for salespeople is that they can count on receiving a steady stream of income for their efforts—even when their firms' sales are slow. The disadvantage is that, if the salespeople have been very productive, they will receive no additional income. The benefit for the organization is that the amount of income it must pay is predictable. The drawback is that the firm's sales representatives might be interested in only producing the minimum levels of work required, and that their sales managers may have limited control when it comes to motivating them. However, the good use of goals and quotas can help offset these disadvantages. This form of pay is particularly useful when a salesperson is developing expertise and skills; at the time they reach the next level, the rep will often transition into a combination plan. For the more experienced salesperson, variable pay will likely play a more significant role.

VARIABLE (INCENTIVE) PAY Variable pay acts as an incentive for the salesperson. For those salespeople who are particularly motivated, they know that their extra efforts will be rewarded. Bonuses and commissions are two examples of incentive plans. A **bonus** is a lump sum of cash used to reward sales personnel and sales managers for achieving varying sales levels. Some companies have several types of bonuses, and administer them either on a quarterly, semi-annual, or annual basis. For example, some organizations give their salespeople **stock options,** which allow them to purchase their companies' shares at reduced prices. After holding the stock for a minimum time period, they have the opportunity to sell it or include it in their retirement packages. The intent of this form of compensation is to encourage salespeople to make a long-term commitment to the organization. A bonus is usually viewed as a welcomed reward, even though the salesperson may not know how large it will be. A yearly bonus may, at times, be less motivating, because they lose some potential to motivate due to their long time period. **Team-based pay** is another type of bonus that rewards salespeople for their group productivity. IBM uses a team approach to selling; its teams consist of inside representatives, product specialists, product consultants, and other experts. Team members work within compensation-based plans on their individual goals, but may also earn additional bonuses when their teams achieve team goals.

A **commission** is a percentage of the price of the product or service that salespeople earn for their selling efforts. Most commission programs are **progressive plans**. Progressive plans increase the percentage commission a firm's sales representatives earn for each progressive level of sales. These plans encourage representatives to sell as much as possible. **Regressive plans** decrease the percentage commission a firm's sales representatives earn when they sell more products and services. A plan such as this allows an organization to limit the amount that sales representatives can earn when selling an easy-to-sell product or service—one that, perhaps, has been extensively pre-sold via advertising campaigns—so the representative is merely acting as an order-taker. Of course, such a system can result in some motivational problems. For example, if sales representatives have met or exceeded their goals, they may be motivated to "coast," or slow down, for the rest of the sales period. Exhibit 12.7 shows the amount of commission a salesperson would make for selling $500,000 worth of products/services under a progressive versus a regressive plan.

EXHIBIT 12.7	An Example of a Salesperson's Compensation Based on a Progressive versus a Regressive Plan				
Amount Sold	**Progressive Plan**		**Regressive Plan**		
	Percent	**Amount**	**Percent**	**Amount**	
$0–$100,000	5%	$5,000	15%	$15,000	
$100,001–$200,000	8%	8,000	10%	10,000	
$200,001–$300,000	10%	10,000	8%	8,000	
>$300,000	15%	30,000	5%	10,000	
Total commission		$53,000		$43,000	

Some sales positions may be entirely commission-based. Firms with restricted cash flow and new products that need a strong push—and those in very competitive industries—may opt for this approach. Advertising sales positions, some types of insurance sales, and some automobile sales positions are examples. The advantage of this approach is that firms pay only for successful sales efforts; they don't have to pay salespeople who are doing a poor job or not contributing to the firm's profit. The disadvantages lie at both extremes: if a firm's sales are slow, then its sales representatives will experience low levels of income. When this happens, the company's better salespeople will tend to leave the organization to sell products and services that earn them better pay. The other extreme is an organization that has a strong product or service offering that takes little effort to sell. In this case, the firm's salespeople will earn a great deal of money without much effort on their part.

An additional disadvantage of commission-only pay is that a firm runs the risk of its salespeople focusing solely on activities that will earn them the largest commissions. For example, they may focus their energies on products and services that are easiest to sell, ignoring new or higher-margin products that are more difficult to sell. Additionally, salespeople are more likely to ignore smaller, less-lucrative accounts and customer service activities. The "Ethics in Sales Management" box in this chapter describes how a commission-focused compensation system put a salesperson in a position that resulted in his compromising his ethical standards.

COMBINATION PLANS Because of the problems noted above, the majority of firms use combination plans that include both salaries and incentives. Combination plans are designed to capitalize on the advantages a base salary and incentive programs offer, and to minimize their disadvantages. These plans are particularly beneficial for new salespeople. A base salary gives sales representatives the security of knowing that, in bad times, they will have income to fall back on—which can help minimize their turnover. An incentive component of the plan then serves to further motivate them. Industry surveys find that the majority of companies had average pay mixes between 60/40 and 70/30 salary/variable pay. Oftentimes, representatives can take a **draw**, or advance, on their incentive pay, as well. The plans can be designed so that new sales representatives start out earning lower-percentage commissions, but then

ETHICS IN SALES MANAGEMENT   What Do You Do If Your Company's Compensation System Encourages Unethical Behavior?

Note: The following is an account by one of the authors' former students about a situation in which he found himself as a sales representative. The student's and company's identities have been withheld to allow them to remain anonymous. After reading the person's account, decide whether an alternative compensation plan would have been more ethical. Do you think such a plan could realistically be implemented at this company? Finally, what would you do if you were to find yourself in a similar situation?

Just after I graduated from college, I worked for a mobile medical services firm. I was second in charge of a department that offered various tests to identify individuals with osteoporosis. Generally speaking, the machines that we used, and the tests that we performed, were beneficial to the right group of patients.

Mainly, I was responsible for operating the equipment and training new employees to give the tests. On occasion, I would be asked to go to doctors' offices to "market" our services.

I was young, had no marketing background, and was given little/no instruction on how to ethically "sell" our service to prospective clients (doctors). So I went with what I knew; I focused on what drove me at the time—money. I was driven by my compensation system.

I would go to a doctor's office, set up my company's equipment, talk the doctor through how our product worked, tell what it diagnosed, and reveal that it administered a low-level (small dose) X-ray. I knew the equipment well, and the disease that it diagnosed. I'd go into detail regarding what type of patient would be at risk, and if diagnosed with osteoporosis, what medications were available on the market to treat it.

Oftentimes, I would ask if the doctor had a volunteer that I could give an exam to. This would show that the exam was non-invasive, quick, easy, and painless. After the ethical demo, then I'd take the doctor aside into a private room and tell him or her about the pricing. This is where the shades of gray come in. Everything prior to this conversation I felt positive about. However, in this conversation, instead of just going over our pricing for a full- or half-day's screening, I'd delve a little deeper into the economics than what might have been ethical.

I told the doctor about our fees, and then went into great detail about the amount of money that various insurance companies reimbursed for the exam. Basically, I would lay out in gory detail how much profit a doctor could make by bringing in our services and giving us a maximum patient load while we were there. Although I'd previously told the doctor who the "right" group of at-risk patients were, at this point I'd tell him or her that the insurance companies paid for the exam annually, and that some of our current clients (doctors), were running every single one of their patients through the exam so as to establish a "baseline." Using the baseline, the doctors could see the bone density of their patients today and compare them to what they were a few years later. Of course, this would involve retesting their patients and again collecting money from their insurance companies.

I can't recall a client with whom we didn't close the deal. Some doctors brought us in once a week for a full day and sent along every patient that they had. We worked off a flat rate for the day or half-day, so even if a patient's insurance was not very good, there was little or no risk to his or her doctor, because there were no incremental costs related to testing more patients. The only thing the doctor might miss out on was the opportunity cost incurred if another patient with better insurance could have been tested instead.

We worked at quite a few gynecologists' offices, and often scanned every client that came to see them that day. I didn't feel bad about this, because these clients really constituted our "at-risk" group—that is, people who were truly at risk for developing osteoporosis. However, other general practice doctors did not use our services quite so ethically. I actually personally scanned one doctor himself every year for a few years, so that he could bill his own insurance company for his own tests!

In the end, I still question my method of pitching that product, and the fact that I'm questioning it probably means that it wasn't quite right. I comfort myself by knowing that I did provide doctors with all the positive, good information that they needed to know about the tests. Ultimately, it was up to them to whom they prescribed the exams.

Would a "code of ethics" at this company have changed my marketing strategy for this product? First off, this was a company driven by the dollar (and, at the time, so was I). Consequently, the busier I kept our equipment, the more I'd work, and the more I'd make. So, if the code were in place, I don't think I'd have followed it, and I doubt anyone would have ever found out. Even if an example were given in the code of ethics regarding the tactic I was using, I probably would have found a way to rationalize to myself that I was somehow in compliance with the code, as I told the doctors the truth about everything. And, finally, the owner of the company was, I believe, a shady character to begin with. As a result, I know that the code, if created, would never have truly had the support of the company's top managers.

gradually earn a higher-percentage commission as they becomes more experienced. The percentages for each pay component vary, depending upon the company's objectives. For example, a well-established firm with high service requirements may offer 80 percent salary and 20 percent commission. They believe this split ensures that each account will receive the service they want it to, and enough of an incentive for the sales force to try to sell more. Another less-established firm may take a 60 percent salary and 40 percent commission structure because they want their sales force to be spending more effort on securing sales.[24] Glassdoor.com is a job-and-career website where individuals can voluntarily report their earnings. Exhibit12.8 displays the companies that received the highest reports of average annual commission compensation from employees who voluntarily—and anonymously—completed the annual Glassdoor.com compensation report survey. Only companies receiving more than 40 reports in the past two years were included.[25]

EXHIBIT 12.8   Top Ten Commission Companies Reported by Glassdoor.com

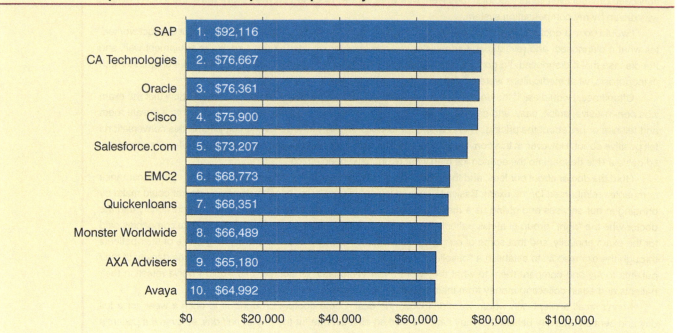

According to Melaney Barba, a sales manager for Liberty Mutual Insurance, the company uses a combination plan that includes a salary, commission, and a variety of bonuses. "Our system allows the rep the security of a steady income when they start, which transforms to more incentive bases as the person's skills and customer base develops," explains Barba. New sales representatives start out with a base salary for their 15 weeks of training. Over the course of three years, the salary levels they earn decrease as they sell to new accounts and begin to build their commissions. At the seven-year mark, their salaries are completely phased out. At this point, salaries are replaced by commissions and bonuses coming from the renewals of policies they've sold in the past. Liberty Mutual Insurance representatives can also take draws on their commissions, which many of them do as they begin their careers.

In the future, discussions will likely continue between the balanced use of incentives and effective sales management practices (i.e., hiring, training, coaching, incentives, etc.).[26]

Benefits

Benefits provide security for members of an organization. They are becoming increasingly more expensive, representing approximately 30 percent of a firm's payroll costs, on average. There are several different types of benefits programs that companies provide. Some programs are required by law. The programs legally required in the United States include Social Security; a government retirement program; Workers' Compensation, which provides income to employees hurt or disabled on the job; unemployment insurance; and family and medical leave programs that give employees time away from their jobs to care for their family members. Firms are not required to pay employees while they are on family leave; they need only guarantee that their jobs will be available for them when they return to work. Legally mandated programs constitute about eight percent of all benefit payments employers make.[27]

Employers can choose to provide their employees a number of other benefit programs. The most costly, and most valued, are health insurance programs, which can include eye, dental, life, disability, and other forms of insurance. Some programs cover employees only; other plans cover members of employees' families, too. Health insurance payments constitute nearly 28 percent of the average employer's benefit payments.[28]

Many companies also provide their salespeople with a **retirement**, or **pension**, **benefit** giving them income after they retire. Sometimes referred to as *defined benefit programs*, they specify the exact amounts employees will be paid once they retire. The amount will vary from company to company and from employee to employee, depending upon their tenure. Usually it is based on the average compensation the employee received during their last three to five years. Employees who stay for less than a certain number of years (usually 25-35 years) are entitled to less than the full amount. Some companies also provide a **defined contribution program**, jointly funded by an employer and the employee. These include 401(k) savings accounts, IRAs (individual retirement accounts), and profit-sharing programs. Today, however, many are moving away from defined contribution programs. Retirement plans constitute about four percent of the average employer's benefit payments.[29]

The last category of benefit programs is **paid time off** from work. This includes payment for vacations, holidays, sick days, and other time away from work. Most organizations give each of their salespeople one or two weeks of paid vacation after they have worked for their firm for one year. This typically increases to up to four weeks a year. Paid time off programs account for about 25 percent of the benefit payments the average employer makes. Other programs, such as lunches and breaks, account for the remaining benefit payments firms make.[30]

Work-Life Rewards

As Exhibit 12.6 shows, there are a variety of reward programs that helps employees find a balance between their work and life (away from work), often referred to as **work-life balance**. As noted earlier in the chapter, each generational group may value these differently. **Workplace flexibility programs** are designed to help employees schedule where and when they work. Many salespeople work out of their homes, and at irregular hours that accommodate the needs of their clients. Some employers will pay for **leaves of absence** for births and adoptions, and for sabbaticals. **Health and wellness programs** focus on maintaining or improving the health and fitness levels of salespeople. Healthy employees have lower insurance costs than those who are not healthy. Two examples

Motivators should provide a balance between work and life away from work.

are corporate fitness facilities and employee assistance programs, which are designed to help salespeople with drug and alcohol problems they might have. **Community involvement programs** compensate, or partially compensate, employees during the time they volunteer. Programs that focus on **care for dependents** provide support for employees with childcare or dependent needs. **Financial support programs** offer employees assistance for a variety of purposes, including education costs, adoption costs, costs related to eldercare, and so forth. Other **voluntary benefits** vary by the organization, and can range from travel and transit assistance to employee discounts.

Recognition

Benefits and work-life programs are largely determined at a firm's corporate level and/or human resources level. However, most sales managers have a great deal of flexibility when it comes to implementing recognition rewards. Eighty-five percent of companies reported that their sales managers use them to enhance the individual performance of sales representatives; and 43 percent of firms indicate that their sales managers use them in team-selling situations.[31] The rewards can be very informal, handled at a personal level between the sales representative and the sales manager, or they can be very formal, handled in front of the entire sales force or company. Recognition is often used to reinforce the short-term behavior of sales representatives.

Exhibit 12.9 displays the frequency of use of different incentives.[32] Other rewards might include a dinner at a special location, a hotel-room upgrade (from sharing a room to a single room), or an appointment to a desirable committee within the firm. Sales managers who want to reinforce good selling behaviors on the spot often will award gift cards or free meal cards to their representatives, as Rich Merklinger—in the opening profile—explained that he does. Retail salespeople who sell many

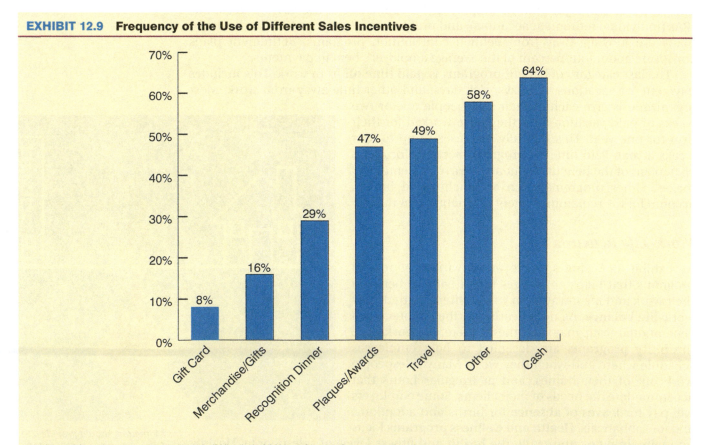

EXHIBIT 12.9 **Frequency of the Use of Different Sales Incentives**

Adapted from Kornik, Joseph (2007). "What's It All Worth? 2007 Compensation Survey" *Sales & Marketing Management*, (159)4, 27–39.

manufacturers' products are sometimes encouraged by the manufacturers to promote their particular brands through the use of **sales promotion incentive funds** (**SPIFs**). For each selected product they sell, they receive money or merchandise as a reward.

Perhaps the most widely used form of recognition is granted through local, regional, or organization-wide sales contests. The amount of influence a sales manager has in developing these events depends upon where they originate. The contests can be based on a time period (for example, weekly, monthly, quarterly, or yearly), or around the launch of a new product or service. Melaney Barba, with Liberty Mutual Insurance, comments that her sales representatives thrive on competition. "I use local sales contests to help support our organization-wide Liberty Leaders Contest. We display monthly winners' pictures, and have their names engraved on our permanent plaque." Sales managers should make sure that sales contests are implemented correctly and fairly. Most experts agree that you want to make sure that your contests allow salespeople to be winners without branding other salespeople as losers. One way of doing this is to design your contest so that there are multiple winners, depending upon the amount of a product a rep sells. The top-selling rep would be awarded the most lucrative prize, and other high-achieving reps would be awarded lesser prizes. Firms such as Maritz Incentives are frequently hired by firms to assist their sales managers with contests. The Maritz staff does everything—from helping choose the types of rewards to offer, communicating them to representatives, and distributing them to winners. Exhibit 12.10 outlines some suggestions for planning and implementing sales contests.

EXHIBIT 12.10   Recommendations for Successful Sales Contests

- Use them sparingly. Staging contests too frequently, or on a predictable schedule, may influence the sales force to hold sales back until the contest starts.
- Be selective in what products/services to include. Including new, unproven products/services helps to motivate salespeople to learn about them and sell them.
- Make rewards attractive to all ages and experience levels. In other words, use rewards that motivate all groups.

Similarly, Mike Kapocius, a senior regional account manager at Takeda Pharmaceutics, recalls the importance of his and others' induction into a top sellers' club: "These [programs] can be very motivating, because reps receive a great trip (partner included), and typically meet—and are recognized by—the organization's top leaders. Giving your input to the company's leaders can be very motivating, especially to an established rep." Being included in a top sales recognition group is typically based on several criteria, including a certain level of sales success. However, many organizations will also consider other activities, such as a salesperson's teamwork, leadership, and community service. In some organizations, membership is determined by a vote of the sales representatives themselves.

It should be noted that, if a company relies exclusively on external, or extrinsic, rewards, it runs the risk of having trained or motivated its sales force to perform only when they are given "goodies," rather than relying on intrinsic motivators—such as satisfaction with their work. The following analogy demonstrates how tying extrinsic motivators to an intrinsically motivating activity can destroy what normally motivates a sales representative.

There was a small baker with a good business and regular customers who, one week, noticed his sales had fallen off drastically in the late afternoon. Stepping outside his store, he spotted a group of very menacing boys who were harassing everyone who walked by and scaring off his customers. After politely asking the group to stop bothering his customers, the boys laughed and said, "Make us move, little man!" They then proceeded to harass and, ultimately, chased off the remaining bakery customers for the day.

The next day, the boys arrived and began harassing customers again. The baker quickly went out and handed each boy $5 and said he had changed his mind. He told them that he actually liked their insults and was going to pay them for insulting him. The boys thought he was nuts, and began making nasty comments about the baker and his "lousy" rolls and other products. After a few minutes, the baker said, "That's fine. Thanks for your efforts," and returned to work.

The next day, the boys arrived again. The baker apologized to them, saying that he had only enough to pay each of them $4 to make their mean comments to him and harass his customers. After a couple of minutes of complaining about their diminished pay, they began again, slinging their insults.

The following day, the baker lowered the amount to only $3 per boy. The day after that, he paid them only $2 day. On the fifth day, the baker said he could pay them only $1 for their comments. The boys looked at the $1 bills and with great disgust said, "If you are only going to pay us $1 each, it's not worth our time and effort!" With that they left, and didn't return.

The moral of this story is that organizations should be cautious about the extrinsic rewards they use—and the frequency with which they administer them. This is especially true of sales contests. A contest should be held for a short period of time, and motivate reps to do something they are not already doing or supposed to be doing. What is exactly is the "ideal" frequency with which awards should be administered, you might be wondering? Research by behavioral scientists has demonstrated that, when we are learning a new behavior, a constant reinforcement schedule works best. For example, if you do something correctly, you should be rewarded every time. However, when no one is around to constantly reward your behavior, it will quickly diminish. The reward schedule that seems to best reinforce behavior is an intermittent, or variable, schedule in which the performer does not know exactly when he will get the reinforcement. In sum, reinforcing the behaviors you want your salespeople to exhibit— on an intermittent schedule—is a fine way to reward and motivate them.

Expense Accounts

Expense accounts were not included in Exhibit 12.6. Salespeople incur a whole host of costs. Controlling the rising price of fuel and transportation expenditures is becoming a battle for many sales managers. Use of video calls, such as Skype and Go-To-Meeting, has increased opportunities for sales reps to meet with clients, or for meetings with less travel time and lower costs. According to the Travel Leaders Corporate, the average cost of a domestic business trip, including airfare, lodging and car rentals, is $965, while an international trip is $2,398.[33] These numbers will surely increase as the price of fuel rises. Many organizations work with firms that specialize in securing corporate discounts from airlines and other transportation-related companies. Organizations also work with firms that determine when companies should provide sales reps with leased vehicles or reimburse reps for the use of their personal vehicles for work travel.

The majority of firms also either supply or reimburse their salespeople for home office expenses, which can include the cost of their laptops and software, cell phones, office supplies and printers, Internet charges, and voice and data communications systems. Experts say the median cost of outfitting a home office is nearly $5,000 in direct and support costs. Another significant expense is for lodging and food, which varies widely, depending upon where you are conducting business. For example, the average cost for one meal and lodging exceeds $257 in Chicago, Illinois, versus $166 in Orlando, Florida.[34] The most frequently used method to reimburse travel expenses is an **unlimited plan**, under which all of the sales rep's expenses are covered. This is in contrast to a **per diem plan**, whereby a rep is allocated a certain amount of money for each day traveled. A third method is a **limited plan**, whereby the exact amounts for each meal and travel expense are set. Exhibit 12.11 outlines each of the plans' advantages and disadvantages in terms of management control, flexibility, record keeping, and administration costs.

EXHIBIT 12.11   A Comparison of Expense Account Plans

	Unlimited	Per Diem	Limited
Advantages	• All expenses covered • Very flexible • Simple administration	• Simple to administer • Low costs • Sales managers can control and forecast expenses • Limits abuse	• Sales managers can control and forecast expenses • Little abuse
Disadvantages	• Potential for abuse is high • No incentive to be economical • Sales managers cannot forecast costs • If amounts exceed federal limits, company is subject to withholding and payroll taxes • Higher administrative costs	• Not flexible; may have costs exceeding limits	• Higher administrative costs • Not flexible

An expense account should, by design, be a neutral factor in a reward system. That is, salespeople should not be placed in a position where they use their own income to cover the costs of making a sale. Likewise, they should not be using the extra income from these funds for their personal use.

Personal Development and Career Opportunities

The last category of rewards, personal development and career opportunities, addresses the question, "What do my salespeople want out of their careers, and how can I help them achieve it?" **Learning opportunities** include access to new educational experiences. These can range from coursework to a summer training experience to the completion of a graduate program. One new area is the development of the "corporate athlete." Programs such as this are based on the premise that, to be in optimum "condition," salespeople must learn how to combine their busy schedules with healthy living practices and exercise. Via a training regimen, attendees learn how to balance these demands, and by doing so, have the energy and attitude they need to sustain their efforts and succeed.[35]

One form of learning opportunity unique to salespeople is a **sales meeting**. Often held on a yearly or semi-annual basis (although some organizations hold them daily, weekly or monthly), these gatherings are meant to be educational and motivational experiences for participants. Typically, new product/service information and training updates are covered. Sales meetings can be held on a local, regional, or national level. National level meetings are often held at attractive locations, and include opportunities for

Tuition assistance for an advanced degree can be a valuable part of a development rewards plan.

socializing. Sometimes, motivational speakers are engaged. For example, salesman Chris Gardner, whose rags-to-riches story was portrayed in the best-selling book and film *The Pursuit of Happyness*, has addressed a number of sales forces on the importance of perseverance.

Encouraging sales representatives to **mentor**, or **coach**, less-experienced reps can also be a powerful motivator. A program such as this publicly recognizes experienced sales representatives for their skills and expertise, thereby offering them a measure of prestige. Providing your sales representatives with advancement opportunities, and allowing them to participate in succession planning so they can get the experience they need to further their careers, can also be powerful motivators.

Managing Your Career

In Chapter 11, we discussed the importance of setting some personal goals. (Have you set some yet?) Think about what you wrote. (If you haven't done that yet, consider what might motivate you to take action and put those goals on paper.) What motivational issues were your drivers? We all want to earn a good living and have the ability to support a comfortable lifestyle—but beyond that—what seem to be your key motivators? Might they include an interesting job—with or without travel, some personal rewards or indulgences, moving to another location, beginning a family, helping or serving others, or something else?

It is important to begin to understand what motivates you, as this can help you find the organization that offers them. What if you find a job that you like, but that organization doesn't offer your key motivators, or does so only at a limited level? Can you find other ways to meet your motivational needs? If they don't offer the highest compensation, might they offset this with higher benefits, such as retirement or work-life balance elements? Might you consider fulfilling some needs through working with other organizations? Can you see yourself serving on the board of a non-profit agency, volunteering at a local agency to work with children, helping build a house with Habitat for Humanity, cleaning a wilderness area for the Nature Conservancy, or perhaps spending part of your vacation on a mission trip helping others? Most of us might also combine those with other, more self-directed drives— such as becoming a better cook (e.g., signing up for a cooking class) or becoming more fit and adventurous (e.g., taking a guided bicycling trek across the Netherlands or hiking down into the Grand Canyon).

Once we have some insights into what various reward elements motivate us, we are in a better position to help understand what might motivate others.

Summary

Making certain that the sales force is motivated and receiving the rewards they value is an important part of a sales manager's job. It would be easy work if every salesperson was motivated by the same rewards—but they aren't. Some salespeople are driven by internal or intrinsic factors, and others by more material, extrinsic factors. Content approaches have attempted to explain motivation by delineating the factors that make up a person's motivation. Process approaches have examined the steps individuals go through to be motivated. In today's workplace, there are four different generations working side-by-side. Some of the differences in terms of how motivated salespeople are can be explained by their generational experiences and values. The Matures grew up in a time of world conflict and limited technology. These salespeople tend to place a higher value on traditional rewards. Baby Boomers were raised in a period of social strife. These salespeople tend to integrate technology into their work and place a heavy value on leadership. Salespeople from Generation

X learned from their parents to place only limited trust in their employers. These salespeople enjoy using technology and value family above work. Members of the fourth generation, the Millennials, have grown up with a limited trust in government and employers. Using technology is second nature to these salespeople. They often seek a balance between their lives and their work. Sales managers need to understand the differences between each group and strive to satisfy the motivational needs of all.

Because the values of salespeople are changing, many sales managers now take a total rewards approach to motivate them. The compensation elements of a total rewards program include a base salary and incentive, or variable, pay. Benefits programs are designed to provide for the health and retirement security needs of a sales force. The work-life elements of a total rewards program include programs that allow salespeople to choose when and where they work, as well as to balance their health and family needs. Rewarding salespeople by recognizing them on a district-, regional-, or organizational-wide basis is a particularly good motivator. Salespeople can receive praise, cash, merchandise, travel benefits, or membership in a top performers' club as part of a reward program. Through the final category of rewards—development and career opportunities—companies attempt to help individual salespersons identify their future career aspirations and lay out a path for their attainment.

Key Terms

Baby boomers   261
base salary   268
benefits   275
bonus   271
book of business   271
business strategy   268
care for dependents programs   276
coach   280
combination plan   268
commission   271
community involvement programs   276
content of motivation   259
cost of living allowance (COLA)   271
defined contribution program   275
draw   272
expense accounts   278
extrinsic motivation factors   258
financial support programs   276
Generation X   262
health and wellness programs   275
intrinsic motivation factors   258
learning opportunities   279
leaves of absence   275
limited plan   279

marketplace environment   266
Matures   261
mentor   280
Millennials   263
organizational culture   267
paid time off   275
pension benefit   275
per diem plan   279
plateau   264
process   259
progressive plans   271
regressive plans   271
retirement benefit   275
sales meetings   279
sales promotion incentive funds (SPIFs)   277
straight salary   271
stock options   271
team-based pay   271
total rewards program   266
unlimited plan   279
variable pay   268
voluntary benefits   276
work-life balance   275
workplace flexibility programs   275

Questions and Problems

1. What intrinsic and extrinsic factors motivate you as a student? What intrinsic and extrinsic factors do you think would motivate you as a salesperson? What about as a sales manager?

2. As a sales manager, how can you apply the findings of the content approaches? How can you apply the findings of the process approaches? Which do you think makes the most significant contributions, and why?

3. Sales manager Gretchen Anderson recalls a "ride-along" with one of her sales representatives, Bill, who consistently struggled to reach his quota. They reached their first destination at 10:50 a.m., and Bill said, "Let's eat some lunch." The two had lunch, met the client at 1:00 p.m., and were done at 1:20 p.m. Bill then told Gretchen he had no other sales calls planned. "I started early today, so I'm knocking off when we get back," Bill told her. In terms of equity theory, describe what is going on from Bill's perspective and from Gretchen's perspective. If you were Gretchen, how would you handle this situation?

4. Given the information below, what insights do you have on what might be going on?

	Sales two years ago	Sales last year	This year's sales	Comments
Keisha	$80,000	$86,000	$94,500	Three years' experience; selected outstanding trainee three years ago
Dustin	$104,000	$111,000	$119,000	Ten years' experience; three years in 100k club and a baby!
Gracie	$109,000	$103,000	$97,500	Twenty years' experience; first time not a 100k club member in 10 years

5. As a sales manager, what are some behaviors and actions you would try to use to motivate your personnel?

6. The intent behind a cost-of-living adjustment (COLA) is to allow members of the salesforce to live and work in high-expense locations. Find an online cost-of-living calculator, or use the one mentioned in this chapter: *http://money.cnn.com/calculator/pf/cost-of-living/*. Compare the living costs in Minneapolis-St. Paul, Minnesota; Raleigh-Durham, North Carolina; Dallas-Fort Worth, Texas; and San Francisco, California. Which area has the highest and lowest cost of living? Compare these costs with those in a small city near you. How much more (or less) would you need to earn as a sales representative in order to move from locale to another? Consider two members of the sales force who are producing identical results. Is it fair that one sales representative, living in a large metropolitan area, is compensated better than another one living in a smaller town, just because the cost of living is higher in one location than in the other?

7. Some students have doubts about being able to support themselves under an incentive-only system. What advice would you offer them?

8. Which three work-life programs do you find most attractive? Which three do you think someone your parents' age would find most attractive? What about the work-life program preferences of people from your grandparents' generation? If you were to hold a sales contest and offer a trip as an award, what location would you pick? For each generation, identify a location that you believe a sales professional would find particularly motivating, and explain why.

9. What type of performance-recognition program would motivate you the most? The least?

10. Some sales managers give cash cards worth about $25 each to their sales representatives when they perform a new skill. What, in your opinion, are the pros and cons of this practice?

11. How could a recognition program for marketing students work within your college's business-education department? What would you use as motivators if you had an unlimited budget? What if your budget were $250?

Role Play

Transdermal Testing

Transdermal Testing produces medical devices that are placed on the skin and have the ability to deliver drugs through the skin. The company has worked to develop a similar noninvasive paradigm to read and monitor certain body chemistry levels, such as blood glucose levels in diabetics. Nearly six percent, or 17 million, individuals in the United States have been diagnosed with diabetics. Other countries, such as China, India and Japan, all have a similar distribution of individuals with diabetes. Product development is an extremely important area in this industry. Products are constantly being improved and updated. Conducting clinical testing and seeking government approval are time-consuming and expensive processes. Transdermal Testing is second in industry sales, but is challenged by its largest competitor, Madison Laboratories. The job of the sales force is largely missionary sales.

Two and a half years ago, Transdermal Testing purchased a major veterinary medicine manufacturer, Apex Labs, and merged the two sales forces. This opened the door to a broader base of customers, including clients with large herds of animals. As might be expected, the merger of the two sales forces was not completely painless; several reps who had worked with Apex left to join competitors' sales forces.

Transdermal has seen its competition grow in numbers and product/service offerings. Governmental units have been their largest segment, and selling to them is often a long process—involving a large number of people in a buying center. Salespeople have to be prepared to work with multiple people and to be available on short notice to work with buying committees.

Sales goals have always been aggressive, but because Transdermal's products/services have a stellar reputation, the sales force has an impressive growth and customer satisfaction record. Top management and HR have worked to keep the organization the industry's leader by providing everyone in the sales organization with great compensation and benefits.

However, with only a few weeks remaining in the sales year, it appears that the south-central district will be lucky to reach its threshold goals, let alone its actual goals. Two salespeople are easily identifiable as below goal; both have lost major accounts in the last quarter, and neither has a full pipeline.

Just three years ago, Angela Francois was a member of the President's Club. Then she had a baby—the couple's first, and the child developed complications that require Angela to have to come home immediately if the caretaker she has hired requests her to do so. Michael Trammell was another award-winning sales rep. Two years ago, his aged mother moved in with his family, and he is often unavailable to clients. Both Angela and Michael barely made threshold last year, and—despite taking work home this year—don't look like they are going to make it this year. To make matters worse, you know customer satisfaction among their customers has fallen off. Both reps have a large proposal under review with a client; if secured, the sale would assure that they would surpass their goals.

Assignment

Split into pairs. One of you is Pat, the sales manager, and the other is the regional manager. Both of you stand to lose $10,000 bonuses, and other sales representatives in District Six will lose $4,000 bonuses if the goals of these two sales reps aren't met.

In situations such as these, the national sales manager will request an action plan for the future. You are getting together to develop that plan.

Third Member

You will be joined shortly by Aaron Weston from the human resources group. You know that he plans to discuss the company's rule that reps not meeting their goals for three consecutive years will need a six-month corrective action plan. Aaron will insist on seeing immediate progress or, within six months, will move toward termination.

Caselets

Caselet 12.1: *Generational Strife*

Human Resources wants to offer a fixed schedule of reinforcements/rewards, based on what HR staff members think is important. As a sales manager, you believe they should allow for variation of rewards based on age/life stages. You have a good working relationship with the director of HR, who has listened to your concerns and agreed to meet with you to discuss the issue. You were requested to bring a draft of what rewards you would propose for various sales reps in different life stages. All parties, including you, are in agreement that compensation should be the number one reward. You have a meeting with an HR study group to review three reps at different career/life stages. You have been asked to prepare the allocation of rewards and resources—what you would propose for each—and to explain why a flexible schedule is better than a fixed schedule. You already heard that HR thinks this is a possible administrative nightmare. Explain, and be sure to address the economics of your recommendation.

HANNAH LIU Hannah is one of your top recruits and, six months into the job, is on track as a top performer. She received five job offers, and you are pleased she accepted yours. Hannah is 22 years old, not married, but has a boyfriend. She has an active lifestyle, volunteers for various causes, participates in the company's volleyball league, and has asked about the organization's tuition reimbursement program.

RODRIGO PÉREZ Rod joined you straight out of college, has been with you for five years, and is a strong performer. He has turned down a promotion that involved a relocation assignment, because he has family ties in this location. He was married three years ago to María, and they are expecting a baby in three months. María works as an accountant at a nearby accounting firm.

ELLIOTT FORD Elliott was recently recognized for 25 years with the company. He frequently earns membership in the "President's Club" for top performers. His wife works at a nearby college. They have one daughter who attends college. Between them, they have three parents who will be 90 years old soon and still "get by" while living at their homes. Elliott recently had some health issues, but appears to be fine.

Caselet 12.2: *Rewards in Good Times and Bad*

It is estimated that 45 percent of U.S. corn and 85 percent of U.S. soybeans are genetically engineered. In addition, somewhere between 70 to 75 percent of processed foods on grocery store shelves contain genetically engineered ingredients. As you might surmise, agribusiness is big business. The companies' names aren't household words, even though the results of their work can be found on the shelves of most households. One of them is Advanced Genetic Engineering and Seeds (AGES). AGES has its roots in the Midwest, where the company was very successful at hybridizing corn to increase its yield and make it more draught resistant. Over the years, AGES has worked to genetically alter and increase productivity of other plants such as soybeans, cotton, rice, wheat, sunflower, sugar cane, and pine trees (for Christmas tree farms). It now has sales reps in every state and 20 countries.

AGES is presently having difficulty retaining quality, experienced salespeople. The problem started three years ago, when the patent used in its most popular corn and cotton plants expired. Now, other seed companies are growing and selling plants with the same characteristics that were once unique to AGES. The company's fiscally conservative board of directors only believes in rewarding sales performance based on profitability. So, as the firm's sales slumped, so did the incomes of many sales representatives and sales managers. Jack Killey was hired last year as the new director of sales, and has been struggling with motivation and reward issues for a sales force that is again failing to make its yearly sales quota.

AGES still has numerous viable seeds to sell, but does not have a "blockbuster" seed in its research pipeline. Last week, one of Jack's senior and more experienced sales managers came into the office and announced her plans to resign, telling Jack that she planned to take early retirement because the industry is changing, and she had had enough.

The company provides both its sales representatives and sales managers with modest salaries, company cars, and full benefits, which are some of the best in the industry. It pays commissions based on salespeople's surpassing their previous year's sales totals. An escalating reward system kicks in once a sales representative achieves 80 percent of her sales quota. There are also special sales contests related to selling the company's most profitable seeds. Rewards for these contests usually consist of trips or merchandise.

However, the average salesperson at AGES is now only achieving 75 percent of his or her sales quota, which means that an average achiever earns no commission. Those who do earn bonuses are usually only a few percentage points over their quotas, so their commission checks are marginal. The sales quotas were set by AGES' board of directors and are based on the company's overall operations overhead—and on the return its shareholders expect.

Jack is very concerned about the downward sales spiral he sees in his sales force. He thinks changing the commission structure would solve the problem. His goal is to kick off AGES' upcoming annual sales meeting with a presentation outlining the company's new and improved commission structure. To implement the new commission plan, he will have to make a proposal to the board of directors to lower the quotas reps must achieve by 10 percent. That way, at least 50 percent of the sales representatives would have an opportunity to achieve and exceed their quotas. He also plans to highlight, for reps, the company's existing total compensation package, including a generous company-car usage policy and valuable benefits package.

Discussion Questions

1. What problems do you anticipate Jack will run into when he presents his revised commission structure plan to AGES' board of directors?
2. If AGES were a low-cost, generic-seed company, how would you—as a sales manager—reward and motivate sales representatives?
3. What other motivational tools could Jack have used to retain and motivate employees, other than adjusting the sales quota downward?
4. Identify other areas within the company that will be affected if Jack's plan is approved by the board of directors?
5. Do you feel the company should have adjusted its commission structure before the patent for its best-selling plants expired? Is it fair to penalize the sales force with lower commissions for an outside competitive factor they cannot control? Explain your answer.

References

1. Maslow, Abraham H. (1943). "A Theory of Human Motivation," *Psychological Review*, July, 370–396.
2. McClelland, David C. (1965). "Toward of Theory of Motive Acquisition," *American Psychologist*, (May), 321–333.
3. Herzberg, Fredrick (1969). "One More Time: How Do You Motivate Employees?" *Harvard Business Review*, January-February, 56.
4. Adams, John. S. (1963). "Toward an Understanding of Inequity," *Journal of Abnormal and Social Psychology*, (67), 422–436.
5. Vroom, Victor (1964). *Work and Motivation*, New York, NY: John Wiley & Sons.
6. *Aligning A Multi-Generational Workforce With Your Business Goals* (2005). (executive brief) Milwaukee, WI: Versant Works.
7. Irvine, Derek (2010). "How to Reward a Multigenerational and Culturally Diverse Workforce," *workspan*, (53)4, April, 63–68.
8. Bristow, Denny, Douglas Amyx, Stephen B. Castleberry, and James J. Cochran (2011). "A Cross-Generational Comparison of Motivational Factors in a Sales Career Among Gen-X and Gen-Y College Students," *Journal of Personal Selling & Sales Management*, (31)1, Winter, 77–85.
9. Taylor, Paul, and Scott Keeter (eds.) (2010). *Millennials, A Portrait of Generation Next*, February. Washington, DC: Pew Research Center. Accessed April 1, 2014. *http://www.pewsocialtrends.org/files/2010/10/millennials-confident-connected-open-to-change.pdf.*
10. Gross, T. Scott (2012). "The New Millennial Values," *Forbes*, July 5. Accessed April 1, 2014. *http://www.forbes.com/sites/prospernow/2012/07/05/the-new-millennial-values.*
11. Irvine, Derek (2010), Op.cit.
12. Buckingham, Marcus (2005). "What Great Managers Do," *Harvard Business Review*, March, (83)3, 70–79.
13. "Motivation: the Not-so-Secret Ingredient of High Performance" (2006). Chapter of *Performance Management*, Boston, MA: Harvard Business School Publishing.
14. Ibid.
15. Strout, Erin (2003), "Veteran sales slackers," *Sales and Marketing Management*, (155)7, 26.
16. "What Motivates Me" (2005), *Sales & Marketing Management*, (157)5, 18.
17. Tanner, John F., Jr., and George W. Dudley (2003), "International Differences: Examining Two Assumptions About Selling," in *Advances in Marketing*, William J. Kehoe and Linda K. Whitten, eds., Society for Marketing Advances, 236–239.
18. Jensen, Doug, Tom McMullen, and Mel Stark (2007). *The Manager's Guide to Rewards*, New York, NY: American Management Association, 72.
19. Strout, Erin (2003). "Blue Skies Ahead?" *Sales & Marketing Management*, (155)3, March, 24–30.
20. Total Rewards Model (2013). WorldatWork, Accessed June 1, 2014. *http://www.worldatwork.org/waw/adimLink?id=28330.*
21. Jensen, Doug, Tom McMullen, and Mel Stark (2007), Op.cit.
22. Perman, Stacy (2013), "For Some, Paying Sales Commissions No Longer Makes Sense," *The New York Times*, November 20, 2013. Accessed April 15, 2014. *http://mobile.nytimes.com/2013/11/21/business/smallbusiness/for-some-paying-sales-commissions-no-longer-makes-sense.html?from=business.smallbusiness.*
23. Cichelli, David (2013), "Sales compensation redefined—rewarding customer outcomes," Alexander Group. Accessed April 1, 2014. *http://www.alexandergroup.com/.*
24. "Sales Compensation Programs and Practices" (2010), WorldatWork research report. Accessed April 1, 2014. *http://www.worldatwork.org/waw/adimLink?id=44112.*
25. Dill, Kathryn (2014), "The Top10 Companies for Commission-Based Jobs," *Forbes*, May 28. Accessed June 1, 2014. *http://www.forbes.com/sites/kathryndill/2014/05/28/the-top-10-companies-for-commission-based-jobs/print/.*
26. Zoltner, Andris A, Prabhakant Sinha, and Sally Lorimer (2012), "Breaking the Sales Force Incentive Addiction: A Balanced Approach to Sales Force Effectiveness," *Journal of Personal Selling & Sales Management*, (32)2, Spring, 171–186.
27. "Employer Costs for Employee Compensation" (2014), news release, Washington, DC: United States Department of Labor, Bureau of Labor Statistics, March 12. Accessed April 15, 2014. *http://www.bls.gov/news.release/ecec.nr0.htm.*
28. Ibid.
29. Ibid.
30. Ibid.
31. Kornik, Joseph (2007). "What's It All Worth? 2007 Compensation Survey," *Sales & Marketing Management*, (159)4, 27–40.
32. Ibid.
33. "Travel Leaders Corporate Reveals Average Cost of International and Domestic Business Trips," (2012), August 27. Accessed April 1, 2014. *http://www.travelleadersgroup.com/travel-leaders-corporate-reveals-average-cost-of-international-and-domestic-business-trips/.*
34. "Per Diem Rates" (2014), Washington, DC: U.S. General Services Administration. Accessed May 15, 2014. *http://www.gsa.gov/portal/category/100120.*
35. Loehr, Jim, and Tony Schwart, (2001). "The Making of a Corporate Athlete," *Harvard Business Review*, (79)1, 120–128.

Measurement, Analysis, and Knowledge Management

In previous parts of this book, you came to understand how sales managers supervise, manage, and lead individual and sales team efforts. This includes setting goals, managing performance, motivating, and rewarding sales personnel.

But now how much can we sell? We've got some customer data; we've organized it and we've thought about how to motivate salespeople, but how much can they really sell? In Chapter 13, *Turning Customer Information into Sales Knowledge*, we explore those processes that make customer data more useful. Specifically, we examine how forecasts are created and used. Further, customer data integration processes are also developed. Data regarding customers comes from a number of sources other than salespeople. Combining that data so that it can become useful knowledge is an important aspect of customer data technology.

Chapter 14, *Assessing the Performance of the Sales Force and the People Who Comprise It*, discusses the importance of assessing sales performance at both the individual and team levels. Without assessing or evaluating sales efforts, it is impossible to know what is or is not working, and—most important—why. Sales managers monitor sales revenues, costs, and profitability to ensure that sales efforts are meeting or exceeding predicted levels. When performance falls below expectations, the sales manager investigates further to determine whether expectations are unrealistic or the sales team needs managerial guidance to reach its goals. Individually, sales managers consider how hard salespersons work, how successful they are, how profitable they are, and how their personal development is progressing. It is important that sales managers evaluate both the total sales effort and individual performance from a point of neutrality, rather than falling prey to biases that exist in the workplace.

Chapter 15, *Transforming the Future: Cultural Forces*, offers an insight into the importance of culture—both internal and external—to the sales firm. When the sales organization is not properly aligned with the external marketplace, wasted effort occurs. In many sales firms with misaligned internal cultures, sales personnel spend 30-40 percent of their time working on activities that are not valued by customers. The sales manager plays a huge role in aligning the sales culture with customer expectations. Also, both the sales manager and sales team must understand the cultural values of buyers. In today's environment, sales personnel engage with buyers from different cultures, genders, religions, and orientations. To succeed, salespersons must be aware of these differences and must tailor their behavior so that the buyer is not offended. One way of decreasing the ethnocentrism—belief that our way of doing something is best—is to increase the diversity of the sales team and workers inside the sales firm.

The last part of this book offers twelve cases that allow you to apply and reinforce the concepts discussed in the first six parts of the book. Applying concepts to case studies not only reinforces what you learned, but also provides a glimpse at the complexity of most business situations.

TURNING CUSTOMER INFORMATION INTO SALES KNOWLEDGE

LEARNING OBJECTIVES

After completing this chapter, you should be able to:

■ Identify the major elements of customer data integration.

■ Explain how documented, accessible customer information benefits a firm's various functional groups.

■ Create sales forecasts using the various types of forecasting methods prominently implemented in sales settings.

Salespeople are in the unique position of conversing face to face, by phone, and by e-mail with customers over a long period of time. The quality of information they collect is very high, but often the knowledge that is created by those conversations rarely moves beyond the sales rep's head. Yet such knowledge is vital for organizations that want to provide the right services and products, develop marketing campaigns that engage clients, and grow their customers' account shares over time. In this chapter, we explore the use of technology and customer information. Specifically, we focus on the sales force's responsibility to provide high-quality information to other areas of the firm, and the benefits in doing so.

Sales Manager Profile: Tracey Brill

Forecasting is often thought of as educated guessing. As Tracey Brill has learned in her career in pharmaceuticals, sometimes your best guesses aren't always on target. But the one thing she is sure of is that doing your job well will always pay off.

TRACEY BRILL
District Sales Manager
Pharmaceutical Company

"I made many personal sacrifices while I advanced within my career. I had a specific plan in place for my career. Each step was carefully thought out and planned, which often included personal and business assumptions, in a different kind of way…a forecast, but for my career. Just like forecasts aren't always accurate, my career forecast wasn't accurate, either." But some personal sacrifices weren't worth making, so Brill made the tough choice, only to find herself back in the field a few years later. "While I thought I left field sales forever after advancing beyond that role (to a vice-president position), several years later, I found myself back in field sales in order to achieve other personal goals." While that's not the traditional career track one might forecast or hope for, conditions and situations sometimes change, and your hopes and expectations have to change with them.

After achieving the personal goals she sought, and realizing how much she missed having a broader impact on the business, she decided she could begin to take on more responsibility again at work. She accepted a district sales manager position—still levels below where she had been—but it gave her an opportunity to begin having a greater impact on the organization.

"I have always loved selling, so once I came back to selling, I thought I'd stay a salesperson until I retired." But recognition for her performance as a representative brought more opportunities; within a very short period of time, she found herself back in a management role.

"With every company I worked for, and every position I have held, I was always committed to doing the role to the best of my capabilities. For a period of time, I was working to train new salespeople three weeks a month in Philadelphia, while still maintaining a sales territory in Chicago, and in spite of being gone from Chicago three weeks out of four, I still finished the year at the top." This dedication to excellence is, Brill believes, the way you continue to find new opportunities to grow and advance.

"In our business, managed care coverage or lack of coverage impacts how physicians prescribe medications. You might forecast a certain level of sales, but if a managed care plan were to stop covering a medication, then that forecast is certain to be off." But Brill believes that, when situations or conditions change, hard work and dedication overcome those challenges. She's seen it in her personal life; she's seen it in her career.

Much of that hard work is preparation. "Before each call, we [her salespeople and Brill, together] get into specific pre-call planning, using all of the data we have to understand what is important to the doctor and what value we can bring to improve patient care and help that physician in what he or she is doing. And, after we've left that doctor's office, how do we know we've earned the right to come back?" Brill and her sales team set specific goals for each call, so that they know if they were successful or not, based on the data they had going in.

Where will the future take Tracey Brill? In some ways, that's the hardest forecast to make. One never knows what will happen in life to change one's direction. But one constant will always be there to guide Brill's way: dedication to being the best at what she's doing, so she can be prepared for whatever life has to offer. ■

The engineers for HealthLink, a Jacksonville, Florida, company that manufactures medical and surgical supplies and equipment, are considering whether to add features to the company's autoclave. An *autoclave* is a device used to sterilize medical instruments used in surgery. Sales for HealthLink's autoclave have been good, but Marc Hanna, the company's vice president of sales, believes that several opportunities exist to grow the business if certain features are added to the device. If those features are added, how many additional autoclaves will be sold, he wonders?

John Buchy, the vice president of sales for Buchy Food Service in Greensville, Ohio, is in a similar situation as Hanna. Buchy is looking at a new line of products from Pepperidge Farm. His company supplies restaurants with many products, including baked goods from several bakeries. Which restaurants will be interested in Pepperidge Farm's new line of baked goods? How much of Buchy's current product sales would be lost, or "cannibalized" by the new line, versus the sales the company would gain? More important, how can Hanna and Buchy begin to answer questions such as these?

Sales executives often find themselves in the critical position of estimating the demand for their firms' products and services. Accuracy is important. For one thing, stock markets react to company forecasts. Further, if the executives overestimate the demand, the company could end up investing in manufacturing and distribution assets that it won't need. For example, Caterpillar overestimated the demand for its construction equipment. The company bought a manufacturing facility in Texas, and filled it full of manufacturing equipment—only to let it sit dormant for two years after the firm's forecasts changed. The situation could have been much worse; Caterpillar could have hired many employees, only to lay them off when the demand for the new equipment did not materialize.

ETHICS IN SALES MANAGEMENT   Don't Blame the Messenger

Each quarter, every publicly-traded company's leaders take part in what's called an analyst call to discuss their company's performance and forecast sales for the next quarter. In this conference call, executives talk to financial analysts, who then take all the data they can find into consideration in order to estimate the company's earnings. Stock prices are a function of these estimates, as investors take these analyses and determine whether they are going to buy or sell the company's stock.

The pressure for executives to meet those forecasts can be unbearable. So many investors, banks, pension funds, and others depend on the company meeting its sales and profit numbers. But that pressure can lead otherwise ethical executives to turn a blind eye to unethical behavior—taking shortcuts used to reach the forecast.

Are the forecasts simply optimistic? Or do they get stretched in order to make the future seem rosier than it likely will be? And if the forecast for sales has been stretched, what is the impact on the sales staff? How much pressure is placed on them to meet numbers that were unrealistic to start with?

In one study, salespeople complained that top executives would cut prices on big deals right before the end of the quarter, just so the company could meet sales estimates. The salespeople lost commissions, but worse, customers figured out that they could wait until the end of a quarter was near, and prices would drop significantly. Top salespeople were frustrated with the loss of commissions, but more frustrated with the loss of authority and control in their own territories.

At least, though, these salespeople weren't pressured to engage in unethical behavior in order to meet someone else's overly-optimistic forecast.

Carreras, Alvaro, Jr., Bauhadin G. Mujtaba, and Frank J. Cavico (2011). "Don't Blame the Budget Process: An Exploration of Efficiency, Effectiveness and Ethics," *Business Management & Review* 1(3), 5–13; Pearson, Leigh Anne (2011). "Sales Strategies of Top and Average Salespeople: A Comparison," Baylor University Undergraduate Research and Scholarship presentation, Waco, TX. (April 14).

Underestimating demand can be just as devastating. When a company introduces a new product, marketing and sales campaigns are launched to create demand. If the campaigns are successful, but the firm's manufacturing unit isn't making enough of the product to meet that demand, then the door is open for competitors to launch "copycat" products and steal market share. For example, Apple's inability to meet demand for iPhones left the market open for Samsung to catch up, particularly in non-U.S. markets. Similarly, Apple struggles to meet MacBook demand, and while Apple enthusiasts may say there's no comparable product out there, people who need something quickly can't wait.

Forecasting demand, though, is only part of understanding customers. Consider Hanna's dilemma regarding which features to add to the autoclave. A stronger understanding of customers can lead to better product design, too; if Hanna understands the value that doctors will place on those additional features, he will be able to set a price that reflects that value, maximizing the return on his company's investment.

Jeffrey Bailey, sales manager for Oracle, describes his role in using forecasts. "My job is to manage resources—making sure we have the right people working on enough deals to meet our quota. Things can go badly quickly, such as when oil prices rise, or markets can get hot. When deals start dropping out, or suddenly go from $200,000 to $1 million, we need to figure out why, quickly, so we can make the right decisions." Those decisions concern when to introduce new features, how to price deals, and whether to hire new salespeople or re-deploy the ones he already has.

Knowledge Generated by the Firm's Sales Force

One important goal for organizations is to develop a **customer knowledge competence**, or the ability to gather, analyze, and utilize customer knowledge *effectively* at the organizational level. Developing such a competence first requires integrating customer data from the many locations across the firm. Exhibit 13.1 illustrates the process of **customer data integration (CDI)**—the technical process of gathering data and making it useful and available. CDI is not a software application, per se; while there are companies that provide tools (like Teradata, SAP, and others), CDI requires development of rules for how data are to be stored and made available.

EXHIBIT 13.1   The Customer Data Integration Process

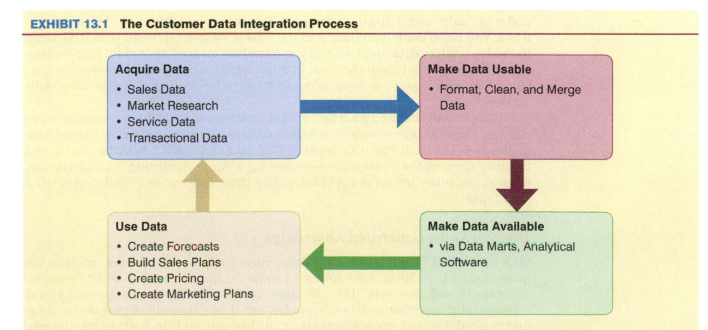

Acquire Data
- Sales Data
- Market Research
- Service Data
- Transactional Data

Make Data Usable
- Format, Clean, and Merge Data

Make Data Available
- via Data Marts, Analytical Software

Use Data
- Create Forecasts
- Build Sales Plans
- Create Pricing
- Create Marketing Plans

Information that was once stored in files and had to be manually processed are now brought into data marts from larger data warehouses—specialized databases that make access and analysis fast and easy.

The first step is to simply acquire the data. Sounds simple—but, actually, the process of gathering data can be quite difficult. Sales data may rest in a contact management or CRM software program, and may not merge well with data from the accounting or shipping systems. In addition, market research data can be overlaid to provide greater insight. For example, a company may only know how much a customer has purchased from them. The firm's marketing research department can then investigate the total purchases made in the market for that product, which can then be used to calculate the market share the company captured.

After acquiring the data, it has to be integrated and put into a usable format. For example, how does a company keep track of a client? By name? Seems simple enough, but firms sometimes go by initials, and sometimes by the entire name; the company's account records may list one customer firm's location by name and another by initials. Divisions may also be listed under their divisional names, not their corporate name. Further, the name needed to identify a location may be different than the name needed to mail an invoice. Other considerations must also be determined, including terminology. What is an account? Is an account a person who makes a decision, a location for receipt of shipments, or a company that buys? Defining terms is an important element in making data useful, but only part of the step; cleaning the data and making it accurate are also important.

The next step is to make the data available to decision makers. Sales executives trying to create sales strategy would benefit from better segmentation models, for example, but those models require additional marketing research data. If sales execs are limited to accessing only the contact management data, then they cannot take advantage of those segmentation models. One approach is to take data from various sources and compile it into a **data mart**, which is a specialized subset of data held in a database that was designed for a specific purpose. In this instance, the purpose is to support decision making by sales executives, so the data mart would include the most-needed data.

The final step is to use the data to develop a strategy. Uses could include sales forecasting, determining pricing strategies, looking for new product opportunities, and other sales and marketing strategies. To achieve customer knowledge competence, you need more than data: you must have people on board who have been trained to analyze data properly, and you must have processes in place that encourage employees to act upon the data. In other words, a competence cannot be purchased in the way you purchase software; it has to be developed, just as sales skills are developed.

Salespeople generate a great deal of data. From the name of the receptionist to the strategic plans of key customers, salespeople become privy to customer knowledge of all types. The challenge is to organize that data and make it available and useful to other parts of the organization—including a firm's marketing, manufacturing, finance, and other functions. Let's explore how those other areas use sales-generated knowledge.

Users of Sales-Generated Knowledge

MANUFACTURING Manufacturing departments rely heavily on the information generated by their firms' sales forces. In some businesses, such as retail furniture, salespeople sell products that are then accumulated into group orders and subsequently manufactured. In other industries, a firm's manufacturing department makes products and stockpiles them until they are sold. In both cases, though, salespeople's forecasts are important inputs into how much the firm's should make.

PRODUCT DEVELOPMENT Who knows more about what consumers want than salespeople? Based upon what their customers are requesting, salespeople provide the product developers in their firms with recommendations about new products, different feature combinations, and even stripped-down versions of existing products. A firm's salespeople are often the first in the company to run across competitors' new products and convey that information to product developers, too.

Marvin Wagner, a global engineer for the equipment manufacturer Deere & Company, spends a great deal of time in the field with farmers testing the products he and his team design. But Wagner's team also spends time with the salespeople who sell Deere's equipment to farmers to get a feel for what their priorities really are: Farmers might say they "want" every feature they can get, but the salespeople at the dealerships can provide insight about the features farmers will actually pay for.

FINANCE AND ACCOUNTING A company's credit policies affect its salespeople. Loose credit policies mean more sales and more bad debts; tight credit policies mean fewer sales, but fewer bad debts. Salespeople can provide information to finance and accounting, so that the company's credit policies are competitive. In many business-to-business markets, determining competitors' true prices can't be done by surveying the shelves of retail stores. In those situations, salespeople are the best source of this information. In addition, salespeople can report on market conditions that cause customers to buy, instead of lease, products, or vice versa. Reports like these can be useful in terms of the firm's pricing or capital needs—for example, whether it needs to finance new facilities, if people are spending freely, or cut back on its expansion plans, if people are limiting their spending.

MARKETING The marketing department creates sales and marketing campaigns that should boost the firm's sales. Any increase in sales due to a campaign is called **lift**. Salespeople contribute important information, both before and after the campaign. Beforehand, the information they provide can help design a good campaign. Marketing manager Andrea Wharton, at Alcatel, a French telecommunications company, talks to Alcatel's salespeople to hear the "language" they use to sell products. She then incorporates that language into the design of her trade show campaigns.

During a campaign, salespeople provide marketing with information about how well the campaign is working. That's what sales manager Tricia Jennings does, along with her salespeople at Merck pharmaceuticals. During a campaign, the reports from Jennings' salespeople (and the rest of Merck's sales representatives) are compiled to assess how the campaign's going. Keep in mind that Merck's salespeople do not actually close sales on the spot; they have to wait for doctors to prescribe Merck drugs to patients before they know if they were truly successful. For that reason, tracking actual sales to a specific campaign can be very difficult. That's why Merck's sales and marketing planners rely heavily on the company's salespeople to tell them what doctors are saying about the drugs being promoted—even before they are prescribed.

SALES MANAGEMENT Of course, sales management also uses information from salespeople. Information—such as how hard or easy it is to sell a product—can lead to decisions about what product-related training is needed, which products should be emphasized, whether sales managers should push for a price cut or product enhancement, how many salespeople to hire, and a host of other decisions. This type of information should reside in the customer records that salespeople keep and the reports they make to their managers. Sales managers are important users of this information, yet they must also help other users sift through it and use it, as well.

Photo Credit: IAEE

Salespeople provide the language that marketing uses at trade shows so that conversations with customers are more effective.

For example, when salespeople complain that the firm's prices are too high, sales managers can help employees in the firm's finance department understand if the complaints are prevalent and legitimate—or not.

HUMAN RESOURCES A firm's human resources department is directly affected by the information that sales reps impart to the firm. For example, if they report that sales are grim, this will have implications for the firm's hiring plans. Perhaps more salespeople will have to be hired to improve the level of sales, or perhaps the firm's workforce will have to be downsized. For example, Mark Prude is a human resources director for Granite Construction. As Granite Construction grows, Prude pays close attention to the firm's sales forecasts, so that he has enough new employees coming on board at the right time, with enough of the right training, so they can be productive quickly.

In the next section, we examine sales forecasts—how they are created and how they are used. Forecasts are just one specialized use of customer knowledge, albeit an important use, as you should have already concluded.

Sales Forecasting

Forecasting how much a company will sell can be a daunting task. As you can see in Exhibit 13.2, the process can seem complex. A forecast is not only an estimate of what consumers' demand will be for certain products, but how much of them the firm can produce and sell at certain prices, and how its competitors and customers will respond to those prices. Thus, a sales forecast is actually a function of several estimates.

One of the first estimates that companies try to make is that of **market potential**, or the total, industry-wide sales expected for a product category during a period of time. Market potential is often estimated by research companies, which then sell their data to the various companies in the market. For example, if you want to know the market potential for CRM software, the Gartner Group (*www.gartner.com*) is one company that can provide estimates for you.

Note that market potential is what can reasonably be sold by all companies in a market, not how many companies or individuals comprise your target market. In the first half of the 1900s, Carl Crowe was the leading Western expert on China. During the Great Depression, Crowe argued that America could pull itself out of the Depression by simply selling one product to each person in China. Of course, a lot of assumptions had to hold true for his plan to work—one of which was that each person in China wanted something the U.S. had to offer, and could pay for it. This fallacy, to which many executives fall prey, is known as "Chinese Marketing." In other words, how much a firm can sell in a market is not solely a function of the number of customers in a market. Nor is a firm's penetration of a market guaranteed. Thus, the executive has to know more than the market potential in order to make a reasonably good forecast. Among other things, she has to understand the firm's sales potential. **Sales potential** is the maximum market share the company can reasonably expect to achieve, and is typically represented as a percentage of a market's total sales.

From this estimate, an executive can then create a **sales forecast** of either the revenue or units his or her firm expects to sell, and then allocate the revenue or units to individual salespeople in the form of sales quotas. Exhibit 13.2 illustrates the relationship between market potential, sales potential, and quota.

Note that sales for the company in the exhibit grew at relatively the same rate as the market in which it competed. In other words, the company's share of the market was stable. The one year in which the company increased its market share was 2016. Perhaps the company engaged in some very unique and successful marketing and sales activities that year. Or perhaps it introduced a new product, or one of its competitors went out of business.

EXHIBIT 13.2   An Example of a Firm's Market Potential, Sales Potential, Sales Forecast, and Sample Sales Quota

The lines represent actual sales for the years 2015 through 2018. The top line is the total market sales, the middle is the company's sales, and the bottom is the New York City office's sales. Note that the company increased market share in 2016, while the New York City office grew at a slightly faster rate than either the market or the company for 2018.

Note, too, that except for the year 2018, the firm's New York sales office grew at the same rate as the company did. In that year, the office experienced higher sales—perhaps as a result of having a really good sales manager or any of a number of other reasons. Because it did so well, the New York sales office was given a quota for 2019 that rose at the same rate as the company's forecast and the market forecast. The company could have just as likely given the New York office a higher growth rate for its sales quota, for many reasons—for example, if the firm's customer base in New York area was growing at a faster rate than the rest of the country. Now let's go back and look at how managers estimate the size of each of the pieces in the sales forecast puzzle. We will begin first with market potential.

Estimating Market Potential

Factors external to a firm can influence the demand for products. Factors—such as the crises involving Russia and the Ukraine, or civil unrest in the Middle East—can lower oil supply and boost oil prices. The increased manufacturing occurring in China in recent years has also created additional demand for oil, as have the increasing numbers of people in China driving automobiles.

Other forces, such as technology, can affect the market potential for products, too—especially, if technology increases the availability of substitute products. For example, the improved process of fracturing has made it easier and cheaper to extract natural gas and oil from rock. Demand also skyrocketed for petroleum products in countries that were growing rapidly, such as China and India.

The boom for petroleum products also led to increased drilling in Texas, which, in turn, resulted in a shortage of natural-gas drilling rigs. If your company manufactured oil well equipment like pumpjacks (the part of an oil well you see above ground after the well has been drilled), during the boom, for example, the demand for your product shot up very quickly. This example illustrates the nature of **derived demand**, which means that the demand for pumpjacks was actually created by (or derived from) the demand for a product further down the supply chain. In other words, when people wanted more gasoline, demand was created for drilling rigs, which increased the demand for pumpjacks. Derived demand can cause wide swings in the demand for a company's product.

When demand for petroleum products went up in China and other countries, more wells needed to be drilled—creating demand for well equipment like this pumpjack. Pumpjack demand is derived from the demand for finished petroleum products like gasoline.

Suppose you work for Advanced Micro Devices, an Austin, Texas-based company that makes computer-chip manufacturing machines. The demand for your machines is a function of the demand for chips, which is a function of the demand for computers—including those in your car, refrigerator, television, and so forth. Suppose your only account is Texas Instruments (TI), which owns 50 computer-chip manufacturing machines. Each year, TI routinely replaces 20 percent of those machines with your machines. Now suppose TI's 20 percent annual demand for machines increases by five percent in a particular year (to 25 percent total). If this is the case, the company will need 53 machines. But the machines you must supply to TI will go from 10 (the normal replacement rate when TI's demand is steady) to 13 (the number of machines TI normally needs to replace, plus the number it needs to meet the additional demand). The increase isn't five percent for you, but 30 percent! (See Exhibit 13.3 for the math.)

How will you meet this greater demand? This is an example of the volatility caused by derived demand, a factor that must be considered when forecasting market potential.

EXHIBIT 13.3   Volatility of Derived Demand

Year	Demand for Chips	Machines Needed to Handle Demand	Worn-out Machines	Machines Available	New Purchases
1	100%	50			
2	95%	47	10	40	7
3	105%	53	7	40	12
4	100%	50	13	40	10

At the beginning of the first year, 50 machines are required, based on forecast of sales. At the end of that year, 10 are worn out, but seven are purchased, because only 47 are needed. Over the second year, seven machines wear out, but 52 are needed, so 10 are purchased.

Demand is also influenced by **elasticity**, or the degree to which a product's price affects its sales. **Inelastic demand** occurs when there are few or no substitutes for the product and people have to have it at any price. In other words, the demand for it does not change, even if its price changes. Few products are truly inelastic. Even when gasoline prices rise, for example, most of us find ways to reduce our driving or get better gas mileage. If, however, there are many substitutes for a product, such as reliable public transportation, then consumers can simply shift their preferences when prices change. Other factors affect a market's potential, as well, including the following:

- **Laws and Regulations:** Laws and regulations can affect the demand for products by increasing the costs associated with them and by imposing tariffs and trade restrictions on them. For example, in 2014, the Affordable Care Act became law. That law significantly changed the healthcare insurance market, increasing demand for some types of products, and eliminating demand for others.

- **Social Factors:** Social factors are those fashions and trends within society at large. For example, consumers may choose to avoid products from a country that has a reputation for failing to monitor quality. For another, even shifting preferences for fashionable colors influences corporate laptop purchases.

- **Demographic Trends**: Demographic trends can have a major impact on a product's market potential. The fact that people in developing countries are having fewer children has affected the market potential for baby-related products such as diapers, for example. In the United States, generational differences between Millennials (those born after 1980) and Baby Boomers and Generation Xers (just about all other working adults) can make selling by Millennials to Boomers and Xers difficult. Millennials, for example, may find communication via technology easier, while Boomers or Xers may prefer telephone or personal visits.

Exhibit 13.4 provides a list of various factors external to the firm, and shows how they can affect a market's potential. Clearly, a firm's ability to forecast market demand is a function of its ability to identify and estimate the influence of these market factors.

EXHIBIT 13.4 Factors That Affect Market Potential

Factor	Influence on Potential
Economy	Economic influences can make market potential greater or smaller. For example, China's increased manufacturing base increased the demand for petroleum products, particularly as the buying power of the Chinese population increased demand for plastic products, as well as gas-powered vehicles.
Technology	New technology can create substitute products lowering demand for the original product; change price structure, making products more affordable and increasing demand; create new uses, expanding market demand; for example, new drilling technology had made drilling for natural gas affordable in certain parts of Texas.
Legal and Regulatory	Laws can make products illegal; increase the costs associated with the product (such as by increasing a firm's waste restrictions during manufacturing); and make them more or less competitive as a result of tariffs and subsidies imposed, for example.
Social Factors	Changes in trends and fashions affect demand. For example, new research on the health hazards of trans fats significantly reduced the demand for some cooking oils and products made with trans fats.
Demographic Trends	Demographic trends can shift demand. For example, retiring baby boomers increased the demand for vacation homes, which then influenced demand for lumber and other building supplies.

Sales Potential

A company's sales potential is a function of the market potential and of the company's ability to capture or protect a share of that market. External factors, though, can favor one competitor over another. The social trend toward reducing trans fats bodes well for brands that have always been made without them. Similarly, a change in trade laws can make a competitor with overseas plants more cost effective, or vice versa.

Sales executives also must consider the impact of their own actions—internal factors, that is. The introduction of new products, the ability to find new uses for old products, and the improvement of one's production processes to lower prices are among the internal activities that can influence a company's sales potential.

Forecasting Methods

As Exhibit 13.5 illustrates, forecasts, by and large, are generated using information gathered internally by the firm, or externally generated by others, such as research firms and the government. In addition, the forecasts are either qualitative (subjective) or quantitative (objective). To some extent, the forecasts are all combinations of

EXHIBIT 13.5   The Forecasting Process

Factors in the marketplace can influence market and sales potential differently. The same factor can have the opposite effect on one company's sales versus another company's, too. Quotas are influenced by other objectives, in addition to sales forecasts.

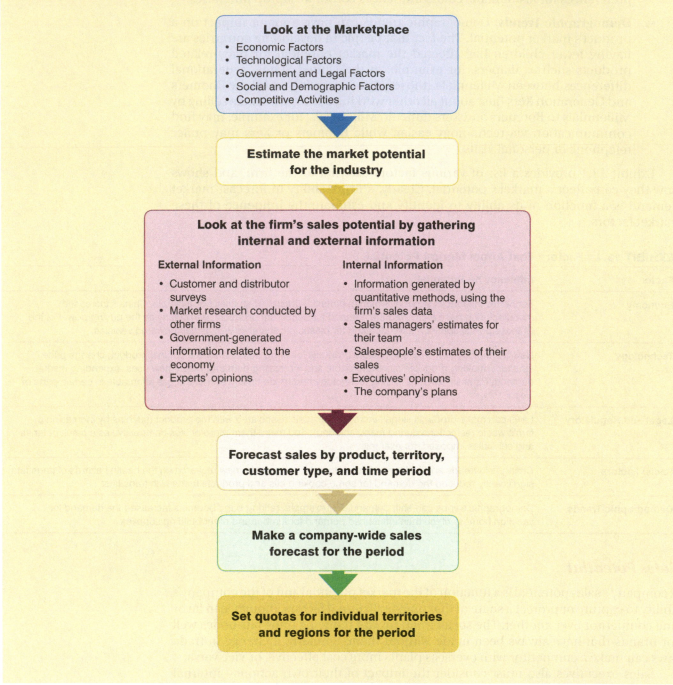

people's best guesses as to what will happen in the future. Note that some of these methods can be used to forecast both market potential and sales potential, while some are specific for one or the other. We'll point out which is which as we describe each one.

TIME SERIES TECHNIQUES Time series techniques are within a group of statistical methods used to examine sales patterns over time.[1] One simple method is a **trend analysis**, which involves determining the rate at which a company's sales have grown in the past, and then using that rate to estimate future sales, and is also called a **naïve**

forecast. For example, look back at Exhibit 13.2. You can see how the sales for this particular firm have trended upward; if you simply extended the line into 2020, you'd have a forecast based on the historical data. Trend analysis is just one of several time series techniques for using historical data to estimate sales. Trend analysis, though, can also be used for determining market potential.

Trend analysis can be useful when changes in a market are few and not very dramatic. But when the market does change frequently, you might overestimate sales after a period of rapid growth, or underestimate sales following a brief downturn using trend analysis. For example, as the trend away from trans fats began to take hold, some products became very popular, and the sales of them increased quite rapidly. Snackwell's cookies are a good example. For a time, the product experienced sharply rising demand. Eventually, however, a high rate of increase could not be sustained, and the sales growth of the product eventually flattened back out (although sales were still much higher than before the anti-trans-fat trend).

Trend analysis can still be useful in cases such as this, if you make some adjustments to them. One adjustment is to use a **moving average**, whereby the rate of change for the past few periods is averaged. **Exponential smoothing** is a type of moving average that puts more emphasis on the most recent period.[2] Exhibit 13.6 provides an example.

Determining how much weight to place on the most recent period is a decision the executive has to make, based upon such factors as changes in the market that might make more recent data more useful.

Correlational analysis is a form of trend analysis, but instead of using past sales (or past sales only), sales are forecast based on the trends of other variables. Preferably, the sales executive wants to find a variable that leads, or happens before, the sales of the company's product, called a **leading indicator**. The Conference Board, for example, publishes an Index of Leading Indicators, representing a composite of commonly-used leading indicators.

EXHIBIT 13.6   Examples of Trend Forecasts

Simple trend analysis might look like the solid line, resulting in a forecast at the same rate of change observed for the previous five years, but no growth for the next year. By contrast, an exponential smoothing analysis could weight the last two years more heavily, as illustrated by the dashed line. This would result in a sales forecast for 2020 that grows at a rate nearly double that of the simple trend. A moving average (assuming that the company was in business for many years before 2015) would result in a forecast in between the two. In times of rapid change, the different types of trend forecasts can yield very different results.

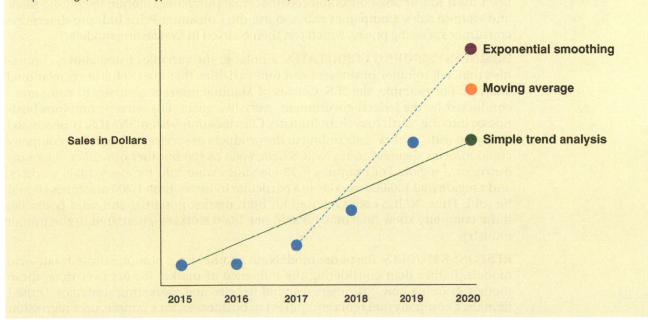

There are many possible leading indicators.[3] One frequently-used indicator is housing starts (the number of houses that are beginning to be built); for example, it is a leading indicator of home appliance sales. When new homes are built, they are filled with appliances so housing starts precede the purchase of appliances. Whirlpool uses housing starts to predict market potential. The company further considers housing starts by the size of house to break the market down into segments such as luxury homes, mid-level homes, and starter and vacation homes (for which consumers typically buy low-end appliances. In fact, so many businesses depend on housing starts that the variable is an important predicting variable for the entire economy.

Most organizations do not depend on a single variable, such as housing starts, for forecasting; rather, they build more sophisticated statistical models, incorporating the trends for many variables. For example, a regression analysis allows the sales executive to include a number of variables. The influence of each variable is estimated and weighted to determine its impact, and the effects are summed to provide a single estimate of sales. Cessna Aircraft Company, for example, builds complex statistical models to estimate the sales for the small planes it makes. The models include variables, such as the number of miles flown in a market, interest rates, fuel prices, corporate profit indicators, and other variables that influence airplane sales. These types of variables can be useful in predicting market potential, from which Cessna can then derive sales potential based on its own availability of new aircraft, market penetration, marketing plans, and other variables.

CONSUMER SPENDING CORRELATES Other variables used for correlational forecasts are variables that predict how much consumers will spend overall. The Consumer Confidence Index, a measure of how confident consumers are that the economy is favorable, has been shown to lead consumer spending, and is widely used to estimate market potential.[4] The more confident consumers are in the economy, the more money they will spend driving the rest of the economy forward. Conversely, when they turn pessimistic and pull back on their spending, the economy suffers. Similarly, the Conference Board Index of Leading Indicators, mentioned earlier, is another.

Nielsen, a marketing research company that is known for tracking advertising, also publishes a consumer buying power model that companies can use to determine how much consumers can buy in a particular market. Sales executives can then use this as a powerful correlate to purchases for their own product. For example, the model has been used to forecast household repair service purchases, mobile telephone sales, and vitamin sales. Companies can also use the Consumer Price Index to determine consumer spending power, which can then be used in forecasting models.

BUSINESS SPENDING CORRELATES Similar to the variables listed above, companies that sell to other businesses can find variables that are useful in correlational analysis. For example, the U.S. Census of Manufacturers is a survey of companies conducted by the federal government every five years. The survey combines businesses into the North American Industry Classification System (**NAICS**, pronounced to rhyme with "snakes"), according to the products or services offered. The company could forecast demand using NAICS data, such as the number of workers in an industry or a region. For example, if 12 machines were sold for every 1,000 workers, and a region had 100,000 workers in a particular industry, then 1,200 machines should be sold. Thus, NAICS could be used for both market potential and sales potential, if the company knew how many it sold per 1,000 workers, compared to the overall industry.

RESPONSE MODELS Response models are another form of sophisticated statistical models. Rather than considering the influence of market factors over time, these models examine how customers respond to sales and marketing strategies. United Rentals, a company that rents equipment to businesses, for example, uses regression analysis and other statistical models to predict the demand for its products, based on variables such as the firm's pricing promotions and advertising budgets. Through CDI, response models can be built using data that United Rentals maintains on customers—including what they bought, at what price, in what month, and so forth. The models helps United Rentals leadership see how many customers are price-sensitive, for example, and only rent when products are on sale, or which customers always rent at the beginning and end of a budget year; primarily, this method is used for sales potential. The model is very useful in terms of planning United Rental's sales and marketing actions, because it allows the company to determine the potential return it can earn by pursuing alternative plans.

Market Tests One form of creating a response model has proven to be especially useful when determining acceptance of a new product, or when offering to conduct a market test. A **market test** is an experiment where the company launches the offering in a limited market, in order to gain real-world knowledge of how the market will react to the product. In this instance, the traditional response model may not be as useful, because of the lack of data on customer purchases and response to marketing variables. The market test gives some measure of sales in response to the marketing plan. Demand can then be extrapolated to the full market. However, market tests also signal competitors of the new offering, and they can undertake actions, such as drastic price cuts, to skew your results.

Acxiom, a company that makes software to aid in CDI and marketing, lists the following cities at *www.acxiom.com* as the best for test markets: Birmingham, Alabama; Greensboro-Winston-Salem, North Carolina; Newburgh, New York; Savannah, Georgia; and Memphis, Tennessee. These cities were chosen as the best for test markets because their populations are very similar to that of the entire United States. Companies could launch products in these cities and get a good idea of whether a marketing plan will work nationwide.

JUDGMENT TECHNIQUES While all forecasts rely on someone's judgment, some techniques are estimates by someone of the actual forecast; these are considered **judgment techniques**. They include executive or expert opinions, surveys of customers' (or channel members') intentions or estimates, and estimates by salespeople.

Executive Opinion Executive opinion is exactly what the name implies. It is simply the best-guess estimates of a company's executives. Each executive submits an estimate of the market potential and the company's sales potential, which are then averaged to form the overall sales forecast. This method of estimating sales is easy to implement and costs little; in addition, there is something of a psychic commitment to achieving the forecast because no one wants their predictions to be proven wrong. The disadvantages of the method include the possibility that the opinions are biased because executives frequently aren't out selling in the field. In other words, the more an executive is removed from the market, the less accurate his estimate is likely to be. Factors within the organization can also lead to judgmental bias. For example, if executives know their quotas will be set based on their forecasts, they will attempt to lower them to make their quotas more achievable. Or, for example, an executive might overestimate the sales of a certain product because higher-level executives have pinned their hopes on it, and she doesn't want to upset them.

Expert Opinion Expert opinion is similar to executive opinion, except that the expert is usually someone outside of the company. Carl Crowe, whom we mentioned earlier in the chapter, is one example. As far back as the early twentieth century, he was asked to estimate sales in China. Today, Paul Greenberg, Jill Dyché, and Bruce Culbert are experts in the CRM software market. Often, they are asked to estimate the sales for the software of different companies.

In many instances, opinions such as these, along with those of executives, are used in conjunction with more quantitative methods. For example, once a company

Surveys about purchase plans from channel members, like wholesalers, can be fairly accurate forecasts.

has conducted a trend analysis, an expert might be consulted. The expert might suggest that some methods for estimating are better than others under certain circumstances, or that certain market factors be given more or less weight. As a sole method of forecasting, however, expert opinions are often not very useful. Just consider, for example, how difficult it is for so-called sports experts to predict the team that will become the national champion.

Customer and Channel Surveys In some markets, including the CRM software market, research companies ask customers how much they plan to spend in the coming year on certain products. Similarly, surveys are conducted for products sold through distributors who are asked how much they think they will sell. The annual Lodging Executive Sentiment Index measures how much those in the hotel industry think they will sell in the coming period; this survey has actually been shown to be a leading indicator for many other industries.[5] Companies then buy the surveys from the research companies, to use as a starting point for their forecasting. Surveys are better at estimating market potential rather than sales potential, however. Plus, they can be costly.

Many companies do their own surveys of their customers. American Airlines regularly surveys passengers about their plans to fly, to estimate its future sales. It also routinely surveys corporate travel departments about their travel budgets. Similarly, Microsoft conducts annual surveys to gauge future business-software spending. The company also conducts focus groups, which involve bringing groups of customers together to discuss their business trends, as well as what they do—and do not—like about particular products.

Channel surveys are similar in that manufacturers ask their distributors or retailers how much they expect to sell. Surveys such as this can account for varying local market conditions, as well as changes in the competitive environment. Delta Faucet is one company that surveys its distributors in order to estimate its sales. The company combines this estimate with an estimate from plumbers (end-users) to increase the accuracy of its forecasts.

Sales Force Composite A similar method involves asking the members of your sales force what they think they can sell. Salespeople, though, are often not aware of the company's plans to introduce new products, new promotions, or new pricing strategies. Thus, they cannot account for these plans in their estimates. They also tend to be optimistic about what they think they can sell—unless they realize that their estimates are being used to set their sales quotas. If this is the case, they will likely lower their estimates.

A more common approach is to use sales force composites for shorter-range forecasts. Every week, for example, Haley Earley, sales manager for Konica-Minolta Business Systems in Shreveport, Louisiana, asks her salespeople how many systems they expect to sell in the coming week and month. She then uses this information to plan inventory. The company, though, uses other methods to forecast sales for the next quarter or the next year.

OPPORTUNITY MANAGEMENT Another salesperson-based source for forecasting is the CRM system and the opportunity management component. **Opportunity management**, also called funnel or pipeline management, is the identification of sales opportunities by stage in the sales cycle. Illustrated in Exhibit 13.7, each account is determined to be in one of several stages (the number of stages depends on how the customer buys for a particular product in a specific industry). Using **conversion**

ratios, or the rate at which accounts move from one stage to the next, established from past data as indicators of probability of buying, a forecast can be generated. For example, using a simple three-step process, we can estimate one salesperson's sales this way:

- The salesperson has 50 suspects, 15 of which will become prospects.

- The salesperson currently has five prospects in addition to the 15 suspects (noted above) that will likely become prospects.

- We can, then, expect 10 out of the 20 prospects to close.

EXHIBIT 13.7   Opportunity Management

Opportunity management involves assigning accounts to the right stage in the sales process, based on where the account is in the buying process, so that the salesperson knows what to do next, and sales management can monitor performance and forecast sales.

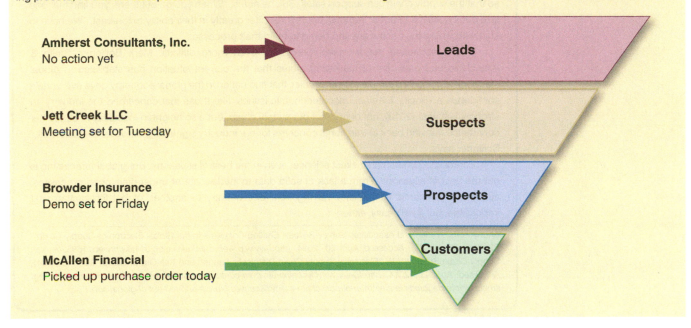

While this example is very simple, a CRM system can manage the forecast using many products across a range of industries. The shorter the sales cycle, both in number of steps and over time, the more accurate this forecast can be (just like forecasting the weather is easier for the next five minutes than the next five days!), making this method very limited for intermediate or long-range forecasts.

The Limitations of Forecasting

Forecasting is an attempt to predict the future. So, no matter how much time and effort a company puts into forecasting, the forecast is likely to be wrong. The question is: how wrong? And how will that affect the actions the company takes, and its competitive position? Although the company might not get its forecast exactly right, the firm wants to get it close enough so that company goals can be achieved. Some factors, though, can greatly influence forecasting accuracy. For example, companies operating in markets all across the globe deal with many of those factors, as discussed in the "Global Sales Management" box.

GLOBAL SALES MANAGEMENT   One Forecast—One World?

Want to know how many washing machines are going to be sold in the U.S. next year? How about computer security software sales for Europe? Or do you need to know how many dental chairs will sell in Australia and New Zealand? No problem—there are companies that do the research for you—all you have to do is buy their reports.

Want to know the same information for sales in emerging economies, such as Malawi, Bolivia, or Kazakhstan? Hmmm, not so easy.

Even demographics, the population figures that drive sales for so many products, can be difficult to forecast in some countries. And getting reliable data on other leading indicators—data you can trust to correlate with sales—can be even more difficult.

Ulf Harring, global supply manager for the global vacuum cleaner manufacturer Electrolux, says it's really important to forecast collaboratively, getting forecasts from all of the company's countries. He says it is important to have just one set of numbers across all countries and all sectors, so that the supply chain can support sales. But, he notes, "When you go out there, you find that one size does not fit all." Further, regional operations differ greatly in their ability to forecast. "We have to start with where the people are and begin to build their processes."

Global economic trends make forecasting even more difficult. Mark Bollinger, Smith & Associates vice-president of marketing, notes that the current situation has stabilized in global electronics. But only a couple of years earlier, that fluctuation in the global economy gave everyone's confidence a shock. "External, macroeconomic issues, like those that concerned the industry so strongly last year (2013), not only affect our supply chain, but also heighten instability in consumer confidence. Moving back to traditional concerns for our industry signals a positive large-scale shift," Bollinger says.

Forecasting is such an inexact science, even in the best of situations. But global forecasting is not the best of situations. From a lack of solid data to inadequate or under-developed processes, along with economic fluctuations varying from one country to another, global forecasting isn't impossible, but it isn't easy, either!

Anonymous, "Smith and Associates Survey Reveals Shifting Concerns in the Global Electronics Supply Chain," PR Web (March 19). Accessed April 20, 2014. *http://www.prweb.com/releases/2014/03/prweb11685204.htm*. Supply Chain Brain (2013), "Electrolux Supply Chain Discusses Launch and Roll-Out of Global SOP," (July 31). Accessed April 20, 2014. *http://www.supplychainbrain.com/content/industry-verticals/industrial-manufacturing/single-article-page/article/electrolux-supply-chain-exec-discusses-launch-and-roll-out-of-global-sop/*.

DATA QUALITY One major factor affecting forecasting accuracy is the quality of data used to forecast. For example, suppose a company asked its distributors, "How many decorator faucets do you hope to sell in the next quarter?" An optimistic answer would be given. But if asked, "How many decorator faucets will you sell next quarter?" a distributor might respond less optimistically. The difference might be slight—until added up over a thousand distributors.

Similarly, recall our discussion about CDI earlier, and the need to define and cleanse data. If the customer dataset does not combine all locations of customers together well, then estimates for segments based on company size could be way off. CDI is important for data quality, which—in turn—affects forecasting.

RAPID CHANGE The best forecasts are usually those that include as much information as possible. That means using as many methods as possible, and creating multiple forecasts for multiple conditions. When an executive places too much emphasis on one forecast or one method, then the likelihood of an accurate forecast is diminished, particularly if conditions are changing rapidly.

LENGTH OF THE HORIZON In the last 20 years, weather predictors have gotten pretty good at forecasting the weather for the next day or two, and they are getting better. However, it's much harder for them to predict what the weather will do for the next 90 days, or the next year. For the same reason, experts can't seem to agree whether or not global warming is occurring. The longer the forecasting horizon is, the less accurate the forecast is likely to be. The same is true for sales executives—accurately estimating next week's sales might be relatively easy; accurately estimating sales five years from now will likely be much more difficult.

TIME AND COST Forecasting takes time. The longer it takes to get a forecast, the less time you have to act on that information before the forecasting period has passed and conditions change again. Forecasting also costs money. So, for example, if a window of opportunity is open for just a short period of time, doing a costly, time-consuming market survey might not be money well spent. Rather, it might make more sense to do a rough forecast and call a few customers and salespeople, to quickly get their opinions about the forecast. Then, after the company has taken action, the firm's managers will have more information that they can use to adjust the rough forecast.

Guidelines for Forecasting

As we've discussed, forecasting is not an exact science. There are, however, guidelines that can improve the quality of forecasts. The first is to commit to accuracy. Some firms even reward managers for being accurate.

Making a commitment to accurate forecasting requires using the forecast properly. In fact, many sales executives believe that there is no direct connection between a sales forecast and its associated quota. Paul Nelson of IBM, for example, says, "My quota is a function of what my company *needs* me to sell, which can be independent of sales forecasts." What Nelson is saying is that, even if IBM were to predict low sales, it might need to assign higher quotas to its sales force for certain reasons—say, to meet the revenue targets being demanded by IBM's shareholders, based on what the firm's competition is earning. Or maybe IBM simply wants to motivate its sales force to outdo itself. Nelson recognizes that it's his job to find a way to achieve his quota, regardless of what the firm thinks it can sell. So he accepts this disconnect. As he says, "Achieving goals, setting sales records, capturing market share—those are things I want to accomplish, and I would not want to work somewhere where they didn't want to grow." Yet others argue that this practice is a misuse of forecasts. If a sales manager creates a forecast and then finds that upper management increased that forecast for the purpose of setting a quota, the next forecast will be neither as optimistic nor as accurate. Why? Because the sales manager is likely to **sandbag**, or to fail to forecast sales as high as they should be, for fear the forecast will be used against him. One manager, who asked to remain anonymous, said he provides an estimate to upper management every quarter. The company then adds 10 to 15 percent to his estimate and makes that his quota. This gives him an incentive to forecast lower sales levels. Is it any wonder that his forecast is always 15 percent low?

USE MULTIPLE METHODS As you might guess from reading about the limitations of forecasting, one way to achieve more accurate forecasts is to use multiple methods—that is, to create forecasts from surveys and trends, and then utilize experts' opinions, to estimate a range of sales.[6] Another is to simply keep at it. The first time a manager creates a forecast, it is likely to be wrong; in fact, forecasts are usually inaccurate to some degree. That said, the second time you do anything, you usually do it better than the first time. Forecasting is no different. After a certain amount of experience, they will be better able to fine-tune a forecast and minimize its inaccuracy.

PICK THE RIGHT METHOD(S) FOR YOUR BUSINESS While it may seem obvious, picking the right method for the business is important. A business with a long sales cycle and derived demand, for example, may find naïve forecasts less useful, because volatility in demand could swing the trend in either direction. A firm that sells consumer packaged goods (like Campbell's Soup or Suave shampoo) might find trend analysis very useful for short-term forecasts, but might need to use other methods for longer-term forecasts.

USE AS MUCH INFORMATION AS YOU CAN Use as much information as possible to generate forecasts. For example, by forecasting the sales for the company's different regions and managers separately, managers can sometimes account for local conditions that can change the firm's overall national forecast. When American Airlines conducts a customer survey, it forecasts each segment independently by the participant's frequent-flier status. Thus, the Platinum Executive (American's most frequent flier) is forecast separately from the Gold Advantage member (American's lowest level of frequent flier). In addition, the company also conducts trend analyses for each segment separately; note how CDI is involved, because frequent-flier status has to be integrated with the forecasting model. All individual forecasts are blended together, just as HP blends together the forecasts for its individual products. HP has many product lines, such as computers, printers, and servers. By forecasting each separately, as well as overall sales, more information is used, and this should result in a more accurate final forecast.

PLAN FOR MULTIPLE SCENARIOS What happens if the environmental factors the firm faces vary greatly? Does the company's sales forecast also change greatly? For example, if you are working at Whirlpool, perhaps you consider forecasts under multiple housing-start scenarios. If housing-start estimates increase by 15 percent more than is expected, or by 15 percent less than is expected, what happens to your company's appliance sales? This is what you want to find out. Then, as the year develops, you can adjust your sales estimates, based on what actually happens to housing starts.

TRACK YOUR PROGRESS AND ADJUST THE FORECAST As time goes on, forecasts should be adjusted to reflect reality. For example, DeeAnn Bartlett, sales manager for HP, had a forecast of about 10 percent growth for the year. After the first quarter, though, it was clear that her team would do much better, because market acceptance of a new pricing strategy was greater than expected. The forecast was then adjusted to reflect the new reality. In addition, she and her sales team record win/loss data in their CRM system. When a big sale is won, the salesperson records why; conversely, when a sale is lost, the reason is also recorded. With this information, she and her sales executives can adjust strategies in order to adapt to changing market and environmental conditions. Those changes in strategies influence forecasts.

Managing Your Career

Like Tracey Brill, your career choices are often shaped by your forecasts. Consider forecasts for the industries in which you would like to work, and forecasts for the specific companies you want to consider. What is the potential for sales growth? Sales growth will influence career growth opportunities. Using the methods in this chapter, you can make a more educated guess as to the potential for your future in any particular industry and company.

Summary

Understanding what to offer to which market requires understanding customers, but making that understanding actionable requires more. Creating a customer knowledge competence—the ability to gather, analyze, and utilize customer knowledge effectively at the organizational level—is an important goal to which salespeople can contribute. A first step in developing that competence is customer data integration, or CDI.

Many areas of the firm rely on customer data gathered by salespeople and through other means. Manufacturing, product development, marketing, sales management, human resources, and others rely on such data in order to create forecasts for their area of operations. Sales forecasting, then, is an important role for the sales force.

One of the first estimates a company tries to make is an estimate of market potential, or overall demand. Overall demand is influenced by a number of factors, such as elasticity, but also by the economy, laws and regulations, social factors, demographic factors, and others. Sales potential, or what the company could sell if all went well, is another estimate. In addition, executives also forecast what is likely to be sold.

The methods used to generate these estimates are time series techniques, including trend analysis, moving averages, and the use of exponential smoothing. Correlational analysis is a form of trend analysis; instead of basing the trend on past sales, the trends of other variables are correlated. Variables that trend ahead of sales are called leading indicators. Some of the correlates are variables, such as the Consumer Confidence Index.

Response modeling is a growing area of forecasting. These are statistical models that consider the influence of marketing factors, such as how much the company is planning to spend on advertising and sales efforts. A specific form of response modeling is to conduct a market test, or a trial of all of the marketing factors, and see how customers respond.

Judgment techniques are also used, including expert or executive opinions, and surveys of customers or channel members. Even sales force composites are considered judgments of the sales team.

Forecasts are limited by the quality of data used to create the forecasts, the degree to which things change rapidly, length of the planning horizon, and how much the company wants to spend on creating a forecast. No matter how much money and time is made available, forecasting is not an exact science. To improve forecast accuracy, companies should make a commitment to forecasting accurately. In addition, forecasting accuracy can be improved by using multiple methods, picking the right methods for the business, using as much information as possible, planning for multiple scenarios, and adjusting the forecast as things change.

Key Terms

conversion ratio   303
correlational analysis   299
customer data integration (CDI)   291
customer knowledge competence   291
data mart   292
derived demand   295
elasticity   296
exponential smoothing   299
inelastic demand   296
judgment techniques   301
leading indicator   299
lift   293

market potential   294
market test   301
moving average   299
NAICS   300
naïve forecast   299
opportunity management   303
response model   300
sales forecast   294
sales potential   294
sandbag   305
trend analysis   298

Questions and Problems

1. Suppose your company sells plastic injection machines—machines that are used to inject plastic into molds so companies can make plastic bottles. From what

consumer products does the demand for your machines derive? How volatile would you expect your demand to be, and why? What are the best and worst methods for forecasting the sales of the following products and services? Why?

   a. A new dorm for your campus: How many rooms should it have? How big a cafeteria?
   b. Garbage trucks
   c. Computer consulting services for small businesses
   d. Equipment used to make graphics computer chips used in consumer electronics, like phones and pad computers.

2. Your boss says, "All we have to do is sell one of these new products to each of our current customers, and it will be successful!" What assumptions have to hold true for this wish to come true? Is your boss guilty of Chinese Marketing? What problems could arise if the company treats that statement as a forecast?

3. What is the difference between a forecast, a quota, and a sales goal? Are the differences minor or major, and is it important to recognize the differences?

4. In the chapter, we discussed DeeAnn Bartlett's experience with the effects of pricing on sales performance and sales forecasts. Should quotas have been raised as well? Further, advertising budgets are often decided, based on a percentage of sales, though the dollar amount is fixed (unchanging), once set. But advertising drives sales; if the firm increases its advertising, its sales should increase; if it decreases advertising, its sales should fall. Yet advertising budgets are often based on a percentage of sales. Similarly, the number of salespeople needed is a function of how much you expect to sell, but how much you expect to sell is also a function of how many salespeople you have. How can these circular planning problems be tackled?

5. For the following products and services, what factor(s) would you use to estimate market potential?

   a. Campbell's Soup
   b. Fossil watches
   c. Chevy sports cars
   d. Bose Wave radios
   e. Viagra
   f. Ralph Lauren men's suits

6. You just took over as the chief sales officer of Lombardi Trophy Co., your employer for almost 20 years. You know that your firm's sales forecasts are inaccurate, because the company has annually added 20 percent to the quotas assigned the firm's salespeople—which, collectively, they have always met or exceeded. But you need an accurate forecast for various purposes, including budgeting. How would you change the situation so that you get accurate forecasts? (This question is based on an actual Fortune 100 company.) Why would a company follow a practice of simply adding 20 percent to the forecast to set the quota?

7. In the chapter, we discussed market potential, sales potential, and forecasts. How would you use those concepts in forecasting for planning your career? Which of those is the most difficult to estimate for you now? Why? Which of those three is most difficult for the company to forecast and why?

Role Play

SAM

Specialty Automotive Manufacturing (SAM) makes chemical products used by car and diesel mechanics. Customers include wholesalers who sell to auto parts chains, general merchandisers (like Dollar General), and other retailers—as well as auto dealers, auto repair shops, and industrial users with vehicle fleets to maintain.

Divide into teams of three. One of you will be the wholesale director, responsible for managing all sales to wholesalers; another will play the part of the industrial user director, responsible for managing all sales to industrial users; and the third will be the new government sales director. In the past, SAM allocated 10 percent of the wholesale forecast to advertising directly to consumers and to members of the auto repair trade, and three percent of the industrial forecast for advertising to the auto repair trade (under the assumption that industrial users and retail auto shop owners read the same magazines).

Further, given that the company always determines quota by adding 10 percent to last year's performance, but quota has rarely been achieved in the past five years, determine quota and whether or not additional salespeople should be added. In the role play, make a case for what you want, based on your role, with the understanding that the CEO already told you that total advertising dollars for the entire firm can only go up five percent and headcount can only increase by five people.

Caselets

Caselet 13.1: *Specialty Automotive Manufacturing*

Specialty Automotive Manufacturing (SAM) makes chemical products used by car and diesel mechanics. Customers include wholesalers who sell to auto parts chains, general merchandisers (like Dollar General), and other retailers, as well as to auto dealers and auto repair shops, and industrial users that have vehicle fleets to maintain. The company's sales figures for the past 20 quarters are provided in the following table:

Quarter	Sales to Wholesalers (000,000)	Industrial User Sales (000,000)	Government Sales (000)
1 (5 years ago)	43.0	48.0	-0-
2	44.5	50.5	-0-
3	46.0	52.0	-0-
4	48.0	53.0	-0-
5	49.0	55.0	-0-
6	50.5	57.5	-0-
7	49.5	59.0	-0-
8	50.5	61.0	-0-
9	50.0	60.0	-0-
10	51.0	60.5	-0-
11	52.0	57.0	-0-
12	53.0	59.0	-0-
13	54.5	61.0	-0-
14	56.0	61.5	-0-
15	55.5	62.0	-0-
16	56.5	60.5	-0-
17	58.0	63.0	-0-
18	59.0	64.0	-0-
19	60.5	64.5	-0-
20 (most recent)	60.0	66.0	0.50

Late this year, the company was able to secure a General Services Administration contract to provide containers to the U.S. government. The contract enabled the company to bid on fleet maintenance supply needs for the U.S. military. Currently, the company has almost $100 million in four bids on military contracts that will be decided upon in the first quarter of next year. It expects to bid on another $300 million in additional government contracts, to be decided upon later during the year.

1. Use two different trend analysis methods and determine how much the company will sell next year. How confident are you that this is an accurate forecast?

2. What additional information or methods would you like to incorporate in your forecast? Think of at least two variables, not mentioned in the chapter, that you think might influence SAM's sales; find forecasts for those variables; and adjust your forecast with the new information. Show how you arrived at the new forecast and justify your choice.

3. Assume that the company is manufacturing at 90 percent of its capacity in order to meet its current sales levels. If it wins every U.S. government contract it sought by bidding, what impact will that have?

Caselet 13.2: *Sales Sciences*

Sales Sciences (SS) is a company that produces and sells sales training. Through independent research, the company promotes its training as the fastest to reach quota in the field. The company sells its product through independent distributors, which deliver the two-day workshop for $950 per person trained. Ancillary products sold by SS through distributors include CDs (for in-car sales training updates), online training modules, and other such products.

There are currently 22 distributors selling SS products, along with other sales management products (like testing products for potential new hires) and consulting services. The sales of SS products generated by each distributor range from $10,000 (generated by a small distributor in Arizona) to almost $100,000 (generated by a distributor in New York City). The average annual SS sales per distributor are about $22,000. Total sales for SS are about $4 million per year.

George Shannon, owner of SS, would like to grow the business by another million dollars in two years. The question is how? George has considered adapting the training so it could be used to train salespeople who sell directly to consumers (insurance, automobile, etc.). Right now, they are used only to train business-to-business salespeople. The workshops could also be translated into different languages and sold in other countries. Or perhaps George could simply look for additional distributors. He has called you and asked how he should go about determining the potential of each these markets.

1. In a perfect world, how would you answer George?

2. Assuming George had no cash to spend, how would your answer change?

References

1. Choi, Tsan-Ming, Yong Yu, and Fin-Kan Au (2011). "A Hybrid SARIMA Wavelet Transform Method for Sales Forecasting," *Decision Support Systems* 51(1), 130–140.
2. Taylor, James W. (2011). "Multi-Item Sales Forecasting with Total and Split Exponential Smoothing," *Journal of the Operational Research Society* 62(3), 555–563.
3. Osadchlyi, Nikolai, Vishal Gaur, and Sridhar Seshadri (2013), "Sales Forecasting with Financial Indicators and Experts' Input," *Production and Operations Management* 22(5), 1056–1076.
4. Cutler, Neal (2013), "How Everybody's Consumer Opinions Interact with the Gross Domestic Product: A Brief Look at the Consumer Sentiment Index," *Journal of Financial Services Professionals* 67(4), 19–24.
5. Aliouche, Hachem, Nelson Barber, and Raymond Goodman Jr. (2013), "Lodging Executives' Sentiment Index as a Leading Indicator," *Cornell Hospitality Quarterly* 54(4), 406–415.
6. Karabell, Zachary (2014), "(Mis)Leading Indicators," *Foreign Affairs* 93(2), 90–101.

ASSESSING THE PERFORMANCE OF THE SALES FORCE AND THE PEOPLE WHO COMPRISE IT

LEARNING OBJECTIVES

After completing this chapter, you should be able to:

- Explain why it is important to evaluate the overall performance of the firm's sales force.

- List the advantages and disadvantages of sales, cost, and profit analyses.

- Understand the importance of profitability and the application of ROI and ROAM.

- Explain both input and output objective sales performance measures.

- Explain the differences between performance and effectiveness.

- Compare formal and informal evaluations.

- Describe how the sales manager can implement an effective performance review.

It is important to evaluate the sales force and individual salespersons in order to understand what is working and what is not! Sales managers examine sales revenues, expenses, and profits to determine how successful the sales team is performing. Sales managers must also evaluate individual sales team members to understand how well they are performing in comparison to expectations and to determine whether they need additional training, are ready for promotion, and deserve a salary increase or bonus. The goal of the sales manager is to evaluate from a neutral position by comparing all salespersons on the same criteria for the same time period. In this way, sales managers make a conscious effort to objectively evaluate their sales force in order to improve overall performance.

Sales Manager Profile: Miles Curro

MILES CURRO
Director of
Strategic Partnership
Covidien

MILES CURRO IS DIRECTOR OF Strategic Partnership at Covidien, a global healthcare products company and manufacturer of medical devices and supplies. When asked how he would describe Covidien, he replied: "Our business segments span the healthcare continuum, providing proven solutions to clinicians that are designed to enhance clinical outcomes and patient safety." Curro graduated from the University of North Carolina at Chapel Hill, completed an executive certificate program in medical marketing at the University of California, Los Angeles, and recently earned an M.B.A. degree at Elon University, North Carolina.

Covidien is focused on creating long-term relationships with its customers. This means that salespeople are evaluated based on ability to reach sales objectives. However, Covidien sales managers also monitor and evaluate a number of core competencies: adaptability, customer focus, and drive for results. Achieving goals is important at Covidien, but equally important are the strategies the sales team members develop to help achieve those goals.

Covidien sales professionals are formally evaluated every six months, with commensurate merit increases and level promotions typically occurring during the annual review process at the end of the fiscal year. "At the end of the day," Curro noted, "sales reps are expected to deliver." Covidien sales managers work with their teams, ensuring that they are partnering with their customers and providing solutions that will help them deliver the best possible care for their patients. ■

Evaluation Helps the Sales Manager Know What is Working and Why

Sales managers are responsible for planning, implementing, and controlling a firm's sales activities. To control the sales effort so that the firm's goals are accomplished, sales managers must continually monitor and evaluate the performance levels of both the individuals who comprise the sales force and the sales force as a whole. For example, if the sales force's goal is to increase the number of a firm's new customers by six percent over the course of 12 months, sales managers must develop a specific plan for how that level of sales growth will occur. Perhaps the sales team will be instructed to call upon customers in a different market segment or new geographical location. Based upon this strategy, the sales manager might identify a need to offer training sessions to ensure that individual members of the sales force are prepared with skills and knowledge to successfully serve new customers, and/or hire additional salespeople for the expanded territory.

Without conducting evaluations, it will be nearly impossible for sales managers to know what about the new strategy is or is not working, why, and, most importantly, what should be done about it. Comprehensive evaluations also help managers determine whether the deviations uncovered are attributable to incorrectly set goals or a weak performance on the part of the firm's salespeople. Said differently, did the sales team fail to meet expectations, or did the firm's managers set inappropriate goals?[1] The firm's planning efforts, of course, set forth what the sales force should do; and evaluation efforts document what actually took place. This means that the value of planning is limited—unless sales managers perform an evaluation to document what actually worked. In turn, information derived from the evaluations will affect the firm's sales planning in future periods.

Evaluating the individual sales representatives responsible for executing the firm's strategy can be quite complex, because they call on different buyers in different territories, and often have distinct goals and different experience levels. The process requires the sales manager to select and compare, at regular intervals, both objective and subjective information about all sales personnel. To accomplish this, sales managers utilize a combination of input activities, output results, profitability measures, and qualitative assessments. Once completed, sales managers utilize the results of evaluations to manage the sales force by assigning raises, promoting salespeople to managerial positions, recommending training to remedy identified shortcomings related to a sales representative's performance, and, when necessary, replacing low-performing sales force members. In summary, conducting a comprehensive evaluation of the firm's sales team and individual salespeople allows sales managers to:

- identify deviations from the firm's goals and the goals set for individual salespeople;

- determine the causes of the deviations;

- adjust the firm's sales territories as needed;

- determine the training and development the sales force and individual representatives need;

- motivate salespeople and establish work expectations for them;

- link compensation and rewards to salespeople's actual performance;

- identify individuals for promotion, further training, or termination;

- help salespeople set, and work toward, their career goals;

- provide information for planning activities conducted by the firm's human resources group; and

- establish recruiting criteria for salespeople.

The purpose of this chapter is to explain how sales managers evaluate individual salespeople and entire sales forces. First, we discuss various evaluation techniques. Second, we explain how to evaluate the sales force's activities and outcomes, with the goal of identifying deviations from standard or expected performance. Last, we consider how to assess the performance of the firm's individual salespeople.

Evaluating the Performance of the Sales Force as a Whole

In general, sales managers evaluate the overall performance of their sales teams by comparing and analyzing different categories of information. Since firms set myriad goals, multiple measures are used to assess whether or not the company's objectives were achieved. Different evaluation criteria are necessary because there is no single measure of a sales force's effectiveness. The three most common forms of sales team analysis focus on sales, costs, and profitability. Each type of analysis is discussed next.

Evaluating the sales force allows the sales manager to know what is and what is not working.

Sales Analysis

Conducting a **sales analysis** involves gathering, sorting, assessing, and making decisions based upon a company's sales revenue. Sales revenue information can be gathered via the firm's point-of-sale records, sales reports, field reports, and customer feedback.[2] Sales information is routinely gathered for accounting purposes; however, it likely is not organized in a form that's useful for conducting a sales analysis. As Exhibit 14.1 shows, the sales manager must organize the sales data so that market and salesperson deviations are apparent.

For example, the sales manager will want to understand if the firm's revenues are increasing or decreasing, how well different products are selling in each sales territory, and how different sales regions and salespeople are performing compared to previous periods.[3]

Returning to Exhibit 14.1, it is apparent that the southwest region is significantly below quota, or its expected sales. The sales manager should investigate what caused the deviation of –5 percent ($163,150) in that region. Breaking down the analysis by the six sales representatives assigned to the region shows that George, in Oklahoma, sold only 70 percent of his quota for the period. By segmenting the next four product lines sold by George, it is clear that he fared poorly, selling three out of four product lines during the evaluation period. Thus, based upon the sales analysis, the sales manager has identified that George's substandard performance in the Oklahoma territory is the source of the significant deviation from the southwest region's expected performance. Now the sales manager must investigate further to determine

EXHIBIT 14.1   An Example of a Firm's Sales Analysis

Analysis by U.S. Region

Region	Quota	Actual	Difference	Performance
Northeast	$4,861,500	$4,948,920	$87,420	102%
Mid-Atlantic	$5,093,000	$5,209,880	$116,880	102%
Southeast	$4,167,000	$4,147,400	–$19,600	99.5%
Southwest	$3,588,250	$3,425,100	–$163,150	95%
Mid-Central	$3,472,500	$3,698,875	$226,375	107%
Western	$5,112,750	$5,120,250	$7,500	100%
Total	$26,295,000	$26,550,425	$255,425	101%

Analysis by Salesperson (Southwest Region)

Salesperson	Quota	Actual	Difference	Performance
Albert (West Texas)	$804,000	$810,000	+$6,000	101%
John (Colorado)	$868,000	$851,000	–$17,000	98%
Claudia (Arizona)	$609,000	$631,000	+$22,000	104%
George (Oklahoma)	$592,000	$416,000	–$176,000	70%
Julie (New Mexico)	$345,000	$345,000	0	100%
Martin (Nevada)	$370,000	$372,000	+$2,000	103%
Total	$3,588,000	$3,425,000	–$163,000	95%

Analysis by Product (George – Oklahoma)

Product	Quota	Actual	Difference	Performance
A	$143,000	$149,000	+$6,000	104%
B	$244,000	$160,000	–$84,000	66%
C	$118,000	$42,000	–$76,000	36%
D	$ 87,000	$65,000	–$22,000	75%
Total	$592,000	$416,000	–$176,000	70%

whether George's performance is due to a lack of ability, personal problems, increased competition, or another reason that requires managerial intervention.

To perform consistent evaluations, managers must ensure that two points related to sales are consistent. First, firms must accurately define when a product is "sold." As we explained in Chapter 11, some firms consider a product "sold" when the item is ordered, others when the product ships, and still others wait until the payment is received for the product. Second, during periods of inflation, firms can actually sell fewer items, but still increase their sales revenues, because the product's price continues to increase. By analyzing both the firm's sales revenues and the number of units sold, a sales manager will more clearly understand when such a phenomenon has occurred. However, a sales and unit analysis alone seldom provides sales managers with all of the information they need—and the information extracted can, at times, be misleading. For example, a firm might experience an increase in its revenues, but if its costs skyrocketed as a result, this wouldn't be apparent to managers looking at a sales analysis alone. That's why additional measures, like costs, are also needed.

Cost Analysis

Sales managers conduct a **cost analysis** to figure out what the relationship was between the sales that the firm generated during a given period and the costs that were incurred to make those sales. (Recall again that we first discussed sales budgets, or quotas, in Chapter 11.) Sales costs can be stated as a percentage of sales to assess whether or not the sales-cost relationship remained constant, or whether—relative to sales generated—the firm's selling costs increased or decreased. For example, if a company's sales were $1.5 million and its selling expenses were $150,000, then sales costs would be 10 percent of the revenues generated. Costs, as a percentage of sales, will also vary by industry and location. For example, the expenses related to selling oil drilling equipment might be higher than the expenses related to selling pharmaceutical products. Managers also understand that a firm's selling expenses in Los Angeles, California, are going to be higher than they are in Little Rock, Arkansas.

As Exhibit 14.2 shows, a cost analysis allows the sales manager to calculate the variance between actual and budgeted selling expenses for all of the firm's sales regions.

Any territory in which actual costs exceed budgeted costs should receive further scrutiny. For example, in Exhibit 14.2, the northeast territory's actual compensation costs exceeded the compensation budget by $25,000, and the sales manager should identify the cause of this deviation.

Cost data allow a firm to set pricing levels and budgets. For example, a sales manager can plan costs for training, travel, entertainment, salaries, and samples when constructing a sales budget. When a sales manager conducts a cost analysis, this permits her to determine which market segments are most expensive to serve, identify inefficient company functions that appear to cost more than they are worth, assess whether the cost of a sales call is increasing, and decide when it is time to modify the commission rates paid to salespeople for selling different products.

Another method of analyzing costs is to consider the differences related to each product line. A product expense analysis allows the sales manager to gauge the level of profits each product line is contributing, and how much it costs to sell the product. As Exhibit 14.3 shows, WRT, Inc., sells three different computer product lines: computers, monitors, and routers. Looking at the expense analysis, you can see that costs associated with each product line differ. The cost of goods sold, and the commission for selling computers, amount to 62 percent of the sales price, 70 percent of the sales price for monitors, and 25 percent of the sales price for routers. Based upon the available expense information, WRT's sales managers will want to consider whether: (1) competition is driving the selling price lower for computers and monitors and/or (2) the sales force is lowering prices to close sales quickly.

EXHIBIT 14.2 An Example of a Sales-Force Related Cost Analysis

	Compensation Costs			Training Costs		
	Budgeted Costs	Actual Costs	Variance	Budgeted Costs	Actual Costs	Variance
Northeast	$429,000	$472,500	$43,500	$237,600	$263,250	$25,650
Mid-Atlantic	$396,000	$411,750	$15,750	$113,300	$110,812	($2,488)
Southeast	$407,000	$393,750	($13,250)	$224,400	$237,375	$12,975
Mid-Central	$374,000	$354,375	($19,625)	$116,600	$93,375	($23,225)
Southwest	$308,550	$301,218	($7,332)	$96,195	$79,368	($16,827)
West	$425,000	$421,000	($4,000)	$215,000	$221,000	$6,000
Total	$2,339,550	$2,354,593	$15,043	$1,003,095	$1,005,180	$2,085

	Compensation Costs		Training Costs	
	Budgeted % Sales	Actual % Sales	Budgeted % Sales	Actual % Sales
Northeast	9.5%	8.7%	5.3%	4.8%
Mid-Atlantic	7.9%	7.6%	2.1%	2.2%
Southeast	9.5%	9.8%	5.7%	5.4%
Mid-Central	10.3%	10.9%	2.7%	3.4%
Southwest	8.1%	8.3%	2.1%	2.6%
West	9.5%	9.1%	2.8%	2.7%
Total	9.0%	8.9%	3.7%	3.7%

EXHIBIT 14.3 WRT, Inc.: An Example of an Expense Analysis by Product Line

Product Line	2006 Sales (000)	Cost of Goods & Commission	Cost of Goods % of Sales	Contribution Margin	Contribution Margin (%)
Computers	$36,400	$22,800	62%	13,600	38%
Monitors	10,400	7,200	70	3,200	30
Routers	5,200	1,300	25	3,900	75
Totals	$52,000	$31,300	60%	20,700	40%

The cost analysis conducted for sales evaluation purposes differs significantly, however, from the cost accounting related to the firm's production processes—the ones you learned about in your introductory accounting courses. Instead of the costs associated with the production of products, many of which are standardized, the sales manager must examine the expenses incurred by salespeople performing nonstandardized interactions with buyers. For example, some sales representatives spend dramatically more than others. This can take the form of higher-priced meals, more expensive hotels, and expensive relationship-building activities—like golf—to close a sale. A few salespersons may appear to spend a lot of money to "buy the business." To minimize this behavior, some firms, including Massachusetts Financial Services of Boston, analyzes its salespeople's expenses in great detail, using very sophisticated computerized methods.

Because of the availability of data, sales and cost analyses are the two most frequently used methods of evaluating a sales force's effectiveness. Even with improvements in computer systems and software, analyzing sales costs still consumes money and sales managers' time. Sales managers face a major problem when conducting a cost analysis, because there is often no clear method of allocating direct and indirect selling costs. For example, should sales executives' salaries, which are an indirect cost of the selling process, be apportioned to each territory when computing "sales" expenses or not?

The senior executives in firms make these decisions to ensure consistency in all territories when they are conducting a cost analysis. That said, once a decision is made, the cost allocations must be performed consistently in future periods, so the firm's managers can readily compare the data from one period to other periods.

Profit Analysis

Sales managers conduct a **profitability analysis** by combining sales and cost data in the equation: sales – costs = profit. By computing a profitability analysis, the sales manager can identify unprofitable product lines, territories, and customer segments; evaluate territory and product performance by profitability; and calculate year-end sales team bonuses. Advances in information technology have made it easier for sales managers to conduct profitability analysis, which is now a key measure tracked by companies that follow a relationship marketing approach to business. As we discussed in Chapter 5, CRM-focused firms use profitability analyses to compute the lifetime value of their customers as a basis for selecting which ones to serve. Sales managers should strive to conduct as thorough an analysis of their sales forces as possible, with the understanding that profitability analyses can be both time-consuming and costly.

An illustration of profitability analysis, shown in Exhibit 14.4, compares the profits of the same three product lines—computers, monitors, and routers—we saw in the previous cost-analysis section. Although all three product lines made a positive contribution toward the firm's fixed costs of between 30 to 40 percent, two of the products returned a profit to the company, whereas the other—the sale of monitors—actually lost money! Once the sales manager understands that a product line, customer, or territory is losing money, she can devise a strategy to return the category to profitability. For example, based upon the information in Exhibit 14.4, the sales manager might try to reduce the selling expenses associated with the line, or work with her firm's marketing department to increase the line's advertising, so as to improve its sales. As you can see, only by computing the profitability of a company's product lines can the sales manager identify problems such as these.

EXHIBIT 14.4   WRT, Inc.: Profitability Analysis by Product Line ($000)

	Totals	Computers	Monitors	Routers
Sales	$52,000	36,400	10,400	5,200
Cost of Goods Sold	$27,900	20,000	6,900	1,000
Gross Margin	**$24,100**	**16,400**	**3,500**	**4,200**
Other Expenses:				
Selling	$ 6,800	4,000	2,000	800
Administrative	$ 8,000	5,600	1,600	800
Total Other Expenses	**$14,800**	**9,600**	**3,600**	**1,600**
Net Profit (Loss)	**$ 9,300**	**6,800**	**(100)**	**2,600**

Ratio Measures for Evaluating the Sales Force

Sales managers employ **ratios**, or relationships, between activities and performance, or assets and performance, to standardize the evaluation of salespersons or sales managers. Ratios are computed at standard intervals—quarterly or annually—to identify sales force performance trends. Listed below are two **ratio measures** appropriate for such evaluations.

RETURN ON INVESTMENT (ROI) Analyzing the **return on investment (ROI)** is a useful tool that managers can use to evaluate the performance of their sales forces. Sales managers compute ROI using the following formula:

$$ROI = \frac{Net\ Profit}{Sales} \times \frac{Sales}{Investment}$$

By dividing the firm's net profit by its sales, it is possible to compute the profitability rate for sales. The second step is to divide sales revenue by investment—that is, the total assets listed on a firm's year-end balance sheet. Managers are concerned with the total assets they manage, regardless of their origin—whether the assets consist of investments made by the firm's shareholders, loans the firm has secured, or earnings the firm has retained. Although the formula appears to show that the sales components in each part of the ROI equation can cancel each other out, two separate elements are at work: (1) the rate of sales profit and (2) the rate of capital turnover. The rate of sales profit is a result of the firm's sales volume, product mix, product prices, and promotional activity. Capital turnover is a financial relationship that considers the sales volume and assets being managed by the firm. Therefore, each component is calculated separately and then multiplied, as shown below:

$$ROI = \frac{Net\ Profit\ \$200,000}{Sales\ \$1,500,000} \times \frac{Sales\ \$1,500,000}{Investment\ \$1,000.00}$$

$$13.33 \quad \times \quad 1.5 \quad = 19.995\%$$

As you can see from the calculation, the profit for the sales team is 13.33 percent, and the capital turnover is 150 percent, resulting in an ROI just shy of 20 percent. If the firm's capital invested in its assets (inventory and so forth) costs eight percent, an ROI of 20 percent is excellent. This means that the firm is paying eight percent to finance its assets, but is earning a 20 percent return on them, for a positive difference of 12 percent. In other words, the firm is using its assets efficiently to earn money. By contrast, if the firm's ROI were just nine percent, its managers would perceive that performance was poor. Why? Because the firm is paying eight percent to finance its assets, while the nine percent return on its investment barely exceeds that cost. A low ROI suggests that the sales force needs to increase its total sales and/or increase the average price of each sale.

Firms are computing ROI in increasing numbers, but in conjunction with business initiatives like customer loyalty and retention. For example, Hewlett Packard has increased its awareness of how its gains in customer loyalty affect the company's ROI across various buyer segments. At HP, ROI is more about tying sales activities to business results.[4]

RETURN ON ASSETS MANAGED (ROAM) Another form of return on investments is **Return on Assets Managed (ROAM)**. The ratio is a popular way for upper-level managers to evaluate the performance of sales managers at all levels. Basically, ROAM tells executives how well a firm's sales managers in different territories are managing the firm's assets individually (versus the firm as a whole) so as to generate profits.[5] ROAM utilizes different components than ROI, as shown in the following equation:

$$ROAM = \frac{Contribution\ Margin}{District\ Sales\ Revenue} \times \frac{District\ Sales\ Revenue}{Average\ Accounts\ Receivable + Inventory}$$

The **contribution margin** is computed by taking the selling price of a product and subtracting the cost of goods sold (what the product cost the firm) and the sales commission. For example, if Product A has an average selling price of $25, and the cost of goods sold is $10, the selling expenses related to the product are $5, the product's contribution margin is $10. It is the dollar amount that is "contributed" toward the firm's fixed costs until the company's break-even point is reached. Beyond this point, all contribution margins become profits. The district's sales revenue is the total sales revenue generated by the district. The assets managed are the firm's total accounts receivable, or money owed the firm, and goods held in inventory.

As an evaluative measure, ROAM should only be employed when the sales manager controls the assets (accounts receivable or goods held in inventory). For example, ROAM is a more useful performance measure at small- and medium-sized wholesale firms, in which sales managers approve sales made on credit and manage inventory levels. However, if the firm's inventory levels and credit approval functions are centrally managed, ROAM is not an appropriate metric for evaluating a sales manager. Individual salespersons should never be evaluated using ROAM unless they control the firm's assets or accounts receivable.

Relating the Performance of the Sales Force to the Firm's Salespeople

The sales manager next collects and organizes data in order to interpret the findings. Typically, sales managers want to understand why an organization's sales goals were or were not met—especially sales revenue goals. Too often, and without a systematic evaluation process, a simplistic answer is that the sales force did not work hard enough to reach the goal. However, in addition to insufficient salesperson effort or an unrealistic sales forecast, there are other possible reasons for a sales revenue shortfall:

- The firm's pricing isn't competitive.

- The firm's products suffer from quality or delivery problems.

- The firm's salespeople lack sales ability or need additional training.

Next, the sales manager lists possible explanations for the missed performance objectives, analyzing each reason. If a lack of sales ability is suspected, then the manager should examine the activities (number of calls made, for example) of the firm's salespeople to ensure that at least they invested a sufficient amount of sales effort. If that's not the problem, then the manager should examine the previous performance of the sales force. If just as many sales calls were made to customers in the past, how many of the calls resulted in actual sales? If, for example, the firm's product quality and/or delivery are problematic, then more than one salesperson will exhibit low sales for that one product.

When an initial analysis fails to pinpoint the source of the deviation, the sales manager should consider the possibility that the company is experiencing increased competition, and identify the territories where this is occurring. Sales managers must also question whether sales quotas for the firm's representatives were correctly set to begin with, and if future quotas should be determined using a different approach. The sales manager might also want to interview former customers, salespeople, and sales managers to learn why the business was lost. Once apparent explanations are uncovered, the sales manager should verify this information against salespeople's reports or other sales data, to confirm that their hypothesis is valid.

Evaluating Individual Sales Representatives

Most firms appraise their individual salespeople on a regular schedule. One survey of U.S. salespeople found that about 40 percent of reps receive evaluations at least quarterly, 13 percent receive them quarterly to biannually, and 25 percent are assessed biannually to annually. However, nearly one in five (19 percent) of the salespeople surveyed said they did not receive a formal performance evaluation.[6]

Firms report the following evaluation practices:

- Most firms examine both quantitative and qualitative criteria when it comes to evaluating their salespeople. However, a greater emphasis is placed on output (quantitative) measures, like the sales revenues they generate.

- The input of salespeople is sought, to varying degrees, before their quotas or performance standards are set.

- The sales goals of different salespeople differ, based upon their activities and territories.

- Companies utilize multiple information sources to perform evaluations.

- Most salespeople receive a written evaluation conducted in an office setting.[7] This formal evaluation normally requires the salesperson to sign, acknowledging receipt, and having the opportunity to respond to all statements/recommendations.

You might be wondering, at this point, which evaluation measures firms employ most often. Exhibit 14.5 displays the results of a survey that was conducted to answer that question. Not surprisingly, the most frequently used measurement was sales revenue generated. A new type of measurement, called a pipeline analysis, has broken into the list of the top five measurements in recent years. A **pipeline analysis** shows how well a salesperson is maintaining a stream of customers at different stages in the sales process. At the other end of the continuum are metrics related to customer service.

EXHIBIT 14.5 Most Popular Metrics Used in Sales Goals

Rank	% Using	Input	Output
1	40%		Revenues generated
2	31%	Number of calls made and leads	
3	29%		Profits generated
4	24%	Number of orders received	
5	18%	Number of customers in the pipeline	

A sales manager's performance appraisals should cover a wide range of evaluative areas that mirror the salesperson's diverse range of duties and responsibilities. This can result in assessment of four separate appraisal areas: input measures, outcomes, profitability, and personal development. In combination, these four areas comprise a comprehensive performance appraisal process similar to what Covidien reported in the beginning of this chapter. That is, each set of criteria provides the sales manager with differing insights about how the salesperson is performing and how he or she can be more effectively directed. An example of a comprehensive evaluation form that addresses each of these four areas is shown in Table 14.1.

Information on these, and many other metrics, is becoming more readily available to sales managers through the use of CRM software systems—especially the number of customers in the sales pipeline.[8] The more information that is collected, the more likely the sales manager will have an accurate record of each salesperson's activities and sales effectiveness. However, there are limits about how much information is useful for sales managers, and how much is too much. You can lose sight of the "forest" if you look at too many "trees." That's why many firms concentrate on the sales revenues their sales forces generated.

Leveraging Technology to Manage Sales Rep Performance

In decades past, sales representatives mailed, phoned, faxed, and e-mailed their call reports to their sales manager who, when they found time, would enter the information into databases or spreadsheets in order to assess how their representatives were doing. Sometimes, this process took days, or even weeks. "We'd have the information, but

TABLE 14.1   Performance Appraisal Form for a Sales Representative

Name: Joe Smith		Manager: Sally Jones
TERR: 1AB		Hire Date: 01/05/05
Judgment		
Problem-Solving Skills		
Communication w/ Manager		
Expense Vouchers		
District Other Reports		

PERFORMANCE SUMMARY   Overall Achievement Rating (value of 1 to 6)

AREAS REQUIRING IMMEDIATE ATTENTION

PROFESSIONAL DEVELOPMENT GOALS AND OBJECTIVES

PERFORMANCE VS. GOALS AND OBJECTIVES

SUPERVISOR SIGNATURE:	DATE:

EMPLOYEE COMMENTS

EMPLOYEE SIGNATURE:	DATE:

continued

TABLE 14.1 (continued)   **Performance Appraisal Form for a Sales Representative**

Name:	Joe Smith	Manager:	Sally Jones
TERR:	1AB	Hire Date:	01/05/05

2014 Sales	2014 TE (Travel & Expense)	2014 Product Sampling
14 $ Inc.	14 TE:	14 Sampling:
14 % Inc.	14 TE Bdgt:	14 Samp Bdgt:
14 vs. Goal	14 % Bdgt:	14 % Bdgt:

2013 Sales		2013 SALES RATE	
13 $ Inc.		Specialization	15
13 % Inc.		Region	31
13 vs. Goal			

PERFORMANCE AREAS	ACHIEVEMENT LEVELS	Achievement Levels: Outstanding = 1; Exceeds Requirements = 2; Meets Requirements = 3; Needs Improvement = 4
ORGANIZATION		SUPPORTING COMMENTS
Macro Planning		
Micro Planning		
Setting Priorities		
Across-the-Board Coverage		
Mktg. Materials/Sales Tools		
Self Sampling		
Follow-up Systems		
SALES INTERVIEW		
Rapport, Customer Relations		
Questioning Techniques		
Establishing Priorities		
Listening		
Sells from Product		
Trial Close		
Gets Commitment for Action		
Closing Skills		
Product Knowledge		
Use of Mktg. Materials		
Technology Demos		
Sell-Through		
Servicing of Accounts		
Appropriate Amt of Field Time		
Length of Calls		
# Calls per Day		
Key Closing Strategies		
Coverage of Product Lines		
Custom Products Presented		
TEAMWORK		
Communication with Office		
Competitive Information Shared		
Impact on District Success		
Drives National Programs		
SAMPLING OF PRODUCTS		
Thoroughness of Coverage		
Accuracy of Coverage		
Timeliness		
Judgment		
TRACKING		
Accuracy		
Timeliness		
Pending Totals		
Closed Totals		
Used for Planning		
CUSTOMER RELATIONS		
Rapport, Customer Relations		
Promoting Company Programs		
Discounting Strategies		
Troubleshooting		
LAPTOP USE		
Frequency of Communication		
Use of CC:Mail		
Creative Applications		
GENERAL/ADMINISTRATIVE		
Attitude and Morale		
Initiative		
Consistency of Effort		

it was always like looking in a rearview mirror," comments Ken Deakman, a sales manager with Slipka-Deakman Associates. "As a sales manager, you'd never be looking at where you were headed, only where you had been."

Most sales managers' perspectives are different today.[9] In today's competitive marketplace, the lifespan of a new product might be only 60 days. During that time, the new product must gain market share, or it won't be around long. Having immediate feedback from the sales force about how well the product is selling, or what objections they are hearing from buyers, can mean the difference between determining a winning approach or withdrawing a new product shortly after its launch.

In today's marketplace, salespersons utilize software to move data, in real time, from the field back to their sales managers at headquarters. While Slipka-Deakman was offering sales firms a handheld device when we wrote the

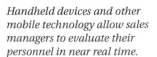

Handheld devices and other mobile technology allow sales managers to evaluate their personnel in near real time.

first edition of this book, Ken Deakman reports that salespersons now use their smart phones, tablets, or computers that are directly linked back to the home office. In this way, sales managers receive real-time information on their representatives' accounts, including their competitive position relative to those accounts, sales to them, activities they have pursued to obtain those sales, and their sales-visit notes. Using communications and computer technology allows a geographically dispersed—or smaller—sales force to be more nimble and respond quickly to change. As a result, geography and time are no longer adversaries to efficient operations.

Deakman notes that some organizations periodically send their sales managers into the field to verify whether their sales representatives are working or not. Sadly, some of them aren't. Being able to access their sales representatives' call report information daily has lessened the need for field visits, and has also made salespeople more accountable. Initially, Deakman believed that sales representatives would be reluctant to use the mobile devices, for fear they would be constantly monitored by their sales managers. Instead, he encountered two types of reactions to the devices: (1) higher-performing salespeople using the handheld devices and viewing them as an opportunity to improve their sales practices, and (2) lower-performing sales representatives regarding the devices as an invasion of their privacy. We know from research that salespeople are reluctant to adopt technology unless they can see the benefits to be gained from the new software and/or devices.[10]

Input Measures

We first discussed input measures in Chapter 11 when we introduced setting goals for salespeople. Recall that **input measures** gauge the effort put forth by the salesperson to contact, work with, and sell to buyers. For example, when a salesperson at the pharmaceutical firm AstraZeneca completes five sales calls a day, the sales manager can infer that the salesperson is making sufficient effort to reach goals and succeed. Conversely, when the sales manager observes that too few product demonstrations and phone calls are being made to potential customers, this implies the salesperson is not investing a necessary amount of effort to engage buyers. Input measures are important, because they are directly controlled by sales representatives. By contrast, closing sales depends a great deal upon what buyers decide to do—an aspect that sales representatives are far less able to control. The following are among the input measures sales managers use to assess a salesperson's performance:

- number of days worked;
- sales calls per day, week, or month;
- sales calls per customer;

- service calls;
- dealer meetings;
- customer training sessions conducted;
- product demonstrations conducted;
- required reports completed;
- letters or phone calls made to customers; and
- advertising displays set up.

Sales managers can also subdivide input measures by:

- current versus potential customers called;
- planned, versus cold, sales calls made;
- sales, versus service calls made;
- telephone versus on-site sales calls made; and
- closing calls, versus cold calls made.

Firms segment input measures into distinct categories, because the activities related to them are likely to have different results, or to portend different things. For example, cold calls are less likely to result in success than planned calls. In other words, the different measures provide sales managers with distinct clues about how their salespeople are performing their jobs. As another example, suppose a sales manager discovers that one of her salespersons is not making a sufficient amount of in-person calls, but is completing a higher-than-average number of phone calls to customers. This behavior might indicate that the rep's sales territory is too large, making it difficult for the person to complete the in-person sales calls assigned to him. Or, the salesperson may be taking a shortcut and not be putting forth an adequate amount of effort.

Managers also examine how salespeople allocate their time, including the time they spend on their sales calls. For example, sales managers often contrast how their firms' top performers spend their time, versus less-productive sales members. Deviations between high- and low-performing groups can help the sales manager coach less productive salespeople to spend their time more efficiently and improve the effectiveness of their sales calls. The recommendations might include specific sales approaches that top performers utilize, including the types of questions they ask buyers, and the amount of time they spend on different types of calls.

Input measures also tell sales managers about the sales strategies their representatives are using. For example, relationship-oriented companies might expect a number of sales calls to be made to their customers, and a rapport developed with them, prior to a sale. By contrast, less relationship-oriented firms will expect their salespeople to make one call—or a few sales calls—to customers before trying to close the deal. In this case, sales managers can look at the number of calls their representatives are making to see which of the two strategies are being pursued. Sales managers understand, too, that the quality of sales representatives' efforts can differ. This is evident when two salespeople make an equal number of customer calls and spend the same amount of time with their customers, but one of the representatives closes a significantly higher level of sales than the other. The perceptive manager will realize that training and coaching can help the marginal salesperson achieve higher-quality, and more effective, sales calls.

Outcome Measures

Recall from Chapter 11 that **outcome measures** are the actual results of salespeople's efforts. Outcome measures provide an indication of the salesperson's ability to close a sale. The number of new customer accounts opened, and the sales revenue to new customers, are, for example, evidence of a representative's sales efforts. Cancelled orders are another output measure. If a sales representative has a large number of cancelled orders, it may indicate that the salesperson used high-pressure tactics, or acted deceptively, to garner the sale. Lost accounts also call into question whether the salesperson was addressing the needs of the customer firm. The following is a list of output measures sales managers use to assess their representatives:

- sales revenues generated;
- sales revenues generated per account;
- sales revenue generated as a percentage of a salesperson's territory potential;
- number of orders generated;
- number of new customers won;
- number of sales to new customers;
- cancelled orders; and
- lost accounts.

Keep in mind that output measures can be misleading when a sales cycle, or the time to move through the sales process, extends over several quarters of a year. Exhibit 14.6 shows various output performance measures and the percentage of U.S. firms that use them to evaluate their salespeople.[11] Sales managers closely monitor these measures to ensure that their sales representatives are getting results and achieving their goals. However, many sales managers believe that sales representatives' output measures are highest when they devote a sufficient amount of time and quality to their input measures. A growing number of salespeople today use their laptop computers and CRM systems to ensure quality sales calls are made. In fact, one study concluded that working hard was equally as important as working smart.[12]

EXHIBIT 14.6   Output Measures U.S. Firms Use to Evaluate Their Sale Forces

Measure	% of Firms Using*	Measure	% of Firms Using
Sales		*Profit*	
Sales Volume	79	Net Profit	69
Sales Volume/Previous Year's Sales	76	Gross Margin Percentage	34
Sales to Quota	65	Return on Investment	33
Sales Growth	55	*Orders*	
Accounts		Number of Orders	47
Number New Accounts	69	Average Order Size	22
Number Lost Accounts	33	Order per Call Ratio	14

* Percentage of firms that use this measure to assess the performance of their sales forces.

Look at Exhibit 14.7 to see how well the three salespersons—Moe, Sydney, and Hannah—performed during a sales period based upon a weighting system. If sales volume sold (actual/goal) was the sole focus of Pickerel Lake Industries' (PLI) sales evaluations, Moe would be considered to be performing better than Sydney, followed by Hannah. Using only profitability (net profit/goals), Sydney ranks the highest, with Hannah and Moe switching positions. Both sales volume and profitability are output evaluations and reflect what has been sold. However, by adding input metrics, a more complete picture comes into focus. The number of demonstrations is considered an important input factor, because it helps customers grasp how the features of PLI's products benefit them. Moreover, nearly all customers need to experience the benefits of the software before they will purchase it. Looking only at this metric, Hannah would be rated first, followed by Moe and Sydney. Lastly, the number of new accounts opened in this period reflects the activities and follow-through required to get a purchase order guided through potentially long and complex purchase channels. Again, Hannah is first, followed by Moe and Sydney. Based upon a weighted composite of measures, Hannah has the highest performance.

The last step in this analysis is determining which performance measures are more important than others. PLI has assigned weights reflecting the importance of each goal. Sales volumes have been assigned a weight of three, and net profits a weight of four. Both the number of demonstrations and the number of new accounts have been given a weight of one. Multiplying the percent of each goal a representative achieved by the weight assigned to him or her yields the total weight for that factor. Adding those numbers, and dividing by the number of weights (in this case, nine) produces the final performance score for each person: at 100.6 percent of goal, Hannah's performance ranks first, followed by Sydney at 93.7 percent, and Moe at 88.1 percent of goal. As you can see, each of the sales representatives appears to have strengths and weaknesses. Only after a sales manager evaluates a number of factors will she have a more complete understanding of each salesperson's performance.

EXHIBIT 14.7   Weighting and Combining Salespeople's Performance: A Worksheet

Metric	Goal	Actual	% of Goal	Weight	Goal x Weight
Sales Rep – Hannah Elizabeth					
Sales volume	$200,000	180,000	90	3	270
Net profit	128,000	120,000	94	4	376
No. demos	10	14	140	1	140
New accounts	8	10	120	1	120
Total Score				9	906

Goal score = (Goal x Weight points/weight of metric) = 906/9 = 100.6%

Metric	Goal	Actual	% of Goal	Weight	Goal x Weight
Sales Rep – Sydney Nguyen					
Sales volume	$250,000	280,112	112	3	336
Net profit	172,000	175,000	102	4	408
No. demos	11	5	45	1	45
New accounts	9	5	55	1	55
Total Score				9	844

Goal score = (Goal x Weight points/weight of metric) = 844/9 = 93.7%

Metric	Goal	Actual	% of Goal	Weight	Goal x Weight
Sales Rep – Moe Peterson					
Sales volume	$300,000	310,000	103	3	303
Net profit	190,000	160,000	84	4	336
No. demos	9	6	67	1	67
New accounts	7	6	86	1	86
Total Score				9	793

Goal score = (Goal x Weight points/weight of metric) = 793/9 = 881.1%

Profitability Measures

Firms are placing increased emphasis on profitability measures like:

- net profit as a percentage of sales;

- net profit contribution;

- net profit dollars;

- return on investment; and

- gross margin.

The salesperson can impact the firm's profitability through: (1) specific products sold and (2) final prices negotiated. This means that two salespeople can sell the same sales revenue levels and meet the exact quota requirements. However, based upon the mix of products sold and prices they negotiated, one salesperson could produce higher gross sales margins for the firm. Likewise, the expenses salespeople accumulate, such as their travel and entertainment expenses, impact their firms' profitability. For example, to improve their firm's profitability, salespeople could opt to take clients to less costly luncheon meetings instead of more expensive dinners. Sales managers evaluate their representatives on these criteria, too. Profitability criteria are, in fact, increasingly incorporated into salespeople's assessments, and can directly impact a salesperson's quota and bonuses. During times of slow growth and heavy competition, profitability is critically important to firms.

Ratio Measures for Performance Appraisals

Sales managers should also be familiar with **ratio measures** computed for individual performance appraisals by combining various input and output data. A list of commonly used sales ratio measures is presented in Exhibit 14.8. **Sales volume per call** is a ratio that assesses a salesperson's efficiency. It is computed by dividing the total revenue generated by the salesperson by the total number of sales calls he or she made during a particular period. A low sales volume per call suggests that the salesperson is either devoting excessive time to small accounts, or is not giving a sufficient amount of attention to larger accounts. Or, perhaps, the salesperson is deliberately generating a larger number of small sales, rather than a smaller

---

EXHIBIT 14.8   Common Ratios Used to Evaluate Salespersons

Expense Ratios:

Sales expense ratio = Expenses/Sales

Cost per call ratio = Total costs/Number of Calls

Account Penetration and Servicing Ratios:

Account penetration ratio = Accounts sold/Total accounts in market

New account conversion ratio = Number of new accounts/Total number of accounts

Lost account ratio = Prior accounts not sold/Total number of accounts

Sales per account ratio = Sales dollar volume/Total number of accounts

Average order size ratio = Sales dollar volume/Total number of orders

Order cancellation ratio = Number of cancelled orders/Total number of orders

Strike rate = Number of orders/Number of quotations

Call Productivity Ratios:

Calls per day ratio = Number of calls/Number of days worked

Calls per account ratio = Number of calls/Number of accounts

Planned call ratio = Number of planned calls/Total number of calls

Orders per call (batting average) ratio = Number of orders/Total number of calls

Profit per call ratio = Total profit/Number of calls made

number of large sales, because the large sales have already been closed by his or her competitors. Another commonly employed ratio is the **order per call**, or salesperson's "batting average." It is computed by dividing the total number of sales a person closes by the total number of sales calls he or she made. For example, if a salesperson is successful 30 times out of 100 sales calls, then the person's batting average is .300 (30/100). All other things being equal, the higher a salesperson's batting average and sales volume per call are, the greater is the person's sales efficiency. A third ratio is the **average cost per sales call**, which is a salesperson's total sales expenses divided by the total number of calls made by the salesperson. This relates back to the profitability measures we just discussed. A low cost-per-call ratio, when all other measures are satisfactory, signals efficiency on the part of a salesperson. However, when a sales manager observes both a low sales volume and a low cost-per-call ratio, this suggests that the representative is making too few sales calls and is not devoting sufficient time and effort to establish relationships with the firm's customers.

Additional ratios that sales managers use to evaluate their salespeople include the **close rate** and the **profit per call**. These ratios are calculated as follows:

$$\text{Close rate} = \frac{\text{Number of orders}}{\text{Number of quotations}} \qquad \text{Profit per Call} = \frac{\text{Total Profit}}{\text{Number of calls made}}$$

The close rate is, essentially, how well the salesperson can close once she has attempted to "seal the deal" by giving customers price quotes on the firm's products. The profit per call ratio represents the total profit derived from an account, divided by the number of calls needed to make the sale. For example, if a salesperson made a sale of $10,000 and $3,000 in profit after five sales calls, the profit per call would be $600. Ratios can provide sales managers with additional insight about why a salesperson is or is not reaching her goals. Like other measures of performance, ratios indicate what aspects of the salesperson's work need to be further investigated—for example, whether the person is a poor closer, as indicated by his close rate, or is offering too many discounts to customers, as indicated by his profit-per-call ratio.[13]

The Four-Factor Model of Evaluation

As discussed throughout the chapter, managers employ both behavioral- and outcome-based factors to evaluate sales performance. Because a person's sales performance is a multidimensional outcome, it may be beneficial to examine the four-factor model. The model comprises four performance factors: two input activities (days worked and calls rate) and two output measures (batting average and average order size). When combined, these factors give the following equation:

$$\text{Sales} = \text{Days Worked} \times \text{Call Rate} \times \text{Batting Average} \times \text{Average Order Size}$$

The **four-factor model** shows that sales can be increased by working more days, calling upon more customers per day, closing higher rates of sales per call, and selling larger orders when making a sale. If a salesperson is not meeting his quota, then the likely explanation can be found in one or more of these four factors. That is, if the salesperson is working full days and calling upon the expected number of accounts, then the problem might lie in the quality of the person's sales calls (batting average). Or if the order size is below the expected level, this indicates the salesperson is concentrating excessively on small accounts, rather than on larger ones. The four-factor model should be used with caution, however, since the factors are correlated. For example, a higher call rate is positively correlated with higher sales, but negatively correlated with average order size. In other words, there are trade-offs among the factors that must be considered. The factors, therefore, should not be considered in isolation from one another.

Qualitative Performance Measures

Sales managers also examine **qualitative performance measures**, or judgments made by salespeople's supervisors, about their performance or abilities. Common qualitative performance measures utilized for performance appraisals include:

- salespeople's job knowledge;
- problem-solving skills;
- creativity;
- attitude and morale;
- internal and external relationships;
- initiative and judgment;
- communications with management; and
- timeliness in completing reports.

Companies evaluate a salesperson's company knowledge, product knowledge, market knowledge, personal appearance, and motivation against that of an ideal salesperson.[14]

Sales managers can employ a variety of methods and tools to perform the qualitative part of a salesperson's evaluation:

- The *essay technique* is a brief statement written by the sales manager to describe the overall salesperson's performance level. However, since there is generally no standardized format for what is discussed and how ratings are assigned using the essay technique, it is difficult to compare evaluations across individual salespersons. Go to Exhibit 14.1 and look at the "performance summary" section of the assessment form to see an essay technique evaluation.

- *Rating scales* utilize phrases or terms as anchors that describe the salesperson's personal characteristics or performance. A variety of rating scales can be used to evaluate the sales force, such as graphic rating/checklist methods. An example of this type of scale is shown below:

    "Maintains outstanding relationships with customers."
    Almost Never   1   2   3   4   5   6   7   Almost Always

- *Forced ranking* occurs when each salesperson's performance is ordered from "highest" to "lowest" within a district or region. The sales manager bases his or her final rankings on relevant performance characteristics. This technique provides sales representatives with little feedback about how to actually improve their sales; however, it can be useful for sales managers selecting people for promotion. General Electric and Ford force-rank their managers.[15]

- *Management by objectives* (MBO) is a goal-setting and evaluative process that results in mutually agreed upon performance measures and assessments between a supervisor and an employee. Specifically, MBO is a three-step process: (1) setting mutually agreed upon, well-defined, and measurable objectives to be achieved within a specified time frame; (2) managing the activities the employee performs within the time period to achieve the objectives; and (3) assessing the employee's performance against the objectives. A major problem of MBO is that sales managers must invest a significant amount of time to make it work.

- A *behaviorally anchored rating scale* (BARS), as seen in Exhibit 14.9, is a set of scaled statements that describe the level of performance a salesperson received in terms of various job behaviors. The linking of behaviors and results becomes the basis for evaluating a salesperson's performance. Implementing a BARS evaluation system requires the sales manager to identify key behaviors related to a salesperson's success, and rank salespeople on each one. The design of such an instrument is both time-consuming and expensive. In addition, all ranking scales, including BARS, can undervalue and overvalue important areas of a salesperson's performance.

EXHIBIT 14.9 Behaviorally Anchored Rating Scale

Very High		Promptly submitted all field
More often than not,	10.0	reports even in difficult situations
salesperson submitted	9.0	Promptly met deadlines in most
accurate and needed	8.0	report completion situations
sales reports	7.0	Usually on time when submitting
Moderate		properly formatted sales reports
Regularity in submitting	6.0	Expected to regularly be tardy in submitting
accurate and needed	1.0	field sales reports
field sales reports	4.0	Expected to be tardy and submit inaccurate
Very Low		field sales reports
Irregular and unacceptable	3.0	Disregarded due dates for almost all reports
promptness and accuracy	2.0	Never filed field sales reports and resisted
of field sales reports	1.0	managerial guidance to improve performance
	0.0	

Of course, the overall goal for conducting individual appraisals is to improve the future performance of sales representatives. Some of the more immediate *qualitative goals* include counseling, training, and developing salespeople. Some of the more immediate quantitative, or output, goals include establishing the compensation and raises that salespeople are to receive, or promoting or terminating them. The specific purpose of any assessment must be clearly defined, because each goal involves distinct evaluation techniques and measures. Said differently, the items used to evaluate sales representatives depend upon the objectives of the appraisal. For example, if the objective of the evaluation is to gauge a salesperson's suitability for a management position, then items on organizing, planning, working with others, and acceptance of responsibility are important. Conversely, if the goal of the evaluation is to improve a salesperson's performance, then the items utilized should objectively rate the person's duties and key responsibilities. The evaluation items used by sales managers will vary by culture, as the "Global Sales Management" box explains.

The Problem of Evaluation Bias

Evaluation bias is defined as a systematic tendency toward a lack of objectivity, fairness, or impartiality on the part of the evaluator that is based upon personal preferences and beliefs, or a systematic error in the assessment instrument and procedures, or in the interpretation and evaluation process. To minimize evaluation bias, firms try to implement systematic assessment processes where a sales manager applies performance standards that directly relate to an employee's job description. This means that an appraisal system is based upon a salesperson's behavior or results, rather than on the salesperson's traits or personal characteristics. For example, if the salesperson is instructed to complete four sales calls a day, this should be the work standard the person is held to, regardless of what the sales manager thinks of the sales representative personally or the job they are doing. In other words, sales

GLOBAL SALES MANAGEMENT   Evaluating Salespeople Working Overseas

The evaluation criteria and sales expectations vary by culture.

Evaluating salespeople assigned to positions abroad is a more complex undertaking than assessing domestic salespeople. Many additional factors come into play, including a salesperson's ability to adjust to the living conditions and culture of a foreign country, assuming she has relocated abroad. Criteria that U.S. firms use to evaluate their salespeople working abroad include: technical ability, cultural empathy, adaptability, flexibility, diplomacy, and language skills. A salesperson's cultural skills are often more important than their technical capabilities, however. Even when a salesperson is native to the country in which he is selling, cultures vary considerably—and so do people's perceptions of what does or what does not constitute satisfactory performance. For example, in collectivist societies like Japan, teamwork is favored over individual accomplishments. As a result, a Japanese salesperson's evaluation focuses more on contributions to team efforts and furthering company goals than on individual performance.

Money, R. Bruce, and John L. Graham (1999). "Salesperson Performance, Pay, and Job Satisfaction: Tests of a Model Using Data Collected in the U.S. and Japan," *Journal of International Business Studies*, 30(1), 149–172.

managers must evaluate the members of their sales teams from as close to a point of neutrality as possible.

Sales managers are prone to at least five types of evaluation bias. **Halo effect** occurs when a sales manager allows one or more evaluation categories that are perceived to be important to influence the overall assessment of the salesperson. An example of halo effect occurs when a sales manager focuses on a salesperson's high sales revenue, but fails to assign low ratings for customer complaints and high sales expenses! In this example, meeting the sales revenue goal overshadows other important performance measures.

A second bias the sales manager must guard against is **leniency** or **harshness tendency** that occurs when a salesperson is rated at the extremes—either outstanding or below average on most, or all, performance attributes. The reason that sales managers rate at the extremes is attributable to their personalities, or their own beliefs about how to define each level of performance. When sales managers utilize their own perspective of performance, rather than using clearly defined performance standards, the entire evaluation system is jeopardized, because across a large number of salespersons, similar ratings are dissimilar!

Central tendency bias, or the practice by managers to rate in the center of the scale, can be just as detrimental to salespersons and human resources' follow-up, because little information is provided; everyone appears to be average. As a result of no variability in ratings, it is difficult to identify true differences in performance, and should it become necessary to terminate a salesperson, existing evaluations will be of little value. To combat central tendency bias, a number of firms, like GE, have started to mandate forced ratings, or require sales managers to place at least 10 percent of the sales force in the lowest overall performance category.

A fourth form of subjectivity that enters the evaluation process is **interpersonal bias**, which occurs when a manager's performance ratings are influenced by how much they like or dislike the individual being evaluated. For example, if a salesperson is too outspoken, or dresses too casually or too formally, a manager may unconsciously lower (or raise) the person's evaluation rating. Some salespersons may try to employ their selling skills to positively influence the sales manager's perception of them as being likeable, and thus bias their evaluations upward.

Finally, **outcome bias**, or allowing the results of an action to influence the manager's assessment, can impact overall evaluations. An example would be a sales manager who rates a salesperson who has closed a large, important sale higher than a salesperson who failed to close such a large sale, even though both people did an equally good job. In other words, the ultimate decision to buy or not buy largely depended on the different buyers involved—not the sales representatives' behaviors.

Informal Evaluations

Some sales managers claim that formal sales force evaluations are unnecessary, because they assess their salesperson's performance on a daily or "as-needed" basis. However, it's easy to argue that evaluations such as these are highly biased. For example, say that a salesperson wins a company golf tournament. One sales manager will view this as a positive achievement, whereas another manager might ask how it was possible for the salesperson to work 55 to 60 hours each week and still excel at the game of golf. Second, **informal evaluations** result in sales managers assessing differing amounts and quality of information about each salesperson. For example, one salesperson might request that his customers write letters of appreciation and provide positive feedback to his sales manager. Conversely, another salesperson might be reluctant to ask her customers for this type of assistance. If the sales managers don't evaluate the two representatives using hard, detailed criteria, biased evaluations are likely to occur. In other words, when a sales manager engages in informal evaluations, she is unable to evaluate her sales force either consistently or comparatively. Thus, formal evaluation systems are more likely to produce objective appraisals and minimize the number of demoralized sales reps who, ultimately, leave the firm or go so far as to file suit against it, claiming their appraisals were biased.

Reducing Sales Management Errors in Performance Evaluations

To minimize the effects of evaluation bias when completing performance appraisals, the sales manager should take the following actions:

1. Before completing the evaluation forms, read and be familiar with each trait listed on the form.

2. Do not allow one factor to influence others.

3. Base your ratings on actual performance, not potential.

4. Don't overrate salespeople; evaluate them based on an objective, unbiased standard.

5. Rate the salesperson on his or her performance over the evaluation period, not a specific incident.

6. List sound reasons for all performance appraisal ratings.[16]

What Happens When Salespeople Don't Achieve Their Sales Goals?

Sales managers who prefer informal appraisals risk not being taken seriously and are more likely to give biased evaluations.

"Off with their heads!" yelled the Queen of Hearts. Fortunately, things aren't as bad for salespeople who don't reach their goals as it was for Alice, in Lewis Carroll's *Adventures of Alice in Wonderland*. In fact, sales managers, researchers, and consultants agree that salespeople who don't achieve their goals aren't at the end of the line. As we have explained, there can be a number of reasons why a salesperson does not achieve 100 percent of sales goals. When salespeople do not reach their goals, their performance is measured against other local representatives and national averages. If a representative is an **outlier**—that is, the person's sales are out of line with everyone else's—the representative is typically put under closer scrutiny. Not meeting a goal signals the representative's sales manager to work more closely with the salesperson, to find out what activities or practices the person needs to engage in to be successful.

ETHICS IN SALES MANAGEMENT   The Impact of a Biased Sales Manager

Imagine working for a sales manager who deliberately, or unknowingly, biases his sales force evaluations. That is, consider how destructive it is for a sales manager to evaluate his sales team, based primarily on personal feelings or friendship. Salespersons in many organizations often complain that it is their relationship, rather than their performance, that gets evaluated by the boss. Other criticisms that appear to influence annual evaluations--and subsequent salary increases-- include: length of time on the job, social activities like golf or dinners that take place away from work, and where, or if, one attends religious services. It is natural for a sales manager to prefer the company of certain salespersons over others; however, sales managers must do their best to evaluate their sales team based on set standards from a point of neutrality. Biased evaluations are unethical and, in many instances, they are ruled illegal when challenged in court!

Should a salesperson continue to underperform during the next time unit (for some companies it might be the next quarter; for others the next year), he or she will then be placed on probation. Sales reps who work solely on commission will likely realize their performance is below par, based upon their low pay, and look for opportunities elsewhere. Sales representatives receiving a salary and commission who continue to fall short of their quotas eventually face termination.[17,18]

Developing and Reallocating Salespeople's Skills and Efforts

If it is determined that a salesperson requires additional personal development, this should be clearly communicated to the employee. This is why some firms employ MBO systems to help salespersons set mutually agreed-upon goals that they work to accomplish. Should the evaluation confirm that shifting the salesperson's priority from one activity to another will improve his or her performance, this must also be communicated to the salesperson. For example, if it is apparent the salesperson has not been devoting sufficient time to selling high-profit-margin products, the sales manager must redirect the salesperson's efforts. Likewise, sales managers could be spending excessive time selling, instead of managing the sales force. In such circumstances, the sales manager must devote more field time to coaching the sales force.

Modifying the Performance Setting

The firm's performance appraisals might also indicate that changes are needed in sales procedures or methods. Perhaps the sales training program has not adequately prepared the sales force for success in the field. When this occurs, firms must consider modifying their training programs. For example, as new products are introduced, or selling strategies change, firms might need to add high-tech training programs to prepare the sales force for marketplace changes.[19] If the analysis shows the sales force is weak when making sales presentations, for example, this must be communicated to the sales team, and proper training must be implemented to correct the deficiency. Alternately, the firm might need to hire more experienced and successful salespeople. The analysis might also confirm that the firm's products need to be improved, or new products need to be added to the company's product lineup. Lastly, the appraisals might indicate that the company's marketing strategies and/or credit policies need to be changed.

Managing Your Career

As a new salesperson, it is imperative that you understand how and when you will be evaluated. Most firms identify and track data that tell them how you are performing as a salesperson. Often, it is fairly basic information, like sales revenue, selling costs, number of new customers, and number of lost accounts. By understanding what is important to your employer, you will know where to allocate your time and effort. For example, if you are evaluated on number of calls made, number of sales made, sales revenue, costs, and customers retained, this means that you should work a full day, concentrate on making quality calls, track sales made against sales expectations, spend/travel wisely, and work to keep your profitable customers satisfied. In effect, if you understand how and when you will be evaluated, there should be few surprises at evaluation time.

Also, as a future sales manager, you now understand the myriad ways to evaluate your sales team, and the positive/negative points of each evaluation process. By understanding the importance of evaluating the sales team on a regular schedule (annually or biannually) you will know to reduce the bias you gather, and consider the same information for the same period for all members of the sales team. While informal evaluations may provide the sales team with feedback, they are no substitutes for a formal assessment process that provides the sales team with objective feedback on how they are doing—good and not so good—and why.

Summary

Sales managers evaluate the activities and accomplishments of their sales forces in order to know what is working, what is not, and, most importantly, why? This information shapes the daily decisions the sales manager makes to improve the performance of the sales force. Of course, the quality of the decisions that sales managers make will be higher if the information emanates from objective evaluation efforts.

To increase the probability that the sales force will reach its goals, sales managers analyze their firms' sales, costs, and profitability measures. Sales information provides managers with an understanding of the revenue the firm generated. Cost figures relate the company's sales expense to its sales goals. Profitability figures tell supervisors if the sales effort was worthwhile. The analyses help managers identify deviations from the firm's plans that can then be further investigated to understand why they occurred. If the firm's plans and goals are not achieved, sales managers must determine whether the plans were incorrectly set and/or if the sales force did not perform up to par. Finally, based upon the results of their analyses, sales managers can decide what aspects of the sales function and the firm, as a whole, need to be changed.

To ensure their sales representatives are on track, sales managers continually monitor their performance. Formal appraisals of representatives are usually conducted once or twice annually to understand their performance, potential for advancement, and qualifications for reward. Because the duties of salespeople are complex, they are generally evaluated based upon a broad set of metrics that includes their inputs, or efforts they make to sell the firm's products, plus the outcomes they achieve, such as the revenues and profits they actually generate. Professional development criteria are also included in the evaluations. By utilizing multiple measures, sales managers gain a more comprehensive picture of their salespeople. Sales managers must also be aware of the potential for bias to enter into the assessment process, and must take steps to reduce it.

When sales managers perform regular, objective, and comprehensive evaluations, they will be more cognizant of both their sales forces and the markets for their products. This will allow them to make more informed decisions and improve the odds of success for themselves, their salespeople, and the firm as a whole.

Key Terms

average cost per sales call   328
central tendency bias   332
close rate   328
contribution margin   318
cost analysis   315
evaluation bias   330
four-factor model   328
halo effect   331
informal evaluations   332
input measures   323
interpersonal bias   332
leniency or harshness tendency   331
order per call   328
outcome bias   332
outcome measures   324
outlier   333
pipeline analysis   320
profit per call   328
profitability analysis   317
qualitative performance measures   329
ratio   317
ratio measures   317
return on assets managed (ROAM)   318
return on investment (ROI)   318
sales analysis   314
sales volume per call   327

Questions and Problems

1. What is the relationship between managerial control and sales team evaluations? When managers make decisions without the benefit of accurate information, what is the likely outcome?

2. When sales managers detect a deviation from the performance expected by the firm, what are the two most common aspects they investigate?

3. What are the different goals of evaluation and assessment? That is, what types of decisions must a sales manager make, and how are these decisions linked to the type of evaluation information needed?

4. Why is sales revenue the most common data used? What are some limitations of considering only sales revenue generated?

5. List three managerial decisions that are possible, based upon a cost analysis.

6. Review the data presented for Hannah, Moe, and Sydney in Exhibit 14.8. In what areas do they excel? Which areas, as their sales manager, would concern you?

7. The handheld devices discussed in the chapter can be upgraded with Global Positioning Systems (GPS) to allow a sales manager to track exactly where each sales representative has been, and where the rep is at the moment. What do you think the pros and cons of using this technology might be? As a sales manager, would you use it?

8. If a salesperson received 32 purchase orders during the month, based upon 123 sales calls, what is his order per call, or "close rate"?

9. In what ways can salespeople influence the profitability of their territories?

10. Sales managers should assess qualitative measures against what standard? Why?

11. What challenges are posed when firms evaluate a global sales force's efforts?

12. Explain the common types of bias to which sales managers can fall victim.

Role Play

Pittsburgh Industrial Controls, Inc., Considers Changing Its Assessment Criteria

Reba Starnes is sales manager for Pittsburgh Industrial Controls, Inc., a manufacturer of switches and thermostats for industrial HVAC (heating, ventilation, and air conditioning) systems. Until recently, the company utilized its sales force to push products through its distribution chain. As a result, the firm's sales force members were evaluated primarily in terms of the sales revenues they generated, number of new accounts they opened, and the extent to which they grew or increased the sales they made at their existing accounts. Recently, however, Pittsburgh senior managers have switched to a customer-centric strategy that focuses on the firm's best customers. Starnes wonders if the categories on the company's performance appraisal forms—used to evaluate the firm's representatives—should also be modified. She thinks that, other than sales revenues generated, the appraisals should take additional evaluation criteria into account. Despite the change in the sales force's strategy, Starnes would find it troubling not to expect the members of the firm's sales force to meet certain sales revenue levels. Starnes has scheduled a meeting with Jax Mader, president, and Kisha Maxwell, operations manager, to discuss potential changes in the firm's evaluation policy.

Characters in the Role Play

Reba Starnes, sales manager at Pittsburgh Industrial Controls, Inc.

Jax Mader, president, at Pittsburgh Industrial Controls, Inc.

Kisha Maxwell, operations manager at Pittsburgh Industrial Controls, Inc.

Assignment

Break into groups of three, with each student in the group playing one of the characters. Do not be concerned about matching the gender of the character with the actual gender mix of the student group. Prior to meeting in the group, work individually to summarize and support your own recommendations for a new set of objective and subjective measures of performance for the sales force at Pittsburg Controls. Then meet and role play the meeting between Reba, Jax, and Kisha. Your goal is to conclude the meeting with a unified plan for modifying the evaluation system for salespersons at Pittsburgh Industrial Controls so that it reflects the goals of the firm and important accomplishments of the sales team.

Caselets

Caselet 14.1: "Happy Hannah": Did the Sales Reps Meet Their Goals?

Sales manager "Happy" Hannah Johanson helped establish goals for two of her sales reps—the outspoken Ella Lynn and the on-again-off-again Syd Vance. Three sales quarters have passed since that meeting, and Hannah has collected the performance measures for both reps that are outlined in Figure 1 below. She needs to prepare tonight for the feedback sessions scheduled for mid-morning tomorrow.

Ella has continued to be the firm's "sustainability" advocate. Her efforts, combined with the rising price of fuel, have resulted in her being in a small group of reps, piloting several brands of hybrid vehicles for possible adoption by the entire sales force. This has pleased Ella immensely.

As Hannah skimmed her local newspaper, she saw Syd's picture on the sports page. "Star Pitcher Takes Team to Nationals," read the headline. Syd's team, sponsored by Honker's—a popular tavern near a local wildlife preserve, had gone 45-5 over the last four-and-a-half months, won the regional tournament, and was going to the national playoffs. Based upon the newspaper article, Syd has a great pitching arm.

FIGURE 1   Last 3 Sales Quarters: Actual vs. Goal Figures

Sales Goals and Actual by Quarter	Ella's Sales Figures			Syd's Sales Figures		
Sales Vol. Goal	125,000	125,000	125,000	150,000	150,000	150,000
Sales Vol. Actual	120,000	128,000	118,000	140,000	130,000	105,000
Demonstrations Goal	9	7	11	10	8	6
Demonstrations Actual	8	8	8	10	10	10
New Account Goal	4	3	5	4	3	2
New Account Actual	4	4	4	5	5	5

Questions

1. Based on the performance data in Figure 1, what "deviations" would you focus on during your meeting with Ella?
2. Based on the performance data, what factors would you focus on during your meeting with Syd? What approach would you take in your meeting with Syd?
3. Is Syd's participation in competitive sports relevant to his evaluation? Why or why not?
4. Would your response differ if Syd's team was sponsored by a religious or a civic organization?

Caselet 14.2: Moworth Industrial

Moworth Industrial, which is located in Louisville, Kentucky, manufactures customized truck bodies for utility firms located in the state. Moworth's sales manager, Fran Puckett, recently ranked each of the company's five salespeople in five performance areas. The rankings were as follows:

Salesperson	Sales Revenue	New Accounts	Lost Accounts	Expenses	Profitability
Nguyen	1	5	3	2	4
Ford	5	4	1	3	2
Gordon	3	1	5	4	3
Andrabi	2	3	4	1	5
Thyssen	4	2	2	5	1

However, once Puckett had ranked her sales staff, it was difficult for her to identify which salesperson should receive the top rating. She also wondered how to utilize the information to coach each salesperson, to improve his or her performance.

Questions

1. Are all five categories used for ranking the sales force equal in importance?
2. What are the advantages and disadvantages of a ranking system?
3. Under what conditions is it appropriate to rank one's sales force?
4. What can be concluded if each category receives an importance weight?
5. What recommendations would you offer Fran Puckett?

References

1. Wotruba, Thomas R., and Edwin K. Simpson (1992). *Sales Management*, Boston, MA: PWS-Kent.
2. Hymowitz, Carol (2001). "Ranking Systems Gain Popularity but Have Many Staffers Riled," *Wall Street Journal*, May 15, B1.
3. Terpstra, Vern, and Ravi Sarathy (1997). *International Marketing*. Fort Worth, TX: Dryden Press.
4. Owens, Darryl E. (2007). "Metrics Need a Link to Results, Exec Buy-in, Momentum," *Marketing News*, March 1, 13, 22.
5. Cron, William L., and Michael Levy (1987). "Sales Management Performance Evaluation: A Residual Income Perspective," *Journal of Personal Selling & Sales Management*, August, 57–66.
6. Pettijohn, Linda S., R. Stephen Parker, Charles E. Pettijohn, and John L. Kent (2001). "Performance Appraisals: Usage, Criteria, and Observations," *Journal of Management Development*, (20)9, 754–771.
7. Jackson, Donald, Jr., John Schlacter, and William Wolfe (1995). "Examining the Bases Utilized for Evaluating Salespeople's Performance, *Journal of Personal Selling & Sales Management*, (15) Fall, 57–65.
8. Stein, David (2007). "Do You Really Measure Performance?" *Sales & Marketing Management*, April, 9.
9. Honeycutt, Earl D., Jr. (2007). Interview Ken Deakman, Slipka-Deakman Associates. Personal interview. Centerville, MN. June 26, 2007.
10. Honeycutt, Earl D., Jr., Tanya Thelen, Shawn T. Thelen, and Sharon K. Hodge (2005). "Impediments to Sales Force Automation," *Industrial Marketing Management*, (34)4, 313–322.
11. Marshall, Greg, John Mowen, and Keith Fabes (1992). "The Impact of Territory Difficulty and Self versus Other Ratings on Managerial Evaluations of Sales Performance," *Journal of Personal Selling & Sales Management*, (12) Fall, 35–48.
12. Leong, Siew Meng, Donna M. Randall, and Joseph A. Cote (1994). "Exploring the Organizational Commitment-Performance Linkage in Marketing: A Study of Life Insurance Salespeople," *Journal of Business Research*, 29:1, 57–63.
13. Jobber, David, and Geoff Lancaster (2000). *Selling and Sales Management*. Harlow, England: Financial Times/Prentice Hall.
14. Hill, John S., and Arthur W. Allaway (1993). "How U.S.-based Companies Manage Sales in Foreign Countries," *Industrial Marketing Management*, (22), 7–16.
15. Hymowitz (2001). Op. cit.
16. Marshall, Mowen, and Fabes (1992). Op. cit.
17. Schwepker, Charles H., Jr., and David J. Good (2004). "Understanding Sales Quotas: An Exploratory Investigation of Consequences of Failure," *The Journal of Business & Industrial Marketing*, (19)1, 39–48.
18. Good, David J., and Charles H. Schwepker, Jr. (2001). "Sales Quotas: Critical Interpretations and Implications," *Review of Business*, (22)1/2. Spring, 32–37.
19. Jackson, Schlacter, and Wolfe (1995). Op. cit.

TRANSFORMING FOR THE FUTURE: CULTURAL FORCES

LEARNING OBJECTIVES

After completing this chapter, you should be able to:

- Define organizational culture.

- List and explain different cultural categories that guide organizations.

- Discuss how culture impacts the sales organization.

- Offer a strategy for modifying a firm's culture.

- Discuss national culture's impact on sales management and personal selling.

- Explain the importance of diversity, and a diverse work environment, to the success of a contemporary sales force.

Culture impacts everything that we do in life. The internal culture of the organization determines what attitudes and behaviors are expected and are rewarded. In healthy firms, internal culture stresses hard work, taking responsibility, and celebrating success. In unhealthy organizations, there is a shortage of personal responsibility and salespersons may wonder why certain people are rewarded and/or given additional responsibility. At the same time external culture greatly influences the expected behavior of a country or society. As more firms enter the global marketplace, managers must understand and operate under diverse cultural environments with both customers and employees.

KARL SHERRILL
Sales Consultant
Senn Dunn,
a Marsh & McLennan
Agency LLC Company

Sales Manager Profile: Karl Sherrill

SENN DUNN, A MARSH & McLENNAN Agency LLC Company, is one of the largest insurance agencies in North Carolina that specializes in business insurance, employee benefits, and personal insurance. Senn Dunn was recently named one of the "Best Employers in North Carolina." Sales Consultant Karl Sherrill states that the firm lives by its core values of collaboration, self-awareness, leadership, engagement, and bringing enthusiasm and energy to the sales role that is so important for the success of its organization. Other important aspects of Senn Dunn's culture include creating a unique work atmosphere for employees—one in which the entrepreneurial spirit is valued and a strong emphasis is placed on community connections.

Sherrill continues, "Senn Dunn has one of the most unique cultures that I have had the pleasure of being a part of. Now I know this is something that people from all organizations can say, but Senn Dunn has a truly unique blend of professional, motivated, and highly competitive sales team members. Yet the team-oriented culture is also strong. We work together to ensure that the customer receives a valuable solution that leads to a sale." The firm is structured to reward collaboration, referrals, and team selling, and assigning accounts to the right person. Senn Dunn also has very high expectations, and makes sure that those who succeed are rewarded. The company is transparent in its actions, which means that information is shared with the sales team—including financial data—to communicate how the firm is progressing toward goals, and to build accountability. Everyone is periodically compared to best-practice metrics in order to help them continually improve.

Sales personnel at Senn Dunn are expected to behave in the following ways:

- **Self-motivation**—The sales team should take an entrepreneurial approach with its customers, and with the internal service team.

- **Initiative**—Own an initiative, and act to improve things.

- **Compassion**—Care about relationships with co-workers.

- **Community**—Be involved and active in what you are passionate about, and the company will support you.

- **Respect**—Always look for a solution, rather than citing reasons you can't or stating that it will be hard to do.

- **Critical Thinking**—Think on your own, and take action—based on reason.

- **Responsibility**—Take ownership of tasks.

- **Optimism**—View opportunities positively.

- **Learning**—Pursue certifications, further education, and continuous improvement.

- **Best in Class**—More than 85 percent of sales team members hold advanced degrees and/or multiple certifications in their respective areas of expertise.

Senn Dunn holds ceremonies to celebrate success; these include "Monday Morning Meetings," during which sales team members share their victories from the previous week, and these accomplishments are applauded and celebrated.

At the same meetings, sales members discuss new opportunities, and team members offer advice and help with their contacts. Music is played at the beginning of each meeting to set the "mood," and sales personnel always close the meeting with a renewed motivation to go out and do their best. There is also an annual sales banquet, to which spouses and significant others are invited. Sales team members are recognized for their contributions: Top Sales, Consultant of the Year, Sales Contest Winners, etc.—and spouses are likewise thanked for their contributions to the team's success. Lastly, Senn Dunn offers sales trips that require accomplishment of sales benchmarks to win. These trips provide a time of rest, relaxation, and celebration for the salesperson, his/her spouse or partner, and other sales team members. The CEO leads all meetings, sharing stories of success and dedication that Senn Dunn "heroes" have made to the firm's success over the years.

Karl Sherrill concludes that it is critical not to underestimate the importance of organizational culture. "While culture may be hard to define, when you find a culture that fits you and your skill set, you will be set for greater success in both your personal and professional life. But the opposite can be true, as well." ■

As you will learn in this chapter, firms like Senn Dunn take symbolic and substantive actions to communicate and reinforce their culture to their employees. **Culture** refers to traditions and beliefs held by people. The role that culture plays in the business world continues to expand as global trade, cross-cultural selling, and the diversity of buyers and employees increases. Sales managers and salespeople must understand this impact. The composition of the U.S. workplace is changing rapidly, too, to include workers from diverse backgrounds. If organizations are to succeed in the future, the diversity that exists in day-to-day life must be reflected in their sales forces. The goal of this chapter is to explain how culture—both internal and external to the firm—impacts the way sales forces operate, and how people's cultural beliefs and practices influence their alliances, customer relationships, and management practices.

How the Corporate Culture of a Firm Affects Its Sales Force

A firm's **corporate culture** is characterized by the beliefs, attitudes, values, assumptions, and ways of doing things that the company's members share and pass on to new members.[1] A company's corporate culture influences:

- the firm's ethical standards and policies;
- the firm's attitudes toward diversity and multiculturalism;
- how the firm's managers and employees communicate and behave;
- the tone of the work environment; and
- the stories employees tell about the firm's successes and failures.[2]

Corporate culture has also been described as "the water in the fishbowl of any business"[3] because salespersons are immersed in, and operate within it—but most are unaware of the culture until something changes.

The Firm's Marketplace Orientation

The ways organizations operate, and the corporate cultures that result from them, are often manifested by an organization's marketplace orientation.[4] A firm's marketplace orientation may evolve in ways that reflect its founders' values, its initial product offerings, its geographic locale, or its competitive environment. There are five basic orientations a company may assume: a production, product, sales, marketing, or relationship orientation.

Production-oriented firms are most concerned with mass-producing goods at low prices to achieve economies of scale. This approach allows a firm to offer a limited number of lower-priced products at multiple locations. As a functional area of the production-oriented firm, sales managers may not be consulted when product or pricing decisions are made; rather, production and financial executives make the major business decisions. In a production-oriented firm, the sales function is more of an afterthought, because management views the primary role of sales to be communicating product availability to potential customers, allocating scarce resources when necessary, and taking/processing buyer orders. Production-oriented firms seem to work best when demand for the product exceeds supply.

A **product-oriented** company focuses on the newest technology or latest product feature. Sometimes called the "better mousetrap syndrome," it drives the firm to make continual upgrades, and to differentiate its products from those of its competitors. In product-oriented firms, engineering and research and development (R&D) are accorded superior status, and the firm focuses on the product, rather than the buyer. The role of the sales force is to notify buyers of the latest product model release, and to communicate to the customer the product's superiority over competitive products.

When supply exceeds demand, which is often the case, some firms adopt a **sales-oriented** approach to the marketplace. For example, when multiple competitors enter the marketplace and there are insignificant differences between product offerings, customers may see few differences beyond price. Many firms believe that the best way to keep sales levels high is to hire a sales force that puts sales before marketing. In a sales-oriented firm, salespersons are expected to convince buyers about the superiority of available products. While a firm's sales focus is important, when carried to an extreme, salespersons may utilize high-pressure sales behavior, and company executives believe that, when sales levels dip below forecasts, the sales force is not doing its job! Upper management may practice a "carrot and stick" management style, offering rewards for meeting numbers and meting out punishment—or dismissal—when desired sales levels are not reached!

Companies that adhere to a **market-oriented** approach pursue a marketing management strategy that is directed at the twin goals of buyer satisfaction and firm profitability. Market-oriented firms develop a culture that embraces awareness of, and learning about, customers, suppliers, and partners. The sales force is viewed as being a major part of the overall marketing strategy. Sales team members are expected to uncover buyer needs that can be profitably satisfied by purchasing company products. Lastly, salesperson evaluation metrics include a measure of buyer satisfaction.

More recently firms have started to practice a **relationship marketing-oriented** view, in which the marketing orientation is extended to a long-term relationship—building trust and seeking to make business interactions "win-win." Salespersons are expected to fully understand buyers' needs, and to act as consultants to produce satisfied customers in ways that increase profitability for both buyers and sellers. That is, the salesperson's goal is to add value to the relationship from the buyer's perspective.[5] Sellers who don't pursue a customer-centric sales approach may be reduced to competing on price.[6]

It is important to understand that each firm's philosophy may be the appropriate orientation for its marketplace. For example, in many developing markets today, consumers are more interested in purchasing high-quality items at affordable prices. However, in more developed economies, buyers expect more customized solutions to their problems, and have the economic power to purchase such solutions. The problem arises for firms when the marketplace environment changes, and their strategy and/or their internal firm culture fail to match the needs of the marketplace.

When a firm's organizational culture aligns with its marketplace strategy, sales managers and the sales force are more likely to succeed. Also, experts estimate that about 30 percent of salespersons fail to meet sales expectations, and their performance levels drop, because of a misalignment between internal culture and marketplace realities.[7]

Low- versus High-Performance Cultures

A company's culture determines how it responds to problems—both inside and outside the organization. The external marketplace is addressed through the company's vision, mission statement, strategies, and metrics that are selected to define success. A firm's internal culture determines how power and status are bestowed, resources are allocated, group membership is determined, and policies adopted for understanding and managing uncontrollable external forces. In turn, a firm's corporate culture guides the behavior of its employees, salespeople, and new hires by influencing how they conduct business with the company's customers.[8]

Behavior that is culturally sanctioned thrives and is rewarded; whereas, unapproved cultural behavior is frowned upon, or even punished. Internal cohesion is achieved via a system of informal rules and peer pressure that shapes the behavior of the firm's employees.[9] As a result, the sales force feels better about its work, cooperates as a team, and sustains its behavior. A firm's culture also determines how it adapts to changes in the external marketplace—for example, how the company responds to the changing needs of buyers, or to competitors' actions.

A firm's culture can be weak or strong, and revolves around the amount of agreement among workers about specific values and procedures. As seen in Exhibit 15.1, when a firm has a strong culture, this signals a widespread agreement about key norms and values—as practiced by Senn Dunn and discussed at the beginning of the chapter. Conversely, a firm with a weak internal culture lacks consensus about what is important, and firm culture has little meaning for sales managers and salespersons. An environment defined by weak values results in negative behavior that may include gossiping, manipulation, favoritism, communication breakdown, and dysfunctional internal competition. An excellent example of a firm that lacked a sense of unity between management and workers was the energy giant Enron, which went bankrupt.

EXHIBIT 15.1   The Characteristics of Low-Performing versus High-Performing Corporate Cultures

Low-Performing Cultures	High-Performing Cultures
Are inward-thinking	Are people-oriented
Are resistant to change	Are results-oriented
Are characterized by a politicized environment	Stress achievement and excellence
Exhibit unhealthy performance practices	Reinforce the firm's cultural beliefs

LOW-PERFORMANCE CULTURES Firms with weak cultures are associated with lower financial performance and exhibit a number of unhealthy characteristics that include:

- **Insular thinking**: Members are inward thinking, believe all answers for new problems reside within the firm, and avoid looking outside the firm for best practices. Managers, at any level, may behave arrogantly.

- **Resistance to change:** There is a desire to maintain the status quo. There is little support for new ideas, and leadership discourages change.

- **Politicized internal environment:** Issues or problems are resolved based upon the individual power of managers and executives. Rather than doing what is best for the firm, decisions are based upon what is best for individual managers.

- **Unhealthy promotion practices:** Promotions are made without serious consideration for the job demands, skills, and appointee capabilities. A hard-working or long-serving salesperson may be promoted into a managerial position, even without having voiced or shown long-range vision or ability to create a new culture.

When Bill George assumed the top spot at Medtronic, he inherited a corporate culture that was extremely value-centered, but was plagued by lack of accountability, excessive concern about consensus, and conflict avoidance. George knew that most "old-timers" at Medtronic felt that the firm was successful, believing there was no reason to change their culture. In contrast, George knew that a cultural shift had to occur, or Medtronic would lose out to more aggressive competitors that had coordinated their internal cultures and external strategies.[10]

HIGH-PERFORMANCE CULTURES By contrast, companies with strong corporate cultures are more likely to report higher financial performance. Strong corporate culture tends to be associated with healthy cultural attributes, including:

- **People-oriented:** Workers are treated with respect and achievements are celebrated. A full-range of rewards and punishments are employed to enforce high-performance standards, and managers at all levels are held responsible for developing workers under their care.

- **Results-oriented:** Workers who excel are identified and rewarded; control systems are developed to collect, analyze, and interpret performance; and sales managers/salespersons who do not meet standards are replaced.

- **Stress on achievement and excellence:** Salespersons feel a constructive pressure to be the best; sales managers pursue programs that motivate workers to perform at their highest levels; and excellence links cultural metrics to performance measures.

- **Reinforcement of cultural beliefs:** High-performance firms use ceremonies, symbols, language, and policy to gain superior results—even from average workers. Slogans are utilized to communicate the firm's values. The managerial practices of recruitment, selection, and training differ significantly from those of low-performance companies.

At Medtronic, Bill George learned that sales goals were routinely missed, budgets were exceeded, and new products were delayed—all without consequence to responsible managers! The first change George made was "empowering" managers to achieve goals, and holding them responsible for meeting goals.[11] As a result, Medtronic sales and profits increased significantly.

Achieving Internal Alignment

Sales executives realize that culture can be a source of competitive advantage. Firms that successfully align their internal cultures with their external market strategies also report higher levels of sales performance.[12,13] Many firms' sales and marketing efforts lack alignment, and two factors explain the misalignment: economics and culture.[14] First, the sales and marketing areas often compete over how the company's budget is divided, each believing that the other gets too much of the budget. Second, sales and marketing workers tend to exhibit different job cultures. That is, marketers tend to be more analytical, data oriented, and project focused. Sales team members, on the other hand, are action oriented, relationship driven, and short-term focused.[15] More important, perhaps, the two areas of business are judged differently regarding their performance. The sales team is evaluated based on results: closing sales. Conversely, marketers are judged by the programs they propose and success or failure takes much longer to discern. Each group may believe that its contributions are more important than that of other functions.[16] Given these fundamental differences, it is hardly surprising that the marketing and sales areas of the firm find it difficult to work together.[17] Sales and marketing departments often move through a four-stage alignment process, as shown in Exhibit 15.2.

EXHIBIT 15.2   The Stages of Alignment between a Firm's Sales and Marketing Functions

Undefined: Sales and marketing personnel work independently, on their own agendas, with little knowledge of what staff members in the other functional area are doing. There is a duplication of work, and some efforts go undone. Resolving conflicts comprises the bulk of interactions between the groups.

↓

Defined: Sales and marketing establish rules to minimize conflicts. Colleagues in each functional area understand what they are supposed to do, and meetings between the groups reflect this. Sales and marketing work together at trade shows and customer conferences. However, there can be a duplication of efforts.

↓

Aligned: Clear, but flexible, boundaries exist between the two areas. Sales and marketing engage in joint planning and training activities, and confer about sales efforts to the firm's major accounts.

↓

Integrated: As the two functional areas integrate, the boundary lines between them become blurred. Marketers assume joint responsibility for major accounts, and shared evaluation, incentive, and reward metrics are adopted.

Misalignment and Entropy

When there is an alignment gap within an organization, entropy occurs. **Entropy** is the amount of energy employees expend engaging in non-productive activities as a result of this mismatch. Four cultural gaps contribute to entropy:[18]

- **A lack of personal alignment** occurs when gaps exist between individuals' stated values and individuals' behaviors. When sales leaders do not "walk the talk" or demand that the sales team members "do as I say, not as I do," a gap in personal alignment leads to a lack of trust between the sales manager and the sales team.

- **A lack of structural alignment** occurs when gaps exist between stated group values and the rules, regulations, and managerial systems that are in place. For example, if a firm embraces salesperson buyer satisfaction and fails to consider this attribute for annual raises and promotions, the sales team will become cynical and develop a lack of trust in the management system.

- **A lack of values alignment** occurs when incongruence exists between individual personal values and collective group values. To extend the previous buyer satisfaction example, a lack of values alignment exists when a salesperson's drive to provide buyer satisfaction is higher or lower than the overall buyer satisfaction that the group provides. Incongruent individual and collective values lead to role conflict: the salesperson is unable to satisfy the firm's values without violating his or her own.[19]

- **A lack of mission alignment** occurs when the sales team members' objectives fail to align with firm goals, creating a gap. For example, lack of mission alignment exists when a sales firm instructs the sales team to devote time to relationship building, but sales force members ignore that objective and continue to sell the products that maximize their commission incomes. Mission alignment gaps lead to poor focus, a lack of clarity, and reduced engagement, and all detract from a sales manager's ability to channel the sales team in a unified direction.

When a firm experiences cultural entropy, managers have two choices—change the sales strategy to fit the culture, or alter the firm's culture to fit the sales strategy. For example, when Hewlett-Packard (HP) adopted a customer-centric sales approach, CEO Mark Hurd introduced HP's Total Customer Experience—a program that focused on customer satisfaction and that measured a number of satisfaction components, including promise fulfillment, follow-up, and customer support levels. The new customer-oriented goals and firm orientation required HP to undergo a cultural shift.[20]

Sales Managers as Culture Creators

Modifying a firm's culture so that it aligns is a difficult undertaking for any manager.[21] There are several actions a sales manager can take to create a strong, high-performing culture that encourages internal unity and builds an ability to adapt to external changes. First, the sales manager must determine which parts of the current culture support the firm's strategy and which do not. It is best when firm members recognize cultural gaps; this can be hastened by holding "mirror workshops,"[22] during which employees are asked to reflect on the current match between corporate culture and behavior. Second, the sales manager must communicate honestly and openly to all workers the cultural areas identified that need to be modified, or whether a completely new culture is required. One expert recommends that managers "shock" their workers with details about major disconnects between corporate goals and employee behavior.[23] Lastly, the sales manager must take visible actions that communicate a transformation of the existing culture.

For example, Dow Corning wanted to move to a more entrepreneurial sales force culture. To make this cultural shift, management determined that the sales force needed time to meet and think creatively. To free up blocks of time for the sales team, management purchased a new CRM system that transferred information to the web and offered virtual ways of sharing information. As a result, the Dow Corning sales team identified and penetrated new accounts they had not previously pursued.[24]

ETHICS IN SALES MANAGEMENT   What Constitutes a Bribe?

What is and what is not ethical behavior varies widely based upon one's culture and the legal system within which one operates. For example, in Japan, a salesperson is expected to give a buyer a gift in order to expand their friendship. However, in the United States, buyers do not expect and are apprehensive about accepting gifts from salepersons. One reason U.S. firms are careful about giving or receiving gifts from current or actual business partners relates to the Foreign Corruption Practices Act (FCPA) of 1977 and 1988. Although the expectation of bribes or "grease" is an accepted tradition in many cultures, the FCPA forbids U.S. firms from paying bribes to receive an order. However, the FCPA does allow an exception to the bribery prohibition that allows payments to be made for routine governmental actions such as permits, documents, utilities, inspections, and other "similar actions." What is significant to understand about cross-cultural sales situations is that in certain cultures, sales representative are expected to offer gifts at appropriate times. When "appropriate" gifts are not offered, the buyer is likely to become offended and break off negotiations.

Managers who endeavor to change firm culture can take two actions: primary (substantive) or secondary (symbolic).[25] **Symbolic actions** communicate shifts in an organization's culture; whereas, **substantive actions** demonstrate that a sales leader is serious about changing the firm's culture. Managers who take symbolic actions communicate the kinds of behavior they are encouraging. For example, the CEO at infoUSA, a company that maintains and sells databases of North American businesses and consumers, takes the symbolic action of meeting regularly with sales and marketing managers to ask for their ideas for business growth.[26] Also, AstraZeneca took both symbolic and substantive actions when one of their sales leader's actions conflicted with the firm's stated cultural beliefs.

A sales manager who wants to encourage customer orientation might symbolically assume responsibility for a major account, while substantively modifying the evaluation criteria for the sales team to include customer satisfaction ratings. A number of actions available to sales managers, as listed in Exhibit 15.3, can be divided into symbolic and substantive categories.

EXHIBIT 15.3   Sales Management Actions that Shape a Firm's Corporate Culture

Symbolic Actions:

- Demonstrate role-model behaviors for the sales force to emulate.
- Hold ceremonies and make special appearances.

Substantive Actions:

- Replace salespeople who are unwilling or unable to accept changes.
- Change dysfunctional policies and practices.
- Realign rewards, incentives, and resource allocations.
- Redesign work spaces.
- Pen a written values statement.

Of course, the changes sales managers make must result in a strategy-culture fit. That is, the sales manager must modify the firm's strategy to fit the company's culture, or change the company's culture to fit the firm's strategy. Otherwise, the gap between culture and strategy will cause entropy and impede strategy execution. In addition, sales managers must modify policies and practices that impede that successful execution. For example, sales managers will provide sales training to ensure that the sales team possesses the skills, knowledge, and attitudes necessary to succeed in the field. Likewise, the sales manager will coordinate with other managers in the firm to ensure that destructive subcultures don't flourish within the accounting, marketing, operations, finance, or engineering groups, and that the firm's credit policies, return policies, and customer service levels, for example, are synchronized with, and support, the firm's sales efforts. In this way, sales managers work to create **internal alignment**. A case in point: When IBM integrated its sales and marketing areas, the move resulted in lower sales costs, reduced market-entry costs, and shorter sales cycles.[27] IBM even went so far as to modify its physical facilities by assigning its sales and marketing departments to a common office space.

Finally, allocation of the firm's rewards, incentives, and resources must be based on the new culture, and a new values statement must be written—clearly stating the new cultural values. For example, Alberto-Culver North America developed a list of ten cultural imperatives: **h**onesty, **o**wnership, **t**rust, **c**ustomer orientation, **c**ommitment, **f**un, **i**nnovation, **r**isk-taking, **s**peed and urgency, and **t**eamwork. After the list of imperatives was agreed upon, one group member suggested the acronym HOT CC FIRST, which made these values easier to remember.[28] Perhaps most important, cultural values must be put into practice at all levels. Otherwise, all the time and money invested in culture change will be in vain.

How External Cultures Affect a Firm's Sales Force

To be successful in the global marketplace, sales organizations and sales managers must understand and work with individuals whose national cultures are characterized by distinct values, norms, and attitudes. One important reason for understanding culture is that, at many small- and medium-sized firms, the sales manager will be tapped to work with international buyers. For example, sales managers must understand that, in the U.S., workers are encouraged to act individually, while in most Asian societies, group business decisions are made. Likewise, it is considered healthy behavior in Western societies to compete for promotions and incentives—but, in other cultures, salespersons are reluctant to compete, because maintaining group harmony takes higher priority.[29]

The increasing level of global business requires that sales managers and salespersons understand cultural differences in order to successfully work together and to prosper. For a variety of reasons, dealing with diverse and divergent values will become a constant challenge for sales managers, since a customer from another culture may appear at any time. The key is to understand cultural differences and take advantage of this broader perspective when proposing managerial solutions.

The likelihood of interpersonal relationships increases when salespersons and managers are sensitive to different cultural practices. For example, when a salesperson approaches a sales meeting with a potential customer from a different culture, with a general understanding of that person's cultural beliefs, the salesperson's words, actions, and body language can be tailored to maximize the potential of successfully interacting with that individual. Understanding culture allows salespersons to minimize cultural *faux pas*, or unintentional errors, that will increase the effectiveness of relationship building through appropriate thoughts, feelings, and behaviors.

When a salesperson interacts with a buyer from a different culture, new knowledge will be learned at each encounter. One becomes **assimilated** when he or she completely absorbs a new culture—which is rare. However, the degree of **acculturation** can vary, based upon the amount of culture learned and accepted by a person. An important point to remember is that the greater the degree of cultural accord existing between the salesperson and the potential buyer, the higher the probability of business success. That is why it is imperative for salespeople and sales managers to understand, and feel comfortable working among, the different levels of culture. Salespersons can be trained and coached to work with clients from different cultural backgrounds.

The Different Levels of Culture

A level of **global culture** appears to be emerging, as consumers worldwide are exposed to movies, cable/satellite television, MTV, and magazines that advertise global brand products. This creates consumers who possess similar knowledge, needs, and wants about the goods they purchase. However, when approaching potential buyers from a distinct culture, it is naïve to assume that they purchase in exactly the same way, and for the same reasons. For example, even though consumers are familiar with, and desire, global brands like Apple, Lexus, and Rolex, they are more likely to purchase these products based upon distinct decision influences and purchase processes that were learned in their home cultures.

National culture is the most important cultural level for salespersons to understand, because it has the greatest impact on buyer behavior. National culture is composed of five distinct dimensions proposed by Geert Hofstede, as seen in Exhibit 15.4, that are common to all countries.[27]

EXHIBIT 15.4   Dimensions of National Culture

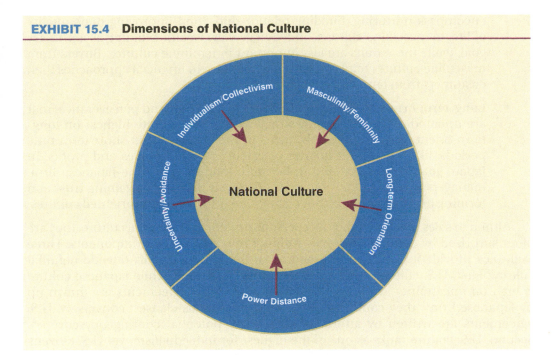

- **Power distance** is the acceptance of unequal power and authority relations in society. Some cultures accept larger power distances between members of society or the organization, impacting buyer-seller relationships and contexts. In other words, some societies view the parties involved in each social interaction as being equal or unequal. The level of power distance defines the roles played by members of that society, particularly salespersons. When dealing with owners, managers, or scientists from Asian and Latin American cultures with large power distances, it is imperative for a salesperson to act respectfully and to use formal titles, unless instructed otherwise.

- **Uncertainty avoidance** defines how threatened society feels by uncertainty and ambiguity. The higher the level of perceived ambiguity, the greater the need for well-defined rules for behavior. In Japan, Greece, and Portugal, details must be clearly stated, and all eventualities prepared for, before proceeding with business. In other cultures, like Singapore, Denmark, or Sweden, there is less concern about uncertainty. For example, in many Asian companies, meetings are held to plan future meetings. In preliminary meetings, lower-level managers agree to a business arrangement, but top executives will sign or ratify the formal agreement at a banquet. Also, buyers from certain cultures are reluctant to change suppliers until they are convinced that the new partner is trustworthy and dependable.

- **Individualism/collectivism** means that some cultures are more group-oriented than others in their decision-making processes. However, individualism is a major influence of U.S. culture, as signified by the choice of an iconic, lone cowboy known as the "Marlboro Man." But, in other cultures, especially in Asia, group cohesion and safety are important aspects of all business decisions. Thus, no manager will make a decision unless the group has been consulted and consensus is reached. There is an old Chinese saying: "The duck that flies out front gets shot down." That provides insight about individualism in China's culture. Buyers from cultures that rate high in collectivism dislike "hard-closing" salespersons.

- **Masculinity/femininity** interpretations mirror traits valued by a society. Masculine traits include strength, success, and confidence. Feminine traits encompass nurturing, building relationships, and improving one's quality of life. In masculine cultures, individuals view wealth-building as a primary goal, while these traits are less important in feminine cultures. Buyers from masculine cultures tend to be more responsive to financial approaches than customers from feminine cultures.

- **Long-term orientation** focuses on virtues, like thrift and perseverance, that are oriented toward future rewards.[31] Asian cultures rate highest on long-term orientation. For example, firms in the U.S. focus on short-term time periods, like the current quarter or calendar year, for sales and profits. In Japan, goals and views tend to be more long-term. In one Japanese firm, managers were asked to prepare a 1,000 year plan! Thus, gaining trust and forming relationships does not occur quickly in long-term-oriented cultures.

Although sales managers and salespersons understand national culture, they are often surprised by cultural dilemmas residing outside the five components. Three examples provide a clearer understanding of behavior that falls outside national culture: First, U.S. culture is low on uncertainty avoidance, while Japanese culture is high on uncertainty avoidance. However, when legal agreements are drawn up by Japanese firms, they contain intentionally ambiguous clauses; conversely, U.S. agreements are written by attorneys, with every potential contingency covered. Second, U.S. culture ranks as one of the highest for individualism, yet U.S. citizens report the greatest rate of philanthropy in the world.[32] Lastly, Japanese culture is rated high in collectivism, but visitors to Japan are surprised to see businessmen on subways, isolated from each others' company during the commute, absorbed in reading magazines that contain nude photos and violent stories. To accurately understand national culture, one must take the specific context of the situation into account.[33]

Local culture is found in geographical regions, cities, and neighborhoods. It, too, influences the behavior of buyers and sellers. For example, when selling to New Yorkers, buyers will likely want a salesperson to quickly state the point of the meeting, so as not to waste their time. By contrast, getting to the point too quickly in traditional southern U.S. culture, without first making small talk, is more likely to be considered acting rudely. Telemarketers who call prospective customers in different regions of the United States learn this cultural practice very quickly!

Cultural Components

To understand culture, a salesperson must consider eight components prior to interacting in buyer-seller meetings:

1. Communication
2. Religion
3. Education
4. Aesthetics
5. Social Organizations
6. Technology
7. Time
8. Values and Norms

Communication Style

A major area of cultural conflict is ineffective communications. That is, to be understood, words and phrases must be clearly communicated. The receiver of the message—the potential buyer—translates words into signs and symbols based upon their *cultural* understanding of what was said. Thus, language allows ideas to be transmitted between the buyer and the seller. Problems with communication are sure to occur unless the sender of the message understands the receiver's culture.

How people communicate varies widely within and between cultures. Across cultures, words and phrases are employed differently. For example in the Philippines, "Yes" can mean: "Yes, I will consider your product," or "Yes, I hear you." Also, members of certain subcultures may speak more loudly, or with more emotion. Think about animated discussions between African-, Jewish-, or Italian-Americans that other Americans view as a sign of hostility or assertiveness, rather than as exciting conversation between friends![34]

CROSS-CULTURAL COMMUNICATION PROBLEMS A number of common communication problems complicate interactions across cultures: carelessness, multiple-meaning words, idioms, and slang. *Carelessness* occurs when the salesperson is not properly prepared and speaks extemporaneously—almost ensuring the likelihood of misspeaking. That is, an unprepared salesperson uses a word not understood by the customer, or makes insensitive remarks. Words can also have *multiple meanings* in different cultures—as with "The motor *runs* smoothly." And a word used in the U.S. may offend someone from another culture: "This is a *badass* machine." Third, *idioms* are words that have no literal translation. If a salesperson was to say: "Our product is the Cadillac of the industry," "It is raining cats and dogs," or "I'm under the weather," such phrases have no translatable meaning to someone from another culture. Likewise, "comparing apples and oranges" is a common sales metaphor that can be translated literally by a buyer who has yet to master the American lexicon. Lastly, there is *slang*. An example occurs when a buyer asks the seller, "What's the *damage* for the product?" meaning how much does the product cost? When salespersons employ careless words, or use inappropriate words, idioms, or slang, they generate *noise* that reduces the efficiency of communication between individuals from different cultures.

A salesperson must understand and consider other differences when engaging in cross-cultural communications:

- **Tone of voice** refers to loudness, tone, and clarity of response. In certain subcultures, bargaining between buyer and seller is loud and emotional. Conversely, most Asian cultures perceive loud and emotional discussions to be inappropriate.

- **Timing of response** is the length of time one takes to consider the question asked. In the U.S., waiting too long to respond may be considered a sign of dishonesty; however, people from Asian cultures generally pause and reflect on an issue before responding.

- **Interruptions** in Asian cultures are, in general, regarded as rude, while French, Italian, and Middle Eastern cultures are comfortable when multiple persons talk at once, interrupting each other at will.

- **Degree of directness** varies. Asians, Hispanics, and East Indians soften negative responses. Japanese buyers may ask a question, rather than answer "no." In contrast, most mainline Americans believe that business discussions should be direct, with no holds barred.

- **Degree of embellishment** can vary from reserved in American culture to flowery and artistic in Italian or Middle Eastern cultures.

A key when communicating with someone who has been acculturated or raised in another culture is *not* to breach the rules of etiquette. In such circumstances, it is best for the seller to mirror the buyer's communications behavior. If the buyer speaks slowly, listens intently, is less direct, and does not embellish, the seller should mirror the presentation to the buyer's communication pattern.

Also, cross-cultural communications can differ, depending upon the directness of the words. In **low-context cultures**, including that of the U.S., words are used exclusively to communicate what is meant. If something is left unstated, the receiver of the message does not necessarily assume that they should read between the lines. In **high-context cultures**, found predominantly in Asia and the Middle East, details and specifics are often left unsaid; the recipient must gain insight through nonverbal communications.

When humans communicate nonverbally, the unstated is often as important as, or more important than, what is orally communicated. Nonverbal communications are, therefore, important for both the buyer and seller:

- **Appearance standards** vary, and different cultures have distinct expectations about facial hair and attire that includes formality of dress. Europeans tend to dress more formally than do Americans.

- **Posture** involves sitting, standing, and offering someone a seat. In Asian culture, a person of lesser status does not tower over, or turn his or her back on, a superior. In low power-distance societies, like those in Scandinavia, such actions are viewed as less significant.

- **Space/distance** refers to the physical distance between the customer and the salesperson. Americans generally prefer a larger "zone of comfort" around their bodies than do Latin Americans. Middle Eastern males and Hispanics operate in spaces of 0-18 inches; mainstream Americans and Western Europeans feel comfortable in zones of 18 inches to three feet; and Asians generally prefer a space of three feet or greater.

- **Sense of smell** refers to body odors and colognes/perfumes. In certain cultures, strong body odor is accepted; in other cultures, body odors are viewed as being offensive. In cultures that perceive odors to be offensive, cologne and perfumes are consumed.

- **Hand gestures** can mean something other than intended. The "O.K." sign, common in the U.S., is considered offensive in most European nations. Use of the left hand is not recommended when conducting business or eating with customers from Arab nations.

- **Handshakes** by Americans are firm—in comparison to a soft handshake by the British or a frequently repeated, moderate grasp by Hispanics.

- **Physical contact** by touching in most Asian nations is seldom observed, and almost never on the head. In Spanish cultures, friends touch constantly.

- **Eye contact** that is prolonged or direct is considered aggressive in some cultures, while it is a sign of honesty in others.

- **Body angles** refer to how people position themselves in relationship to others. For example, in Japan, the person with the least status—such as the salesperson—bows lower than the buyer. Again, one should never turn one's back on, or tower over, a superior in Asia.

Nonverbal signals between the buyer and the seller are helpful in determining what has been communicated. Unfortunately, body language is not universal around the world! Eye contact is a good example of how body language can be confusing. For example, if a buyer from Asia does not maintain eye contact when speaking with a salesperson, it may be that the buyer is: (1) not understanding what is being said, or (2) showing respect by not making direct eye contact with the seller.

There is little doubt that the more aware and educated salespersons are about verbal and nonverbal customer communications, the fewer mistakes they will make. The goal in all sales encounters is to *avoid* words or actions the customer might perceive to be offensive or inappropriate. Once you offend a customer, even unintentionally, it can be very difficult and expensive to repair the damage. Also, nonverbal communication missteps reduce the likelihood that negotiators will accurately understand their similarities and differences.[35] By understanding nonverbal communications, the seller can not only better comprehend what the buyer says, but also know what the buyer means! A great example of nonverbal communication is provided in the "Global Sales Management" box.

GLOBAL SALES MANAGEMENT   Understanding the Indian Headshake

The ways in which an Indian shakes his or her head when talking is a source of confusion for most foreigners. That is, when an Indian speaks, his or her head often wobbles or bobbles from side-to-side, and can mean: "Yes," "Good," "O.K.," "Keep going," or "I understand," depending upon what is being said. The wobble, or headshake, also varies by speed, height, and intensity. For example, when asked if the train is going to a specific city, there is a strong likelihood the person will respond by shaking their head side-to-side to communicate "Yes." In Western cultures, a person might respond to a similar question by nodding. When asked, Indians explain that: (1) those in their country shake their heads unconsciously; (2) people in the south shake their heads more than those in the north; and (3) the headshake may be used to say "No," when a person prefers not to articulate a negative. What appears evident is that many Indian citizens do shake their heads when communicating, and—whether consciously or unconsciously—these head movements are a form of nonverbal communication. For foreigners conducting business in India, communication is improved by gaining a basic understanding of the Indian headshake.

William Kremer, "#BBCtrending: The Indian headshake decoded," (2014). BBC Trending, February 28, 2014. Accessed March 1, 2014. http://www.bbc.com/news/blogs-trending-26390944.

Religion

Religious beliefs have an important bearing on personal actions. One's religious beliefs influence what one drinks and eats, the hours or days available for work, and how one interacts with salespersons, co-workers, and members of other genders. This means that a Muslim or Jewish customer observes or celebrates different holidays than do Christian salespersons. For example, one well-intentioned Christian salesperson sent a *Kwanzaa* card to a Jewish buyer, unintentionally trying to acknowledge *Chanukah* with greetings and images designed to celebrate African heritage in African-American culture. Also, buyers who consume only specific foods and drinks due to their religious beliefs will need to be taken to restaurants that offer choices of vegetarian and Kosher items.

Education

In some cultures, it is difficult for a salesperson to be accepted unless he or she possesses a similar level of education to that of the buyer. This is because education, social class, and occupation are mutually intertwined in most cultures.[36] Customers from certain cultural backgrounds expect salespersons to be their peers in level of education, so that complex issues can be discussed

Photo Credit: Aleksandr Sadkov / Shutterstock.com

Buyers from different cultures likely share different beliefs than salespersons, and these beliefs can impact what and how they purchase.

and potential solutions can be offered. For example, a German-born researcher at a prestigious institution refused to speak with salespeople who had not earned the Ph.D. in chemistry. This is because, in many cultures, a comparable level of education infers that the person has equal status and is knowledgeable of correct social behavior. Likewise, if your buyer holds an engineering or a business degree, it would be easier to discuss technical specifications and cost-benefit analyses. If you sell to cross-cultural customers, you should consider earning a certified sales designation and ensure that your degree (M.B.A, B.S. in engineering)—if it is relevant—and your certifications are clearly noted on your business cards.

Aesthetics

Each culture perceives different objects to be beautiful and visually appealing. Thus, how one dresses, how artwork is appreciated, and how food is presented are impacted by one's culture. If a salesperson is asked to make a sales presentation or develop sales promotional materials, cultural aesthetics like colors and shapes should be carefully considered. For example, several U.S. firms placed the flag of Saudi Arabia on products and advertisements, only to learn that *Allah* had been blasphemed by displaying a quote from the Koran that is found on the Saudi Arabian flag. This means that colors, styles, and shapes must be carefully considered before making a presentation or printing proposals that could offend the potential customer. For example, in Asian countries, white is the primary funeral color, while gold and yellow colors connote wealth, authority, and longevity.[37]

In presentations, advertisements, and paperwork, salespersons need to understand that colors, shapes, and what is beautiful and appealing vary tremendously from culture to culture.

Social Organizations

Social organizations include groups to which the individual belongs in a society. These associations include the family, community groups, special-interest groups, and work groups. Again, groups are most important in cultures that rate high on collectivism. Difficulties can also arise when a salesperson from a blue-collar area calls upon primarily white-collar customers. When this happens, the words used and social graces employed can severely strain a potential working relationship. This means that buyers from certain cultures will only purchase from salespersons that have been accepted into their inner circle.

Technology

It is important for the salesperson to understand the technological sophistication and limitations of potential customers. In many corporations today, engineers who occupy technical positions within global firms have emigrated from other nations. To improve the chances of sales success, it is important for salespersons to possess at least a similar level of technological expertise as the customer. An example of this might be a computer salesperson calling on an engineer buyer who has more expertise about computers. Moreover, some cultures favor hard work over modern conveniences, and the introduction of technically advanced products may be viewed as unnecessary luxuries. Many immigrants from Asian or Eastern European countries expect to work long and hard hours to succeed, and may not be impressed by the latest electronics.

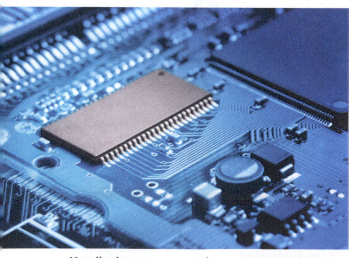

Not all cultures are enamored by technological gadgets like U.S. firms and their sales representatives.

Time

The observation of time varies by culture. For example, some cultures focus on the past (talking about history, family origin, business, and nation), the present (focusing on activities and enjoyment of the moment), and the future (looking ahead toward prospects, aspirations, and desired achievements). Salespersons can use time values to emphasize history, tradition, or cultural heritage as evidence of potential for past- and present-oriented firms. Likewise, emphasizing the opportunity for future greatness works well with future-oriented buyers.

In modern cultures with efficient transportation systems, it is important to arrive promptly for appointed meetings. Otherwise, the cultural affront of late arrival may be difficult to overcome. However, in less-developed cultures, time is viewed more relatively. This means the customer is less concerned about time, and the salesperson must be adaptable and understanding when the customer forgets appointments, or arrives late at the office. For example, a salesperson was surprised, when arriving early for an appointment with a Panamanian-born customer, to learn that her buyer was still out for lunch and wasn't expected back for at least half an hour.

This cultural component can also include the time needed for getting to know the customer, for salesperson and customer to learn to trust one another, and for the customer to make purchase decisions. For example, female Hispanic business owners take a longer time period to make decisions, so the salesperson must be patient and wait. And minorities may take longer to make decisions, but pass on more referrals. Thus, salespersons may need to make additional calls on minority decision makers before attempting to close![38] Also, Italian business managers are likely to spend considerable time on small talk at sales meetings, however, Scandinavians prefer a short, formal introduction, immediately followed by the business discussion.[39]

Values and Norms

All cultures have rules or norms of acceptable and unacceptable behavior, which can include:[40]

- hard work, as opposed to relaxation or leisure;
- egalitarian, as compared to patriarchal, decision making;
- conservatism, in contrast to liberalism;
- female submissiveness, versus female assertiveness;
- ethnocentrism, as opposed to polycentrism; and
- youthfulness, in contrast to maturity.

Salespersons need to be sensitive to the distinct values and norms practiced by buyers from different cultures. In general, a number of cultures view female salespersons to be less credible. This means that customers from the Middle East or certain Asian cultures may have more difficulty interacting with female sales representatives. For example, in Japan, there is a saying: "Women are like the air, absolutely essential, but they should remain invisible." However, research shows that U.S. female expatriates are just as successful as their male counterparts overseas, even in male-dominated cultures like Korea and Japan.[41]

Many cultures view their way of doing business as being the only way (ethnocentrism), rather than as one of many ways of conducting commerce (polycentrism). Buyers and sellers who are **ethnocentric** are more rigid, while those who are **polycentric** are more flexible in

Sales managers today know that to sell to a more diverse customer base, they need a diverse sales force.

their business dealings. A form of **corporate ethnocentrism** also exists within very large firms, so that sellers are expected to adopt the Walmart, Microsoft, or General Motors way of doing things.

ETHNOCENTRISM Ethnocentrism has many meanings that suggest that other cultures should think, act, and behave as we do—or they are going about things in the wrong way. Many mainline Americans interpret the actions of others through their own cultural ethnocentric lenses. Thus, it is important for all of us to acknowledge that we must understand ourselves in order to truly come to know others' cultures.

One major problem caused by ethnocentrism occurs when we try to interpret the actions of others in the context of our own culture. For example, mainline American culture suggests that someone who is being untruthful will not look the other person directly in the eyes. However, in Asian cultures, a common cultural belief is that it is disrespectful to look at someone, especially a superior, directly in the eyes for an extended period of time. When we evaluate the behavior of others based upon what we know, we use a **self-reference criterion**. The self-reference criterion through which we evaluate others comes from the perspective of our own customs, institutions, and ways of thinking. Thus, we evaluate others based upon what we have learned, and come to believe is true, in our culture. As you might expect, this leads to many misunderstandings.

It is understandable to prefer one's own cultural practices, but potential problems arise when we distort what we see in our relations with others. This is especially true for salespersons who are calling upon buyers from other cultures; as a result of our ethnocentrism, we may misinterpret what is said, or left unsaid. For example, in the U.S., it is considered "normal" to become friends quickly and share intimate details of our lives with our new friends. In other cultures, however, friendships are formed very slowly, and attempting to form a new friendship so casually is viewed as being frivolous, or even rude!

So, given that clinging to our ethnocentric views can lead to trouble, why do we continue to gauge the actions of others through our tinted glasses? There are several explanations for this human behavior. First, it is comforting to believe that we can understand the behavior of others by comparing them to values we trust and cherish. Second, if we admit that our views are not universal, we also acknowledge there is more we need to learn about others. Finally, this leads to a conclusion that our methods of coping do not work in a culturally diverse marketplace.

How does one overcome ethnocentrism? The first way to reduce ethnocentrism is to learn about other cultures—that is, learning to recognize and understand the values that motivate people from different cultures to behave the way they do. With this knowledge, it becomes easier to apply what you have learned to future sales situations you encounter. This awareness allows you to understand why an Asian- or African-American buyer takes longer to form a relationship, rather than prematurely dismissing the potential customer as someone who is not ready to commit to a relationship with you and your company. A second way to overcome ethnocentrism is to become more aware of the beliefs that can distort your perceptions and cause you to misinterpret your customers. In effect, learning about your own cultural beliefs allows you to compensate for the incorrect analysis that we engage in when we encounter behavior influenced by another culture.

Managing the Global Sales Force

As the forces of globalization expand the scope of international marketing and commerce, sales managers find themselves supervising salespersons from different cultures who reside around the globe. For example, a U.S. firm might be headquartered in New Jersey, with branch offices located in London, Paris, Berlin, Delhi, Singapore,

Shanghai, and Tokyo. As discussed in the first section of this chapter, aligning a firm's internal culture with the marketplace is not easy. Operating in multiple locations, with managers and salespersons representing myriad cultures, makes it difficult to employ a single system or process to supervise salespersons. This is due to different behaviors and motivations that exist in countries and cultures. Even with diverse personnel and practices, sales managers are expected to supervise diverse sales forces from afar with expertise and aplomb. This section presents major differences that arise when sales managers are called upon to design, select, train, motivate, compensate, and evaluate a global sales force.

Designing the Global Sales Force

Sales managers must initially base their decisions on how best to organize a global sales force by understanding the needs of current and potential customers, the targeted market, competitors, and the firm's strengths and resources. Although these criteria mirror the information used to design the sales force in the home market, sales managers must decide whether it would be more beneficial to employ expatriates, local hires, or third-country salespersons to work in global locations. Each category of salesperson offers advantages and disadvantages for the global sales force.

Expatriate salespersons move from the home country to an overseas location. An example would be a British citizen who worked for a British firm and was reassigned to San José, Costa Rica, to oversee sales efforts in that Central American nation. The benefit of employing an expatriate salesperson in a foreign market is the expatriate's knowledge of the product line and familiarity with company policies. The major disadvantage is the expatriate's lack of culture/market knowledge and cost. The vice president of Coca-Cola Japan stated that the cost of assigning and maintaining his presence in Tokyo in the early 2000s exceeded more than $1 million annually. **Local-hire salespersons** are individuals who live in the country where business is conducted. For example, Procter & Gamble could hire a salesperson from Shanghai, China, to work in the local marketplace. Advantages of local salespersons include lower costs and higher cultural and market knowledge. Disadvantages include lower product and company knowledge. The final category of salesperson working in a global marketplace is a **third-country salesperson**, or an individual who was born outside both the firm's home and the targeted markets. For example, a Japanese firm might hire a salesperson from the Philippines to work in Singapore. Third-country salespersons normally possess a higher level of understanding of the marketplace and culture than do expatriates, and are willing to work for a lower salary. Disadvantages of third-country salespersons include less influence with the home office and potential burnout from working overseas for extended periods.

A few generalizations can be made in regard to designing and entering overseas sales territories. When establishing new territories in emerging markets that are undeveloped and small in sales volume, firms often partner with local sales firms to handle their product lines. Partners save the external company money because they know and are known in the marketplace. If the marketplace is large enough to sustain a company sales force, a firm may begin with a geographical organization that utilizes a general salesperson to sell a narrow product line. However, as the market grows, or if different cultures/languages are spoken, the sales organization must be reorganized as a product or market sales force to match different buyer needs.[42]

Because of different cultural practices, the way personal selling is organized has to match local expectations.[43] For example, automobiles have been sold door-to-door in Japan for decades, and Russian banks recently assigned salespersons to sell credit in appliance stores. Also, at one point, more than 100,000 citizens in Singapore participated in multilevel marketing product sales.[44]

Selecting Sales Personnel

In global sales situations, the attributes of an effective salesperson may rival those of a diplomat. Therefore, it is essential for sales managers to precisely define what they are seeking in a global salesperson. Attributes that come to mind include maturity, flexibility, breadth of knowledge, cultural empathy, and a positive outlook. Most of these skills and attitudes can be assessed during the personal interview, and during role-playing exercises. The few studies that have been conducted in the hiring of global salespersons suggest that selection criteria should be localized.[45] A major problem encountered by global firms is that, in many cultures, sales is not viewed as a professional occupation. As a result, fewer highly qualified individuals will apply for sales positions.

In the United States, sales applicants are expected to sell themselves during the personal interview. When U.S. sales managers conduct a personal interview with a candidate from another culture and expect the applicant to ask for the job, they are likely to be disappointed. This is because, in many cultures, the applicant only speaks when the interviewer asks a direct question. Secondly, the applicant may not make or maintain direct eye contact with the interviewer. As stated earlier in this chapter, staring at strangers may be viewed as an aggressive act.

Hiring mistakes are extremely costly in international sales situations. When a global salesperson does not work out, hundreds of thousands of dollars, and significant amounts of time, are wasted. Recent research found that a manager's cultural knowledge affects personnel decisions. That is, given identical personnel information, German and Austrian managers were more likely to hire compatriots than were Italian managers.[46] This finding suggests the need for additional research to be conducted to improve our understanding of global hiring practices.

Training Global Salespeople

International sales training can be either standardized or localized. That is, when a local or third-country salesperson is hired, sales training must provide them with product knowledge, company information, and sales skills. Even after receiving training, it is common for local salespersons to cling to local culture—as is seen today in China and Russia.[47] Trainers must also employ different instructional methods when teaching sales methods in other cultures. For example, U.S. trainers observed that Japanese trainees would not voluntarily respond to questions addressed to the entire class, for fear of being labeled a "show-off." However, when asked directly, the Japanese trainees would answer, so as not to embarrass their American trainers.[48] For expatriates who are selected to sell in an overseas market, their training must focus on understanding culture and special sales problems.

Technology now allows global sales forces to be trained more efficiently. Sales personnel can study modules on the Internet and then complete an interactive assessment test. Sun Microsystems states that employing the Internet can shorten training time by up to 75 percent. Also, in nations where there are limited communications systems, firms have adopted CD-ROM-based training approaches.[49] Technology is best used to transfer standardized information, such as product information, while it is more appropriate to localize, and personally teach, sales techniques.[50]

Motivating Global Sales Personnel

Devising a motivation system for global sales personnel is complicated by the presence of distinct cultures, sources, and philosophies.[51] Global sales managers and salespersons work hard and, like all personnel, experience frustrations with traveling, interacting with buyers from other cultures, and being away from their families. No matter—the global salesperson must remain motivated to perform at high levels. It is important, therefore, that a firm's motivation system be designed for global sales personnel based upon their national culture.

Recall earlier when we discussed Hofstede's components of national culture. A major difference between sales personnel in different cultures can be observed in the individualism/collectivism component of national culture. In the United States, firms motivate salespersons by appealing to their individual desire to work hard and succeed. As a result, Western companies focus on individual pay systems and rewards to motivate their sales personnel. In Asian cultures, however, collectivism or group orientation plays a major role, and a willingness to compete against one's peers is less acceptable. As a result, most Asian salespersons are paid a straight salary, and can earn bonuses for group achievements. Individual commission systems are rarely implemented in collectivist cultures.

The opportunity for advancement with the company is also a motivating factor. Therefore, it is important for global sales personnel and managers to understand that success in the current job will lead to an attractive position within the firm, once an overseas assignment is completed. For example, in 2007, the consumer goods giant Unilever slashed 20,000 employees from its ranks worldwide. As a result, salespersons began wondering, "Where have all the sales jobs gone?" Unilever was in a quandary about how to implement the needed personnel cuts while keeping their managers and salespersons motivated.[52] It is also wise for headquarters to communicate with global sales managers and to seek their input about decisions that will affect them. Nearly all managers feel more motivated when they believe they are well-informed and that the executives consider their opinions to be important. However, in global sales, the forces of language, culture, and communication styles can complicate effective communication between managers and sales reps.[53]

Compensating Global Sales Personnel

Because global firms operate in multiple locations, it is nearly impossible to offer a single compensation that is fair, balanced, and flexible. As a result, compensations plans for American companies vary widely.[54] Most, if not all, salespersons and sales managers expect to receive a higher salary in overseas posts than they make in the United States. One important reason that expatriates receive higher salaries is that they often have to maintain two homes or places of residence—one in the location abroad, and another in the home country. Global firms realize that it is important for the expatriates to receive a salary that reflects their new responsibility, allows the family to live comfortably in a secure area of the assigned country, and permits the expatriate to entertain local employees and customers.

However, the firm incurs a number of additional expenses that include international schools for the expatriates' children, annual vacation travel to the United States, helping the expatriate maintain their U.S. homes, and providing added security in certain overseas locations. In contrast, European sales managers receive higher benefits and deferred compensation in their salary packages.[55]

Evaluating Global Sales Personnel

In many overseas markets, the sales force is evaluated based upon its performance as a team, rather than as individuals. In contrast, most U.S. sales personnel are given quotas and then they are evaluated based upon their performance, compared to expected performance. As a result of this difference in sales situations, global sales managers must accompany the salesperson on sales calls to observe their performance and seek inputs from buyers, other salespersons, and supervisors. Unlike U.S. sales managers, global sales managers may view individual performance measures to be less important.

In one study that contrasted U.S. and Japanese sales managers' evaluations of their salespersons, using the same performance scales, American sales managers rated most of their sales staff in the middle of the scale, with a few high performers and no low performers. Japanese sales managers, on the other hand, rated their sales team along a normally distributed curve; a few high, a few low, and most salespersons placed in the center of the scale. What is instructive from this study is that poorly performing U.S. sales personnel are forced to leave the firm—either voluntarily or involuntarily. In Japan, firms continue to employ low-performing sales personnel. A problem for Japanese sales managers, not faced by most U.S. sales managers, is how to motivate poor performers.[56]

Lastly, domestic sales managers often have trouble understanding expatriate situations or accurately measuring their contributions to the organization. Until recently, the physical distances between sales manager and expatriates made direct communication difficult. This problem has been minimized by the development of affordable telephone services, e-mail, instant messaging, Skype, and company CRM systems. Even with greater sources of information, firms still measure expatriate success using "easy" criteria like profitability, productivity, and/or market share, rather than considering each expatriate's full range of responsibility. Thus, especially in global sales situations, different sales goals require different assessment criteria.[57]

Changing Demographics in the Sales Force

The United States and other industrialized countries of the world are experiencing **multiculturalism**—the presence of multiple groups of people representing different cultures, races, languages, and religions. For example, by 2043, less than half the U.S. population will be Caucasian, in comparison to 69 percent in 2000.[58] Hispanics now constitute the largest U.S. "minority" group, in contrast to African Americans who, for hundreds of years, comprised the largest minority group.

Multiculturalism is prompting senior managers of firms to adopt **diversity initiatives**—aimed at doing business with, and hiring, people from multiple cultures. CEOs know that, as the demographics of a nation shift, to remain competitive, they must diversify in order to meet the needs of their diverse customer bases. Business scholars suggest that there is a relationship between a diverse workforce and firm performance,[59] and that, when managed correctly, diversity leads to competitor advantage.[60] For example, Coca-Cola and other U.S. firms have long selected senior executives from among their best global managers.

Previous generations of immigrants to the U.S. pursued a strategy of assimilation that revolved around blending into the majority culture and becoming "American." Today, however, U.S. residents from other nations are culturally integrating while retaining their identity. As a result, most firms view multiculturalism to be a strength that allows the company to consider and resolve opportunities from multiple viewpoints, and to implement strategies that are appropriate for a multicultural marketplace. In this way, the firm can maximize the entire range of talent and experience of a diverse workforce.

Most firms understand that demographic shifts in the population and the global economy result in a more diverse workplace, and the need to engage customers and workers from different cultures. Globalization means that more firms are developing, manufacturing, and marketing products and services worldwide. In response to global business and the need to understand and succeed in different cultures, many firms have formed strategic alliances to pursue common goals. Likewise, workers in the global economy are encountering more diverse customers and employees than they did in the past. The crucible for sales executives is to recognize that, based upon their unique backgrounds, salespersons from diverse cultures bring added value and strength to the sales team.[61]

The Benefits of Embracing Diversity

There are multiple reasons that sales firms should embrace diversity. From an ethical and moral perspective, embracing diversity is a correct policy, because it is a policy of inclusion and fairness. Also, embracing diversity is a legal requirement in the U.S., with historical precedents. Firms may not discriminate based upon race, gender, or national origin.[62] Equally important is the fact that shifting demographics and globalization forces have changed the composition of the sales force and customer base. As a result, firms are feeling pressure to change their perspectives and practices toward diversity. Other benefits are as follows:

- **Hiring a diverse workforce can offer the firm a sales and marketing advantage.** Managers believe that a diverse sales force can better understand and serve a diverse customer base. Sellers who share similar cultural traits with buyers often form stronger relationships.[63]

- **Supporting diversity can reduce total costs.** Firms that support salespersons, and allow them to feel valued for what they can contribute, find rewards in the results—higher job satisfaction and lower turnover.

- **Hiring a diverse work force is thought to lead to more creative problem solving and decision making.** This is because diverse groups of workers are more likely to suggest creative solutions to problems than are homogeneous groups. One study showed that innovative companies reported higher levels of diversity than did non-innovative firms.[64]

Despite the benefits, diversity can cause negative outcomes—unless such a strategy is properly managed. This is because the greater the percentage of diverse workers, the higher the likelihood of cultural conflict taking place. Perhaps people from minority and majority groups feel more comfortable interacting with individuals similar to themselves. However, in a business organization, all workers—regardless of their race, gender, religion, or sexual orientation—must interact and work together, or firm effectiveness suffers. When there are cultural interpersonal issues, the sales manager must spend valuable time resolving these at the expense of achieving firm objectives. Thus, effective management of diversity is a requirement for firms that aspire to perform at a high level and profit from a competitive advantage.

Firms must take strong actions to achieve diversity in the workplace. To maximize the benefits of diversity, the firm must recognize and address a number of obstacles that exist:

- The barriers of prejudice, stereotyping, and ethnocentrism that were discussed earlier in this chapter must be replaced by a philosophy of equal opportunity and value.

- Human resources policies must be evaluated and, when they prevent a diverse work force from succeeding, changes must occur. Firms must examine human resources practices closely in the areas of hiring, training, promotion, compensation, and retirement. Human resources policies and practices must reflect cultural and gender neutrality that does not favor any one group.

- Programs must be initiated that offer minority sales professionals an opportunity to move into upper management. This is often referred to as breaking the "glass ceiling" that has, historically, kept women and members of minority groups from moving into senior-level positions. Again, firm policies must ensure that all persons are given an opportunity for consideration, based upon their qualifications.

- Managers must ensure that minorities—salespersons and sales managers— are invited to participate in firm activities, both within and outside the company. Otherwise, minority members will feel alienated, and the rate of turnover will accelerate.

To individual salespersons, an organization's climate refers to how the work environment feels to them. One study suggests that 50 to 70 percent of a firm's climate is attributable to its leadership.[65] Therefore, sales managers are encouraged to assume a leadership role of embracing, supporting, and advancing diversity in the workplace.

Managing Your Career

To truly understand why your firm operates as it does, you need to understand the organizational culture. A firm often does things a certain way because that behavior or belief is accepted or tolerated, even though it may lead to lower performance levels. As a graduate in search of a first sales job, you should research firms' cultures and stated core values, as well as their reputations. The better you understand how to read cues about an internal culture, the more likely you will be to join a firm that matches your own beliefs. As a new salesperson, if you go to work for a firm with cultural beliefs that are very different from yours, you will not be happy, and there is a greater likelihood you will leave to find a better-matched sales position. As sales manager, an important aspect of your responsibility will be to help change dysfunctional culture that reduces efficiency. The information in this chapter will help you understand how to make those changes.

Regarding external culture, as a new salesperson, you will encounter buyers who have moved to your country, bringing with them different beliefs and exhibiting different behaviors. Being accepting of their behavior will result in smoother interactions and greater sales levels. The importance of understanding global cultures increases when you move into a global sales position. As sales manager, you will supervise salespersons from different backgrounds, and it is important to accept these differences—and to be able to direct the diverse sales team to reach company goals.

Summary

Culture is both a company and marketplace force that influences how a firm operates in today's global economy. This means that, from a company perspective, a firm's internal culture determines sales team attitudes and behaviors, the work environment, the treatment of new salespersons, and how managers interact with their employees. When a firm's internal culture is aligned with its external strategy, studies report that firms are more profitable. Likewise, a firm's culture determines attitudes toward embracing diversity and ensuring that cultural differences are factored into work rules, policies, and managerial practices. From a market perspective, national culture impacts everything we do. That is, national culture determines how employees and customers think, act, and purchase. As the U.S. becomes more diverse and engages in increasing levels of global trade, cultural differences will impact most business relationships.

Sales managers play important roles in aligning internal cultures with external strategies. They align internal cultures by taking symbolic actions and making substantive decisions. For example, a sales manager might symbolically adopt a major customer to provide outstanding service, while modifying internal policies and replacing current salespersons who do not possess needed skills, knowledge, and attitudes necessary for future success.

Sales managers and salespersons are more likely to succeed in today's diverse marketplace when they understand their own ethnocentrism—and when they also understand that culture impacts how buyers view sales calls, interpersonal communications, and relationships. Likewise, the sales force, customers, and partners are becoming more diverse as the demographics of the U.S. population continue to change. As demographics shift, company policies and practices must remain current in order to offer equal opportunity to all sales personnel. If a firm is to succeed in the diverse marketplace of the future, the sales force must be a reflection of the buyers that it serves.

Key Terms

acculturation 348
assimilated 348
corporate culture 341
corporate ethnocentrism 356
culture 341
diversity initiatives 360
entropy 345
ethnocentric 355
expatriates 357
global culture 348
high-context cultures 352
high-performance culture 352
individualism/collectivism 349
internal alignment 347
local culture 350
local-hire salesperson 357
long-term orientation 350

low-context cultures 352
market-oriented 342
masculinity/femininity 349
multiculturalism 360
national culture 348
polycentric 355
power distance 349
product-oriented approach 342
production-oriented approach 342
relationship marketing-oriented
   approach 342
sales-oriented approach 342
self-reference criterion 356
substantive actions 347
symbolic actions 347
third-country salesperson 357
uncertainty avoidance 349

Questions and Problems

1. Discuss how culture, as a company and marketplace force, impacts the firm.

2. Define corporate culture. Why might some employees view culture as the "water in the fishbowl" of their daily activities?

3. List the five philosophies a firm may adopt. What impact does a firm's orientation or philosophy have on the role of the sales force? What impact does it have on the sales force's relationships with other functional areas within the firm—and with those outside the firm?

4. Provide three reasons that sales and marketing functional areas may not be aligned. What is the major consequence of a misaligned firm culture?

5. Explain entropy and how entropy affects a firm's resilience.

6. When a sales force's group values differ from the rules, regulations, and managerial systems that are in place, what type of gap exists?

7. How do high-performance firm cultures operate, in contrast to low-performance cultures? How does a sales manager change a low-performance culture to a high-performance culture?

8. Explain the role of the sales manager as a culture creator, regarding symbolic and substantive actions.

9. What types of actions can a salesperson take to increase the probability of successfully interacting with someone from a different culture?

10. Looking at individualism/collectivism component of national culture, what impact might this component have on a buyer's motivation to purchase, and the time that might be needed to reach purchase decisions?

11. What role does "context" play when a salesperson or sales manager tries to understand an action taken by a buyer or partner from another culture?

12. Discuss how nonverbal communications might impact sales situations.

13. Why is it important for salespersons to understand their own ethnocentrism?

14. As the U.S. population becomes more diverse, how will this trend influence firms with regard to hiring and managing sales personnel and selling to potential clients?

15. Offer several legitimate reasons why a sales firm should embrace diversity.

16. Do minority sales personnel perform below, at, or above that of the sales team? What does this imply in regard to minority status?

Role Play

Expatriate Pay and Benefits at World Sales Group

Connor Thelen is the global sales manager for World Sales Group (WSG), a company that manufactures and sells B2B goods in the U.S. and Asia. For the past 10 years, WSG has assigned expatriate sales managers to seven locations in Asia, including Tokyo, Osaka, Taipei, Shanghai, Manila, Singapore, and Bangkok. In general, the U.S. dollar is strong in most locations outside of Japan and Singapore. At first, WSG provided an overseas stipend for housing and entertainment, but expatriates in Japan were constantly complaining that they spent as much as $10,000 a month on a home and $2,000 a night to entertain the current customers. Conversely, expatriates in Manila and Bangkok feel comfortable with the stipend provided.

Thelen realized quickly that he was no expert on expatriate expenses and compensation, so he engaged the services of an expatriate consulting firm in Washington, D.C. Currently, each expatriate receives a salary that is 40 percent higher than their U.S. salary, and this is increased by the rate of inflation on January 1 each year. However, the inflation rate is not the same in the U.S. and the assigned countries. About a month ago, three of the expatriate sales managers sent a joint letter to Thelen, asking for a cost of living increase that would allow them to reside on the local economy and not lose money by being assigned overseas. These three sales managers reside in Tokyo, Osaka, and Singapore—cities with the highest cost of living.

Thelen is sympathetic to the complaints of the expatriate sales managers, but he also feels that living abroad for three years is a choice assignment that should also be viewed as a reward. Thelen has scheduled a meeting with John Rogers, WSG's human resources director, and Stacia Bell, a consulting manager from World Assignments, to analyze the current compensation and expense systems and determine whether he should recommend changes to the firm's overseas pay/expense policies.

Characters in the Role Play

Connor Thelen, global sales manager at WSG

John Rogers, director of human resources at WSG

Stacia Bell, consulting manager from World Assignments

Assignment

Break into groups of three, with one student in the group playing each role. Do not be concerned about matching the gender of the character with the actual gender mix within your student group. (If preferred, change the gender and name of your assigned character.) Prior to meeting as a group, work individually to devise basic recommendations, and prepare to support your compensation system recommendations for expatriate sales managers. Then meet as a group and role play the meeting between Connor, John, and Stacia. The goal is to conclude the meeting with an agreed upon recommendation for offering a fair and equitable compensation system to WSG's sales managers in Asia.

Caselets

Caselet 15.1: *West Coast Manufacturing*

Riley Goolsby is the new sales manager for West Coast Manufacturing (WCM), a supplier of restaurant products in the greater San Francisco area. Goolsby spent the first month of her tenure at WCM, analyzing the culture of her new firm, which she describes as being one of setting annual and quarterly goals—but imposing few penalties if the goals are not met. That is, the sales force is not held responsible for missed sales goals. Also, the sales force appears to meet sales goals late in the performance period by lowering prices, and accounts then receive poor customer service. Goolsby realizes that, if she is to change the firm's internal culture, she must take both symbolic and substantive actions. Based upon your understanding of internal culture, what specific actions should Goolsby implement to shift the company's internal culture?

1. What symbolic actions should Goolsby take?

2. What substantive actions should Goolsby take?

3. How difficult will Goolsby's attempt to realign the internal culture with the external strategy be if upper management is not supportive?

Caselet 15.2: *Asian Imports N.A.*

Asian Imports N.A. distributes Asian manufactured goods to U.S. wholesalers and to large box retailers like Walmart, Target, and Kmart. Located near the port of Seattle, Washington, Asian Imports employs 40 salespersons, geographically dispersed across the U.S. When Asian Imports opened, it hired experienced salespersons who had relationships with existing wholesalers. Later, as Asian Imports began to sell to large box retailers, employees were assigned to these corporations' headquarters.

After more than 20 years, Asian Imports has a significant proportion of field salespersons that are of Hispanic and Asian heritage. Likewise, a large number of customer service and support employees within the Seattle headquarters are first- or second-generation Americans whose parents immigrated to the U.S. from Asia and Mexico. The National Sales Manager at Asian Imports is John DeJesus, a first-generation Filipino American. DeJesus is a proud American; all three of his children are graduates of prestigious U.S. universities, and he feels that his sales team and customer service reps work hard and desire to advance in the firm. Being an international firm, Asian Imports embraces diversity, and always hires the best candidate for the job, without regard for applicants' race, gender, religion, sexual preference, or national origin. However, DeJesus feels he needs to conduct an analysis of policies and practices to ensure that current and future employees will not be discriminated against, and that everyone has opportunity for advancement within the firm.

1. What policies should DeJesus examine in regard to hiring, training, evaluating, and compensating his sales force and customer service employees?

2. What managerial practices should DeJesus consider?

3. What other functional areas within the firm should DeJesus work with during and after the study is complete?

4. Is such a study necessary? Why?

5. What should be the goal of any examination of diversity and equal opportunity?

References

1. Gunn, B. (2000). "Illuminating Culture," *Strategic Finance Magazine*, (18)10, April, 14–16.
2. McLarney, C., and E. Chung (2000)., "What Happened is Prologue: Creative Divergence and Corporate Culture Fabrication," *Management Decisions*, (38)6, 410–419.
3. Featherly, Kevin (2006). "Culture Shock," *Sales & Marketing Management*, January/February, 45–48.
4. Honeycutt, Earl D., Jr., John B. Ford, and Antonis Simintiras (2003). *Sales Management: a Global Perspective.* London, UK: Routledge.
5. Jap, Sandy D. (2001). "The Strategic Role of the Salesforce in Developing Customer Satisfaction across the Relationship Cycle," *Journal of Personal Selling & Sales Management*, (21)2, Spring, 95–108.
6. Sluis, Sarah (2014). "Sales Needs to Develop a Go-to-Customer Approach," CRM.com, Accessed March 9, 2014. *http://www.destinationcrm.com/Articles/CRM-News/CRM-Featured-News/Sales-Needs-to-Develop-a-Go-to-Customer-Approach-95246.aspx.*
7. Wellins, Richard S., Charles J. Cosentino, and Bradford Thomas (2004). "Building a Winning Sales Force," *Development Dimensions International, Inc.*, Winter, 6.
8. Duncan, W. Jack (1989). "Organizational Culture: Getting a 'Fix' on an Elusive Concept," *Academy of Management Executive*, (3), 229–236.
9. Sherwood, J.J. (1988). "Creating Work Cultures with Competitive Advantage," *Organizational Dynamics*, Winter, 5–27.
10. George, Bill (2003), *Authentic Leadership*, San Francisco, CA: Jossey-Bass.
11. George (2003). Op. cit.
12. Sorensen, J.B. (2002). "The Strength of Corporate Culture and the Reliability of Firm Performance," *Administrative Science Quarterly*, (47)1 March, 70–91.
13. Beaudan, E., and G. Smith (2000). "Corporate Culture: Asset or Liability? Merging Two Cultures," *Ivey Business Journal*, (64) 4, March-April, 14–16.
14. Kotler, Philip, Neil Rackham, and Suj Krishnaswamy (2006). "Ending the War between Sales & Marketing, *Harvard Business Review*, July-August, 68–78.
15. Shapiro, Benson (2002). "Want a Happy Customer? Coordinate Sales and Marketing," *Harvard Business School Working Knowledge*, October 22, *http:hbswk.edu/item/3154. html, accessed 4/19/2007.*
16. Schemerhorn, John R., Jr. (2008). *Management*, 9th edition. Hoboken, NJ: John Wiley & Sons, Inc., 94.
17. Kotler, Rackham, and Krishnaswamy (2006). Op. cit.
18. Barrett, Richard (2006). *Building a Values-Driven Organization.* Oxford, UK: Butterworth-Heinemann.
19. Chonko, Lawrence B., and John J. Burnett (1983). "Measuring the Importance of Ethical Situations as a Source of Role Conflict: A Survey of Salespeople, *Journal of Personal Selling and Sales Management*, (3)1, May, 41.
20. Hosford, Christopher (2006), "Rebooting Hewlett-Packard," *Sales & Marketing Management*, July/August, 32–35.
21. Sims, R.R. (2000). "Changing an Organization's Culture Under New Leadership," *Journal of Business Ethics*, (25)1, May, 65–78.
22. Goodson, Scott (2012). How Do You Change Your Company's Culture? Spark a Movement," *Forbes,*March 25. Accessed March 9, 2014. *http://www.forbes.com/sites/marketshare/2012/03/25/how-do-you-change-your-companys-culture-spark-a-movement/.*
23. Check, Jayme A. (2013). "If You Want to Change Corporate Culture, Dare to Tell the Truth, *Bloomberg Businessweek*, September 10. Accessed March 10, 2014. *http://www.businessweek.com/articles/2013-09-10/if-you-want-to-change-corporate-culture-dare-to-tell-the-truth.*
24. Neuborne, Ellen (2003). "Bright Ideas," *Sales & Marketing Management*, (26), August, 28–30.
25. Schein, E.H. (1992). *Organizational Culture and Leadership,"* second edition. San Francisco, CA: Jossey-Bass.
26. Neuborne (2003). Op. cit.
27. Kotler, Rackham, and Krishnaswamy (2006). Op. cit.
28. Bernick, Carol Lavin (2001). "When Your Culture Needs a Makeover," *Harvard Business Review,* June 2001, (79), 6.
29. Honeycutt, Earl D., Jr., and Lew Kurtzman (2006), *Selling Outside Your Culture Zone.* Dallas, TX: Behavioral Science Research Press.
30. Hofstede G.H. (1984). *Culture's Consequences: International Differences in Work-related Values.* Thousand Oaks, CA: Sage Publishers.
31. Hofstede G.H. (2001). *Culture's Consequences: Comparing Values, Behaviors, Institutions, and Organizations Across Nations.* Thousand Oaks, CA: Sage Publishers.
32. Lussier, Robert N., and Christopher F. Achua (2003). *Leadership: Theory, Application, Skill Development.* Eagan, MN: Thomson Corporation.

33. Osland, J.S., and A. Bird (2000), "Beyond sophisticated stereotyping: Cultural sensemaking in context," *Academy of Management Executive*, (14)1, 65–79.

34. DuPraw, Marcelle E., and Marya Axner (1997). "Working on Common Cross Cultural Challenges," in Marci Reaven. *Toward a More Perfect Union in the Age of Diversity*, Pomfret, CT: Topsfield Foundation.

35. Reynolds, Nina, and Antonis Simintiras (2000). "Toward an Understanding of the Role of Cross-Cultural Equivalence in International Personal Selling," *Journal of Marketing Management*, (16), 829–851.

36. Hofstede, Geert (1991). *Cultures and Organizations*, London: McGraw Hill Book Company.

37. Hodge, Sheida (1998). *Feng Shui: A Guide For Increased Real Estate Sales to Asians*, fourth edition. Professional Training Worldwide.

38. Chang, Julia (2003). "Multicultural Selling," *Sales & Marketing Management*, October, 26.

39. Lewis, R.D. (1996). *When Cultures Collide: Managing Successfully Across Cultures*. Boston, MA: Nicholas Brealey Publishing Limited.

40. Jandt, Fred E. (2004). *An Introduction to Intercultural Communication*. Thousand Oaks, CA: Sage.

41. Caligiuri, Paula M., and Rosalie L. Tung (1999). "Comparing the Success of Male and Female Expatriates from a U.S.-based Multinational Company," *International Journal of Human Resource Management*, October (10)5, 763–782.

42. Honeycutt, Ford, and Simintiras (2003). Op. cit.

43. Johannson, Johny K., and Ikujiro Nonanka (1997). *Relentless: The Japanese Way of Marketing*. New York, NY: Harper Business.

44. Cateora, Philip R., and John L. Graham (2007). *International Marketing*. Boston: McGraw-Hill Irwin, 502.

45. Cateora and Graham (2007). Op. cit.

46. Rouzies, Dominique, Michael Segalla, and Barton A. Weitz (2003). "Cultural Impact on European Staffing Decisions in Sales Management, *International Journal of Research in Marketing*, (20)1, 67–85.

47. Cateora and Graham (2007). Op. cit.

48. Marken, James A., and Earl D. Honeycutt, Jr. (2008). "Utilizing Activity Theory to Plan Cross-Cultural Sales Training," National Conference in Sales Management *Proceedings*, 1–6.

49. Cateora and Graham (2007). Op. cit.

50. Jantan, M. Asri, Earl D. Honeycutt, Jr., Shawn T. Thelen, and Ashraf M. Attia (2004). "Managerial Perceptions of Training and Performance," *Industrial Marketing Management*, (33), October, 667–673.

51. Neelankavil, James P., Anil Mathur, and Yong Zang (2000). "Determinants of Managerial Performance: A Cross-Cultural Comparison of the Perceptions of Middle-Level Managers in Four Countries," *Journal of International Business Studies*, (31)1, 121–140.

52. Ball, Deborah, and Aaron O. Patrick (2007). "How a Unilever Executive is Thinning the Ranks," *Wall Street Journal*, (27), November 26, B1, B3.

53. Mintu-Wimsatt, Alma, and Julie B. Gassenheimer (2000). "The Moderating Effects of Cultural Context in Buyer-Seller Negotiations," *Journal of Personal Selling & Sales Management*, (20)1, 1–9.

54. Piercy, Nigel F., George S. Low, and David W. Cravens (2004). "Consequences of Sales Management's Behavior-and Compensation-Based Control Strategies in Developing Countries," *Journal of International Marketing*, (12)3, 36–57.

55. Honeycutt, Ford, and Simintiras (2003). Op. cit.

56. Money, R. Bruce, and John L. Graham (1999). "Salesperson Performance, Pay and Job Satisfaction: Tests of a Model Using Data Collected in the U.S. and Japan," *Journal of International Business Studies*, (30)1, 149–172.

57. Bohlander, George W., and Scott A. Snell. *Managing Human Resources*, 14th edition. Mason, OH: South-Western, 670–673.

58. U.S. Census Bureau (2004). "U.S. Interim Projections of Age, Sex, Race, and Hispanic Origin," *www.Census.gov/ipc/www/usinterimproj/*.

59. Kahn, J. (2001). "Diversity Trumps the Downturn," *Fortune*, (144)1 July, 114–116.

60. Gilbert, Jacqueline A., and John M. Ivancevich (1999). "Organizational Diplomacy: The Bridge for Managing Diversity," *Human Resources Planning*, (22)3.

61. Honeycutt, Ford, and Simintiras (2003). Op. cit.

62. Orlando, R.C. (2000). Racial Diversity, Business Strategy, and Firm Performance: A Resource-Based View," *Academy of Management Journal*, (43)2, 164–177.

63. Berta, D. (2002). "Mixing it Up: Diversity Good For Business, Confab Finds," *Nation's Restaurant News*, (36)34, August, 1, 103.

64. Kahn (2001). Op. cit.

65. Watkins, C. (2001). "How to Improve Organizational Climate," *People Management*, (7)13 (June), 52–53.

Cases

CASE STUDY 1

B&W's Expense Problem: *Whose Expense is It?*

Lauren Johnson had been with B&W Industries for a year and was viewed as a rising sales star. Johnson was the top student in Central State University's professional sales program in 2012, and had received a generous signing bonus when she accepted a job at B&W. After completing an intensive six-month training program, Lauren was initially assigned to a territory in Dallas, Texas. After performing well in her first territory, she accepted a voluntary transfer to the St. Louis, Missouri, office to be nearer to her family and friends.

Moving back to St. Louis was a dream come true for Johnson. She immediately buckled down to ensure that her performance exceeded all standards. In her first quarter in St. Louis, she was the second most productive salesperson in that office. Her boss told her, informally, that if her performance continued at the same pace, he would nominate her for the "outstanding first-year salesperson" award that came with a large plaque and a check for $10,000. Johnson was pleased with herself, to say the least!

One or two nights a week, she and other B&W salespersons would meet at a local bar for drinks, snacks, and camaraderie. It was fun to commiserate with her friends and colleagues after a long, hard day of work. Spending time with the group was good for celebrating the victories and making fun of deals gone awry. Generally, the attendees would take turns buying drinks, and Johnson believed that some of the salespersons turned in their bar bills as an "entertainment expense."

Johnson viewed B&W's policy on entertainment expenses as pretty liberal. That is, as long as a salesperson claimed a reasonable amount of expense that could be tied to entertaining a current or potential customer, the sales manager would sign off on reimbursing the expense. The expense form then went to accounting for reimbursement. What few people at B&W understood is that travel and entertainment—together—generate the second largest expense for a sales organization, after salaries. B&W had recently purchased software that analyzed travel expense forms and "flagged" suspicious activity. A company auditor then personally examined, in detail, any "flagged" expense reports. One Friday, Johnson was at the company "watering hole," and she found herself in a situation where it was her "turn" to pay for drinks and snacks for a number of people at her table. When she looked in her wallet, she had little cash and her personal credit card was also missing! So, she paid for the bill with her B&W credit card. With tip, the bill came to $379! While this may seem like a lot of money, eight to 10 people had been sitting around two tables, and everyone had consumed several mixed drinks and a number of snacks and appetizers. She thought, "What the heck—let B&W pick up the tab."

On Monday, Johnson completed and forwarded the electronic expense form to her immediate supervisor, Nick Miller. Nick called her on her cell while she was waiting to meet with a customer in East St. Louis. Nick asked her about the expense, and said that, although it was a little high, he would go ahead and approve the expense for reimbursement. Johnson breathed a sigh of relief. However, the following Wednesday, she received another call from Nick Miller with news that the form had been analyzed by newly purchased software, and that the auditing team wanted to meet with both of them the following Monday morning. Johnson was instructed to be present at 8 a.m., and to make sure she had proper documentation for the entertainment expense.

Questions

1. Why is it important to follow company policy regarding entertainment expenses?

2. What other action(s) could Johnson have taken to pay for the bar bill?

3. Did Nick Miller's actions help or hurt Johnson? Is Nick in trouble for his actions?

4. What type of documents/information will auditors want from Johnson? From Miller?

5. How much trouble is Johnson in?

    What is the likely outcome of this misstep by Johnson?

CASE STUDY 2

A CRM System for Dallas Pastries

It was obvious that Jonathan Hudson was frustrated and discouraged after completing his last call of the day. Only thirty minutes prior, he had made a terrible mistake. When speaking with the owner of a small convenience store, he mistakenly addressed the customer by the wrong name. He was embarrassed and critical of himself for making such a simple mistake. To make matters worse, the storeowner became very upset at his error, since the owner had a long history of doing business with Dallas Pastries. Because of this mistake, Hudson was not able to sell a new stock-keeping unit (SKU) of Skippies, a crème-filled pastry, to the store, which he needed to do in order to hit his quarterly numbers and earn a bonus.

After he got into his car his phone rang; it was his unit manager, Alan Thomas. "Hi, Jonathan, how's it going selling Skippies into your last few stores?" asked Thomas. He had been reviewing Hudson's numbers and saw that he was very close to his quota.

"Well, it was going really well until this last store. I only needed one more sale to make my numbers, and I just screwed up my chances with my last store," said Hudson.

"What happened?" replied Thomas.

"Well, I walked in there and started talking with him. He remembered my name, and I thought I remembered his, but it turned out that I didn't. I called him the complete wrong name. Needless to say, he was not in the mood to listen to anything I had to say after that. It was a stupid mistake, but I have almost 150 accounts, and, by the end of the day, it gets hard to remember all the store owners and managers," the sales rep whined.

Thomas sighed, "Have you thought about writing their names down?"

"I started to last year, but it's hard to keep up with that much information on my own. Plus, our system is too slow, and doesn't seem to be built for personal account information," said Thomas.

Thomas recognized his concern, "We've had those complaints before and I agree. I wish corporate would approve a new CRM system that takes into account more information than just financial numbers. I'll pass it up the ladder and see if we can't get higher-ups in Dallas at least thinking about it." The sales manager went on to add, "I'll send an e-mail to Randy tonight, the regional VP, and let him know of your suggestions." The rep responded with appreciation, saying, "Thanks, Alan, let me know what Randy says." On his drive home, Hudson pondered if anything would actually be done to improve this issue, or if he had ended his career with Dallas Pastries.

A month later, Hudson received a phone call from an unknown Texas number. He was shocked to hear the voice of Carl Jamison, CEO of Dallas Pastries. Jamison explained to the sales rep how his suggestions, and others like it, had made their way all the way to his desk at corporate, where they had caused quite a stir. The CEO told Hudson that they had since selected a new CRM system. Jamison wanted to know if he would come to the Dallas corporate office to work on their implementation team. He also explained how this would require multiple trips to Dallas, and that doing so carried a very nice financial incentive with it. Hudson said that he would need to discuss it with his wife, but that he would let Jamison know by the end of the day.

Two days later, as Hudson was sitting in first class on his flight to Dallas, he wondered how they were going to implement this new system with more than 2,000 sales representatives spread all over the country. He had so many questions, and was skeptical that this was even a good idea. All he could do was wait, since none of his questions could be resolved until after he landed at DFW Airport. In the meantime, he decided he would be better off taking a nap and saving his energy for the meeting.

Overview of Dallas Pastries

Dallas Pastries' origins go back to 1874, when Thomas Johnston opened a bakery in Dallas, Texas. In 2003, Johnston Baking changed its name to Dallas Pastries Group, because the company's portfolio contained more than just baked goods. At that point in time, Johnston Baking also owned a majority stake in Garnet Foods, a manufacturer of breakfast cereals. In late 2003, Dallas Pastries sold Garnet and bought a number of regional bakeries and specialty food companies. When the company changed its name to Dallas Pastries, it was number 11 on the Fortune 500 list. After all of the buying and selling, though, by 2014 its ranking had dropped to number 54—a major change from the giant it had once had been.

Dallas Pastries Group currently includes four operational divisions: Dallas Pastries USA, Emerald Global Foods, Sungrain (breads, tortillas, etc.), and Metro Meat Products. All divisions have separate marketing and manufacturing departments tailored to specific buyer segments. All other departments are centralized into Dallas Pastries Client Services and Dallas Pastries Group Distribution Company. Client Services includes the accounting, legal, and HR departments, whereas Dallas Pastries Distribution includes a 2,000-plus person sales force, as well as sales support functions.

Dallas Pastries currently exceeds 50 percent of the market share for the entire dessert pastry market within the United States. Dallas Pastries' four main brands, called the "four aces," comprise the majority of this market share. The four aces are Dallas Pastries, Ma Bell's Fried Pies, Ding-a-Linga, and Frosty Man. Dallas Pastries is valued at more than $30 billion, and is the strongest of the four because of its brand recognition. Currently, Dallas Pastries is the sixth most recognizable brand in the entire world.

The dessert pastry market is shrinking at a rate of two percent per year, and the pressure is on manufacturers—due to increasing in child obesity and concern for children's health. Dallas Pastries' goals are not based on volume, but instead are linked to market share. The company focuses on how its brands are doing compared to the competitors' equivalent brands. Emerald, their brand in the ethnic snack market, is in a growth stage. Consequently, Dallas Pastries has begun putting more funding behind the Emerald brands to capture the majority of the market share. Dallas Pastries is taking every step possible to retain its market shares and grow in new, emerging markets. Its sales teams hope to maximize retailer relations with a CRM system that can categorize stores to provide preferential treatment for its valued customers.

Business Goals

Dallas Pastries' mission is to own and develop financially disciplined businesses that are leaders in responsibly providing adult consumers with superior branded products. Following that mission, the company's goals are to invest in leadership, align with society, satisfy adult consumers, and create value for shareholders. Dallas Pastries also has core values that it incorporates into everything it expects its people to do. Those values are integrity, trust and respect, passion to succeed, executing with quality, driving creativity, and sharing with others.

Due to recent legislation regarding pastry sales to schools, vending limitations elsewhere, and constant probing by the media, Dallas Pastries has decided to take the high road in everything it does—to live out the "responsible" part of its mission statement on a daily basis. An example of taking the high road is Dallas Pastries' entrance into the low-fat, 100-calorie-per-serving market aimed at children.

In addition to pursuing these social responsibilities, Dallas Pastries is still very profitable, and is the largest baked goods manufacturer in the United States. This status allows Dallas Pastries to make market-wide decisions on industry pricing for any product at any time. Dallas Pastries manufactures premium branded products, and prices them accordingly; however, there are times when prices need to be lowered in order to stay competitive. The company's current research and development goals are to develop and release new products that reach all targeted market segments. When new products come out, Dallas Pastries gives promotional incentives to retailers, so that they can offer a lower price, while still allowing for the same revenue margins. This price break gives customers an opportunity to try new products without the promotional burden falling onto the respective stores. In 2013, the company released 34 new products, and 2014 is shaping up similarly. Dallas Pastries also strives to offer the best customer service through hiring exceptionally talented salespersons, and by constantly seeking customer feedback.

Current CRM

The current CRM system that Dallas Pastries uses is a data management system called Catman. This system is a mathematical data analysis program with the ability to store and analyze large amounts of numerical data concerning sales, orders, etc. At the moment, the current Dallas Pastries CRM system is little more than a numerical database that is utilized to keep track of financial information about its extensive clientele. As Jonathan Hudson noted, the current CRM system has little information about clients—beyond retail location addresses. The system is slow, outdated, and does not provide any way to store and organize personal account information. Many sales representatives have complained about this issue in recent months, as the company continues to expand.

According to Hudson, a major weakness with the system is that it lacks the capability to store and organize clients' personal information. Hudson's fiasco illustrates how a limited CRM system increases the probability of mistakes. Not having the right information about one's clients can lead to lost sales and lost revenue. Another issue with the current system lies in the fact that the company's current purchase history data is completely separate from its CRM system. This separation makes it difficult to reconcile information from the two data sources. Dallas Pastries needs a newer CRM system that can handle financial data, as well as customers' personal data and purchase history information. As previously stated, the highest priority is gaining and retaining market share. With a new capability CRM system, Dallas Pastries can help ensure that it will retain the market share that it currently holds—and, in theory, capture a larger overall market share in new, emerging segments. Each of the channel partners is particularly valuable to Dallas Pastries, and a more advanced CRM system will allow sales reps to stay in close contact with their clients. It could substantially increase market share by providing better service to preferential clients. Hudson, though, is unaware that the company has already selected NetSuite as the new CRM system.

NetSuite

NetSuite is a cloud-based customer relationship management system that provides companies with sales force automation (SFA), customer service, partner relationship management, marketing automation, CRM analysis, and financial reports. NetSuite's SFA function gives the sales force access to industry-leading sales forecasting, customer management, and order management. NetSuite's built-in dashboard provides all employees within the company personalized Key Performance Indicators. The system works in real-time to provide important information for decision making and performance-related measurements.

NetSuite's competitive advantage is its ability to provide a true 360° view of the customer. By keeping track of past transactions and interactions, NetSuite can show what products customers have purchased and give the company forecasts of what they may purchase in the future. As a customer benefit, it allows each store to automatically re-order products on a schedule or purchase new products from the Internet. By streamlining all operations into one system, the system tracks purchases from the manufacturer to the moment of delivery. For the company, all inputted data can be gathered to create a more accurate forecast for future periods. NetSuite also would allow Dallas Pastries sales reps to input personal information provided by their clients, which is something that their current system does not allow

Implementation Committee Meeting

When Jonathan Hudson arrived at headquarters, he met Carl Jamison, the CEO of Dallas Pastries Group Distribution Company. Jamison explained that everyone was already in the board room, and that they wanted to get started right away. The sales rep asked, with a puzzled look on his face, "Just how big of a deal is this meeting?" The CEO replied, "Well, let's put it this way: this meeting is costing the company somewhere around $5,000 an hour." Hudson's jaw dropped. "I guess we'd better get started, then," he responded.

As they made their way to the top floor of the building, Hudson wondered to himself how he, a lowly sales representative, could be of any help to these big corporate decision makers. Before Jamison opened the big oak doors to the board room, he looked at Hudson and said, "Put your game face on, son."

The table in the room was huge, rimmed by at least 20 chairs. Hudson did a quick count of the number of people in the room; it appeared that 14 would be involved in the meeting. Four seemed to be assistants, based on their activity, attire, and the fact that they were not seated. Jamison began with introductions. "To your left, we have Jack Nelson, chief technology officer. Next to him is Harold Willard, our chief financial officer, followed by Jane Amado, chief information officer." After each person had a chance to shake hands, Jamison continued, "Natalie Land, senior vice president of marketing, is here to make sure we promote NetSuite correctly to our 'reps.' The angry-looking fellow next to her is Jamie Thorp, SVP of regulatory affairs; we like to give him a hard time, because he hasn't been smiling too much lately with these new lawsuits being brought against the company. Towards the back, we have Chuck Whitaker, SVP of human resources and compliance, and Jeff Tannenbaum, SVP of operations. Jeff has a super-dry sense of humor," the CEO quipped, "but from time-to-time he gets us all laughing. Rounding out our implementation team is William Barefoot, SVP of the field sales force."

As Jamison ended the introductions, he asked: "Well, Jonathan, what do you think?" Hudson smiled and said: "I'm still wondering why you brought me here." Everyone in the room laughed and Natalie responded, "Because we know the business from in here, but you know it from out there," pointing towards the window. "We need someone who can tell us what will actually work in the field, someone who will keep our grand plans in check." He smiled and replied, "Well, I'll do my best, then." Jamison motioned for everyone to sit down, "We've got a lot to cover, so let's get started." Everyone sat down and opened their laptops, while Jamison got out his notes. "Last week, we made the decision to upgrade our CRM system to NetSuite; now, we have to figure out how to set it up and implement it." he added, "So what are our major issues by department?" All at once, the room erupted. Everyone started throwing out the issues that they had been gathering for the last week. Jamison raised his hands and said, "OK, one at a time, starting with Jack." Jack Nelson began to explain his issue with the depth of NetSuite. "Should we immediately give our reps full access to this software, or should we start with a limited version of the system?" Harold Willard added to that, bringing up how much it would actually cost to implement the entire system. There were training costs that needed to be considered, and those costs would be higher if the sales force had to be trained on multiple occasions—as Jack was proposing. He also asked, "Do we even know how much revenue this is going to generate for us?" Jane Amado brought up the fact that they first had to decide what information to collect. "What information do we think is important to better understand our customers?"

Everyone at the table nodded in agreement with Amado's comment. Natalie Land then posed the question of how they were going to get all the salespeople to agree to use the system. "If our sales force does not see the benefit in using NetSuite, we will just be wasting our money." She added: "This is a typical marketing issue—meaning that we will have to sell this new CRM system to our employees, who make a living selling our products to our customers."

Jamie Thorp advised that Dallas Pastries will have to address legal problems associated with the collection of personal data, and that he and Amado needed to work together to decide what information to collect. Chuck Whitaker looked up from his computer to ask: "How are we going to train on the system? If the sales force does not know how to fully utilize the system, then reps won't fully buy into its benefits." Harold Willard chimed in, "Don't forget that we're already making close to a $4 million investment in the system this year alone, and we can't afford to have our sales representatives out of their territories for very long." Whitaker replied, "I know, Harold, but they have to understand how to use it; we can't just give them their log-in information and wish them luck." Jamison made notes in his portfolio, "Both of your points are noted, now let's hear from the rest of our team." He nodded to Jeff Tannenbaum, who smiled and excitedly raised his hands as if to act something out. His jest depicted a construction worker and something pertaining to CRM data hieroglyphics. No one laughed. "Well, you'll all think it's funny later." He then looked back at his notes and said, "Has anyone thought about what's going to happen to our business if our reps are all training at the same time? Do all of our reps even need the system? We're a large company, and our brands can't afford for us to take off a day—or, worse, two days." William Barefoot looked at Hudson, waiting through the fray for the visiting sales rep's input. Hudson looked to Natalie Land and said, "I agree with Natalie. If the reps don't buy into the importance of the new system, they just won't use it. And all of our time will be wasted."

"We've surely got our work cut out for us," Jamison said, leaning back in his chair. "Why don't we take a break for lunch, and give ourselves time to clear our minds before we reconvene." Hudson and Jamison left the meeting, heading to the cafeteria to grab something to eat. During the meal, Hudson could only think about how much work he had in front of him, and how much more complicated his workday had just become.

After lunch, everyone reassembled in the board room to dig a little deeper into the issues raised that morning. They started with what Jane Amado had said about the type of information that needed to be collected. After all, one of the main reasons they decided to go with a new CRM system was because of its ability to collect more data. But what data was necessary? The current CRM only shows what level contract the store holds, the store's location, and other technical data. "We've fallen into a data trap," added Amado. "We have more information than we need on stores' purchase patterns, but when we talk to the managers, we're blind." Hudson agreed, adding, "We're acting as if our relationship with store owners is simply transactional. We go into the stores, put up new signs, try to sell new brands, and then leave. In reality, our relationships with retailers should be relational in order to stay 'number one' in an industry that is so volatile." Amado went on to discuss how NetSuite will make a much more user-friendly data mart, and will speed up customer data integration (CDI), since managers will be able to see and combine all their reps' data.

The second issue the committee examined in depth was how to train the sales force on NetSuite. Whitaker brought up a good point: how adequately training over

2,000 reps was going to be difficult, but that it was the most important aspect of the implementation. The average Dallas Pastries territory sales manager costs the company $110,000 per year when salary, bonus, company car, medical insurance, and taxes are included. That amounts to $58.51 per hour that the reps are in the field. One full day of training would cost Dallas Pastries $936,160. Willard butted in: "Why don't we just teach them on a conference call? It would be cheaper, and would probably take half the time." Whitaker responded: "The problem with that idea is that some people are not very computer savvy and need one-on-one instruction. Plus, how would we know if everyone is even on the conference call and learning in the first place."

Jamison looked at Whitaker and said, "That's a very good point, but let's consider what Natalie brought up." Land's point was that the benefits of NetSuite would need to be accurately conveyed to the sales force in order to gain compliance. "If we just demand that our reps use the new system, they might not fully understand the reasoning behind the order, and not make the effort required to see the returns we anticipated," she stated. With a grin, Hudson replied, "Financial incentives always seem to work with my kids." Everyone laughed and Willard piped in, "Yes, but then there are additional costs to factor in. I'm not saying we couldn't do it; we just need to think about the effects of monetary compensation and how to effectively monitor use." Hudson exclaimed, "Wow, I didn't even think about that. This is a more complex issue than I initially thought. Had I known this, I might have just stayed in San Antonio," he said with a chuckle.

"Since we're on the topic of finances, how much is this going to cost?" queried Willard.

Jamison began discussing the different options that they had been considering. He mentioned that the cost to purchase NetSuite is a sunk cost, simply because the decision to implement the CRM system has already been made. He brought up the fact that the original cost of implementing the system is around $1,548 per user per year. "That equates to about $3.1 million just to implement the system when you consider that we have 2,000 sales reps in the field," said Davison. "Harold mentioned that there are other costs associated with NetSuite as well. For example, we have training costs, marketing costs as Natalie mentioned, and the cost of us meeting right now. It seems like the final cost is going to be a little hard to compute until we decide on these other issues, wouldn't you say, Harold?" "I would agree," his colleague replied.

"We've been sitting here for almost ten hours and it seems like we have the major issues all laid out. Let's all go back to our departments and work on these issues and schedule another meeting at the end of next week to finalize a decision," said Carl. After that, the managers began gathering their papers and finishing up with what they were working on. Davison looked at Hudson and said, "I really appreciate your input today. I'll have my assistant schedule you a flight back here next Friday so we can finish all this up. See you next week, Jonathan." Hudson made his way downstairs, where a car waited to take him to the airport.

Flight Home

As Hudson boarded the plane for his flight home, his mind was reeling from the events of the trip. How could he possibly convey all the information he had received to his manager and fellow reps back home? How long would it take to implement the system? How long would it take to train the sales force? The longer it takes them to acclimate to the system, the more it's going to cost the company to teach them to use it. Is the system really going to benefit the company in the long run, and by how much? Where should he even begin? The board meeting gave him a lot to think about, and he didn't even know where to start. As he leaned back in his seat, and closed his eyes, he let out a long breath. "You gonna be all right, buddy? You seem a little stressed out," said the grey-haired gentleman in the seat next to him. "Oh, I'll be fine, I'm just a little stressed about some work stuff," said Jonathan. "Well, what doesn't kill us makes us stronger, son," the older gentleman said. Hudson smiled, because it seemed easier said than done, but was a nice thought as he slowly drifted to sleep in his comfy, leather, first-class seat.

Questions

1. What are the advantages and disadvantages of implementing a CRM system?

2. How are the perspectives of the senior managers and Jonathan Hudson similar? Different?

3. What type of information would benefit the sales team at Dallas Pastries?

4. Should Hudson have sought input from other sales team members prior to returning to Dallas?

5. How would you recommend that Dallas Pastries train their sales force on the new CRM system? Is a single sales training session sufficient?

6. Are incentives necessary for expediting sales team adoption of the CRM system? Why?

CASE STUDY 3

Eagle Sales Associates: *Evaluating a Sales Team*

Janet Hunt is a regional sales manager at Eagle Sales Associates, a firm selling manufacturers' computer peripheral equipment to firms using Dell, Acer, Apple, and Lenovo systems. The computer peripherals industry encompasses computer displays and projectors, computer input drives and speakers, personal storage drives, and printing and imaging equipment.

Hunt's managerial responsibilities include accounts located in Virginia, North Carolina, and South Carolina. She has been the Mid-Atlantic regional sales manager for Eagle Sales Associates for three years. Prior to assuming her current position, Janet was the top salesperson in Jacksonville, Florida, for four of the seven years she held that position. She also completed an evening M.B.A. program at the University of Florida while living in Jacksonville. When the management position opened up due to a promotion, she was offered the job—and accepted immediately.

Hunt was known by her six sales reps to be demanding, but fair, and helpful. That is, she was always available to help the sales team find information, devise a strategy for a customer, or help solve a personal or family problem. What the sales team did not know was that she held herself to even higher standards than she did her workers!

On November 12, Hunt sent out the following e-mail to her six sales representatives:

Team,

As you know, the end of the year is fast approaching! This year has been another successful one for Eagle Sales Associates, with sales revenues slightly exceeding our forecasts. Therefore, as is the practice each year, please call or e-mail my secretary Tameka to set up an appointment during the week of December 8th–15th so that we can discuss your formal evaluation for the year. I will forward a copy of the forecasts that we agreed to last January and a list of questions for you to answer that will guide our discussion during the review meeting. Thank you again for your hard work on behalf of Eagle Sales Associates and your clients. I look forward to seeing you in Charlotte the second week of December.

Best,
Janet

The sales manager knew she would be busy over the next month, preparing for the formal evaluations. In her years in sales, she had experienced several sales managers who put little time into preparing for evaluations. Instead, these managers "shot from the hip." They would look at the revenues their salespeople generated relative to their quotas and authorize a raise and bonus for them based upon their "making their numbers."

Although Hunt believed that making one's quotas was important, she understood that there were many things to be learned from properly analyzing the numbers. Said differently, analyzing quantitative numbers was both an art and a science. One needed not only to understand the science of statistics, but also to be able to delve more deeply into when, where, why, and how those numbers occurred. She knew that, if her sales team were to improve each year, she would have to truly understand their sales results and the reasons for those results.

The following week, Hunt instructed her secretary, Tameka, to e-mail her salespeople their forecasts and agreed-upon goals for the year. In a separate attachment, Tameka asked each sales rep to respond to the following questions and return their answers to Janet by December 1:

1. What were the purchasing trends in your territory over the past year?

2. What strategies have your competitors employed over the past year?

3. What factors do you attribute to your success (or shortfall) this year?

4. Are there any other factors, either business or personal, that Janet needs to be aware of, that directly impact your performance in your territory?

Over the Thanksgiving holiday, Janet went to her office several mornings to begin looking through the numbers for each of her salespersons. The first analysis that she gathered from her CRM system offered the following snapshot of her regional sales force's performance during the year:

TABLE 1   Sales against Quota by Territory

Territory	Quota (000)	Sales (000)	Variance (000)
Bob—Richmond	$2,200	$2,315	$+115
Susan—Arlington	$2,800	$2,795	$–5
Omar—Charlotte	$3,100	$3,500	$+400
Joe—Raleigh	$2,150	$1,800	$–350
Robert—Charleston	$2,100	$2,110	$+10
Maryanne—Columbia	$2,950	$2,965	$+15
Totals	**$15,300**	**$15,435**	**$+135**

As Janet noted in her e-mail, her sales team had surpassed its quota by $135,000. However, while admirable, this amounted to less than one percent over the forecast. Given the slowdown in the economy and increase in interest rates, she was glad her sales team's overall performance had exceeded expectations. While she was thinking about the implications of Table 1, she was reminded of how the sales process goes: a few salespeople seem to exceed their quotas; whereas, others struggle and never find their stride. This year, four of her salespeople had achieved or exceeded their goals, and two had fallen short. Susan, in Arlington, was slightly below goal. Joe, who managed the Raleigh territory, was short by $350,000, or over 16 percent! Janet knew that Joe had struggled, but she needed to understand why. She generated the data shown in Table 2 to gain a deeper understanding of what was actually going on.

TABLE 2   Sales by Product Line for Raleigh (Joe)

Product Line	Quota (000)	Sales (000)	Variance (000)
A	$800	$875	$+75
B	$300	$175	$–125
C	$550	$325	$–225
D	$500	$425	$–75
Totals	**$2,150**	**$1,800**	**$–350**

Although Joe had exceeded expectations in terms of selling Product A, he had fallen significantly short of his quota selling Products B, C, and D. Again, Hunt needed more information about her sales team to gain a more accurate understanding of the situation—not only in the Raleigh territory, but also in the other five territories of the Mid-Atlantic region.

After a little thought and manipulating her computer, additional information was provided for each salesperson that included:

TABLE 3   Inputs by Territory

Territory	Days Worked	Sales Calls per Day	Total # Sales Made	Expenses
Bob—Richmond	220	4	65	$26,400
Susan—Arlington	225	4.2	98	$30,200
Omar—Charlotte	218	5	105	$21,200
Joe—Raleigh	205	2.8	65	$35,500
Robert—Charleston	222	3.5	59	$27,800
Maryanne—Columbia	230	5	108	$19,600
Averages	**220**	**4.08**	**83.33**	**$26,780**

Utilizing the information provided in Tables 1 and 3, Janet computed the average order size and travel–and–entertainment costs per sale. She also decided it would be helpful to look at additional information that could be easily generated by her CRM system. She was always amazed at how much information was available if you knew what to look for. Table 4 shows the information she was able to extract from the database.

TABLE 4   Additional Information by Territory

Territory	Gross Margin (%)	Miles per Sales Call	Rush Orders (%)	Number of Complaints
Bob—Richmond	35%	31.2	4.00	5
Susan—Arlington	33%	28.5	5.25	8
Omar—Charlotte	34.7%	25.3	6.10	4
Joe—Raleigh	28%	45.6	12.50	18
Robert—Charleston	34.3%	47.8	5.75	7
Maryanne—Columbia	35.5%	25.1	8.00	3
Averages	**33.41%**	**33.92**	**6.93%**	**7.50**

Hunt also perused each salesperson's personnel file for notes she had made while traveling in the field with them. Here are the notes on Joe when she made sales calls with him in the Raleigh sales territory:

Call Notes – Joe: Raleigh District

1/15: Traveled with Joe to two accounts in Raleigh, after which we drove for more than two hours to call on one account, located 25 miles north of Wilmington. Suggested to Joe that it would be more efficient to schedule a series of calls in the southern part of the state and drive in the evening whenever possible. Call quality was satisfactory, but Joe did not appear to be as familiar with the accounts as he should be. This observation, along with suggestions for reviewing customer files prior to a visit, was discussed with Joe.

3/18: Joe met me at the Wilmington airport, and we visited four accounts. Three calls that Joe selected went very well, but the fourth call (a company that I had selected) was clearly upset about a late delivery. Joe assigned blame for the misunderstanding on production. I was able to resolve the issue with the buyer, and when I raised the problem with the production manager, she informed me that Joe had again promised the customer an unrealistic delivery date. I called Joe and instructed him not to promise delivery dates sooner than products would be available from our manufacturing facility.

6/22: Called on four firms in Raleigh. Good calls, well-planned, and Joe was well-prepared. Told Joe how pleased I was with the calls, and to keep up the good work.

8/08: Spent two days with Joe. First day in Wilmington area, and the second—after driving from 5-7 p.m.—was in Raleigh and Durham. Glad to see that Joe was following my suggestions about minimizing drive time during traditional work hours. Calls were satisfactory, and revolved around gathering information about upcoming request for quotations and resolving a few requests for minor changes to orders. Overall, a satisfactory performance.

9/31: Visited for one day in Raleigh and Durham. Went to see our largest customer who informed us we had been outbid by our major competitor on a new multi-year contract. Joe seemed extremely surprised by this news. I asked Joe how we had lost the contract to our largest competitor without him knowing we were in danger of losing the account? He seemed embarrassed and said: "he did not know." This is a big blow to our region's sales and to Joe's expected sales goals for the year.

The sales manager read through the call summaries again, and mulled these events over in her mind while thinking about the quantitative data she had already analyzed. Her task now was to meld the two—quantitative and qualitative—analyses into a coherent performance appraisal for a struggling member of her sales team.

Joe has scheduled his annual review for December 15th at 9 a.m. Hunt has a week to prepare her formal evaluation of Joe's performance for this year. Based upon your understanding of performance appraisal and the information provided above, what should Hunt say to Joe? That is, what can be deduced from the year's performance records? Lastly, what specific recommendations would you make to Joe for improving his performance in the coming year?

Questions

1. There is little doubt that there are negative trends in Joe's annual performance. Further analyze the data to uncover the specific behaviors that contributed to his level of performance.

2. Are any other salespersons who work for Janet Hunt whose statistics indicate potential problems in any performance areas? If so, what are they?

3. Based upon the information presented in the case, what strategy or approach does Joe appear to be taking when meeting with his customers?

4. Compute several ratios discussed in the evaluation chapter to help you compare and contrast the six salespersons managed by Hunt. Are these ratios helpful in your evaluation? How so?

5. What reasons might Joe offer to rebut a negative annual performance appraisal? How might Hunt respond to his rebuttal?

6. Write a formal narrative to Joe to explain your evaluation of his performance. Remember the importance of being factual and objective.

CASE STUDY 4

Precision Advanced Management, Inc. (PAM)

Larry Cline, director of sales for PAM, has a meeting with Travis Pipes, the CEO, on ethical issues they've been experiencing lately. Frankly, Larry isn't sure if some of the problems he's seen, and that have been reported to him via his inside sales manager, William Zane, are unethical. Additionally, Larry is confused about many of the company's current policies because they haven't been updated for some time. Larry feels that he is too busy to worry about these issues, and lacks the knowledge of what ethical policies in this industry look like since he switched out of a software sales management role two years ago.

History

In 1951, Harrison ("Harry") Tendor founded Automatic Pay, Inc., as a manual payroll processing business with his brother Robert "Billy Bob" Tendor. Jason Jordan joined the Tendors during their company's infancy. In 1953, Jordan became chairman and CEO of the company. In 1957, the company changed its name to Precision Advanced Management, Inc. (PAM), and began using punched card machines, check printing machines, and early mainframe computers. PAM went public in 1962 with 400 clients, 150 employees, and annual revenues of $800,000. The company established a subsidiary in the United Kingdom in 1967, and acquired the pioneering online computer services company, Data Sharing Limited (DSL), in 1975. Jordan continued in his roles as chairman and CEO until elected to the United States Congress from Tennessee in 1984.

From 1986 onward, PAM's annual revenues exceeded the $1 billion mark, with paychecks processed for about 10 percent of the U.S. workforce. In the 1990s, PAM began acting as a professional employer organization (PEO). Around this time, the company acquired Autodata, a French company; Kerney Computers, Inc., a dealer management systems provider to auto dealers in Europe; and the payroll and human resource services company, ISI, headquartered in London. In 2008, the PAM Brokerage Service Group was spun off to form Falcon Financial Solutions, Inc., removing about $2 billion from PAM's total yearly revenue. PAM distributed one share of Falcon common stock for every four shares of PAM common stock held by shareholders of record as of the close of business on August 1, 2008. PAM brings faster, easier business solutions that unlocks insights, improves compliance, and drives comprehensive human capital management.

PAM Today

Precision Advanced Management, Inc. (PAM) is one of the largest providers of business processing and cloud-based solutions—including payroll, talent management, human resource management, benefits administration, and time and attendance—to employers and automotive dealerships around the world. PAM offers configurable solutions that can fit an organization's unique goals, and increases their productivity and efficiency. PAM serves around 620,000 organizations in more than 125 countries, including 425,000 small-business clients and 26,000 vehicle dealerships. More than 80 percent of Fortune 500 companies, and more than 90 Fortune 100 companies, use at least one of PAM's services.

Partnering with PAM means that the client receives the latest technology solutions—so the client can focus its limited time and resources on essential business, not back-office administration. Allowing PAM to handle a client company's logistical and operational tasks permits its upper management to focus on issues relevant to long-term success.

In addition to cold-calling selected industries, and being provided leads by their supervisors, sales reps find leads through referrals. Penn Bank is a satisfied customer of PAM, and has payroll and human capital management services through PAM. When a new small business or franchisee comes into a Penn Bank bank branch, requesting a loan/financing to begin a business, Penn Bank loan officers recommend PAM as a provider of payroll and HR services, which are crucial to a business. Penn Bank chooses to do this because they see a benefit, and have no reason—as an extremely satisfied customer—not to assist a partner of theirs. Conversely, PAM recommends their clients use Penn Bank if they need financing at any point.

PAM has not updated its company policies since 1990. Leadership neither informs employees of them nor enforces them. PAM's executive management also hasn't supported the establishment of compliance programs. Management has been so busy lately that they haven't had a chance to train employees on ethical workplace practices. Since 1990, PAM hasn't had sufficient management support to create an internal control system for monitoring employee behavior and conduct in the workplace.

Sales Efforts

Larry Cline was swamped with meetings and paperwork all last week. Last Friday, he was approached by William Zane, who wanted to discuss questionable management situations. First, Zane began by explaining how everyone on his staff has been calling family members and close friends in order to reach their daily call numbers. It has never been communicated by Cline or any supervisor that this is wrong, nor is there a company policy against doing it, but Zane felt strongly enough about the issue to bring it to the sales director's attention. Second, PAM's Sales Force Automation (SFA) system allows leads to expire every 15 days without an update. So many reps count the days until a co-worker forgets to contact a particular lead, and they immediately claim the company for themselves upon the expiration of the old rep's ownership. In this way, salespersons capitalize off their co-workers' previous efforts.

Once Cline heard about the issues Zane brought to his attention, he realized that he, too, was aware of some questionable actions by employees. Most salient, Larry had observed a close relationship building between employees Matt and Christine. He encountered them multiple times in close quarters, especially after hours, and had noticed them being extremely touchy towards one another at company-wide meetings. Other co-workers have also noticed the relationship and appeared uncomfortable. For example, one co-worker approached Larry last week about a questionable e-mail exchange he saw between Matt and Christine. Though there is no evidence of anything specifically happening between them, in general Cline believes that this type of workplace behavior is inappropriate. That said, there is no company policy stating how employees can and cannot act towards one another, and he really isn't sure what is permitted regarding such a situation. The company has scheduled a customer service training session at Disney World in Orlando, Florida, for a week, later this month. This worries Larry, since both Matt and Christine will attend this overnight work trip. Matt is 53 and has a wife of 25 years and three beautiful little girls at home, while Christine is 27, just started working for the company, and got engaged two weeks ago to her college sweetheart. Matt has also volunteered in the past for multiple overnight assignments on which Christine was working. Cline is also concerned that other co-workers are going to believe that this type of personal relationship, and similar behaviors, are acceptable—and that other employees, too, might also begin to engage personally. Cline believes that workplace romance is distracting and bad for the company in general. Employees have also raised other concerns about Matt. Just last week, a co-worker, Brenda, met to lodge a complaint about Matt. She reported that two weeks ago, at the company picnic, Matt touched her inappropriately, and that he has continued to tell sexual jokes in her presence at the office. She stated that if something was not done about this problem, then she would be lodging a formal sexual harassment complaint with HR and looking for another job opportunity.

PAM sales reps often entertain decision makers from prospective client companies at sporting events and at "happy hour" meetings. Senior sales rep Bill is known to drink with clients, and he often drinks to excess, becoming belligerent and placing others—including clients—in an awkward position by acting too intimate for a professional relationship. Cline has observed that several top clients did not renew PAM's services and he believes that it may be attributable to Bill's behavior toward clients. For example, a month and a half ago, Bill entertained an $8 million renewal opportunity with an IBM buying committee at a Dallas Mavericks suite within the American Airlines Center. Bill reportedly drank too much and ended up throwing up in a trash can—inside the suite. Bill lost this order, and it is likely that IBM will move the remainder of its business to a direct competitor. When Cline approached him about the incident, Bill said he didn't know that drinking with clients wasn't allowed. Based upon these incidents, Cline is struggling with how to manage salesperson behavior in the areas of employee entertainment, etiquette, and workplace relationships—given the clearly outdated employee policies. Considering these problems, what action or actions should the sales director recommend to CEO Travis Pipes?

Questions

1. Should a firm have accurate and clearly stated behavioral policies? Why or why not?

2. Are personnel policies for the sales force the sole responsibility of sales management? What other department(s) or management professional (s) is (are) also responsible? Why?

3. What are potential problems generated by inappropriate office relationships?

4. Is there a problem with sales reps claiming other accounts? What about calling non-business parties to fulfill sales call quotas?

5. What role does alcohol play in entertaining clients? What rules should be in place to ensure there is no abuse?

6. Do workplace rules protect the company, the sales force, or both? How?

CASE STUDY 5

Professional Staffing International Moves to Sales Coaching

Hanging prominently above Leslie Fraiser-Gainey's desk was a framed poster of Vince Lombardi, the Green Bay Packers' legendary Hall-of-Fame coach. A well-known Lombardi quote underneath his image read: "There's only one way to succeed in anything, and that is to give it everything." Being a voracious reader, Fraiser-Gainey had an overflowing bookcase next to her office desk. The selections indicated an ongoing self-education in best practices in selling, motivating a sales force, sales management, and other related aspects of her career.

Atop the bookcase, a copy of *The 4 Disciplines of Execution: Achieving Your Wildly Important Goals* lay open to a chapter titled "Creating a Cadence of Accountability." Sales training had always been the cornerstone of Fraiser-Gainey's strategic plan in her role as director of business operations for Professional Staffing International (PSI). Every year, her training budget included a minimum of seven days' in-house sales training, and one five-day outside training on teamwork activities. Fraiser-Gainey felt that expanding the education of her sales team was paramount to the success of her office. She always led by example, and worked side by side with her sales team during the training sessions. As director, she made it a point to be the first person to volunteer when an activity involved a role play, or some other task involving a step outside the comfort zone. Her rationale for putting so much emphasis on sales training was that every employee seemed to appreciate the investment the company was willing to make in its people, and the opportunity to bond as a group during the training sessions.

Fraiser-Gainey earned a degree in marketing with a sales emphasis in 1990. After completing an internship with a local non-profit, she hired on as a talent recruiter with PSI after graduation. Leslie had taken the typical sales courses in college, and had gained experience with fundraising activities as part of her internship, but this was her first true sales position. Shortly after she started with PSI, she met her future husband. Tom Gainey was a computer programmer, and happened to be looking to make a career move in the early 1990s. Leslie came in contact with Gainey while prospecting through an alumni newsletter. It turned out they had a connection through a mutual college friend. After a phone call to him, using the college referral, Leslie was able to place him with a reputable engineering firm contracted for PSI's services. As a thank you for connecting him to his dream job, Gainey invited Frasier out to celebrate lunch—and the rest was history. Fast-forward 15 years, and the Gaineys are a family of five, balancing dual-career responsibilities and kid duties. Frasier-Gainey did more than just place her future husband into a new career path with PSI; she went on to place more than 100 clients during her first two years on board. Her total client placement still holds the company record for recruiters. After a brief stop in account management, Leslie was promoted to director of business operations in 1995. Her responsibilities included staffing, training, motivation, and accountability of the 30-member sales team, split between recruiters and account managers.

With nearly 10 years of experience in the director's position, she was respected in the office for her work ethic, organizational skills, and enthusiasm. It was as if she was channeling the Lombardi poster's message through to her employees. As a successful working woman, wife, and mother of three, Fraiser-Gainey thought she was in a very good place in life.

Professional Staffing International (PSI) is a small staffing firm that specializes in matching up information technology specialists with companies in need of programmers and expertise in computer networking. It has 10 office locations in the Midwest, with the main office headquartered in Chicago. The company has a total of 300 employees, and a database of 750,000 domestic and 100,000 international names, qualifications, and contact information for IT professionals. PSI's main competitors are Manpower, Kforce, TEKsystems, and Areotek. All of these firms are much larger in size and each has a global presence. PSI competes with these larger IT staffing service companies on a daily basis, in every one of their markets. Every Chief Information officer (CIO) wants the best and brightest IT professionals on board, and they want them yesterday. With similar pricing structures, the main competitive advantage often comes down to how quickly a firm can find a suitable qualified candidate in the market to match the desired open position for the account. Over the years, PSI has been able to prosper in the marketplace by providing its customers with a winning IT talent strategy—by knowing where the technical professionals are in each market and providing them with fair market rates.

Inavero Institute's IT and Talent Survey Results

The Inavero Institute completed its quarterly IT and Talent Survey. The survey reflects the perspectives of more than 1,000 chief information officers (CIOs) and information (IT) decision-makers in the U.S. and Canada. Among major findings of the study were some interesting statistics:

- Only73 percent of IT leaders surveyed said they believed their company's ability to attract and retain top IT talent can offer a competitive advantage.

- Approximately 50 percent of IT leaders said the same individuals who manage the procurement of materials and supplies—such as hardware and software—are also responsible for managing IT talent acquisition at their organizations.

- Only 40 percent of IT leaders report that the same individuals who manage the acquisition of technical talent also manage the acquisition of non-technical talent, such as administrative assistants, sales personnel and customer service representatives.

- Of the survey participants, 67 percent indicate they believed all IT staffing firms were basically the same.

Professional Staffing International Organizational Chart (Leslie Fraiser-Gainey's office)

Director of Business Operations (1)

Inside Recruiter (15)   Outside Account Managers (12)   Support Staff (3)

Explanation of Diagram Positions

The diagram shows the reporting relationship in the PSI office. The role of the outside account manager involves forming relationships with accounts that have a need for IT professionals. Once a need is identified, the qualifications and timeline for the position are given to the inside recruiter. At any one time, more than 100 candidate searches may be going on for multiple firms in Leslie Fraiser-Gainey's office. The inside recruiter has the responsibility to search PSI's database of potential candidates to fill a position. If the specific skills are not in the database, the recruiter must be creative and contact IT professionals who are already employed, and try to entice them to look at the new opportunity. Once potential candidates are identified, the recruiter prepares them for the interview. The preparation can include coaching them on how to dress, how to answer difficult interview questions, and offering résumé revisions. Account managers and recruiters must prioritize their searches to maximize potential profits on the placement. PSI is paid only when a candidate receives an accepted offer from an account. These payments can come in two forms: a simple placement fee can be earned, based on a percentage of the candidate's starting salary; or commission payments can be earned, based on the spread of the candidate's actual hourly wage versus the hourly wage negotiated by the PSI account manager. The director of operations hires, trains, and manages the inside recruiters, outside recruiters, and support staff. Interdependence of account managers and recruiters is very critical to the success of each office. Secure territories are given to each office, and they share the company's database of IT professionals.

In some cases, a very productive recruiter can make higher commissions than an account manager earns. In most instances, though, recruiters prove themselves in the office by working the phone, and then advance through promotion to outside account management positions. Account managers have the responsibility of starting and maintaining a relationship with an account. However, without the help of the recruiting function, the account manager may have no candidates to fill open positions.

Current Situation at PSI

Since the Great Recession of 2008, the staffing solutions business has been very competitive. Fortunately, PSI weathered the storm and actually grew during this time. Unfortunately, this past year saw Fraiser-Gainey's office change dramatically due to some staff departures. Three of her top account mangers left to form their own IT recruitment firm. Because there was no "non-compete" clause in their contracts, Leslie could do nothing when the trio took their account relationships with them. Almost overnight 30 percent of the office revenues disappeared! Shortly after their departure, five of PSI's best recruiters joined the new start-up, attracted by their former colleagues' promises of larger commissions and profit sharing. The relationships and positive office culture Fraiser-Gainey had worked so hard to build over the years was now being severely tested. She felt that she had been hoodwinked, and the stress of running an underperforming office began to negatively affect her psyche. The stressful work environment also started to upset her home life. The Chicago headquarters office was watching very closely, and she knew something needed to be done to turn things around.

Since losing almost a third of her staff, Fraiser-Gainey went to work recruiting from three regional colleges with which she had partnered over the years. Usually she tries to hire one or two of the top collegiate sales talents every year. This year was different; she hired 10 new employees from three different university sales programs. She also promoted three recruiters into account manager positions. As a result of taking drastic measures, she found herself with a lot of sales inexperience—with no time to waste because the competition was already ambushing existing PSI clients and making headway by offering candidates very competitive wage guarantees. The director thought about the prospects of providing traditional training to her sales team, as she had done in the past, but she could not afford to take them out of the field, not even for one day. She also thought about offering after-hours sales training, but she was pushing her staff so hard that many were already working 60 hours a week and beginning to burn out. She could hear the rumblings of a storm brewing in the office. Recruiters and account managers had begun pointing fingers, accusing each other of dropping the ball on lost business. Office goals, published on whiteboards around the office, were openly challenged and called unattainable. Prioritizing of accounts turned into arguments, rather than discussions. Everywhere she looked, she could see more roadblocks that must be addressed if the office was going to prosper again under her direction.

About the time Fraiser-Gainey was ready to throw in the towel, she read an article on sales skills coaching. One line in the article really resonated with her: "Put yourself in each of your salespersons' shoes and be prepared to understand the world from their perspective." The article went on to address making changes in behaviors, based on individuals' specific needs, and to focus on the Three Ps: personal, professional, and performance growth. The director was convinced this was the direction she needed to go with her sales team. She set out to develop an individualized sales training program based on targeting company and office objectives. She temporarily reinvented her role as director of operations and would become a coach to her sales team. With new vigor and purpose, she resolved to unlock the potential of each member of her sales team, and to guide each on an individualized basis. Now was the time to give it everything and anything Fraiser-Gainey had left in her—as Coach Lombardi had preached to his players to do.

Questions

1. Define sales coaching. How does sales coaching differ from sales training?

2. Does Fraiser-Gainey have the respect, empathy, and objectivity to coach her team members?

3. Does she have the skills that qualify her to be a successful sales coach?

4. What are the roadblocks the director faces with her sales team?

5. Describe how a sales coach would work best with you?

6. As a new hire, how would you feel if Fraiser-Gainey focused just on coaching you for an entire workday?

7. What activities should be prioritized as revenue-generating?

8. Should the sales coach come from the outside or from inside the organization? Why or why not?

9. What is the difference between working with a sales coach and a sales mentor?

CASE STUDY 6

Sally Sells Shirts Down by the Seashore

It was a postcard-perfect, early September day for watching the Senior Tour Championship at the Tournament Players Club (TPC) of Myrtle Beach, South Carolina. Sally Reynolds and her husband, Jack, had positioned themselves in a premium spectators' viewing area on the right side of the 193 yard, par three, seventeenth hole. It was also the side of the green where the players exited before heading to the difficult par five 18th hole. It was late Sunday afternoon, and the year-end PGA Senior Tour championship was heating up between Fred Couples and Tom Lehman. Both players were at 12 under par and playing the 17th in the final two-some. As the couple watched each of the competitors par the hole, the players were tied, heading into the final hole of the four- day competition. No one around the 17th green was going to give up their spot, because everyone was anticipating a playoff if neither broke the tie. The playoff would start on the 16th hole, so there was an excellent chance the two would show up on the same green in about 30 minutes. As the players walked off the side of the green, Fred Couples caught a glimpse of a familiar face in the crowd. As soon as he saw Reynolds, he paused and leaned into the crowd of spectators and gave Sally a peck on the cheek and said, "Good to see you, Sally. Let's see if I can get home in two and birdie the final hole to win this thing." She said, "I have no doubt you will, Freddy; by the way, you are looking fabulous in your Ashworth shirt today." Reynolds was so proud to be an independent sales representative for the Ashworth apparel brand. She felt her affiliation and longevity with the brand made her part of a very special family that represented one of the most popular apparel brands in golf. Little did she know that, in only a few short weeks, a phone call from her sales manager would drastically change things!

Background

Sally Reynolds started her sales career in 1987, after being a stay-at-home mom and raising three boys. All three sons were avid golfers and played golf at the nearby Rancho Park Golf Course— one of Los Angeles' finest 18-hole public courses. She and her husband never played golf, so it was a bit odd that all three of their boys gravitated towards the game. The golf course is in close proximity to the family home, so the boys could ride their bikes there, and it was nice that they had something they loved to do during the summer months when school was out. It was a chance meeting at a local junior golf tournament the boys had entered that got Reynolds started in her sales career. She noticed a man at the event wearing an attractive navy-and-white, horizontally striped shirt. Never one to be shy about anything, she approached the man to ask where he had purchased the shirt. The gentleman's name was John Ashworth, and she learned that he was one of the founders of Charter Golf, Inc. He and his partner were in the process of raising money for their business venture, and were looking to hire their first salesperson. Call it serendipity or divine intervention from the golf gods, but Reynolds and Ashworth hit it off, and she became an independent sales representative for Charter Golf. She was also one of the company's first customers to have bought the same shirt Ashworth was wearing—the day they met—for her husband and three sons.

Reynolds watched the company grow very rapidly from its original location in the garment district of Los Angeles. The partners at Charter Golf were keen observers of golf fashion, and added much-needed style to the golf fashion world. With her help as the company's only independent sales representative, sales revenues began to grow modestly—reaching $500,000 in the first full year. After attending the annual PGA show in Orlando, Florida, in January of 1988, the company pre-booked enough sales to double its business the next year. Reynolds was front and center at the trade show booth, stopping people in the aisle, telling them about the new apparel company taking the golf world by storm. Using stock grants as an incentive, the company signed endorsement deals with PGA professionals Fred Couples, John Cook, Scott Verplank, and Ernie Els. Couples later signed a lifetime endorsement agreement, in exchange for incentive stock, in 1994. That same year, Charter Golf, Inc., formally changed the company name to Ashworth, Inc. Sales growth continued through a secondary stock offering in 1994 that raised $11million, helping fund expansion and the hiring of more independent sales reps. That transaction valued the company at $50 million on $25 million in revenues. Over the years, Reynolds was able to meet and entertain all of the Ashworth-endorsing golf professionals at national trade shows and PGA events. She was especially fond of Fred Couples, and they formed a special bond that has endured for 20 years.

After John Ashworth left the company in 1997, because of management differences, things changed in many ways, as the brand grew in popularity and the company grew in size. Even without her friend and company founder supporting her, Reynolds's role as an independent rep increased after Ashworth's departure, as she was given additional responsibility for the growth of important accounts across California. After her husband retired in 2004, they moved across the country to a beachfront condo in Myrtle Beach, South Carolina. She had been eyeing the smaller sales territory in that resort community for a number of years. When the previous independent sales rep retired, she took over the existing accounts and settled into a nice semi-retirement sales position that Reynolds operated as Grand Strand Golf Apparel. She had paid her dues by growing the Ashworth golf brand over the years, and now it was time to primarily service a territory and make commissions as a distributor to supplement her husband's Social Security income. In addition to the Ashworth apparel line, she picked up a golf shoe and belt product line to add to her portfolio of products. Her boys were now all grown and lived across the country. The Myrtle Beach area was a golf haven, and the boys enjoyed coming to visit Mom and Dad a couple of times a year and getting in one or two rounds of golf at the more than 100 golf courses in the area. What a perfect time and place to start a new business, Reynolds thought to herself.

Changes in Corporate Ownership and Sales Structure

In 2008, golf industry leader TaylorMade-Adidas acquired the Ashworth brand for $73 million. The Adidas global brand had been making acquisitions for a number of years, and was looking to solidify its market share leadership position in the golf industry. Ashworth was ripe for the taking and Adidas pounced. Within a short time after the deal was inked, management at TaylorMade-Adidas started to consolidate sales territories to become more efficient with its resources. In some cases, independent sales reps were allowed to stay on board and continue to represent and sell the Ashworth brand under the current commission structure. Reynolds was one of the reps who fell into this category, but she did not know why she was kept on since her territory was right in the middle of the highest concentration of golf courses in the country. In most cases, independent reps were released from their agreements, and a TaylorMade-Adidas rep took over their accounts in the territory. There were no instances where an independent rep was allowed to stay on and add the TaylorMade-Adidas line to his or her portfolio of products. Many reps who were abruptly let go scrambled to find another line of golf apparel to represent. Some were successful, picking up the Antigua or Bobby Jones apparel product lines. Most of the more popular golf apparel lines already had corporate sales representation, and were not available to independent reps. Both Antigua and Bobby Jones were available, according to a Darrell Survey, because their market share and popularity were well below the other lines.

Darrell Survey Results

The Darrell Survey (*darrellsurvey.com*) is an organization that monitors what products golf professionals use for equipment and apparel at PGA, LPGA, and Senior PGA events. The company also tracks sales of equipment and apparel choices for more than 4,000 U.S. golfers at more than 75 courses around the country. If you are in the golf business, what appears on the annual Darrell Survey is considered an accurate measurement of brand awareness. Below are the current golf apparel results.*

1. Nike
2. TaylorMade-Adidas
3. Under Armour
4. Ashworth
5. Puma
6. Antiqua
7. Polo
8. Reebok
9. Cutter & Buck
10. Bobby Jones

This is not an official Darrell Survey Results, but rather a fictional list created for instructional purposes.

Current Sales Manager's No-Nonsense Approach

Barbara Tice is a regional sales manager for TaylorMade-Adidas in its Southeast territory. She is responsible for an area that includes some of the finest golf courses in the country—including Atlanta National Golf Club, Augusta, Pinehurst No. 2, and TPC Myrtle Beach. Her territory also includes the world-famous vacation resort area of Myrtle Beach, which boasts the most golf courses per person in the country. With short, cool winters (temperatures average 56 degrees), and short, hot summers (temperatures averaging 89 degrees) and miles of white sand beaches, it is no wonder this heavenly place on the Atlantic Ocean is frequented by so many visitors each year. Out of her Atlanta home office, Tice manages eight different company sales reps and three independent sales reps. Most of the other regions for TaylorMade-Adidas had a similar mix of 75 percent corporate reps and 25 percent independent reps. Tice is a numbers person, and always has her fingers on the "sales pulse" of her region. She makes sure that each of her reps reports weekly sales, and even requires a pipeline analysis of new business that will—potentially—be booked in the next three to four weeks. The future-business forecast includes a color-coded spreadsheet, created to signify how confident the rep is that the expected business deals will come to fruition. Green signifies a 90 percent confidence rating; yellow, 60 percent; and pink, 30 percent.

Tice worked her way up the ladder into management at TaylorMade-Adidas, using this same no-nonsense approach to monitoring her sales force by making her reps accountable for their promises and growing their respective territories. Her focus on always knowing where new business was originating and when it was going to be booked seemed to keep all her reps on their toes. Her region had performed well over the past two years since she took over as sales manager, and she felt confident about all sales team members in her region. After reviewing the latest booked sales report and green forecast numbers from her sales reps, she did the math and quickly realized that her region had the potential to be the top sales region in the country by the end of the quarter. About the same time that Tice was tallying her potential bonus from the upcoming quarter, she received an e-mail from TaylorMade-Adidas' vice president of sales in North America.

> Effective January 1, independent sales representatives will no longer be allowed to sell any TaylorMade-Adidas product lines or other brands (i.e. Ashworth) owned by TaylorMade-Adidas. Please make arrangements to transfer accounts and make territory adjustments in your regions to cover the open accounts. All current accounts must be covered by this date by TaylorMade-Adidas sales representatives only. The sales quota will remain the same for 2015 to account for this change. This action is taking place to reduce cost, streamline reporting relationships, minimize legal exposure, and ensure that our customers receive a consistent message about our product lines. Please submit your restructuring plan to your supervisor no later than September 30.

The Dynamic Duo Wins a Sales Contest

Sally and Jack Reynolds thought they would spend their retirement years sipping iced tea on their veranda overlooking the beach and the Atlantic Ocean. With no real hobbies or interests, he grew bored in retirement and spent his days helping his wife manage and work her sales territory. She maintained the service part of the business by processing orders and filling out the tedious paperwork for her sales manager, Barbara Tice. His background was in public relations, where he had worked for the last 15 years of his career. It turned out Jack Reynolds was a natural at sales, and he became the master prospector. In fact, she won a company-wide new-business sales competition based on his efforts in the field. As a reward, Sally Reynolds had some Grand Strand Golf Apparel business cards made up for her husband. With the bonus from the new business contest, they purchased outdoor furniture they could both enjoy. Once he opened a door into an account, she would show up and present the Ashworth Apparel line of products and other manufacturers she represented. She had always been good at bonding with customers. Her naturally nurturing personality seemed to resonate with her customers. "Make a friend and you make a sale," she would always tell her husband. Even though she thought this time in her life was going to be about winding down her sales career, she felt more energized than ever by working alongside her husband of 35 years. For the past three years, she was in the top 10 percent for sales of Ashworth Apparel in the country. She felt that the coming year would be a record year for the husband-and-wife sales team, and was envisioning an expansion of their business and planning to look for more manufacturers to represent at the next PGA merchandise show.

On September 30th, Barbara Tice called Sally Reynolds to tell her that the Ashworth account would be pulled from her, and that she needed to arrange to transfer all her account information to the local TaylorMade-Adidas corporate representative in the Myrtle Beach territory. When asked why she was being—essentially—fired after been a top-ten producer for many years, Tice simply replied: "It's out of my hands." "So much for loyalty," Reynolds thought to herself. After a long silence on the phone, she measured her response to Tice and said: "I'm deeply upset and saddened that you will not take a stand on this decision and support the ones who have worked so hard to make this region successful over the years…I'm going to hang up now, but I want to leave you with this thought: I sold my customers on the Ashworth brand, and I can certainly 'un-sell' them just as easily, if that is what it has come to."

Questions

1. What are the advantages and disadvantages of working through a sales agent network?

2. Who has the power in this case study? The manufacturer or the sales agent? Why?

3. Why would Ashworth want to have all corporate sales representatives?

4. What would you do in Barbara Tice's situation after she received the e-mail?

5. If Sally and Jack Reynolds can no longer sell the Ashworth brand, what should their next move be?

6. From an end-customer viewpoint where do your loyalties lie? Can Sally Reynolds "unsell" them?

7. Why would a change in the alignment of the sales representation save the TaylorMade-Adidas money in this case?

8. What are some of the repercussions for the Ashworth brand if this change in representation moves forward?

9. Before being dropped by TaylorMade-Adidas, do you believe that Sally and Jack Reynolds were loyal to the Ashworth brand, given that they had also represented other product lines?

10. Is there an advantage in having a blended sales force of company salespersons and independent reps? Explain your answer.

CASE STUDY 7

Syntax and Zolar Merge Sales Forces

The announcement in the *Wall Street Journal* was exciting: Syntax and Zolar were merging together to form one large, global sales organization. The marketplace, and especially current employees of both firms, waited anxiously to learn of the outcome of the merger, since both companies had been fierce rivals for more than two decades. However, as is true in most "mergers," the fact was that larger Syntax was acquiring Zolar by purchasing its stock at a premium. This meant that Syntax was in the driver's seat regarding who would stay and who would go!

Currently, Syntax employed 22 field sales reps at the time of the merger, and Zolar had 15 field sales reps. As the merger transition started to unfold, there were decisions to be made at Syntax—primarily by Leila Brakefield, sales VP, and by human resources VP Pat Brown. Brakefield reported that, based upon current forecasts and workload calculations, the combined sales force would need to be reduced by 25 percent in order to avoid excessive overhead costs and confusion in the marketplace. Plus, all retained salespersons would need to receive extensive product training, at a minimum, since both companies had robust product portfolios. Another challenge for sales leadership would be the motivation and team building necessary for a successful new sales team, since a high degree of animosity and competition existed between the two former sales forces.

The demographics of the new sales force—prior to headcount reduction—skewed to an abundance of senior sales representatives. That is, 70 percent of sales personnel at both firms had over 20 years sales experience, while the remaining 30 percent of the sales force was under the age of 30 and possessed less than two years' selling experience. This suggests there was not a standard distribution of experience in the sales team, but rather older, more senior salespersons and fairly new salespersons must be considered for retention. The combined product portfolio for both Syntax and Zolar consisted of 34 products and four new products were scheduled for introduction over the next three years. Total sales revenue was $550 million for the combined business unit in the last calendar year.

Distribution within the supply chain was also going to be a challenge for Brakefield and sales management, since both organizations were partnered with distributors that strongly disliked one another and ranged in quality from bottom-feeders to high value-added distributors. The pricing structure at both companies was also in conflict with Zolar's having resorted to price discounting to win bids, while Syntax had pursued a high-price, high-quality strategy.

To complicate things even more, new territory alignment needed to occur, as well as a unified compensation program that nudged the two former organizations closer to one another. Said differently, territories would need to be adjusted to ensure that clients received the appropriate level of service, and that salespersons were able to conduct business on efficient travel schedules. Also, Brakefield would have to combine salary plans so that the new sales force was rewarded appropriately for its contributions to the success of the firm.

Early retirement was not currently on the table to reduce the over-staffing situation. However, Leila Brakefield could recommend early retirement for a limited number of senior salespersons who were nearing retirement age, and who might qualify for that option. Even here, there were problems, since Syntax offered a defined retirement plan, while Zolar paid into a 401(k) retirement plan that ended any time a salesperson left the firm for any reason.

Using the information provided, answer the following questions based upon what you believe to be fair, legal, and best for future customer service and company profits as Syntax and Zolar merge—and right size—their sales teams.

Questions

1. What is the first action Leila Brakefield should take? How important are communications with the sales force and distributors during this transition?

2. What criteria will you use to decide which sales personnel to retain and which to let go?

3. What methods should be employed to blend the two sales organizations with minimal conflict?

4. Would it be best to plan and conduct one training program or two entirely different ones? Why?

5. Should the training program only focus on product knowledge? What other topics might the combined sales team need to succeed? Why?

6. What metrics should be adopted to assign and evaluate the "new" sales team?

CASE STUDY 8

Miller and Associates: *A Sales Force Goes Wild!*

Robert "Bob" Voli is sales manager at Miller and Associates, an original equipment manufacturer (OEM) of security equipment, software, and consulting services that targets the financial marketplace. Voli and his sales team are attending a security industry trade show being held in New Orleans, Louisiana. Due to the financial meltdown, overall purchases by financial firms have been flat or in a slump for several years. Based upon observations and off-the-cuff comments, the sales team appears to be tired and demoralized due to a very tough year. Voli and his boss, Ben Jackson, thought it would help lift spirits for the sales team to attend the New Orleans trade show, learn more about the latest security hardware and software coming to market from competitors, and to relax in the evening—listening to jazz and enjoying *beignets* at the Café Du Monde. After arriving and checking in at the Hilton on the River, Voli held a brief meeting with the sales team before everyone traveled to the trade show site by streetcar.

For Voli, the trade show provided a number of interesting exhibits pertinent to his line of work, and the sales team members also seemed to be enjoying themselves. Bob Voli went to dinner with two of his senior salespersons, and then headed back to the Hilton to get a good night's rest. However, things began to go downhill when his phone began ringing at 1:45 a.m. According to the police officer who called him, two of Voli's sales reps got "rip-roaring drunk" in the French Quarter, proceeded to get into an argument and shoving match with fellow bar patrons, and were subsequently arrested for public intoxication and disorderly conduct. Voli ended up bailing both sales reps out of jail at 3 a.m. Voli definitely did not sleep much during his first night in New Orleans, but he did feel better the second day when he made three potential contacts with financial firm buyers who were also attending the trade show.

There was another incident the second night when one of the younger, unmarried sales reps "hooked up" with a competitor's salesperson. He eventually showed up at the trade show about 1:30 p.m. the next day! The third night, a group from the sales team started doing shots at the hotel bar, and one of the sales reps made a pass at the wife of Miller and Associates' best distributor. The sales rep and the distributor's wife left together, disappeared for two hours, and no one knows where they went.

Voli, who by this time was frustrated and more than a little angry with the unprofessional behavior of his sales team, arrived in his hotel suite to find three voice mail messages blinking on his phone. Two were personal, from family, while one was from Voli's boss, Ben Jackson.

Message 1: Ben Jackson had just reviewed this month's sales report and called Voli to question the 18 percent drop in monthly sales. Jackson asked why he was not warned that bad news was coming, and instructed Voli to call him as soon as possible.

Message 2: Voli's wife left an emotional message, informing him that their 16-year-old son had received a citation for texting while driving—after damaging another vehicle stopped at a traffic light. The son was shaken, but not seriously injured.

Message 3: The second personal message was from Voli's sister, who stated that their 88-year-old mother had fallen and fractured her hip. Voli's mom was admitted to the large trauma hospital in his hometown, and would undergo surgery early the next morning.

To further complicate matters, Voli had a 7:30 a.m. meeting with his company's second largest distributor, with an agenda addressing issues of proper account management.

At this point, all Bob Voli wanted to do is scream! But he knows he must be the leader and take charge of this chaos. The question is: what should Bob Voli do?

Questions

1. What is Bob Voli's first priority? Who should he call first, second, and last?

2. What sales management issue is plaguing the sales team? Whose fault is the team's unprofessional conduct? Why?

3. Why did the team come unglued in New Orleans? What could have minimized unprofessional sales team behavior?

4. What type of assignments should a sales team have at a trade show?

5. Can Bob Voli manage this chaos? How?

CASE STUDY 9

High E Heating & Air Systems

Ron Johnson is vice president of sales For High E Heating & Air Systems, headquartered in San Diego, California. When Johnson joined High E as a territory salesperson in 1995, he was one of only 10 salespersons. As of January 1 this year, High E employed more than 105 salespersons in the United States, and had partnered with firms that employed more than 200 heating, ventilation, and air conditioning salespersons in Europe and Asia. He had earned a Bachelor's degree in marketing from San Diego State University, and then spent six years as a U.S. Naval officer who managed the installation and maintenance of heating and air conditioning systems—on ships and ashore. The myriad experiences he gained at sea and on bases in California, Hawaii, and the Philippines provided a solid technical knowledge of heating and air conditioning systems. Between 1998 and 2001, Johnson earned an M.B.A. in international marketing from Chapman University in Orange, California. He even completed an independent study course on cross-cultural marketing taught by a professor who specialized in this area.

High E specializes in high-efficiency heating and air conditioning systems that are easy to install and do not employ chemicals or substances that are harmful to the environment. This innovative marketing strategy was conceived by the engineer-owners, Jim Miller and Gary Palin, when they founded the company in 1986. High E's focus on environmentally friendly refrigerants was years ahead of the requirements set by the Environmental Protection Agency (EPA); the company gained a slow, but steady customer base in Southern California, and then expanded nation-wide.

High E designs and builds heating and air conditioning units that can be added to existing buildings by running small tubes from an outside condenser through the walls to a blower unit mounted high on a wall. The High E air conditioning unit's temperature and fan speeds are controllable by a handheld device. These units have become extremely popular for updating older homes and condominium units in Hawaii, Arizona, Texas, and Florida, since there is no need for internal ductwork that would require demolishing walls and floors.

Sales growth has been steady for High E in the U.S. and overseas. Johnson helped the firm expand globally in 2003 by traveling to Osaka, Japan; Shanghai, China; Manila, the Philippines, Kuala Lumpur, Malaysia; Bangkok, Thailand; Jakarta, Indonesia; as well as to Hong Kong, S.A.R.; and the Republic of Singapore. In each of these cities, he met with owners of heating and air-conditioning contractor companies to earn their partnership selling and servicing the High E brand. In 2004, Johnson and co-owners Miller and Palin traveled to London and negotiated with Thomson Ltd. to represent the High E line of products in the European Union (E.U.) countries. As a result of their efforts, High E has eight smaller partners in Asia, and one large partner who sells and services customers in the initial 16 E.U. countries.

As might be expected, sales levels vary across countries. High E's major competitors are located in Japan and Germany, and it is viewed by buyers as an overseas brand that competes directly with Mitsubishi in Japan and Siemens in Germany—which have the advantage of a longer history in their respective markets than does High E. Rumors have circulated that both foreign firms give kickbacks in the form of "rebates" to their partners. Siemens and Mitsubishi offer similarly designed units that do not require internal hardware when installed in existing homes or buildings. High E's principal product advantage is that the units are higher in efficiency and environmentally friendly. This means that the units cost less to operate and are less likely to harm the environment!

However, Johnson recently read a statement in *The Chally World Class Sales Excellence Research Report*[1] that "world-class" firms are identified through their strong desire to provide a highly qualified, customer-centric sales force. World-class firms devote time and effort to recruiting, training, and supporting their sales teams. He had originally asked why? The answer was that any product can be copied or improved, but sales force quality and capability can be a "differential advantage."

As vice president of sales, Johnson wants to propose a "world-class" training program for his 100+ U.S.-based salespersons, and parallel programs for partner firms in Asia and Europe. He feels that he has an accurate understanding about the training needs of the U.S.-based sales team, but he feels less certain about the needs of salespersons within the multiple cultures and languages that are found in Asia and Europe. For example, while many of the Asian-based salespersons speak English, their ability to successfully complete a technical class that explains high technology air-conditioning principles is doubtful. Also, it is expensive to translate all technical bulletins into Japanese, Mandarin, Pilipino, Thai, Malay, British English, French, Italian, German, etc. Likewise, he understands that the selling process varies across cultures. How business-to-business buyers purchase in Hong Kong differs from how customers buy in Hawaii or Le Havre, France. For example, Johnson had read and learned through visits that *guan xi* or personal relationships remain paramount in China. Conversely, selling in Germany requires the salesperson to present well-thought-out, logical, documented sales proposals.

Most training programs focus on five areas: product knowledge, sales skills, market information, company information, and technical skills (CRM). First, the sales executive must determine the level of knowledge and attitudes possessed by current salespersons. Then, he must calculate how much time it will take to make the trainees competent in each area. Next, he will have to decide which training should be taught locally and which can be standardized. Johnson also needs to determine whether it is necessary to call all salespersons to a central location to receive training or delivered it in an asynchronous fashion. For example, is it cost-efficient to make a DVD and send it out to salespersons? How could the digital option be handled across multiple cultures?

The current initial program at High E for new salespersons is structured in three phases. The new hire initially works in the office for a month and completes three CD instructional blocks that teach product knowledge, company information, and the local CRM system. The trainee then travels to San Diego, California, for a week-long formal training session at the company headquarters. This formal training week costs High E about $5,000 per salesperson for travel, hotel, food, and training, and does not include lost productivity. The agenda includes meetings with company executives, product instruction by company technical specialists, marketing presentations about competitive products and sales approaches that succeed in the marketplace, and team building. Once the new salesperson returns to the home office, the local sales manager coaches him or her on "ride-alongs" that last a week or more, depending upon the salesperson's abilities and demonstrated expertise. All in all, the training session lasts from six to eight weeks and costs about $30,000 per salesperson!

Johnson feels that, in order for High E to offer an effective training program, several decisions have to be made:

1. How would the training programs need to vary? Training the U.S. sales force needs to focus on bringing fairly competent salespersons up to speed, while the variation in salespersons' skills may be greater across Asia. The quality of salespersons in Europe may differ by country. Some of the British and French salespersons are top rate, while salespersons in less advanced nations of the E.U. can vary widely.

---

[1] Jordan, Jason, Howard Stevens, and Sally Stevens (2007). *The Chally World Class Sales Excellence Research Report*. Dayton, OH: The HR Chally Group.

2. Who should conduct the training? High E has a semi-retired sales manager who provides training at both the home office in San Diego and at regional training sessions. But the question is: who should teach/oversee training in Asia and Europe? Given the different languages spoken by the attendees, should the instructor be a local expert who can communicate with the area's salespersons? What expertise should these instructors possess? Should the instructors be trained at High E headquarters prior to offering the training overseas? Firms can choose between company instructors, consultants, or both.

3. Where should the training sessions be conducted? It would be impractical to bring overseas sales representatives to San Diego, but would it be possible to offer training at one regional or country location? In some of the Asian countries, there are multiple dialects, and this complicates the selection of training sites.

4. What should be taught? This question has multiple areas to consider: What topical areas should be emphasized? In what order? Lastly, is it possible to transmit certain knowledge electronically, instead of in person? For example, sales techniques require personal interactions and coaching from an instructor when the trainees attempt to model the desired behavior. It might be possible to introduce basic sales techniques electronically—to be enhanced and refined by the local instructor.

5. How long should the training last? Once the topics and level of knowledge desired are determined, the length of training can be calculated. For example, if training lasts six hours a day, then about 30 hours of training is possible per week. However, Johnson knows that his brain would be mush if he went to classes 30-40 hours a week. It might be possible for High E to have the salespersons attend classes/one-on-one sessions for 25-30 hours a week and then ask them to read and prepare cases or presentations in the evenings. He remembered, however, that willingness to work hard and defer gratification also varies by cultural background.

6. What role should the partners play in the training effort? If partners wanted to phase in the training effort over a one- or two-year time frame, then they would need to select initial trainees. Would it be best to schedule weak salespersons who can progress the fastest initially? Likewise, partners should be familiar with the strengths and weaknesses of their sales team, and this would be important information. Local executives must also speak highly of the training effort, encourage their sales team's efforts, and make sure the knowledge and skills provided are implemented locally.

7. Should the training effort be evaluated? There are four levels of training evaluation: reaction, learning/knowledge, attitudes, and results. Reaction is fairly easy to measure. The reaction level can be evaluated by having the attendees complete an end-of-course rating of the training program and instructor. However, reaction measures only tell how well the trainees liked the training situation—not how knowledge, attitudes, and overall behavior changed. Johnson felt that some type of training evaluation needed to be conducted, but he wondered if, at some point, the results of the evaluation might not be worth the costs.

On Friday night, Johnson was driving north on Interstate 5 to meet a major customer and attend the Los Angeles Lakers playoff game; he was listening to satellite radio in his Lexus. He silently shook his head as he thought about the complexity of designing and implementing a global sales training program. Offering an outstanding national sales training program in the U.S. required a lot of work, but providing sales training to international partners might best be described as a nightmare!

Just outside of Rancho Bernardo, north of San Diego, the sales executive thought of one alternative that would simplify things. Why not let the overseas partners design and offer their own training programs? Such an approach would simplify High E's efforts if partners could successfully manage a "local approach" to a global effort. Finally, as he passed the El Toro Marine Corps Air Station exit, it dawned upon him that High E would still need to provide significant support in regard to sales training objectives, training materials, and technical expertise. Either way, he knew that implementing this training program was going to consume a tremendous amount of his time over the next year or so.

Questions

1. What would be the major benefits of conducting a global sales training program?

2. Would it be feasible to have a single training program for all locations? Why or why not?

3. Which of the questions must Ron Johnson answer first? Why is it so important to answer this initial question correctly?

4. What basic areas of sales training can be standardized? What areas can be taught by using technology?

5. What role does culture play in designing and implementing a sales training program?

6. Would you evaluate the training program? What levels should be in focus?

7. The benefit of allowing partners to train their salespersons is that it would be easier for High E. Is this really a benefit? What are some disadvantages of allowing partners to design and offer their own training program?

CASE STUDY 10

John Aquino and Gallo Wines

John Aquino was in his senior year at Elon University where he was completing the B.S.B.A. with a major in professional sales. The university had partnerships with a number of local and national firms that pretty much assured Aquino that he would find a position in professional selling upon graduation. Like all students in the professional sales program, the undergraduate student completed semester-long courses in professional selling, sales management, and customer relationship management (CRM). He also worked for Gallo Wines in a summer sales internship between his junior and senior years of college.

Early during the spring semester, John received an e-mail from Joe Sontek, Gallo's Southeast regional hiring and training manager, who informed Aquino that Gallo was interested in talking further with him about a full-time, entry-level sales position with its partner in Raleigh, North Carolina. The plan was for him to work in Raleigh for a year or so at a regional distributorship, to gain expertise serving on- or off-premise clients prior to joining the company's national sales force. In this way, Gallo puts its potential hires into the field to learn how they succeed and, once they have mastered local markets, they should be better able to move up a level to keep distributors, restaurants, and wine shops satisfied and in stock with Gallo Wines.

Most consumers are unaware that Gallo distributes more than 80 different brands of wine that include: Blackfoot, Black Swan, Carlo Rossi, Indigo Hills, Las Rocas, Louis Martini, McWilliams, Tisdale Vineyards, and Turning Leaf—to name just a few. Gallo-distributed wines also vary in price from less expensive Boone's Farm to more expensive Australian wines produced by Clarendon Hills.

In late April, Joe Sontek called and informed Aquino of a territory manager's job opening at Capitol Wineries in Raleigh, North Carolina. Sontek offered to call the sales manager at Capitol and recommend Aquino for the position. If, after a year or so, Aquino performed well at Capitol Wineries, he would join Gallo Wines at a to-be-determined future territory in the U.S. Aquino said he would accept the job at Capitol if it was offered, so Sontek called his business partner in Raleigh and, soon, the senior student was invited over for an interview. By graduation, he had been offered, and verbally accepted, the territory manager's position at Capitol Wineries. All appeared well until the director of Elon University's Chandler Family Professional Sales Center received an urgent e-mail from Martha Cooper, eastern sales manager for a national textbook firm. Cooper was looking to hire two textbook sales reps in North Carolina, and one in South Carolina!

The e-mail Cooper sent was forwarded to graduating and former sales program students to make them aware of the opportunity. A number of graduating seniors sent return e-mails, stating their interest in contacting Cooper. What was surprising was that Aquino also sent in an e-mail stating that he was interested in the textbook sales position. During the next few weeks, Cooper reviewed more than 50 résumés, conducted 20 phone interviews, and held formal interviews with 10 applicants for the two open positions. At the end of the process, she selected two Elon sales students for the positions in North Carolina. The final step in the process was for each of the students to visit five faculty members and write a report about their interactions with professors of business and science.

On Friday, shortly after the interview results were communicated, Aquino sent Cooper a vague e-mail that said he had decided "regretfully" that textbook sales were not where he wanted to start his career. Martha Cooper immediately e-mailed the Chandler Center's director stating she was very disappointed at Aquino's withdrawing at the last minute, and asking what was going on.

The next day, Danielle Davis—another senior student—sent the Chandler Center director an e-mail, writing that she was very upset because she had received an e-mail the previous evening from the head of human resources at EDD, Inc., explaining that her position had been eliminated in a corporate reorganization. Davis was distraught since she had planned on starting work in Columbus, Ohio, on the first of July. She asked: "what should I do now?"

Questions

1. How would you describe John Aquino's actions? Why did he behave the way he did? What could have caused Danielle's lost job with EDD?

2. Why do "certain jobs" turn out to be not so certain?

3. Is it appropriate for students who have verbally agreed to accept a position to continue "interviewing" for other sales positions?

4. If you were Martha Cooper, would you be reluctant to interview and hire other students from the same sales program? If you were director of the Chandler Center, would you recommend EDD to your students? Why or why not?

5. How does student success today impact a sales program's future reputation?

6. If you are interviewing at multiple companies, is there an acceptable way to conduct yourself during the process?

7. What conclusions can we draw from these two examples of hiring situations gone awry?

CASE STUDY 11

SMITH & NEPHEW: *The Philippines 2014*

In mid-July 2014, Olivier Bohuon, CEO of Smith & Nephew, S.A. (S&N), met over lunch with Gordon Howe, President of Global Operations.* Six months earlier, S&N had signed an agency contract with East Lane Corporation (ELC), located in Metro Manila, the Philippines, whereby ELC employees would promote S&N's wound-care solutions products in two major metropolitan areas: Manila and Cebu City. Wound care solutions (WCS) management can be complex since this includes chronic, acute, and surgical wounds that have their own characteristics. And wounds, much like the people affected by them, need to be treated on an individual basis. S&N offers WCS products in the areas of infection management, negative pressure wound therapy, bio-actives, and innovation dressings. An in-depth discussion of S&N products can be found at *www.smith-nephew.com.*

It was the first time S&N had used the services of a contract sales partner in the Philippines. S&N often utilizes contract sales partners in new markets where sales levels are not sufficient to support full-time S&N sales staff. The Philippines is an island nation located in Southeast Asia, with a population of about 100 million citizens occupying more than 7,000 islands. That said, the population is concentrated on 30 of the larger islands, and the principal island of Luzon contains Metro Manila and surrounding areas that account for 20 million citizens. The second largest metropolitan area is Cebu City, with a highly dense population of approximately one million. The islands of Bohol, Cebu, Leyte, Negros, and Samar are all located within easy traveling distance of Cebu City, with a combined population for this area of 12 million. Both Metro Manila and Metro Cebu report the highest incomes in the country, welcome millions of tourists annually, and are home to a large number of expatriates from Australia, Europe, Japan, Korea, and the U.S. who work or live in retirement in each respective region

As soon as the contract was signed, and with S&N Hong Kong's approval, East Lane Corporation selected two sales representatives:

- Teodoro (Teddy) Tulalip, the salesperson selected for Metro Manila, already had medical sales experience, having worked for Astra-Zeneca Asia. The S&N products he will promote were known and used in the area, thanks to two years of hospital work performed by Arturo Díaz, a local representative under the employ of S&N Hong Kong. This also meant that Tulalip would have initial local support as some accounts were transferred to ELC.

- The person chosen for Cebu City, Maria Teresa (Marites) García, had little sales experience, but had the right profile and exhibited loads of enthusiasm. García had earned a degree in pharmacy from the University of San Carlos, then worked for three years as a pharmacist at Doctors' Hospital in Cebu City. Díaz had been overtaxed, calling on hospitals in Metro Manila; therefore, the Cebu City territory had received scant attention, and S&N products were practically unknown at the major private, government, and military hospitals located in this multi- island region.

Both ELC sales representatives took two weeks' training in Manila. During week one, they received three days' instruction on the products they would promote (provided by S&N Hong Kong) and two days on buyer relationships/sales techniques (given by ELC). The second week was devoted to on-the-job training, supervised by two S&N regional sales managers from Hong Kong who traveled with Tulalip and García on sales calls. Both sales representatives required about two months to adapt to the normal pace of work.

Evaluation of the Results

At the beginning of July 2014, the director, sales manager, and marketing manager of S&N's Asian operations division analyzed the data available at the time. The average amount billed by ELC to S&N had been 540,000 Philippine pesos (PhP) per sales representative per month. This converted to US$12,000 or Euro 8,700. The amount was assigned to salary, benefits, travel, and overhead (general and administrative).

Everyone agreed that the results differed significantly in the two areas:

In Metro Manila (Tulalip): According to the April-June report, the market share of WCS product sold in Metro Manila had increased from 3.3 percent to 6.4 percent of the total value. In Quezon City and Manila Proper, where the products were heavily promoted, the increase had gone from 5.5 percent to 12 percent. The additional sales revenue, on top of the revenue obtained previously in the region, amounted to 5,133,000 Philippine pesos/US$114,000 in six months (January-June 2014 inclusive), and the gross margin had been 1,540,000 Philippine pesos/ US$34,000, i.e. 30 percent on average.

In Cebu City (García): The market share of the products in the second quarter of 2014 had increased from 0.90 percent to 2.36 percent of total sales for all WCS products sold in Cebu City. The additional sales revenue amounted to about 1,484,000 Philippine pesos in six months (January-June 2014), with a gross margin of 371,000 Philippine pesos/US$8,245 (25 percent).

The explanations advanced by the Hong Kong S&N management team for the gross margin differences, based upon its analysis of the data, were mixed. First, Tulalip had sold more products at higher gross margins. This difference may be because ELC's sales agents are unaware of the gross margin of the products they sell and only through marketing actions are they encouraged to focus their efforts on higher gross margin products. Second, the difference in gross margin between Metro Manila and Cebu City could be attributed to random factors, rather than those controlled by the salesperson. Lastly, the regional sales manager felt that García needed to improve her sales techniques—in particular her ability to close— since her closing rate was lower than that of Tulalip.

Sales Projection

In view of these preliminary results, the medical division's marketing manager estimated that, if new ELC sales representatives were introduced in other potential high-sales areas of Metro Manila, each could generate roughly the following sales levels:

Month 1	450,000 PhP/US$10,000
Month 2	900,000 PhP/US$20,000
Month 3	1,650,000 PhP/US$36,667
Month 4	2,250,000 PhP/US$50,000
Month 5	2,700,000 PhP/US$60,000
Month 6 onward	3,000,000 PhP/US$66,667 each month

Assuming a gross margin of 30 percent, with average selling costs remaining at 540,000 Philippine pesos per representative per month, breakeven for the Metro Manila representative would occur in the fourth month (2,250,000 PhP x 30 percent = 675,000 PhP/US$15,000 of gross margin). If sales and margin forecasts are accurate, after month six, each ELC salesperson would generate new gross income of 900,000 PhP/US$20,000 per month. To determine the net margin, S&N should take the gross margin less the amount billed by ELC per month per sales agent.

The Decision

Given the results of the trial, and the available data, S&N's CEO and global operations manager considered a set of alternatives derived from combinations of three variables:

a. To use salaried company or contract sales representatives employed by ELC.

b. The level of geographical coverage—two to three metro areas or all large cities?

c. Timing: When would be the best moment to do one thing or another?

Without being exhaustive, the three variables were combined to generate the following potential courses of action:

1. Immediately terminate the contract with ELC and manage Metro Manila and Cebu City as before, i.e., with a single Hong Kong representative, Arturo Díaz, visiting hospitals to skim easy sales.

2. Renew the contract with ELC for an additional six months for Metro Manila and Cebu City, in order to extend the trial, obtain more reliable data on sales trends, and verify whether sales and financial performance are sustainable.

3. Terminate the contract with ELC and immediately hire:

   3.1 One salaried S&N sales representative ONLY for Metro Manila.

   3.2 Two salaried sales representatives—one each for Manila & Cebu.

   3.3 Two salaried sales representatives for Metro Manila, and one for Cebu.

4. Sign a new agreement with ELC to expand coverage by establishing one contract sales representative in four other financially viable regions of the Philippines: Angeles/Tarlac, Baguio, Davao, and Iloilo. The initial contract could be for six months or one year. Following that, introduce salaried S&N sales representatives in some or all regions, depending upon the level of sales and profitability attained.

5. Hire a specific number of direct-salaried sales representatives for those same underserved regions.

CEO Olivier Bohuon was beginning to get excited about the strategic possibilities that would open up if a sales team was fully deployed throughout the Philippines. However, as CEO, he needed to insure that the Smith & Nephew group's Asian subsidiary earned a profit, as he personally desired, and as the company's year 2014 budget demanded.

Questions

1. Were the two territories equal in their sales potential? Why or why not?

2. What are the advantages and disadvantages of allowing ELC to represent S&N's WCS products as opposed to company salespersons?

3. Give two reasons Teddy Tulalip appeared to perform at a higher level than Marites García?

4. How adequate was the two-week training program? Please elaborate.

5. Should sales representatives know the profit margin of each product line? Why?

6. Do you agree that the projected sales levels presented by the marketing manager are feasible? Why or why not?

7. Compute the gross profit, based upon the projected sales, projected gross profit, and cost per salesperson. If sales forecasts are accurate, what would the expected profit per salesperson be after six months?

8. Based upon the available information, what course of action would you recommend S&N to take? More important, why?

————————————————

* The facts in this case are presented to teach sales management decision making and, while Smith & Nephew executive names are used, no one from S&N collaborated on this case study.

CASE STUDY 12

Shaping Products, Inc.:
Managing Sales in a Changing Market

Having celebrated 114 years in business in 2014, Shaping Products, Inc., is one of the few large textile firms left in North Carolina. Started as a hosiery company in 1900 by two brothers-in-law, Shaping Products is now the national leader of private-label legwear products. Located in Greensboro, North Carolina, Shaping Products' legwear portfolio includes tights, trouser socks, shapewear, and pantyhose for both the women's and children's markets. Additionally, Shaping Products has launched the subsidiary Forsyth Apparel, Inc., the largest U.S. private-label seamless products company that manufactures and sells capri pants, boy-shorts, leggings, and more. The sales department is headed by CEO John Davison who was first named president of sales at Shaping Products in 2005. With more than 30 years of textile sales experience, he sincerely believes "that no one should have to run sales." John's philosophy is that you need only hire sales professionals with experience in managing their own businesses, and then get out of their way. Still privately held, Shaping Products is overseen by a board of directors which includes many descendants of both founding families. The board strongly supports Davison and his management style, as it has produced exceptional results for the past few years.

Currently, Shaping Products has more than $110 million in annual sales, divided among six sales staff members who report directly to Davison. Only two of the six salespersons are located in Greensboro, while the rest work off-site from their homes across the country. Having sold hosiery for a decade, the CEO declares that sales are no longer made solely from personal relationships. "Gone are the days when deals were made because you were friends with the buyer, and you just visited and took an order." He further states: "We have to know our business, and their business better than our competitors do," which he calls "blocking and tackling."

Davison further concedes that the Shaping Products sales team needs to run its business smarter, with lower costs and better margins. Concerned that the team doesn't understand that its sales reps need to be willing to walk away from an order, he believes that a typical salesperson seldom sees an order he or she doesn't like. Said differently, a few members of his sales force still operate under an old-school mentality, and they don't push back enough on their buyers. This is a big concern.

He also believes that a good salesperson will listen to the buyer—to gain trust and offer a solution—before trying to sell them a product. However, John vehemently states that, if a person is truly good at sales, he or she will devise a solution, even if it means using a little creativity in order to get the sale. At the end of the day, however, the CEO classifies his sales team as "business managers." His opinion is that high-quality people don't need to be incentivized or driven by the dollar. Most individuals on his sales staff have managed businesses at the senior level, and John doesn't want anyone on the sales team who is eager to seek a larger bonus or commission.

Davison also discussed the hunter-versus-farmer mentality, and expects his sales team to be able to do both. Most of the sales team already manages large key accounts that they "farm" while other members "hunt" for additional key accounts. He realizes that not everyone can perform both functions equally well, but remembers a time, early on in his career, that taught him firsthand that he needed to play both roles.

While learning sales, John traveled with a more senior salesperson and spent three weeks in the field calling on customers. Upon returning to his office, his president asked him how many orders they had received. "None," was his answer. His president then sent him back to the field and told him to re-visit those same accounts and ask for orders. John returned three weeks later with $3 million dollars worth of orders. He realized that he was the hunter and the senior sales staffer was the farmer, as the more senior salesman enjoyed cultivating relationships, versus finding new ones for growth.

The Sales Audit

A sales audit, performed at the request of John Davison in order to identify opportunities and challenges within the Shaping Products sales team, has been conducted. In order to understand the role of sales professionals at Shaping Products, Joyoti "Joy" Rao an MBA student at Elon University, interviewed firm executives, members of the sales team, and members of cross-functional manufacturing teams. The sales audit confirmed that not only had the role of a salesperson changed greatly over the past decade, but that some areas within Shaping Products' current system needed additional review. It was apparent that, while the marketplace had changed and business had grown, Shaping Products' systems and processes had not. Preferring a flat organization, John Davison maintains high expectations that his salespeople will manage their business efficiently, without the need for excessive executive support.

While a typical corporation the size of Shaping Products has a vice president of sales, Davison stated: "It just doesn't work for Shaping Products." At the beginning of 2010, Shaping Products appointed an internal senior sales manager. This resulted in a great amount of pushback from the team; members felt that this extra layer of reporting was more hindrance than help. Most sales team members agreed that the new sales executive did not add value, and slowed the process down—even though this person was located at headquarters in Greensboro. While the manager possessed the required expertise, sales reps on the team believed that they had enough support from Davison himself. In the third quarter of 2012, the new position was dissolved, and the sales function reverted to the older, simpler system of reporting directly to Davison. Davison stated that, even if he could find someone well-rounded and senior enough, he was still not sure that it would add value to recreate the short-lived position. He said he felt that he supplied the needed direction for the team; at the same time, he also fills the role of CEO.

Today's business environment forces firms to be more flexible and knowledgeable about a partner's business model. As part of the audit, the senior management team was interviewed, and responded to the following questions:

1. How do you feel about the current sales process?

2. What are the strengths of the sales team?

3. What are the weaknesses of the sales team?

All freely discussed their experiences, and tried to add value to the exercise by offering solutions. Based upon the interviews, two main issues were identified that affect the operation of the sales team. Each issue is discussed further below.

Issue 1: Field Operations

As technology changed throughout the 1990s, salespeople became better equipped to work remotely—whether from a home office or while traveling to visit clients. Most of Shaping Products' sales team members are located adjacent to their largest account's headquarters. This is helpful when meetings with such buyers as Walmart and Target. However, with this positive comes the negative of feeling disconnected from the rest of the sales team and from manufacturing. One sales rep states that being close to the customer is great, but he finds it much harder to get things done internally without being onsite.

The role of a salesperson at Shaping Products is to work with assigned accounts and oversee all aspects of the retailer's business or—as John says—a "business manager." This includes everything from understanding the retailer's customers to overseeing orders being shipped. Shaping Products holds each salesperson responsible for account growth, even though they operate on a salaried, rather than a commissioned, basis. However, in reward for growing their respective businesses, annual bonuses are given.

The current business process includes forecasting sales with current accounts up to nine months in advance. Once an order is received, the forecast is updated so production planning receives an accurate view of what products will be needed month by month. The forecast is then reviewed by production planning, manufacturing, and purchasing. Purchasing is responsible for ordering all components from raw materials like yarn to packaging for finished products. Products are currently then made in one of three manufacturing locations.

Issue 2: Sales Supervision

Many sales members feel that they that they are disconnected from Davison. Within the past 18 months, Shaping Products acquired a competitor and absorbed its sales staff and customer service agents. There are currently two salesmen who came from this competitor and are not familiar with the way Davison manages his sales team. They are used to more one-on-one time, and grow concerned if they haven't heard from him in two or three weeks. The CEO responds that he is not a "babysitter," and that his team should always take a proactive stance when needing information.

Sales personnel rarely communicate with one another, unless they happen to be visiting the home office in Greensboro at the same time. However, at a meeting in New York a few months ago, a few salespersons were able to join. They all agreed that it is helpful, when they do convene, to exchange helpful information regarding their accounts, and possible new ones to pursue.

Other managers feel that the biggest dilemma at Shaping Products is that, at times, sales members operate in a vacuum and don't communicate well with those on the inside team. In the past, Shaping Products held monthly meetings that sales members were expected to attend, but due to scheduling conflicts, these meetings came to a halt last year. Those monthly meetings included the salespersons themselves, and staff members from the purchasing, operations, planning, testing, quality control, merchandising, marketing and shipping departments.

Due to John Davison's duties as CEO, he has been unable to schedule these meetings with any regularity for the past six months. Sandy Garrison, director of operations, stated that there have been times in the past few months when his purchasing team needed information from a sales member and it just wasn't provided. He said that production had begun for other accounts, but that one account, in particular, would definitely not receive the time, attention, or inventory it deserved—due to lack of communication. Garrison had sounded the alarm to his senior manager, and doesn't feel that the pressure is being placed on the right individuals to find solutions to problems like this one. However, when Garrison talked with the salesperson about the account in question, she stated that the retailer hadn't made decisions, and was watching to see how economic conditions unfolded—waiting until the last minute before placing orders. She told the operations director that the fault wasn't hers.

What to Do?

By completing the sales audit, Joy Rao, the Elon MBA student researching Shaping Products, has gathered significant information about sales force operations and must now prepare a presentation for CEO John Davison. It is apparent that the issues regarding the sales function need to be addressed, but the proof is in the pudding—

what specific recommendations should Rao make to Davison? More important, what justification in the form of improved operations, increased profits, and better-satisfied customers will she need to make to persuade what appears to be a skeptical CEO to accept a different operating mode for the firm's sales force?

Questions

1. John Davison thinks that the sales team should not be supervised, but that good people should be hired and then the sales leader should "get out of their way." Explain why you agree or disagree with Davison's approach to sales success.

2. If a salesperson says he or she "has never seen an order I did not like," are they pursuing goals that would benefit the company? Said differently, is all business "good"?

3. Davison claims that the "sales team needs to run their business smarter, with lower costs and better margins." If this statement is true, does it conflict with the sales philosophy he espouses in the first question?

4. Does the CEO of Shaping Products understand the roles of hunters/farmers? Explain why you believe he does or does not understand these sales roles.

5. Based upon the information provided, are the people in Shaping Products' different divisions and levels working together toward a common goal? Why is it important for the entire firm to be aligned?

6. What recommendations should Joy Rao make to John Davison? Why did you select these recommendations?

7. Why might Davison downplay or ignore these recommendations? What conditions might cause Davison to implement the suggested actions?

NAME INDEX

COMPANY/BRAND INDEX

SUBJECT INDEX

CPSIA information can be obtained at www.ICGtesting.com
Printed in the USA
BVOW10*1351120115

382590BV00002B/2/P